Going Pro

Scholarships, Student Athletes and the Money

By
Donald C. Moss

Crooked Island Publishing, Inc.

Copyright © 2004 by Donald C. Moss. Published by Crooked Island Publishing, Inc. 15030 Ventura Blvd., Ste. 19–850, Sherman Oaks, CA 91403. All rights reserved. Printed in the United States of America. No part of this book may be reproduced in any manner whatsoever without written permission except in the case of brief quotations embodied in critical articles and reviews.

Publisher's Cataloging-in-Publication
(*Provided by Quality Books, Inc.*)

Moss , Donald C,
   Going pro : scholaships student athletes and
the money -- / Donald C, Moss. -- 1st ed.
   p. cm.
   Includes bibliographical references and index.
   LCCN 2004092066
   ISBN 0-9747260-0-1
     1. Sports--Economic aspects--United States.
   2. Professional sports--Economicaspects--United States.
   3. College sports--Economic aspects--United States.
   4. College sports--Moral and ethical aspects--United States.
   5. School-to-work transition--United Statcs.
   I. Title.

GV716.M67 2004   338.4'7796'0973
                        QB133-2090

CONTENTS

Acknowledgments

It has truly been a blessing to spend the last eight years researching, writing and producing this book. It is impossible to thank everyone who contributed to the finished product and I will do my best to include the names of the people who are in my collective memory.

First and foremost, I would like to thank my wife Elainna, who put up with more crazy ideas on this project and others, all the while providing the encouragement and support to see me to the end. To my children, Dijorn and Karina, all of my love.

I would like to thank my family, including my parents, Sam and Dorethea who taught me to persevere and not give up. My sisters, Frankie and Olivia who continues to embody the spirit of what family is all about. To my aunt Catherine who gave me the seed money to travel half way around the world to pursue my dream of attending the University of Southern California. To my grandparents who will forever remain in my heart, especially my grandfather Daniel, for whom the main character is written.

To my literary partners in crime, thanks to Regina Brzozowski for straightening out the manuscript I thought was good writing. Bridget O'Brien for her line editing. Nancy Tsai for assisting with the layout of the book. Heather Rothman for keeping me straight on who and whom. Veme Anya for helping to soften the rough edges. Thanks to Allegra Newman and Andrew DeFrancis for reading on Saturdays and giving the needed insight to the strengths and weaknesses. Thank you focus group, Scott Schiff, Christopher Thell, Guiselle Torres and Cassandra Lamb.

A special thanks to Margaret Akerstrom, Marvin Mitchell, Mary Johnson, Tom Kowolski, Richard Lapchik, Ronnie Carter, Bob Moore, Stacy Slaughter, Jim Pedone, Pascal Andre, Francis Narron, Gary Bernato and Russ Palmer.

To the professional coaches and athletes who took the time to patiently answer my questions, I owe a debt of gratitude: Grant Hill, Calvin Hill, Oscar De La Hoya, Marcus Allen, Junior Seau, John Wooden, Earvin

"Magic" Johnson, Ken Carter, Tyrone Willingham, Leigh Steinberg and Mike Krzyzewski.

My thanks to all of the high school athletes, collegiate student athletes and other aspiring athletes who contributed to the thesis of this book.

I would like to thank the wonderful journalist around the globe who are exceptional writers and provided clarity to the stories that contributed to the book. Thanks to Crooked Island Publishing for having the insight to connect the dots. For those of you reading this book, I thank you.

INTRODUCTION

GOING PRO is a term we hear from time to time and it is generally associated with athletes seeking to make the transition from amateur to professional athlete. However, too many wonderful athletes have left home with a scholarship and the promise of a brighter tomorrow, only to return to economically depressed neighborhoods with nothing more than "if only I could have. . ." indelibly etched in their consciences. University presidents with athlete graduation rates that number in the teens look the other way when it comes to athletes not showing a sincere effort to earn a meaningful degree, all while the universities collect millions of dollars as a result of these same athletes. If the general student body graduation rates were commensurate with that of the athletic departments in some schools, the presidents would be run out of town before the fight song was over.

Of course there are two sides to this story. The second includes the athletes themselves being offered a chance to improve their lives through education as well as the exposure to showcase their talents, often on national television. The student athlete and his parent(s) as a whole, is equally responsible for taking advantage of every opportunity a college scholarship has to offer.

Cash payouts under the table to student athletes, fictitious courses or grades being offered to keep players academically eligible and players filling up the police blotter with various assaults. As long as the hostile feeling exists that "the universities are getting rich off of the sweat of our brow," we will continue to read about one scandal after another.

One day I opened the newspaper and I saw that a student athlete who graduated from Arizona State University with a 3.84 GPA in marketing decided to walk away from the millions of dollars being offered by the Arizona Cardinals (the team that drafted him in 1998). Pat Tillman left the NFL to serve his country in the Army's elite Rangers. He did not want the riches, fame and glory, though he could have swept it up without batting an

1

eye. Sadly, Tillman lost his life in Afghanistan defending the freedoms we enjoy. This, in my opinion, epitomizes what a student athlete is all about.

Undoubtedly, the position that you take on this hotly debated issue will depend on your personal experiences and whether or not you were an athlete growing up. It may also depend on your socio-economic status. It was personal for me and my experiences were directly connected to why I chose to write about this subject. My intention in writing this book is to bring an awareness to the youth in this country who strongly believe that they too will someday earn a living through his/her athletic abilities. It is not my job to persuade the reader or anyone else who has an influence on athletes throughout the world to come to the same conclusion I did.

These are some of the stories that came across my desk as a journalist and information brought to my attention as a result of the nature of my profession. I will admit up front that my choices in life and, more importantly, my lessons in life, will be reflected throughout the book. It may appear to the reader at times that I am being heavy-handed one way or the other, and it is with this understanding that I will not be able to please everyone, nor will I try.

The battle over how to keep collegiate athletes from crossing the threshold legally or illegally into professionalism without jeopardizing their amateur status was lost long ago. In fact, by the NCAA's own definition, athletes are currently being paid, albeit by the institutions that control their futures, through "grant-in-aid" or scholarships.

What is fair compensation for athletes who help bring in revenue through gate receipts, merchandising and television contracts for their respective schools?

The book gives examples of both pros and cons to this contentious debate and offers viable solutions for this conflict.

For those who read this book and look beyond the material things in search of balance—press forward, this book is for you.

PART I

LEARNING LIFE'S LESSONS EARLY

A Good First Lesson

I am not sure when this subject became so deeply ingrained in my soul, but at some point in 1995 I made a conscientious decision to pursue the subject of student athletes. Particularly, the lack of education given to students recruited by colleges for their athletic programs.

The ubiquitous post-it note pad caught my attention. "Dan, I need to see you as soon as possible, Jim."

My five years as a beat sports reporter for the Orange County Post told me something was in play I wasn't quite ready to digest. I placed my notes from an earlier interview with an injured All-American running back from UCLA on my desk, and I proceeded directly to my boss' office. Jim Teckerman was a thin, tanned man who could have doubled for the comedian Billy Crystal—he even had a similar laugh.

This particular morning, I could tell by his hastily scribbled note, this meeting was not going to be swept away in humor.

Jim offered coffee, and I graciously declined. "What's up?" I asked.

"I hear you are currently working a story on why universities are not held to a higher standard for ensuring the same success rates off the field as they are on the field." I felt my blood pressure start to climb, so I decided to take a deep breath before I blurted something out I would later regret. As a collegiate walk-on student athlete in the late 1970s, I saw first hand what happens to athletes who get caught in the hype of playing professional sports and do not attend class. I also remembered how universities were willing to throw athletes into courses that offered very little academic substance, certainly not enough to justify credits toward a four-year degree. "Keep them academically eligible so they can play on Saturday," seemed to be the collegiate mindset.

I had known this conversation with Jim would eventually take place, but I didn't think it would happen so quickly.

"I have decided to do a background investigation of an incident involving a kid whose scholarship was revoked because he became academically ineligible for the upcoming football season," I said.

"Let's just drop that one off in the round file cabinet on your way out. I'm sending you to Phoenix on Thursday to do a cover story on Grant Hill." Jim, usually comedic, was very dismissive in his tone.

As I got up to leave the meeting, I knew deep down, like a fish that had ingested a hook, that I was not going to be able to let go of this story so easily. As I walked back over to my office (more aptly described as a 7x10 cubicle), I felt as though I had been in a smoke-filled theater trying to focus on the screen, but barely able to see the big picture.

The Post was having some difficult financial years because of the advent of cable television and various other start-up print publications. Jim was feeling the pressure to print articles about coverage & stars of the NBA, NFL, NHL and MLB games. This middle-of-the-road stance was what Jim believed the majority of our readership looked for in our sports coverage. My boss' position was who cares if athletes go to class or not? My proposed story was definitely bumping up to the edge of controversy.

It was time to head home and pack my bags for Phoenix.

At home, my wife and I got into a lengthy debate about how much responsibility schools should accept for athletes who end up, after four or five years of playing sports, without the benefit of a good education.

I argued there needs to be more university mentoring and less hand wringing because their student athletes are responsible for helping bring in millions of dollars. My wife believes student athletes are using the schools to showcase their talents in front of thousands and in some case, millions on television. We called it a draw and decided to continue the debate later.

The next morning I arrived in Phoenix to a picture-perfect 70-degree desert greeting. Winters can be a real prize for a reporter covering sporting events in this town. I received some covetous glares from colleagues upon hearing the assignment I drew.

* * * * * * *

My most memorable recollection of Arizona is driving with a high school friend from Miami to Los Angeles for college. We took off driving in a 1980 Ford Thunderbird, a college gift from my dad. It was four years old but needed body work. Just outside of Phoenix, I awoke from my slumber and suddenly realized it was 2:30 A.M., but the ambient air temperature outside the car was hovering somewhere around 95 degrees.

Suddenly it occurred to me that if it was this hot and the sun wasn't even up yet, we must have taken a wrong highway and ended up in Death Valley! I suppose it was the naiveté of two young teenagers.

That was a long time ago, and now I was here to cover one of the NBA's most promising new superstars since Michael Jordan.

Most assignments are of the one-night turnaround variety, no need for more than a carry-on bag. Customarily, I check into my hotel, check my phone messages, e-mail, etc. After a brief shower and clothes change, it is time to review my notes. In order to get as many details as possible, I organize my questions starting with the things I absolutely have to have to complete my assignment, then end with more mundane questions.

Entering the America West Arena through the "Media Relations" door, a very attractive blonde named Heather greeted me with my media packet, which included my laminated press credential and the all-important meal ticket. It's one of the perks that come with covering college and professional sports, but I try not to let it go to my head or my waistline. Some nights it consists of a ham and cheese sandwich and a bag of Fritos. On those nights, I defer to my $50 per diem. On this particular night, it included baked lasagna, a tossed green salad and unlimited dinner rolls.

As I completed the gauntlet of fine dining, I spotted a friend of mine, AP reporter Ted Zimmardo, who is considered one of the top sports writers in the country. "It figures I would find you around the food," he quips. We both broke into that "guilty as charged" laugh.

We took our designated seats at the media tables courtside, and it hit me how so many kids could easily become intoxicated by the electrified atmosphere of playing in front of 20,000 screaming fans and millions of television viewers. The roar of the crowd is deafening. My mind drifted back to the earlier conversation I had with my boss about my interest in scholarship athletes and their respective universities. There were only 12 uniformed players on each team. What happens to all those others who try to make this atmosphere their reality, but fail? My pragmatic boss would argue there are over 18,000 fans in attendance and tomorrow morning, the rest of the fans not in attendance will want a recap of the game. For the moment, I focused my attention back on the game, and it did not take long to forget the debate after the opening tip-off of the game between the Phoenix Suns and Detroit Pistons. Even though I've covered all kinds of sporting events, I am always amazed by the speed and agility of players 6 foot 2 and taller, racing up and down the hardwood court. I often begin to feel guilty for being paid to watch an NBA game in person. This feeling doesn't last long after the realization hits me that I have a story that I need to file electronically with an 11 P.M. deadline. The game's pace see-sawed, ranging from players hitting shots from the top of the free-throw line to making baseline shots players like Jordan, Bird and Magic made famous.

Totally immersing myself in the game, I focused directly on my subject. Grant Hill, the Pistons' (currently with the Orlando Magic) all-star forward stands 6 feet 8 inches tall and is a handsome guy with a caramel complexion and a smile that is unmistakable. Hill was selected by the Detroit Pistons in the first round of the 1993 NBA Draft out of Duke University. Hill's mother was a college dorm-mate of former First Lady and current New York Senator Hillary Rodham Clinton at Wellesley College. Hill's dad, Calvin Hill, is a Yale graduate and former NFL running back.

As luck would have it, I saw Calvin Hill seated at courtside, just opposite the scorers' table.

Being the opportunistic journalist that I am, I decided to see if I could get two stories instead of one.

Starting the fourth quarter, the game took on the appearance of an indoor track meet, with players fast breaking at a break-neck pace. With 7:42 left and a television time-out, both teams' players grasped for that last breath of air their bodies would take in. Both coaches shouted unheard, unintelligible instructions appearing like they were merely lip-synching their words. The deafening roar from the crowd kept the euphoric intensity at a peak, rivaling a 747 during takeoff.

With the score tied at 103, Phoenix was attempting to inbound the ball. The pass was deflected, and suddenly Grant Hill took the errant pass and made a thunderous dunk shot. Even the opposing team's fans appreciated the highlight. I knew post game there would be a mob scene in front of Hill's locker.

Post game, my fears were realized as hoards of print and television media formed a semi-circle around the star of the show, Grant Hill. Because I needed to ask specific questions other than the proverbial, "So how does it feel to be the hero of tonight's game," I had to wait out the crowd, which was threatening to smash my deadline like a piece of Waterford crystal thrown against the wall.

I patiently waited in the corner of the locker room reviewing my notes as a man with an imposing 6-foot-3 frame walked into the room and glanced around. It was none other than Calvin Hill, mid 50s, still looking as if he could drag a few would-be tacklers around the football field. He was engaging the Pistons media relations' representative, David Dubrof, in friendly conversation.

I approached Hill and Dubrof with an outstretched hand to introduce myself as Dubrof said, " Hey Calvin, this is Dan Christensen. He's a writer for the Orange County Post, out here to do a personal profile on Grant." Dubrof was very familiar with my assignment because I had an earlier encounter with Dubrof when I attempted to scoop a private one-on-one at the Hyatt Hotel pre-game. Unfortunately for me, Grant Hill was scheduled to shoot a PSA (Public Service Announcement) for the NBA's Reading is Fundamental program earlier that same afternoon.

I began to tell Calvin Hill what an honor it was to meet him, but I quickly got the impression that he had heard this yada yada stuff from the adoring public before, so my professional instincts kicked in and I stuck to the script. I explained I would like to get his take on the importance of student athletes taking advantage of the opportunities their God-given talents had provided for them. My first question was, "I know that you graduated from Yale and your wife from Wellesley. What did you and your wife say to Grant to make him understand how important it was to get a good education?"

"Grant understood early on that education is the great equalizer. For those believing their athletic skills will be the only answer, I say this: we are moving into a new century where only the educated will survive," Calvin Hill replied.

We continued to converse on this subject for about 10 minutes. Finally Grant Hill made his way over to where we were standing. After Calvin introduced me, I asked Grant what he thought about athletes who had opportunities to earn a degree, yet chose to only pursue the athletic avenue.

"It's hard for me to understand why some athletes choose to pursue only athletics. I had wonderful role models in both my mother and father," said Hill. "I was taught early on my parents expected me to do well in school."

As I concluded my interview with the Hills, Grant turned back toward me and said, "It's just like jumping out of an airplane with two parachutes: if one fails, at least you have another option to fall back on."

Just shy of the deadline, I e-mailed my story back to the office and I headed back to the airport for the one-hour flight back to LAX.

The next morning at the office, Teckerman appeared mildly pleased by the article I wrote on Grant Hill, but he wasn't sure why I chose to include the quote from Calvin Hill. Teckerman let me know I was edging ever so close to insubordination, based on the comments I included about academics and sports.

I couldn't help but admire Calvin Hill. Here was an African American who attended one of the most distinguished academic institutions in the country and excelled in amateur and professional sports. Not only was he a great athlete, but a beacon for others who left home to become a complete person in both sports and academics. Calvin Hill's wife Janet also attended a prestigious university. Their son not only graduated from Duke with a degree in history, but was now one of the NBA's star attractions. This was the story I believed more Americans should be reading about. Instead the media is focusing too much on athletes who get themselves into trouble with the law. It may sell newspapers, but in my opinion, it offers distorted truths and taints successful student athletes.

I carefully hid my feelings and I tried to appeal to Teckerman's journalistic faith, but he wasn't buying it. His response was, "Dan, we have enough political fires to put out without you starting another one."

I was certain my next assignment would be something along the lines of interviewing the guy responsible for cleaning up the dog poop after the Westminster Dog Shows or maybe talking to Hugo the water-skiing chipmunk. To Teckerman's credit, he gave me a peach travel assignment.

Traveling to River Falls, Wisconsin, my assignment was to cover the Kansas City Chiefs NFL training camp and do a feature about Heisman Trophy-winner Marcus Allen. I knew Marcus from my college days at USC where he was a star running back and I was a defensive back who donated my body to research on the practice field as a walk-on (a non-scholarship player). I often wondered what if anything would have changed in my life had I been given a "full ride" at USC. Would I have hit the books any less had I been given equal treatment to scholarship players? A moot point at this stage of my life, I dismissed it as I always did.

Making my customary phone calls to the team's media relations office, I got an interesting response from Bob Moore, the media relations director.

"Hey Dan, you can interview Marcus, but he has already stated that he is limiting his time with the press this week," said Moore. Bob Moore was a very pleasant man with a warm disposition. Some media relations guys act as if they are the ones putting fans in the seats, but not Moore. He was very accommodating. My response was, "Hey Bob, let Marcus know I will be coming strictly to talk about his professional football career with a brief look back to his USC glory days."

With the ground rules of the interview intact, I headed to LAX to catch a Northwest red-eye to Minneapolis, Minnesota. River Falls is situated on the Minnesota/Wisconsin border, just over the Minunga River. I find it easier to fly directly to Minneapolis and drive the remaining 70 miles over the border to River Falls, Wisconsin.

River Falls is a beautiful Wisconsin community filled with small, close-knit neighborhoods, shops, majestic farmlands and large barns and silos. While driving to the training facility I kept thinking to myself, this seems like an odd place for an NFL team to hold training camp, out in the middle of the heartland. Of course this is the ideal place; with no big-city distractions, teams can concentrate on nothing but football.

At the training camp, I headed over to the media office, situated inside a conference center. The facility was actually part of the University of Wisconsin, River Falls campus. Yearly, the Kansas City Chiefs take over the dorms and practice facility for about six weeks during July and August.

I was issued my press credential, given last-minute instructions about the day's schedule, and directed when I could and could not be out on the practice field.

A person who has never seen an NFL training camp practice session can believe me when I say that they have not missed much. Most of the workout is centered on a labyrinth of monotonous drills executed over and over until it becomes second nature.

I decided to position myself at the edge of the practice field to catch Allen's attention. That way when the players headed to the locker room, I could snag M.A. (His friends and close associates called him by his initials).

Like a guided cruise missile, I zeroed in on Allen just after he left the practice area.

"Hey M.A., Dan Christensen, remember me? I played ball with you at USC." He clearly remembered me, however, there was this parenthetic pause that came over him. I quickly kicked into my inquisitive reporter posture and proposed a tentative meeting right after lunch.

"I really need to run some errands after lunch, why don't you catch up with me tomorrow." I have seen every kind of brush-off invented. He was trying to throw me off stride. I acquiesced, and we agreed to sit down right after tomorrow's morning practice.

Fatigued from the red-eye, I decided to bee-line back to my hotel to catch a quick nap and prepare for my interview with Allen. One of the things I enjoy doing when I travel to an unfamiliar city is to drive around or take a bus or a train. After my nap, I decided to visit the famous Metropolitan Stadium in Bloomington, Minnesota, the site of some of the best pro football games ever played. As a child, long before the Dallas Cowboys were graced with the title of "America's Team," I was a Cowboys fan of epic proportions. I cried the day Jim O'Brien kicked the winning field goal in Super Bowl IV, as the Baltimore Colts defeated the Cowboys 16–13. Conversely, I will always remember celebrating the last-second touchdown play known in the NFL history books as the "Hail Mary," thrown by Roger Staubach to Drew Pearson. It happened at Metropolitan Stadium, so I decided to go pay homage to this cherished tundra. After driving around and burning expensive octane, I decided to stop and ask for some directions. Pulling into the local gas station, I approached an attendant who closely resembled Erik the Scandinavian Viking. Ah ha, now I realized why the Minnesota mascot was a Viking. The attendant (a.k.a. Erik) instructed me to turn around and take a look at the very large shopping mall.

"Do you see the Mall of America right there? That replaced the stadium." Uncertain whether to feel surprised or embarrassed, I thanked the man for his gas and history lesson, and I headed back to my hotel. Sightseeing over!

The next day I woke up to a beautiful summer day in the Twin Cities. At 70 degrees, the sky had a beautiful majestic blue hue to it. As I made the trek back across the bridge to Wisconsin, I began to grow apprehensive about my interview. Almost 15 years since I had any real dealings with M.A., I wasn't sure if my good will had sustained such a time lapse. In the majority of my interviews, I just take a very "you need me more than I need you" attitude.

This was different. For one thing, the last time I saw M.A., he was driving a late model Nissan 260 Z with a missing hubcap. Now he had reached that top financial echelon in the world of professional sports. Tragically, some of those who are blessed to ever reach that plateau often change.

I arrived at training camp around 9:30 A.M. and took a seat up in the bleachers, paying about as much attention to what was going on down on the field as a drill sergeant watching paint dry. The foghorn sounded signaling the end of the morning practice session. I hurriedly made my way down to catch the players who now had spilled onto the asphalt path leading back to the locker room. I caught up to M.A. only to hear him say, "Hey I know I promised that interview right after lunch, but I need to run to the bank. Honestly, we'll do it as soon as I am done with the afternoon practice." Well what could I say? That afternoon we finally sat down inside the office of one of the team's assistant coaches, and the interview began. I began asking him questions about the old days just to break the tension and within a few minutes we were in what I call a "journalistic swing." That's when my questions are flowing and the responses are coming back with the same fluidity.

After the interview, I e-mailed my article to the assistant editor. I waited a couple of hours to adjust to the difference in time zones, then decided to call and check up on my story's status. The article ended up being a big hit back at the office. Teckerman was across town, meeting with one of the paper's biggest board members. Jonathan Wentworth was president of the local college, and Wentworth had called an important meeting that afternoon on campus. When I called in, Teckerman's secretary, Linda, made it clear Jim was smiling after he read my story. Linda was a short, garrulous woman who grew up in the New England states and was very protective of Teckerman.

"Well, is it safe for me to come back to the office?" Linda was more than encouraging. "Jim is sending you to interview Oscar De La Hoya who is preparing to fight former middleweight champion Julio Caesar Chavez." For De La Hoya, this would be the biggest fight of his young career and what many boxing fans were referring to as the "fight of the decade."

The article was scheduled for The Post's Sunday Sports (boxing special edition) section that was supposed to run the week leading up to the fight. De La Hoya was training at his facility in Big Bear, a mountain town in Southern California. I was assigned to do a personal story about this local hero known as the "Golden Boy" who had won the gold medal in boxing at the Barcelona Olympic Games in 1992.

Boxing promoter Bob Arum headed the De La Hoya training camp. Arum arranged for the media to come up by chartered bus. Arum was a sharp and intelligent promoter who was congenial toward everyone. He made De La Hoya available for the throngs of reporters who had converged at this unusual setting for a boxing training facility. Winding our way through the San Bernardino Mountains, I was formulating my questions to ask the Golden Boy. Oscar De La Hoya grew up on the tough streets of East Los Angeles. With boyish good looks and a wonderful smile, this son of Mexican immigrants was struggling to garnish support from the Mexican-American community that was squarely behind the Mexican challenger, Julio Cesar Chavez. De La Hoya was viewed as a "sell-out," someone who, through his or her hard work, made it successfully and then moved out of the neighborhood to a better life. This sounds exactly like the American Dream, but when one starts from humble beginnings, people expect them to stay in crime-ridden communities so they can "keep it real." Arriving at the top of Big Bear Lake, the narrow streets, featuring estate homes dotted in between the majestic pine trees, were swelled with parked cars. The wooden structure De La Hoya shared with his family and boxing handlers sprawled across about two acres of land. The large garage positioned just behind the residence was converted into a boxing gym equipped with an official boxing ring and all the training equipment a champion would need.

As the media exited the chartered bus, a young woman, identifying herself as Dena, Oscar's publicist, immediately greeted us. I introduced myself and asked how much time I would be allotted to interview the champ. Dena, an attractive woman in her early thirties with short, dark hair, had a very assertive disposition. Exactly who they wanted to handle the hundreds of requests from adoring fans in search of autographs and the insatiable media that sensed that this could be the biggest fight of the decade. All of us were given an outline that detailed the schedule for the day, with lunch being identified as the first order of business. One of the few benefits of this job is the ability to mooch food at various venues. Today was no exception. Upon wolfing down the sandwiches and chips, I took my position to corner the champion De La Hoya to find out what his feelings were about being snubbed by the very group he grew up around. De La Hoya was somewhat at a loss to explain why people from Southern California would be so supportive of Chavez.

We also spoke about kids that looked up to him and what it means to be a role model. Of course I couldn't help but ask where he would be if his career as a boxer had not materialized. "I have always wanted to become an architect and my goal is to box another six or seven years, then who knows, maybe I will go to college and study architecture," said De La Hoya. De La Hoya is warm and very charismatic, and I wondered why he was subjecting his body and those good looks to the pounding that prizefighters take. Then I overheard someone say the De La Hoya camp was guaranteed $20 million for this fight. With that kind of money, he could buy an architecture school. Once again, I wrote my article around my concern for athletes, projecting the theme of staying in school and pursuing one's dreams in conjunction with pursuing an education. The media watched Oscar simulate a boxing match with timed three-minute rounds, sparing with his boxing partner as mariachi music blared in the background. I was completely impressed with the training facilities and the number of handlers associated with "Team De La Hoya." I knew that Julio Cesar Chavez was in the twilight of his career, while De La Hoya was in the budding prime of his. The problem was, did Chavez fans realize these things?

✳ ✳ ✳ ✳ ✳ ✳ ✳

I met Kim, my wife, at a banquet for the USC vs. UCLA cross-town rival football game in 1985. It was the annual coaches' luncheon held at the Pasadena Ritz Carlton, and my future wife was an assistant in the food and beverage department. I found her smile very flattering and her olive complexion and almond-colored eyes captivating. We connected right away and dated for about 18 months before I asked her to marry me. With the exception of my occasional business travel, we kept very precise hours. We always managed to meet every evening at the dinner table, to share in each other's daily tribulations. The escalating and continuing tension between my boss and I was beginning to give Kim an uneasy feeling. She was very much aware that I had strong convictions about my principles and beliefs that not enough was being done to stress the importance of education first or to get this message out to athletes, particularly young impressionable kids who couldn't see past the multi-million-dollar professional contracts and the millions being earned in endorsements.

Now finished with the meal and the dishes put away, I informed Kim I would be prepared to spend some of my spare time researching why I felt that universities were remiss in their responsibility to ensure that the athletes they recruit receive a proper education and instead were just keeping them "eligible" to satisfy some NCAA guidelines. I had personally witnessed highly recruited ballplayers who never took more than 30 credits toward a bachelor's degree and after their four years of eligibility were used up, they were exiled back to communities that held little or no opportunities for them to grow economically. I certainly wasn't naïve enough to believe that it was solely the responsibility of the university. After all, these young players were adults and hence needed to be self-motivated to pursue a degree in their field of choice. But most of these kids come from neighborhoods where people know very little, if anything, about collegiate studies. The results of my initial findings confirmed a number of factors which I felt were key to identifying some solutions to the problem. The statistical analysis of athletes going on to the pro ranks would need to be exposed to a wider audience to adequately address the issue. But first, I had to convince my superiors that my research was compelling enough to sell newspapers. I was getting excited thinking about the story that our newspaper could do: a three-part expose on what colleges are doing to bridge the gap on what athletes achieve on and off the playing field. In my mind, the issue was more than just measuring athletic programs by the number of players who received degrees (although that was very important); I wanted (and I am sure the majority wanted) to see athletes come out with the tools to compete in every facet of society. Be it computers, law, business or engineering, a new world paradigm was quickly evolving and it was time for ballplayers and colleges alike to get serious and get their game on.

My Oscar De La Hoya article made the front page of the Sunday Sports section that featured the big upcoming fight.

Over brunch, I gave Kim a three-page outline detailing how I would approach Teckerman the next business day with the synopsis for the Expose' on Student Athletes. She dismissively glanced at it for a moment and set it aside. Kim then peered over the Calendar section of the Sunday Post and said, "Could you stand being unemployed with a mortgage and all of the trappings that we have come to enjoy? Perhaps you're just going through that mid-life crisis I hear men go through." I shot back with "yeah, just give me the afternoon to get over it." The terse exchange put a damper on the rest of the day.

The next morning upon entering my office several congratulatory messages were left on my voicemail about the profile I did on Team De La

Hoya. I had spent the better part of the weekend preparing how I would approach Teckerman. Armed with the voicemails reassuring me of my abilities, I headed for the conference room where my boss was seated near the entrance. As I got closer, my heart began racing about how this meeting would turn out.

Teckerman was combing through a set of notes when I asked if he could spare a moment.

"Sure what's on your mind?" As I handed him my outline, he bristled and began to show signs my proposal was about to face some stiff opposition. As Teckerman flung off his glasses and turned to face me, "What the .,." I cut him off and explained that this was a subject long overdue, and I was determined to see it in print. By now both of our voices escalated, causing a couple of co-workers to stare in from outside the conference room that we were occupying. We both dug our heels in; neither one of us willing to concede our position. Teckerman slammed his hand down on the table and emphatically told me "No!"

I was completely stunned. I knew that there would be some resistance to my doing this story, but I never thought it would get to this type of vituperative standoff. After all, I'm the reporter who just had a Sunday front-page byline. I collected my outline and like a child who had been rebuked by his father, I managed to stagger back to my desk. I was angry and winded and in need of getting outside to grab some fresh air and figure out what my next assignment would be. My creative conscience had just suffered a severe blow … I needed to regroup. Now what? I knew that I was not assigned to cover the Chavez / De La Hoya fight, so I collected my thoughts and tried to figure out what would be my next move.

Not wanting to let anyone know how hard I had taken it on the chin, I tagged along with staff writer Jeff Brower who was headed out to the Great Western Forum to cover a high school basketball championship game between Orange County perennial champion Mater Dei and a school from Fresno, Clovis West. It had been about 10 years since I covered high school sports for my school newspaper, and I figured it would do me some good to go out and watch high school players who play the game for free.

Brower was a throw back from the era when stories were written on a Smith Corona. He was a mentor to me, and I took advantage of his eagerness to give me pointers about the news business.

Watching those young kids dive for loose balls and play a team game lifted my spirits. The heated argument that had consumed my mind earlier was, for the moment, hidden away. The kids playing looked so young to me, or maybe it was just that I had aged. The first half was a very close contest, with both teams showing a great deal of talent. I could see why so many young basketball players want to jump past college and into the NBA. With the exception of some of their bodies not being strong enough to pound out a grueling 82-game schedule, it was conceivable that a couple of ballplayers were good enough to warrant a look by pro-scouts, though I would of course encourage them to go the collegiate route first. Each year, I may see three high school players throughout the country good enough to be invited to compete at the big league level. Since I was along strictly as a spectator, I didn't feel the looming deadline to file the story, and so I just put my feet up and enjoyed the ride.

After the game was over, Clovis West edging Mater Dei by three, Brower filed his story and asked me to join him for a late night cup of coffee. After a quick call to Kim to notify her of my plans, Brower and I met over at the Starbucks in Westwood.

"Do you know why Jim has been stonewalling you on your proposed feature story?" asked Brower. A bit perplexed by the question, I indicated that Teckerman felt that the piece wasn't timely enough and therefore wouldn't sell.

"Well, that's certainly the corporate line they are feeding you. The real reason has to do with Jonathan Wentworth and that transfer player they picked up from back East. It turns out the transfer student had someone falsify his records so he could get admitted into the university and Wentworth is neck deep in it. Your exposing them is the last thing they need," Brower continued.

By now my cup of decaf was turning cold while my blood pressure jumped. "Jeff, if what you're telling me is true, we need to go over Jim's head to the senior editor," I exclaimed.

Jeff Brower looked directly at me with those distinct hazel eyes and said, "Dan, I like you like a son, but if you mention any of this to the 'powers that be,' I will deny this conversation ever took place." With that, Jeff got up and headed out the door into the cool crisp evening.

When I got home that evening, Kim was not pleased to hear about the office discussion between me and Teckerman. She indicated that I needed to let this one go and continue covering stories on players that the public wanted to read about and not some ideological diatribe about why colleges should do more to compensate their athletes. I began to explain to Kim the conversation I had with Brower an hour earlier, when she interjected, "So now you are going to take on the president of the university and your boss at The Post?" I was beginning to wonder if my motives were sincere or if this was some type of power play on my part to exert my wishes to cover the kinds of story I felt I was hired to write. Was I that far off base, or was it a case of my wife wanting to make sure that our mortgage payments would not be jeopardized? I fell asleep that evening watching "Nightline" and when I woke up the next morning, I was no longer tense. A strange calm had descended on me.

2

THE R LETTER

I hustled into work that morning eager to get a fast start to my day. As I headed to my office, I crossed paths with Teckerman and we gave each other very cordial smiles and greetings. After returning a couple of phone calls and looking at my complimentary Sports Illustrated magazine, my phone started ringing and it was Teckerman on the other end asking me to give him an update on what I was working on. I strolled over to his office to show him the memo that I had drafted shortly after arriving that morning. The memo read as follows:

```
To: The Orange County Post
Attn: Mr. James Teckerman, editor
Subject: Letter of Resignation

Dear Mr. Teckerman,

  After careful consideration, I have decided to tender my
resignation effective immediately. I would like to thank
this organization for giving me an opportunity to develop
my professional journalistic skills.

  I would also like to personally thank you for giving me
the drive to pursue my passion of always searching for the
truth at all cost.

  It has been a pleasure working here, and I will miss you
all.

Sincerely,
Daniel A. Christensen
```

I could tell that my boss was surprised. He didn't see this one coming. After clearing his throat, he said, "You know you should really reconsider this letter of resignation. I realize that we had a dispute yesterday but this …this is not necessary." I wanted to tell him that complacency has its place, but not with me when it comes to the lives of young, unsuspecting, innocent athletes. Truth be told, I wanted to call him a liar. But I didn't. It was simply time to move on. For the past year I'd felt that way, I just never found enough courage to do it until now. I just turned and walked away.

Formulating what I was going to say to Kim, I went home and embarked on a cleaning spree. I then started cooking dinner while getting my game face on for what I knew would be a difficult conversation. I needed all the bonus points I could muster up, and I needed them in a hurry. My wife usually arrives home around 5:30 P.M., and according to my watch, I had about two hours to complete my task. I cooked and cleaned the house anticipating that she was not going to take the news very well.

When Kim opened the door, her bemused look immediately gave me a feeling that this explanation would not be easy. We embraced, and she asked if I was feeling all right. I assured her that I was fine and quickly explained that I had handed in my resignation earlier that day. After dropping her bags, she asked, "You're kidding right? Tell me you are not serious!" This was going to be tougher than I had figured. I tried to plead my case, but Kim would not hear of it. She demanded that I go back to work the next day and rescind my resignation. I couldn't do that, and I needed to find a way to help her understand that this was not going to be an option. I never wanted to work in a profession where it was just about a paycheck; it had to be fulfilling. Otherwise, I could just as easily take a freelance position working my own hours, travel, and not be too concerned about storing up treasures for retirement. By now dinner was an afterthought, and I finished it alone at the dining table. I was the perfect person, having witnessed it first hand, to pursue the story surrounding athletes and what should be done to improve the educational validity of athletic scholarships, even if it jeopardized my marriage. I made another attempt that evening to help my wife at least see the importance of this decision, but all she was interested in was what I would do to earn a living. At that moment, I felt she looked at me and only saw a paycheck.

The next morning Kim was out the door a little earlier than normal, indicating that she was still very upset with my decision. I headed off to my office for the last time to turn in my laptop and collect my small box of mementos that I had collected working at The Post over the last six-plus years. The guard at the entrance to the employee parking garage instructed me to "park on the side of the building in the visitors' lot." I had turned in my resignation not even 24 hours earlier, and already this was reality—I was no longer part of the family.

I said goodbye to the group of people that had taught me a lot about being a good journalist. When it came time to say goodbye to my boss, Teckerman extended his hand and wished me luck. I almost became emotional, and then I thought about why I was leaving and bated the moisture that had pierced my eyelids. Turning and walking through the doors of the L-shaped newsroom, I waved at my mentor Jeff—he passed me a note to "keep in touch."

Not having a job to go to was a strange feeling for me. For the past 10 years, I had always maintained steady employment, including summer internships and a stint as a tour guide at the Los Angeles Museum of Science and Industry in Exposition Park. Now I was on a mission: I would research, write and expose what I saw as a travesty of justice on the families whose children received a scholarship and emphasized athletics over academics with no real interest in taking advantage of the opportunities that a degree would afford them. Now the question was, where do I start? I had accumulated a modest savings account of $10,484.32 along with a Money Market account that had $26,342 as of my most recent statement. I would need some real capital in order to truly do a good job of researching this information to make a plausible attempt at writing a book that would address the issues, and more importantly, provide solutions to the issues at hand.

At home, I immediately began outlining what it would take to produce a book on this subject and the cost. The initial numbers were a bit overwhelming. By conservative estimates, I was looking at a minimum of three months on the road to conduct interviews, do research, etc. Not counting the cash flow need for superfluous things, my basic hotel, meals and fuel allowances would be at least $130.00/day. Multiply that by 90 days, and it totals $11,700. I had not factored into account the cost of phone calls, photocopying and the occasional milkshake. I came to the conclusion that some serious cost cutting was needed to produce a quality manuscript. The Money Market account belonged to both of us, and I knew that wasn't an option. This would be a tremendous gamble. Not only was my journalistic reputation on the line, my marriage would most certainly be stretched to the matrimonial limits as well. Sharpening my pencil, I decided to see if there was some place I could cut corners to save money. I could certainly cut some of my food allowance and lose weight at the same time, but I focused on the biggest expense of the budget, the hotel costs.

If I converted my truck into a motel on wheels that would certainly cut my costs and possibly give me a shot at pulling this project off. I could shower at the YMCA after working out and park the truck in the parking lot of shopping centers or on public streets where there wouldn't be night parking curfews. For safety's sake, I would have to park in areas that were brightly lit, but not so bright as to draw attention to myself. This idea was starting to sound a bit farfetched. Not only did I give up a promising career as a sports journalist, but now I was contemplating driving around the country, living out of the back of my five-year-old Chevy truck with a camper shell on the back.

I was now brushing up on how I would break the news to my wife Kim. I was certain she was expecting to come home and hear how I prepared my resume to re-enter the job market to write for another news publication.

When Kim arrived home, she handed me a form with the name of a personnel placement service and suggested that I give them a call the next day. I knew trying to make my pitch would be foolhardy at best, so I took the information and decided to table my "exciting proposal" for a more opportune time.

I went to bed that evening frustrated by the lack of opportunity to reveal my next assignment. I knew that if I abandoned the idea of going out on the road, I would probably experience a lot more frustrating nights.

Leaving home at 8:45 the following morning, I headed out to the local library to start my research on stories related to the subject of athletes and academics. I started searching back 15 years to get a feel for what information would be available. The *Los Angeles Times* had an extensive archive and I began with searching for the key words: athletics, academics, collegiate, sports and NCAA. The volume of information was so daunting, I decided to just get started and separate what was important from the things that were not germane to the story. I worked well into the afternoon and began photocopying and cataloging the voluminous information that would be the foundation for my book.

When Kim came through the door that evening, I pitched my idea about traveling around the country to write "the book." Initially, she sat quietly and listened to what I had to say. Then she stood up, turned around and walked out the front door and drove off. She didn't say a word, but her actions certainly conveyed everything that I needed to know about the support I would get from my wife. I was starting to feel like I was the only person who thought this was a good idea. When Kim returned, she had some take-out Chinese food and she said, "I can't go through this with you. Eat as much Chinese food as your heart desires, and when you are finished, if you still insist on continuing with this project, proceed on without my blessing." So that was that. Something that was truly important to me was just a "project" to her. I felt hurt and relieved at the same time. I sat the paper plate with the fried rice and orange chicken on the kitchen counter and grabbed my travel bag and began packing my clothes and personal toiletries. I told Kim that I needed some quiet time to think and I would call her in the morning. She didn't even look up at me when I headed out the door.

I checked into the local motel and felt the weight of 10 small pick-up trucks on my shoulders. It was a little more comforting to know that at least there were no children in our home. Who knows, maybe that's what made my decision to walk away from my job a bit easier.

The first night in the motel was as difficult a night as I had experienced in a long time. I'm sure I didn't get 20 minutes of sleep. If I didn't go back home by the end of the following day, I would reach a point at which I probably wouldn't be able to turn around. I tossed and turned all night contemplating what my next move would be. Was Kim giving me an ultimatum or was this her way of adjusting to the idea that I was not heading out to find a 9 to 5? My dad once told me that "Success has a thousand fathers and failure is an orphan." I felt the pressure to succeed had just been ratcheted up by a factor of 10. As night slowly began to transition into a new day, I gave up on the idea of getting any sleep and got started converting my plans into action. After all, if I was going to travel around in my truck, I figured I had better stop getting used to what a comfortable bed felt like.

In order to truly understand how I got to this point, I needed to go back to the very athletes who got me thinking about this delicate balance between getting a solid education versus chasing a dream of living the good life through professional sports.

* * * * * *

To truly understand the nexus of underclassman eligibility with professional sports, one has to go back to over 30 years ago when Spencer

Haywood, a college sophomore sensation out of the University of Detroit, was a star on the 1968 U.S. Olympic team in Mexico City. When the Olympics ended, he continued to play college basketball at the University of Detroit. After competing in his junior year at the University of Detroit, Haywood opted to sign a professional contract with the lesser-known American Basketball Association (ABA), which, unlike the National Basketball Association (NBA), had no rules against signing players that had not completed their NCAA collegiate eligibility.

After playing one year for the Denver Rockets, Spencer Haywood was offered a large financial incentive to switch leagues and accept an offer to play for the Seattle Supersonics of the rival NBA—which at the time was the more lucrative league to play in. Because the Supersonics did not acquire Haywood through the NBA draft, other owners in the NBA objected and moved to block the acquisition. Feeling that his right to earn a living through his acquired basketball skills were being violated, Haywood filed a suit against the NBA owners in federal court. A federal judge agreed with Haywood's position that the NBA's draft rules were improper because they did not allow for players who had a need to play basketball to earn a living—hence the "Hardship Ruling." The Hardship Ruling means that all an underclassman has to prove is that it would be detrimental for him and his family if he did not turn professional early. If no state or federal laws are being broken, a player could now enter the NBA draft straight out of high school, rather than wait until after four years of college competition had been completed. This 1971 landmark ruling by the U.S. Supreme Court became known as the Spencer Haywood Ruling. It was used by players like Michael Jordan, Isaiah Thomas, Magic Johnson, Kevin Garnett and Lebron James, just to name a few. A lot of the young players today have never heard of Spencer Haywood and do not care about his accomplishments. To them, it's all about the shoe deals and other endorsements, along with that large NBA contract.

Up until 2003, no one had seriously challenged the National Football League's position on underclassmen being drafted. Unlike basketball and baseball, football is a very physical contact sport, and it would be suicidal for a kid to want to suit up against mentally and physically superior athletes in a violent collision sport like football.

That all changed this past year when Ohio State running back Maurice Clarett, through legal counsel, got a federal judge to strike down the league's longstanding policy of not allowing underclassmen the right to participate in the NFL draft. The policy was that in order for a player to be eligible for the NFL draft, he must wait three years after his high school graduation date.

Clarett was the first true freshman in the school's history to start at running back. That same year, the Ohio State Buckeyes won the national championship. The following spring Clarett was accused of lying to campus police after he filed a theft report for items stolen from a car that was on loan to him. After an internal investigation, Ohio State suspended the freshman phenom, alleging Clarett had violated NCAA rules by accepting gifts and money, then complicating matters by lying to investigators.

Many insiders felt Clarett's federal court challenge was a move by him and his supporters to keep him from sitting out the suspension handed down by Ohio State. Whatever the reason for this bold move, U.S. District Judge Shira Scheindlin, in a 71-page opinion, ruled that the NFL was in violation of the Sherman Act and thus denied underclassmen the opportunity to earn a living. The NFL announced they would file an appeal.

Clarett was not the first athlete to consider challenging the NFL's ban on underclassmen.

In 1994, Florida State wide receiver Tamarack Vanover gave serious consideration to challenging the rule. One month before Maurice Clarett announced his decision to take the NFL to court (January 2004), I met up with Vanover for lunch in San Diego. Now after nearly nine years, Tamarack Vanover was nearing the end of his football career and didn't want to say something that could be misleading. He graciously answered my questions about why he elected not to challenge the NFL ruling back in 1994.

"I felt that I was ready to play at that level, but after flying out to Los Angeles and meeting with my attorney, we decided to hold off and play out my option with the Las Vegas Posse of the Canadian Football League (CFL)," said Vanover. So poorly received in Las Vegas, the team ended up playing their last two home games on the road. The Canadian Football League found out, like so many other leagues that have come and gone, just how difficult it is to compete with the NFL.

According to Vanover, someone has to be the first to pave the way so others can follow. "To me, the hardest part of anyone making it as young player coming out of college early is . . . can he handle the mental stress that they will put him through. For sure the veteran players are going to test him, and he will need somebody who is willing to take him under his wing and guide him."

After playing one season in Las Vegas, the CFL's Winnipeg Bombers acquired Vanover's rights in the dispersal draft as a result of the defunct Posse. The Kansas City Chiefs purchased Vanover's rights from the CFL and drafted him in the third round of the 1995 NFL draft. At the time of our meeting, Vanover was still hoping that some NFL team would be giving him one more opportunity to play. When I asked him what was next in his career path should his playing days with the NFL be over, he shrugged and said, "I might try to go back up and play in Canada."

* * * * * *

Shortly after joining the *Orange County Post* back in 1994, I got an opportunity to interview a player that elected to leave school a year early to be drafted into the NFL by the San Diego Chargers. I was sent down to do a story about the increase in football players whose ancestry was from the tiny Polynesian country of Samoa. After shaking his hand, I could see why this athlete was an exception to the college football players who stick around for the duration of their eligibility. Junior Seau was 6'3" and weighed about 220 pounds without an ounce of fat anywhere on his frame. Seau was a standout linebacker and destined to be an All-American out of the University of Southern California, and he opted to turn pro after his junior year in college. What made his story so special was that he was the fifth player taken in the draft that year. Most teams do not take a chance on underclassmen, especially when their first selection is in the top 10 picks on opening draft day.

When I arrived at the San Diego Chargers training facility, which was about a quarter mile from where the Chargers play their home games at Qualcomm Stadium (at that time it was called Jack Murphy Stadium), I caught up with Seau in the weight room where he was building onto those rock hard pectoral and deltoid muscles. It helped that we had the common bond of both having worn the Cardinal and Gold uniform (although he played and I watched). I found him to be very approachable. Most athletes who reach this level of super-star status require you to "kiss their ring" and something else before they will sit down and grant you a one-on-one interview. We immediately began by talking about people whom we had common friendship with, and it helped to break the ice for the questions I had constructed. Junior Seau came across as a very caring person and one who felt strongly about giving back to the community in which he grew up. He was raised about 25 miles north of downtown San Diego near the Camp

Pendleton Marine Base, and it was as if some of the tough character-building traits rubbed off on him. After a sparkling junior season in 1989 as the Trojans' leader on defense, Seau decided to roll the dice and declared himself eligible for the 1990 NFL draft. He had accomplished all of the goals he had set except for graduating from college. I asked him about that. Some questioned his decision to leave school early and labeled it risky, but not Seau and his supporters.

"It worked out for me . . . whether it's something that statistically is proven good for the student athlete? I doubt it. The stock was high, we took the gamble and my family and I discussed it, and it was something we wanted to do. Overall, it's not something that everyone ought to look into," said Seau. It was well past the time that he normally granted the media, and I could tell that he was eager to get back to his workout. I thanked him for the hour access at a time when I needed to prove to my superiors that I could pull off the big interviews. If I had to point to one defining moment for the idea to write on athletes and educational opportunities, I can say that it was that morning in the Chargers' weight room. Junior Seau had accomplished a lot. I couldn't help but sense he was still not comfortable with leaving school early, even though it worked out for him and his family professionally.

* * * * * *

The rest of my morning on my new quest was spent measuring the rear of my truck and finding a futon to sleep on while I traveled around the country. A discount mattress store was in the process of moving some of their inventory to make room for the new material, and I was able to get a good deal. Another sign, in my mind, that my decision to go out on my own and write a book was a good thing. It had been 24 hours since I had last spoken to Kim, and I decided to call to see if things had improved since our last conversation. My voice was quivering as I asked her how she was doing. Kim has always been good at hiding her feelings, but she didn't hesitate to let me know that I was in need of a good soul searching about who I really wanted to be. I was now becoming incensed at the thought that she was discounting my commitment to this very important issue. I realized that this was certainly not a cure for cancer or the answer to world peace, but it was my crusade, and I was now determined to see this to what ever end it would take me. What happened to richer or poorer? I could not believe she was not backing me on what I truly wanted to pursue to make me feel like a complete journalist. I took my marriage vows seriously, and I truly loved my wife, so I wasn't ready to put my marriage on the line for this cause. However, it was starting to take on that appearance.

Before heading east to begin my cross-country venture, I made a quick trip up to Palo Alto and Stanford University. Stanford is often called the Ivy League of the West and unlike the Ivy League schools on the East Coast, Stanford offers athletic scholarships. The Ivy League concluded long ago that a university had to decide whether or not they were fully committed to athletic excellence or academic excellence—rarely can one have both. Stanford was coming close to proving that postulate false. I wanted to interview the head coach of the football team that had just completed a dream season and came within a couple of big plays from winning the 2000 Rose Bowl.

When I would identify myself with the Orange County Post, people would return my calls. Now I was just Dan Christensen and it was going to be a lot tougher to get people to accept my calls and grant me interviews.

Fortunately, I was granted an interview with then Stanford Cardinal head football coach Tyrone Willingham. He has since moved on to the high-pressure zone of coaching up at none other than one of the elite programs in the country, Notre Dame. Driving up north on Highway 101, I was struck by the beauty of the trees and coastal beaches that made the trip up a paradox. Here nature reveals her innermost beauty along this peaceful stretch of road that winds its way up through Northern California, and yet I was headed for a time in my life where things weren't going to be as tranquil as the scenery in front of me.

Arriving in Palo Alto around 1:30 P.M., the casual, relaxed atmosphere on the campus affectionately called the "Farm" revealed why this setting is perfect for college studies. Students seem to stroll effortlessly from one building to the next with backpacks closely in tow. A young man walking in my direction stopped to give me succinct instructions on how to get to the athletic offices in the Arrillaga Sports Center. Arriving in the athletic offices overlooking the football practice field, I was impressed with a board honoring student athletes with a grade point average above 3.0. Ordinarily, this would not be hailed. Normally these would have been the National Championship awards and individual achievements perfectly placed at the entrance to the athletic building. Not that accolades should not be prominently displayed, but potential athletes are getting mixed messages when they see this on one hand and then are asked to maintain "acceptable" academic standards to remain eligible to participate in their respective sport.

I sat patiently just outside Coach Willingham's office as I checked my watch to confirm that the coach was running about 10 minutes late. This was a little bit surprising because I remember an article written in the *Los Angeles Times* about the Stanford coach emphasizing how he is a stickler for running on schedule. Recently jobless, I was in no big hurry, so the delay gave me a chance to go over my notes to prepare me for any contingencies. Minutes later, a thin but fit coach came out and greeted me with a warm smile and a firm handshake, profusely apologizing. I gave coach Tyrone Willingham a brief overview of what I was working on and how I felt he would be just the person to help me with connecting the dots between the commitment to athletes and their success after their playing days were over. Being an African-American coach made it all the more important because of his high- profile status coaching at one of the country's most prestigious universities. There is also a disproportionate number of African Americans who are affected by not taking advantage of the educational aspect of being a student athlete. I sensed his caution flag going up, because he was not sure what types of questions I would ask.

I started with what sets Stanford apart from the other schools competing in the Pac-10 conference and around the country when it comes to keeping the players focused on and off the field. Coach Willingham stated the first thing he insists on from his players is respect. "Once you can have mutual respect from and for your players, then you can begin to make things happen. I insist that each one of my football players takes advantage of the alumni association that this school brings and what it represents to the world."

Now it all made sense. If the school represents more than just the athletic program that it is working to build and nourish, then its athletes will take away more than just the cherished memories of playing on a team. If there is a choice between Stanford and a school with a good sports reputation, a person who is more concerned about his athletic future will probably pick "U of Jocks." That's not to say that this athlete will not get as good an education, but when he or she graduates, the doors will be wider for that student athlete from Stanford to walk through because of Stanford's reputation for academic excellence.

The interview was transitioning from cautious responses to now free-flowing discussions that resembled a chat session more than an interview.

Coach Willingham pointed out that "We are so conditioned to seeing the winning touchdown or the last-second shot to win the game, we have failed to also give equal attention to that player who stays after practice to work on sharpening his skills or the basketball player who is in the gym until midnight practicing that jump-shot."

As it turned out, he and I were born not very far from each other and we both agreed the way our parents were raised and the values that they passed on to us are key to the success and happiness that we experience. There was a time if a kid did something wrong in his neighborhood, he got into trouble with the neighbors who witnessed the folly and who weren't afraid to chastise him and then pass on the deeds to his parents for additional punishment.

Discipline is needed in order for today's athlete to master the skills of pursuing his college education and preparing for sports. It is also very difficult for a coach to be asked to win games or else face the consequences of losing his job. Adding to that pressure is the need to be sure every athlete brought into the program is indeed taking advantage of a free education—in this case, Stanford would cost a parent close to $125,000.

Concluding the interview, we sat and talked about how different things are today in sports as opposed to the way they were. Coach Willingham and I talked about the importance of religion and how it played a very important part in our upbringings. We both agreed a spiritual balance and belief in the Lord help a person handle the difficulties that life can throw your way. I really enjoyed the interview; in some ways it was like going to visit a friend I hadn't seen in years. I sensed sincerity about Tyrone Willingham's program and more importantly the true essence of what coaches should want and expect out of their student athletes. You don't read about athletes beating up girlfriends or agents paying players under the table on the "Farm." That's not to say that it could not happen, it's just that Stanford's approach to winning on the field and off is one that I think should be emulated. Stanford is internationally recognized as a leader in education and also has a basketball program that is expected to compete year after year for the Pac-10 Championship along with being ranked during most of the 2000–01 and 2003–04 seasons as number one in the country. Stanford has earned 87 NCAA championships in a variety of sports (second only to UCLA, which has won 91). This program convinced Tiger Woods to accept a scholarship to play on their golf team. If this sounds like a promotional for Stanford, it's because I looked at most of the schools around the country and I felt that this program exemplified the most well-rounded achievements in the classroom and in athletic competition.

Satisfied with the information I received from one of the top college football coaches in the country, I traveled back south to Los Angeles to tie up a few loose ends before I headed out on the road.

3

THE OMNIPRESENT
NCAA . . .

The NCAA is the official governing body for intercollegiate athletics. The acronym stands for the National Collegiate Athletic Association, but for some, it could mean "Nope Can't Accept Anything." The very initials strike fear and terror in the hearts and minds of many athletes, coaches and administrators. It was established in 1906 as a voluntary association to help govern intercollegiate sports and to establish and enforce fair guidelines written and voted on by member colleges and universities. The NCAA enforces a labyrinth of rules and regulations that are maintained at its headquarters in Indianapolis, Indiana. With over 1200 colleges, universities and affiliated organizations under its jurisdiction, the NCAA is the central entity responsible for establishing and enforcing the rules and regulation of fair athletic intercollegiate competition. It also negotiates lucrative television contracts and corporate sponsorships associated with NCAA member schools.

The NCAA strives to maintain the highest standards of academics and athletics through tough guidelines established through members of the association. It is one of the most powerful governing bodies in the country with the exception of the United States federal government. It's no wonder so many people quake at the thought of an NCAA investigation.

The NCAA's theme is "To Strive To Maintain Intercollegiate Athletics As An Integral Part Of The Educational Program And The Athlete As An Integral Part Of The Student Body." But at times this mantra has come in direct conflict with universities achieving their highest mandate, which is to educate above all else. To truly understand the NCAA as a whole, you first have to go back to how it originally came into existence.

At the turn of the 20th century, the game of football was becoming very popular in the United States. The game, which had its roots in Europe, where it resembled both soccer and rugby, was hailed as a sport that was too violent for the young aristocratic boys to play in the preparatory schools in England and Scotland. As Ivy League schools like Harvard, Yale and Princeton began to participate in the sport, a league began to form to adopt a set of rules to govern the game. There was no equipment used at that time to protect the players from injuries and as more and more schools became interested in participation, so too the number of injuries and deaths increased. In 1905, the game claimed 18 lives and 149 players were injured. The public uproar forced some schools to rethink the game, while others resisted changes. To offset legislation that had been drafted to eliminate the sport, President Theodore Roosevelt called for a committee to reform the game. The president (being a former student-athlete at Harvard) summoned representatives from Princeton, Yale and Harvard to the White House to discuss the game's future. After considering the public's concerns, United States Military Academy Captain Palmer E. Pierce suggested forming an association with other member schools to establish the necessary power to reform football. The Intercollegiate Athletic Association of the United States (IAAUS) was formed, and new rules were implemented to improve the game.

In 1909, with well over 70 member schools enrolled in the association, the IAAUS was renamed the current National Collegiate Athletic Association (NCAA). The biggest threat then and today is keeping its athletes under amateur status. Amateurism is defined by the NCAA as "one whom athletics is an avocation."

Although the NCAA is only officially concerned with participants in colleges and universities, its long arm has also reached out into the high school sectors and beyond. A high school athlete approached by someone offering tangible gifts for services involving an NCAA-sanctioned sport has a tough decision to make. Even though he/she is not yet enrolled in any college, accepting any such gift would jeopardize his/her eligibility to compete in college athletics.

Without a doubt, the most contentious fights between the NCAA and potential student-athletes are the net results from the guidelines that were established within the last 20 years to try and eliminate the embarrassing stories about athletes attending college for four years and not being able to read or write at a seventh grade level.

In 1983, under intense media scrutiny, the NCAA adopted a resolution called Proposition 48. This legislation, effective 1986, called for incoming freshman student athletes to have a minimum grade point average of 2.0 in 11 "core classes" in high school and score at least 700 points out of a possible 1600 on the Scholastic Aptitude Test (SAT) or 15 out of a possible 36 on the American College Test (ACT) entrance exams. Athletes who could not meet these minimum requirements were classified as Prop. 48 students, or "partial qualifiers," and were not eligible to play in their respective sports their freshman year. That meant they lost a year of eligibility and a real possibility that they would not receive financial aid. The athlete in question had to score high enough on one of the two requirements—GPA or SAT—to receive financial assistance. Needless to say, this touched off a heated debate that still rages today. While the NCAA was applauded for initiating tougher guidelines holding athletes to higher academic standards, many believed this was nothing more than a move to decrease the number of African-American students entering college. The standardized tests colleges and universities used to evaluate applicants for enrollment were viewed as biased against students who came from underprivileged environments, and therefore it was argued that the test(s) were not a true measure of academic ability.

In 1989, under intense pressure to modify the new mandates to improve the image of the NCAA and athletic educational reforms, the NCAA passed Proposition 42 at its annual meeting. It was designed to close what some members of the governing body saw as a loophole in Proposition 48. Remember, Proposition 48 still technically allowed those "partial qualifiers" to receive financial aid. Proposition 42 prohibited anyone who did not qualify as a freshman with a minimum 2.0 grade point average and 700 SAT or 15 ACT score from receiving any financial aid, be it an athletic or academic scholarship. It went so far as to ban a student from receiving financial aid who would otherwise be offered aid had it not been for the fact that he/she was an athlete who did not meet the NCAA Proposition 42 guidelines. In essence, it held athletes to even stricter financial aid standards than non-athletes.

John Thompson, then Georgetown University's basketball coach, was one of the most vocal critics of the new Proposition 42. Thompson, a former basketball player at Syracuse and a five-season player for the NBA's Boston Celtics, walked off the court in protest to the edict just prior to the Georgetown Hoyas' game against Boston College. To many African-American coaches and administrators, the introduction of Proposition 42 bolstered their belief that the issue of improving the educational standards was racially motivated. Those who opposed using the standardized test as a part of the qualifying criteria pointed to the concerns by the Educational Testing Service (which administers the SAT) that the test was in fact not suitable to be used in the "cut-off" manner in which the NCAA was applying it.

A major blow to those favoring the standardized tests was the Princeton Review Course. Developed by John Katzman, it is a tutoring program designed to help students prepare for the SAT and ACT, providing the students can afford to pay for the course. Many students from affluent backgrounds use the courses to improve their test scores. Once again proof students whose parents had money had an advantage.

In a July 4, 1989, *Los Angeles Times* article titled "Crash Course," reporter by Dan Le Batard interviewed Kevin Drexel, the executive director of the Princeton course in Beverly Hills. Drexel stated, "You give me anything other than a corpse, and I can coach them to at least a 700. It's kind of ironic. We didn't teach them any academic skills. We taught them test-taking skills applicable only to the SAT. These kids really aren't any smarter."

This was the kind of fuel opponents to Proposition 42 were looking for. Admission of proof there was a bias based on economic advantages. The following year at the NCAA convention in Dallas, delegates from Division I schools voted overwhelmingly 258–66 to support Proposition 42 with the exception that non-athletic financial aid be given to non-qualifier freshman (based on need) as long as the aid did not count against a schools' scholarship limits in football and basketball. It would only count against a schools' scholarship limit where the athlete was practicing with his/her team. This aid, based on need only, was small consolation to the opposition. Even with this goodwill gesture, concerns started to be voiced that some schools could exploit this situation and begin stockpiling players because the aid would not be counted against the school's athletic budget.

There was clearly a power struggle within the NCAA between the Presidents Commission and those who believed only the minority athletes were coming out on the short end of the stick. To understand the motivation behind the Presidents Commission, one needs to look back at its formation.

In the 1980s, as was the case in the very beginning of the NCAA, public concerns about the way colleges were running sports programs and the casualties left in their wake demanded a change. Instead of physical injuries and death, the problem was psychological and was manifesting itself in the form of athletes who spent four or sometimes five years attending a university without earning a modicum number of credits toward a degree. This scandal threatened the reputation of the NCAA and its chairman, Richard D. Shultz.

"The scope or even the existence of the problem no longer is relevant. The fact is that the public perceives college athletics to be in serious trouble. Perception has become reality in our case. We must do something to change that perception," said Shultz as he addressed NCAA members. In 1989, a commission was formed within the NCAA called the "Knight Foundation" to look into the matter and make recommendations to reform the student-athlete image that had taken substantial blows. This commission, empowered by a $2 million grant from the Knight Foundation (which has made numerous grants in journalism, education, arts and a host of community initiatives to improve the quality of life), called for the presidents of the universities to have a more active hand in deciding what the NCAA should do to put the "student" back into student athlete. The chairman of the foundation, James Knight, stated, "We hope this commission can strengthen the hands of those who want to curb the abuses that are shaking public confidence in the integrity of not just big-time college athletics but the whole institution of higher education." The Knight Foundation Commission on Intercollegiate Athletics came up with a plan that was called the "one plus three" plan. The commission, co-chaired by president emeritus of the University of North Carolina Chapel Hill, William C. Friday, and Theodore M. Hesburgh, president emeritus of the University of Notre Dame, issued three reports that helped to usher in the college and university presidents' involvement in the reshaping of athletics in the last decade of the century.

First, the plan called for presidential control in academic integrity, financial integrity and accountability through independent certification. To obtain this, the commission believed the NCAA member institution's trustees had to unequivocally back the reaffirmation of total presidential control over the running of athletic departments rules, finances and personnel. The commission also recommended the presidents should have control over the NCAA.

At the 1991 convention, in an address to NCAA members, NCAA Executive Director Richard Shultz stated, "I don't think this is just a shot in the dark for the presidents. I think they have genuine enthusiasm to see that important changes are made in intercollegiate athletics and that intercollegiate athletics takes its rightful position in higher education."

Armed with power to make sweeping changes in their hip pocket, the university presidents went on to form the Presidents Commission and began implementing what they perceived was their mandate to strengthen the NCAA's academic requirements for athletics eligibility, hence Propositions 48, 42, 16 . . .

The 1991 NCAA convention was a watershed year for college and university presidents. It was known as the Reform Convention. It was the first time that president commission reform measures were implemented into law by the NCAA members. The Presidents Commission began listening to the student athletes themselves. An NCAA Student Athlete Advisory Committee was set up to hear concerns from the athletes about any issues they wanted to speak on. The Athletes' two biggest concerns were more money for student athletes, and time demands on student athletes. To address the time demand issues the committee created the "20 hour rule." This rule limited athletes to 20 hours per week of competition or required practice time during the season. It sounded like a hollow ruling because if a coach asked a player to "volunteer" some time to the film room, what was that player suppose to say? No?

The cost containment legislation, designed to cut costs, ended up hurting the NCAA in more ways than one. The proposal called for a limit to coaching staffs and phased in a 10 percent reduction in scholarships. The limit in coaches' salaries set up something called a "restricted-earnings" coaching position. It was supposed to induce more graduate athletes to consider going into coaching. Essentially, a salary cap was placed on coaches that limited their salaries to $12,000 during the school year and an additional $4,000 during the summer. Coaches with varying years of experience filed suit against the NCAA for restraint of trade. This was a case that truly exposed just how much power the NCAA felt they had with anything to do with collegiate sports. It would be the equivalent of the National Football League telling the Tampa Bay Buccaneers to go out and hire first-year coaches for under $16,000. In May of 1995, a federal judge ruled in favor of the coaches and found the NCAA in violation of the Sherman Antitrust Act and lifted the earning restrictions. Three years later, the same Federal judge awarded $67 million in damages to the coaches, and the NCAA appealed the ruling. In 1999, the NCAA dropped its appeal and agreed to pay $54 million in damages to the plaintiffs.

This was somewhat condescending considering that one would be hard pressed to find anyone to take an administrative job at the NCAA with such a restrictive salary. The coaching positions being offered were targeted for the very same athletes who worked to bring in millions of dollars to the NCAA.

The Presidents Commission began drafting legislation to strengthen the academic integrity of the schools throughout the country. In 1993, the NCAA welcomed a new executive director, Cedric W. Dempsey. With new leadership, the NCAA Presidents Commission drew legal fire from various fronts as it forged ahead with more sweeping changes to the eligibility standards that were already in place.

In 1996, the commission re-shaped the initial eligibility standards by requiring a minimum 2.5 grade point average in 13 instead of 11 core subjects and a sliding SAT score based on the grade point average. Example: If a student had a 2.5 grade point average, he would have to score at least 810 on the SAT. If the grade point average was 3.0, this meant the student only needed to score 750. This was supposed to give students who worked hard to achieve high grades but were poor test takers an opportunity to still qualify under the new requirements now identified as Proposition 16. What started out in 1973 by simply requiring that an athlete earn a high school diploma and a 2.0 grade point average had come full circle and now administrators would need a Cray super-computer to determine which athletes qualified.

The tougher academic guidelines were definitely having an effect on some athletes. But was it working to improve the academic standards the Presidents Commission set out to achieve? Opponents felt it would be better to give athletes an opportunity to at least attempt to compete in the classroom even if they were not academically eligible by NCAA standards. One of those in favor of this belief is former USC basketball coach George Raveling. In an article written in 1989 by *Los Angeles Times* writer Mike Downey entitled "Raveling Takes a Stand Besides Thompson," Raveling is quoted as saying, "In 1984, the NCAA commissioned a study which revealed that had Proposition 48 existed back in 1977, 70 percent of the black athletes who by 1983 had graduated or were still in college studying, would never have been admitted into college in the first place."

Clearly both sides are interested in improving the standards of higher education among athletes—the breach is without a doubt a result of ideological differences. Some of the most contentious debates over the tighter eligibility requirements have come from those losing a year of eligibility due to the partial qualifier. Because partial qualifier athletes are not allowed to compete during their freshman year, that first year is lost. Some NCAA members considered adopting a resolution called Proposition 38, which would allow partial qualifiers to gain back that lost year (granting a fourth year), providing the athlete had completed at least 105 units toward a degree. Delegates at the convention initially approved Proposition 38, but after reconsidering the legislation, defeated it. It was a clear signal the Presidents Commission was transfixed on its own agenda. According to Bob Oliver, an NCAA executive, "Our legislation does not permit a non-qualifier to get a fourth year of competition back, unless they fit into the category of a student with a diagnosed learning disability."

The NCAA found even adjusting for athletes with learning disabilities proved to be a lightning rod for lawsuits. In 1995, Chad Ganden was a standout swimmer at Naperville North High School in suburban Chicago. The 17-year-old senior and state swimming champion had been diagnosed with a learning disability, which put him at odds with the NCAA for early-recruiting visits to potential colleges. The problem stemmed from classes Ganden took in high school that were basic courses taught at a slower-than-normal pace. Ganden's parents disagreed with the NCAA's position and filed a federal lawsuit charging the NCAA with discriminating against learning-disabled students. In a letter sent to the NCAA in May of 1994, the Department of Education Office on Civil Rights warned the NCAA that it was "concerned" that its eligibility rules may violate section 504 of the Federal Rehabilitation Act.

Ganden met the grade point average and the required SAT scores, but the NCAA ruled his 3.5 core credits he earned during his freshman and sophomore years were unacceptable to meet the 13 core classes as required in the tripod eligibility process. The NCAA granted Ganden a partial waiver in a landmark case for student athletes who have been diagnosed with learning disabilities. Ganden signed a letter of intent to swim for Michigan State University. However, the waiver did not allow him to compete his first year in swimming competitions, only to practice. In a 1996 *New York Times* article written by Tarik El-Bashir entitled "Learning Disabled Man Gains N.C.A.A.

Victory," Ganden's father, Warren Ganden, said, "The whole program is absurd. He is allowed to practice for five hours a day but is not allowed to compete. It doesn't make any sense. Practicing for five hours a day will not interfere with his studies but competing eight times a year will? They don't know sports and they don't know disabilities."

The number of students who are identified as learning disabled is on the rise. In a 1994 survey, about 3 percent were identified compared to the 1 percent back in 1988. With the increase in the number of students identified as learning disabled, this issue will have to be addressed more and more in college athletics.

The concern to ensure that qualified athletes enter the universities of their choice took a turn that almost was a public relations catastrophe. Tougher academic legislation was being passed with every annual NCAA convention. When the 1994 Presidents Commission focused on the creation of an "initial-eligibility index" that tiered grade point averages with test scores, things became very tense with the 3,000 members Black Coaches Association (BCA). The new guidelines were affecting African-American athletes by far more than any other group. Athletes from disadvantaged communities had trouble getting past the minimum required SAT and this more than anything else made the BCA grow incredulous about the Presidents Commission's promise for improved academics for everyone. This, along with the defeated legislation to increase the number of grant-in-aid scholarships from 13 to 14, caused the BCA to consider a boycott of men's college basketball in 1994. The decision to boycott was shelved.

The cornerstone of any organization is its ability to enforce the rules and govern according to the laws it enacts. The NCAA is committed to enforcing the laws that have been meticulously voted on for over 90 years. According to Walter Byers, former executive director of the NCAA from 1951 to 1987 and author of *Unsportsmanlike Conduct*, "Whatever our problems in achieving an honorable workplace for college athletes, enforcement is the bedrock upon which the NCAA's edifice is based—from a cramped hotel room in Chicago with one part-time administrator and one full-time secretary, to a multimillion-dollar profit distribution center with about 230 full time employees authorized as of 1994–95."

By the 1960s, colleges were becoming very competitive in a game of "one upsmanship." The need to use the school's name to promote athletics was as hot a race as the "space race." Wealthy university donors were lining up to line the pockets of top-recruited athletes from all over the country. No longer was it as important to brag about academic achievement as it was to be able to say that your alma mater was the national champion in the popular revenue sports of football and basketball. Winning coaches wielded as much clout as high-ranking government officials.

It was not unusual for freshman football players from underprivileged neighborhoods to drive up in brand new cars that were purchased by school boosters. The trick for the boosters was to make sure that the banks that financed the transaction would not become complicit with the chicanery. The sad commentary is that if it had not been for the students' athletic abilities, these same financial institutions would not even offer these kids' parents a cup of coffee. When was the last time an athletic administrator or booster proposed funding an inner-city library or school with computers or textbooks? Yet when it comes to competing to see who will represent a conference in the next big corporate-sponsored bowl games, here comes "big bank Hank" with a fat wallet and a pat on the back.

This rush to sign big name high school prospects from rival schools knew no boundaries. The parents of these athletes were offered everything from relocation expenses and jobs to outright kickbacks, just to have the opportunity to bring a top prospect into the school.

A very well known NFL football player (who wishes to remain anonymous) was courted so heavily in high school that the university he ultimately signed with was bold enough to offer a monthly check to his family, which was definitely not part of the "official" grant-in-aid that he should have received. Each month, a stipend was mailed to this ballplayer's family home. When the ballplayer left school and entered the NFL draft, a family member actually called the university to find out why the payments had stopped coming.

As television contracts for NCAA events continue to stream skyward, the ever-increasing pressure to win will undoubtedly raise the stakes on the recruiting war.

Today, it is much more difficult to catch these elaborate schemes, in part because the NCAA was somewhat neutered by a landmark case that all but stripped the organization of its powers to truly govern college athletics.

The case involved a prominent college basketball coach by the name of Jerry Tarkanian. He was known by his nickname of the "shark." Coach Tarkanian was a figure who had developed a strong bond with inner-city basketball stars and to look at him, you could easily mistake him for some-body's dad or uncle. He was often seen biting towels on the bench to help calm his nerves during ballgames. He also happens to be one of the most winning coaches in collegiate history. In 1968, coach Tarkanian was hired by Long Beach State to coach its men's basketball team. Early on, rumors surfaced Tarkanian was providing athletes whom he recruited with free airline tickets and had not executed proper Letters of Intent, the legal docu-ments every athlete must sign to contractually bind them to a school, thus ending the recruiting process. Whether these rumors were founded or not, the NCAA launched an investigation to determine what, if anything, had happened. Under intense pressure from school officials, coach Tarkanian decided to leave Long Beach State and take a job at the University of Nevada Las Vegas (UNLV) which, according to the NCAA, was already being investi-gated for infraction violations. According to Tarkanian, the NCAA just picked up its investigation and followed him to UNLV. After reviewing the findings of the NCAA's investigative reports, the Infractions Committee levied a two-year suspension on Tarkanian from coaching UNLV basketball. The NCAA decided to use a "show cause" provision in the rules book that demanded UNLV suspend the coach or else be in direct contempt of the Infractions Committee's authority and face possible consequences. The university stood firmly in opposition to the rulings and refused to suspend coach Tarkanian.

This was the gauntlet being thrown down and now it was time for the NCAA to demonstrate just how much power it truly had in enforcing its written laws. The suspension would have allowed coach Tarkanian to remain as an active faculty member in the physical education department, but that was unsatisfactory to the university and especially to Tarkanian. Lawyers for Tarkanian argued that the NCAA had denied Coach Tarkanian his constitu-tional rights to due process. UNLV sought to find fault with itself and assume the brunt of the penalties without admitting any wrongdoing on the coach's part, but the Infractions Committee wasn't buying it, and so the case dragged on through the state of Nevada's judicial system and ultimately ended up on the floor of the United States Supreme Court. In December 1998, the U.S. Supreme Court ruled the NCAA was not governmental or "state" action, and therefore it did not need to answer to federal due process standards. In other words, the NCAA due process issues would have to be resolved in the Nevada state courts which had ruled the NCAA did in fact violate Tarkanian's constitutional right to due process. Now UNLV was told that it did not have to adhere to the suspension handed down by the NCAA. This was a major blow to the authoritative power the NCAA felt it had to enforce its laws within the states.

This signaled the beginning of the change in power always assumed by the voluntary organization. Twenty years after the first legal battle began, the NCAA decided to drop its case against Tarkanian and UNLV. A negotiated settlement was reached between the NCAA and university officials which amounted to UNLV being levied a one-time suspension from playing in the 1992 NCAA basketball tournament. In 1998, the NCAA finally agreed to pay coach Tarkanian $2.5 million in a settlement. In the end, there were no winners. Tarkanian had to personally battle over 20 years one of the most tenacious organizations in college sports. The University of Nevada Las Vegas had to air out some embarrassing laundry, from which it still is trying to recover. Most importantly, the NCAA was exposed to legal vulnerability that continues to challenge its true authority when enforcing existing laws related to collegiate athletics.

By 1972, another key issue facing the NCAA was an initiative to bring balance into the way colleges promoted women's athletics. The United States Congress voted into law landmark legislation that banned any discrimination on the basis of sex (either academically or in athletics). That decision, which was part of the Federal Education Amendment Act, became known as Title IX, and it had far-reaching effects on interscholastic athletics. Specifically, Title IX states: "No person in the U.S. shall, on the basis of sex be excluded from participation in, or denied the benefits of, or be subjected to discrimination under any educational program or activity receiving federal aid."

Prior to enactment of Title IX, women's athletics was considered secondary to the men's programs. Budgetary considerations for women were considered after the men's programs were complete. With the exception of crew, golf and tennis, it was not likely for universities to field a competitive team of women, and this was keeping in tradition with the NCAA. The question of whether or not a school could develop a women's athletic program and remain financially solvent seemed to constantly rear its ugly head. Title IX changed all of that, and statistics showed a growing interest in women's sports.

From 1971 to 1973, there was a 57 percent increase in the number of women participating in intercollegiate athletics. There was a strong push for administrations to turn the women's programs over to women athletic departments to run. No longer should mostly male-dominated athletic directors have complete control over how the budget would be divided when it came to funding competitive women's sports.

Leading the charge for change was the Association for Intercollegiate Athletics for Women (AIAW). In 1973, the Association began holding championship competition for women in basketball, volleyball, swimming, track and field, golf and gymnastics. The competition was in direct conflict with the NCAA, which was seeking to bring women's athletics under its jurisdiction.

The AIAW interpreted Title IX to mean whatever the colleges devoted to their overall collegiate athletics, half should be contributed to the women's programs.

The sporting events dominated by men felt that if their programs were responsible for bringing in the revenue, then they should at least have some say in how the revenue would be divided. The AIAW would counter and say that if the same dollars were spent in female athletics, it would be just a matter of time before there would be parity in male and female sports.

Title IX governs the overall equality of treatment and opportunity in athletics while it gives the respective schools the flexibility to choose the sports based on college enrollment, budget restraints, popularity of sports, and the ratio of men to women. Whether women chose to play football or not was not at issue here, but rather, are they given the same opportunities and afforded equal facilities.

To determine whether federally funded schools are in compliance with Title IX, there are three primary rules to consider.

1. Financial assistance must be rewarded proportionally based on the number of male and female athletes.

2 If there is under-representation by a sex, that institution should demonstrate program expansion responsive to the interest and development of the abilities of that sex.

3 Any benefits, opportunities and treatments given to all athletes competing, must be equivalent, but not necessarily identical.

The AIAW, armed with these federal guidelines, set out to gain the same media attention that was afforded the men's programs. In a showdown with the NCAA, the AIAW filed a lawsuit against the NCAA charging it with anti-trust. Specifically, the AIAW felt that the NCAA used its extensive resources to promote NCAA women's championships and the networks were then naturally drawn to NCAA sanctioned sporting events, thus undermining the AIAW's efforts to gain the all-important television contracts that are essential to compete on a level playing field, both literally and figuratively. In the cases where men's athletics foots the bill, women's competition is and should be an integral part of the athletic program because it teaches women the same important virtues. Teamwork, leadership and competitive spirit should not be limited by gender.

* * * * * *

No one can argue the point that sporting events are more exciting to watch live than on television. The sheer excitement from the number of spectators in the stands gives the game an added dimension. Hence "home court" advantage is predicated on the vociferous buzz that cannot be duplicated in any other form. Today, it would be hard to imagine any great sporting event that would not be globally televised. The strange truth is that at one time, there was a strong resistance to televising collegiate sporting events.

Around 1939, before World War II, when most homes did not have a television set, the NCAA felt televising games would be detrimental to the live gate receipts that represented the majority of the revenue. If spectators were shown the game for free, there would be no incentive to go out and pay to watch it. The end of the war saw an explosion in the popularity of the television and its effect on viewers in this country. Broadcasting sporting events was unheard of and the NCAA wanted to keep it that way. In 1950, concerned members decided to form a Television Committee to study the effects that television, or the "electronic free ticket," as it was called, would have on attendance.

The Television Committee, chaired by University of Pittsburgh President Thomas J. Hamilton, concluded television was potentially a boost to collegiate sports, provided the NCAA could control the product. The Television Committee also proposed a moratorium on live telecasts during the 1951 season to test certain market areas and "black-out" dates to do comparative analysis.

The declining attendance in 1952 led to the Television Committee's decision to pass a plan that limited live television events controlled and directed by the NCAA. No school would be allowed to monopolize the airwaves, so a once-a-year limit was placed on all schools. The plan ignored the powerful schools that dominated in the revenue sports and geographical locations. 30 years later, this decision would come back to haunt the NCAA.

By 1954, the best of both worlds was finally coming into view. Television ratings and gate attendance for college sports were headed for new highs. This was the beginning of a 20-year increase. The television networks were lining up to bid for the right to broadcast the weekly college football games. The plan passed in 1952 saw NBC plunk down $1,144,000. In comparison, by 1982, the development of cable networks had pushed the asking price by the NCAA to $31 million. The allure of television was beginning to change the way universities marketed themselves to prospective students. No longer was a game just a sporting event, but a marketing tool to showcase the schools and their respective degree programs. The two-minute halftime pieces the universities produced were straight out of Madison Avenue. This pushed the stakes to compete in Division I sports to another level. Get in the game at all costs. Colleges had tasted the sweet success of sports on television and were not about to turn back.

The concerns of television broadcast suppressing gate receipts were long behind the NCAA. But the lucrative television contracts by the major networks were creating new challenges the NCAA would soon learn about.

With the networks anteing up tremendous sums of money to broadcast college football and basketball, a subversive current was now threatening to break the long-standing authority the NCAA had enjoyed with member schools. At the heart of the issue was the way in which conferences were sharing the revenue from televised games. The schools that had long-standing traditions of winning championships weren't eager to give the non-prowess schools an equal share of the conference take.

Schools like Penn State, Michigan, USC, Alabama, Oklahoma and Notre Dame, long on winning tradition, were now poised to entertain proposals for independent television contracts, which would remove obligations to the NCAA and respective conferences and thus negotiate to appear on any network that could deliver the best offers. But there was a problem with this plan.

The NCAA television plan usurped the notion schools had their own authority to strike deals independently from the governing power of the NCAA. Upstart cable companies were eagerly courting the colleges to "enlighten" them on the millions of dollars being lost in regional sales from local retailers.

To make these deals a reality, the College Football Association (CFA) was formed to coordinate the efforts of those member schools that felt the need to create a new way of doing business. Led by Chuck Neinas from the Big 8 conference, Reverend Edmund Joyce of Notre Dame and Fred Davison from the University of Georgia, the CFA spearheaded the charge to change the way football would be viewed on Saturday afternoons.

This new way of doing business was a direct challenge to the authority and leadership of the NCAA. If successful, the new CFA could undermine the delicate balance college conferences had developed over years. With reduced revenue, the non-profit NCAA would be nothing more than a paper tiger trying to enforce the rules it had established over the 70-plus years of existence.

But if the NCAA was now fighting for its collective life, the CFA had some formidable hurdles to cross as well. For one thing, it was an organization that was new to the game of negotiating TV rights and, more importantly, it would need to sign the powerhouse schools in order to promote the credibility needed to get the major networks to the bargaining table.

The NCAA's offensive strategy was to secure the best television contracts in the history of college sports. This would leave the CFA out in the cold.

Like championship prizefighters, the NCAA and the CFA took turns diminishing each other's position in an attempt to win support for their collective organizations. Statistics on numbers of viewers and financial projections flew back and forth to support each of their positions for control of the coveted television rights.

ABC and CBS had already secured television contracts with the NCAA, leaving NBC as the odd person out. The CFA—recognizing that there were hard feelings by NBC toward the NCAA—set out to develop a partnership and draw the national interest that it needed to convince the schools who were "still on the fence" in deciding whether to stay the course or usher in a new era.

Now that the partnership of NBC and the CFA was well under way, it was time for the CFA to call in their markers and check off what schools would commit to the new merger.

In December 1981, concerned that the CFA was fracturing the NCAA's solid membership support, the NCAA called a special convention. The convention promised to address the concerns core members had about issues: the growing number of schools in Division I determined to get a piece of the television pie and the number of grant-in-aid scholarships that was burdening some of the universities that struggled financially to keep pace with their fellow schools.

After the NCAA held its special convention, schools that were leaning towards joining the CFA turned and overwhelmingly got behind the NCAA and the deal it signed with ABC, CBS and TBS.

The wind was let out of the sails of the CFA. Feeling like the NCAA had torpedoed them, the CFA sought legal recourse and filed a federal antitrust lawsuit. The University of Georgia and the University of Oklahoma were identified as the plaintiffs in the case and the case was brought to trial in Oklahoma City, Oklahoma. At issue was whether or not the NCAA, through coercion, blocked the CFA's ability to generate substantial profits by denying them valuable business property rights. By controlling the number of games broadcasted and limiting the teams' number of appearances, did the NCAA set out to raise prices by limiting the output of the product?

The NCAA argued TV controls increased competitiveness and balance by lesser schools by increasing publicity, morale and fund-raising activities. This was supposed to bring parity back into the collegiate ranks. However, Judge Juan Burciaga decided these controls did not lend themselves to competitive balance. The NCAA lost on appeal to the 10th Circuit in Denver, Colorado. In June 1984, the case moved all the way up the ladder to the Supreme Court, which heard the arguments.

In a 7–2 vote, the justices ruled in favor of the CFA and found the NCAA, through its members, did in fact restrict trade as well as violate a number of antitrust laws due to limited output of televised games.

Ironically, absent in these legal proceedings was the mention of improving the quality of the people who were ultimately responsible for bringing in the revenue. This was supposed to be about student athletics, but it was lost somewhere beneath the millions being tossed around in those smoke-filled conference rooms.

The student athletes' rights to a fair education were being jeopardized by the demands put on them through this collective bargaining. Athletes are merely pawns on a grander scale of political chess, completely manipulated by administrative financiers.

Like two Bengal tigers determined to gain control over the territory, both the CFA and the NCAA came away from their legal entanglements bloodied. Almost twenty years later, it is hard to say who suffered the most. The legal defeats over the years have left the NCAA vulnerable to another power struggle by disgruntled athletic directors looking to boost revenues by negotiating independent deals without NCAA approval—thus rendering the NCAA weaponless. Conversely, the CFA has never really recognized the full potential that it sought to achieve at its inception.

Notre Dame certainly fired a hollow tip at the CFA in 1990 when it quietly broke ranks from the CFA and signed a deal with NBC. The move ultimately cost the CFA approximately $35 million.

In a nationally distributed article in NCAA News, June 26, 1994, the executive vice president of Notre Dame, Reverend Beauchamp, stated that student athletes' compensation of grant-in-aid is fair compensation for participating in collegiate athletics. According to Reverend Beauchamp, "20 or 30 years after a playing career, the enduring memory for most athletes will be of the competition and camaraderie—not the cash."

Contrary to what Reverend Beauchamp wrote in his article, most student athletes whom I interviewed over the last seven years have more memories of lost opportunities and a sense of being exploited by a system that has enjoyed billions in revenue. For those athletes who dedicated their college days to the game more than to the classroom, the everyday reminders of struggling to make ends meet will never be eclipsed by those memories that the Reverend describes.

My game plan called for me to first drive to Boston, Massachusetts, then make my way back to California, zigzagging from state to state while conducting my interviews and choreographing the research with the final product my book.

Even though Kim and I had a few days to talk about my schedule and when I would be in touch with her, we spent the last few days in disagreement about my resignation, or as she called it, "my mid-life crisis."

Kim was not used to living in an unstable relationship. Growing up the only child, her father was a CPA for Price Waterhouse and her mom was a traditional stay-at-home mom.

Kim grew up in the Northern California community of Sebastopol, just west of the lush wine country of Napa and Sonoma. Her parents were always in attendance to all of her extracurricular activities, from piano recitals to high school cheerleading. Having children was something she wanted and I convinced her to wait until we were able to afford a house in a better community, one with a better school system than the one in our district.

I think Kim saw this latest venture as a way in which I may have reneged on some of our previous plans. I needed a little time and space to prove to her I was right all along on this one. I attributed the difficulty of not sleeping the last three nights prior to leaving to being overcome by the excitement of launching off into what I considered to be a very important endeavor.

I departed from California on a crisp spring morning heading east on I-10. The send-off was as cool as I had anticipated from Kim. Traveling across the California desert into Arizona and New Mexico, I kept the car in the fast lane and made very good time. As nightfall descended upon me, a severe thunderstorm greeted me at the New Mexico/Texas border town of El Paso. The fatigue that had initially threatened to delay me by several hours had long passed, and now I was determined to make it to my first planned stop in Fort Stockton, Texas. Second thoughts about the project were starting to creep in when I received a phone call from a man name Tony Segretti. He was my first scheduled interview the Monday after I arrived in Boston. Segretti was the father of a 15 year-old tennis player who was ready to step up and play on the pro circuit. Apparently Segretti had called to confirm our appointment and he accidentally called my old number at the Orange County

Post. My former boss, Jim Teckerman, spoke to Segretti and tried to convince him that it would be detrimental to his daughter's career if the interview took place. I convinced Segretti to at least listen to what I had to say, and if after that he still wished to cancel, I would understand. It was clear that my former boss was not taking my resignation and this project as graciously as I hoped he would. My conversation with Segretti was proof that Teckerman had every intention of shutting me down. I would have to wait until I reached Boston to see if my first subject would back out.

Pressing through state after state, I made it through the East Coast within four days of my departure from Los Angeles. Since I had the whole weekend before I needed to make it to Massachusetts, I decided to take a detour and spend the day up in Cape Cod on Martha's Vineyard.

The drive up I–95 through Connecticut and Rhode Island was coming back to life. A view of the leaves reappearing after the lengthy winter in New England, were now coming into focus. The last time I had been up this way was fall, the foliage had been so explosively red, orange and yellow, it almost looked unreal. I really adored the juxtaposed rock formations that seemed to protrude out like God had intended them.

I arrived in the town of Falmouth around 1:45 PM and was a bit embarrassed to discover that Martha's Vineyard was an island out just beyond the Nantucket sound.

I parked my car in the ferry's parking lot and elected to take my bike across and tour the island by bicycle. The afternoon was cool and overcast with the forecast calling for the possibility of light showers that evening. I thought the best approach was to begin riding away from the ferry landing and just "explore." About 15 minutes into my ride, I came across a posted sign that said "Gayhead" with an arrow indicating to follow that road. Immediately, my thoughts shifted to John F. Kennedy, Jr., who was killed 18 months earlier along with his wife Carolyn and her sister, Lauren Bisset. Reports stated the trio was headed to John's cousin's wedding. Their plan was to land at Martha's Vineyard to drop off Lauren, who was visiting for the weekend, then continue on to Hyannisport where the wedding was to be held. I suddenly found myself determined to make it to Gayhead, situated on the southwestern side of the island. As a child, I had visions of being an airline pilot. After college, I saved enough money to actually take flying lessons, and on more than one occasion, found myself inside a stratus layer of clouds on the verge of falling prey to vertigo. As the Bible scripture says,

"There but by the grace of God goeth I." John F. Kennedy, Jr., was born 17 months after my birthday, and although I never came close to understanding the nobility and fortune his family possess, I still felt like we were kindred spirits as I went out to the bluffs where he fell and paid my respects to a fallen hero, his wife and his sister in-law. The bike ride was a true delight as I cruised up, down and around the beautiful countryside. Homes were marked with posts that read "Zone and Plot" as opposed to the traditional number and street name. Forty-five minutes into my ride, it dawned on me that I was not sure how far I had ventured out. After a few near misses, I finally decided to stop and ask someone. A nice elderly woman informed me that I was quite a distance from Gayhead, perhaps as far as 12 to 13 miles. By now I was not only winded from the bike ride, but was beside myself at the thought that I was not even half way there. Nevertheless I persisted. By now, a light rain was beginning to fall steadily as I continued to press onward toward my destination. The steeper the hills, the more determined and buoyed I became. The ride past beautiful seaside cottages was amazing . . . as if they were positioned like a Norman Rockwell painting. Onward I rode past countryside landscapes with rolling hills and golden ponds. It absolutely took my breath away.

The area had once teemed with Native Americans whose presence was palpable to me as I surveyed the majestic fields stretching out to the Atlantic. As nightfall was beginning to approach, I contemplated calling over to the ferry landing for a taxi ride back to the dock. I had been riding for over an hour and a half, and I knew that whatever lingering strength I had in reserve would surely be consumed by the ride to Gayhead. Now lurking deep inside my innermost thoughts was the sign I had just passed indicating 23 miles back to the ferry landing. It would be 23 miles of steep inclined hills that would dispel me of the grandiose misconceptions I may have had of making the return trip by bike back to Indian Point. Approaching Aquinna, the town next to my destination, I passed by a descendent no doubt of the original settlers. He greeted me as I rolled onward on my road bike heading past the local police and volunteer fire station. As I pulled up past the lighthouse on my right, it all became very clear why this tranquil ride that began innocently enough was etched deep inside of me and why I was drawn to this hallowed spot on Martha's Vineyard. In front of me was the most peaceful sight that I had witnessed in a long time. The air was damp and the initial phase of a classical "Nor'easter" was beginning to form. The Atlantic was very calm, almost paradoxically calm given the forecast for the area.

The small snack kiosk that was just up ahead looked out of place. The rotating illumination of the beam from the lighthouse pierced the gray low cloud cover that had now blanketed the island. I sat there quietly for a few minutes and prayed.

There are some things that inextricably tie us together as human beings. There is an understanding that we are on this earth but for a relatively short period of time and some souls are called home before others. Nevertheless, it is a call that all must answer at some point.

I was exhausted and lost. I prayed to the Lord for strength to make the long journey back to my point of disembarkation. By now, dusk had overtaken day and the recrudescent sun had finally slipped below the horizon. I pedaled with more vigor, continuously extinguishing the thought of calling a taxi. Having no discernable light other than the occasional headlight from a passing motorist to navigate the trip back, I pressed onward and rode with determination. With every steep hill that I climbed, weariness began to settle into my legs making the return trip that much more difficult. Darkness was all around me, and the thought occurred to me that I had not seen any cars passing for quite some time. Could it be that I was on the verge of making a full circle that would bring me back to Gayhead? It was not a pleasant thought, but it did energize me to find something that looked remotely familiar to me from the outbound leg of this journey. As I approached a junction point, I noticed a couple of cars headed in a direction that appeared like it might get me back to the center of town. The sun had set to my left so I knew I was headed north. As I began to merge with the flow of traffic, the soft raindrops falling on my head were a reminder that I had left my riding helmet back in California. Tired, dazed but not broken, I rode into the landing point overjoyed that my spiritual mission had finally concluded. Safe, secure and now on the voyage back over to the main land, I realized that this was an epiphany—a metaphor for this entire book-writing tour. Faced with difficult odds, could a recalcitrant spirit summon the courage and the determination to see the project to fruition? I would not have to wait very long to find out.

4

THE PROFESSIONAL
VORTEX

The allure of professional sports has reached an all-time high in this country. Professional athletes earn more money than almost any other occupation.

Billionaire H. Ross Perot once said that if the United States Congress allowed the North American Free Trade Agreement (NAFTA) to pass, the giant sucking sound that you hear would be the loss of jobs headed south of the border.

We are now starting to hear a different sound that makes a whoosh. That sound is coming from the number of teenage ballplayers who are going over and around the colleges and universities in this country en route to the promise of financial bliss.

However, the sad truth is that only an infinitesimal number of players successfully make that leap.

The odds of a high school football player making it into the NFL are 1 in 6000. Even if he makes it into the NFL, the average player's career is 3.4 years. You say you want to dunk over Shaq, or take Allen Iverson "to the hole," statistically speaking, the likelihood of that ever happening is pretty small—perhaps as low as 1 in 10,000. Undoubtedly, there is a long list of young athletes that feel they are the 1 in that coveted group.

Daryl Dawkins, a.k.a. "Chocolate Thunder" entered the NBA draft out of high school back in the early 1970s and made an impact early. He defied the odds and played for eight seasons. Dawkins was the exception, not the norm.

Although high school lottery players like Kevin Garnett, Kobe Bryant, Jermaine O'Neal and Tracy McGrady have made impressive contributions to their respective teams, they all, to a certain extent, lost a valuable part of developing as young men.

Los Angeles Lakers coach Phil Jackson was a guest on the pre-game Laker Report on KLAC 570 Radio (01/12/04) speaking about the number of high school athletes coming into the NBA each year when he stated, "the NBA is for men, not for boys. By not going to college, they [high school NBA draftees] miss out on the life experiences that college life offers." Lebron James, the Cleveland Cavaliers' newest high school graduate top draft pick, could be the exception and not the rule. Nike signed James to a shoe deal before he ever played a minute in the NBA. Lebron James will have the best financial and legal team assembled. That does not happen with most young athletes trying to make it out of high school.

Ever since Spencer Haywood successfully sued the NBA on its rule against drafting underclassmen, it has been illegal to deny anyone the right to apply for any job, providing they are not violating other state or federal employment laws.

With a sheet of paper and a fax machine, an 18-year-old kid can transmit a letter to the NBA headquarters in New York, declaring himself eligible to be drafted. That's exactly what a high school player out of a San Fernando Valley high school did.

Ellis Richardson was a 6-foot-4 guard who averaged 21 points a game for Polytechnic High School, but he really didn't turn many heads with his streaky shooting skills and limited defense. "Ever since I was little, I've wanted to be like Magic Johnson dribbling the ball up court," said Richardson. The Los Angeles Times first reported the story in April of 1998 because Ellis Richardson sought the draft without even being listed as one of the top 100 high school players in the state of California.

Richardson joined the ranks of thousands of high school athletes who have limited options because they lack the grades and test scores to qualify for an NCAA scholarship. The logical progression is usually for athletes to enroll in junior college to improve their grades and get a chance to sharpen their skills against players in some cases with "marginal" talent. The NCAA will allow high school athletes limited range with exploring options for professional opportunities providing they do not sign with an agent or declare themselves eligible for the various professional drafts. As an example, a high school athlete may compete in a professional competition provided he/she does not accept any monetary or compensation for participating in the event.

Somehow Richardson was convinced that he was an NBA-caliber player. Unfortunately, that encouragement was coming from his family and a person who was all too familiar with lost NBA dreams. Richardson was hanging out at the Stonehurst Recreation Center where he enjoyed playing pick-up games when he was befriended by a man name Red. Taj "Red" McDavid is someone who, like Richardson, decided to declare himself eligible for the NBA draft after his senior year in high school in 1996. Red was a guard from Palmetto High School in Williamston, South Carolina. When the NBA didn't draft him, he ended up bouncing from tryouts to Anderson Junior College. Red's high school basketball coach, Lanton Williams, wasn't at liberty to comment specifically about Red McDavid's situation at McDavid's mother's request. She was concerned that the negative publicity could possibly hurt her son's chances at getting his opportunity to play in the NBA. Coach Williams did say that he felt that it was a mistake to risk the NBA chance. "I see maybe two kids per year in our league who are good enough to play Division I college basketball", said Williams. "They all think that they can, but they can't—as for the NBA . . .zero."

People had warned Ellis Richardson that the same fate awaited him, but he wasn't hearing it. After playing in a local all-star game, Richardson scored five points, which ranked him 16th among scorers in that game.

"I'm not letting anyone take my dreams," says Richardson. "The NBA just appeals to me too much."

Red convinced Ellis Richardson to file that request with the NBA. Four years have passed since this application was filed. To the best of my knowledge, neither one ever played a minute of collegiate or NBA basketball. The reality, sad though true, is that for every Kevin Garnett, there are thousands of Ellis Richardsons and Taj McDavids. The high school lottery continues, egged on by stage parents hoping against hope that their son or daughter will defy the almost insurmountable odds and provide the financial windfall that could transform their lives.

The NBA hasn't exactly been exonerated from some of the blame for so many teenagers seeking employment on one of the most exciting world stages. Millions of dollars are being spent to market the product in such a way that it beckons anyone with a dollop of talent to test the waters of the draft.

Teams have personnel scouts all over the world in search of the next great player—desperate to keep another team from beating them to the "diamond in the rough." When you throw in a few less-than-scrupulous sports "reps" filling some of these vulnerable kids' heads with the notion of expensive cars and big bank accounts, you have all the elements in place for emotional anguish and endless hardship.

The slogan "NBA Action Is Fantastic," may help put more fans inside the arenas, but it also puts false hope in the minds of many who may blow their chances at a good education and end up as low-skilled labor. It is analogous to a fishing vessel trolling the open waters in search of the big fish in the sea. Invariably, you are going to suck in some small ones that are unsuspecting. It is an unfortunate byproduct of the process.

* * * * * *

Teams eager to grab players at an early age are finding that it is often at a steep price. In June of '99, the Dallas Mavericks drafted a high school basketball player from Chicago who was a ward of the State of Illinois.

When Leon Smith was five his father left, and with his mother now consumed with her own personal hell, Leon and his five siblings were shuttled to various foster homes. Despite connecting with some of the people in charge of his well-being, Leon retreated to the inner sanctity of his personal thoughts. He refused to connect with most of the other young boys in the foster home and only felt comfortable communicating with his brother Jerry.

Separated from their sisters, the boys lived at a foster home called Lydia Home for almost eight years. They began adjusting to the regimen that was so comfortable that they fought and won a court battle against their mother when she sought to regain custody. As Leon approached the age of 13, the state ordered him to move to a home called Sullivan House for teenagers, again throwing him into an unstable situation. His brother Jerry, being a year younger, remained at Lydia Home.

The solitary confinement that Leon had experienced over the previous eight years caused him to slowly drift to a place where basketball would be the only ray of hope for this young teenager to ascend from the abyss.

Leon's basketball talents were apparent, and high schools from all over the city of Chicago were interested in recruiting him for their program. Confused and socially insecure, Leon bounced from Mount Carmel, a Catholic high school, to Martin Luther King High, a powerhouse in basketball. His skills sharpened, and colleges and professional teams from coast to coast coveted him. In order to thwart the attention from so many interested parties, Leon agreed to play for the legendary Coach Tarkanian at Fresno State University. That promise became as vaporous as some of the other decisions that Leon Smith was making as once again agents and hangers on helped to change his mind as Smith continued to scan the horizon for someone he could have faith in.

By now, the 6-foot-10, 235-pound player had decided not to go college, and he felt the only option available was to declare himself as a candidate for the 1999 NBA draft.

It is customary for teams interested in drafting players (particularly players being drafted in the first round) to have potential draftees go through a series of workouts so that all of their strengths and weaknesses can be properly evaluated. Fearing that other NBA teams might show interest in Smith, the Dallas Mavericks opted to draft Leon Smith in the first round sight unseen. What made that move particularly puzzling is that all first-round draft picks are given a guaranteed salary. This means that with rare exception, every player drafted in the first round will be paid whether or not he plays one minute in an NBA game.

The Dallas Mavericks had to trade two second-round draft picks to the San Antonio Spurs in order to have the opportunity to select Smith in the first round.

Hearing the news in Chicago, Smith was ecstatic and he celebrated with some of the people who knew him from childhood. In a very short period of time, he had gone from being a ward of the state to one of the most sought after basketball players in the country.

As predictable as bad news and taxes, the troubles of Leon Smith were ignited after being assured of a three-year, $1.45 million contract and guaranteed money for being drafted in the first round. Not many high school kids could handle a million dollars without proper mentoring, let alone a young man who has bounced from one state-sanctioned boarding home to another.

As a condition of drafting Smith, the Dallas Mavericks had asked and gotten assurances that Smith would agree to play in a developmental league like the Continental Basketball Association or play in Europe to sharpen his skills and mentally develop during his first year. Smith later denied having agreed to play in the developmental leagues and he begged Mavericks' coach Don Nelson to keep an open mind and at least allow him the chance to make the team and become an impact player immediately. Nelson relented and agreed to allow Smith to report to training camp six weeks later.

It didn't take long for trouble to arise as Coach Nelson's son, Donnie Nelson (an assistant coach), got into a shouting match with Smith after demanding the young temperamental player run some extra conditioning sprints. Smith stormed off the court, ignoring the instructions and leaving the team with a dilemma about what to do with a player who was extremely talented but clearly lacked the discipline to handle the rigors of an NBA lifestyle.

Now Leon Smith's agent, Dan Fegan, was feeling the pressure to convince Smith to reconsider playing in the developmental leagues during his first year. Leon responded to Mr. Fegan's request by firing him. Now that Fegan was no longer in the picture and the Mavericks were unable to legally enforce the prearranged deal that they initially struck with Smith, the Mavericks pursued efforts to trade Leon Smith—with no takers.

Leon Smith was once again in a situation that he was all too familiar with—alone and uncertain of his future.

A broken relationship with a former girlfriend left Smith so despondent that he rammed his former girlfriend's mother's car. After spending the night in jail for that infraction, Smith agreed that he was in need of psychiatric evaluation.

Dot-com magnet Mark Cuban purchased the Dallas Mavericks and attempted to salvage the young Smith's NBA career, but in the end, Dallas had to cut its losses and negotiate a buyout settlement with Leon Smith. The irony was that as Dallas was severing ties with Smith, they were simultaneously signing the enigmatic Dennis Rodman—a situation which lasted all of one month.

Ten months after the Dallas Mavericks released Leon Smith, the St. Louis Swarm of the International Basketball League gave Smith his release after he averaged seven points and nearly eight rebounds in only three games. Smith did not play in his last game due to personal reasons. The once proud high school player who felt that he was too good to play in the developmental leagues was now being rejected at that level as well.

Where does the sanity stop and the insanity begin? For young players like Leon Smith, it is a curse more than a blessing that their physical stature is an invitation to be exploited by so many who only have their own interest in mind. It is extremely difficult for a young kid who has both parents at home to help guide him through the difficult decisions related to professional sports, let alone a kid with no one but the State of Illinois and a small, caring contingency to fall back on.

The amount of media coverage focused on teams that win championships and the financial windfalls associated with the winners is creating a predatory appetite to devour any and everything that stands in the way of the crowning victory. How else do you explain why teams are willing to take a young person who is ill-equipped to manage a convenience store and put him in charge of managing millions of dollars plus enough pressure to cause a stock broker to grimace.

There has to be a point where as a society, we wake up and say no more. No more teenagers in professional sports unless they are being chaperoned by their parents or legal guardian.

* * * * * *

In order to begin to understand this rush to send young athletes into the higher echelon of professional sports, we need to go back to a period of time when young sports fans were wide-eyed hopefuls, practicing the jump shot, serve and volley or the leaping catch in backyards all across America. Our parents were supportive, but tempered our exuberance with a reminder of how it was important to enjoy playing the game and to "just have fun." We knew that the difference between good and great was clearly discernable. No matter how good you were, you understood that there were others who could play just as well if not better.

Then came the advent of cable television and high-priced sneakers, and suddenly the structure of sports changed. The race to find young, gifted athletes took on a whole new meaning. Almost overnight, parents of gifted high school and college athletes were inundated with the promise of highly paid contracts and instant fame and fortune if their kids would just put more effort into their game. Stories about athletes foregoing their senior year in college and opting for the draft are incessant. The NBA is brazen enough to even draft kids out of high school. Most high school students are not quite mature enough to handle living on their own in an apartment, let alone adapting to the rigors and pressures of a career in the NBA. There are a few players who come to mind who were able to make the leap across that vast chasm. Tracy McGrady, Kevin Garnet, Jermain O'Neal and Kobe Bryant are but an infinitesimal small number who can claim a partial victory in this effort. I say a partial victory, because we see the legal entanglement that Kobe Bryant is currently facing and at the time of this book's printing, we are uncertain of Bryant's future.

Money can make up for certain shortcomings, but the advantage of financial knowledge that a student athlete can acquire by going to school cannot be taken for granted. I know that I am making this much more simplistic than it is; financial hardships and the need to "strike while the iron is hot," have to be considered. When Tiger Woods opted to leave Stanford after his sophomore year, he made a conscientious decision to leave a nurturing academic environment for the high-profile, high-profit earnings of the Professional Golfers Association (PGA) tour.

Ironically, Tiger's father, Earl Woods, had to make a similar decision on whether to continue his education at Kansas State University or leave school for a shot at playing professional baseball for the Kansas City Monarchs of the old Negro Baseball Leagues. Earl chose to remain at Kansas State and later he became an officer in the U.S. Army. Obviously their circumstances were quite different, but it underscores the point made earlier—the need to take advantage of potentially high-earning sports contracts before this ephemeral opportunity disappears. In the case of Tiger Woods, his earning potential had reached a point where it would have almost been foolhearty to ignore.

Stanford has been in the same location since 1874 and I'm sure it will be there when and if Tiger decides to resume his studies. It is important to note that highly intelligent family members and advisors surround Tiger Woods. Also, Tiger had already established himself as a top athlete in his sport. There is no draft in the PGA, taking away a lot of the risks/uncertainties that are associated with the NBA & NFL. Golf happens to be a sport that is based on an objective score. Tiger already knew what score he could shoot on a professional golf course.

This is not always the case with other athletes who are looking to abbreviate their education in search of the "big dollars." The pressure from family members to leave school and declare themselves eligible for the draft of their particular sport is often too overwhelming to refuse. Athletes who come from lower income communities that face financial hardship on daily basis are able to identify more with the professional ballplayer who comes into their living room on television than they are with educated working professionals in society. The teacher or the accountant isn't projected in front of millions of viewers. Our society puts a higher premium on sports, therefore, the salaries commanded receive headline news. Often the parents of these athletes are without college experiences themselves, therefore they have no gauge to measure or determine what is best. More and more professional athletes, even after overcoming insurmountable odds, are locked in bitter lawsuits with their sports agent or financial planner because of poor or fraudulent advice on money matters has been given. I will be discussing this subject in greater detail in the chapter on sports agents.

With a solid education, athletes can discern between substantial investment advice and the underhanded ponzi schemes or "charitable organizations" that are devised to subjugate unknowing participants. Examples of such deals will be detailed in the next chapter.

In years past, parents acted as the rooting section with a hug and encouraging words when their kids' team came up short. It was also clear that before playing sports, schoolwork had to take priority over everything else. Coming home with a bad report card meant the bat and glove stayed up in the closet until the child demonstrated sincerity back in the classroom. No one talked back to the teacher for fear of the repercussions with the burly vice principal or physical education instructor.

Recently, there appears to be a parental shift. Parents see their athletically talented offspring as commodities to be used to reap financial gain at the opportune time.

There are certainly exceptions to the rule, but these exceptions are few and far between. Freddie Adu became a professional soccer player at the age of 14. John McEnroe became a professional tennis player at age 17. Tracy Austin won the U.S. Open at the age of 16. Muhammad Ali became the heavyweight champion of the world in boxing at age 21.

For every Austin, Ali, Adu, McEnroe or Woods, there are tens of thousands of athletes who never got their names on the front page of the sports section of the newspaper.

Parents are at times inadvertently their kids' worst support group. There is an inherent bias that blinds them to their kids' shortcomings and weaknesses. To illustrate this point, in 2001, there was a T.D. Waterhouse investment commercial that featured former NFL great Calvin Hill and his NBA superstar son Grant Hill. The commercial shows Grant giving a little kid named Bobby pointers and encouragement to help him improve his basketball skills. Little Bobby is missing shot after shot with Bobby's mother cheering him on. Suddenly Bobby's mother looks at Calvin and says, "I'm thinking about finding an agent for Bobby!" Calvin exclaims, "AGENT? What Bobby needs is a good retirement plan."

Parents see something in their youngsters that most others fail to notice. By not being honest with your child or yourself, a parent may deny opportunities that may not present themselves again.

A parent's unfulfilled desire to live out aspirations to be successful in sports is transferred unfairly to the next generation, manifesting itself in the local community park and recreation leagues. Parents often engage in verbal and physical altercations over a kids' sporting event.

In a Boston suburb, a disgruntled father was charged with fatally beating another parent at a hockey rink. According to the Middlesex County District Attorney's office, Thomas Junta, a 42-year-old truck driver with no previous criminal record, confronted Michael Costin, who was acting as a referee during the play of a youth hockey match. Because of what Junta (pronounced Zhun-tah) perceived as rough play by the 10-year-old sons of the two fathers, Junta shouted from the stands to Costin to stop allowing the "body checking" and fighting. A short time after the match was over, the 6-foot-2, 275-pound Junta began assaulting the 5-foot-11, 170-pound Costin as he left the rink. After being ordered out of the facilities, Junta returned and slammed Costin onto a concrete floor which caused Costin to become brain dead almost instantaneously.

Now charged with manslaughter, Junta pled not guilty and got 10 years in prison. The final result is two families torn irreparably because of some rough housing by 10-year-old kids.

Parents have become so violent at youth sporting events, it is now mandatory in several states for parents as well as the youngsters participating in youth leagues to sign a promise not to verbally or physically abuse the players, officials or other persons participating/viewing these events.

This is little consolation for Michael Costin, the victim in this brutal assault.

The impetus behind a sharp rise in such violence can be directly linked to the billion-dollar sports industry that is tied to athletic scholarships, lucrative salaries and the need to brag to others about our kids' athletic accomplishments.

What kind of message is sent to the young people when they look up in the stands and see parents nose to nose over silly calls during a game that in the overall context of things, is insignificant?

There are a lot of good people who dedicate their lives to coaching baseball, soccer, football and basketball. Unfortunately, not enough of those stories make the headlines. For every story about a parent who becomes unglued or a coach who exercises poor judgment, we should be equally ready to report about the unsung heroes who give of their time and resources without giving it a second thought.

For some parents, coaching is a way to assure their child gets to play regardless of their level of talent. There is the burning question of when to put into the game the child who is lacking in talent. Should everyone play, risking the chance that someone could make a mistake that costs the team a victory? Should coaches take the position that if you pay to play, everyone plays, regardless of talent level? Participating in sports competition will teach kids more about teamwork, sportsmanship and fair competition, values that will stay with them long after the cleats are hung up for the last time. This is with out a doubt the foundation for positive and successful futures in or out of sports.

Parents, as coaches or spectators, need to remember it is just a game. Children are impressionable. They want to emulate what they see. The fundamentals of good sportsmanship and not winning at all costs should be taught and stressed much more than how to throw a curve, shoot a jump shot, or score from a corner kick.

The urge to leave school or forego the college education will always be a challenge for most gifted athletes. The money is too enticing not to at least give some consideration to it. The common denominator that many athletes who have won championship rings state is that long after the money has be spent, the title of Champions always stays with you. To a certain extent, that is how the educated think. Long after the wealth and the material things grow old, education is something that can never be taken away.

PART II

THERE ARE NO
FREE LUNCHES!

I spent the weekend finding my bearings in Boston. I had been to the city on numerous occasions to cover the great Laker / Celtic basketball match-ups, but then my assignments were clear. Now I had to fly by the seat of my pants. It had been three days since the Martha's Vineyard bike ride, and the soreness that I had been expecting, turned out to be negligible.

I had briefly checked in with Kim the previous evening and got the impression she was starting to come around and realize that this wasn't some "scheme" I had conjured up to keep from sending my resume to the local job procurement agency.

I hustled over to Cambridge where I met Tony Segretti for lunch. He was tanned and slender with a thin mustache in his mid 40s. "You have 10 minutes, that's it," said Segretti.

Taken aback by his introduction, I agreed, and we began talking about the Junior Circuit.

"I know there are a lot of temptations that my daughter can fall into, but believe me, I am not just throwing her out there like some piece of meat. She has one of the best coaches in the game and we are making sure that she studies five hours a day."

I wondered if they were rushing his daughter, Lisa Segretti, into competition too soon against the best in the world, particularly since Wimbledon was just three months away.

"I can tell you this, Lisa will be number one in the world before her 18th birthday, that you can print in your book," said Segretti. She was just three years away from that target date. I had to ask this next question, which I saved until the end of the interview.

"Is there any truth to the rumor that your daughter is using anabolic steroids?" Pushing back from the table, Segretti pointed his finger and said, "That's nothing more than lies by Lisa's competition to undermine her hard work. If I see one word about her being on the 'juice' in your book, I will have my attorney slap you with a libel suit. According to my watch, you got two minutes more than you were supposed to get."

As expected, the interview ended. I tried to explain I have to ask those types of question, but the protective father wasn't hearing it.

The rest of the week was spent talking to students and administrators on both Harvard and Boston College campuses. Most of those who were interviewed wanted to either speak anonymously or they gave generic answers like, "yeah, I think there is a problem with student athletes getting privileges that the rest of the students fail to receive. They are pampered beyond belief." A female coed at Boston College spoke enviously about players' training table and the type of food the players received, saying, "Steaks, tossed salads and desserts spanning the length of a board room table. Yeah, I wish sometimes I could enjoy that when I sit down to a tray with pizza and bland fish sticks."

Later that afternoon, I began calling old contacts at the Boston Globe, looking for stories that might help me give some insight to the subject of student athletes and the insatiable desire to play professional sports for a living. As I scrolled through hundreds and hundreds of pages of information on this antiquated piece of equipment called a Gideon 900, countless stories that had been written on the subject were showing up with leads either too old to track down or memories conveniently starting to fade on specific details. Using the Gideon, I was able to view stories from as far back as 1984. I cataloged everything by dates and publication source. The research was slow and methodical, but I wanted to be thorough. The articles kept surfacing one after another. This story was going to be tough to get my arms around. Photocopying everything remotely related to the subject of professional sports and educational tie-ins, it didn't take long for me to build up a sizeable file.

After five days of research and interviews with a few high school coaches and athletes, it was time to wrap up a few loose ends and continue the journey toward my next stop, Connecticut.

The bicycle that I had toured Martha's Vineyard with was locked up underneath the Carpenter Center for Performing Arts on the Harvard University's campus, or so I thought it was. It was a cold Friday evening and I was preparing to pack up and head south. As I drove up the street toward the Performing Arts Center, I knew right away that something wasn't quite right with this picture. Shocked, saddened, violated ..any of these emotions would not have explained one tenth of the way that I was feeling. I could not quite figure out how the bike could have been removed from the bike rack. When I purchased the bike I had invested in a Kryptonite lock and the salesman in the store assured me that it was next to impossible to steal the bike with that type of lock on it. Well I guess he was right about the lock; it never relinquished the tire that it was attached to.

I decided to forget about the formality of walking over to the police station to file a theft report. It wasn't like I was going to be headed for the turnpike and look up and see someone riding it. I had just purchased the bicycle six months earlier so the personal theft was starting to feel like a root canal.

South down the Massachusetts Turnpike, I placed that dreaded phone call to my wife Kim. I knew that it was going to give her something else to worry about and perhaps prompt her to say "I knew you shouldn't have gone on this trip."

After the phone rang for the third time, I was beginning to think that perhaps I could delay this conversation for another time when I heard her voice whisper a soft "hello."

5

SECRET AGENT MEN

Riches certainly make themselves wings; they fly away as an eagle toward heaven.

—Proverbs 23:5

The legal representation of athletes is a relatively new profession that has grown to be one of the most sought-after occupations in sports. Where team general managers and owners once scoffed at the notion of someone representing a player in contract discussions, it would now be considered financial suicide for an athlete to go into salary negotiations without an experienced legal and or financial consultant.

The best way to describe an agent is by its definition (according to Merriam-Webster's Ninth Collegiate dictionary): "a means or instrument by which a guiding intelligence achieves a result." Trying to determine the best person to achieve said objectives is one of the most important decisions an athlete will have to make. Because it is rare that a person is ever in the position to sign a professional sports contract, the privileged few should weigh all of their options.

The media are drawn to the details and are willing to give the specifics about how much and for how long. Because athletes are considered public figures, their financial information is there for the public to comment on.

If you listen to the sports talk radio shows or read the letters to the editor in the local paper, you hear a great deal of frustration over player salaries being blamed on athlete's agents. Often, fans feel agents are more interested in getting the players the biggest contracts and if the team or the game suffers, too bad!

Agents are only doing what they are being paid to do and that is to make sure that management pays their client "fair market value" for their client's skill level.

An agent's leverage over management is only as good as the player that he/she represents. Ballplayers realize early on they need someone who has a feel for the game and where it is going, as well as a working knowledge of how sports and big business coexist.

It wasn't long before sports agents had to negotiate contracts with team owners and with corporate management who wanted the star athletes to help sell their product. Teams only pay so much for a talented player, but Madison Avenue is where the real payday is.

An agent can make or break a career in an instant. For example, Lebron James, the newest basketball phenom out of high school, has taken his God-given talents on the court and converted them into a mega payday in endorsements. James' reported $90 million shoe deal with Nike made his earnings on the basketball court seem modest.

An agent will also receive a percentage of a player's salary, typically 5 to 10 percent of the player's base salary. Agents make the real money in signing up with corporate sponsorship.

It is not by chance that a lot of the high draft-pick players contact an agent like Leigh Steinberg. Many agents seek the most for their clients, even if that may hinder the ability of a team to sign other talented players. But Leigh Steinberg views negotiations as a win-win proposition. In his book *Winning With Integrity—Getting What You Want Without Selling Your Soul,* Steinberg takes the approach that "There are two winners in every negotiation: You and Your Opponent."

His way of thinking goes beyond just the contract that is currently being negotiated and looks much farther into the future at potential deals that will be much more lucrative than the contract at hand.

What measure does Steinberg use to gauge athletes who will be the next marquee sports figure?

"I look for an athlete who understands good fundamental values. Living in a community where people care for each other is a value which will stand the test of time when everything else fades," said Steinberg.

When we think of sports communities and states that produce talented athletes, not many states can boast the same level of success Florida has had in producing top-quality collegiate and professional football players. During the 1980s and 1990s, the state produced six national championships in football.

If athletes are subject to crossing the line and veering off the moral compass heading, then the same can be said about sports representatives where lucrative contracts are at stake.

It was no surprise when a sharp-dressing sports agent, William Black, set up shop down in the Southeast Conference and began a recruiting campaign.

For some athletes, poverty and despair were their neighbors. Anyone who drove a fancy car and wore expensive clothing definitely grabbed their attention.

The Florida ballplayers knew William Black as "Tank," and by 1998 his company, Professional Management Inc., was one of the biggest sports management companies in the country. Tank's client list was impressive; NFL all-pro defensive end Javon Kearse of the Tennessee Titans, Jacksonville Jaguars running back Fred Taylor, NBA superstar Vince Carter, and NFL wide receivers Ike Hilliard and Reidel Anthony. Tank used this list to entice other players to sign on with his agency and more importantly, convince these athletes to believe in his investment strategies.

Tank preyed on young athletes' financial naiveté to lure them into what federal prosecutors claimed was nothing short of bilking millions of dollars in fraudulent schemes and activities. Using middlemen to recruit athletes for his agency, Tank would illegally slip money to collegiate athletes. NCAA rules ban athletes from taking anything not offered to the entire student body of that university.

Upon accepting the cash disbursements from Tank's agency, the athletes would in turn sign over their representation rights to Tank. Then Tank negotiated tens of millions of dollars in sports contracts.

In May 1999, the National Football League Players Association (NFLPA, the league's players union) filed a complaint against Tank, accusing his company of paying players under the table. In August 1999, the NFLPA's disciplinary committee revoked Tank's agent license for three years. Shortly after the NFLPA took action against Tank, he filed suit against the NFLPA claiming its actions were racially motivated. An interesting charge because the NFLPA's president, Gene Upshaw, is also an African American.

What set in motion the torrid federal investigation was not in the form of cash payments, but a brand new white Mercedes Benz driven by an outstanding college football player who was tabbed to be drafted in the first round of the 1999 NFL draft.

After the University of Florida won the 1999 Orange Bowl game, defensive standout Jevon Kearse was spotted driving a brand new automobile on campus. Kearse was still a student enrolled on scholarship so this was in direct violation of school policy. The athletic director, Jeremy Foley, contacted the University Police Department, which had already initiated an investigation into the allegations that some of the football players had in fact received sums of cash from sports agent William "Tank" Black.

By now, the trap had been set and all of the players who thought they had a future in professional sports and would be financially set for life, were about to find out just how much those college perks would end up costing them.

After Tank negotiated multi-million dollar contracts on behalf of his clients, federal prosecutors set out to prove Professional Management Inc. (PMI) abused the players' trust by investing in a series of Cayman Island off-shore companies and elaborate securities schemes to defraud its clients of $12 to 14 million.

It is not uncommon for professional athletes to enlist their sports agent's advice on investments. However, it is unusual for athletes to give their agent total access to their salaries and bonuses. The U.S. Attorney's office documented six transactions from July 1997 to February 1999 that prosecutors claimed showed proof Tank moved earnings from his clients' accounts into his personal bank account.

The Securities and Exchange Commission (SEC) conducted an investigation into a company in San Diego that in 1996 tried to develop a board game—a trivial-pursuit-type game that centered on great accomplishments of African Americans. The developer of the game sought exposure by negotiating player endorsements from PMI clients, in exchange for his free shares of stocks. SEC investigators claimed that Tank (in some instances without his clients' knowledge) took the free shares of stocks and turned around and sold them back to his clients for values greater than the stocks were worth. When some of the players were made aware of what had happened, they demanded their money back, which was returned to them from funds that had been established in Cayman Island off-shore accounts. Essentially, players were paid back with their own money.

Philadelphia broker Michael Chappel said William "Tank" Black instructed him to invest New York Giants wide receiver Ike Hilliard's $1.1 million bonus check into seven highly secured mutual funds offered by reputable investment portfolio companies for Hilliard's retirement.

Chappel told investigators that two weeks after he had set up the investment accounts, employees of PMI instructed him to liquidate the accounts and withdraw the funds. Chappel went on to explain why this was a "horrible idea" and that his client would incur severe penalties for early withdrawal. It was alleged that Black used these funds to set up a Cayman Island title loan company. Promising 20 percent returns on their investment, Tank Black convinced players to put money into what was determined to be a pyramid or ponzi scheme.

A pyramid scheme is set up so that money invested by new members is used to pay out dividends to earlier investors. The system continues until there is no longer an influx of capital, at which time the scheme collapses and the newest investors are left with nothing.

Because these athletes did not have the financial wherewithal to discern solid advice from get-rich-quick schemes, they trusted the person who negotiated their very first professional contract. College-aged players' financial naiveté and trust is understandable, said Richard Berthelsen, NFLPA general counsel. "Consider yourself at the age of 21 or 20 talking to someone who by all appearances is a very successful businessman. You see the limos he's riding in and the private jets he's flying in. They say to themselves, 'Look how well he seems to have done. I've never even seen this kind of lifestyle before; he's my man,'" Berthelsen said.

Arizona Cardinals linebacker Johnny Rutledge summed it up by saying Black "took advantage of guys who didn't have knowledge of money at the time. They always used their physical bodies to make money, but they didn't know how to manage it."

Out of all the clients that PMI burned, no one was hurt more financially than Jacksonville Jaguars running back Fred Taylor. From the witness chair in a Gainesville Federal Courthouse, Taylor testified that William "Tank" Black essentially stole millions of dollars from him.

During an emotional testimony, Taylor stated, "Your client was clearly the one who robbed everyone blind. He handled my money, and he did whatever he wanted to do with it—and now I don't have it." According to prosecutors, Taylor lost nearly $3 million.

In February 2002, William "Tank" Black was found guilty of conspiracy to commit wire and mail fraud, conspiracy to commit obstruction of justice and conspiracy to defraud the government.

This was the latest sentence because prior, in June 2001, William "Tank" Black pleaded guilty to money laundering and was sentenced to six years imprisonment in a Michigan courtroom for helping convicted drug dealers transfer more than $1 million in cash into offshore Cayman bank accounts.

Johnny Rutledge summed it up best when he said, "Tank was a guy who I trusted like a father. I was really hurt by it."

Red flags should go up, especially when it comes to someone else controlling the checkbook. According to Leigh Steinberg, "the real key is to never sign over power of attorney, which is the right of the financial planner to write the checks directly out of the player's account. That is a practice fraught with potential for fraud. Even if executed with perfect discretion, it doesn't give the athletes any skills in terms of self-management of his money. It omits the teaching and learning processes."

Sports agents usually consider a number of factors when deciding to represent a player who they feel will go on to a meaningful career after sports. According to Leigh Steinberg, "a good agent looks for someone who understands that he (the athlete) has a responsibility for his own actions. That is the type of person who not only is going to be successful in sports, but someone who can prepare for a second career from the very beginning."

In 1997, a financial planner in San Diego appeared to be led astray by lucrative contracts from professional sports. It had all of the similar circumstances to PMI. Pro Sports Management International, owned and operated by John W. Gillette, Jr., represented professional athletes including (then San Diego Chargers) Miami Dolphins linebacker Junior Seau, Dallas Cowboys safety Darren Woodson, Washington Redskins Stanley Richards and former San Diego Padres pitcher Greg Harris.

To help create a high level of trust, Gillette took advantage of athletes' strong religious upbringing by conducting prayer sessions and bible study. "Gillette had an effective marketing tool," said Bob Johnson who worked briefly for Gillette, whose son, Tampa Bay Bucs quarterback Rob Johnson, was defrauded $150,000 by Gillette.

John Gillette, a former Shearson Lehman stockbroker, bilked his clients out of approximately $10 million. He commingled athletes' money with non athletes' money. Through a series of proposed real estate ventures, Gillette convinced investors that he would put their money in AA-rated, tax-free bonds to be used to finance construction of a building planned for the use by the Drug Enforcement Administration. He even went so far as to steal City of San Diego stationery and forge the signature of the head of financial services for San Diego, California.

Gillette promised his clients a 50 percent return on their investment through his Impact Investments. Though a series of San Diego real estate developments did make money, his clients, some of whom he convinced to turn over power of attorney to him, never saw a dime. Promising to invest in a water park in a suburb of San Diego called Poway, the only people to get wet were Gillette's clients. One athlete plunked down $500,000 and never even got a receipt.

Gillette enlisted the help of Elaine Terrones —a licensed stripper who served as a key assistant. Allegations swirled and Terrones took off with records after the operations closed. According to the district attorney's investigator, there was evidence Terrones may have transferred money into a Cayman Island tax haven.

Gillette pled guilty to 37 counts of grand theft and one count of forgery and was sentenced to 10 years in state prison.

For every John Gillette and William Black, there are many other highly ethical and honest sports agents and financial planners who handle athletes' high-end income without absconding with their trust or their hard earned money. One solution is to not turn over total access of their income to anyone.

No amount of legislation will change the hearts of people who deliberately seek to take advantage of others who lack the background of financial investing. Looking at the markets today, with top corporations like Enron, WorldCom and Imclone, even the brightest minds are not immune from being stung by investment fraud.

The University of Florida is trying to keep agents from improperly contacting players by hosting a sports representation day on campus. Sports agents and financial representatives are invited to register with the school to introduce themselves to potential professional prospects in a structured, legitimate environment. This gives everyone a level playing field to initiate dialog about what options are best for each athlete.

Another source for professional advice on choosing an agent is the players' association. Representatives from each sport will sit down and answer questions to see if the agent in question is certified. The players' union will have background information on each agent. In most states, financial planners are not regulated. This should be a real concern if a player is considering someone to handle his investments.

A final approach to help eliminate financial abuse is to use separate and unrelated representatives to negotiate contracts and to provide financial advice. Before investing in any ventures, research the proposed plan. If this is a first-time proposal, it is risky and the potential to lose a great deal of money will be high. Invest in entities with a long history or track record. These returns can be verified over several years of growth.

Some proponents believe colleges should require all student athletes to take a minimum of two semesters of finance and accounting while they are in school, regardless of their major. This way, athletes who enter the professional sports world will have some idea of how to handle money, and those who go into other careers will be better off, too.

In some instances, these athletes are receiving sums of money that they would not otherwise earn in five lifetimes. The carefree feeling of "if it's gone, oh well I'll just earn more," puts a lot of players in a very vulnerable spot. When word gets out that these guys are about to sign a big contract, family members are often there to give all kinds of financial advice on how to spend the money. At times, this is the first step to heartache, and it will undoubtedly lead to hard feelings when the athlete doesn't invest in a family member's lifelong dream of owning a clothing store or restaurant.

What happens when someone does invest in another person's dream? More times than not, the investment doesn't prove fruitful and family and friends end up not speaking to one another. Some athletes are coming from an environment where the only successful people they have ever seen are pimps and drug dealers.

This should never be an excuse to get involved with people who are willing to break the law in order to gain an unfair advantage over their competitor. If an agent is willing to bend the rules or break the law in order to sign a player, then that agent is capable of stealing from that player. Once an agent breaks the law to get that superstar athlete, chances are they will do just about anything to keep that player and more importantly, maintain that high lifestyle image that they have grown accustomed to.

Usually, the athlete's family is the best line of defense to prevent unscrupulous agents from contacting the athlete. By setting up a screening process, families can put sports agents on notice that whatever discussions about future plans and representation will have to take place in front of a group of family and friends that has the athlete's best interest at heart. Family members can take this opportunity to talk with their tax accountant or attorney independently from their sports agent. Often members from the local church or civic organizations have experience in the field of entertainment law or finance or might know someone whose son or daughter was represented in contract negotiations. It is not necessary to use someone from within this circle to actually perform the work, but rather to act as an advisory board.

A checks and balance approach keeps the left hand from controlling what the right hand is doing. In the banking industry, every employee is required to take at least one week of vacation every year. This is designed so if there are any questionable transactions taking place, they will generally stand out when someone else closes out the books for that week.

According to sports agent Leigh Steinberg, "Every athlete that I have agreed to represent in the last five years has put me through an interview process so rigorous, I could have probably been confirmed for Secretary of State at the end of it."

Kareem Abdul-Jabbar, the all-time leading scorer in NBA history is the last player most people would believe could fall victim. Nearing the end of his illustrious career, Abdul-Jabbar faced a financial crisis he didn't see coming. A standout player at UCLA and a bright student, he built a small fortune playing basketball in the NBA and earned millions in endorsements. After years of believing that his financial future was set, Kareem Abdul-Jabbar woke up to the realization the investments he thought were solid had in fact eroded away. Some of the earnings had in fact been embezzled, and he filed a lawsuit against his business manager, Thomas Collins.

When the Los Angeles Lakers captain should have been celebrating his 40th birthday, a dark cloud swirled around the investments Collins made on behalf of Abdul-Jabbar and several other NBA players. Using money borrowed from Abdul-Jabbar's personal line of credit, Thomas Collins invested in Orange County Hotels, which went bankrupt, and other extravagant ventures like Arabian horses, oil wells and gold coins.

Initially Collins negotiated the contracts between the Lakers and Abdul-Jabbar. It ended six years later with Abdul-Jabbar suing Collins for $59 million, claiming fraud, negligence and breach of trust.

At the time, Abdul-Jabbar's lethal skyhook shot and dominant post-up game were shadows of what they once were. Fortunately for Abdul-Jabbar, he was playing for the Los Angeles Lakers and owner Jerry Buss. Buss gave Abdul-Jabbar a one-year extension worth $2 million to play for the Lakers, and this helped him recoup some of his losses.

In a 1986 Forbes magazine article, Abdul-Jabbar was quoted as saying that most athletes and their business managers resemble "the blind leading the lame."

In his suit against Collins, Abdul-Jabbar alleged Collins allowed him to spend "excessive sums" of money on personal items. Many athletes are intimidated by financial statements and are embarrassed to admit they don't understand them. It is easier to leave that to the "experts" and stick to playing the sport.

Not all sports agents fall under the heading of "buyer beware." In fact, some sports agents are willing to help their clients setup charity programs to give back to the communities where they or their clients grew up. In the inner city of Los Angeles, a former minor league baseball player turned sports agent decided to invest $1 million of his own money to build a baseball field in an area that saw the last baseball field built some 50 years before. Dennis Gilbert developed a sports marketing firm successful enough to represent outstanding players like Barry Bonds and Jose Canseco. In a business where some representatives would rather take than give, he proved that "it is truly more blessed to give than to receive." In a *Los Angeles Times* article, columnist Bill Plaschke (Jan 27, 2002) states that Gilbert grew up playing on dirt fields in Gardena, California, and it wasn't until he "reached high school before he ever played on a grass infield." The field, named after Gilbert, is a place where kids who would not otherwise have an opportunity to pitch off of a mound and run down fly balls with a warning track are now able to get the feeling of playing on a real baseball diamond, thanks in part to this agent who gave something in return for the blessings that he received. "I wanted them to have the same chances I had. I realized a field was the perfect idea," said Gilbert.

One of the best ways to hedge against fraud is to diversify your investments and invest with multiple brokers/agents. Minimize investing with family or friends. My college roommate once told me, "Money knows no family or friends." If you want to test a family relationship or a friendship, loan them some money.

As the apostle Paul wrote in Philippians 3:13, "Forgetting those things which are behind, and reaching forth unto those things which are before, I press toward the mark for the prize of the high calling of God in Christ Jesus." In other words, we cannot change what has happened to us in our lives in the past, but we can certainly write a new chapter and learn from our mistakes to go on to a prosperous tomorrow.

If you are caught in a bad financial situation, often the best thing you can possibly do is to put the bitter lesson behind you and learn so that you don't repeat the same mistake.

There seems to be a common denominator in every story that was previously identified in this chapter. Greed! Not to imply that everyone that gets burned is greedy, no, it simply is the thread that permeates some business dealings. Either the person putting up the money is convinced that a "killing" is in the making, or the person soliciting the funds has bad intentions fueled by greedy aspirations.

Parents have to work harder at teaching their kids that there is no such thing as a free lunch. Socio-economic status is no excuse for taking shortcuts in an effort to get ahead in life.

Let's take a look at what those "bonuses" that the clients of William "Tank" Black actually cost them in the end. According to Jacksonville Jaguars Fred Taylor, Tank Williams gave him roughly $500 per month spending money and for his birthday an extra $1,000. The information is not clear but we will figure year-round for two years. At five times 12 plus birthday bonuses, Taylor received roughly $14,000. His cost for that illegal stipend ended up totaling almost $3 million. Tank was making a loan to those players against their potential future earnings.

I often think of my grandfather in these situations. An immigrant from a family of simple means, he built a small fortune as an entrepreneur selling plants and trees. His advice I keep with me everyday: "A slow dollar is a sure dollar."

Kim took the news of my bike being stolen as if I had said, "it's 65 degrees and sunny." She mentioned that I had purchased the bike with my gold card, which had buyers' insurance. I was glad to hear her in a better mood than when I left. We talked about the incoming bills and whether I needed her to transfer some funds to pay them. Then she asked how was I coping with sleeping in the back of the truck.

"I am doing pretty good at this point." In the back of my mind, I knew it would be getting hotter and muggy at night—that was going to be the real test.

I settled in Greenwich, Connecticut, the following day. The phone call to Kim had gone a little better than I had expected. I suspected she was missing me and didn't want me to know. Besides, I still loved her very much no matter where the book trail led me. In the end, I was determined to find my way back to Los Angeles to be with her.

Deciding to commute to New York City, daily I caught the Connecticut commuter train in from Greenwich and walked the short distance from Grand Central Station to my scheduled interviews in and around Times Square. The street musician and minstrel shows that often took place on the sidewalks always seemed to entertain me.

Undaunted by the lack of cooperation I received from school officials at some of the local colleges in New York, I continued to pore over copious sections of reports on the NCAA and I researched the index files of the New York Times, Washington Post and USA Today articles to help determine what other sources or leads would be available for my quest.

From one article, I learned about a guy who wanted to be called Hershey. Hershey was a ball player who grew up in Brooklyn. During his senior year in high school, he made a run at the city scoring title in basketball. Now Hershey spends his days working as a maintenance worker for the New York City Transit Authority.

I met Hershey one afternoon when he was leaving his shift to head home. He graciously accepted my invitation to talk with him about what happened that kept him from making a living in the NBA. "You see this limp I carry, that's what did me in. My left knee wouldn't stay healthy."

I could see that Hershey was starting to regret going down memory lane. He was offered scholarships to just about every school from Maine to Wyoming.

"The funny thing about it was, I thought after I blew out my knee I would still get somebody to give me a shot. Every pro team doctor I saw said I will be lucky if I can still walk by the time I turn twenty-five," said Hershey. When I asked him if he ever thought about going back to finish his education, Hershey replied, "Finish! Man I never got started. I put in the bare minimum just so I could continue to play."

I knew there were a lot of Hersheys out in the world, barely getting by. His real name wasn't Hershey and I couldn't help but ask him one more question before he disappeared down into the subway to catch the A-train back to Brooklyn. "Why did they call you Hershey?" I asked. He gave me a motion with his hands as if he was leading a fastbreak and replied, "Because I was pure sweetness when I dribbled down court." With my story in hand, I thanked him and I headed for the train back to Connecticut.

After long city days of research and interviews, I would return each evening to the Greenwich library to enter my research and thoughts into my laptop. It was my office, and everything appeared to be working out smoothly until April 9, 2000. That morning started out with a leisurely approach of preparing my laundry for the week. After the usual preparation of notes and phone calls, I completed folding a few clothes and placed them back into the travel bag. In route to the commuter rail station, I suddenly looked up and found a vehicle moving into my lane and then suddenly stop. I initiated an attempt to avoid the collision. My left front bumper slammed into the late model Buick sedan and rotated that car 170 degrees. The Buick then struck a Mercedes traveling in the opposite direction. After choking on the noxious fumes emanating from the airbags that had deployed, I pushed open the jammed door and exited from my damaged truck. Two elderly gentlemen were standing in the middle of the intersection asking each other if they were ok. By then everyone turned their attention toward the man who was trapped in the rear of the Buick. He appeared to be conscious and alert, however, unable to exit the vehicle because the rear end of the car was compressed. The police and fire rescue appeared within minutes. They used the "Jaws of Life" to extricate the trapped man. With the exception of a small scratch on the back of my leg, I did not suffer any injuries. The three elderly men all went to the hospital for observation. The police report confirmed that everyone was released that evening from the hospital in good condition. The woman passenger in the Mercedes was also not injured. I was cited for "not allowing a safe distance" which didn't make sense to me because I felt that my lane was compromised by the unsafe driving of the elderly man in the Buick in front of me. I had insurance to resolve the car accident, but what happened next was beyond my wildest dreams.

6

HIGH SCHOOL OR
HIGH SCAM

Two roads diverged in the woods, and I—I took the one less traveled by, and that has made all the difference.

—Robert Frost

It was time for me to step back and look at the younger generation, mainly teenagers, and to figure out where they fit into this whole aspect of future student athletes.

There appears to be a very dangerous precedent taking place in high schools all across America. Where once the goal of most administrators and parents was to educate kids above all else, the focus is now beginning to shift to having a winning sports program first, then following up with making sure student athletes get decent grades.

Young athletes today are bombarded with commercials that emphasize that the type of shoes you wear is synonymous with success. "Just do it," has become a way of life rather than a sports manufacturer's moniker. Parents who once proudly bragged their child was on honor role are now silenced by a more prominent boast that their child was responsible for scoring the game-winning touchdown or driving in the winning run with a base hit. There is nothing wrong with championing our kids' sports accomplishments, but there has to be balance in young athletes' lives, otherwise sports will be the only thing they excel in.

Studies have proven students whose parents take an active role in their education go on to more prominent and successful careers. This obviously isn't the discovery of a new planet, but it explains why some parents make it to every sporting event their child participates in but can't find the time to attend the PTA meetings or parent/teacher conferences. At some point, we as parents owe it to our children to demand the same effort they put into sports be given to academics as well.

No one benefits from lowering the academic bar when it comes to the debate about athletics and schoolwork. When a high school in Texas made it mandatory for students involved in after-school extracurricular activities to maintain a 2.0 (a C average or better) and not earn a D or an F in any subject, a firestorm ensued from some of the parents who demanded that the school board eliminate that ruling. A similar situation occurred in Richmond, California, in 1999. A working-class community north of Oakland had a high school basketball team that was rolling along with a 13–0 record. Suddenly, in the middle of the season, the games came to a screeching halt when Richmond High School's basketball coach, Ken Carter, announced that there would be no more practice or games until his entire freshman, junior varsity and varsity teams improved their grades. Some of the players, feeling the pride of an undefeated team, forgot about the contract they had signed with this no-nonsense coach that demanded they maintain a 2.3 grade point average, complete all of their homework assignments, sit in a front-row seat and attend classes on time. The minimum 2.0 set by the school district for after school sports participation was below Carter's standard and he wanted every player to go to college.

"The reason I established the goal of 2.3 GPA was because that is the minimum grade point average you can have in order to receive a college scholarship," said Coach Carter. When the basketball team showed up for practice, a sign read, "Report to the library." The coach was waiting for them with volunteer tutors and teachers eager to help get the players back on the book track. "I told them I was canceling games and practices until the players did better at school," said Carter.

If the coach thought that everyone would agree with his priorities, he would quickly find out who was in favor of this new concept of postponing games in lieu of better grades. Some of the school board members thought that coach Carter had overstepped his authority. "If they are going to be making policy decisions like that, it should be made through the school board," said board member Charles Ramsey. Most of the players' parents were in favor of the lockout. Nevertheless, the firestorm over the decision quickly gained national attention and put the debate between school athletics over academics right in the middle of the media's crosshairs.

School Principal Haidee Foust-Whitmore was somewhat amused by the decision when she first heard the coach's decision. She knew that backing coach Carter would send the right message to everyone that the number one objective is to get these kids to work at their highest potential. With a school that consistently ranked among the lowest in test scores and sending graduates off to universities, who could (with a clear conscience) stand in opposition? When there is a sense of urgency like that at schools with students drifting off to remedial jobs after graduation, sometimes you have to do away with protocol and just make something happen. It appeared that some of the opposition to the plan came from people who didn't get a chance to appear in front of the news cameras.

"On the streets and public basketball courts in Richmond and any other city in America, you see the broken dreams of former high school legends who got left behind by life. I was just not going to let that happen to these boys," said Carter.

So committed was this coach to answer the call of higher academic achievement that he was willing to forfeit the remainder of the season.

Carter's team did resume play after three forfeitures and finished the regular season 19–5. They went on to the playoffs, but lost in the second round that season. Of course Coach Carter took the brunt of the blame from people who wanted a state basketball title. Said Carter, "In the end, my goal was to get these boys into college where they could learn to become leaders and come back to this community as productive citizens."

A big part of the problem for a lot of these kids from low-income neighborhoods is that there is no glamour in studying. You don't see any television stations or writers coming into the library at 4:30 in the afternoon and saying, "we would like to interview your top students here." No highlight footage on the 11 o'clock news with kids getting ready for the big math or science test the next day. The message is loud and clear: score 1500 on your SAT exams, no biggy; score 28 points against your cross-town rivals, and you are guaranteed you will get recognition on several fronts.

In some African-American communities, the students who hit the books hard and make a concerted effort to make honor roll are labeled "Uncle Toms" or accused of "just trying to act white." This mindset dates back to a period in time when only upper-society whites were allowed to be educated in this country. Those feelings have changed as people begin to realize just how far behind you are in life without an education, but in some circles that change has not happened quickly enough. The irony in all of this is that up until the late 1960s African Americans were segregated when it came to education and choices about what schools to attend. If you go back to the turn of the 20th century, it was against the law in some places for people to educate someone who was non-white.

White students fare a little better in lower income communities but also have a fair number of students who do not take advantage of educational opportunities afforded them. It is the area of sports where we see a greater divergence in cultural attitudes.

According to a study conducted by Northeastern University's Center for the Study of Sports in Society located in Boston, 66 percent of African American teenagers who reside in urban America believe that they can earn a living in professional sports as opposed to 33 percent of their white counterparts. When you consider the odds of 1 in 60,000 ever making it to the professional ranks, it leaves you dumbfounded why any parent would hold out hope of encouraging their kids to pursue only the sports dream.

Part of the answer to that rhetorical question comes from the fact that African Americans have never reached the pinnacle of success in the corporate environment like they have in the area of sports and entertainment. Bill Cosby, Oprah Winfrey, Tiger Woods and Bryant Gumbal are all household names that made it as a result of hard work and the power to captivate an audience. If those individuals had had to cut their teeth on the corporate ladder, you probably would never have heard of any of them. When you consider NBA hall of famer Earvin "Magic" Johnson (who is becoming a commercial conglomerate in the retail industry of Southern California), even he used the "hoop dream" to get the initial capital and the political pull to make it happen.

The winds of change are definitely blowing, and you only need to look to the nation's capital to see it. Colin Powell and Condolezza Rice are Secretary of State and National Security Advisor, respectively. These are two of the highest-ranking positions in the United States government and "minorities" occupy them both. Many believe that had Colin Powell chose to run for president in the 2000 election, he would have won and become the first elected Black president in this country. This should be a prime example of how African Americans can succeed without the athletic component, but like the odds of making it in professional sports, Secretary of State and National Security Advisor carry long shots as well.

Statistics have proven that children try and copy what they see, so what they are exposed to is as good a barometer as any to predict the future of our youth. If you grow up in a household where there is a lot of television watching, particularly sports, then there will be a higher regard for games and playing, whereas if you grow up in an atmosphere where books have a prominent place, kids are more likely to seek that avenue.

In 1997, a study funded by a grant from the New Hampshire Charitable Foundation found the level of parental education and parents' ability to earn an income in the upper echelons of society were by far the major influences on students performing at the highest levels on scholastic aptitude exams, and test scores and had very little to do with classroom teaching methods. In other words, kids coming from underprivileged backgrounds really have to play catch-up when it comes to competing for enrollment in colleges and universities across the country. Throw in the need for a student to be the best he/she can be in a sport, it leaves very little time for studies. If students fall behind, it is easier in some instances for the parent to encourage their children toward what they are good at and allow an athlete to play on traveling squads or stay out late and play down at the local parks and gyms when he/she should be preparing to turn in a homework assignment.

Because there is so much competition to earn athletic scholarships in various sports, parents have a tendency to push their kids harder, and in some instances, beyond their kids' athletic abilities or desires. The net result is often disappointment and deep-seeded self esteem wounds that take years to heal. Part of the problem stems from the monetary value of some of these scholarships. With private schools' tuition ranging from $8,000 to $35,000 per year, it's not surprising to see people hire private coaches to help develop their budding star's talents. According to Bob Walsh, a high school coach who has been involved in boys basketball at Haverhill High School in New Hampshire for over 15 years, the pursuit of earning that coveted prize is putting a great deal of pressure on everyone, including the coaches.

"[Parents] have their kids going to summer camps and playing year-round. If a kid isn't getting enough playing time, then it becomes a problem."

In the Northeast and Midwestern parts of the country where hockey is the preferred sport, parents that spend years watching their kids develop on the ice in local league competition find it very difficult when those athletes reach the age where winnowing takes place in junior high and high school. The competitive race to grab those limited spots on the junior varsity and varsity teams can turn lifelong friends into bitter foes.

According to Massachusetts Newburyport High School hockey coach Richard (Spike) Sprague, when the parents intervene on behalf of their child, it makes it that much tougher to coach those participating in sports. Said Sprague, "All parents are great people, but in athletics, they have blinders on and they don't see beyond their own child."

Whenever there is a possibility that a scout or recruiter is present, often times teammates accuse each other of "hot-dogging it" or overzealous play all in an effort to impress that one person who might hold the keys to their future.

And what about the parents who can afford to send their kids to those high-priced boarding sports camps that feature professional players as coaches? The price is higher when you consider some people pay upwards of $50,000 for their sons and daughters to have the chance to learn from and compete against some of the brightest talent in the world. It clearly goes beyond looking for the edge to earn a four-year scholarship—this spills directly over into the big-business side of professional sports, complete with nutritionists and agents. No one promises your child will be the next superstar in golf or tennis, but they drop enough big-name players on their colorful brochures that hook parents into hauling their checkbooks with them to these camps. Let's face the facts, most people know by the time their kid is about age 12, whether or not he/she has what it takes to compete at the high school or college level, but when it comes to believing your child will make it professionally, you really never know. Every community has that great child prodigy everyone proclaimed would be the next great superstar and for whatever reason most never even get to shine on the collegiate level.

We must applaud the parents who can keep the sports monster from gobbling up everything and everyone in its path, all for the sake of a professional dream. Said one parent when asked what his son has learned from competing in sports, "It's been a vehicle to learn about life. That's what competitive sports is for kids. He's learned about teamwork, loyalty and competition."

Too often parents are not realistic about their children's chances because they are not educated about how the scholarship process works. Anyone who feels that their son or daughter is good enough to earn a scholarship should contact high school coaches and college recruiters to get the facts. If your kids are as good as you think they are, it is a sure bet that a college recruiter will find them. The more informed you are about how scholarships are offered, the better chance your child has at earning one. More importantly, be objective about your star athlete. Your evaluation will always be higher than most others, so listen to people who have nothing to gain or lose by giving you a fair and objective analysis of just how good your child is or isn't. Another important factor most child psychologists point out is not to put a pass/fail or all-or-nothing importance on obtaining a scholarship. If children feel that by not getting a scholarship in a particular sport they have failed their parents, then chances are they will begin to doubt other areas of their lives that are successful.

The most important thing a child should learn about playing any sport is sound fundamentals of the game. We see kids that exhibit a certain degree of talent but lack the overall fundamental skills, and when your level of skill is on par with everyone else, the differences between good and great are rooted in the players who built their game on solid technique.

Another very important factor to consider if your child is offered a scholarship is whether or not to attend a big Division I school or drop down a level and play in Division II. If the athlete has the physical attributes to compete in Division I, it is a no brainer because of the high-end media exposure associated with Division I athletics, however, if the talent is average, perhaps Division II is a better choice and most statistics show the study habits and emphasis on education can be more rewarding. Even after earning a scholarship, the pressure to maintain that scholarship can be just as stressful. Most universities issue scholarships on an annual basis to be renewed each year. Some athletes and school officials feeling the pressure to maintain a certain win-loss record have been tempted to "bend their academic records" just to remain competitive for a shot at a state athletic title. An incident took place in South Florida where an investigator by the Miami-Dade state attorney's office was called in to look at the possibility of falsification of student-athletes' grades. Five schools were under investigation for converting lower grades to higher grades so star players would be eligible to compete in the league tournaments.

The *Miami Herald* report stated star athletes at four of the schools under investigation did in fact receive higher grades than they had actually earned. "This goes directly to the heart of the integrity of the educational system," said one law enforcement official. "What message are you sending to students who work hard to get good grades when athletes can get their grades changed from F's to A's?" It was reported by teachers (in some of the schools under investigation) that coaches and administrators routinely pressured them to change year-end grades of some athletes so they would not be rendered academically ineligible to participate in the upcoming sports season. Teachers at one school told stories of failing grades issued to prominent football players that were inexplicably changed to passing grades after the grading period had ended.

Not only is this an embarrassment to the schools that operated in this manner, but it is doubly devastating for athletes, who in some cases were not educated enough to even fill out a job application. This teaches athletes that there is a double standard in place, only to later find themselves wondering why it evaporates once their playing eligibility expires.

Teachers' changing grades is akin to cheating. It is not tolerated in schools by the students, but the teachers and administrators do it when they cheat the athletes out of their own future by changing grades and bending rules.

Teachers reticent to come forward were concerned about administrative backlash if they divulged information that would be harmful to the school. How do you enjoy victories by the football team, basketball team or the swim team when you are aware that you had to break the rules to ensure that victory?

Grades are supposed to be a reflection of a person's knowledge in a particular subject. Instead, some school officials are more concerned with job security and using student athletes like pawns.

Certain high schools are as aggressive in recruiting players as some colleges. Where once schools looked across town to dip into another school district to count on that great player to compliment the well-organized team, now there is a strong focus on recruiting from around the world. In Fresno, California, a high school basketball team came within a pair of free throws from winning the state Division IA basketball tournament in March 2000. What may or may not have been clear at the time was whether their star center, Charlie Rodriguez, was 19 and past the legal age to play high school basketball. The 6-foot-7 center was recruited from the Dominican Republic and had attended Clovis West High in Fresno, California, for two years, but the state department denied his visa when he tried to return for what was at the time believed to be his senior year.

According to documents provided to Clovis West when Rodriguez first enrolled in school, he showed his birth date as December 20, 1982, which would have made him 16 during his first year on campus. His size and muscular build had the opposition questioning his age from the very beginning. The first time I actually saw Rodriguez play, it was quite impressive. He dominated the game and more importantly, controlled the low post against a 6–11 prep All-American the entire game. It got to the point where you actually felt sorry for this kid that had a 5-inch height advantage, but physically couldn't stop Rodriguez.

An ESPN investigation about three basketball players from the Dominican Republic attending another California high school prompted school officials to do a little more checking into reports that Charlie Rodriguez may in fact be older than he first indicated. Inconsistencies in Rodriguez's story about when he first attended high school surfaced and things began to get a bit cloudy. According to school officials, before Rodriguez was ever enrolled, they placed a call to the California Interscholastic Federation (the governing body of California high school sports) and informed commissioner Jerry Laird about their potential star athlete. Initially Laird found no problems but subsequently determined that Rodriguez had in fact turned 19 prior to the start of that school year. According to Clovis West principal Gary Giannoni, the school had received appropriate documents. "I never considered Charlie was older. Even though he was big, Charlie was immature. His social skills were those of a high school freshman."

After completing its investigation, the CIF stripped the Clovis West Eagles of 70 games, including forfeiture of all play-offs and regional titles they had won.

A lot of this type of recruiting is illegal. Because some countries have rudimentary record keeping, athletes are brought into this country to compete against players sometimes two to three years their junior. As proof, look at what took place during the 2001 Little League World Series. A father falsifies his son's birth certificate so that the son can play on a little league team from the Bronx. Because the kid has a physical age advantage, he fires baseballs that appear to the opposition to look like BBs and the team goes on to win the world series. Then the news about a forged birth certificate surfaces and the child who was allegedly taught to lie at an early age is suddenly thrust into world headlines with his unsuspecting country left to shamefully scramble to do damage control. The irony in the story is the young pitcher was probably good enough to shut down kids his true age if not older.

In the past, before there were Fox Sports Net and ESPN, kids played for the fun of it. If you won the league championship, that was the gravy. The main thing was to go out there and have fun. Now with instant television coverage of games from Pop Warner to the NFL, everyone is seeking their Andy Warhol sports moment. They want their fifteen minutes of fame as quickly as possible. Unlike the fame or infamy that comes from the network talk shows and daytime reality television, sports offers big money endorsements if you wear the right sports apparel. Those contracts are only offered to the winners. There's no room in our society for second place. With that type of economic pressure staring many coaches in the face, some are willing to take chances to be number one.

Just like the immigrants who come for the economic opportunities that this country offers, foreign-born hockey, basketball and baseball players will pull up stakes from their familiar surroundings for a shot to make it among the best players in the world. Australian-born Martin Iti was convinced that he had what it takes to make it. At the youthful age of 15, and at 6 foot 11, he certainly had the height. His mother agreed to allow him to come to America only after believing that he could get an excellent education. His guardian took him from one city to another; all in search of getting him the right exposure and coaching that would eventually land him a contract with the National Basketball Association.

Arizona, Florida, Colorado, Nevada and California were places Iti called home in search of basketball bliss. A retired commissioner from the CIF voiced concerns about sports agents and representatives that import players from other countries for the sole purpose of exploitation, thus "resulting in the corruption of high school basketball." When Iti's mother got wind of the fact her son had been shuttled from one state to another, she began to get concerned about her son's education. Foreign students have eight consecutive semesters to complete their eligibility once they enroll in high school. Determined to put an end to the myriad of moves and relocation that would have caused Lewis and Clark to become dizzy, Martin Iti was ordered by his mother to come home. A bizarre showdown at Los Angeles International Airport was complete with dueling documents: one ordering Iti to immediately return to Sydney, the other from his American guardian insisting that he remain here in the United States.

Returning home without a high school diploma or a promising future at a major university, Martin Iti became another statistic in the saga of foreign and domestic promise wasted on the hope of a professional career. Players from around the world are starting to gravitate to the U.S. in search of "fame and fortune" in various sports, but those numbers haven't come close to the players from this country seeking stardom out of high school.

High school was never supposed to be another training ground for future professional ballplayers, but it is steadily moving in that direction. Some kids 11 and 12 years of age have told stories of how coaches from various schools around town have approached them about where they would attend high school.

In 1994, California state legislature passed laws allowing high school students to transfer to a school outside of the school district that they lived in. Known as the open enrollment law, it was designed to give parents more options in deciding where their children could get the best education. The good intentions turned out to be a recruiting blessing for coaches looking to improve their chances at winning a state title.

In 1998, the Oxnard school district tried to address this dilemma by imposing a mandatory athletic suspension, barring transfer students from competing in district-sanctioned sporting events for one year. The move dramatically reduced the number of transfer students the following year by a third. The ruling didn't affect private schools, which continued to recruit and continued to dominate in football and basketball.

Parents whose son or daughter was good enough to earn a starting position sophomore year were suddenly trying to understand why a kid from the inner city could come in and immediately take their starting position away. According to an *L.A. Times* article written by Eric Sondheimer entitled "Too Many Athletes Are Making All the Wrong Moves," one concerned parent wrote, "My son loved playing basketball for his high school and was looking forward to playing varsity his senior year. Unfortunately, the varsity coach told him in June of his junior year that he doesn't take seniors who aren't starters or the first off the bench [on junior varsity]. So even though my son was loyal to his high school basketball program for three years, doing what his coach asked of him, he was not allowed to play.

The player on the varsity team that played the same position was a transfer student who didn't live in the boundaries of my son's high school. My complaint about transfers is that they sometimes take the place of a player who did want to play for their local high school."

If school districts around the country don't nip this in the bud, it will only be a matter of time before the courts will be filled with lawsuits from disgruntled parents who feel that their children's Constitutional rights have been violated on the grounds that they were denied an equal opportunity to earn an athletic scholarship.

Some might feel that this is all about fielding the best teams, but for many it is a way for parents to give their kids access to educational opportunities in the suburbs that may not be available in the inner city.

The landmark Supreme Court case of *Alan Bakke v. Regents of the University of California Davis* in 1977 centered on a white student who, after being denied admission to medical school, sued on the grounds of reverse discrimination. In an attempt to maintain ethnic diversity, the medical school decided to "set aside" a limited number of openings to accept minority applicants with lower grades and test scores than some of the white students that were denied admission.

In June 2003, the issue of using race as a basis for admissions into institutions of higher education was again addressed by the United States Supreme Court. In a 5-4 ruling upholding a University of Michigan's law school affirmative action program, Justice Sandra Day O'Conner wrote, "Effective participation by members of all racial and ethnic groups in the civic life of our nation is essential if the dream of one nation, indivisible, is to be realized."

The court, however, struck down the University of Michigan's undergraduate admissions policy of using a separate point system which placed a higher value on single underrepresented minority applicants, over such factors as writing ability or leadership skills.

This case was by far the strongest challenge to overturn affirmative action policies in our society since 1978.

Perhaps in an ironic twist, we may see the day when there are spots held open for white kids so that they may be given a chance to play on the basketball team. There is definitely a trend in which Catholic preparatory high schools that are recruiting players from other parts of town to give their schools an advantage in sports over other schools in the district. There is an impending case at the U.S. Supreme Court that centers on this very issue.

In the case of *Brentwood Academy v. Tennessee Secondary School Athletic Association* (the governing body for high school athletics in the state of Tennessee), Brentwood Academy claimed that TSSAA's recruiting rules, which barred coaches from recruiting middle school athletes, were a violation of Brentwood's First and Fourteenth Amendment rights to free speech. In a surprising ruling, a district court judge initially ruled in favor of Brentwood Academy. Then the Sixth U.S. Circuit Court of Appeals in Cincinnati overruled the district court ruling.

This case could have profound consequences on how high school coaches conduct themselves in the fierce competitive recruitment of athletes as young as 10 years old. At least 40 states have filed amicus briefs. This is clearly a landmark case and will have tremendous consequences if Brentwood Academy prevails.

"It would destroy the concept of fairness," said Robert Kanaby, executive director of the National Federation of State High School Association.

If Brentwood Academy wins the case, young student athletes may give up on studies all together and the door would be open for the NBA to institute a supplemental lottery system by which they would draft the rights to some kids while they were in middle school just to lock up the future rights to a potential superstar player. One coach told me that he had parents approaching him when their kids were in ninth grade asking if he knew of a good agent.

The Supreme Court reversed the District Court's initial ruling and found TSSAA was in-fact a state actor and sent the case back to be reviewed again by the District Court under the standards for reviewing a case that applies to state actors.

TSSAA was arguing Brentwood waived its right to question the constitutionality of the recruiting rule because it chose to become a member of TSSAA.

"This was our one shot to hit a home-run and not have to defend ourselves against the First and Fourteenth Amendment," said TSSAA Executive Director, Ronnie Carter, "We took our best shot at it and missed."

A final Court ruling could come as early as fall 2004.

Most people don't realize this, but according to NCAA statistics, one half of 1 percent of those athletes competing in high school go on to play in professional sports. That would be the equivalent of lining up 500,000 cars and you having one chance to find the car that has the key that will start that car. The average car is 15 feet in length. That means if you lined up one car after another, you would have cars from Los Angeles to Dallas, with only one shot to find the car that starts. When you look at it in that perspective, no one in their right mind would want to gamble with their children's future. This is tantamount to parents playing the lottery with their kids as the ticket.

It's hope that fuels that kind of wishful thinking. Hope that my kid is the one, hope that I will retire wealthy, hope against hope that my kids have what it takes to reign supreme in their sport. Hope is the helium filled balloon that elevates the dreams from one extreme to another without ever realizing that the game is rigged and you are chasing the proverbial carrot that always stays one step ahead of you. As coach Ken Carter once told me during an interview with him in downtown Los Angeles, "With proper planning, your child stands a better chance of owning a sports franchise than he has playing for one."

No other sport seems to dominate the attention span of teenagers like basketball. It shouldn't be surprising to anyone when you see more players drafted into the NBA out of high school than any other sport. I'm sure some might make the argument that baseball drafts more 18 year olds and younger, but there are stop gap measures that baseball has in place within the minor leagues. Most who are drafted out of high school take on average four to five years before being called up to the majors. There are also more opportunities to pursue post-high school graduation courses because less demands are put on young baseball players.

The NBA has finally seen the light on this subject and is currently underway with a developmental league called the National Developmental Basketball League (NDBL). Players perform not in front of the crowds numbering in the thousands that their elite NBA cousins play in front of, but before smaller audiences closer to 2,000. Players would have to use creative financing to become millionaires (annual salary $27,500) and they travel not by jet but by bus. For some players, this is the last shot at NBA stardom. There is always the Continental Basketball Association or European leagues, but they are at best the last place most aspiring players will ever compete in a semiprofessional environment. After that, it's basically back to the real world of minimal professional opportunities and few prospects.

Instead of playing on popular teams like the Lakers, Knicks and Celtics, NDBL players play for teams like the North Charleston (S.C.) Lowgators. There is career counseling to assist players with resume writing and off-season job placements, but how many meaningful jobs are out there for these high school kids when they've taken a pass on the possibility of a college education and darted off in search of the NBA dream?

Omar Cook is a prime example of this process. After playing his freshman year at St. John's, Cook declared himself eligible for the 2001 NBA draft. He was selected by the Denver Nuggets in the second round and was cut before the start of the regular season. A month later, he signed with the Dallas Mavericks but reported to camp with a lackluster performance and within five weeks found himself unemployed once again. With no education to fall back on, he now works twice as hard in hopes that someone will take notice and give him that elusive shot again.

According to the NDBL's senior vice president, Rob Levine, "Not everybody is going to be an NBA player or star. But you can keep playing ball and we'll give you the opportunity."

The idea of having this developmental league can't possibly sit well with the NCAA. Players who would have gone on to star for a particular university are instead heading for the European and developmental leagues like the NDBL.

The NCAA makes a lot of it's revenue on "March Madness," and anything that potentially dilutes that talent pool could have reverberating effects later when it comes time to renew those lucrative television contracts.

We've all heard the argument some people make when they say, "if an athlete isn't going to go to class anyway, why waste the universities' time with enrolling these athletes. Just let them go off and practice doing what they want to do." As a society, we should have a problem with that because the experiences that a young person will gain while at an institution of higher learning will begin to shape their minds about other career possibilities, even if at the time their interests lie elsewhere. I would even venture to say that once a student athlete realizes he isn't quite as good as he once considered himself to be or if he suffers a serious injury, then the motivation to earn a degree takes on a new meaning, and that could occur even in his senior year. Once the decision is made to launch down that road of pro athlete or bust, the options become limited and that is where the "make it at all cost" mindset is cast.

It's been said that an athlete's career is just like the round bouncing ball that they dribble. When you lift that ball over your head, it symbolizes the greatest potential that you have. Then the ball drops and each bounce reduces its height/value by 50 percent until the ball stops bouncing.

Another source for exploitation comes in the form of summer basketball camps run by AAU in conjunction with sports shoe conglomerates like Nike and Adidas ABCD. Each summer over 3000 high school basketball players and over 600 coaches set up a five-day sports combine to evaluate the cream of the crop. The tournament features several high schools running concurrent games morning, noon and night with college coaches from all of the elite Division I colleges across the country. Pick any name from the college perennial powerhouses of coaching and there is a very good chance that he will be strategically sitting where he can get a birds-eye view of the next great superstars of the NBA.

These tournaments are invitation only and the best of the best are there to prove that they can compete among the talent that they have heard about but have not had the opportunity play against until now. This is as close as some of these athletes will ever come to earning a scholarship to "big-time U," and some are looking for the validation that they are good enough to even bypass college and head straight to the pros.

This environment obviously attracts the kind of attention that could also corrupt a player with a payoff for the right to represent a potential NBA lottery pick (as identified in the previous chapter). The summer leagues are not regulated like at the college level, so there is more room for a player to make a false step and accept something he or she shouldn't. For the NCAA, this can be a nightmare when it comes to avoiding improper contact between students, coaches, agents and anyone else who might have an interest, legal or otherwise. Summer league coaches who are looking for an opportunity to join a major college coaching staff may be tempted to try and steer an athlete toward a particular school. Because high school athletes are off limits to recruiting attempts from college coaches until after their junior year, it can be very tempting for some coaches, who may be under the gun to win because of an off year, to stretch the rules to gain an advantage.

In an attempt to regulate this situation before it turns into a free-for-all, the NCAA can only control the collegiate coaches in attendance. There is talk that the NCAA is considering baring college coaches from evaluating or participating in the summer camps altogether.

At this point, the NCAA has decided to take a more conservative approach and limit the 24-day evaluation period to two weeks.

One thing is for certain, even if the college coaches are barred from attending, there will be other "evaluators" who will take their place. According to Sonny Vaccaro (a founding father of the grassroots summer shoe camps, first with Nike and currently with Adidas ABCD), "If the [college] coaches aren't allowed, there are no rules. It will only open up a Pandora's box."

The proverbial box however, is already open! It was opened the minute sports-governing bodies, schools, coaches and players decided to accept "free" shoes, apparel and money from shoe manufacturers. "No servant can serve two masters." Luke 16:13.

Whether college coaches are allowed or not, this summer mainstay will continue. Too much is at stake, and the train has already left the station. Parents who are desperate to give their kids any edge they can get to help improve the chances that their son will finance the family's "dream" often give permission to AAU coaches to take their children across the country with coaches who are not accredited by any organization.

Some of these coaches defend their position by saying that they are helping some of these kids by keeping them off the streets. Traveling across the country to play in tournaments may very well be a wonderful experience for players who have never been out of their communities and given a chance to see how the rest of the world lives, but for athletes who are failing in the classroom, this is nothing more than a free meal if that coach allows those players to travel when they should be back in summer school.

Because these summer teams bump up against the boundaries of NCAA guidelines about receiving special gifts from coaches and agents, it is certain that the NCAA will institute new laws about what a potential collegiate athlete will and will not be able to accept in the name of maintaining his/her amateur status.

Maybe part of their motive will stem from the fact that the NCAA doesn't make any money off of these camps, but again it is not ready to pull the plug on their potential pool of "March Madness" participants. It's ironic that the NCAA has deals with the shoe companies and the coaches of the major universities have their own multi-million dollar shoe deals, but it isn't in the best interest of the game for AAU and summer leagues to strike their own deals. It begs the question: is this about sports, or is it about corporate domination?

Nike grassroots director George Raveling was quoted (in a book about the shoe wars called *Sole Influence* by Dan Wetzel and Don Yaeger) as saying, "What has happened is that most people are ignorant of economics in America today. When I was growing up as a kid, municipal and state government provided young people with opportunities to grow and prosper in sports. Today, many municipal, state and federal fiscal responsibilities have been transferred to the private sector and so big business is being asked more and more to assume what are governmental responsibilities. But then, what happens in this dynamic—when you transfer that responsibility to big business, they now become criticized for being civic-minded."

Whether you side with Nike or Adidas ABCD, it appears to be the same, just wrapped in a different package. If the shoe companies are truly altruistic, why don't they outfit schools that don't win the championships and don't have blue-chip players? I'm sure they can come up with statistics that show how this school over here or that school over there doesn't have a big name reputation, and yet they receive the same support. If you want to truly test their sincerity, let's see them fund park and recreation leagues run by local municipalities, without attaching themselves to individual players who are featured in summer leagues and scouting magazines.

Not everyone is impressed with the fast-talking sales promotions of these shoe companies and traveling teams. At 5 foot 9, no one would ever mistake James Taylor of being a basketball insider, but he has a great deal of knowledge of how the game is really played. Taylor is the father of a high school standout in basketball who turned away all of the offers his son received to play in a traveling summer leagues and said no to the free shoes that came in constantly. Marcus Taylor, a 6-foot-3 point guard from Lansing's Waverly High School, was being compared to a former standout from East Lansing by the name of Earvin "Magic" Johnson. According to the senior Taylor, they fielded calls and inquiries from all over about his son participating in these summer camps and starring in shoe commercials.

"Right up front I said he's not going to do it, but if you want to talk, I'll listen," said Taylor.

Marcus Taylor continued to play high school ball, and he sharpened his skills working out in scrimmages with the Michigan State Spartans basketball team.

As though it were a selling point, coaches kept approaching James Taylor to talk to him about how the opportunity to travel and play in AAU tournaments would give his son a great deal of exposure.

"My son doesn't need any more exposure," said Taylor. "I don't think there would be as many problems if parents were more involved with their children." Where would you guess his son is in the area of academics? He is number one in his class.

Since so many kids grow up in homes where there isn't much in the way of guidance and emotional support, the situation is rife for widespread abuse. When so many offers are flying through the mail or on the phone, it is difficult to determine who is sincere and who is trying to make a quick dollar. The question that most parents should ask themselves is, would this coach or sales rep have anything to do with me if not for the fact that my son or daughter can hit, throw, catch or shoot a ball. Sincere coaches are usually found at the Boys and Girls Club, the YMCA or at the local Park and Rec Center. They have no monetary incentive to coach in these leagues, whether the kid is a superstar or whether he/she just wants to participate in sports.

Anyone else should be looked at skeptically, especially if they are recruiting from some other part of town or across state lines. Coaches who are willing to spend thousands of dollars to get an athlete to leave home and join that team generally have vested interests. That's not to say that it could not be beneficial for both parties, it just means that statistically speaking, the person doing the soliciting will be interested as long as there is something to gain from the relationship. Once an athlete's useful life has expired, like an empty milk carton in the refrigerator, he too will probably be discarded.

Not wanting to lump the good with the bad, the image of AAU coaching could not have been more tarnished than it did with the much talked about abuse that occurred with Kansas City prep all-star player JaRon Rush. It appears that his name has become synonymous with what is wrong with receiving gifts illegally. Rush, a 6-foot-7 forward, once one of the most sought-after players in the country, parlayed his talents into receiving favors reserved for presidential hopefuls. Flying around in corporate jets and hobnobbing with NBA stars like Michael Jordan and Scottie Pippen, Rush could have made it to the top, but instead he took the easy money, and it ended up costing him a professional career in the NBA.

It all started when he was 11 years old and caught the eye of a wealthy business owner named Tom Grant. Grant, a strong financial supporter of his alma mater, Kansas University, was involved in sponsoring youth sports teams and helping under-privileged kids pay for private schooling.

Grant hired Myron Piggie to coach his summer league team, the Kansas City Childrens Mercy Hospital 76ers. Piggie had had several run-ins with the law, including being charged with selling crack cocaine and shooting it out with a KC off-duty police officer. Piggie, who was now holding a couple of blue-chip players in his short-lived coaching stable, pleaded guilty to federal charges in connection with $35,000 in payments he made to players he coached in the summer leagues.

Some suspected the wealthy businessman Grant was trying to influence Rush's decision about signing with the Kansas Jayhawks. This was due to a quote in the local paper that had JaRon Rush questioning then-popular Jayhawks coach Roy Williams' (now with the North Carolina Tarheels) coaching style. Rush was suddenly left looking at his second choice for college, UCLA. It didn't take long before Grant and Rush's relationship cooled.

After enrolling at UCLA, the Bruins got more than they bargained for when the NCAA suspended Rush for 24 games for his involvement with Piggie. Surely UCLA must have heard the rumors that there were improper gifts coming to Rush while he was a star at the tony Pembroke Hills prep school. The UCLA Bruins were ordered to return $45,321 from their 1999 tournament earnings for playing with an ineligible player.

Following the suspensions during his sophomore year, Rush decided to declare himself eligible for the NBA draft. Snubbed by all teams in the draft, Rush, now battling personal demons with alcohol, found himself languishing in the ABA with dreams of making it in the NBA. Three weeks after the ABA Kansas City Knights signed him to a minor league contract, JaRon Rush missed a practice and was released.

This story is a facsimile of that of so many other stories of athletes who once had promising careers only to find themselves wondering how the things could have changed so quickly.

After checking into a substance abuse program, Rush renewed his friendship with Tom Grant. Grant agreed to help Rush by paying for his abuse-counseling program.

It would be convenient to blame the AAU coaches or the shoe companies or even the system itself. The truth is everyone needs to examine his own motives. If people can look themselves in the mirror and honestly say that they would do what they do even if they didn't get paid, it would begin to address the problems. At this point, there is an incredible amount of money to be made in amateur basketball, partly due to the mammoth battle between the two shoe giants to sign the next superstar. Because one player can turn a program around, basketball is the most vulnerable to these types of abuses. Ultimately parents have to take back their children's future. Sometimes saying no can be the best thing that can happen to the so-called "superstar." When they are no longer superstars, the only people who will return their calls will be mom or dad.

A large number of the homes where some of the great players come from tend to be single-parent homes. At times the father is in jail or deceased and the child is left to be raised by mom or grandma. It is imperative that kids are shielded from getting filled up with the hype that begins with a quick first step and ends in the pile of what could have been.

Mayday! We are Taking on Water

As my truck was being hoisted up on the back of a flat-bed tow truck, the police officer informed me I had to collect my possessions, go down to the police station and post a bond for the traffic citation. Since I was from California, there wasn't a guarantee that I would return in the event of a legal matter, so Connecticut required that I go to the police station and post a $78 bond. After returning to my truck, I began collecting my personal belongings, including a checkbook, leather valise, and a plastic carrying case containing my German-made Sig Saum 9-millimeter handgun.

The gun case caught the attention of one of the officers. "Do you have a permit for this weapon?" officer Reeves inquired. I proceeded to my truck where I had all of the paper work that was presented to me at the time of the purchase. I began getting this sinking feeling that this situation was starting to move from a simple question-and-answer session to something more legally problematic. The higher-ranking officer at the scene quickly took control and indicated we were going to take a ride to the police station to post the bond on the accident and then finish the necessary questions on the gun issue.

It didn't take long for the police officers to reveal their position on my traveling through their state without a permit issued by the Commonwealth of the State of Connecticut.

Officer Reeves read the Miranda rights and informed me I was officially being charged with section 44–306—entering the state armed without a Connecticut Firearm Permit.

The conversation suddenly shifted from a very informal discussion about my knowledge of handguns to me acknowledging that I understood what my rights were. I was asked if I would be willing to give a statement to the officers about my "Sig 9." At this point, I thought it best to assert my Fifth Amendment right not to incriminate myself, and politely terminated their interrogation on the matter.

I was now in the custody of the Greenwich police department. I had been placed in an interrogation room, less handcuffs, and questioned for over two and a half hours. After having my bags searched and being questioned about the need to travel with a gun, there was no doubt in my mind that an arrest was imminent.

I was escorted down the hall where I was fingerprinted and my photograph was taken, just like on television. I must say that the officers were quite professional and courteous throughout the ordeal. It was as though they were willing to bend over backwards to assist me in my dilemma, although my being a journalist certainly did not hurt my situation. Later, officers Reeves and Smith were kind enough to escort me around the corner from the police station to the city bank to withdraw the bond money I needed to post. As we left the ATM machine, a blue-haired elderly woman gave me a look as if to say that either I was a VIC—very important criminal, or I must have had a lot of money in my possession to require not one, but two uniformed police officers flanking my sides. We finished the necessary paper work, and I was released three and a half hours after this bizarre ordeal began. I was ordered to appear in the Stamford Superior Court on November 17, 2000, to answer the charge of the weapons permit violation.

I didn't know how serious the charge was or whether it was considered a small infraction or a felony. I was naïve enough to think that maybe if I appeared in front of the judge on the 17th and explained my side of the story, he or she might be willing to dismiss or reduce the charges. I was perhaps residual disorientation from my accident that prompted me to think that a judge would throw out a gun possession charge in today's society where there are over 5000 people killed yearly from the use of a firearm. The gravity of the situation became perfectly clear after I was informed that in order for me to get my gun back, a licensed federal firearms dealer would have to (through a court order) take control of the gun and ship it back to California to the place where I purchased it.

After locating a licensed dealer over in Norwalk, Connecticut, I decided to stop by and explain my predicament to the owner. He was a gentleman in his late thirties wearing wire-rimmed glasses and didn't seem that receptive to my scrape. As I was explaining my situation to him, in mid sentence he interrupted me and blurted, "So what you are telling me is that you are a felon." Completely taken aback, it was all I could do to defend myself and stumble through a sentence of, "well not exactly, you see I still have to have my day in court." The gun dealer's response was all the impetus I needed to find an attorney and a good one at that! I thanked the gun dealer for the "pep talk," and immediately began making inquiries about a good defense attorney in the area.

7

MAYDAY! WE ARE TAKING ON WATER

Tomorrow People, Where is your past? If you don't know your past, you can't know your future.

—Ziggy Marley

For a long time in this society, sports was something viewed as a pass-time like watching a play or looking up at the stars. This was not necessarily true among the African Americans in this country, because for a long time colored people didn't have the same privileges their white contemporaries enjoyed. So from the very beginning, African Americans viewed sports as a defining point in the hope of what could be. When you consider the fact that Jack Johnson back in the early 1900s was given an opportunity to fight for the prestigious heavyweight championship of the world in boxing, it gave Blacks in American something that they could never achieve in the board rooms and businesses—a sense of accomplishment and national pride.

During the 1932 Olympic games in Berlin, Nazi leader Adolf Hitler had already proclaimed that the Aryan race was superior in every aspect, including strength and speed. So when Jesse Owens shattered that myth on German soil, people from this country were euphoric in his success, particularly in the black neighborhoods.

In 1946, the same could be said when Joe Louis defeated Max Schmelling and captured the heavyweight title. These were examples of how by being superior athletes, these men rose to a level of adulation that wasn't seen in any other area of society.

Sports has always played a major role in the black community. The difference is, in earlier times it was never viewed as a cure-all for the various social ills that black people faced before the time of civil rights and integrated schools.

There was a time in this country when black parents had to walk three miles each way to make sure their kids got some form of education. It was a mark of pride to tell their neighbor that their son or daughter was admitted to a college or was graduating from one of the many prestigious black institutions of higher learning. An education was looked upon as the pinnacle of success one could achieve. No longer would black folks have to settle for assignments as cooks, servants and porters. Long before young impressionable kids wanted "to be like Mike," parents instilled the virtues of how far education could take those who pursued it. Asking black children in the 1930s and 1940s what they would like to grow up to be, an overwhelming majority would have yearned to be educators or administrators in a professional environment. Today, its been statistically proven that over 50 percent would probably mention some form of professional sports or entertainment.

For the past 20 years, there has been a slow and methodical transformation, not only in black America, but in white America as well. The classroom has been transformed into 30-second sound bites. Reality television has taken over the airwaves in which families are airing their dirty laundry in a sort of cathartic cleansing that drives ratings and pushes the envelope of decency. Where once there were only three major networks carrying sporting events, now there is around-the-clock coverage of games ranging from European football (soccer) to boxing on the Spanish channels to highlight footage from all of the day's sporting events.

Television has changed the way sports is covered and has changed the way we see ourselves as a society in sports. Cable sports networks are on 24 hours a day and cover everything from fly fishing to monster truck pulls. It is not unusual to turn on the television and watch a high school sporting event complete with play-by-play and slow-motion analysis.

Some might argue that the success of many athletes is directly related to their ability to perform on the field and so what does it matter if kids aspire to make millions of dollars playing their favorite sport. After all, if it had not been for that sport, many would not have been given the opportunity to attend college in the first place.

The media has done an excellent job of showcasing the well-to-do and not nearly enough attention is given to what happens when players fail to successfully leap that chasm to reach the pot of gold on the other side. At the bottom of that pit, lies tales of broken relationships and wasted opportunities.

When we turn on the news, we are fed endless information about how much money an athlete is paid, or how big a contract an organization signed with a network or cable company, or how much money the owners of sports franchises are making. Of course everyone wants their fair share of the rewards, and so salaries continue to escalate in order to ward off any labor disputes between the players associations and the leagues, which consist of team owners. It is sort of the Marie Antoinette "let them eat cake" theory. If the players are busy eating cake, they won't pay attention to how much money the owners generate from lucrative television contracts, corporate sponsorship, and the millions generated from stadium rights, personal seat licenses and public tax money.

There was a time a family of four could go to a professional football game or hockey match and come home with money left in their pocket. Today the average family of four won't come home with money left in their pocket, and chances are, they won't even be able to afford to attend the game.

When attending a NFL football game, be prepared to pay $80–$100 per ticket. Parking -$15, hotdog and drink- $8.00. An average family of four can expect that outing to cost roughly $350–$400.

The need to keep up with the burgeoning salaries of today's top athletes has put the squeeze play on corporate sponsorship as well. And, in order to see a professional sporting event, be prepared to spend upward of $150–200 a night or sit in the nose-bleed sections and not eat or drink anything while there.

In the "letters to the editor" in the sports sections of the major publications, a lot of this disgust is pointed directly at the athletes in part due to their high salaries, while very little attention is focused on the owners. Whenever there is a labor dispute between the players union and management, take a look at where most of the fan resentment is focused.

Coincidence or merely a reflection of society? The owners are mostly white, the athletes in the major sports are predominately African American or Latino—with the exception of tennis, hockey and golf.

Sports, like so many other aspects of our society, has a history interwoven with how most people see each other. Slavery has often reared its ugly head in our inner psyche and still has a very profound way of shaping how people behave on and off the athletic field. Some people would say "Oh no, not another history lesson on slavery, let's just move on." If only it were that simple, surely we wouldn't be having the problems that we see in our day-to-day living. Sports has transcended a lot of the racial issues confronting us on the 6 o'clock news, but even sports cannot completely escape the stain that exists some 150 years after the abolishment of slavery. As the great civil rights leader Martin Luther King Jr., once wrote, "If the inexpressible cruelties of slavery could not stop us, the opposition we now face will surely fail."

When attending a sporting event, it is one of the rare moments in which people who would otherwise not spare each other so much as a glance if they crossed paths in public, are drawn together for a common goal of rooting their team to victory. People with different ethnicities hug, high five and embrace in a way that makes you stop and ponder what can and should be the norm.

Could winning be a more powerful motivation to end discrimination? In some cases the answer to that question is a definite yes. We love associating with winners, and it matters not what a winner looks like. This could explain why so many schools of higher learning won't consider students without exceptional grades and test scores for admittance into their classrooms, but are willing to look the other way if an athlete can bring notoriety to the school through exceptional athleticism. Then and only then is an acceptance letter issued to a student with marginal grades and test scores.

Perhaps this type of thinking is precisely why former Green Bay Packers Hall of Fame quarterback Paul Hornung speaking on the subject of Notre Dame's need to return to its winning tradition, said in an interview with a Detroit radio station WWJ-AM.

"We can't stay as strict as we are as far as the academic structure is concerned because we've got to get the black athlete," said Hornung. "We must get the black athlete if we're going to compete. We open up with Michigan, then go to Michigan State and Purdue—those are the first three games, you know, and you can't play a schedule like this unless you have the black athlete ..you just can't do it." Hornung, who is a broadcast analyst for Notre Dame football on the Westwood One Radio group, openly criticized the university on its academic requirements. In the process albeit unintentionally, he undermined the dedication and commitment of many student athletes who work very hard to achieve the grades necessary to gain admittance into Notre Dame or any other school with high academic requirements. Notre Dame University quickly spoke out against these comments stating: "We strongly disagree with the thesis of his remarks."

Having in the past, interviewed Notre Dame football coach Tyrone Willingham, who happens to be the first African American coach hired at Notre Dame in any sport, must have been deeply troubled by those comments. As a former head coach at Stanford, Willingham (as mentioned earlier in this book), is a firm believer in recruiting only the finest athletes, both on and off the field, in order to win. If he did it at Stanford, he can certainly do it at a school that hardly has to sell blue-chip prospects on the idea of playing football at Notre Dame.

The same issues were brought up in 1996 when California voters passed Proposition 209, which prohibits state and local government agencies from giving preferences to women and minorities in contracting, hiring and COLLEGE ADMISSIONS.

This was a problem for the UC Board of Regents, the board that governs the University of California's nine campuses throughout the state. How would they justify allowing kids with lower grade point averages and test scores into the UC schools to participate in the highly profitable athletic programs, while at the same time flashing the "No Vacancy" sign to the non-athletic minorities who were applying for admissions with equal or better grades and or test scores?

Here is how the game was played. Since 1996, the UC admissions policy has been set up with a two-tiered system that considers between 50–75 percent of all the students admitted to each campus. These students are judged solely on the basis of academic grades and college entrance exams. That leaves at least another 25 percent of the students to be considered for admittance by other factors like overcoming adversity, special circumstances and, of course, athletic ability. This rule allows schools like UCLA and UC Berkeley the opportunity to recruit players who would not otherwise qualify under the new Prop. 209 guidelines, and thus skirt the anti-affirmative action legislation.

This new admissions policy so effectively decreased the number of minorities being accepted to the UC schools that the UC Board of Regents had to revise its policies for admitting minority students regardless of their athletic abilities.

It would be nice to think that this decision was based on concerns that every student in this country be given at least a chance to gain an education and improve their quality of "life, liberty and the pursuit of happiness." However, it stood to reason that if minority students weren't made to feel welcomed at the admissions office, how long would it take before some of the top high school athletes got the message that the UC schools had a "need not apply" sign at the entrance to the school?

The private schools in the state were under no such mandate, and schools like the University of San Diego, University of Southern California and Stanford were surely going to take advantage of such a misguided policy.

Similar opposition forces against affirmative action admissions in the states of Texas, Louisiana, Mississippi and Washington have successfully won court rulings against preferential treatment when it comes to university admissions policies.

African-American students make up about 3 percent of the undergraduates at the University of Washington, and about 54 percent of the football team—the team that happened to have a won a national championship title during the 1997-98 season.

It leaves one to wonder what is really going on in the upper echelons of legislative and judicial offices to want to bar people from opportunities of higher education unless there are financial benefits to these schools. For those people who think this argument doesn't hold water, a closer look at the elementary or grade school level would be in order. If you go into the classrooms of these schools in affluent communities, look at the number of non-white students in these schools that have no competitive sports programs, where sports exist only in the physical education classes. Only a small number of minority students would be counted in those classrooms.

It isn't until you get to the grade levels where the schools are competing for city and state recognition that many schools are recruiting players from all over the place.

We are subconsciously creating a generation of young sports mercenaries who will play anywhere, anytime, if the money or the perks are right.

This nation could agree in principle with doing away with admissions quotas if two things were to happen:

1. Every kid in this country would have equal access to the books, computers and quality teachers throughout America, regardless of socio-economic or ethnic background.

2. We eliminate the special-ruling quotas straight across the board for athletes as well.

I know that some would argue that a lot of kids who might otherwise end up in jail or in the grave, are given a "second chance" through their athletic abilities.

Every child has the ability to learn. Therefore, if as a society we set the bar high enough, everyone can achieve if given the opportunity.

African American author Randall Robinson, who wrote the national bestseller, *The Debt*, eloquently identifies numerous factors to help us understand why African Americans have been "disenfranchised" in this country for so many years.

"We hardly ever in life exceed the expectations set for us by the general society," says Robinson. "Some of us are conditioned to excel. Others are conditioned to fail. Few of us, however, are conditioned to give much conscious thought to where the bar has been set for us."

Before we can talk about leveling the "playing field," we must first do something about leveling the educational system. To bolster the points made earlier about equal access to text books and learning materials, Randall Robinson makes note of the fact that his daughter is a high academic achiever and that she scored academically higher than the majority of her white contemporaries "because of the stimulating intellectual environment of her home generally and, more specifically, because her mother taught her the rudiments of reading before she had set foot in kindergarten." There can be no substitute for the fundamentals of reading, writing and arithmetic. No amount of income can make up for a fundamental lack in this area, regardless of what the box scores may state the following morning in the sports section.

By allowing children the opportunity to spend more time playing outdoors or watching television instead of balancing their daily routine with studies, parents are essentially denying their children a valuable weapon needed to win the war against educational complacency.

In the 1950s, conventional wisdom said that educators could only do so much for students who lacked the strong educational upbringing to succeed in the classroom. If parents were unwilling or unable to participate in their children's studies, it was widely believed those students could not possibly compete with their peers.

Then along came a professor from the University of Chicago by the name of Benjamin Bloom who challenged that way of thinking with revolutionary research that proved "all children can learn" en route to developing the foundation for the government's "Head Start" for early childhood education program. Government reports stated that educators had very little to do with the level that a child would grow educationally. In other words, scholastic achievement could be traced back to that child's social and economic characteristics.

Professor Bloom contradicted those theories and proved that if you could improve the countenance of the educators and tailor the lessons to the need and level of the students, then you could minimize the effects of socioeconomic influence.

Professor Bloom's research found that about half of the intellectual capacity of an adult is developed by the time the person is four years of age and about 80 percent by the time that he or she is eight.

An emeritus professor at the University of Chicago, Bloom helped to define how educators, combined with demanding but affectionate parents, could push young people to achieve at the top levels in academics, arts and sports. His signature "mastery learning" techniques are utilized in schools and halls of higher learning throughout the world.

In September 1999, this education pioneer passed away, but not before he left us with a better understanding of what we could be regardless of our background.

In my quest to find a story about someone who exemplified the essence of professor Benjamin Bloom, I stumbled across a young man who grew up in Jamaica.

Floyd Wedderburn struggled mightily with academics when his family moved here in the early '90s. Large in stature, this gentle giant (6 foot 5 and 335 pounds) enjoyed playing football and basketball. So gifted was this young man that Penn State football legend Joe Paterno offered him an athletic scholarship to play at Happy Valley, Pennsylvania. The only problem was that Wedderburn struggled with English and posted a low SAT score, which sidelined him his freshman year.

Three years of struggles with injuries and position changes left the Penn State tackle contemplating where to go from there. The team had a mediocre season in 1997, and it looked like football would be over for Wedderburn. Then one afternoon, he received a call from his mother inquiring about the rumor she had heard that he would be quitting football.

"You are not a quitter," Pauline Wedderburn told him. That was the kick-start that Floyd Wedderburn needed to get it going. During his freshman year, when he was ineligible to play football due to NCAA's minimum grade point average/ SAT scores, Wedderburn got some academic tutoring from a very special teacher.

Head coach Joe Paterno enlisted the services of his wife Sue to help out with Wedderburn's academics. "She was tough, just as tough as Joe," Wedderburn said. This speaks to the heart of why coaches like Joe Paterno are so successful. There are a lot of coaches who can draw X's and O's, but how many of them truly care if the players who they recruit—all of them— succeed after their eligibility has expired?

Remembering that afternoon while on the Stanford campus inside the office of then-head coach Tyrone Willingham (now the head coach at Notre Dame University) and talking about this very subject, I posed the question: "Could you feel comfortable inviting every player that you recruit into your home?"

"If you don't have mutual respect for one another, then it will never work. If I don't have a great deal of personal respect for a player, a strong sense of values, not only would I not invite that young man into my home, but I would not invite him into my program," said Willingham.

The player who came to Penn State struggling to find his place there finished his college education with a degree in Human Development & Family Studies and is currently an offensive tackle for the Seattle Seahawks in the NFL.

* * * * * *

Not long after I had completed my research on Floyd Wedderburn, a fire-storm ignited down in Fayetteville, Arkansas. After leading the Arkansas Razorbacks to the 1994 national basketball title along with three final four appearances and five conference championships, head basketball coach

Nolan Richardson was fired after a down season in which his team finished 13–14. It wasn't necessarily the weak performance that drew attention to the firing although it was rumored that the Arkansas administration had begun considering other coaches to replace the 17-year head coach—the first African-American head coach in the conservative South Eastern Conference.

Identifying what he thought was unfair treatment from the media with regard to his program, Nolan Richardson must have felt boxed in, and so he decided to go on the offensive.

Turning the bright lights and cameras back toward the media, Richardson held a press conference and lambasted the media for its lack of diversity in hiring minorities as reporters from the various agencies in Fayetteville and other media outlets around the country.

"When I look at all of you people in this room, I see no one who looks like me, talks like me or acts like me. Now, why don't you recruit? Why don't the editors recruit like I'm recruiting?" said Richardson. "My great-great grandfather came over on the ship, not Nolan Richardson. I didn't come over on that ship, so I expect to be treated a little different. Because I know for a fact that I do not play on the same level as the other coaches around this school play on. I know that. You know it. And people of my color know that. And that angers me."

Needless to say that after coach Richardson unleashed that "heater," his days were numbered, and I think that was what he wanted. He wanted to be able to go out on his terms and in doing so, bring to the forefront an issue that largely goes unreported.

Some of the people there were in agreement with him, although they never expressed their feelings in the same forum or manner. The appeal would have gotten a more favorable reception if not for the fact that it came on the heels of a losing season and it appeared to those in attendance that it was reflexive—a result of his failures, not theirs (media).

In a March 5, 2002, an article by *L.A. Times* sports writer J.A. Adande, "Media Diversity Worth a Question," Adande wrote, "I've read some tired columns that sarcastically lament poor Nolan Richardson and his $3-million buyout. These writers will never even have a chance of considering Richardson's perspective. They'll never write in a newsroom in which they're the minority." It has been well documented that coach Richardson was very instrumental in bringing positive recognition to the University of Arkansas through his charitable work and helping to pave the way for other minority coaches to have an opportunity to coach because of his on and off-court successes. Somewhere along the line, all of that was reduced to the banal measurements of wins and losses.

Nolan Richardson had more to concern himself with than just the media that had congregated that afternoon at his press conference on the Arkansas campus.

ESPN's documentary series called "Outside The Lines" ran a story about 36 NCAA men's basketball programs that had allowed a zero percent graduation rate during the period of 1990–1994. Arkansas under coach Richardson was identified as one of the 36 programs, and this was obviously a concern for everyone. In an interview taped prior to his being let go, Richardson was quoted as saying, "I think the responsibility doesn't necessarily rely all on the coach. The important thing is, who's in control here? Are the parents in control? The kids are in control of their life some. Where do you stop putting the blame on the coaches, the institution?"

I would agree with Nolan Richardson on the fact that it has to start with the parents, but it is the parents who put their faith in these institutions and coaches to make sure that their sons and daughters are given every opportunity to excel inside the classroom and out.

How many coaches or administration representatives would be willing to sit a kid down and leave them off of the upcoming roster if they were not completing their assignments?

In researching this book on colleges that ranked highest and lowest statistically on graduation rates, it was very disappointing to see that some of the traditional African-American colleges ranked among the lowest schools in the category of graduating their athletes.

The once-proud beacon that was the only place where descendents of slaves were welcome was now allowing some of its finest athletes to compete one-dimensionally.

Statistically, one could make an argument that some of these athletes were academically non-qualifiers for some of the big name colleges, therefore they opted to accept scholarships from traditional non-white schools, but that doesn't cut the mustard. The NCAA sets the minimum bar to compete in intercollegiate sports, so every school has to adhere to the same standards.

Howard University, a historically black college, set the standard by successfully graduating all of its 24 scholarship athletes who entered in fall 1991. However, in the mid 1980s, Howard had a 34 percent graduation rate among its athletes on scholarship. A senior point guard from the women's basketball team summed up the key to success.

"Coaches [here] give more than lip service to academics," said Kimberly Ford. "In some programs [elsewhere], the coaches don't enforce academics." Ford finished a five-year program in civil engineering a year earlier than scheduled.

The plain truth is that any school that allows an athlete to matriculate in their program for four to five years without so much as declaring a major or accumulating enough credits to at least be within a semester of earning his diploma, is nothing more than an academic façade showcasing talent for the various professional franchises.

When the NCAA announced putting stricter requirements on high school athletes earning scholarships, the proposal was viewed suspiciously. However, there has to be a point where we begin to make some hard choices about what's important and decide where our children's futures lie. The Black Coaches Association is strongly against any stricter academic standards for high school athletes.

A possible solution to the problem could be for every athlete who does not meet the minimum guidelines, there would be a rule that they are not allowed to play in their freshman year and must meet a minimum grade point average in order to compete in their sophomore year.

Everyone wins! Think about it, if that student doesn't qualify, then he/she is required to continue to hit the books at the school's expense. The schools will have a huge incentive along with the coach at that school because they have committed funding to that person's education and will want to ensure his/her success on the field and off.

If athletes decide after their sophomore year that college isn't what they had hoped it would be, the school would not have to cough up the rest of the scholarship money and the athletes would be free to pursue other educational goals or professional endeavors.

I can hear coaches around the country saying what a terrible idea that is, and they would be right if they are only interested in what that athlete could do for them.

This chapter started off by addressing the emotional issue of slavery in America. There are very few subjects that make people feel more uncomfortable than the tragic ambivalence of one group's fettered hold over another. Is it racism every time an African-American coach is questioned about his team's lackluster performance? Is it racism if a white coach decides to drive through the south side of Chicago, Harlem or South Central L.A. looking for athletes to play for him, when he would not otherwise set foot in those communities?

Situations are not always black and white. There are times when we need to take a step back and look at it from a completely different perspective. Mistrust on the part of African Americans because of age-old stereotypes of the haves and the have-nots has created a sense of entitlement. The late Arthur Ashe refers to this in his 1994 best-selling memoir *Days of Grace*, where he poignantly identifies a debilitating mindset that exists in some of the African-American neighborhoods today.

After visiting a high school in Stamford, Connecticut, and meeting with some of its varsity athletes (many of whom were black males), Arthur Ashe recalls a spirited debate that unfolded on the subject of whether or not athletes should be required to earn a minimum grade point average in order to qualify for scholarships. Many of the black players had argued that since blacks had been discriminated against and they had spent so much time training and developing their athletic skills, it would not bother them if they [the athletes] were given scholarships over students who were academically more qualified. In other words their "sense of entitlement."

"On display was the increasingly dominant African-American adolescent ethos of entitlement, 'you owe me,' which I consider monstrous. One can be sure that an adolescent with such an attitude will make no particular effort at scholastics," said Ashe. "Why should he? His teacher (black or white) owes him a passing grade."

The 2002 NCAA college basketball tournament gave us more than the usual last second buzzer beaters and tournament upsets. This tournament showcased two of the brightest participants that exemplify what you can achieve regardless of your background. Duke University All-American guard Jason Williams and University of Maryland fifth-year- senior guard (ACC player of the year & first team All-American) Juan Dixon, both earned National Championship rings (last year Duke, this year Maryland) along with their diplomas, and they couldn't have traveled a more different path en-route if they had scripted it themselves. Juan Dixon grew up in the rough streets of east Baltimore with both of his parents "chasing the dragon" —a colloquialism for shooting heroin. Juan and his brother Phil tried to occupy their time by playing basketball. Phil, now a Maryland police officer, was the stabilizing force in Juan's life, especially after not one, but both of the brothers' parents died within a year of each other from AIDS.

"My parents weren't bad people," said Juan Dixon. "They just found themselves in a bad situation with the wrong crowd."

Phil Dixon, a Division III All-American star athlete at Shenandoah Valley College in Virginia, had to step up and raise Juan, his other brother and his younger sister.

Juan was a 6-foot-3, skinny kid who had to beg his basketball coach (Gary Williams) at the University of Maryland to even give him consideration to make the squad. On many nights when UM coeds were out on dates, Juan was at Cole Field (Maryland's historic gymnasium) shooting baskets late into the evening. What was most impressive about this young man was not what he accomplished on the court, although that was extremely impressive, but at a time when most young kids from areas of impoverishment would have contacted the NBA about coming out of school early, Dixon decided to use all five years of his college eligibility to earn his degree and develop as a player and mature as an individual.

Jason Williams was blessed to have both of his loving parents at his side throughout his basketball career. Highly recruited by just about every school in the nation, Jason Williams had the educational background to excel at any school, and he chose Duke. Williams was a consensus All-American and was the runner-up in the 2001 prestigious John R. Wooden award for the most outstanding player in college basketball. He too could have taken his national title ring (2001) and headed for the bright lights and big paydays of the NBA, but like Dixon, he decided to stay in school and finish his degree in an impressive three years. This was a testament to the parents who stressed education above all else, and Jason wasn't about to disappoint them. Duke, considered by many to be the Ivy-League school in the south, has the reputation of producing some of the finest scholars and a few good basketball players as well.

After Duke defeated Arizona in the 2001 men's NCAA title game, I had the opportunity to meet Jason Williams along with his teammate Shane Battier, who ended up being crowned the recipient of the John R. Wooden award that year. I could see why Duke's basketball coach, Mike Krzyzewski, (affectionately called Coach K), was so successful. He not only recruited great basketball players, he recruited great young men—players who are highly educated, well spoken and, more importantly, well mannered. Meeting

Coach K at the Wooden Award ceremony in Los Angeles, I asked him about how difficult it is to coach in a period when athletes are looking to leave school early for that shot at the NBA.

"We encourage all of our ballplayers to pursue their dream of someday playing professionally. I think that is why some of them come to Duke," said Krzyzewski.

To get a better understanding of the percentage of sports fans who thought it would be more advantageous to side-step a college education for the chance to earn a living in professional sports, I conducted an informal study. At a state championship high school tournament, I asked people at random this simple question: "Should a talented high school athlete pass up a four-year scholarship to a university if he feels that he is good enough to turn pro?" Those responding to the survey gave answers that were reflective of their socio-economic backgrounds. An overwhelming number of them agreed that the young prospects should pass on the college experience for the chance at the "big money," based, in part, that some of the respondents had not attended at least two years of college themselves. It was not unusual to hear comments like, "What do they need to go to college for? Even if they get an education, they're going to have a hard time getting a job." The gentleman admitted that his response was influenced in part by having grown up during the Depression and experiencing first-hand the shift in automotive manufacturing to other countries. A woman in her early sixties stated that young black males have little or no hope of growing up in the inner cities and attending college.

"The people that they associate any success with are pro athletes and drug dealers. If we saw more professionals in our neighborhoods, then maybe we wouldn't have to have this discussion," she lamented.

When we approached some of the high school coaches who were there to watch and perhaps pick up a few pointers on how their counterparts reached the finals, not a single coach wanted to go on record and respond to the question. Why? Because of the fear that the next great blue-chip player might read their comments and not want to play for that particular coach.

The spectators whom I spoke to who were in favor of guiding these talented athletes toward college first were people who had college degrees or who had at least attended junior college. They were more apt to speak in terms of long-range plans of earning money and keeping it, and not just instant success.

It is often disconcerting to hear mature adults speaking about getting rich through sports when they are witnesses to the infinitesimal number of players who actually make it. Ask yourself this question: How many people do you personally know who made it into professional sports? Of that number, how many played professionally for more than five years? Now, how many of them are millionaires as a result of their professional careers?

Statistics show that less than one half of one percent of the entire population will ever retire with any significant wealth from playing professional ball, but we live in a society where people pretend that it is an every-day occurrence.

This brings up another point that one of the respondents in the survey alluded to. When people of color succeed, whether it be in professional sports, entertainment or as a result of a well paying career, the urge to move into the affluent suburbs is insatiable. To move to the suburbs or wealthy communities is proof that you have, indeed, succeeded. Who can blame them? Perhaps that is what's contributing to the problem. How can young impoverished kids look up to educated people who have "made it" if they don't see any of them? Let's take a look at what they do see on an ongoing everyday basis:

Mom gets up early every morning to catch public transportation to a job that pays just enough to cover the basic expenses. Dad, if he is around, is struggling with two jobs, because one job pays the rent and nothing else. Teachers are underpaid and overburdened with the responsibilities to be teacher and social worker all at once. The teacher drives a car that was paid off six years ago, but he/she doesn't make enough to keep up with everyday expenses to trade that one in for a newer model. The parents think the local corner merchant is charging too much and partly to blame for the strain on the household. Illicit drug dealers or numbers runners always seems to have plenty of everything. Last, but not least, pro athletes on television sell everything from the latest sporting gear to fast food.

It shouldn't be a surprise to anyone when young kids see these types of scenarios played out on an ongoing and everyday basis and want to take a shot at the professional sports endgame.

Now that we have identified the problems, what's the solution? First and foremost, there has to be an educational revolution in this country. Not the kind where politicians running for office will make mention in their litany of campaign promises only to push them to the back burner once in office. No, we need to bring the same resolve for destroying terrorism and eliminating the country's fiscal deficit back into the classroom.

There is also a problem when public schools are forced to cut funding for textbooks and eliminate school programs while taxpayer funds are used to build brand new stadiums for wealthy ballplayers and extremely wealthy team owners.

There are other ways of building new stadiums without having to siphon off precious tax dollar needed for renovating schools, repairing roads and policing neighborhoods.

The city of San Francisco proved that it could still build a 21st century ballpark without making the city drain its coffers. In the early 1990s, the San Francisco Giants baseball team tried unsuccessfully four times to pass a bond initiative to have a new stadium built. The owner at the time was literally dying a slow financial death at wind-swept Candlestick Park. Fed up with the voters of San Francisco and Santa Clara county, the team threatened to sell the ball club and move to Tampa / St. Petersburg, Florida. But a local group of investors came up with a plan to purchase the team and build a new stadium at the edge of the downtown bay-front and do it without begging the public for the money. The investment group, led by grocery store and investment tycoon Peter Magowan, set out to do what most analysts thought would be "economic suicide." The two largest lending institutions on the West Coast, Bank of America and Wells Fargo, refused to fund the project, so the Giants looked to Chase Securities to syndicate a $170,000,000 loan. According to San Francisco Giants public relations manager Stacy Slaughter, "We decided to take on the construction project ourselves. We had to make sure that since we were funding the project ourselves, there wouldn't be any major overruns in cost or scheduling, and so we got built-in guarantees against construction overruns."

The Giants put the revenue from their personal seat licenses (PSL's) into an escrow account to help offset the cost of construction as they built. The stadium cost roughly $350 million to build and required the team to raise half of the money up front from corporate sponsorship, PSLs, naming rights and any other creative financial ideas they could come up with. One of the largest telecommunications companies in the world, San Antonio-based SBC communications, which owned at the time Pacific Bell, was approached about purchasing the rights to naming the stadium after the lucrative telecommunications giant (no pun intended). SBC paid $30 million to put its name on the stadium. It is very common now for ballparks to sell the use of the stadium's name to a private corporation.

As you might expect, most cities and team owners pooh-poohed the idea as unrealistic, but in April of 2000, the Giants organization opened its gates to over 40,000 fans at the beautiful new Pacific Bell ballpark. Some critics pointed to the fact that the team was fortunate to have the robust economy in San Francisco right about the time the team was selling sponsorships and season tickets, but the team implemented sound business decisions on and off the field. They encouraged individuals to pool their resources to purchase season tickets and share the home dates so that if one person in the group experienced financial hardship, the others could go out and find a replacement season-ticket holder. Timing was certainly in the Giants organization's favor. The second year after the team opened in their new facility, San Francisco outfielder Barry Bonds went on a home run tear, and everyone wanted to see if he could surpass Mark McGwire's 1998 single season home-run record of 70. To the delight of the San Francisco fans, Bonds blasted 73 homeruns that year and broke Mark McGwire's single season home-run record which had stood for only three seasons. Prior to McGwire's record year, the single season home-run record of 61 was held by Roger Marris set back in 1961. Bonds is currently on pace to break Babe Ruth's all-time career mark of 715 and the current record of 755 held by Hank Aaron. The Giants have sold out almost every game for the past three seasons.

Officials from various sports organizations have come to the ballpark to get a glimpse at how the San Francisco franchise did what many (particularly owners of sports teams) thought could not be accomplished in today's economic climate.

Is the Giants' organization assured that this will work even if the ball club starts losing? Who knows, but one thing is for sure. You have to feel good about any team that is willing to try and honor the public's right to use tax-based revenue on more pressing issues.

Just as corporations and the private sector are searching for alternatives to solving fiscal shortfalls, the public side of government has to be equally diligent in coming up with alternatives to address deficit spending. "60 Minutes" ran a story on how the Department Of Defense (DOD) has jurisdiction over some 200 K–12 schools in the United States and abroad. The story focused on why students in these schools were excelling in all subjects and in many cases, scoring higher on the standardized tests than their public or private school counterparts. The story went on to show how the military has an open-door policy and encourages parents to come into the classroom at anytime to observe how the class is being conducted, something that is clearly discouraged in the public schools in this country. The military superintendent felt that this type of approach to learning could easily be adopted in the public sector if parents took a more direct involvement with their children's schoolwork. One parent stated that she was not going to re-enlist in the Army until she saw how well her daughter was doing in the military-sanctioned school; she then changed her mind and felt it was well worth the financial sacrifice to help her child continue to make great strides in her studies. The bottom line is that the big "D" word. Discipline. With it, anyone can achieve their full potential in sports, education, or anything else.

I spent the rest of the afternoon on my cell phone contacting potential attorneys to handle my defense. After consulting with a legal referral group, I was given the name of two criminal attorneys in the area. The first one I called was matter-of-fact and appeared to be interested in my case, however, he was clearly too busy. He indicated that he would be willing to send his assistant to represent me at the pre-trial hearing if I could get a check over to him in the amount of $2,500 by the following business day.

The next attorney I called was immediately responsive to my concerns, and invited me to his office the following day. When I arrived at his office, this articulate man who appeared to be fresh out of law school greeted me. After a few minutes of legal questions and answers, my fears were allayed. Charles Abate appeared to be a very competent criminal lawyer with a deceptively boyish appearance. We discussed the specifics of the case, and he enlightened me about the penalty should I be convicted. I was facing the possibility of five years in prison and a fine of $1,000, not to mention the fact my record would permanently reflect a felony conviction. We concluded our discussion with my feeling a sense of relief. I let my attorney know, after some prayerful consideration, I felt he would be the right person to represent me in court. An unexpected expense not in the initial budget, I now had to find the $2,000 retainer fee needed to cover my legal defense.

It was now time to place that phone call that I knew would not go as easily as my last call about the stolen bike. I caught up with Kim at work. She was busy setting up for a corporate luncheon featuring some big wigs over at General Motors.

"I can't talk to you right now, I've got some last-minute details that I have to finish before 11 o'clock," she whispered. As an afterthought she asked, "Are you all right?" I didn't want to add to her pressures, so I told her I would call her later that evening at home.

After securing a rental car and finding an inexpensive hotel, I decided it was best to sit down and develop a schedule to continue conducting my interviews and researching the information needed to write about the fate of student athletes. The Thanksgiving Day feast was fast approaching, and I had decided to head south to Miami for the holidays. I knew that I desperately needed to sleep in a comfortable bed and eat a decent meal for a change. The fast food appeal had long worn off, but the extra pounds from consuming such a diet had not.

That evening I told Kim about the accident. She began crying and asked me to reconsider what I was doing. I was too far down the tracks to head back to the station at this point. I reassured Kim this was just a small setback, and that I would soon turn the corner and start to experience some good luck pretty soon. When I mentioned I needed her to wire $2,000 to my defense attorney, she reminded me there was no provision in my budget for "going to jail." That was precisely why I needed the money. "Besides," Kim quipped, "since your father convinced you to take that gun after I said not to, you should call and ask him for the money."

Friday, November 17, started like most mornings. Early morning scripture reading and prayer followed by the mundane practice of preparing for work was all I could do to simulate the start of a "normal" day. But this day was going to be anything but routine as I headed over to Stamford to appear in court on the weapons charge. After passing through the metal detector, I found myself standing in the hall outside the courtroom listening to public defenders and high-priced attorneys alike go through arcane discussions with their clients on the particulars of their cases.

One story that particularly caught my attention dealt with a father who was there to help his son overcome an assault. This father, like many other fathers, really didn't seem to be interested in the guilt or innocence of his son, he just wanted the public defender to get the judge to release the boy into his custody. The next statement from the public defender is what really sent me into a tailspin. "O.K., what we will do is make the prosecutor bring in the victim and let him testify."

In this case the victim was a man who happened to be a homeless person whom the son was accused of hitting over the head and taking a dollar from. I wasn't sure whom I had more acrimony toward, the public defender or the father. Incarceration was probably what the young man in question needed at the time. I certainly understood why the parent was looking out for his son's best interest. I also felt that although flawed in some respects, I was dealing with the greatest legal system in the world, and was about to find out first-hand how it all worked.

My attorney, Charles Abate, greeted me and began explaining how his initial pre-trial maneuver to get the prosecutor to reduce the charge to a misdemeanor was unsuccessful. Now we were going to go through the process of requesting the judge to allow me the opportunity to go through a program called Accelerated Rehabilitation (AR). AR is a program set up for first-time offenders who have never been arrested before for a felony; I could get a probationary sentence and upon successful completion, have the conviction expunged from my record—a second bite at the apple if you will. I wasn't overly zealous about the idea of facing a judge who might not be sympathetic to my claim of ignorance of the weapons laws in the State of Connecticut, so I reluctantly agreed with the recommendations of my attorney. Abate explained in detail to me what the procedure was and what he wanted me to do when my name was called. After some last-minute instructions, I proceeded into the courtroom and found a seat.

"All rise. This courtroom is now in session. Anyone who by law having business with the court shall remain seated and come to order. The Honorable Lawrence Kester presiding." The judge entered the room, an aging figure, somewhat short in stature—but long in mete—took his seat as the room collectively resumed their seating. As the docket was called, individuals walked up in front of the bench and had their charges read aloud to the courtroom. At one point, a group of jailed detainees were brought into the room, handcuffed and placed before the bench to enter their plea. A young male was brought in, and I noticed right away that his beige t-shirt and green camouflage pants were fitting him rather loosely. As he walked up to the bench, a sudden burst of laughter came over the room. As I looked up to see what caused the sudden levity in the courtroom, I noticed the bailiff helping this young man pull up his pants. They had completely fallen down to his ankles, and the only thing he had on was his skivvies. At that moment, I actually felt more sympathy than any other emotion. It was the same feeling I had when they brought the cohorts who were handcuffed together in earlier. What had happened that caused these young men with bright futures to become entwined with a judicial system rife with broken aspirations? I knew deep down inside that fate had somehow brought me to this place so that I could see first hand the people I was probably researching. These were the same young men who were filled with so many promises of playing on some college or professional team, now mired in the bonds of the judicial system. To understand what I thought I was witnessing, I thought of the famous quote, "Gentleman we have faced the enemy, and the enemy is ourselves."

Then my name was called. As I approached the bench, my attorney simultaneously merged with me from his seat abeam the court reporter's box, where all of the attorneys were positioned. "Your Honor, Charles Abate representing my client Mr. Daniel Christensen."

With those words uttered from my attorney, I knew that I would have been tossed right into jail had my first thought of representing myself prevailed. We entered a plea of not guilty and stipulated to the judge that we would be seeking the AR program. The judge, in his authoritative voice, said, "Permission is granted to apply to the program provided the defendant notifies the victim—who in this case was the Greenwich Police Department—and is cleared through the initial background checks. Mr. Christensen, have you ever been arrested in this or any other state in the U.S.?"

Answering truthfully, I indicated that I had not, and with that declaration, I was given permission to pay the fees necessary to apply for the program. As my lawyer and I exited the courtroom and made our way to the court's bursar window, I turned my thoughts to heading to Indianapolis, and, for the moment, putting this legal nightmare behind me. To make sure I wasn't about to do something that would jeopardize my case, I asked my attorney if I would be allowed to leave the state until my next court appearance. My attorney indicated that the AR program did not restrict my movement.

"Just remember if you fail to appear, the state will issue an arrest warrant and the gun charges along with others will be brought against you," said Abate. My attorney didn't have to worry. I was in enough hot water without adding to my dilemma. Abate and I agreed to keep in touch after the holiday period. We were given a return-to-court date of December 7, 2000. With information and court documents in my briefcase, I shook Abate's hand, and set off for Indianapolis, Indiana.

Indianapolis was a transitional point. My plan was to go Monday directly to the NCAA headquarters (which had recently moved to Indianapolis from Kansas) and conduct interviews with top administrators in the organization. It would also give me an opportunity to conduct statistical research on student athletes, specifically, the graduation rates for intercollegiate athletes competing in sports at Division 1A institutions. Upon completing my interviews, I would be off to Miami for some warm rays and little of mom's home cooking.

8

SEOREH!

If there be any truer measure of a person than by what he does, it must be by what he gives.

—Robert South

"I am not a role model." After uttering those six words, basketball superstar Charles Barkley set off a very contentious debate about whether or not athletes should be considered role models. Barkley had a very valid point when he stated that teachers, parents and grandparents are the real role models and that athletes are more or less entertainers. But when you stop and think about it, most youngsters who view their favorite ballplayers through the screen of a television set feel a kinship to these players and will emulate their every move in an attempt to become as good a player or better. Madison Avenue is all too aware of this and has developed a savvy approach to marketing. If youngsters see their favorite ballplayers drink a certain brand of soft drink or fly through the air in a pair of sneakers, they will pressure mom, dad or even grandparents to buy that particular brand.

Professional athletes are also human and as such, they have shortcomings just like everyone else. The difference is, when the average person walking around has a drug problem or is racked with the demon of spousal abuse, their escapades are not exhibited on the front cover of the morning news. Not so for the heralded athlete, as it should be. When you ask the public to cough up a percentage of their take-home pay to view a sporting event, it should be expected that the celebrated figure will make an effort to be a model citizen. We all sin and fall short of the glory of God, but when some people who are looked up to as sports heroes dismiss their boorish conduct as "boys being boys," then the public should withhold adulation for such behavior.

As stated earlier, the odds of any student athlete making it into the professional sports world are stacked against them. Even those who do make it have a tremendous burden to maintain the corporate side as well as perform at the highest level in their sport.

There are a few coaches and athletes who have successfully been able to manage the balance, but not many.

JOHN WOODEN

In this post 9–11 era, we often use the term heroes to describe the men and women who sacrifice so much for the good of mankind. One such person is legendary basketball coach John Wooden. Considered one of the greatest coaches in any sport, Coach Wooden, from 1948 until his retirement in 1975, accumulated a winning percentage of .808. This included capturing 10 national championships, seven of which were consecutive, from 1967 to 1973. Three of those championship teams went undefeated and at one stretch, UCLA had a home-court record of 60-1. Yet for all of those winning seasons, the paradox is that Coach Wooden would be the first one to tell you that it wasn't about winning. "Focus on effort, not winning," is a trademark for Coach Wooden.

Long before the NCAA had developed academic guidelines for athletes, Coach Wooden demanded equally of his players both to attend class as well as perform on the basketball court. A piece of paper that he kept in his wallet carried a simple message from his father. It is from Shakespeare's *Hamlet* as Polonius speaks to Laertes: "This above all, to thine own self be true."

Coach Wooden enjoys epigrams like this one: Talent is God-given; be humble. Fame is man-given; be thankful. Conceit it is self-given; be careful.

Two years ago, looking for an opportunity to interview John Wooden, I contacted the Los Angeles Downtown Athletic Club to cover the John R. Wooden Award ceremony held every year in April. The award is given to the most outstanding college basketball player in the country.

Seated in the reception hall just outside of the room where the ceremony was being held, I got the opportunity to watch on a television monitor the crowning of the John R. Wooden award to Duke University forward Shane Battier. Most of the local media was on hand to take pictures and ask the core questions required of them by their bosses. Suddenly this elderly gentleman walked into the room assisted with an aluminum cane and a small entourage. I recognized the gentleman as none other than the guest of honor. Slowed by father time, John Wooden was seated at the front of the room and I decided to make my way over to him before the rest of my colleagues recognized I was sitting there conducting an exclusive. Impeccably dressed he had a full head of salt-and-pepper hair and baby blues positioned right at me. I introduced myself. He was as gracious toward me as if I had played on one of his championship teams, but couldn't quite call me by name. I was impressed with how mentally sharp the coach is at 94. We discussed the mindset of young ballplayers in college and why their interest in leaving school at such an early age (if they go at all) is a major concern for most college programs. Coach Wooden jumped on the subject immediately. "In my opinion, I think it is a mistake when any young person has an opportunity to go to college, and they let that opportunity pass them by," said Wooden.

John Wooden puts such a strong emphasis on education that he stated, "I wanted to attach a cap and gown to my award, but I was overruled on that idea."

An overzealous reporter decided to press in on my interview and ask the coach if he felt anyone could come close to coaching a college team to 10 national titles again? "Well I never thought that Lou Gehrig's record for consecutive games played would be achieved in my life time, and certainly not be broken by a short stop," said Wooden. Under the watchful eye of his daughter Nan and her husband Stan, the coach was whisked away to take part in the dinner portion of the ceremony, and this reporter was left pinching himself to make sure he wasn't dreaming.

JACKIE ROBINSON

There have been several student athletes who have made their mark at the collegiate level, then gone on to make a major impact within society. Jackie Robinson starred at UCLA and lettered in baseball, basketball, football and track. He was a gifted athlete who elected to leave school early to join the Armed Forces and pursue a professional career in sports. Robinson of course, went on to fame and notoriety as the first Negro to be allowed to play professional baseball in the Major Leagues.

JACKIE JOYNER-KERSEE

Another student athlete with the same first name Jackie, excelled at UCLA in track and field. Jackie Joyner- Kersee, from 1984–1996, won every heptathlon she ever competed in. In all, Jackie Joyner-Kersee finished her career with the six highest scores in the history of the sport with two World Championships and two Olympic gold medals and she rewrote four different world records.

After retiring from world-class competition in track and field, Jackie Joyner-Kersee had one more major accomplishment left in her sights. Determined to give something to the community that was responsible for most of her accomplishments, Joyner-Kersee raised several million dollars to build East St. Louis a new community center. Unlike some athletes who reach that level of success, Joyner-Kersee wanted to give something back to the community so that other youngsters could have the same opportunities to reach their full potential.

ROBERTO CLEMENTE

Greater love hath no man than this, that a man lay down his life for his friends.

—John 15:13

There are but a handful of great athletes who never had the opportunity to attend college and compete in student athletics, yet go on to achieve tremendous success. Pittsburgh Pirates right fielder Roberto Clemente was a man who exemplified what it means to truly be a hero.

In October 2001, I flew to Phoenix to catch Game Two of the World Series between the defending World Champion New York Yankees and the Arizona Diamondbacks. As a reporter, I have had the privilege of covering two World Series in the last seven years, but this was my first time purchasing a couple of tickets from a scalper who charged me twice their face value. The pre-game festivities particularly caught my attention because seated along the infield were the widow and three sons of Hall of Fame Pittsburgh Pirates right fielder Roberto Clemente. Every year since his tragic death on that fateful day in December 1972, The Roberto Clemente Award for the year's outstanding humanitarian baseball player in the Major Leagues is given to the player who demonstrates the compassion and tireless efforts to improve the lives of others.

On December 23, 1972, Roberto Clemente received word that a major earthquake had struck Nicaragua, killing 6000 and injuring more than 20,000 people. Scores of people were left homeless.

After receiving an award in San Juan that evening, Roberto Clemente was approached by a local television producer named Luis Vigoreaux, asking if Clemente would help in a relief effort to send necessary food, blankets and medicine to the Nicaraguans who were in desperate need.

Clemente made the ultimate sacrifice when the plane he was on, carrying the relief aid, crashed shortly after take-off, killing everyone on board. Athletes who strive to make a mark on the game can certainly take pride in personal achievements; the Roberto Clemente Award should be one of the most honored.

EARVIN "MAGIC" JOHNSON

It's not very often that you see a collegiate basketball player lead his team to a national championship as well as a world championship, but Earvin "Magic" Johnson did it in 1979. In my opinion, it doesn't happen very often, but here again you had a sophomore in college who had everything to gain by leaving school early. With the national title and a guaranteed contract worth millions of dollars in his favor, Johnson almost turned down then Los Angeles Lakers owner Jack Kent Cooke's offer to play for the Lakers and return to Michigan State. Cooke increased his offer, and the rest is basketball history.

I was fortunate to meet one of the greatest basketball players to ever play the game on a red-eye flight coming home from Hawaii. A few years earlier, my wife and I had just completed a beautiful weeklong vacation on both the Big Island and Maui, when we boarded the 8:30 P.M. United flight bound for Los Angeles. My wife and I were seated in 4A & 4B, window and isle respectively. Just prior to the cabin doors being locked and secured for the flight, this very tall gentleman suddenly appeared at the overhead cargo bin, securing his belongings and taking seat 4F. It was basketball legend Magic Johnson.

He is Magic Johnson to the millions of fans and followers around the world, but I knew from my previous research that his family and close friends knew him as "EJ" or Earvin. In my assignments to cover various sporting events, I had never met Earvin before, and it was fitting that the first time we met, it was as if we had known each other all our lives. We talked about how our lives had paralleled, both of us born in the year 1959, we both attended the same church, and we earned our living off of sports.

I have had the opportunity to get to know great athletes on and off of the playing surface, but very few have ever come across to me as down-to-earth as Earvin "Magic" Johnson. We sat for the first two and a half hours and talked about everything from family to politics and beyond, with my wife interjecting at every opportunity.

He was returning from Kapalua where he and his wife Cookie had decided to sell their vacation home so that their kids could come to Hawaii and play with other kids staying at the resorts.

I got to interview him in a way that really wasn't an interview at all. Johnson gave me a better understanding of why he was able to accomplish so much during his phenomenal career in the NBA and still became one of the most successful businessmen in all of sports. What made this chance encounter such a blessing was that I had already selected Johnson as an example for this book as a student athlete who overcame the odds of making it in professional sports, transcending his or her sport as a contributor and more importantly a humanitarian. Rarely does a reporter interview a famous celebrity without going through their publicist, agent or media relations representative, so this was unique, a veritable coup.

ARTHUR ASHE

Arthur Ashe is another name that comes to mind when I think of the consummate student athlete. "Many young athletes are probably doomed, tragically, to return to the poverty from which sports almost saved them." This prophetic statement by Ashe sadly is still very true today.

To say Arthur Ashe was one of the greatest tennis players to ever hit a cross-court shot could be arguable; to say that he was one of the greatest ambassadors of the sport would be irrefutable.

Arthur Ashe grew up during the late '40s and early '50s in this country when it was difficult for blacks to enjoy those of life's pleasures whites had always taken for granted as everyday living, particularly in the south. The "Jim Crow" laws of segregated housing and shopping areas left an indelible impression on Ashe, and he decided at a very early age to try and change things for the better.

Intent on becoming an architect after his tennis career was over, Ashe received some sound advice from his mentor and tennis coach J.P. Morgan who told him to major in something a little less time consuming. Ashe took it to heart and changed his major to business administration.

Ashe wanted to make a difference in this world in his own way. Along with the social programs combining tennis and self-esteem, the Arthur Ashe Foundation reached out to improve the lives of minority children who may not have had some of the same opportunities he had. This period in his life was what he called his "middle passage," where he began to speak out on issues such as AIDS, Apartheid, inequalities of Haitian refugees and the need to improve graduation rates among student athletes. Arthur Ashe understood very well, perhaps better than most associated with sports and education, that to be black and uneducated was surely the closest thing to be handed a poverty-filled death sentence in this country. His concern and passion led him to reach out and take a stand that, although unpopular among most African-American communities, nevertheless was the proper position to take. Ashe believed by raising the educational expectations of young kids in the poorer communities, the focus would shift from athletics to spending more time within the books, thus giving them a better chance to succeed in society whether they played sports professionally or not.

For Ashe, the battle lines were clearly drawn with the NCAA's Propositions 48 & 42 (which were extensively detailed earlier in the book). This issue became such a force in his life that Arthur Ashe decided to co-found an organization called AAAA, the African American Athletic Association to assist in the nurturing and counseling of young athletes to perform academically and to assist with job placement once their playing days were over. With the assistance of Gloria Primm Brown of the Carnegie Corporation and a host of others, Ashe got personally involved to try and prove that, given the proper setting and with the right people involved, young people could excel regardless of their race or their parents' financial status. In his quest to find material on past and present contributions from African-American athletes, Arthur Ashe was surprised by the lack of material written by black or white historians on the subject. With a high percentage of African Americans having competed in various sports throughout this country's history, (given the paltry literary record of the legacy), Ashe invested $300,000 of his own money to research and write three volumes on the "History of the African

American Athlete" called *A Hard Road to Glory.* This was one of Arthur Ashe's proudest accomplishments on or off the court.

While conducting research throughout various libraries and news publications, Ashe was astonished to find information about athletes whom, up to that point, most Americans did not know existed. The book was a success both spiritually and commercially. Ashe made back more money than his initial investment had cost. He felt he had finally created an archive that people could truly research to glean the rich history of African Americans in sports and their accomplishments in the United States and beyond.

Arthur Ashe believed that family is the central point in our lives and we should not prejudge anyone. He demonstrated his belief that good will always overcomes evil by the example he led in sports and in life.

On February 6, 1993, Arthur Robert Ashe, Jr., died from complications related to AIDS in New York City.

Ashe writes in his autobiography, *Days of Grace,* "The morning after winning Wimbledon, I should have asked, 'why me?' If I don't ask 'Why me?' after my victories, I cannot ask 'Why me?' after my setbacks and disasters."

His faith sustained him until the end as evidenced by the scripture that was presented at the beginning of his book:

> *. . . since we are surrounded by so great a cloud of witnesses, let us lay aside every weight, and the sin which so easily ensnares us, and let us run with endurance the race that is set before us.*
>
> —Hebrews 12:1

TIGER WOODS

If ever there was an athlete ready to skip college and turn pro straight out of high school, it would be Tiger Woods. Though not yet mature enough to handle the rigorous day-to-day challenges a professional golfer faces, Woods certainly had the talent.

In 1994, Tiger Woods signed a letter of intent to compete on the golf team at Stanford University. For Woods, the academic reputation of Stanford was the deciding factor over such schools as UNLV, Arizona and Virginia. There, he felt he could pursue both his athletic and academic excellence simultaneously.

By 1996, fed up with the imposing restrictions the NCAA placed on its athletes, Woods opted to turn professional and proceeded to win two titles and finish in the top 10 in five out of his first eight PGA tournament events. The following year, Tiger Woods became the youngest player to ever win a Masters.

Whenever there is a child prodigy showing signs of greatness, the overwhelming urge to push and drive can consume most parents. This is particularly true in the area of financial commitment. Some parents are willing to mortgage their life savings and the family home just for the opportunity to develop a superstar athlete.

The Woods family came to the realization that in order for Tiger to continue developing and achieving his potential, financial sacrifices would have to be made. According to Earl Woods in the book he wrote about teaching Tiger lessons on golf and life called *Playing Through* with Fred Mitchell, "We weren't necessarily sacrificing so he could become a professional golfer; we just wanted to be there for our son and to facilitate his happiness. And golf was certainly making him happy."

Woods also stated he and his wife never argued about the money they spent on Tiger's development, a point many parents initially agree on, but few ever adhere to.

The success of Tiger Woods has brought with it a new generation of parents looking to replicate the complete athlete from the marketing makeover to the total dominance of their sport. They call it the "Tiger Formula." First you have to find youth, add one part hard work, one part unquenchable drive (there is no substitute for this ingredient), two parts financial commitment and a whole lot of sacrifice, and you begin to see what it takes to bring kids from the local tournaments to the world stage of competition.

There are millions of dollars at stake for the few who are successful, not only in tournament purses, but more importantly, in corporate endorsements.

After his sophomore year at Stanford, Tiger and his family decided it would be in his best interest to leave school and pursue his dream of becoming a professional golfer. It was a tough decision for Earl and Tida who had a simple rule: "no schoolwork, no golf." The constant battles the Woods had with the NCAA from country club memberships to receiving a free lunch with golfing legend Arnold Palmer, forced the elder Woods to "reassess something I had believed throughout my entire life: that education came above everything."

Matt Kuchar became the next amateur world champion following Tiger Woods, and he was bombarded to quit school and turn pro like Tiger did. Kuchar didn't bend to the heavy, lucrative deals offered to him and elected to finish his degree at Georgia Tech. Mark Kuchar's name is not a household one at this point on the tour, but even if he had quit school, there is no guarantee that he would be any closer to winning a PGA tournament.

"60 Minutes II" profiled such a family last year that decided to test the formula. When Sean O'Hair was 15 years old, his father, Marc O'Hair, decided to move the family from Arizona to a golf academy in Bradenton, Florida. The senior O'Hair wanted to give his son Sean the opportunity to train and compete with young kids looking to reach the same success levels that Tiger Woods, Phil Mickelson, Sergio Garcia and V.J. Sing have achieved. Prior to the "60 Minutes II" piece, almost no one had ever heard of the name Sean O'Hair, and it's a strong possibility that we may never hear his name mentioned again on television. It's not that the young O'Hair isn't a talented golfer, he may very well be. It is the Atlas-like pressure that often erodes these young athletes to the point of drug addiction, alcoholism or worse.

A female version of Tiger Woods has certainly burst onto the scene. Michele Wie (pronounced We), the 15-year-old female golf sensation, is a hit on the Ladies Professional Golfers Association Tour. Wie is also a very gifted athlete and she already has the talent and maturity to turn pro after high school, but she is currently not focusing her attention in that direction.

Although her parents are investing as much as $50,000 a year on golf, they are keeping their daughter's feet firmly planted by limiting the number of tournaments she plays in and keeping her academics as the number one priority. Like Tiger, Michele Wie plans to attend Stanford.

According to NCAA Bylaws, an amateur can participate in a professionally sponsored tournament like the LPGA as long as there is no cash compensation or any equivalent. Also, an athlete cannot sign with an agent or express intent to turn pro through a contract or receive compensation of any kind for endorsements. (For more information about these and other rules regarding amateur status, go to www.ncaa.org)

By being the three-time defending US Amateur Champion and the reigning NCAA Division I Men's individual champion, Tiger Woods assured himself of a solid financial footing, long before he ever made the decision to leave school early. Is it right for an athlete to leave school early and turn pro?

It's probably best answered on a case-by-case basis. A decision that works for one athlete could turn out to be another athlete's worst nightmare.

For others, there is always the "safety net" for a kid whose parents are successful and who know people in positions to make others successful. Kids growing up in poverty, however, face a completely different reality.

There are a lot of successful people in the world who are highly educated, but lack a diploma from an accredited university. The real tragedy comes when an athlete has neither.

The beginning of this chapter is titled "SEOREH," which is "heroes" spelled backwards. The title of this chapter was selected because often in society we have our heroes reversed. It is easy to see why people who perform marvelous feats of agility in sports on a world stage can captivate our imagination to the point that we hold them in the highest regard. In reality, heroes are people who go out every day and make a difference in the lives of others by doing the very things that don't require super athletic ability or super human strength. Heroes accomplish things that don't always reach the headlines, but are every bit as important as the things that do. Schoolteachers, firefighters, law enforcement officers, librarians, emergency medical personnel and parents/grandparents are the real heroes in life.

LEGALIZING INTEGRITY

The trip from Connecticut to Indiana was thankfully uneventful. My plans that I had so carefully laid out before I left California seemed to change by the hour. Now that I didn't have my truck to sleep in, I located a relatively inexpensive motel and began to organize myself for the following business day.

I had been playing phone tag with Kim over the weekend, and we finally connected at the end of the weekend. I told her my plans for the upcoming Thanksgiving holiday, and I tried to convince her to fly to Miami and join me and my parents. I guess the gun charge had put a damper on those plans, and now Kim wanted to remain on the West Coast.

"I've decided to drive to San Francisco and spend the holiday with my family, besides, my mom's not doing very well, and I want to check up on her." Kim's mom had been diagnosed with the early onset of Alzheimer's, and her father was pulling double duty running the household and caring for her mom. I certainly agreed with her wanting to go up to the Bay Area, and I even gave some thought to canceling my trip to Florida and spending Thanksgiving in San Francisco, but then I would have disappointed the other important woman in my life.

I woke up Monday morning to a weather advisory for all of the upper Midwest. The forecast included snow showers for Indianapolis. I walked outside to my car and was greeted by temperatures in the low twenties with a wind chill below zero. The shock of the crisp air nearly took my breath away, but I was determined to continue my journey. I entered the NCAA's underground parking lot that was positioned adjacent to a beautiful man-made lagoon running the length of the property. As I entered the main lobby area past the Hall of Fame building, a security guard greeted me and inquired about the nature of my visit. After the initial perfunctory call to the research desk, I was given a nametag and escorted to the library by a very jovial assistant named Mary Jennings. She was extremely helpful in pointing out the books I was in need of to commence my search and even placed a phone call to a researcher in Kansas City who was able to answer some questions on how the NCAA calculates its graduation rates. As I pored over the compiled data submitted by member university athletic departments, I began to get the feeling that there was more to this story than just graduation rates. Could a number really explain what these universities were doing to ensure a good education for these kids whose parents entrusted them to the care of their respective colleges?

I had seen first-hand how some athletes had such tunnel vision when it came to the belief that their scholarship was their ticket to the pros as opposed to the entrance to a brighter future into the corporate world. Some universities have pulled strings to qualify certain players, knowing the odds are high that some of these recruits will probably never finish with a degree. In fact, I would from time to time run into former teammates from school, working jobs that they certainly didn't need to go to college to obtain. It would be a little embarrassing to hear them try and explain away what happened to lead them into these positions. One evening on my way to cover a San Diego Chargers—Denver Broncos game, I saw a scholarship athlete from my junior year in college hustling tickets outside the stadium. I recognized him right away, but I doubt seriously if he ever saw me.

There are schools with very high graduation rates for student athletes in which the emphasis is on balancing schoolwork with athletic competition. These are the schools that you would expect, mainly Ivy League schools which do not offer athletic scholarships and schools that generally finish at the bottom of the list in their respective athletic conferences. There were a few surprises in football. Northwestern and Stanford, having competed in the 1996 and 2000 Rose Bowl games, respectively, were also very high on the list of schools that graduate their overall student body along with their students athletes. In basketball, Stanford, Duke and Georgetown also make strong showings in the classroom and in the NCAA basketball championships.

A statistic that smacked me square in the face was the number of African American basketball players from the University of Louisville who failed to graduate during a period from 1989–1993. Not a single African American player was awarded a degree in any field of study. I thought there must have been a misprint, so I called over to the athletic office at Louisville and requested to speak with the academic coordinator for athletics. I was directed to a gentleman by the name of Marvin Mitchell. After a brief introduction and a quick synopsis of what I was working on, I proceeded to ask for an explanation for an academic record that was, by any standards, abysmal. Mr. Mitchell informed me he had just recently been hired there as the Associate Athletic Director and had only been involved in the past year with trying to get the ship turned around and headed in the right direction. I could tell he was sincere in what he was saying, so I requested and got an interview to sit down face-to-face to hear what factors led to the problems at Louisville. Our meeting would have to be delayed for a week. It was just three days before Thanksgiving, and I had a plane to catch down to the "Magic City."

I spent the rest of the afternoon compiling the results of all of the Division I schools' graduation rates for freshman players and transfer students in each major sport. It was clear that the decision makers were not interested in going on record, as my request to interview the executive director was denied. With that, I thanked the NCAA research staff and I headed for the Chicago O'Hare Airport for my two hour and 43 minute flight to Miami.

I arrived in Miami around 4 o'clock in the afternoon. The balmy sunshine and 74-degree temperatures were beginning to agree with my countenance. I arrived at my parents' house and immediately made myself comfortable. After spending the last five weeks on the road, in and out of roadside motels that could only be called motels by the most far flung of definitions, it didn't take long to get reacquainted with familiar surroundings. My father and I chatted about the latest: what was going on with my legal predicament and how the book-writing tour was shaping up. My mother had not yet arrived home from work, so we continued our chat. Just prior to the dinner hour, my mother entered and gave me a big hug. I could tell that my cross-country researching adventures were wearing thin on her nerves as a concerned mother. About an hour later, we all gathered around the dinner table, and I had my first decent meal in nearly two months.

Ten minutes into the meal, the phone rang and my mother spoke cordially to the caller. Within a few seconds, I could tell it was Kim calling from California. My mother asked about Kim's mom's health and sent them her love and with that handed me the phone. I could tell Kim was excited about telling me some "good news." She had spoken to my friend over at the Post, Jeff Brower, and he had a proposition. I could hardly wait to hear what this was about.

9

LEGALIZING INTEGRITY

Question! When was the last time you were able to pick up a newspaper and read about a famous athlete, politician or entertainer who was not in trouble with the law? It seems like every time we open the sports page, we immediately do a double take to make sure that we didn't accidentally grab the front page by mistake.

The simple truth is athletes and entertainers are just like anyone else, except for those God-given talents and a lot of media coverage you simply can't buy. In other words, they too are sinners and subject to the same pitfalls as everyone else.

If the average person goes over to First National Bank and robs it, you may or may not hear about it. If a prominent athlete or well-known celebrity tries it, everyone with a television, radio or computer will know about it inside of 20 minutes.

We live in a world where seconds, not days or weeks, are the barometer for measuring/updating information. The competitive edge to grab the story and be the first to break the news has put us in this frenetic pace to head hunt for celebrities at odds with the law. Often celebrities believe since adoring fans have put them on such a high pedestal, the law doesn't apply to them. Strangely enough, it seems the fans who lift their favorite athlete or entertainer to that rarified stature, are just as quick to bring them crashing back down to reality. Of course there is no shortage of victims willing to take the leading role in this tragic Shakespearean play, center stage of life.

The perception is if you can make it in professional sports, then all of your problems magically resolve themselves. In many instances, the problems start with the fame and exorbitant salaries most young people aren't ready to handle. Even if student athletes are successful enough to navigate the various mines that await them, the temptations will continue to grow as the success escalates.

A case in point would be the O.J. Simpson story. Here is a person, who, by most accounts was not viewed as a criminal, let alone a knife slashing double murderer. There he stood charged with the double murders of his ex-wife, Nicole Brown Simpson, and her friend Ronald Goldman in the tony section of Los Angeles called Brentwood.

This was not just another athlete on trial for murdering his ex-wife; this featured a Hall of Fame NFL superstar who had also appeared in television and movies. The first reaction most people felt when they heard the news of the murders was shock and sadness and probable certainty that the man who once ran through the airports as the All-American pitch man for Hertz Rent-A-Car was in no way involved. However, it would be safe to say that the majority of people today who witnessed the trial and the evidence, have very little faith in O.J.'s innocence. Found "not guilty" in the criminal trial, he was later found guilty in the civil suit brought by the parents of Nicole Brown and Ronald Goldman.

Subsequent to the Simpson trial, we have seen other athletes go on trial for murder. In January 2001, former NFL Carolina Panther wide receiver Rae Carruth was convicted on three charges relating to the shooting death of his pregnant girlfriend Cherica Adams. The district attorney's office contends that on November 16, 1999, Carruth, learning his girlfriend was pregnant, decided he did not want to provide financial support to Adams. The state laid out its case that Rae Carruth along with three co-defendants conspired to lure his girlfriend into an ambush as he boxed Cherica's car in between himself and the shooters. Cherica Adams was shot four times after attending a movie with Carruth. She died a month after the attack. Carruth avoided being convicted on the more serious charge of first-degree murder. However, he was convicted of conspiracy to commit murder, shooting into an occupied vehicle and using an instrument to destroy an unborn child. The defense claimed the shooting was the result of the co-defendants' retaliation because Carruth would not give them drug money. In a sad twist of irony, the child was delivered by Caesarean section while Carruth's defense was paid for by the state because he was indigent. Rae Carruth is now famous for being the first active NFL player to be charged with murder. Unfortunately he would not be the last.

Following the St. Louis Rams' victory over the Tennessee Titans in Super Bowl XXXIV in January 2000 in Atlanta, Baltimore Ravens All-Pro linebacker Ray Lewis was involved in a fight outside of an Atlanta nightclub where two men were fatally stabbed. Conflicting eyewitnesses stated initially Lewis threw punches during the altercation. Lewis was initially charged with murder, but he eventually pled guilty to a misdemeanor charge of obstruction of justice for not cooperating with the police investigation. At the time this book went to press, the murders had not been solved.

Often the difference between some of the players playing professional sports and the buddies they grew up with is money. If you grow up hanging out on the corner and getting into mischief, that mindset is still there. It doesn't suddenly disappear just because a talented ballplayer signs a multi-million dollar contract.

For most athletes, the question of who you can trust and who is out to get inside of your pockets is always a concern. The guys whom you grew up with knew you when you had nothing. It goes without saying that they are not there just because of your new-found fortunes, although that certainly adds a hook to the relationship.

Professional sports teams are now investing a great deal of financial resources into investigating athletes and their backgrounds. The statistical charts that track the vital athletic profiles used in an effort to predict a superstar are now being put to the test to analyze a potential problem child. No matter what psychological profiling professional teams use, they will continue to have someone who defies logic and snaps as a result of the pressures to maintain that coveted lifestyle.

At what point do teams start to look ahead and recognize the early warning signs and place a higher emphasis accountability. Winning games should never take priority over strong character when the immoral flags go up prior to draft day? How many times are we made aware of a player's checkered past being overlooked in order for the club with first draft rights to claim him, all in the quest for the championship title? The bottom line is that moral character is taught long before draft day. It begins at home from the time you are too young to know your ABC's.

And it's not just the players who are crossing the ethical line. More and more, coaches, general managers and even owners are taking liberties with the law. In an age where corporate accounting is very closely scrutinized, we are reminded of the former owner of the Los Angeles Kings NHL hockey team, Bruce McNall. He had it all during the late 1980s and early 1990s, so much so he single-handedly put LA hockey on the map by acquiring undoubtedly the greatest hockey player to ever lace up a pair of skates. Wayne Gretsky was McNall's prize possession, and at first it appeared to be working brilliantly. Gretsky helped the Los Angeles Kings to their first Stanley Cup final in 1993 while the owner continued to find creative ways to finance the journey.

At one point, Bruce McNall's financial empire was worth hundreds of millions with such extravagant acquisitions as thoroughbred racehorses, rare coins and even the Toronto Argonauts of the Canadian Football league. By the mid 1990s, the financial house of cards began to collapse under the weight of debt that drove McNall to the point of falsifying bank documents and using horses as collateral.

When the dust settled, Bruce McNall pleaded guilty to four counts of bank fraud, which totaled $236 million. In 1997, the once-highflying corporate exec was sent to prison. In McNall's defense, he never pointed the finger at anyone but himself. Long after some of his family and friends (including his wife) left McNall, Wayne Gretsky still remains his friend and credits McNall for looking out for the best interests of hockey. In some ways, Bruce McNall was instrumental in brokering a deal which ultimately paved the way for the existence of the Anaheim Mighty Ducks. He felt the ends would have justified the means.

Look at what transpires when athletes feel the need to take performance enhancers to win. With the increase in steroid use among athletes around the world, it's no wonder that people are questioning any athlete's success. What price do you put on your reputation?

At the 1988 Summer Olympics in Seoul, in the so-called fastest human competition, the 100 meter Canadian sprinter Ben Johnson exploded past then-reigning champion Carl Lewis at about the 70-meter mark of the race. Like he had been shot out of a cannon, Ben Johnson left the competition behind en route to a gold-medal finish in the 100-meter race. After the customary drug testing was performed, it was determined that Johnson had used a banned substance and was disqualified and stripped of his gold medal. In the years since that embarrassing moment, Ben Johnson has never come close to the level that he displayed in the Olympics, and it is certain that he will forever be remembered for that one mistake.

In the fall of 1998, Mark McGwire and Sammy Sosa launched an all out assault on Roger Maris' single season home-run record of 61 established coincidentally back in 1961. Previously, Babe Ruth held the title of 60 set back in 1927. As the 1998 season ended, Mark McGwire edged out Sammy Sosa and stood atop the mountain with a new single season homerun record of 70. Some of the fans questioned the validity of the record in light of McGwire's admission of using androstenedione, subsequently banned the following year by MLB. His title only lasted three years when San Francisco Giants slugger Barry Bonds hit 73 homeruns during the 2001 season.

Now the controversy swirls around the current single season homerun champion, since Bonds' personal trainer, Greg Anderson, along with the founder of Balco, Victor Conte, were indicted on distribution of banned drugs. Barry Bonds has always maintained he has never taken steroids and never will. "They can test me anytime they like," he said.

If you are going to accuse someone of using banned drugs and besmirch that athlete's accomplishments and more importantly, good name, it is imperative to have the "goods" on them. Speculation and assumptions will not do. If wrong, how do you put the toothpaste back in the tube?

Confession is the first step to recovering one's self-esteem whenever athletes' misdeeds are uncovered. However, denial has a way of somehow stepping up instead, as if the public has no clue about someone's shenanigans. If all else fails, start pointing the finger in another direction. It is almost like the emperor who has no clothes on. If an athlete says that he or she didn't do it, that should be good enough. But when gifted athletes have always had someone there to step up and resolve what ever conflicts may arise, it doesn't take long before some athletes come to expect that. That's where the lines between right and wrong begin to get blurred. It may start out with someone writing a note because the high school all-city player decided to skip school. Before long, transcripts are doctored up so that the athletically gifted one is accepted to the state university. From there, term papers that are written by a tutor and credit given for classes and class work that's not performed. This is the starting line for trouble, and if we don't recognize it for what it is, we fail not only the athlete, but more importantly, society.

In 1976, best-selling author James Michener wrote a book about student athletes and sports in society called *Sports in America*. In it, Michener writes how "a distressing number of college athletes" are woefully unprepared to leave the campus environment and deal with the real world of adulthood. Said Michener, "For them, the adulation of college athletics was . . . an albatross they could never shake off. [It] was not character building, it was character destroying." Almost thirty years after Michener's prophetic observations, sadly, things have not changed.

Until you have spent your whole life preparing for the world stage, you can't really begin to understand the pressures put on athletes to be the best. How else can you explain what happened during the qualifying trials at the 1994 figure skating championships in Michigan? During the Winter Olympic trials in Detroit, Tonya Harding, a 23-year-old figure skating champion was involved in a bizarre incident in which her former husband, Jeff Gillooly, along with other cohorts, planned and carried out the infamous "clubbed knee" incident against leading Olympic skating contender Nancy Kerrigan. Harding always maintained that she knew nothing of the plan to try and injure her toughest competitor from the United States. Through a series of legal maneuvers, Harding was allowed to compete in the 1994 Winter Games, but she was plagued with a malfunctioning skate and finished well out of the medal ceremonies.

After pleading guilty to hindering the investigation into the attack on Nancy Kerrigan, Tonya Harding, looking to avoid jail time, agreed to be stripped of her 1994 national championship by the U.S. Figure Skating Association and accepted a lifetime ban from any U.S.-sanctioned skating events.

Just prior to this book going to print, the Associated Press released a story about NHL St. Louis Blues forward Mike Danton being charged for allegedly conspiring with his 19-year-old girlfriend to commit murder by hiring a "hit man." In this bizarre story, Danton fought with a male acquaintance (rumored to be his agent) over Danton's "promiscuity and use of alcohol." According to the FBI, Danton hatched a plot to have a male friend murdered by a "hitman" because [Danton] feared this acquaintance would go to St. Louis Blues management, thus ruining the hockey player's career.

What happens to athletes who are falsely accused of crimes and allegations? Once the information is released, it is very difficult for the public not to "rush to judgment." In some cases, the athletes certainly have a track record of misconduct. But what about the ones who were truly innocent?

It is just like the elected official when he held a press conference on the steps of the courthouse after being completely exonerated by a jury of his peers and asked, "Where do I go to get my good name back?" It takes years to build a good reputation and just a fleeting moment to lose it. Just ask Richard Jewel. A young man in his twenties working as a security officer during the 1996 Summer Olympics in Atlanta, Jewel was assigned to Security Detail near Olympic Park. Just before midnight, a bomb exploded in the park, killing a woman and injuring others. As Richard Jewel ran to assist the wounded, he was unaware that his actions made some law enforcement officers suspicious. Jewel was detained and questioned for several days while media pounced on him as the prime suspect. It later turned out that Richard Jewel was simply a good samaritan who was put through a living hell just because the media was in a hurry to report and ran with allegations before they were checked out conclusively.

In some instances, a whole state can be tarnished by improper behavior. The state of Utah, which is almost synonymous with higher moral standards and strong Christian beliefs found itself embroiled in a tangled web of bribery and improper influence when it made a strong bid to host the 2002 Winter Olympics in Park City. It had been a customary practice for the cities vying for the opportunity to host the world for the Olympics to give "gifts" to a group of hand-chosen officials from the International Olympic Committee. Of course, many IOC officials denied that it was "business as usual" to conduct the search for the host city by accepting any monetary or gratuitous favors to obtain swing votes, but when it was all over and the shouting ended, there was a tremendous shake up in the IOC, including with the president. A panel formed to investigate the wrongdoing concluded that there was improper behavior by some officials, and the recommendation also included a suggestion that the head of the governing body retire.

Often, we in the media will gravitate to stories that are at times sensationalized. More stories should be written about the positive aspects of sports and the athletes who give without looking for recognition. I am happy to report that there are still a lot of very good athletes who donate their time and financial resources everyday, but you rarely ever read about it. Perhaps that's why there was joy on the part of a lot of sports fans during the 2002/2003 NBA season when the San Antonio Spurs won the NBA championship. This team truly has one of the greatest humanitarians to ever play any sport. David Robinson is just like, well, Mr. Rogers. A devout Christian who not only speaks about living a wholesome Christian lifestyle, he is symbolic of what every man or woman of faith should strive for.

As a midshipman in the Navy, he was truly a gifted big man on the court and clearly was a favorite of every NBA team's draft selection. Instead of chasing the million-dollar contracts the league would have offered, Robinson served his country and fulfilled his commitment just like Naval graduate Roger Staubach, former NFL All-Pro quarterback for the Dallas Cowboys. Both showed why they led their respective teams to multiple championships.

Steve Smith, a talented player in his own rights who gave his alma mater Michigan State a million-dollar grant, was a player who had not touched a championship trophy. He too was on that Spurs team, and for once, you felt like the good guys won. That's not to say that the other teams aren't full of guys who give back as well, it's just that these guys stand out among the rest.

Warrick Dunn and Kurt Warner are NFL players who also have decided "It is more blessed to give, than to receive." They have come up with a program to help low- income mothers by providing the down payments on new homes along with furnishings and groceries. The idea came to Warrick Dunn as a result of his own mother's struggles to raise a family as a single mom. One night while she was working as an off-duty police officer, she was tragically shot to death, leaving Warrick with the tremendous task of caring for his siblings. Dunn accepted a scholarship to play football at Florida State University in Tallahassee. Not only did he take on the pressures of performing on the field and in the classroom, he also insisted on making the four hour commute home on weekends to check on his brothers and sisters.

Arizona Diamondbacks pitcher and future Hall of Famer Randy Johnson has been actively working within the various communities to help shrink the homeless and hungry population that sadly seems to keep growing.

Kip Kaino, an Olympic long distance runner from Kenya, has taken on a noble task of raising several hundred orphans who've lost their parents to war, famine and AIDS.

Another Olympian, decathlon champion Rafer Johnson, teamed up with Eunice Kennedy Schriver, to form the Special Olympics to give children born mentally and physically handicapped an opportunity to compete in athletic competition.

Former NFL Cincinnati Bengals quarterback Boomer Esiason, has committed tremendous time and resources to help find a cure for Cystic Fibrosis (CF). His son was diagnosed with the disease early in life so this cause is near and dear to the Esiason family.

There is no doubt that there are countless other professional athletes and everyday people from all walks of life who give of their time and resources to make it better for those who are less fortunate. Am I saying that all of these athletes are perfect? Of course not. We are all humans and as such we are subject to making numerous mistakes. It's what happens after you have fallen that truly shows the character and integrity of a righteous person.

An entire book could be devoted to the subject of proper behavior and the professional athlete—those who are and are not truly heroes and role models. If you never play a single second of professional sports, you can still make a great impact on society by getting involved in a philanthropic cause that will undoubtedly change lives long after we remember who won the MVP in a Superbowl or a World Series.

I Bet You. . .

It had been a while since Kim was this excited about something—I knew it was probably something good. Kim indicated that Jeff Brower, my friend at the *Orange County Post,* called and asked how to get in touch with me. Apparently, the word was out I was on the road researching the subject of student athletes, and the local television station was interested in hiring me to develop a piece on the very same subject for their 5 o'clock sports edition. I agreed with Kim I would speak with the station manager about the freelance assignment, but I wouldn't make any promises, and I certainly wasn't about to abandon my current project on the road.

"Dan, just hear them out and see what they have in mind," Kim chided. I knew she wanted me to leap out of my chair at this opportunity and come running home and a couple of years earlier, I would have. For now, the phone call to the station manager would have to wait until the following Monday after the holiday.

I spent the rest of the Thanksgiving weekend reading and making notes to help organize the schedule of interviews I had lined up. Kim, still miffed as to why I didn't fly back to San Francisco for the holiday, spoke to me extensively over the phone during that time, and she slowly came around. We made arrangements for her to come down to Miami on Christmas Eve, and afterward, spend New Years down in the Bahamas. With Kim's mom in poor health, I knew those plans were tenuous at best. If there was ever a time in our marriage when we needed some quality time together, it was now.

After a wonderful Thanksgiving feast with my family, Monday morning rolled around and it was time to make the trek back to Chicago to the winter that had arrived prematurely. I said my goodbyes in the pre-dawn hour, and headed off to Miami International. The flight back was uneventful if you didn't count the sardine like conditions I experienced on the return leg. A high school soccer team playing in a holiday tournament in South Florida was trying to get back home from competition.

My mid-morning arrival in Chicago was a chilly reminder that I was no longer in the "Sunshine State." I quickly grabbed a car and headed out for my first interview.

During my research, I had come across an article about a DePaul University group that had developed a consortium to help athletes who had not finished college go back and complete their degree program. I discovered this was an extension of the Northeastern School of Sports in Society group out of Boston. After a couple of phone calls, I made arrangements to meet with the consortium Director, Tom Kowolski. We scheduled a meeting out at DePaul's Lake Forest satellite campus. The area was going through some continued development, and I managed to get myself thoroughly lost. After finally making my way over to Kowolski's office, I was greeted by this tall All-American guy who had the stature of someone who played either basketball or football. Tom has that Midwestern handshake, firm, and he looks you directly in the eye. We exchanged pleasantries and Kowolski, with his broad smile, asked how could he help me. I knew right away that I had found someone who understood the scope of the problem, and we immediately hit it off. I gave him an overall view of what I was working on, and I began asking him questions about how his program worked. He informed me their group was under contract with the NFL and NBA leagues to assist former players who are currently in different cities from where they did their initial undergraduate work. In essence, the consortium researches what classes a player needs to graduate and finds the equivalent curriculum an athlete attended at a participating school in the city where the athlete is currently living. Thus, the professional player graduates from the school he originally matriculated in with the transfer credits, even though he completes the remaining credits from a different university.

I could tell from our discussion we both had a similar interest in assisting athletes who at one time possessed an opportunity of a lifetime, but for whatever reason were now trapped in circumstances that had not allowed them to complete their education. I explained what I most wanted to accomplish with this book and the steps that I was taking to try and give a balance to the subject. I shared how I had previously interviewed professional athletes who were successful on and off the field, and now it was time to shed some light on those less fortunate who were working for a living and did not have a career. We spent the better part of an hour discussing his program along with other programs available to student athletes who have exhausted their NCAA eligibility. Tom Kowolski also indicated Major League Baseball has one of the best programs through their minor leagues for players who would like to earn a degree while competing at a shot for the Majors. However, it is a little unrealistic for minor league ballplayers to enroll in a four-year college degree program while playing baseball because as a player advances through the three levels (single A, double AA and triple AAA), he is continuously being uprooted and moved to different cities. That dilemma notwithstanding, I took down the director's name for Major League Baseball and felt it would be a good source to present to all potential baseball hopefuls. After collecting as much data as I could from Kowolski, we agreed to continue sharing information on the subject. Kowolski also indicated that he was interested in getting schools like Northwestern to join the Consortium. Because they pride themselves on providing a top-notch education, he didn't feel his program would align itself with what Northwestern believes is their edict for students enrolling at their University. I wanted to look at Northwestern's program a little closer to see what the secret for success was in and out of the classroom.

10

I BET YOU...

Gambling, by definition, is the wagering of money or anything of material value on the uncertain outcome of an event. In the United States, legalized gambling is a multi-billion (with a b) dollar industry. That amount doesn't begin to address the illegal bets that take place either through various community numbers games or off-shore betting. It is estimated that one out of every seven Americans are involved in some form of gambling, be it casinos, racetracks or state-run lotteries. The idea of get-rich-quick schemes is not new to this country. It has been around since ancient civilization. And if some local officials, private corporations, and a small number of Native American tribes have a say in it, gambling will be here for a lot longer.

Take a drive down the main drag of Las Vegas, and you will see why towering hotels and casinos are popping up like mushrooms in an open pasture. A friend once told me, "Money won is twice as sweet as money earned." I beg to differ with him. There is a second part to that equation, and that is that no one ever talks about the money lost. Based on the size of those hotels, there appear to be a whole lot more lost than won.

With the number of casinos and gaming establishments being built today, gambling could become one of this country's biggest financial crises, right behind the lack of affordable health care and housing. It seems like every time you turn on the television, glitzy ads are running to convince you that if you don't play, you can't win. Even the networks are in on this by running the winning lottery numbers during the evening newscast.

That's what casinos and "bookies" are counting on. Betting on sporting events is quickly becoming the most popular form of gambling. The practice of betting on sporting events is not new, and it has obvious pitfalls. By virtue of someone directly or indirectly altering the outcome of a game, gambling is one of the biggest threats to fair competition in sports. As far back as the beginning of the twentieth century, people have had nefarious ideas when it comes to sporting events and money.

If the casinos suddenly start booking a lot of action on a particular game with no clear explanation for the occurrence, in all likelihood they will be placing a call to the FBI. As long as the house is controlling the odds and keeping the winning edge, no problem, but if there is any chance that their odds may be in jeopardy, they will move quickly to preserve their interest.

This brings us to the point about student athletes and wagering or gambling. There is a general consensus there is at least one bookmaker on every college campus in America—this includes divisions II and III as well. In 1995, *Sports Illustrated* magazine ran a three-part series entitled "The Campus Gambling Epidemic," which highlighted the rampant nature of college students' involvement in on-campus gambling rings. Students who had never gambled before in their lives were telling chilling stories of how they gambled away tuition money on college and professional ballgames. In 1995, those discoveries appeared to be shocking allegations and limited to some misguided coeds and fraternity brothers. Today, not a single student on campus is immune to the endless bets that are placed either through the campus bookie or on the Internet.

The advent of the Internet has taken gambling to another level. Offshore accounts are now taking at least 15–20 % of the gambling action. By one estimate, there are over 1800 Internet sites set up to take bets. When the *Sports Illustrated* article was written nine years ago, there were only 250. All that is needed is a credit card to set up an account. Go on any college campus during the first week of classes and you will literally stumble over the voluminous stacks of credit card applications banks bombard the students with. In most instances, banks rarely make loans to 19-year-olds without full- time employment, but that's not the case if you are a full-time university student. Even if you don't currently have a job, the lending institutions are aggressively competing for the future earnings of college students in this country. Easy access to cash is contributing to the problem that is showing no signs of diminishing.

A Harvard medical study found that almost 5 percent of college students admitted to having a gambling problem. Other studies have shown that almost 1 in 5 students between the ages of 18 and 26 have gambled on at least one sporting event in their lives.

Gambling is quickly becoming the "drug du jour," surpassing the more conventional stimulants like alcohol, pot and cocaine. The biggest problem with intercollegiate gambling is that if not brought under control, it will surely undermine the pure essence of college sports. Where would the joy be in watching a sporting event if every time you saw a player miss a shot or fumble the ball at the goal line, you had doubts about the validity of the game?

We've seen no less than five universities dragged through the scandals because of point-shaving in games where players were paid to throw the game. Arizona State, Boston College and Northwestern were all sullied in recent years by this type of scandal. All are fine institutions of higher learning that find themselves having to explain to their alumni why they had players in their program who thought more about their personal needs than the reputation of the university.

I once interviewed a former collegiate bookie who is now a cardiologist living in Southern California. He thought that there was nothing wrong with betting on amateur sports. He only took bets from friends and he would "lay off" any big bets that he was afraid to cover in case that person won. He felt like he couldn't enjoy watching the game as much unless he had some "action" on it. He points out, "who's going to sit there and watch a game that is 24 to 'zip' in the fourth quarter, unless your bet is in doubt?"

The sad truth is that lives are being destroyed and families broken up over the need to place bets on sporting events. Students will give their parents a line about needing money to cover school expenses, then put it on the upcoming home game. Once that trust is broken, how long does it take to earn it back?

The NCAA is concerned about this growing trend and is pushing to pass legislation that would eliminate wagering on collegiate and amateur sports.

Spearheading the NCAA's efforts to eliminate betting is William S. Saum, Director of Agent Gambling and Amateurism Activities. Saum has taken the initiative for Congress to pass legislation to ban betting on all amateur sports. It is currently legal to bet on collegiate sporting events in Nevada. Saum has solicited help from Senators John McCain, R- Arizona;

Sam Brownback, R-Kansas, and John Edwards, D-North Carolina in this regard.

Lobbyists representing the state of Nevada oppose such legislation, stating that the loss of revenue from such a ban would jeopardize the state's economic growth. Nevada felt the majority of money wagered on amateur sports in this country comes from the illegal side of bookmaking and parlay/Internet betting that takes place outside its jurisdiction.

In other words, Nevada believes there will continue to be large sums of money placed on collegiate games that are televised or not, and why should the black market rake in millions of dollars while the state of Nevada stands idly by and watches?

This poses an interesting dilemma for the NCAA. As stated earlier in the book, the majority of revenue the NCAA and its associated universities receive comes from television rights to broadcast games. It is widely known that television viewership of intercollegiate competition is tied to betting. In 1995, the FBI estimated that at least $2.5 billion was wagered on that year's NCAA Men's Division I basketball tournament, only second to the Superbowl. The NCAA basketball tournament is one of the largest revenue-generating events. If you stop and ask the question, "why would so many people be interested in the collegiate basketball tournament?" It simply is the unpredictability of picking a winner. There are so many first-round upsets in the tournament that it helps to give betters a bigger financial incentive to pick a long shot and then watch it unfold. No other collegiate sport gives you that kind of unpredictability. With football, you have a good idea of the dominant teams, whereas with basketball a shot at the buzzer can be the difference between winning and losing.

The networks understand this concept, and they are willing to pay for the privilege. By some estimates, the ratings for amateur sporting events broadcast on television would drop by as much as 50 percent if not for the wagering factor.

As much as the NCAA needs to take a moral position and attempt to try and pass laws to eliminate betting on all games sanctioned under their banner, the obvious truth is their coffers would begin to dry up if the networks didn't have that hook.

So now the NCAA finds itself caught between a rock and a hard place. It cannot continue to allow member schools to play in tournaments and bowl games in Las Vegas while continuing to beat the drum against gambling.

Ultimately, it will have to clean house or else face the certainty of more student athletes being caught up in point-shaving scandals and betting infractions that will threaten the credibility of college sports. Some student athletes already upset with what they feel is improper compensation for the amount of money generated by their talents may very well be tempted to accept money to help "balance the books."

To counter any thoughts that a student athlete might have of engaging in point shaving or providing any inside information that can tip the odds in a sporting event, the NCAA is taking a proactive position. By adopting Bylaw 10.3, the NCAA has issued a stern warning that prohibits any athletic department and its staff members and student athletes from "engaging in gambling activities as they relate to inter-collegiate or professional sporting events."

That hard-line position may very well have cost former University of Washington head football coach Rick Neuhisel his job. It appears Neuhisel was involved in one of those popular men's college basketball tournament pools when he was called in for questioning by his athletic director. If true, the very nature of being involved with wagering on collegiate sports makes one wonder what Neuhisel was thinking. After being confronted with the evidence, Neuhisel was terminated by Washington Athletic Director Barbara Hedges.

The NCAA spends millions of dollars producing videos and posters on their "Don't Bet On It" campaign, only to learn that one of the top football programs in the country has a coach who may have been involved in a questionable gambling parlay.

Professional sports teams have long understood the very nature of sports and gambling. The NBA, NHL, NFL and MLB have all teamed up with the FBI to produce an anti-gambling program to eradicate the connection between professional sports and gambling. A videotape entitled "Gambling With Your Life" shows an athlete how his career can be taken away from him in an instant. The chance a professional athlete would throw away his career on a point-shaving incident is less likely given the amount of money professional ballplayers make. Somehow gambling and professional sports have found a way to coexist without experiencing the numerous scandals that have plagued the amateur level.

Will there ever come a time when we will no longer see wagering on sporting events? Certainly not in the near future. What about those who say it should not be taken away from fans who want to gamble just because of a small group of people that can't control themselves? Many would have you believe there is no difference between out-of-control gamblers and those who do not know when to quit drinking alcohol or eating too much. The difference is what is at stake when gambling takes place on sporting events: the integrity of sports is in question.

Ultimately, stadiums will continue to fill to capacity crowds, and ratings on network and cable television will reach record numbers, but unless the gambling is brought under control, the game will eventually become a victim of its own successes.

PART III

MOVING FORWARD
FROM HERE

Eureka It's the Choices!

I kept my promise to Kim and found a moment to call KTZC television studios in Hollywood. The director of sports was a fellow by the name of Robbie Dietz. I explained to him the details of the project I was working on and indicated that I had resigned from the *Orange County Post* as a result of my dissatisfaction with not being able to do in-depth reporting on the subject of student athletes.

As I was about to explain to Dietz that I probably wouldn't get a good recommendation from my former employer, Dietz cut me off and asked, "Have you ever heard of a player by the name of Donnel Bradshaw?"

"Yes, as a matter of fact I have," my excitement becoming ever more difficult to contain. "Well, we have a good lead on a story that Bradshaw was academically a non-qualifier for acceptance into Coastal College of the Pacific, but the President, Jonathan Wentworth, pulled strings and got him enrolled."

My excitement quickly turned to nervousness, as I was not sure who leaked the story. Not wanting to reveal the source who had given me the initial scoop, I pretended to be surprised by the accusation. "Are you sure of your facts?" The conversation was starting to be more like an interrogation rather than a job interview, so I played along with Dietz's analysis. He informed me his source was a local journalist and an administrator at the college had corroborated the story.

Finally the station director asked me straight out, "I hear you are in the Midwest right now. Would you be willing to fly back for the assignment of uncovering the truth about what happened down at the college?" I told him I would have to think about it, talk it over with my wife. "I'll be in touch with you by the middle of the week," was my reply. This was too tempting. The subject matter that caused me to resign from the newspaper was now staring me square in the face.

Dietz reminded me in news things change quickly, and I needed to give him an answer by 5 o'clock the following day. This was pressure I had not felt in quite some time. I knew once Kim heard the offer she would be beside herself if I didn't come home and go in for the interview. I also had to call my friend Jeff Brower. I needed to know from him if he had, in fact, leaked the story to the network. I also still had a legal issue to deal with, and if KTZC got wind of the weapons charge, I could save myself the trouble of flying home.

I immediately called Brower to find out what, if anything, he knew about who leaked the Donnel Bradshaw story.

"Hey Jeff, it's your pal Christensen. I just spoke with Robbie Dietz over at KTZC, and he is on to that story you and I spoke about after the high school basketball game a few months ago."

There was a pause and then Brower answered, "Yeah, I decided to give him that lead, and I recommended you to do the investigative part. This was right up your alley, and I had been thinking about it for a while. This story had to be told. I thought about running with the story myself, but decided I was too close to retirement to start 'shaking the trees.'"

I wanted to assure Brower that I would never reveal who told me about the story, and if I decided to come back and accept the offer to do the investigative piece, I would be willing to go to jail before I compromised his identity. It was a distinct possibility I would be going there for the arms possession anyway. We exchanged our goodbyes, and I mentioned I would call him when I got back to L.A.

Immediately after the Brower call, I placed a phone call to the Northwestern Wildcats sports information office. I was referred to Margaret Akerstrom. Akerstrom is Assistant Director of Athletics, Academics and Student Services. Upon meeting her, it quickly became clear why the Wildcats have a 92 percent "success rate" with their athletic recruitment. I say "success rate" instead of graduation rate for a reason. For the remainder of the book, I am defining success rates as students who not only graduate, but also go on to a meaningful profession. Too often athletes end up with a degree that for all intents and purposes will not put them in the position to take advantage of opportunities other graduates are getting. More on that later. After introducing myself to Margaret Akerstrom, we discussed the college's edict and what sets Northwestern (NU) apart from the other schools in the Big 10 and the country.

"Northwestern believes you are a student first and an athlete second, instead of the other way around. When a potential athlete comes to visit, we pair that individual with another player and they attend a class together. The athlete gets the feel of what academic demands he or she will experience should they decide to attend Northwestern."

Akerstrom also opined potential student athletes usually don't meet with their "position coaches" until after the initial classroom tour is conducted. It starts with an attitude of books first, and then play. What a novel idea. Northwestern is very competitive on the court and field in a conference that will produce national champions in every sport. NU also uses a very comprehensive approach to its student selection process for athletes. "We won't bring a player into our program if we don't think he or she will be able to succeed in the classroom," says Akerstrom. NU's policy also does not allow a student to miss more than four consecutive scheduled classes. This also speaks to the sincerity of the commitment to the quality of education. Northwestern has seen its share of controversy. In 1995, it found itself in the wake of a gambling and points-shaving scandal. It did not take long to see the attitude on that subject. Akerstrom immediately went into an "under no circumstances" posture when we began discussing academic versus disciplinary infractions. "There are certain things that will get you automatically expelled from this university, no questions asked." It's the old adage—"Fool me once, shame on you. Fool me twice shame on me," which has the university in a "no foolishness" mindset.

The school also issued a "Presidential Mandate." This pamphlet takes a step-by-step approach to what the University President is expecting from student athletes. Akerstrom was one of the most polished administrators I had encountered. She was well versed on the subject and provided me with a plethora of information in the form of books, handouts and worksheets. Unlike many people with whom I had set up interviews who eventually stood me up or called and cancelled at the last minute, she maneuvered her schedule to accommodate my request. That told me everything I needed know about the seriousness Northwestern takes toward athletics and academics. I was very fortunate to have spoken to Margaret Akerstrom because, in my mind, she'd set the bar for the standards by which I felt all other schools should try to emulate.

It was time to make a decision about whether or not I would give up this project to head home and take the KTZC job. It was also time to call Kim and inform her of what transpired. Whatever decision I would make, I still had to return to Connecticut to resolve the legal albatross weighing me down.

11

EUREKA IT'S THE CHOICES!

Now that you have taken the time to read this book, I hope you will come to the same conclusion that I have in researching the question of what it takes to ultimately become successful on the playing field and in the classroom. As we have seen in the various stories that have been presented in the previous chapters, it is not just talent that gets one recognized and signed to a multi-million-dollar contract, though it certainly is needed. It's not just luck, although there are many people who would beg to differ with me on that point as well.

As with anything in life, ultimately it comes down to choices. Do we choose to play this sport or that sport? Do we get up and practice for one hour or for four? Should we play for this team here or that team over there? Is this person a better coach, or can I receive superior instruction from another? Is it better to be the big fish in the little pond or should I remain a pup and run with the big dogs? Do I stay in school and achieve something that time cannot tarnish nor take away, or do I listen to the agents and advisors and declare myself fit to earn a living through professional competition? These are just a few of the choices facing those athletes who go on to greater achievements and those who seem to drift into obscurity.

There are no pre-cast molds that sets great athletes apart from the rest. Does the name Leon Wagner ring a bell? How about Raymond Lewis? Each player at one time was at the pinnacle of his sport. Leon Wagner was considered one of the first great power hitters to don a Los Angeles (currently Anaheim) Angels uniform. Wagner was selected in 1961 by the then-expansion franchise Los Angeles Angels and was an impact player for that team immediately. In three seasons with the Angels, Leon "Daddy Wags" hit 91 home runs and drove in 276 runs. In the 1962 Major League All-Star game, Wagner was voted game's MVP.

Three days into the 2004 new year, 69-year old Leon Wagner died virtually penniless. It was reported by the *Los Angeles Times* that his last known residence was an electrical shed behind a strip mall.

—CHOICES—

Raymond Lewis was considered to be one of the best urban legends to ever set foot on a basketball court. If you knew anything about basketball and you lived in the Los Angeles area during the early 1970s, you knew Raymond Lewis. At 6 foot 1, Lewis ruled the local courts with rainbow jump shots and no-look passes. After leading then-perennial powerhouse Verbum Dei High to three consecutive CIF titles, Lewis appeared to be headed to Long Beach State to play for legendary coach Jerry Tarkanian, but in a surprise move, Lewis decided to sign with Cal State L.A. It was rumored that Lewis was given a red Corvette and additional scholarships for a few of his friends as an incentive. Coach Tarkanian once stated Lewis was "the best high school player I have ever seen anywhere."

In Raymond Lewis' freshman year in college, he led all freshmen in scoring, averaging 39 points a game. In his sophomore season, he finished second among all scorers in the nation, averaging 33 points a game. After Lewis' second season in college, he opted to file for hardship and enter the 1973 NBA draft.

The Philadelphia 76ers had the very first pick and they selected guard Doug Collins of Illinois State. That previous summer, Collins was a guard on the infamous 1972 U.S.A. basketball team that supposedly lost to the Russian team in that controversial game in Munich, Germany. According to the game's timekeeper, there was a malfunction with the official time clock in the game, and twice the clock was reset. The third time was the charm as the Russian team in bounded the ball with a pass the length of the court. After contact, the Russian center caught the ball and dropped it into the basket for the go-ahead score as "time" expired. In protest, the men's U.S. basketball team never attended the award ceremony, and to this day those silver medals remain unclaimed in a vault.

The 76ers had one more pick in the first round that year, and they used it to select Raymond Lewis out of Cal State L.A. Lewis had a good rookie camp showing his talents against others including Doug Collins. But Raymond Lewis wasn't happy with his contract after learning that Collins was earning more money. Lewis held out of regular training camp that year, hoping the 76ers would renegotiate his contract. Showing up for an exhibition game in Illinois, still bitter, Lewis left by halftime and didn't return to Philadelphia until his third year of a three-year contract. Whatever talent Philadelphia saw in the '73 draft to choose Lewis 18th overall was now a faded memory. Bouncing from various leagues and pick-up games, Raymond Lewis traveled down that dismal road like so many others. Thrown from one side to the other, strewn with broken promises and untapped talent and skills.

After years of abusing alcohol, Raymond Lewis died at the young age of 48 due to complications from an infected leg. With talent that could have taken him anywhere in the world, he never really moved away from the neighborhood. Raymond Lewis' postscript simply was: Good enough to compete against the finest the NBA had to offer, Lewis never played a single second in an official NBA game.

—Choices—

Years from now, I'm sure sports fans will look back and remember the "Clarett Factor." After helping to lead his Ohio State Buckeye football team to a national championship, Maurice Clarett found himself on the outside looking in as he took on the National Football League. Clarett became the first player to legally challenge the NFL's long-standing rule of not allowing any athlete to participate in their draft if the player has not been out of high school for more than three years.

A lower court ruling stated Clarett and seven other players, including USC's All-American wide receiver Mike Williams, were entitled to participate in the NFL Draft. Among other things, the lower court ruled the NFL was in violation of anti-trust laws.

Two days prior to the 2004 NFL draft, Justice Ruth Bader Ginsberg upheld a decision by the 2nd U.S. Circuit Court of Appeals, which ruled against Clarett and the others seeking to participate in the draft. The ruling left open the possibility that the barred players could be included in a supplemental draft, should a higher court rule in the players' favor.

The player who stands to be the biggest loser in all of this is Williams. An All-American, Williams was projected to be a first-round pick. Barring any last-second heroics, Williams' status will definitely drop as his options quickly dwindle from sitting out a year to playing in the Canadian or European leagues. Ouch! Clarett wasn't even supposed to be picked until after the second and perhaps as late as the third round. Since both players signed with sports agents, the NCAA declared them ineligible to compete at the collegiate level, automatically forfeiting their amateur status. In order to be reinstated, they would have to file a petition to be declared eligible. Neither player completed their second year of academics. Only time will tell how this story turns out.

—CHOICES—

Something not often addressed is career-ending injuries. When athletes are in their prime, it rarely occurs to them that their bodies were not designed to take a pounding. As such, one blow to a vulnerable body part could dash everything an athlete has worked so hard to achieve.

After sustaining a serious injury, some athletes completely give up on both the athletic and academic sides of the equation.

That didn't happen to a former teammate of mine, Andrew Dossett. In 1980, a native of Shreveport, Louisiana, Dossett earned an athletic scholarship to USC. As an outside linebacker for the Trojans, Dossett suffered ligament damage to his left knee and required surgery. Although his football career never really recovered after surgery, Dossett continued onward to lofty aspirations by graduating summa cum laude and was inducted into Phi Beta Kappa.

Andrew Dossett overcame his hardships and went onto become an orthopedic surgeon and serves as a physician for various professional teams, including baseball's Texas Rangers and the NFL's Dallas Cowboys, along with serving as the spine consultant for the NBA's Dallas Mavericks, the NHL's Dallas Stars and PRCA Rodeo Cowboys.

Dr. Dossett is a prime example of how student athletics work if you take advantage of all of its benefits.

—CHOICES—

Senator Bill Bradley was a three-time All-American at Princeton University and a member of the 1964 gold medal-winning basketball team in Tokyo, Japan. After graduating in 1965 with a degree in history, Bradley turned down a professional contract to play for the NBA's New York Knicks.

Instead, he traveled to England and studied economics at Oxford. The second time around, Bill Bradley accepted the invitation to play professional basketball, and in 1967 signed with the Knicks. His illustrious career included two NBA titles and induction into the NBA Hall of Fame in 1983. In 1979, two years after retiring from the NBA, Bradley was elected to the U.S. Senate as a representative of New Jersey. His bid to win the Democratic nominee in the 2000 election came up short, but Bradley continues to work on various committees and projects to improve the lives of the disenfranchised.

You may know others like Dr. Dossett and Senator Bradley who may not appear in the headlines, but proved that their athletic abilities took them on to successful careers in all walks of life.

—Choices—

The University of Georgia is still trying to recover from the scandal in which assistant basketball coach Jim Harrick Jr., whose father was head basketball coach, taught a class called "Coaching Principles and Strategies of Basketball" during the 2001 season.

The 20-question final exam included questions such as:

1. How many goals are on a basketball court?

2. What is the name of the coliseum where the Georgia Bulldogs play?

3. How many points does a three-point field goal account for in a basketball game?

These were some of the tougher questions. Needless to say, the younger Harrick was fired and the senior Harrick resigned. The NCAA released a 1500-page document alleging, among other things, that Jim Harrick Jr. had "fraudulently awarded grades of A to three basketball student-athletes" enrolled in the course, providing an extra benefit to athletes by how he taught the course.

The university agreed with the NCAA's findings and suspended the team from competing in the Southeastern Conference and NCAA tournaments. In the end, there were no winners.

—CHOICES—

Now the NCAA has a new reform package that is being called historic. The proposal is supposed to be an incentive/disincentive plan, which, if approved by its members, will begin penalizing schools whose players do not progress academically in a timely manner.

The new system, if it is approved, calls for a system that awards points to schools whose athletes advance academically from one grading period to the next. Initially, schools will receive a letter stating their current status and how they would score if the new system were in place—a sort of snapshot of whether or not a school is currently in good standing. If those schools that were warned in 2004 don't improve by 2005, they would begin to lose scholarships.

The difficulty will come when the NCAA committee, which is responsible for determining the "cut-off" criteria, tries to come up with a fair and equitable system. The so-called revenue-generated sports (i.e., basketball and football) have always been a source of contention for where the need for reform lies, which no doubt will continue with these new changes.

"A simple one-for-all formula would lead to anomalies and complaints and wouldn't work," said NCAA President Myles Brand.

Detractors of the plan point out that it will put the onus on university professors and administrators to keep student-athletes moving along whether they are progressing academically or not.

If this new legislation helps give student-athletes a good education, wonderful, but it could be just another piece of legislation. The truth is, this could be another form of window dressing. As long as the NCAA and its affiliated universities stand to make millions off intercollegiate athletics, it will still be up to the student-athletes and their parents to make sure they are the ones who prosper in the end.

—CHOICES—

12

NO ONE GRADUATED?

That evening, I called Kim at home and told her about the conversation with station manager Robbie Dietz. I told her I would call Dietz in the morning and thank him for the opportunity, but I needed to pass. In my opinion, if I had helped break that story, it would look like I was trying to embarrass *The Post* and thus rub my former boss' (Teckerman) nose in it. Kim understood. The following morning, I spoke with Dietz and thanked him for the opportunity. "Well, when you get back to California, give me a call ..I can always use someone with the type of conviction that you have," said Dietz.

As luck would have it, I was on my way back to Indianapolis to conclude my research when I got a call from a gentleman who identified himself as the Assistant Athletic Director for the University of Louisville. As I attempted to explain the nature of my inquiry, my cacophonous cellular phone call prevented me from communicating with him. Finally after the third attempt, I decided to pull off the freeway where my conversation was finally transmitted audibly.

The voice on the other end of the phone identified himself as Marvin Mitchell. He offered to buy me a new phone service if it would help me out, but I graciously declined. I cut to the chase and indicated my research found that in a period from 1989 to 1993, no African-American basketball players graduated from Louisville. He was a bit reticent to talk to me over the phone so he agreed to meet me in Louisville that Saturday. I made the journey from Indianapolis down to Louisville in less than two hours. I had never been to

Kentucky before, and the only thing I could relate to was the great Muhammad Ali grew up there. The afternoon was cold and light snow flurries had blanketed the area. I arrived at Marvin Mitchell's residence and knocked on the door. The gentleman who answered the door stood 6 foot 7 and weighed approximately 285 pounds. I was completely thrown off by his presence, but it didn't take long for us to get deep into our discussion. We developed a rapport instantly. He was unpretentious, and answered all of my questions in a forthright manner. It was clear to me he truly had taken this job because he cared. He cared about an athletic program that had reached the pinnacle in college basketball twice in the last 20 years was not achieving the same success in the classroom. As a whole, the entire student body hadn't fared so well, a fact I found ironic in light of the sign I had read posted at the Indiana - Kentucky stateline: "Welcome to Kentucky, Where Education Pays." Somebody forgot to tell that to the people in charge of the academic program for University of Louisville's basketball team from 1989 through 1993.

The interview lasted for over two hours and covered the delicate balancing act of NCAA guidelines and student athletes' needs. Mitchell described how some parents are seemingly helpless to control their kids as teenagers and then expect them to come into a structured environment of restricted sports and academia—it is a recipe for failure. One parent went as far as to ask Mitchell this rhetorical question, " I have trouble getting my son to pick up after himself, how do you expect me to get him to go to class every day?"

We concluded our interview over dinner while some of the patrons in the restaurant stared over at our table from time to time. Marvin was well aware that his size gave people the impression that he was a professional athlete, and he would sometimes play up to the folly. "Yeah I get that look all the time when I am out in public." People want to know what team he plays for and he is quick to answer, "Is the meal complementary if I tell you?"

I was glad I took the opportunity to go to Louisville and get the other side of the story. As a journalist, I feel it is very important to let the story come to you as opposed to developing a theory and then setting out to make the story fit some preconceived notion.

I made the trek back up to Indianapolis to see if I could meet with NCAA officials about a few more loose ends. After placing several phone calls to Bill Saum (the NCAA's point person on Collegiate Gambling), I was told I was welcome to stop by and pick up literature and videos outlining the NCAA's position on gambling by student athletes and other persons associated with any member schools. However, an interview with Mr. Saum would be out of the question. I took the opportunity to stop back by the NCAA headquarters one more time to find out as much as I could on the course of action the NCAA was taking to try and curb what many feel is the biggest threat to amateur athletics.

After waiting in the lobby for about 15 minutes, a woman came down and greeted me with an arm-full of videocassette tapes and some literature titled "Sports Wagering Information Packet." It was the NCAA's official position on gambling. It was definitely a different reception than the one I had received three weeks prior. I didn't even get a name tag this time.

The next morning, I received a phone call from my attorney Charles Abate, inquiring when I would be returning to Connecticut. The only thing the Commonwealth of Connecticut had to assure my return was the $78 bond I posted after the accident. The possibility of being extradited back from California may have played into my decision to return as well. I reassured Abate I had one more stop to make in Pennsylvania, where I would be sitting in on a trial of a basketball player that once ruled the courts in North Philadelphia. He was now charged with murdering a neighbor over crack cocaine.

Howard McNeil was everyone's pick to beat the odds and make it in the NBA. His skills were so polished, they nicknamed him "smooth." At 6 foot 9, McNeil had all of the scouts drooling, and college coaches lined up just for the opportunity to be rejected. In 1973, McNeil, just a kid in the eighth grade, found himself caught in a legal battle over whether he could transfer out to the suburbs and play for a predominately white junior high school. After high school, McNeil chose to attend Seton Hall in New Jersey. In the classic case of one-dimensional student athletics, McNeil struggled with his studies and ended up leaving school early to play in the NBA. Lacking in both playing time and pro-scout exposure due to academic ineligibility his senior year, during the 1982 NBA draft, McNeil was selected by the defending world champion Los Angeles Lakers in the fifth round. After a poor showing in camp, the Lakers released him.

Howard McNeil eventually found opportunities to play basketball in Portugal and Greece. After a 10-year stint in the European Leagues, McNeil returned to Norristown, Pennsylvania, where he struggled to make a living while sinking deeper into the quagmire of crack cocaine. According to prosecutors, Howard McNeil was accused of entering 38-year-old Francis

Brennan's apartment and viciously stabbing and strangling her to death as he left the crime scene carrying a sentry safe containing 40 bags of crack cocaine. It was alleged that the victim's boyfriend was a known drug dealer.

Half way to Pennsylvania via Ohio, I received another call from Charles Abate. "Dan, time's up. I need you in Stamford by tomorrow morning." I had run out of time. Now I had to worry about facing my own legal dilemma. I would have to come back to the McNeil trial after my legal battle was concluded.

After a brief conversation with Abate, I pressed for Greenwich, Connecticut, determined to make it in time for my December 7th court appearance. My anxiety was heightened as I headed back. I felt my clean background was definitely a plus going into the proceedings, but you never know how a slip here or an overzealous prosecutor could make things much more difficult than expected.

Traveling back across Interstate 80, I felt that I was traveling in slow motion. I didn't know what the status of my truck was. I had a bad feeling about the body shop manager based on our last conversation. Originally it was supposed to take just 10 business days to complete the job. It had already been three weeks, and they were just starting to make the basic repairs to the front grill and hood. I was ready to pull my truck into another shop, but with the work that the body shop had already started, it would be next to impossible to switch at that point. The shop manager was a man in his mid to late 50s and he reminded me of Dagwood from the comic strip Blondie. He started out saying all of the right things and assured me he would be able to get me up and running with "limited" down time. My frustration with the whole experience was beginning to spill over into the research trip. I began to have doubts about whether or not I would see my project to its fruitful conclusion. Woody (the name I began calling the body shop foreman), was now telling me it would be another two to three weeks before the work on my truck would be completed.

I began pleading with Woody to no avail. Didn't he realize my budget was severely hampered by this unacceptable timeline he was now insisting on? I quickly realized that I was not a priority and probably never was. The conversation ended with me telling him that I would stop by his shop the following Monday.

On the morning of Thursday, December 7, I tried to get a mental head start on the proceedings that were about to occur. It was time for me to find out if Judge Lawrence Kester would accept a plea of not guilty and allow me into the Accelerated Rehabilitation program. The traffic from Ridgefield, New Jersey, was especially heavy crossing the George Washington Bridge into Manhattan. As I proceeded up I-95 into Connecticut, I couldn't help but think about how a simple fender bender had placed me head-on with the worst legal predicament I had ever encountered. I was determined to beat this thing, and like many other challenges I had faced previously, I came well prepared for all contingencies.

I parked at my attorney's office and proceeded to walk the two blocks to the courthouse. After passing through the security checkpoint, I settled into my familiar corner next to the main door of Judge Kester's courtroom. Nervously awaiting my meeting with Abate, I was approached by a young man who had a foreign accent, perhaps from the nation of Nigeria. He asked me in a broken dialect if I was there to represent him. The question appeared odd at first until I realized that I was dressed rather formally compared to the other defendants in the building. I indicated to him that I was not his legal counsel and accepted the inquiry as a complement.

After a few minutes of brief fidgeting, my attorney appeared and we greeted each other with a quick handshake and the perfunctory exchange regarding our Thanksgiving holiday.

"Dan, I've got some good news and some bad news."

I am one those who likes to eat my vegetables before I get my dessert, so I asked for the bad news first. As it turned out, the District Attorney's office was unwilling to reduce the charge from a Weapon in Vehicle 29–38 charge to a misdemeanor. Also, at the start of the morning's discussion with the DA's office, it was starting to look like my attorney would have to make a strong appeal on my behalf to the judge. In other words, the DA felt that my case wasn't exactly a slam-dunk for the Accelerated Rehabilitation program. It would be up to Abate to prove to the court I was truly a valid candidate for this first-time offender's program. I was so taken aback by this information I forgot that there was still some good news on deck. Abate looked at me and said, "remember how we were ordered by the judge to notify the "injured party?" Apparently the "arresting officer" (I put this in quotes because it was an arrest only in a technical sense) appeared that morning and spoke directly to the prosecutor handling my case. Officer Reeves took the time to come up to Stamford Superior Court to speak on my behalf for the AR program. According to my attorney, not only did Officer Reeves not object to my plea of not guilty with AR, he also indicated to the prosecutor that I was "most cooperative" throughout the police investigation, and that he felt the AR program was designed for people in my circumstances. With that affirmation, my attorney seized the opportunity to ask the prosecutor to relay the conversation to the judge that he had with the police officer. My attorney, being as sharp as he is, recognized the importance of the judge getting the police officer's statement from the prosecutor's side of the bench.

As the court clerk called my name, a bold confident swagger had taken over the insecure gait that I had when I first entered the courthouse.

Charles Abate presented the courts with a brief biography of my background, including the fact that I was currently traveling around the country for work. Judge Kester asked, "What line of work is your client engaged in, trucking?" My attorney pointed out that I was a journalist doing research for a book, at which time the judge looked up and began smiling. It was the first time I saw the judge actually become amused. Then it was the prosecutor's turn to reveal to the judge what was stated in the conversation earlier that morning between the prosecutor, the police officer and my attorney. The prosecutor laid out the facts in the case and indicated that the arresting officer made an appearance on my behalf. However, the state was asking for two years probation and the weapon to be condemned. I was about to see my $800 investment quickly go down the drain. I immediately leaned over to Abate and requested they return the gun to California via a registered federal gun dealer. Judge Kester agreed to revisit this after a satisfactory probationary period was concluded. In the meantime, the gun would remain in Greenwich Police property lock-up. With those instructions, the judge agreed to the Accelerated Rehabilitation program, and I was off to settle the necessary fines and paper work. God had smiled on me in that situation. There were a lot of ways this whole incident could have turned out, most of them unpleasant. I sat down and wrote Officer Reeves a personal note to thank him for doing something that probably only a handful of officers would have done.

Once again, I bid my attorney farewell, and we agreed to keep in touch. At the time, I wasn't aware that I might be in need of his services again if things didn't work out over at the body shop.

I was elated that the legal entanglement, which had had me bound, was finally behind me. I couldn't jump up and down just yet, because just around the corner waiting for me was good ol' Woody and his foolishness. I proceeded directly from the courthouse to the body shop. When I arrived I, was greeted by one of Woody's employees. After a brief wait, Woody took me out to my car and began explaining why the schedule they had agreed to at the start of the project had now doubled. I was furious, but I knew that to blow up now would only delay their actions even more. Besides, I was just told to stay out of trouble for the next two years. Looking down at the ground so he wouldn't have to lie to my face, I asked what was his best guess when my truck would be finished. Emphatically, he blurted out "in a week, I hope." With that I whirled and headed back to my rental car and off to New York.

13

GOING THE DISTANCE

It was Friday, December 17, 2000. I was beginning to run low on money. The budget I left California with was now an afterthought. The accident and subsequent weapons charge was causing me to have to come up with some alternative answers to pay for the rest of the time spent on the road. I began looking into staying in a motel on the outskirts of New York, specifically New Jersey. At the first motel I stopped in, the manager asked me if I needed the room for a couple of hours. Steadying myself I said, "No, I was looking for something a little more long-term and I hope a room that had at least cooled off before I checked in." I finally settled into the Expressway Motel just outside of Bergen, New Jersey. The room wasn't bad if you were willing to ignore the cigarette burns on the dresser and the mattress that was placed on top of a wooden box. I had to affix some aluminum foil around the antennae to improve the television signal.

During my motel stay, I ran into a gentleman from Detroit who was in New York to jump start an R&B singing career. It was interesting that he was pursuing a dream in the recording business and I was in search of a literary career. He indicated he left his family back in Michigan to make a last-ditch effort to break into the recording industry. I could tell the whole experience was beginning to extract a price he was questioning; the viability of a dream yet unrealized.

I had decided to spend a few more days in New York organizing the last three interviews I had remaining before returning home to Florida for the

Christmas holiday. I felt like I wouldn't be able to make any long-term plans without knowing when I would get my truck back.

I continued to comb through the files of the *New York Times* and *Washington Post* to authenticate my story about what made success stories out of some athletes and footnotes out of others. The more I pored over endless articles about student athletes and the need for stricter academic standards, the more I was convinced this story actually had legs. The clock was running, and I knew that in order to complete my work, I would have to find a way to condense the material and limit my search to areas that encompassed only the last five years.

One afternoon as I was headed back to my hotel, out of the corner of my eye, I suddenly I saw a copy of the *Philadelphia Inquirer* with the headline: "Ex-Basketball Star Found Guilty of Murder."

With my curiosity piqued, I grabbed the newspaper and realized it was the Howard McNeil case I was on my way to cover when my attorney summoned me back to Connecticut. All I could think was what a waste. The World Champion Los Angeles Lakers had drafted McNeil in the fifth round in 1982. Now he was convicted of third degree murder and sentenced to life for murdering an alleged drug dealer. McNeil could have been living along the beautiful coast of Malibu or Newport Beach; instead, he was locked up in a Pennsylvania maximum-security prison. It was yet another example of one-dimensional athleticism.

In order to expedite my research, I decided to split my days into two parts. The first half of the day found me combing through old files and stories. My research was coming together with the help of the librarian and the periodicals that contained the most intricate details about my subjects. The second half of the day was set aside to write about the events. Some days the information would take up three to four pages of notes. Other days were noted with a simple paragraph or two.

The Christmas spirit was in the air and I decided to wrap up work early one afternoon. As a child growing up in Miami during the 1960s, I often had the opportunity to travel to New York to visit my mother's parents in Brooklyn. I wanted to take a ride back over the Brooklyn Bridge to my grandparents' old stomping grounds. They had long been deceased, but the memories of visiting them were as vivid as though it had happened last year. The four-story brownstone, located in the middle of Third Street and Fifth Avenue, looked exactly the same way I remembered it. I glanced up at the third floor window facing the park and the memories of the hot summer nights and my sitting on the ledge of the window seal brought tears to my eyes. My mother's parents were not wealthy by any stretch of the imagination, but they had and gave a lot of love, which was worth more than any material things they could have given us.

After leaving my grandparents old neighborhood, I decided to try to find an old friend who is the pastor of Brooklyn Bethel Church. After spotting a cab stand on Fourth Avenue, I stopped and asked directions to the church. It's funny how none of the cab drivers I approached had any idea how to find the address I was in search of since I now had my own transportation. Frustrated, I proceeded toward my car when a middle-aged cab driver wearing flip-up glasses asked me for the name of the street I was looking for. After showing him the address, he indicated it was up in Bedford Stuyvesant.

Something profound happened while we were talking. We began talking about God's Grace and how he moves throughoutour lives. We shared stories about traveling around the city, his more entertaining than mine. It was interesting that even though we came from totally different backgrounds, we were both trying to find our own identity in life. Jerry was concerned about my safety and my being directionally challenged while driving in New York. He gave me his home phone number and insisted I give him a call if I got lost. We both wished each other a good evening, and I proceeded to one of the roughest areas of town. I never did find my friend that evening, but I found a new.

The week of Monday, December 20, 2000, started out with a slower pace than the previous weeks. I was stuck waiting for some good news about repairs on my truck. In the mean time, I continued going through the archives of the *New York Times* and *Washington Post*. Scheduling interviews with people whom I identified prior to traveling on the book tour was proving to be difficult. Often, the person whom I wanted to interview felt the idea of elaborating on what went wrong during a time that should have been their most cherished years was too much to revisit. There was also the problem of getting people to tell me where I might locate my interviewee. This was obviously a concern from a security standpoint. Both theirs and mine.

Later that afternoon, while I was waiting for a call from Kim, I began to wonder if this whole journalistic experience wasn't just some disguised midlife crisis that I was denying existed. I remembered being a kid watching outlandish television stunts and hearing my father exclaim, "some people will do anything to keep from getting a job." Was I the one who was now trying desperately to keep from facing the challenges that life was so desperately trying to reveal to me? Was this what Kim was referring to when she admonished me to "grow up and start acting like a man approaching 40 and not 20." Not wanting to give much credence to this thought, I pressed onward.

14

LET'S GO HOME

I was starting to get antsy about going down to Miami and leaving the truck in Connecticut until after the holidays. I decided to give up on locating my last two interviews until after the first of the year. I was contemplating leaving my truck in the shop until after the holidays and just heading straight for Florida. There were a couple of problems with that plan. First, I was being charged $38 per day for a rental car and I knew my funds were about to run out. Second, I also faced the strong possibility that when I returned after new year's to pick up my truck, the winter weather might trap me on the East Coast longer than I wanted to be there. It was time to turn my attention toward a vacation planned by Kim. We were going to meet in Miami on Christmas Eve and spend Christmas day at my sister's house. Then it was off to the Bahamas for five days on an exotic island. My paternal grandfather grew up in the Bahamas.

Shortly after lunch, my pager came alive, indicating someone had just left a message on my answering service. I managed to retrieve the message from Woody, who had decided that he was finished. I was cautiously relieved. After calling the body shop and explaining to Woody how his actions forced me to delay my research and cancel part of my trip, he sighed and responded with, "Gee Dan, that's unfortunate. So when do you think you will be up here to pick up your truck? And don't forget I need a cashier's check for the total amount." I told him I would let him know within the hour. I didn't want to let my pride get in the way of returning to get my truck, so I scratched the idea of telling Woody to keep it until after the holiday.

I was supposed to pick Kim up from the airport in a few days and my marriage was past the point of strained. The last thing I wanted to have happen was a delay that would prevent me from getting down to the Miami airport before Kim arrived.

I called Kim to give her the good news about the truck and confirm her flight arrival. The hotel concierge where she works, told me Kim had already left for the holiday break the previous afternoon. I tried her cell phone, but again, I got no answer.

I called Woody and informed him I would be in Stamford before 4 o'clock. So there would be no misunderstandings, I asked what time the shop would close. I had just over two hours to get up to Stamford before the crush of rush-hour traffic would delay me getting the truck for another day. Packing the last items, I checked out of my motel and headed back for Connecticut.

I arrived just in time. I looked over, under and throughout to see if I could spot any obvious flaws in their work. Satisfied with what I saw, I paid Woody and started the long trek down to Florida. The winter night was quickly closing in as I approached the rush hour traffic through the Washington D.C. Beltway. The last time I drove through the area, a semi-tractor trailer had collided with a passenger vehicle and the accident shut down I-95 for over an hour and a half.

Passing through Virginia, I was reminded of a story a friend, Frank Norton, told me in college about a property he maintained as a young man for a successful Wall Street banker. The frail banker, well into his eighties, called my buddy over to where he was sitting and inquired whether Frank had gone swimming in the pool the previous afternoon. Frank, concerned he might lose his job hesitated, and began apologizing and was abruptly interrupted. "Son," said the elderly banker, "you got more enjoyment out of that pool yesterday than I got in the 32 years I spent working to maintain it."

I guess sometimes we spend so much of our energy earning a living that we don't take time to enjoy the fruits of our labor.

It was quickly approaching midnight, and I had just crossed over the Virginia/North Carolina state line. So pleased with my pace, I decided to drive all night so that I would be at my parents' home in time for an early dinner in south Florida.

Although I still had 14 hours of asphalt ahead, it was a huge psychological victory to have my truck make it that far without any major incidents. As the beautiful daylight began to break through the cumulus clouds over the east coast of Florida, the morning commute was underway. I knew if I could just hang in there for another eight hours, I would be finished with one of the most unforgettable chapters in my life.

When I arrived at my parents' house that afternoon, I was greeted with a lot of hugs and the unmistakable smell of Chanel perfume. Exhausted, I turned around to see Kim standing behind the door ready to give me a big hug.

"I have been trying to call you all night," I said. Kim decided to fly out a day early and surprise me. I wasn't sure if she was headed to Florida or to a divorce attorney's office. I was glad she chose the former.

The Christmas dinner was shaping up to be more of a family reunion for me than expected. Since I live on the West Coast, it is a bit unusual for me to be home for the holidays. I got to see family members who I hadn't seen in almost 20 years. We dined on traditional family dishes and as usual, everybody brought their specialty. People were a bit reluctant to talk about my adventures and to be honest, I wasn't all that crazy about bringing them up. My sister and her husband flew in from Detroit, and they caught me up on the latest in their lives. As it turned out, they announced to everyone that they were expecting their first child and everyone was euphoric with the news. What made the news even more special was that my sister had just turned 43.

We enjoyed the holidays and the trip down to Nassau. The week flew by and it felt good to spend some quiet time with Kim. We tiptoed around the question of when my research would conclude. The atmosphere was too festive to start down that path, but I knew that within a few days, some tough choices would have to be made. I knew Kim wanted me to head home, but I needed a few more weeks to wrap up my interviews and tie up a few loose ends.

As Kim prepared to head back to California, I began taking the necessary steps to drive back. I drove Kim to the airport and she took the first flight. We agreed to touch base that evening and by then I would have made up my mind as to when I would return.

I had already made up my mind about returning immediately back to Los Angeles. I just wanted to think it through before I informed anyone. I went back to my parents' house and told them I was headed back to L.A. in the morning. Both my mom and my dad knew it was the best decision.

After getting everything packed and put inside the truck, my mother called me to the phone. Kim had arrived home safely and she wanted to tell me about the news from earlier in the day. "Dan, you're not going to believe this. KTZC broke the story about Donnel Bradshaw yesterday. Apparently, Jonathan Wentworth was forced out as the President of the college," Kim shouted.

I casually mentioned that I would be headed home tomorrow. Kim told me to "drive carefully."

It had been several months since I first set off on this journey, and now I was uncertain what if anything I had found. I knew there were certainly a lot of life's lessons sprinkled in for good measure, but what about the subject of student athletes? It was too early to tell and besides, there were at least 250 pages of a manuscript to write before I could begin to answer that question. After years of countless interviews and research, the bottom line is no one knows for certain why some athletes with less talent achieve success, and others with far superior athletic talent end up back in the old neighborhood talking about what happened long ago.

Getting home safely was now my number one priority and I had seen a lot of reminders of just how important that task was. I will probably never forget the number of makeshift memorials that I passed along the many highways of this country. It was a constant reminder that somebody's mother, father, brother, sister, aunt, uncle, husband, wife or child did not get to his/her appointed destination. It was sad because for every time I saw flowers or crosses marking the location of the accident, I was left with the thought of the number of places where there were no visible signs of a memorial. The number of people who lose their lives out on the interstates is staggering and I didn't need to be reminded just how quick such an occurrence could happen.

In some ways the trip had ended just like it had started. The heavy rains that greeted me when I arrived in the Southern California basin, like the trials and tribulations I had encountered on this excursion, were all washing away like the storm. When I walked into the front door of our home, my wife greeted me with a hug that sucked the wind out of my lungs. I wanted to tell her that I would not be going back to work in the field of journalism.

"What would you say if I told you that I am going down next week and apply for a teaching job at the L.A. Unified School District?" I asked. "Who knows, I may decide to coach as well."

Kim looked over at me and said, "Dan, welcome home."

15

CONCLUSION: A FINAL WORD

There is no doubt the issue of what is fair compensation for student athletes and when should athletes turn pro, will continue to be debated. There are no easy answers. The one thing I can say is I've never seen a good education go on the injured reserve list, or go into a slump. In closing, let me leave you with this analogy. A student athlete is like the talented person who walks across the high wire in the circus. Education is the safety net that is perfectly positioned underneath the hopes and aspirations of making it someday in front of the big crowds. I wish you all the best as you prepare for a joyous life of academics and participating in athletic competition.

REFERENCES

The following are presented as references for actual quotes and factual information used in the book and to document source material for proper credit. Any errors of omission are accidental and are not intended to injure said sources. If sources are clearly cited throughout the book within the chapters, it may not be duplicated below.

1: A GOOD FIRST LESSON IN LIFE

Quotes from Grant Hill and Calvin Hill, interview with the author, Detroit Pistons vs. Phoenix Suns, Feb. 1996, America West Arena.

Quotes from Marcus Allen, interview with the author, Kansas City Chiefs, University of Wisconsin at Riverfalls, Jul. 1994.

Quotes from Oscar De La Hoya, interview with the author, Big Bear training facility-media day May 1996, in preparation for the WBC super lightweight title fight with champion Julio Cesar Chavez.

2: THE R LETTER

Facts and information from "NFL Told to Allow Younger Players," (no author) Los Angeles Times, Feb. 6, 2004.

Quotes from Tamarack Vanover, interview with the author, Bennigans Restaurant San Diego, Ca., Nov. 22, 2003.

Quotes from Tyrone Willingham, interview with the author, Apr. 2000, Stanford Athletic Department Coach's o.ce.

Quotes from Junior Seau, interview with the author, Sep. 12, 1994, San Diego Chargers weight room, Jack Murphy Stadium.

3: THE OMNIPRESENT NCAA. . .

Much of the statistics and information for this chapter were taken from: From *The NCAA News & Features,* Nov. 8, 1999 issue: "The NCAA Century Series—Part I: 1900-39"

From *The NCAA News & Features,* Nov. 22, 1999 issue:

"Part I - Sanity Code"

"The electronic free ticket"

"NCAA Answers call to Reform"

From *The NCAA News & Features,* Dec. 20, 1999 issue:

"NCAA Timeline: 1990-99",

"A Presidential Era"

"1990s: A Decade of Litigation"

"Opportunity vs. Exploitation"

Facts and information from "Knight Commission to Assess Impact of NCAA Reforms," Bob Rubin; *Miami Herald,* Jul. 25, 2000.

4: PROFESSIONAL VORTEX

Quote from H. Ross Perot "The Giant Sucking Sound. ," from NAFTA Free Trade Agreement debate with Vice President Al Gore, Jan. 1993.

Statistical Odds of Playing Professional Football, NFLPA received through phone inquiry Feb. 25, 2001.

Facts and information from "Though the NBA, Scouts and Even His Coach Aren't Believers," David Wharton, *Los Angeles Times*, Jun. 24, 1998.

Quotes from Lanton Williams, phone interview with the author, Nov. 16, 2000.

Information on Grant Hill and Calvin Hill, T.D. Waterhouse television commercial, 2001.

Facts and information from "A Fatality, Parental Violence and Youth Sports," Fox Butter. eld; *New York Times*, Jul. 11, 2000.

5: SECRET AGENT MEN

Quotes from Leigh Steinberg, interview with the author, Mar. 2001, Newport Beach, CA.

Facts and information from "He Showed Them the Money," Carrie Miller, Lise Fisher, Lourdes Briz; *Gainsville Sun*, Mar. 12, 2000.

Facts and information from "Gillette Admits He Stole from Pro Athletes," Don Bauder; *San Diego Union Tribune*, Dec. 11, 1997.

Facts and information from "Kareem's Financial Crisis Adviser's 'Family' Torn Apart as Loses Total in the Millions," Gordon Edes, James Granelli; *Los Angeles Times*, Apr. 8, 1987.

6: HIGH SCHOOL OR HIGH SCAM?

Quotes from Ken Carter, interview with the author, Apr. 2002, MGM Sound Stage; Slam Ball.

Quotes and statistics from the Northeastern University; Center for the Study of Sports in Society,Nov. 2000.

Quotes and information from "Too Many Compete, Too Few Scholarships," Coco McCabe, *Boston Globe*, Mar. 1999.

Quotes and information from "Investigation of Dade Players Forwarded to NCAA," Pedro F. Fonteboa, *Miami Herald*, Jun. 21, 2000.

Quotes and information from "Former Eagle's Age in Question..". Terry Betterton, *Fresno Bee*, Mar. 1, 2001.

Quotes and information from "State Probes Whether Schools Altered Grades to Help Athletes," Ken Rodriguez, *Miami Herald*, Jan. 6, 2000.

Quotes from Ronnie Carter, phone interview with the author, May. 7, 2004, TSSAA Supreme Court Trial.

Quotes and information from "Nothing Minor About Their Dreams," (no author), *Associated Press*, Mar. 10, 2002.

Quotes and information from "The Ploys of Summer," Robyn Norwood, *Los Angeles Times*, Aug. 6, 2000.

7: MAYDAY! WE ARE TAKING ON WATER

Quotes and information from "Hornung: Irish Should Still Lower Standards," radio interview on Detroit Station AM-1270, ESPN.com, Mar. 10, 2004.

Quotes and information from "UC's Regents End A.rmative Action Ban," Rebecca Trounson, Jill Leovy, *Los Angeles Times*, May 17, 2001.

Quotes and information from Benjamin Bloom "U. of C. Prof. Who Saw Potential of All to Learn," Meg McSherry Breslin, *Chicago Tribune*, Sep. 15, 1999.

Quotes and information from "Wedderburn Learns Mother Knows Best," David Kenney; *Chicago Tribune*, Sep. 20, 1999.

Quotes and information from "Howard Has Perfect Grad Rate," Mark Asher; *Washington Post*, Nov 16, 1998.

Quotes from Stacy Slaughter, phone interview with the author, S.F. Giants on Paci. c Bell Park, Apr. 2001.

8: SEOREH

Quotes from John Wooden, interview with the author, John R. Wooden Award Ceremony, Los Angeles Downtown Athletic Club, Apr. 6 2001.

Quotes and information from *The Wizard of Westwood*, John Wooden, co-authored by Dwight Chapin and Je. Prugh.

Quotes and information from *A Kind of Grace*, Jackie Joyner Kersee, co-author Sonja Steptoe.

Quotes and information from *My Life*, Earvin "Magic" Johnson, Co-author William Novak.

9: I BET YOU. . .

Quotes and information from Southern California Cardiologist, phone interview with author, Sep. 17, 2004.

Quotes and information from, NCAA Statistics on Gambling and Related Information, "The Gambling Threat," *NCAA News & Features* Newsletter, Jul. 2, 2001.

Statistical Analysis obtained from "Gamblers Anonymous," website: www.gambler-sanonymous.com.

11: EUREKA . . . IT'S THE CHOICES

Quotes and information from Margaret Akerstrom, interview with the author, Northwestern University, Nov. 2000.

Quotes and information from Marvin Mitchell, interview with the author, University of Louisville, Dec. 4, 2000.

Quotes and information from "Urban Legend," and "Bitter Ending," Bill Plachske; *Los Angeles Times*, Feb. 14, 2001, Jan. 25, 2004.

Quotes and information from "Hey Coach, I Aced the Final," (no author); *Los Angeles Times*, Mar. 4, 2004.

14: LET'S GO HOME

Quotes and information from "Hoop Star Sentenced For Murder Over Drugs," Meredith Fisher, *Philadelphia Inquirer*, Aug. 12, 1999.

INDEX

QUICK ORDER FORM

Please make a copy of this form for Fax or mail orders

Fax Orders: (818) 990-6045 Please use the form below

Phone Orders: Toll Free (866) 463-6064

For Credit Cards Orders:

Mail Orders: Crooked Island Publishing, Inc.

15030 Ventura Blvd.

P.O. Box 19-850

Sherman Oaks, CA 91403, USA

e-mail: crookedisland@aol.com

- -
-

Going Pro: Scholarships, Student Athletes and the Money

❏ I would like to order _____ books

❏ Please send me information on Speaking/Seminars

Name: _____

Address: _____

City:_____State:_____Zip_____

Telephone:____(_____) _____

email:_____

Sales tax: Please add 8.25% for all orders shipped to a California residence.

Shipping and Handling: Add $4.50 for first book. Additional books will be charged at UPS book rate.

Evidence For The
Law Enforcement Officer

Evidence For The
Law Enforcement Officer

Third Edition

Gilbert B. Stuckey

Faculty Emeritus, Department of Public Safety and Service
Mt. San Antonio College
Member, Nebraska State Bar Association

Gregg Division
McGraw-Hill Book Company

New York St. Louis Dallas San Francisco Aukland Bogotá
Düsseldorf Johannesburg London Madrid Mexico Montreal
New Delhi Panama Paris São Paulo Singapore Sydney
Tokyo Toronto

The editors for this book were Susan H. Munger and Mitsy Kovacs, the designer was Roberta Rezk, and the production supervisor was May E. Konopka. It was set in Baskerville by Trufont.

Library of Congress Cataloging in Publication Data

Stuckey, Gilbert B
    Evidence for the law enforcement officer.

    Includes index.
    1. Evidence, Criminal—United States.
I. Title.
KF9660.S8   1979   345'.73'06   78-16377
ISBN 0-07-062401-1

EVIDENCE FOR THE LAW ENFORCEMENT OFFICER, Third Edition

2 3 4 5 6 7 8 9 0   DODO   7 8 5 4 3 2 1 0 9

Contents

Exclusion of Confessions Because of Delay in Arraignment
Right of Counsel and Right to Remain Silent
Evidence Discovered through Improper Confession Excluded
Confession Given after an Unlawful Arrest May Be Excluded
Confessions Still Acceptable as Evidence
Proof of the Crime in Addition to Confession
Admissions

What Is the Exclusionary Rule?
Search and Seizure
Search by Valid Consent
Search Pursuant to a Search Warrant
Search and Seizure Incident to an Arrest
Search without an Arrest
Objecting to Introduction of Evidence
Lineup Identification

Direct Evidence Versus Circumstantial Evidence
Admissibility of Previous Crimes and Misconduct
Means or Capability to Commit a Crime
Consciousness of Guilt
Character of the Defendant
Character of Victims

Documents as a Kind of Evidence
What Is Right of Discovery?
Right of Discovery through Preliminary Hearing
Pretrial Discovery
Prosecution's Right of Discovery
Defendant's Right to Original Investigative Notes

What Is Physical Evidence?

Preface

In order that law enforcement and correctional officers may be kept abreast of the more recent appellate court decisions and statutory enactments relating to the admissibility of evidence, *Evidence for the Law Enforcement Officer* has been revised for the third time.

Both the law enforcement and the correctional officers who have been engaged in the prosecution of criminal offenders know the value of evidence. The officers know that the success of the prosecution depends upon their ability to collect and preserve evidence and to testify about that evidence in court. They also know that in the collection and preservation of evidence and in testifying, there are certain rules and regulations that must be followed. These rules of evidence must be known to the officers, and they must abide by them if they expect to do their job in a competent manner. However, officers and preservice students who try to study and read the books in the field to familiarize themselves with the rules of evidence are generally discouraged. These books are written in a highly technical and difficult style intended for the student of law, the attorney, or the judge. *Evidence for the Law Enforcement Officer* was written to fill this gap in information.

This book gives officers and preservice students an understanding of the field of evidence from a practical standpoint. It is designed to give a workable and understandable discourse on the entire field of evidence with particular emphasis on areas of interest and importance to officers in their daily work. Even so, the study of the rules of evidence is not an easy one.

As officers familiarize themselves with the rules of evidence, they gain the impression that many of the rules are continually changing and they feel that it will be impossible to cope with the rules in their work. In a sense, the officers are right. Many of the laws, as they pertain to the admissibility of evidence, have a fine line of demarcation between what is admissible and what is not. Even judges often find difficulty in determining the line of demarcation. Many times a judge will learn as the result of an appeal of a conviction that he or she made an incorrect decision because the decision will be reversed by the appellate court. These decisions often affect the way officers investigate a case.

There have been marked changes in the rules of evidence—particularly in the fields of search and seizure and in the admissibility of confessions. Some of these changes have not been to the liking of the officers. These changes have handicapped the officers in their work. They feel that the courts are more concerned with some technical right of a defendant than with the protection of the whole society. Nevertheless, the officers must adhere to these decisions and work harder to collect and preserve evidence to overcome these added burdens. It might be well for officers to reflect on the appellate court decisions which have been so unfavorable to them. It is highly possible that these decisions would not have been handed down if the officers involved had been better informed in the field of evidence.

Once the officers have mastered the rules of evidence, they will be able to collect evidence that will be admissible in a trial. They will secure witnesses who are competent, and who will testify in a proper and effective manner. With effective pretrial preparation, when the case goes to trial there will be fewer acquittals and fewer criminals will be released to prey again upon the public. The image of the law enforcement officer will be enhanced in the eyes of society. Officers with a thorough knowledge of evidence will go a long way in controlling crime in America.

As officers read through this book, it may appear that such areas as the rules pertaining to "presumptions" and "knowledge of the court" do not concern them in their work. Yet, in order to understand the significance of evidence in the whole judicial process and everything going on at a trial, officers must be familiar with the entire trial procedure. Familiarity will help them to avoid pitfalls and to make a more favorable impression on the judge and the jury.

Also, it should be stated, there is but little difference between the rules of evidence as they apply in one state and another or in local courts as distinguished from the federal courts. Many differences that prevailed in the past have been wiped from the rule books by decisions handed down by the Supreme Court of the United States. Good examples of this are the application of the "exclusionary rule" and the "admissibility of confessions" as covered in this book. For this reason, this study of evidence is as practical for a reader in New York as it is for one in California or Florida or Washington or Hawaii or, for that matter, any place throughout the free world. Hence, this book will be helpful to everyone who wants a practical insight into the rules of evidence. It will be particularly helpful to officers and police and correctional-science students, who must become better and better informed in regard to the rules of evidence. This book is also beneficial to those persons who may become jurors or witnesses and to others with a sincere interest in our administration of justice.

I would like to express my appreciation to LaVelle Anderson, Instructor, Speech Communications and Drama Department, Mt. San Antonio College, and to Ann Posey for their assistance in the preparation of the manuscript for this third edition.

Gilbert B. Stuckey

Trial Procedure

Each arrest of a criminal must be followed by some kind of prosecutive action unless the charge is dismissed. If the criminal enters a plea of guilty to the charge for which the offender was arrested, the prosecutive procedure is comparatively simple. The officer does not become too extensively involved. On the other hand, if the criminal enters a plea of not guilty, the trial which follows can become a very time-consuming, complicated ordeal. The officer plays an important role in the whole process. For this reason, before beginning the discourse on the evidence, it may be well to review briefly the trial procedure. The reader may then have a better understanding of the rules of evidence and their application in the presentation of facts during the trial.

It is not necessary to go into all the details leading up to trial. However, a summary of the stages of the trial procedure as they unfold may give the reader a better understanding of what is taking place throughout a trial and why the rules of evidence were developed.

Basically, any trial, whether criminal or civil in nature, has for its primary purpose the determination of the truth about what happened in the case. The trial is nothing more than a story of the case told in logical sequence in order that the judge and jury may follow it clearly. Each witness unfolds his or her particular chapter of the story while testifying to personal knowledge of the facts. There is very little difference between the rules of evidence applicable in a criminal case and those in a civil matter. Perhaps the most marked difference is in the amount of proof necessary. In a criminal case the prosecution must present enough evidence to convince the jury of the guilt of the defendant beyond a reasonable doubt. In a civil trial only a preponderance of the evidence must be presented on the part of one side or the other to receive a favorable judgment. Another variation is in the voting by the jury in reaching their conclusion. In most jurisdictions, in a criminal case there must be a unanimous decision; in a civil matter a unanimous vote of the jury is not generally necessary in order to award judgment in favor of a particular litigant.

ACCUSATORY PLEADINGS

In order to bring any criminal case to trial, certain legal documents must be filed with the appropriate court. These documents are referred to as "accusatory pleadings." In most instances the first document to be filed is a complaint, and in misdemeanor cases this may be the only accusatory document to be filed. The complaint sets forth the charge against the arrested person, who is now known as the "defendant." It is against this charge that the defendant's defense must be prepared. In felony cases an additional accusatory pleading is filed in most instances. This additional document will be either an information prepared by the prosecuting attorney or an indictment returned by a grand jury.

The Fifth Amendment of the United States Constitution provides that: "No person shall be held to answer for a capital, or otherwise infamous crime, unless on a presentment or indictment of a grand jury." This guarantee is included in the Constitution to prevent persons accused of a serious crime from being held without sufficient probable cause. Because of this guarantee in the United States Constitution, some states have also included in their criminal procedure the presentation of all serious crimes (all felonies and some more serious misdemeanors) to a grand jury.

The grand jury is a body of lay persons selected within a community to hear criminal charges. The body usually consists of nineteen members, but this number may vary in some jurisdictions. The persons selected must possess all the requirements of a trial juror. When a person is accused of a serious crime, the prosecuting attorney will present evidence, primarily through witnesses, to the grand jury to determine if there is sufficient cause to believe that a crime has been committed and that the person accused has committed it and may be held for trial. If they so decide, they will return a legal document known as an "indictment," which will become the accusatory pleading against which the accused must offer defense. If they decide that there is insufficient evidence to show either that a crime has been committed or that the accused has committed it, the grand jury will return a "no bill." If this takes place, generally no legal action can be brought against the accused unless further evidence can be developed and the case again presented to a grand jury and an indictment returned.

Instead of presenting criminal charges to a grand jury, some states have substituted a different type of judicial safeguard for the accused. The procedure is known as a "preliminary hearing," or a "preliminary examination." When a person is accused of a serious crime and is in custody, the evidence is presented to a judge instead of a grand jury. The proceeding is much the same as a trial, except in most instances the defense will not present any evidence.

In view of the United States constitutional guarantee that a person could not be charged with a serious crime except by indictment or presentment, there was some question whether the preliminary hearing fulfilled the right of due process of law as provided by the Fourteenth Amendment to the United States Constitution. But this question was answered in the case of *Hurtado v. California,* 110 U.S. 516 (1883), in which the preliminary hearing, in lieu of a grand jury hearing, was sanctioned.

It is interesting to note that although the grand jury proceeding is considered to be the ultimate guarantee of an accused against being illegally held for trial, some accused persons have challenged this procedure in lieu of the preliminary hearing. The challenge is based upon the fact that neither the accused nor the defense attorney may be present during a grand jury hearing, whereas in a preliminary hearing both are permitted to be present. They may cross-examine the prosecution's witnesses, and in most instances the defense may present evidence of its own. Irrespective of the attack made on the grand jury system, the appellate courts have held that the grand jury procedure fulfills the due-process-of-law guarantee.

Even though some states have adopted the preliminary hearing procedure, in most instances the grand jury system will not have been abolished and will still be utilized in some cases. Whether a case will be presented to a grand jury or to a judge at a preliminary hearing is largely at the discretion of the prosecuting attorney (often designated the district attorney, or D.A.) However, the accused must have been arrested and available to appear at the preliminary hearing either as the result of still being in custody or having been released on bail with the promise to appear. But the facts can be presented to a grand jury without the accused's having been arrested.

Returning to the preliminary hearing, if the judge, after hearing the evidence as presented by the prosecution, decides there are sufficient facts to believe that a crime has been committed and that the accused committed it, the judge will hold the accused for trial. The judge's decision in this regard is referred to as "binding the defendant over" for trial or "held to answer" for trial.

If the judge decides against the prosecution, no prosecutive action can be taken against the accused unless further evidence is developed and the case is again presented to the judge. However, in most jurisdictions the facts could still be presented to a grand jury to determine if an indictment would be forthcoming. Usually the prosecution will not take this action unless it is felt that the judge's decision was arbitrary.

If a judge decides that the accused should be held for trial, the prosecuting attorney will prepare a legal document to be filed with the trial court. This document, known as an "information," will set forth the charge against the accused. The indictment and the information are very similar in wording, and both are very similar to the complaint. Each sets forth the crime which the defendant is accused of committing, the approximate date that the crime was committed, and the place where it was committed.

JURY OR COURT TRIAL

A criminal trial may be conducted in one of two ways. It may be what is known as a "jury trial" or it may be a "court trial," that is, a trial by the judge alone without a jury.

The Sixth Amendment to the Constitution of the United States, as well as provisions in the constitutions of the fifty states, guarantees to a defendant in a criminal trial the right to be tried by an impartial jury. For many years these provisions were interpreted to mean that the defendant must have a jury trial. It was not until 1930 in *Patton v. United States,* 281 U.S. 276 (1930), that the Supreme Court of the United States gave a qualified approval for a defendant to waive the jury and be tried by a judge alone. Most states now permit the defendant to waive a jury. However, usually the prosecuting attorney must agree to this waiver. There are some states that will not permit a waiver of the jury if the crime is one in which the maximum penalty is death. The rules of evidence, with a few technical exceptions, are primarily the same whether the case is tried by a jury or by the judge.

THE JURY

At common law and in most states in this country a jury in a criminal trial consists of twelve persons. Although in the early history of Europe many of the inquisitory councils (also referred to as "juries") often consisted of a number ranging from four to sixty-six, by the thirteenth century twelve was the usual number of an inquisitory council. By the fourteenth century the requirement of twelve had become more or less fixed. Thereafter this number seemed to develop a somewhat superstitious reverence.

When the colonists came to America, juries of England were composed of twelve persons, and so it was only natural that juries in this country should also consist of twelve. Yet the Sixth Amendment to the United States Constitution prescribes no set number for a jury. All that this amendment states is: "In all criminal prosecutions, the accused shall enjoy the right of a speedy and public trial, by an impartial jury." Inasmuch as there appears to be no real significance to a jury being composed of twelve persons, some states have broken with tradition and have passed laws permitting a jury in a criminal case to be composed of less than twelve. In Florida a jury may consist of only six persons in all but capital cases. A jury of this number received the sanction of the United States Supreme Court in the case of *William v. Florida,* 388 U.S. 78 (1970).

Even in those states in which it is required by law that a jury be composed of twelve persons, some deviation of the rule is permitted in most jurisdictions. For example, in misdemeanor cases a jury of less than twelve is allowed if agreed upon by the defense and the prosecution. How many less than twelve is not designated, but the number can not be less than six. Also in felony cases some jurisdictions permit a trial to continue with fewer than twelve if one of the jurors becomes incapacitated to act and the continuance with less than twelve is agreed upon by the defense.

Although the Sixth Amendment provides that "in all criminal prosecutions, the accused shall enjoy the right to a . . . trial by an impartial jury," it has been held that this guarantee does not apply in the prosecution of petty offenses. [See case of *Frank v. United States*, 395 U.S. 147 (1969).] The Court held that since the offense was a petty one, the defendant was not entitled to a jury trial and his rights had not been violated. Indirectly, therefore, it has been concluded that any offense which does not carry a maximum sentence of more than six months' imprisonment is a petty one and does not entitle a person to a jury trial.

■ Qualifications of Jurors

Although the qualifications of a trial juror may vary somewhat among the states, the general qualifications are the same. The person must have reached adulthood, which now in most instances means that the person must be 18 years of age or over. He or she must be a citizen of the United States and a resident within the jurisdiction of the court involved. The prospective juror must have a sufficient knowledge of the English language to understand the testimony and to be able to communicate during the deliberation. The person must have use of his or her natural faculties,

Fig. 1-1. Courtroom scene. (United Press International Photo)

meaning having the ability to see, hear, and talk. A person with a past felony conviction will be disqualified from jury duty in most states.

■ Function of the Jury

In a jury trial the function of the jury is to determine the facts of the case. In other words, they interpret the evidence as it is presented and try to determine what happened. Their ultimate goal is to ascertain whether the defendant is guilty of the crime as charged and brought to trial. This decision is made after the evidence of the prosecution and the defendant has been submitted for their review. A defendant in a criminal trial does not have to present any evidence in his or her own behalf, particularly if the defendant believes that the prosecution's case is so weak that there is already a reasonable doubt about his guilt. On the other hand, the defendant's evidence may be offered in an effort to overcome that presented by the prosecution. This is done in the hope that it will create a doubt in the mind of the jurors, if that doubt is not already present. Although the ultimate function of the jury in a criminal case is rendering a verdict of guilty or not guilty, as will be further pointed out a jury will in some cases determine the sentence to be imposed.

THE JUDGE

It is the responsibility of the judge to see that the defendant gets a fair trial and, from the standpoint of society, that justice is done. To accomplish this the judge has many duties. To list a few: The judge will interpret the law of the case for the jury; will decide what evidence is admissible and what is not; will rule on objections made by the attorneys; will determine the competence of witnesses; and will protect the witnesses from overzealous cross-examinations. In some jurisdictions the judge may comment on the credibility of the witnesses and the weight of the evidence, and, in many instances, may be responsible for imposing the sentence to be served by the defendant.

In a jury trial the function of the judge is much like that of a referee. The judge keeps order in the court, sees that the trial progresses properly and smoothly. It is the judge's duty to maintain control over the conduct of those involved in a trial proceeding. To assist in this regard, the judge may exercise the power of "contempt of court." Contempt of court procedure gives the judge the right to fine or place in jail anyone who acts improperly during a trial. When the trial is a court trial, the judge acts in a dual capacity. The judge not only does the things listed in a judge's normal capacity but also performs the function of the jury in determining the facts of the case. The judge therefore renders the verdict of guilt or innocence.

PROSECUTING ATTORNEY'S RESPONSIBILITY

Once the time of a trial arrives, law enforcement officers' duties are, for the most part, completed. By now they will have collected physical evidence, interviewed the witnesses, and discussed the case in detail with the prosecuting attorney. All that remains for the officers to do is testify in a modest, unbiased, and intelligent manner. The progress of the trial is largely the responsibility of the prosecuting attorney, whose role in the judicial procedure becomes paramount.

However, prosecuting attorneys have many responsibilities far ahead of trial time. First, their duty is to prosecute the guilty and to see that the innocent are protected. As was stated by the United States Supreme Court in the case of *Gideon v. Wainwright*, 372 U.S. 335 (1963), prosecuting attorneys "are everywhere deemed essential to protect the public's interest in an orderly society." In this capacity, prosecuting attorneys must decide which criminal charges should be prosecuted and which should be dismissed in the interest of justice. When the decision is to prosecute, the prosecuting attorney must decide which witnesses will be used and what evidence will be presented. It is not necessary that every witness who has some knowledge of the case be called upon to testify. Neither is it required that every bit of physical evidence be presented. The only requirement is that a sufficient number of witnesses be called and evidence presented to afford the accused a fair trial. In deciding what to use, the prosecuting attorney will consider past experience with the particular charge involved, knowledge of the personality of the judge who will be hearing the case, and the potential dramatics of the situation as the trial progresses. If an officer has an honest belief that some important items have been overlooked, the officer should feel free to mention this to the prosecuting attorney when the court is not in session. The prosecuting attorney may have forgotten some piece of evidence during concentration on the trial, but may, on the other hand, have made a last-minute decision not to use this evidence. In either event the officer, because of familiarity with the case, is justified in mentioning the evidence, but must abide by the prosecuting attorney's decision and not argue about its validity.

■ Reasonable Doubt

It is the responsibility of the prosecuting attorney to present sufficient evidence to convince the jury of the guilt of the defendant beyond a reasonable doubt. Although the term "reasonable doubt" is quite well understood by all, it is most difficult to define.

The following are two examples of legal definitions of reasonable doubt as developed by the courts. In *Holt v. United States*, 218 U.S. 245 (1910), the

United States Supreme Court approved this definition of reasonable doubt as being acceptable for a judge to use as an instruction to a jury:

> Reasonable doubt is an actual doubt that you are conscious of after going over in your minds the entire case, giving consideration to all the testimony and every part of it. If you then feel uncertain and not fully convinced that the defendant is guilty, and believe that you are acting in a reasonable manner, and if you believe that a reasonable man in any matter of like importance would hesitate to act because of such a doubt as you are conscious of having, that is a reasonable doubt, of which the defendant is entitled to have the benefit.

In a New York case, *People v. Barker,* 153 N.Y. 111 (1897), the court approved this definition: "A reasonable doubt is not a mere whim, guess or surmise; nor is it a mere subterfuge to which resort may be had in order to avoid doing a disagreeable thing; but it is such doubt as reasonable men may entertain, after a careful and honest review and consideration of the evidence of the case."

ROLE OF THE DEFENSE ATTORNEY

Among other guarantees, the Sixth Amendment to the United States Constitution provides that "in all criminal prosecutions, the accused shall . . . have the assistance of counsel for his defense." As a result of United States Supreme Court decisions, it has been held that an accused shall have the right of assistance of counsel for defense in all instances, and if the accused cannot afford an attorney, one must be provided (see *Gideon v. Wainwright*). It has also been established that an accused is entitled to the assistance of counsel long before the time of the trial. As was stated in the case of *Escobedo v. Illinois,* 378 U.S. 478 (1964), an accused is entitled to the assistance of counsel at the time an investigation is "focused upon a particular suspect."

Because of this zealousness by the courts to afford an accused the right of counsel through every phase of the criminal proceedings, the defense attorney becomes a most important figure in the administration of justice. His or her primary function is to make certain that all the rights of the defendant are properly protected. The defense attorney will make certain that the charge against the defendant is a valid one and that there was sufficient probable cause to have made the arrest. The defense attorney will advise the defendant concerning statements that he or she may or may not make. At the time of the trial the defense attorney will cross-examine the prosecution witnesses and present the defense that is deemed necessary under the circumstances. Along with the judge, the defense attorney has the responsibility of seeing that the defendant is given a fair trial.

As has been stated, if an accused desires the assistance of counsel in defense, this right may not be denied. But an accused may waive the right to the assistance of counsel and be entitled to self-representation, assuming that the decision to self-representation was an intelligent one. [See *Faretta v. California*, 422 U.S. 806 (1975).]

OPENING STATEMENT

Whether the trial is heard by a jury or by the judge alone, the prosecution will present its evidence first. Most of the evidence will be presented through the testimony of witnesses. If the trial is heard by a jury, the judge will read, or have read, to the jury the charge for which the defendant has been brought to trial.

After reading the charge to the jury, the trial proper commences. Before calling the first witness the prosecuting attorney will make what is known as the "opening statement." This statement is a summary of what the prosecution intends to prove through its evidence about the guilt of the defendant. The defendant's attorney is also permitted to make an opening statement summarizing efforts to prove the defendant innocent. Generally, the defendant's attorney will not make a statement until the prosecution has completed its side of the case.

ADMINISTERING THE OATH

If the defense attorney waives the right to make an opening statement at the conclusion of the prosecuting attorney's statement, the time to call the first witness has arrived. Before the witness takes the seat to testify, which seat is frequently referred to as the "witness box" or "witness stand," an oath is administered to the witness by the bailiff or some other officer of the court. The oath consists of words to this effect: "Do you solemnly swear to tell the truth and nothing but the truth, so help you God?" The witness will—or should—reply in the affirmative. During administration of the oath, witnesses are required to raise their right hand. There are those who object to taking the oath because it requires them "to swear" and "to swear" has the implication that they are using profanity, which is against their beliefs. Likewise, some profess no belief in a deity and object to the oath because of the mention of God. To accommodate those to whom the oath is objectionable, the "affirmation" has been substituted. In other words, all that the witnesses do is to affirm or declare that they will tell the truth. But in any event, all witnesses must either swear or affirm that they will tell the truth before being permitted to testify.

EXAMINATION OF WITNESSES

■ Sequence of Witnesses

The sequence in which witnesses are called to testify will depend largely upon the kind of case involved and how the evidence may best be presented in a logical order. It is not necessary that the witnesses be called in the sequence in which the events of a case took place. For example, if a defendant were being tried on a charge of having burglarized a place of business, the order of calling the witnesses could vary greatly. The first witness might be the owner of the place burglarized. Through the testimony of this witness the first elements of the charge would be established, i.e., that there was an illegal entry and articles were taken without permission. Or the prosecuting attorney may find it more convenient to place the arresting officer on the stand first. Through the testimony of the officer it may be shown that the defendant was arrested near the scene of the burglary during the early morning hours, at which time he had in his possession articles taken from a place of business which had been burglarized. Such testimony alone would be a strong indication of the guilt of the accused.

■ Direct Examination

The questioning of a witness by the side who calls the witness is known as "direct questioning," or "direct examination." Direct examination usually begins by asking the witness his or her name, address, and occupation. Even though this information may be well known to all in the courtroom, it is necessary for the completion of the court record of the case. After these preliminary background information questions are completed, the general questioning of the witness about his knowledge of the case will begin.

During the direct questioning, whether it be by the prosecuting attorney or the defense attorney, the attorney must form the questions in such a manner that the desired answers are not indicated. If the answer desired is implied, the question is known as a "leading question" because it tends to lead the witness to the answer that should be given. For an example, the following might be asked: "It is true, isn't it, that the defendant had a gun?" It is quite obvious from the wording of this question that the attorney wants the witness to answer in the affirmative. On direct examination this question would be objected to by the opposing side, and the judge would sustain the objection because of the leading nature of the question asked. However, this same question could be rephrased as follows: "Did the defendant have a gun?" In asking the question in this manner, the attorney gives no indication whether a "yes" or "no" answer is desired. This question is perfectly acceptable, as it permits the witness to answer freely according to the facts of the case without being led.

The theory behind not permitting leading questions to be asked during direct examination is that if the desired answer is indicated, the witness may be inclined to give that answer irrespective of the truth.

Although leading questions generally may not be asked during direct examination, some limited use of this type of question is permitted during the direct examination. In presenting preliminary matters, such as the identification and the occupation of a witness, leading questions are usually permitted because they refer to noncontroversial matters and save trial time. Restricted use of leading questions is sometimes permitted to refresh the memory of a witness. Also, leading questions are occasionally permitted during the direct examination of children or mentally defective persons to assist them in giving their testimony; however, this must be done with considerable caution because of the possibility that such persons will follow a suggested answer.

■ Objections

During the direct examination of a witness by the prosecuting attorney, the defense attorney will undoubtedly inject many objections to questions asked by the prosecuting attorney. These objections may be based on any one of a number of alleged reasons given by the defense attorney. An objection may be based upon the grounds that it is a leading question, that it asks for a conclusion of a witness, or that it is irrelevant. Objections may be well founded. On the other hand, an objection may be injected for psychological reasons to break a line of questioning by the prosecuting attorney or to lessen the impact of the testimony that is being given. This might be compared with a time-out called by a football team at the moment that the opposing team is making a concerted drive down the field.

In any event, when an objection is made by either the prosecuting attorney or the defense attorney, the witness must remain silent and not answer until the judge has made a ruling, or decision, on the objection. This ruling will be stated by the judge in one of two ways. The judge will either "sustain" the objection or "overrule" it. If the objection is sustained, or upheld, the witness must not answer the question. If the witness inadvertently answers the question before the judge can make the ruling, or if the witness answers the question after the objection is sustained, the witness will undoubtedly be admonished by the judge. If the witness persists thereafter in answering questions prior to the ruling being made, the witness could be held in contempt of court. If the judge overrules the objection, the witness may answer the question asked.

If the witness answers a question to which an objection was sustained, the answer may be "stricken" from the record, which means that the jury must disregard the answer. But it is almost impossible to completely erase a thought once it has been planted in the minds of the jury. The answer to the question objected to may be so damaging or prejudicial to the defendant that the judge will declare a "mistrial." In that case the trial is stopped, and must be started all over again, which is time-consuming and costly. If the responsible witness happens to be a peace officer, there may be serious repercussions, such as being charged with contempt of court, for an officer is supposed to know court procedure.

This review of trial proceedings may assist officers in avoiding this pitfall, as well as others, which might place them in an unfavorable light. Further details on the proper manner in which to testify will be set forth in Chapter 13 entitled "How to Testify Effectively."

■ Contempt of Court

It may be well to consider some of the implications of "contempt of court." It is the duty of a judge to maintain control over the conduct of those involved in a trial proceeding. Contempt-of-court procedure gives the judge the right to fine or place in jail anyone who acts improperly during a trial. Also, a refusal by a witness to appear in court after receiving a subpoena to do so will undoubtedly result in the witness being held in contempt of court. A refusal to answer a question on the witness stand, unless it is a question that would subject the witness to punishment, may cause the witness to be in contempt; misconduct by the attorneys or jurors involved in the case or any unruliness on the part of the spectators may result in contempt.

As a result of this explanation of the contempt-of-court phase of our judicial procedure, the reader may gain the impression that it is a constant threat to those involved in a trial. It should not be so considered. The possibility of punishment for contempt of court should be considered a necessary accompaniment of the judge's duty to assure that the litigants get a fair trial and that witnesses are protected from abuse.

■ Cross-Examination

After the direct examination is completed, the other side has the right to cross-examine the witness. The right of cross-examination is considered essential for the discovery of the truth during a trial. So after the prosecuting attorney has completed the direct examination of the witness, the defense attorney may, as desired, cross-examine the witness. In most instances the attorney will cross-examine the witness. There are several reasons why the defense may wish to do so. One is to try to cross up the witness's story and thereby cause the testimony to be given less consideration by the jury; a second may be to show that the witness is prejudiced and consequently may have testified incorrectly or untruthfully; and a third may be merely an effort to prove that the attorney is earning a fee. In any event the cross-examination is frequently a trying experience for the witness involved.

During direct examination, little or no effort is made to belittle or embarrass the witness, but upon cross-examination the witness may be placed in an unfavorable position because the attorney is endeavoring to overcome the impact of the witness's testimony, particularly when the witness is an officer and is being cross-examined by the defense attorney. The officer frequently will be the most damaging witness against the defendant, and any effort on the part of the defense attorney to lessen the weight of the testimony is beneficial to the defendant.

Asking leading questions during the cross-examination is permitted because the witness is considered to be adverse to the side that is cross-examining; the witness therefore will give the answer that he or she wants to give and will not be led by the cross-examiner.

Jurisdictions vary in the scope of cross-examination. A majority of the states restrict cross-examination to matters testified to during the direct examination. No new matters or facts may be brought out during the cross-examination. For this reason a witness should not volunteer any more information while answering a question than is asked for by the attorney. Occasionally during direct examination by the prosecuting attorney, officers become overanxious to relate some bit of information about the case and go beyond the question asked during direct examination. This should be avoided for several reasons. The prosecuting attorney may be desirous of waiting for a more effective time to convey this information; or it may open up areas for cross-examination which should not have been gone into at that particular time.

About a fifth of the states follow the English rule, which permits a wide-open policy on cross-examination. In other words, the witness may be cross-examined about any fact relevant to the case. The cross-examiner is not restricted to matters testified about during the direct examination.

■ Redirect Examination

Upon conclusion of cross-examination by the defense attorney, the prosecuting attorney may further question the witness in order to clarify certain statements or answers given during the cross-examination. This second questioning on the part of the prosecuting attorney after the cross-examination is known as "redirect examination." The redirect examination is only for the purpose of clarification of matters brought out during the cross-examination. New matters are not generally allowed to be brought out during the redirect examination except by special permission of the judge.

■ Re-Cross-Examination

After a redirect examination has been conducted, the judge may grant permission to the defense attorney to ask a limited number of questions concerning further clarification of statements made by the witness during the redirect examination. This questioning is referred to as "re-cross-examination."

■ Sequential Review of Examination of Witnesses

The sequence described in the examination of witnesses—that is, direct examination, cross-examination, redirect examination, and re-cross-examination—may follow with each witness throughout the trial, whether the witness is for the prosecution or the defense. It is not necessary, however, that each of these steps be taken.

■ Prosecution Rests

After the prosecuting attorney is satisfied that enough evidence has been presented to prove the defendant guilty beyond a reasonable doubt, the prosecuting attorney will "rest" the case. This is a way of saying or indicating that the attorney has presented all that he or she intends to and is ready to rest his or her chances on that which has been brought forth.

If the judge believes that the prosecution has failed to prove the defendant guilty beyond a reasonable doubt, the judge may enter a judgment of acquittal. In some states, the judge does not have the authority to enter a judgment of acquittal but may order the jury to enter a verdict of not guilty.

■ Corpus Delicti (Meaning the "Body of the Crime")

During the presentation of a case by the prosecution, the *corpus delicti* must be established. Establishing the corpus delicti is proving the elements of the crime. Many persons are under the mistaken belief that the corpus delicti of a case consists of locating a major piece of physical evidence of the crime, such as the body in a murder case, but such evidence is not necessary to establish the corpus delicti. To establish the corpus delicti there must be proof that a crime was committed. Finding the murdered victim materially assists in proving that a murder was committed; but it is possible to prove a murder charge without the victim's body being located. Otherwise, a murderer might avoid prosecution by successfully concealing the body of the victim. The crime of murder may be proved by the testimony of eye-witnesses who saw the crime committed or by physical evidence. The identity of the person who committed the crime is not a part of the corpus delicti.

DEFENSE PRESENTATION

After the prosecution rests, the defense will present its side of the case in an effort to prove the innocence of the defendant. However, the defendant does not have to present any evidence in his or her own behalf if it is believed that the prosecution has failed in its efforts to prove the defendant guilty beyond a reasonable doubt. The defendant, therefore, may also rest at this point. But the usual procedure is for the defendant to present some evidence, regardless of how weak it may be.

The defendant may present evidence from one standpoint or a combination of standpoints. Efforts may be made to prove the defendant innocent by way of an *alibi*, that is, to prove that the defendant was in an entirely different place from the area in which the crime was committed and could not, therefore, have committed the crime. Or the proof may be by "character witnesses," who will attempt to convince the jury that the defendant is of such good character that he or she would not be guilty of committing the crime of which charged. In the case of murder or aggravated assault, efforts may be made to prove that the act was in self-defense or by accident.

PROSECUTION'S REBUTTAL

Upon completion of the presentation of all the evidence on the part of the defendant, the prosecution has the right to call additional witnesses or to present evidence to overcome certain matters brought out during the defendant's portion of the trial. Ordinarily, no new evidence is presented at this time except by special permission of the judge. In order to introduce new evidence, it is usually necessary to prove that the evidence was newly discovered and was not known at the time of the presentation of the case by the prosecution.

CLOSING ARGUMENTS

After both sides have presented their cases, the prosecuting attorney and the defense attorney may make closing statements to the jury. These statements are referred to as "closing arguments." These arguments are a summarization of the evidence presented by each side during the trial. The prosecuting attorney and the defense attorney will make pleas to the jury, each asking favorable consideration of the evidence and the verdict each seeks.

INSTRUCTIONS OR CHARGE TO THE JURY

When the attorneys for both sides have finished their closing arguments, the judge will read the "instructions" to the jury. This procedure is sometimes referred to as the "charge" to the jury. These instructions merely consist of an interpretation of the law and the rules of evidence as they may apply to the particular case. The purpose of these instructions is to assist and guide the jury in their review of the evidence in order that they may arrive at a verdict.

DELIBERATION AND VERDICT

After the judge has instructed the jury, the jury will retire to a jury room where they will weigh the evidence presented during trial and attempt to arrive at a verdict. This review of the evidence is referred to as the "deliberation by the jury." To prevent the possibility of any outside influence affecting the jury's verdict, the jury is usually *sequestered*, sometimes referred to as being "locked up," during the deliberation period. In some jurisdictions it is mandatory that they be sequestered during the deliberation. Legally, the judge may sequester the jury during an entire trial, but this is usually not done unless it is required in the particular jurisdiction.

The period of time that a jury may deliberate will vary considerably. It may be only a matter of minutes, or it may be several days. The seriousness of the charge and the length of the trial often play determining roles in the deliberation time. In most jurisdictions the jury in a criminal trial must reach a unanimous verdict, which means all of the jurors must vote for guilt or acquittal. This unanimity frequently takes time, but a judge usually will do everything possible to encourage the jurors to reach a decision. If they cannot, the result is known as a "hung jury." The judge will discharge that jury, and the case will have to be tried over again from the beginning with a new jury.

If, on the other hand, the jury arrives at a verdict, the jury is returned to the courtroom and the verdict is announced. In most jurisdictions after the verdict has been announced in open court, the jury's function is over and the jury will be dismissed.

If the verdict is one of not guilty, the defendant is immediately freed of the charge and custody and may not be tried again on the same charge, as it would be a violation of the double-jeopardy clause of the Fifth Amendment to the United States Constitution.

SENTENCING THE DEFENDANT

If the verdict of the jury is guilty, the defendant must be sentenced. The sentencing procedure varies greatly among the states. In many states sentencing the defendant is the prerogative of the trial judge. The judge will set the length of time that the defendant is to serve. In some states, the jury not only renders the verdict but also imposes the sentence.

SUMMARY

The rules of evidence are primarily the same whether the trial is of a civil or a criminal nature. The degree of proof necessary in a criminal case, as distinguished from a civil case, is one of the most marked differences. In a criminal case the defendant must be proved guilty beyond a reasonable doubt. In a civil matter the plaintiff must only present a preponderance of the evidence to receive favorable judgment. Reasonable doubt has been defined as that state of mind in which the juror after a review of all the evidence still has some conscientious doubt of guilt.

A criminal trial may be heard by a jury or a judge alone. The prosecuting attorney has the responsibility of the trial's progress for the most part. The prosecuting attorney will present evidence first, most of which will be through the testimony of witnesses, one of the most important of whom is the peace officer who investigated the case. Witnesses must swear or affirm that they will tell the truth before they are permitted to testify.

While a witness is being questioned, objections may be raised to questions asked. The witness should remain silent until the judge sustains or overrules the objection. If the witness inadvertently answers before the judge makes his ruling, the witness may be held in contempt of court. The right of punishment for contempt of court is granted a judge to assist in the proper control of the trial's progress.

Witnesses present their knowledge of the case through direct examination, which may be followed by cross-examination. Redirect examination and re-cross-examination may also be conducted.

After the prosecution has presented its side of the case, the defendant may, if desired, present evidence. Following the defendant's presentation, there may be rebuttal evidence offered by the prosecution if deemed necessary, after which the prosecuting attorney and defense attorney make closing arguments. Upon the conclusion of the closing arguments the judge instructs the jury on the law of the case. The jury makes the decision whether the defendant is guilty or not guilty. If the defendant is found guilty, the judge in most jurisdictions will impose the sentence.

QUESTIONS FOR REVIEW

1. In what way does the burden of proof differ between criminal and civil cases?
2. How many jurors must vote for a verdict in a criminal case? How many in a civil case must vote for a judgment?
3. What is the difference between a jury trial and a court trial?
4. May a defendant in a criminal case waive a jury trial in all instances?
5. Explain "reasonable doubt" so far as proving the guilt of a defendant in a criminal trial is concerned.
6. What is the difference between an oath and an affirmation?
7. About what matters may a witness be cross-examined?
8. What is the purpose of redirect examination?
9. What is the purpose of closing arguments?
10. What is the charge to the jury?
11. What is meant by a hung jury?
12. What is meant by sequestering the jury?
13. What is the purpose of sequestering a jury?

LOCAL RULES

In view of the fact that there are differences among jurisdictions on certain rules of evidence, rules of procedure, and points of law, the reader may wish to consult the prosecuting attorney for his or her area and ascertain the answers to the following questions.

1. Is a unanimous verdict of the jury required in a criminal case?
2. Is cross-examination limited to direct examination?
3. May a jury trial in a criminal case be waived?
4. May the jury consist of less than twelve persons?
5. When does a court trial begin?
6. Must a jury be sequestered? If so, at what time during the trial?
7. Who is responsible for sentencing the defendant?

Evidence–Rules and Kinds

DEFINITION OF EVIDENCE

Evidence has been defined in many ways. In its simplest form, evidence is defined as information. In a legal sense it is the information presented during a trial which enables the jury to arrive at the truth about what happened in a particular case. Technically, evidence is the means, sanctioned by law, of ascertaining the truth about a question of fact during a trial proceeding. It has also been defined as the medium of proof in a trial; it is the means by which a fact is proved or disproved in court. To state what evidence is in the language of the ordinary person: It is the testimony given by witnesses, the articles found at a crime scene, and the other things presented during a trial which enable the judge and jury to determine the facts about what happened in a case. It enables them to ascertain the guilt or innocence of the defendant. If this definition were taken too literally, it would imply that everything which sheds some light upon the truth of a fact in question should be revealed during the trial, but because of certain rules of evidence not everything that sheds some light may be presented.

The law enforcement officer has used the term "evidence" with a specialized meaning. To the officer evidence means the articles found at a crime scene, on a suspect, or in the suspect's car or home, or those things developed during an investigation, such as latent prints or a plaster of paris cast. It is those things which, after being found, are transported to the station and deposited in a judicial sanctuary known as the "evidence locker," where they remain until they can be utilized in a criminal trial to assist in a conviction. If they are not so used, there they continue to be stored collecting dust, becoming mildewed, or corroded beyond recognition, as no one dare touch or throw one piece away because of the evidentiary halo which surrounds it. Although the officer's interpretation is not a true definition of evidence, it is not unwise that the officer should place this legal reverence on articles found during an investigation of a crime, because with this attitude the officer is taking the precautions frequently necessary to sustain a conviction. Legally, the articles found do not become evidence until they are introduced in court during the trial.

RULES OF EVIDENCE

"Rules of evidence," or the "laws of evidence," as they are also known, are a set of regulations which act as guidelines for judges, attorneys, and law enforcement officers who may be involved in the trials of cases. These guidelines assist in determining how the trial is to be conducted; what persons may be witnesses; the matters about which they can testify; the method by which articles at a crime scene are collected and preserved; and what is admissible and that which is not. These rules are the product of many years of judicial evolution. They were developed by trial and error, through logic and sound judgment, following the basic needs of a good society. They make for the orderly conduct of the trial, prevent one spouse from testifying against another, except in certain instances, forbid the use of hearsay as evidence on occasions, and prohibit the admission of illegally obtained evidence. The law enforcement officer should not look upon these rules as an interference with his efforts to secure convictions. Instead he must realize that these rules were developed for the primary purpose of determining what actually happened in a criminal case.

We have not always had rules of evidence as they are known today. Such rules are comparatively recent, having been developed mostly within the past three centuries. They were originally designed to assist untrained jurors in arriving at a verdict.

In the days before jury trials, proof of guilt or innocence was decided by ordeal, battle, or compurgation. For the most part, the ordeal was an appeal to the supernatural. Biblical historians credit Moses in 1450 B.C. with describing a method for determining the faithfulness of a man's wife. The accused wife would be brought before a priest, who would mix dust from a tabernacle floor with holy water and force her to drink the mixture. If she were guilty of unfaithfulness, the liquid would cause her "belly to swell and her thighs to rot." If she were innocent, God would see that she suffered no ill effects. Another frequently used ordeal to determine guilt or innocence consisted of forcing an accused person to remove a rock from the bottom of a boiling pot of water. Any accused whose hands became blistered was found guilty. If the hands did not blister, an accused was acquitted. Acquittals under this system were rather rare.

Another kind of trial was introduced in England as a result of the Norman Conquest in 1066. This was trial by battle or combat (also known as "wager of battle"). In this system the victim of a crime and the accused would be forced into a physical encounter. Even litigants in civil matters were often required to ascertain who was right and who was wrong by this method of proof, the one who was right being the winner. It was assumed that God would give victory to the one who was right. In criminal matters if the accused won, the accused was acquitted; and so judicial combat became a prevalent way to establish justice, and it continued to hold sway for a period of time, but did eventually die out as a means of establishing right and wrong.

A more humane method of ascertaining guilt or innocence utilized from time to time was by *compurgation*, also known as "wager of law." By this system the accused would testify in his or her own behalf, pleading innocence. The accused would be supported by helpers known as "compurgators," or oath helpers, often twelve in number. These supporters or helpers would testify to the good character of the accused and particularly his or her reputation for veracity. These persons would not necessarily know anything about the facts of the case, but merely came forth to tell how good the accused was. This system soon furnished fertile grounds for perjury and proved to be as ineffective at determining the truth as the ordeal and combat methods. But it is considered to be forerunner of our use of character witnesses.

Later a trial by jury system began to make its appearance. But it was in no way like the trial by jury as we know it. The first juries had the function of charging the accused with a crime, acting in much the same capacity as a grand jury of today. They served to substantiate an accusation, leaving the test of innocence or guilt to be decided by some other means, such as trial by ordeal, battle, or wager of law. As time passed and the trial by ordeal, battle, and wager of law lost favor, the accusatory jury was given a dual function. Members of the jury would gather information from the countryside, mostly hearsay in form, concerning the alleged crime. They would then meet as a body to present what they had learned and to decide whether the accused should be held for trial. If a trial were held, the same jury would try the accused and render a verdict. Later it was decided that the accusatory jury, known by then as the grand jury, should not also try the accused. Therefore a separate jury, known as the "petit jury," was selected for that function. This jury, like the accusatory jury, relied upon evidence from the countryside. Later the petit jury was composed of persons with personal knowledge about the case. As time passed, witnesses who had information about the case were called to testify before the petit jury. However, much of the testimony of the witnesses was based upon hearsay information. Soon after 1700 A.D. the trial by jury as we know it today was beginning to become a reality, because use was made of sworn witnesses with the right of cross-examination. Hearsay evidence began to disappear from the judicial process. It was then that our rules of evidence began to develop into what they are today.

Fig. 2-1. Medieval duel fought between man and woman to decide marital issue. The man's feet are suspended in a hole in the ground, whereas the woman is permitted to stand free, unimpaired in her movement. Whoever wins the battle is pronounced legally justified by the judge. (The Bettmann Archive)

Today's rules of evidence cover the entire field of judicial procedure. As heretofore stated, in most instances they are equally applicable in civil matters and in criminal cases. The rules are numerous and some are involved. It will be the purpose of this book to concentrate on those most applicable to the work of the officer. As the officer studies them the officer may become confused, because some are difficult to understand, and the line of demarcation between what is admissible and the inadmissible is very fine. The officer may also become discouraged, as some of these rules are constantly changing; they are becoming more restrictive on the officer and his or her work. The officer will also find that it is difficult to abide by some of the rules, primarily because what was perfectly legal and proper one day is completely reversed the following day as the result of some appellate court decision. This is well illustrated by the effects of the exclusionary rule, which prohibits the use of illegally seized evidence in criminal trials. (This rule will be discussed in detail in Chapter 8.)

But in spite of such problems, the rules of evidence enable officers to know at the time of the investigation what evidence will be admissible during a trial. These rules also help officers to understand what evidence is and what information can be gained from it. They reaffirm to an officer that evidence is the information about the facts of the case, and that the effect that this evidence has on the jury is the proof of these facts.

DESCRIBING EVIDENCE

For a better understanding, evidence has been categorized by many writers, as well as in the statutes of some states, into kinds of evidence. These fall within three general categories: (1) testimony of witnesses; (2) real, or physical, evidence; and (3) documents, or writings. Some jurisdictions classify knowledge of the court, or judicial notice, and presumptions as kinds of evidence. Each category has its own important and unique function in the presentation of facts during a trial proceeding. For this reason each will be discussed in detail under separate headings or in separate chapters. In the meantime, there are certain terms and adjectives used to describe or qualify evidence which should be clearly understood.

■ Relevant Evidence

Irrespective of the kind of evidence it is, unless that evidence has some connection with the issues of the case it should not be admitted. If the evidence has a connection, it is said to be relevant. *Relevant evidence* is evidence that tends to prove or disprove any fact in dispute. It must explain or shed some light on the issues involved in the case. Relevant evidence has been described as that evidence which logically, naturally, and by reasonable inference tends to establish some fact. Devising an exact test for relevant evidence is difficult; it has been stated that the best test is one of good common sense and logic. If through good common sense and logic it is determined that the evidence offered will assist in establishing whether a crime was committed and whether the accused is guilty of that crime, the evidence is said to be relevant. The testimony of a witness who saw a man break into a building during the night would be relevant evidence to prove a burglary. The burglary tools found in possession of the man would be relevant evidence to prove intent to commit theft in the building.

Not all relevant evidence is admitted. Evidence that has a tendency to unduly prejudice the jury may be excluded. For example, the prior convictions of an accused may be relevant in establishing his or her guilt. But because of the prejudicial effect of such convictions, they are generally not admissible. Relevant evidence may be excluded because it would tend to cause confusion or create so many side issues that trial time would be wasted if it were admitted. Relevant evidence that is so remote or speculative in time or place that no logical inference can be drawn from it may also be excluded, as in the case described below.

A defendant was on trial on a charge of armed robbery. The victim of the robbery, the defendant, and a codefendant had all been drinking together in a bar when the victim excused himself from the others, stating that he had to pick up his child at school. The defendant requested that the victim drop the codefendant and him off at another bar on the way. The three got into the victim's car with the defendant sitting in the back seat. After traveling a short distance, the defendant stuck a knife against the back of the victim's neck, telling the codefendant at the same time to take the victim's wallet, watch, and other valuables. The defendant then struck the victim on the head with a piece of wood, causing him to lose consciousness, and the defendant and codefendant left. Upon regaining consciousness, the victim reported the robbery to the police. Driving in the vicinity of the robbery 6 days later, the victim spotted the defendant and called the police. At the time the defendant was arrested, a knife was found in his possession. The victim could not identify the knife as the one used in the robbery, as he had been unable to get a good look at it. At the trial, the arresting officer was permitted to testify about the arrest and about finding a knife on the defendant. The knife was offered as evidence by the prosecution but was excluded by the judge as being too remote in time to be relevant. In the opinion of the judge the fact that a knife was found on the defendant six days after the crime was committed had little or no connection with the facts of the case, and whether the knife found on the defendant was the one used in the robbery could only be speculated. The officer's testimony as to finding the knife was struck from the record. Later, in testifying for the prosecution, the codefendant identified the knife found in possession of the defendant as the one used in the robbery. The knife was again offered in evidence, and this time the judge admitted it, as it now had been definitely connected with the facts of the case.

Whether the evidence can meet all the tests of relevancy and admissibility is up to the trial judge. Occasionally, a trial judge will admit evidence which is only remotely connected with the facts of the case and allow the jury to decide on the weight to which such evidence is entitled. Some judges would have permitted the knife just discussed to be offered as evidence even though it had not been definitely identified as the weapon used in the robbery. If a knife has been used to commit the robbery, then a knife that has been found in the defendant's possession will have some connection with the facts of the case.

Relevant evidence may also be excluded because it is inadmissible. For example, a piece of physical evidence may be most relevant, yet it may be excluded because it was improperly obtained.

■ Material Evidence

There is a tendency on the part of many in the field of jurisprudence to use the terms "relevant evidence" and "material evidence" interchangeably, yet there is a difference. *Material evidence* is that which has great significance to the facts of the case. It is evidence upon which the jury places much weight or thinks is important in proving the facts in dispute. It is possible for evidence to be relevant to the issues of the case, yet be immaterial or insignificant in its persuasive power of proof.

■ Competent Evidence

Ordinarily "competency" is used in determining whether a person is competent or qualified to testify in a trial proceeding. However, the term is also used to decide whether certain evidence is admissible or not. *Competent evidence* has been described as evidence which is admissible contrasted with that which is not. For example, a confession may shed light upon the facts of a case, yet because of some irregularity in obtaining it, the judge may rule that it is not admissible. Under these circumstances it is stated that this confession is not competent evidence. Because the term competent evidence is somewhat confusing, some writers believe that the term admissible evidence should be substituted for it, thereby utilizing the term competency only as it refers to the qualification of witnesses. The competency of witnesses will be discussed in detail in Chapter 3.

■ *Prima Facie* Evidence

Prima facie evidence is that evidence which, standing alone, unexplained or uncontradicted, is sufficient to establish a given fact. In other words, *prima facie* evidence is good on its face to prove a fact unless or until it is overcome by other evidence. *Prima facie* evidence is often the result of the violation of a statute. For example, if the operator of a vehicle exceeds the posted speed limit, the excess speed is *prima facie* evidence of a traffic violation and is sufficient to prove the violation unless some evidence is presented by the operator to justify the excess speed. To cite another example: if one individual sees another shoot a third person, this would be *prima facie* evidence that a homicide has been committed. This evidence standing alone, uncontradicted and/or unexplained, would be sufficient to convict the offender of a homicide. However, the offender may attempt to overcome the *prima facie* evidence by presenting evidence that the shooting was done in self-defense.

■ Cumulative and Corroborative Evidence

The terms cumulative and corroborative evidence have sometimes been thought to have the same meaning. However, legally there is a difference. *Cumulative evidence* is evidence which repeats earlier testimony by another witness and in which no new facts are presented.

Corroborative evidence is that evidence which supports and confirms evidence already given. It is additional evidence of a different character about the same point. It has a tendency to strengthen other evidence presented.

To illustrate the difference between cumulative evidence and corroborative evidence, the facts of the following case are set forth. A defendant was on trial for selling narcotics on the night of March 18 at 8 p.m. Testifying in his own behalf, the defendant introduced an alibi defense. He alleged that he could not have committed the crime as he was at a place other than that where the crime was committed and had been mistakenly identified as the seller. The defendant claimed that on the night of March 18 at 8 p.m. he was attending a movie at the Bayou Theater with his wife, mother, and sister. He said they saw the show entitled *The Pink Man.* He also stated that it was a rainy night. The wife testified in behalf of her husband, stating that she recalled the night of March 18 and that at 8 p.m. on that night she was at the Bayou Theater with her husband, mother-in-law, and sister-in-law. She also testified that the movie that they had seen was *The Pink Man,* and that it was a rainy night. The mother and sister of the defendant also testified for the defendant, giving exactly the same facts as the wife. The testimonies of the three women merely repeated the testimony of the defendant. They were a *cumulation* of the same set of facts with no new facts presented.

The manager of the Bayou Theater was called as a witness and testified that on the night of March 18 the movie *The Pink Man* was showing. An official of the weather bureau, also called as a witness, testified that on the night of March 18 it was raining. The manager of the theater and the weather bureau official both substantiated or corroborated the testimony of the defendant. They presented facts that made the same point, but their testimony was not merely a parroting of the testimony of the defendant.

It should be pointed out that the testimony of neither the theater manager nor the weather bureau official placed the defendant in the theater on March 18. It was the testimony of the wife, mother, and sister of the defendant that would tend to prove the alibi defense. But was the testimony of these witnesses, all closely related to the defendant, believable? That was a matter for the judge and the jury to decide. (The believability, or credibility, of witnesses will be discussed in detail in Chapter 5.)

The number of witnesses that may be permitted to present cumulative evidence is within the discretion of the trial judge. The judge will allow a reasonable number to testify, particularly on behalf of the defendant, in order to assure a fair trial. However, attorneys usually keep the number within reason; otherwise a jury could become bored listening to the same set of facts being presented over and over again. The same may be said concerning corroborative witnesses. Corroborative witnesses may present facts of a different character, but these facts still add nothing that is materially new. Therefore some limitation is necessary.

JUDICIAL NOTICE OR KNOWLEDGE OF THE COURT

Perhaps no courts in the world make greater demands for complete accuracy in every bit of evidence offered than those of the United States. Each point must be properly and legally presented and proved. This proof must be presented, with a few exceptions, by witnesses having firsthand knowledge of each fact in the case. The demand for firsthand knowledge of the facts results in a very costly procedure from the standpoint of time, energy, and money.

There are certain facts that may be accepted without formal proof by the way of testimony being presented. These facts, of which a judge may take *judicial notice*, fall within two categories. In the first category are facts so commonly known and accepted by community members of average intelligence that requiring proof during a trial would be ridiculous. For example, it is accepted knowledge that it is light in the daytime and dark at night, and that a rock thrown into a lake will sink. The second category includes those facts which may be accurately and readily determined by referring to available, indisputable, and accurate sources. Examples would be the laws of the United States and certain geographical and scientific facts. The facts may be ones which a judge knows. However, not having personal knowledge of a fact need not prevent a judge from taking judicial notice of its existence. There are some facts that judges may accept immediately and others that they may accept after referring to some record or other source. For example, a judge may not personally know the particular street at which a traffic accident took place. But if this street is shown on an official map to which the judge can refer, its existence may be accepted without further testimony of its location. Note, however that the judge would not take judicial notice of the visibility of this intersection to a driver without further proof.

Judicial notice, sometimes referred to as "knowledge of the court," has been described as a judicial shortcut or as a substitute for formal proof. Facts of which the court will take judicial notice are usually introduced into the trial proceedings at the request of one of the attorneys. Or the judge may voluntarily take judicial notice of a fact without the request being made. Once judicial notice is taken of a fact, that fact becomes a part of the evidence of the case and the jury will be so instructed.

Some jurisdictions list judicial notice as a kind of evidence, whereas others merely consider judicial notice as a substitute for formal proof. In either case, those facts of which judicial notice is taken must be weighed by the jury in arriving at a verdict.

The following are some of the facts of which a judge will take judicial notice. The list is not in any way all-inclusive, but it mentions some that are common to criminal trials.

■ Notice of Public Statutes

Most jurisdictions permit judges to take judicial notice of all public statutes, or laws, of the United States as well as those of their own state; but only about half of them allow judges to take judicial notice of the statutes of other states. This limitation has been criticized and may one day be relaxed since it has no real basis.

In many instances a judge's personal knowledge may not include a particular statute and it will be necessary to refer to the statute books to verify its existence. Once this is done, however, no other proof will be required.

■ Notice of Geographical Facts

There are many well-established geographical facts which fall within the category of judicial notice or knowledge of the court. These include state boundaries, international boundaries, city limits, and the location of streets and highways. The navigability of certain waters is also recognized, as are the differences in temperature between the north and the south. Again, there may be instances where the judge will have no personal knowledge of the geographical fact in question and may wish to consult some official map.

■ Notice of Words, Phrases, and Abbreviations

The court will take judicial notice of commonly known words, phrases, and/or abbreviations. The words whiskey or wine will be recognized as intoxicating beverages. The abbreviations a.m. and p.m. are well known and will be accepted in court. A judge may not take notice of jargon or terms used in the vernacular, since they have different meanings to various persons. For example, the term mic or mike to a law enforcement officer has the immediate connotation of a microphone, but to an engineer mic would probably mean a micrometer. However, there are certain jargon terms that are so well known in a particular community that a judge may take judicial notice of their meaning. Moonshine whiskey is commonly accepted and known to mean illegal distilled liquor. The term grass is so well known in certain areas to mean marijuana that a judge may take judicial notice of that fact.

■ Notice of Time, Days, and Dates

Many facts about time are judicially recognized, such as 24 hours make a day, or 7 days make a week. January first is recognized as the beginning of a new year, and New Year's Day is accepted as a national holiday. Because of differences in religious beliefs, the Sabbath is not accepted as being Sunday.

■ Scientific and Medical Facts

For a scientific or medical fact to fall within the realm of judicial notice, it must be an established fact. Scientific and medical theories progress from the unknown to the debatable and then to the known or established fact.

Perhaps no area of judicial notice is more subject to change than that of scientific or medical facts. With the research and progress made in these fields, what was once an accepted *fact* is now nothing more than an old wives' tale. At one time it was an accepted fact that the earth was flat; flying to the moon was impossible; tuberculosis meant certain death; and tomatoes were poisonous. Likewise many things that were at one time unacceptable are now common, such as the sterilization of milk, immunization against disease, and measurement of heart movements electrically.

The acceptance of certain facts in the fields of science and medicine has worked to the advantage of the law enforcement officer. Many matters pertaining to fingerprints are now accepted as being based on scientifically known facts and are recognized by the courts. For example, it has been determined by medical research that under certain conditions people exude body fluids through the pores on the ridges of their fingers, hands, and feet. It has also been determined that there is a transfer of these fluids to the objects that they touch, thereby leaving patterns of the ridges. Science has developed chemicals and powders to adhere to these patterns, so that they become visible and can be photographed and lifted. Some matters pertaining to fingerprints are subject to proof, but in general, such facts are now accepted and recognized as a science. The structure of a human hair as distinguished from that of an animal is scientifically recognized. It is medically accepted that blood can be grouped and that it can be typed in groups O, A, B, or AB. Acceptance of these proved facts frequently assists officers in obtaining convictions.

The interpretation of the results of a polygraph has not been generally accepted as a scientific fact. However, it is a medically accepted fact that the human body reacts differently under certain circumstances. There may be a change in blood pressure, a variation of the heartbeat, or changes within the respiratory functions of the body. It is also a medically accepted fact that these things can be scientifically measured and compared. From that standpoint, a polygraph is recognized. However, this does not mean that the conclusions of the operator must be accepted as scientific fact. It might be stated that polygraph results are still in the debatable stage. Therefore the criminalist performing examinations in the crime laboratory may not have any conclusions accepted under the rule of judicial notice. However, the ability of that criminalist to make determinations through the use of established scientific facts and principles is recognized.

Courts are now taking judicial notice of radar as a means of determining speed. It has been stated that "radar devices are matters of common and universal knowledge." The court will take judicial notice of the principle upon which radar works, but the accuracy and efficiency of the apparatus will depend upon the officer who uses it and who must convince the jury of this ability during testimony.

■ Matters of Common Knowledge

As stated earlier, a judge may take judicial notice of those facts which community members of average intelligence know to be true. But the court may also take judicial notice of other facts that may not be so universally known. Judicial notice may be taken of facts that are of such common knowledge within the territorial jurisdiction of the court that they cannot be reasonably disputed. Courts must not necessarily wait until everybody knows and understands a fact before judicial notice can be taken of it. Anything which is generally understood by persons familiar with the subject is considered to be common knowledge. This is particularly true in relation to scientific facts.

■ Proof May Be Presented

If a judge refuses the request of an attorney to take judicial notice of a pertinent fact, then that attorney will have to present adequate proof to establish the existence of the fact.

■ Future of Judicial Notice

Because of concerted efforts being made to save trial time, there is a general feeling that greater use will be made of the judicial notice procedure in the future.

PRESUMPTIONS

In addition to facts of which the courts will take judicial notice, there are also deductions which may be made from certain sets of facts which the law will recognize. These deductions are legally known as *presumptions.* Presumptions are recognized because they follow the normal course of events. Experience has proved that each time a given set of facts arises, the end results of the set are almost always the same. Under these circumstances, it is logical to presume that the same results will continue to take place. For example, the law states that it is a logical presumption that a letter properly addressed, stamped, and placed in the mail was delivered to the addressee. It is a logical presumption since that is what normally takes place. It is the probable result. Thus it might be stated that one reason why presumptions are recognized is that they are based on the law of probability.

The acceptance of presumptions is also based on the social habits of human beings. For example, the law states that a person who has been missing and unheard of for 7 years is presumed to be dead. Most people are gregarious creatures with family ties, and they do not normally vanish without making contacts with either friends or family unless a tragedy has taken place. If there has been no information about a person for 7 years, the logical deduction or presumption is that the person is dead. There is nothing particularly significant or magical about the 7-year period. It probably came from old English statutes which declared that a person who went to sea or was otherwise absent from the kingdom for 7 years was presumed to be dead. The laws of the states have continued this criterion. Some people assert that this period is now too long. They say that the 7-year period was appropriate at a time when transportation and communication were much slower than now, but they believe that an absence of 3 years should now be sufficient to justify the presumption of death.

Legally, a presumption has been defined as a deduction which the law expressly directs must be made from a certain set of facts. Or, to state it in another way, a presumption is a conclusion which the law says must be drawn from a particular set of facts which have been brought to the attention of the jury as presented by the evidence. Presumptions, however, must not be confused with knowledge of the court. A presumption is merely a conclusion which the law says must be reached, whereas knowledge of the court is a definitely known and accepted fact.

From the two examples given of presumptions, it can be seen that presumptions may be incorrect. For some reason or other the letter may not have been delivered. Or due to certain vicissitudes of life, the person missing and unheard of for 7 years may not be dead, but instead is possibly quite well and living peacefully in some distant community. It has been held that the presumption of death should not be drawn if there is some known reason, such as a family feud or domestic difficulties, why the missing person has not made any contacts.

The law has categorized presumptions into two classes: (1) conclusive or mandatory; and (2) rebuttable, refutable, or debatable.

A *conclusive presumption* is one which the law demands or directs be made from a set of facts. It cannot be refuted by other evidence. From a practical standpoint a conclusive presumption is not a presumption, but a statement of the law that must be followed. For example, at common law and in some states it is a conclusive presumption that a child under 7 years of age is mentally incapable of committing a crime. Such a conclusive presumption in effect declares that a child under 7 years of age cannot be charged with a crime, or be prosecuted.

Actually, there are very few conclusive presumptions, and not a great deal is gained by discussing them. On the other hand, there are a great many *rebuttable presumptions*. The effect of a rebuttable presumption is that it must stand unless overcome by evidence to the contrary. The jury is bound by a presumption which has not been refuted. Consider the presumption that a letter properly mailed has been delivered. If no evidence is presented to prove that the letter was not delivered, the jury must presume that it was. The burden of overcoming a rebuttable presumption rests upon the side against whom it works.

■ Rebuttable Presumptions

The laws of most states have specifically spelled out many acceptable rebuttable presumptions. Additionally, there are those from the common law which are also recognized so long as they do not conflict with some state statute. The next few pages set forth several rebuttable presumptions with which the officer should be familiar. This list is by no means complete, but it does reflect some of the more commonly encountered presumptions in criminal matters.

PRESUMPTION OF INNOCENCE. Perhaps there is no better known rebuttable presumption than that "a person is presumed innocent until proved guilty," or, as it is sometimes stated, "a person is presumed innocent of a crime or a wrong." This presumption is based upon the needs of a free society; it is a part of our American heritage and has been described as a person's guarantee against injustice and oppression. It is this presumption that the prosecution must overcome if the prosecuting attorney is to prove the defendant guilty beyond a reasonable doubt.

Some writers allege that the presumption of innocence is not a presumption at all, but an assumption. These writers state that one accused of a crime is *assumed* innocent until proved guilty. They justify their position on the grounds that a presumption is a deduction made from a proved set of facts. But in the case of innocence no facts are set forth from which this deduction can be made. They further contend that the alleged presumption of innocence is merely a statement of law or rule requiring the prosecution to prove the accused guilty beyond a reasonable doubt. Nevertheless, judges, in general, in their instructions to the jury include an instruction that the jury is to presume the defendant innocent until proved guilty beyond a reasonable doubt.

PRESUMPTION OF SANITY. There is a general presumption that all persons are sane. This presumption stems from the fact that sanity is the normal human condition. It permits the prosecution to proceed with a criminal trial without having to first prove the defendant to have been sane at the time that the crime was committed. It places upon the defendant wishing to use a defense of insanity the burden of proving the insanity. If the defendant endeavors to prove insanity, the prosecution may present evidence to refute the defendant's allegation of insanity; this evidence is not to refute the presumption, but to strengthen it after the defendant has attempted to refute it. However, there are some jurisdictions which hold that all the defendant must do is raise the defense of insanity and the prosecution has the burden of proving the defendant sane at the time the crime was committed.

CHILDREN UNDER A CERTAIN AGE ARE NOT CAPABLE OF COMMITTING CRIME. At common law it was conclusively stated that children under 7 years of age were not capable of committing crimes. Not all states in this country recognize this presumption as conclusive; some term it a rebuttable presumption. In the statutes of many states, a rule reads in substance that "a child under 14 years of age is not capable of committing a crime unless it can be proved that the child knew that the act was wrong at the time that it was committed." In other words, if a child under 14 years of age is brought to trial, the prosecution must prove that the child had knowledge that the act done was wrongful. In these states age is no barrier to prosecution. It is only a rebuttable presumption that children under a certain age are not capable of committing a crime.

MISCELLANEOUS REBUTTABLE PRESUMPTIONS. The following are some additional better-known presumptions:

1. People intend the ordinary consequences of their voluntary acts.
2. People take ordinary care of their own concerns.
3. Evidence willfully suppressed would be adverse if produced.

4. Official duty has been regularly performed.
5. The ordinary course of business has been followed.
6. A writing is truly dated.
7. A man and a woman deporting themselves as husband and wife have entered into a lawful contract of marriage.
8. A child born in lawful wedlock is legitimate.
9. The law has been obeyed.
10. A ceremonial marriage is valid.
11. The identity of a person can be made by the identity of the name.
12. An unlawful intent is presumed from doing an unlawful act. It has been held, however, that this presumption is not applicable to prove specific intent where the intent is an element of the crime.
13. Things have happened according to the ordinary course of nature and the ordinary habits of life.

■ Knowledge of the Law

There is no established legal presumption that a "person is presumed to know the law." However, there is a maxim or rule of law providing that everyone is assumed to know the law and that ignorance of the law is no defense for a criminal act. Nor is it a defense that one did not know that an act was punishable. This maxim is based on the demands of society. Otherwise-successful prosecutions could be defeated if offenders were able to plead ignorance of the law as their defense.

■ Presumptions as Evidence

Are presumptions evidence? The authorities are divided on this question. Some of them classify presumptions as the fifth kind of evidence. This is based on the fact that a presumption is sufficient to establish a fact unless rebutted. However, it has been said that presumptions are the weakest and least satisfactory kind of evidence. On the other hand, there are those who assert that presumptions are not evidence, and definite statements have been included in statutes to that effect. From a practical standpoint, it is probably not too important whether presumptions are called evidence or not; it must only be understood that a presumption has to be drawn from a given set of facts unless evidence is presented to overcome it. From a legal standpoint the question is important. When a presumption is classified as evidence, it places upon a jury a most confusing task of trying to determine the amount of weight that should be given to a presumption in comparison to the testimony of witnesses or other evidence. By declaring that presumptions are not evidence, the burden of the jury is materially lessened, as the jurors may in clear conscience give greater weight to evidence presented than to the deduction which must be drawn from a presumption.

BURDEN OF PROOF

Burden of proof means the necessity of proving a fact in a trial. As has been stated, the prosecution has the burden of proving the defendant guilty beyond a reasonable doubt. The necessity arises from the fact that a person is presumed innocent until proved guilty. That burden does not shift from the prosecution. It is for this reason that some writers on evidence allege that the presumption of innocence is not in reality a presumption but a statement of fact which the prosecution must overcome. Also the statutes of some states fail to include the presumption of innocence as a presumption but state that "the party claiming that a person is guilty of a crime has the burden of proof on that issue." Since the prosecution is claiming the defendant to be guilty, the burden of proof is cast upon the prosecution to prove the guilt.

The term burden of proof has been often used in a rather loose sense. As was stated, its primary meaning is the burden of proving the facts of the case, but it can also mean the burden of initially going forward with the evidence. Because of this ambiguity the Model Evidence Code has substituted the term "burden of persuasion" for burden of proof.

Technically, the term "going forward with the evidence" means something entirely different from burden of proof. Going forward with the evidence casts upon one side or the other the responsibility of refuting certain facts presented during the burden of proof. For example, a presumption or other fact which works against the defendant may be presented by the prosecution. The defendant may permit the presumption or other fact to stand without refuting it or may present facts to overcome it. More specifically, at the conclusion of the prosecution's presentation, a defendant may do one of two things. Feeling that the prosecution has failed in its burden of proof, a defendant may choose not to present any evidence in his or her own behalf. Or a defendant may choose to present evidence to prove an alibi defense or to show that an act was done in self-defense. This presentation of refuting evidence is referred to as going forward with the evidence.

INFERENCES

Although the reader may find it difficult to distinguish between presumptions and inferences, the two should not be confused. Legally, an *inference* is a permissible deduction or conclusion that the jury may make from the evidence presented. It has been defined as "a deduction which the jury may make from the facts proved without the law directing them to make such a deduction." If evidence is presented that the defendant's fingerprints were found on a safe door after a burglary, the logical deduction or inference would be that the defendant touched the safe. This coupled with other evidence may cause the jury to make an inference or deduction that the defendant was guilty of the burglary. However, there is no law stating that the jury must make this deduction. But in the case of a presumption there are expressed rules of law which direct that, unless overcome by other evidence, a certain deduction *must* be made from the facts which have been presented.

STIPULATIONS

There are other facts that may be presented during a trial without formal proof being required. These are facts upon which the attorneys involved agree or stipulate exist. This agreement may take place either before or during the trial. Once the attorneys have agreed upon them, it will not be necessary to call witnesses to present the facts. Rather they will be related to the jury at the appropriate time either by one of the attorneys or the judge. The jury will be instructed that these facts are to be taken into consideration in arriving at a verdict.

Stipulations are usually made concerning facts that are relatively unimportant to the trial or to facts about which there is little or no dispute. The primary reason for a stipulation is to save trial time and expense.

Occasionally, though, an attorney will stipulate to a fact because of the emotional impact it might have if presented by a witness. Under such circumstances, the opposing side may not agree to the stipulation. For example, in the case in which the defendant alleged that he attended the Bayou Theater on the rainy night of March 18, the prosecuting attorney could have easily stipulated to the testimony of both the theater manager and the weather bureau official. Their testimony did not actually prove any fact of the case. There was no allegation that the movie *The Pink Man* had not been showing on the night of March 18, nor was there any fact indicating that it was not raining on that night. However, the defense attorney might well have desired that those two witnesses be called in order to present corroborative evidence by witnesses who were not related to the defendant. Thus, the defense attorney might not have agreed to the stipulation.

SUMMARY

Evidence in its simplest form is information. Legally, it has been described as "the means in a trial proceeding which enable a judge or jury to determine the truth of what happened in a particular case." This evidence may include testimony of witnesses, physical things presented, documents, and knowledge of the court.

The rules of evidence are the guidelines which enable those involved in a trial to know what is admissible and what is not. These rules also make for orderly procedure throughout the trial.

Evidence can be described as being competent, relevant, material, *prima facie,* cumulative, or corroborative. Competent evidence is that which is admissible; relevant evidence is that which has some connection with the questions at hand; and material evidence is that which has an influence on the judge or jury. *Prima facie* evidence is evidence which is good on its face until overcome by other evidence. Cumulative evidence is evidence which is merely repetitive in nature. Corroborative evidence is supporting evidence of a different character.

Knowledge of the court, or facts of which the court takes judicial notice, are those well-established facts that are commonly known and that are accepted without any proof. They need not be something which the judge knows, but may be something that can be substantiated by reference to some record.

Presumptions are deductions which the law states must be drawn from a particular set of facts, unless evidence is presented to overcome them. Presumptions are classified as conclusive and rebuttable. Conclusive presumptions are few in number and are actually nothing more than a statement of substantive law. Rebuttable presumptions are deductions made from a set of facts, which may be overcome by the side against whom the presumption works.

A stipulation is an agreed-upon fact.

QUESTIONS FOR REVIEW

1. What is evidence from a legal standpoint?
2. Name the kinds of evidence.
3. What are the purposes of rules of evidence?
4. Define the following: (a) relevant evidence, (b) material evidence, (c) competent evidence, (d) *prima facie* evidence.
5. What is meant by the term "knowledge of the court"?
6. Name four categories of things of which the court will take judicial notice.
7. What is a presumption?
8. Name the two types of presumptions and tell how they differ.

9. Name five of the more commonly accepted rebuttable presumptions.
10. What is a stipulation?

LOCAL RULES

As there are differences among jurisdictions on some rules of evidence, the reader may wish to ascertain the answers to the following questions from the local prosecuting attorney, as suggested in Chapter 1.

1. Is judicial notice listed as a kind of evidence?
2. Are presumptions classified as evidence?

Witnesses– Competency and Privileged Communications

3

Most of the evidence in any trial is presented through the oral testimony of witnesses. It is only right therefore that we probe deeply into this facet of the rules of evidence pertaining to witnesses. In general, witnesses are persons who have some knowledge about the facts of a case. A witness has been described legally as a person whose declaration or statement is made under oath or affirmation in a trial proceeding. It is possible for this statement to be made either orally or through a written document, such as a deposition or an affidavit. In criminal trials the use of the written declaration is very limited because, with some exceptions, in a criminal trial the witnesses must appear personally against the defendant. This requirement that the witnesses appear in person stems from the constitutional guarantee embodied in the Sixth Amendment of the United States Constitution, which provides: "In all criminal prosecutions, the accused shall . . . be confronted with the witnesses against him." Therefore, the discussion of the rules of evidence as they pertain to witnesses will be confined for the most part to the oral testimony.

WHO IS A COMPETENT WITNESS?

As has been stated, the primary purpose of a trial is to arrive at the truth of what happened in a case. In these circumstances it is mandatory to have persons who will tell the truth when they testify. At common law certain conditions, it was felt, would cause a person to be unable to testify truthfully. Therefore, certain persons were not permitted to be witnesses, since they were considered to be unable or incompetent to tell the truth. These were (1) persons who did not believe in a God, because of a lack of fear of divine punishment for falsifying; (2) persons who were lacking in mental capacity; (3) persons who had been convicted of a crime, because of untrustworthiness; (4) parties to a civil suit, and both the victim and the defendant in a criminal trial, because of bias; and (5) one spouse testifying for or against the other.

Most of these common-law restrictions have been abolished. Today, in the majority of jurisdictions, a person is competent to be a witness if able to perceive what is going on and to relate these perceptions to others. A witness must also be able to understand the oath or affirmation and comprehend its compulsion to tell the truth. The absence of a religious belief, a lack of some mental capacity, being a party to a suit, or having been convicted of a crime does not make a person incompetent as a witness. The presence of any of these conditions may affect the weight of the testimony in the eyes of the jury, but these conditions will not prevent the person from becoming a witness. A few states hold that a person who has been convicted of perjury may not be a witness.

◼ Children as Witnesses

As mentioned in Chapter 1, all witnesses must testify under oath or affirmation to tell the truth. Formerly, it was held that a child could not testify unless he understood the significance of the oath. This requirement has been generally discarded. Jurisdictions vary considerably with regard to the competency of a child to become a witness. Many states make no reference to age as a restriction on becoming a witness. The only test is that a person be able to understand what is going on about him or her, to relate this knowledge intelligently to others, and to know the necessity of telling the truth. If a child meets this test, the child may testify. In the case of a child of tender years there is the burden of proving to the satisfaction of the judge that the child meets the test, particularly the necessity to tell the truth. The burden is upon the side producing the child as a witness to prove that the child can correctly perceive and relate perceptions truthfully to others. It is not necessary that the child understand the oath as such, but the child must know that the truth is required when testifying. In making the determination whether a child knows that it is necessary to tell the truth, the usual procedure is to ask the child whether it is wrong to "tell a lie," or to make some other similar inquiry. It has been held that if a child has learned that telling a falsehood brings punishment, this is sufficient to prove that the child knows the necessity for telling the truth.

Some states hold that a child over a certain age is competent to be a witness. For example, a child 10 years of age or over may testify. There is no burden of proof of understandability placed upon the side presenting the child if the child meets the age requirement. A child under the prescribed age still may testify, but must meet the test heretofore described.

Age, therefore, is no longer a barrier to becoming a witness. This is as it should be. If the rule were otherwise, most of the child-molesting cases would go unprosecuted because of the unavailability of the principal witness, the victim child. It has been stated that a great deal of caution should be exercised in permitting a very young child to become a witness because of possible injustice to the defendant as a result of some imaginary act of misconduct the child may conceive or have had planted in his mind.

■ Persons of Questionable Mental Stability

In addition to children, persons who are mentally retarded, senile persons, or those who have been declared mentally unbalanced may also become witnesses because they may still have lucid moments. In most jurisdictions, the only requirement is that they meet the same test as any other person, that is, the ability to perceive, retain, relate, and understand the necessity to tell the truth.

PRIVILEGED COMMUNICATIONS

To carry the rule of competence of witnesses further, there are special circumstances which may arise under which a person may refrain, or be prohibited, from testifying concerning certain matters or information. This condition occurs when a person is in possession of information gained as a result of some confidential or privileged relationship. This rule of competency or privilege is based upon the demands of society. There are relationships in which public policy encourages the exchange of confidential information between two persons. It is felt that such exchanges of confidential information should be without fear that they may have to be revealed in court at a later date. Legally, such exchanges of confidential information are known as "privileged communications." Although keeping these privileged communications inviolate may work a hardship in the trial of cases, it is deemed that maintaining them as secrets between those involved outweighs the benefit that society would derive from their disclosure. However, these privileged relationships are limited in number because any privilege claimed against the disclosure of information acts as a block in ascertaining the truth during a trial.

■ Categories of Privileged-Communications Relationships

In several relationships recognized by law the exchange of confidential information is encouraged and is permitted to fall within the privileged-communications category. Included in these relationships are (1) husband

and wife; (2) attorney and client; (3) physician and patient; (4) clergy and penitent; (5) peace officer and informant; and (6) in some jurisdictions, news reporter and news source. Because of the importance of each of these relationships to the officer, each will be discussed in detail.

■ Competency versus Privileged Relationships

These relationships do not necessarily bar the persons involved from becoming witnesses. A relationship may merely restrict what may be related on the witness stand. In other words, if information is gained as a result of the aforementioned relationships, the persons involved may refrain from revealing this particular information to others in court. It is possible for the person in whose favor the privilege has been established to waive its protection and thereby permit the testimony to be given.

It is probably technically incorrect therefore to speak of competency in connection with privileged relationships. Competency refers to whether a person is qualified to be a witness or not, and the disqualification, if any, usually is based upon some mental or physical defect which prevents the person from perceiving, retaining, or relating knowledge. If that defect is present, there is little that can be done to correct it, and so the person does not become a witness.

In a privileged relationship there is no physical or mental defect present that incapacitates the person from becoming a witness. The privileged relationship merely restricts the persons involved from relating certain information on the stand. Whether technically correct or not, the term "competency" still weaves its way into legal dialogue in reference to privileged relationships. One frequently hears the remark that a wife is not competent to testify against her husband. Actually, she is not privileged to testify against him in many instances unless he waives that privilege. But little is to be gained in the discussion here by arguing whether the term "competency" should or should not be used in connection with privileged relationships.

■ Requirements for Privileged Communications

For any confidential information exchanged between two persons to fall within the privileged-communications rule certain requirements must be met. First, the exchange must be between two persons whose relationship is recognized by the law of the particular state as coming within the rule, that is, it must emanate from one of the aforementioned generally accepted relationships. Second, the communication must have been exchanged because of the relationship. Third, the communication was such that the interests of society would be benefited to a greater degree by keeping the information secret than by revealing it. A fourth qualification may well be added: The information exchanged was intended to be confidential.

HUSBAND-WIFE RELATIONSHIP

Perhaps in no other area of evidence is there a wider difference between jurisdictions than in the approach to competency and privileged communications as they pertain to the husband-wife relationship. The courts and lawmakers have been caught in the dilemma of trying to maintain the domestic tranquillity of the home on the one hand and protect society from the criminal on the other. The husband-wife relationship is unique in comparison to the other relationships in which the privileged-communications rule as such is operative. The husband-wife relationship involves more than just the exchange of confidential information between them. Their very status grants additional privileges so far as testifying or not testifying is concerned. So the problem whether one spouse may or may not testify for or against the other is approached from two entirely different viewpoints.

The first approach is that a husband and wife should have some restriction upon their being able to testify because of the damage that testimony may cause to the harmony of the home. How far this restriction should be permitted to go has caused no end of confusion. But it is generally accepted by all jurisdictions that there should be some restriction. It is also fairly well agreed that most of these controls are to remain in effect only during the time that the couple are married.

The other approach to the husband-wife relationship inquires how far confidential information gained as a result of the marriage union should be protected and for how long. Every effort will be made to clarify these points throughout the discussion that follows on the husband-wife relationship.

■ Common-Law Approach

At common law, neither spouse was a competent witness for or against the other. This rule was based partially on the premise that man and wife were one; and at common law a party to a suit, whether civil or criminal, could not be a witness. The rule of preventing one spouse from testifying for or against the other at common law was also established upon the basic needs of a good society, in this instance the need of a wholesome family relationship. Policy demands that a husband and wife should be allowed to live in a state of mutual trust and confidence without fear of being compelled to be a witness against each other. To permit one spouse to testify against the other would endanger that relationship and the tranquillity of the home, and, in turn, society would suffer.

■ Modern Approach

Most states today have by statute abolished the common-law rule which made one spouse incompetent to testify for or against the other and have established rules of their own in an effort to arrive at some equitable solution to the husband-wife relationship problem. These rules vary greatly, and discussion will be confined to those that are applicable only in criminal matters.

SPOUSE MAY TESTIFY IF CONSENT OF BOTH IS GIVEN. One approach, and probably the most restrictive, is the rule which states that one spouse may not testify for or against the other without the consent of both. For example, if while out shopping a wife should see her husband rob a service station, she could not be compelled to testify against her husband unless willing to do so, and in addition the husband would have to give his consent for his wife to testify against him, which is not very likely to happen. But those advocating this rule feel that the harmony of the home is still in danger unless both spouses are willing to permit the testimony to be given.

This rule further implies that even though the husband gave his consent, the wife would not have to testify unless she chose to do so. She still is in a position to judge the harm that may be caused to the family relationship when she decides whether or not she should testify.

SPOUSE MAY TESTIFY FOR BUT NOT AGAINST OTHER SPOUSE. A few jurisdictions have adopted the rule that one spouse may testify for the other spouse in a criminal matter, but not against the other. This is based on the premise that more harm than good would be done in trying to prevent one spouse from testifying for the other. The value of such testimony may be in question as it could be tainted with bias or may permit the prosecution to bring out adverse material on cross-examination which could affect the harmonious relationship. However, these reasons are probably not strong enough to prohibit a spouse from testifying for the other when there is a desire to do so.

CONSENT BY PROSPECTIVE WITNESS ONLY. Some states have endeavored to approach the problem from a more logical standpoint, that of permitting the spouse to testify either for or against the other spouse in accordance with the witness spouse's own desires. In other words, the consent of the defendant spouse would not be required, and the choice of testifying or not would be made entirely by the prospective witness spouse. In this case the perspective witness spouse would make the choice whether the harmony of the home was considered paramount to interests of society in testifying. In either instance, but for certain exceptions, the witness spouse could not be compelled to testify.

However, there is included in the rules of evidence in some states a provision that a spouse has the right or privilege not to be called as a witness against the other spouse. This rule permits the prospective witness spouse to make the choice as to testifying or not testifying against the other spouse. But the rule is silent as it relates to the right to refuse to testify for the other spouse. This silence has been interpreted by some courts as compelling a spouse to testify for the other spouse. For example, a husband who is on trial for having committed a criminal act could compel his wife to testify for him, and she would have no choice in the matter.

■ No Marriage-Relationship Privilege Granted

A few jurisdictions take the viewpoint that there should be no marriage-relationship privilege granted prohibiting one spouse from testifying against the other in criminal matters. This view is based on the premise that a home which is riddled with the knowledge of criminal activity taking place has but little domestic harmony, so that there is no reason to invoke the privilege rule. There are many who feel that this is the most practical approach to the husband-wife relationship.

■ Spouse Commits Crime on Spouse

In those jurisdictions which adhere to the policy of one spouse not being permitted to testify for or against the other, the problem arises what attitude should be taken when one spouse commits a crime on the other, or against the property of the other. Should the rule of not permitting one spouse to testify against the other without the consent of both still remain in effect? Also, what about the rule which prohibits a spouse from being compelled to be a witness when that spouse is the victim of an attack by the other spouse? In the first instance if the rule were to remain in effect, the defendant spouse would be given an undeserved protection because the victim spouse could not testify without his consent. In the second situation the victim spouse may not wish to testify voluntarily because of the fear of further attacks upon the victim spouse. It must be remembered that the basic reason for the rule in the beginning was the protection of the domestic harmony of the home, but when an attack has been made by one spouse upon the other, the harmony of the home has already been interrupted, so to continue to invoke the rule is nothing more than an absurdity.

For this reason most states have passed statutory provisions which permit the victim spouse to testify against the defendant spouse without the defendant's consent being given. In fact, in most jurisdictions the victim spouse can be compelled to testify irrespective of his or her wishes.

This rule has been carried even further in some states in which it is held that not only may the spouse be compelled to testify when he, or she, is the victim of a crime, but also when the child of the spouse, or property of the child, is the victim of a crime by the other spouse. A few states have made a further extension of this rule and held that if, during the commission of a crime on a spouse or the property of the spouse, a third person is injured or the property of the third person is damaged, the victim spouse may be compelled to testify. For example, if a third person should come to the defense of a wife who was being beaten by her husband and the third person were injured by the husband, the wife could be compelled to testify against the husband in a trial charging the husband with an assault and battery on the third person. Some states also hold that the spouse may be compelled to testify if a crime is committed against the child of either spouse, or the property of such child. This situation would arise when stepchildren were involved.

■ Information Gained before Marriage

In those jurisdictions in which the husband-wife relationship prohibits one from testifying against the other, the prohibition relates to all matters, regardless of when the information was gained. It includes knowledge of facts learned prior to the marriage as well as during the marriage. This rule is placed in effect because the persons are man and wife, and not because of any confidential information received or exchange of privileged communications. However, if it can be proved that the marriage took place merely to prevent the testimony, the rule will not be invoked. Since the reason for the rule is to protect the harmony of the home, a marriage for the purpose of prohibiting testimony would have but little harmony. It has also been held that the rule is inoperative where the marriage was void from the outset.

Once the marriage is dissolved by divorce or annulment, the rule prohibiting one spouse from testifying against the other no longer remains in effect. Either spouse may then be compelled to testify concerning information gained prior to the marriage and facts learned during the marriage which did not come as a result of an exchange of confidential information because of the marital relationship. As will be pointed out in greater detail hereinafter, there are certain communications between a husband a wife which may be kept confidential even after the marriage is severed. It becomes most important, therefore, to be able to distinguish between knowledge gained by one spouse irrespective of the marriage relationship and that which was acquired by, and because of, the marital status. This is not always easily done. It is clear, however, that any information or knowledge gained prior to the marriage would not be a privileged communication.

■ Information Exchanged between Husband and Wife

Up to this point, the discussion has been primarily concerned with whether one spouse could testify for or against the other because of the marriage relationship. The issue now is what protection should be given to information that is gained strictly because of the marital status which would not have been gained otherwise. This problem may arise in two different situations; first, in those cases in which a spouse is willing to testify against the other, and second, when there has been a dissolution of the marriage, and one spouse is called upon to testify about some information gained during the time that the marriage was intact. It is an accepted fact that for a successful and wholesome marriage relationship to exist there must be a free exchange of communications between spouses. The law recognizes this relationship as one in which the mutual exchange of confidential information is not only encouraged but must take place. Consequently, the privileged-communications doctrine is made applicable to the husband-wife relationship. The problem is how far the doctrine should be allowed to apply. The age-old balancing of equities presents itself again, that is, the protection of the home against society's protection from the criminal. In attempting to reach some solution to this problem, jurisdictions vary considerably about what a spouse may reveal in court concerning information gained as a result of the status. All agree that there should be some restriction, but how much protection should be afforded has been subject to much debate and court interpretation. There was a time when a few courts held that any exchange of information between a husband and wife was to be treated as a privileged communication, but today it is generally held that for the privileged doctrine to be applicable, the communication must have been intended to be a confidential one, and as such, the privileged-communications doctrine may carry over even after the marriage is dissolved by divorce, annulment, or death. In other words, situations may arise in which a spouse may not be able to testify concerning confidential matters learned as a result of the marriage even though the couple are no longer married. This viewpoint is based upon the philosophy that society is dependent upon strong home relationships, and anything which tends to weaken them even after death or divorce, such as revealing confidences in court, is frowned upon.

It is well known that many conversations take place between a husband and wife which are for their ears and theirs alone. These conversations may pertain to many things, even to crimes committed or acts of misconduct. There is no doubt that these communications would be considered confidential communications, and as such, many jurisdictions will not permit a spouse to reveal this information in court when the privilege is claimed by either spouse even after the marriage is dissolved. There are a few jurisdictions which do not recognize the privileged-communications doctrine when the communication pertains to criminal acts, but others extend the privileged doctrine to all confidential exchanges of information, even though the marriage has been dissolved and the information pertains to crimes. This is based upon the theory that one spouse should not be made hesitant about revealing to the other some secret for fear that it might someday be revealed in court should a divorce take place. It is believed that by this freedom of exchange of confidential information the dissolution of the marriage may be avoided. This is not to be confused with information, which may be gained by one spouse concerning the other, which was not exchanged in confidence between the two. For instance, returning to the previously mentioned example of the wife who observed her husband rob a service station, in many jurisdictions the wife could not be compelled to testify against her husband as long as the marriage was intact, but once the marriage was dissolved, she could be compelled to testify against her former husband, because she did not gain her information as the result of any confidential exchange of communications. On the other hand, if the wife did not see her husband rob the service station but the husband came home and in private revealed to his wife that he had robbed a service station, in most jurisdictions the wife would not have to reveal this confidential information if either she or her husband claimed the privilege, even though the marriage had been dissolved. It is pointed out that the privilege may be claimed by either spouse, as it is considered to be for the benefit of both.

There are a few jurisdictions which hold, as in the case of the privileged marriage relationship, that the privileged-communications doctrine should not be applicable in criminal matters. Many think that this is the better and more practical approach to the problem. It has been stated that any suppression of the truth is dangerous when the security of the community against a criminal is at stake, and that there must be a strong argument presented to allow this suppression to take place. There is a question whether the protection of a crime-ridden home is a sufficient argument.

■ Privileged Communication Not Recognized

The federal government and a few states have abolished all privileged communications between a husband and wife. In these jurisdictions an accused spouse may prevent the other spouse from testifying against the accused spouse. Federal Rule of Evidence 505 provides that "an accused in a criminal proceeding has a privilege to prevent his spouse from testifying against him." This rule means that even though a spouse were willing to testify against the accused spouse, the accused spouse could prohibit the testimony. This rule is not applicable in a proceeding in which one spouse is charged with a crime against the other. Once the marriage is dissolved, a spouse could be compelled to testify concerning all communications and acts which took place either before or during the marriage.

Rule 28 of the Uniform Rules of Evidence, which has been adopted by some states, recognizes the privileged-communication doctrine only during the marriage. Once the marriage is dissolved, the privilege is abolished.

IS AN ACT A PRIVILEGED COMMUNICATION? A problem in the field of privileged communications which has perplexed the courts for many years is whether an act, as well as an oral or written statement, should be considered a privileged communication. In other words, if one spouse observes some act on the part of the other spouse in the privacy of the home, should this act be treated on the same basis as an oral or written communication by the other spouse? Does this act done in the privacy of the home become a privileged communication about which the observing spouse may not testify? For example, assume that a wife observed her husband come into the home and remove a gun and a large amount of cash from his pocket and hide them in a closet. May the wife testify about what she saw her husband do in those jurisdictions which permit the wife to testify without the consent of the husband, or may she testify in all jurisdictions if the marriage is dissolved by divorce before trial? There is a definite split in the decisions of the courts in their answer to this problem. Many jurisdictions cling to the view that any information which comes to the attention of either spouse as a result of the marital status must be protected as a privileged communication. This includes private acts as well as other forms of confidential communications. Those adhering to this view believe that there should be complete freedom of movement in the home as well as a free exchange of ideas and confidences, and all must be protected under the privileged-communications doctrine. An equal number of courts hold that the privileged-communications doctrine, as it applies to the husband-wife relationship, pertains only to written or oral statements and signs communicating a message, and not to acts.

INFORMATION BETWEEN HUSBAND AND WIFE HEARD BY THIRD PERSONS. The next problem as it pertains to the husband-wife privileged-communications rule is: What action should be taken in protecting a communication between the husband and wife which is heard by a third person? It is generally held that when a statement is made knowingly in front of a third person, it is not deemed to be a private matter, and the privileged-communications doctrine does not apply. It has been held that if the statement were made in the presence of small children too young to comprehend what the statement was all about, the information could be considered a privileged communication.

The next matter for consideration is what protection should be given to statements made between a husband and wife which are not made directly in front of a third person, but which are overheard by this person. The decisions in the past generally have held that the privileged-communications rule does not apply to third persons who overhear a conversation between a husband and wife, but there has been a split in the opinions whether there should be a distinction made in the application of the privileged-communications doctrine between merely overheard statements and a deliberate attempt to eavesdrop. Some courts have held that any conversation overheard by a third person is not privileged, even though it was gained as result of eavesdropping. Consequently, the third person may testify about what was heard. This is based upon the theory that if a matter is to be of a confidential nature, the declarant should take the necessary precautions to prevent others from hearing it. If this is not done, the privilege is lost. This would not include conversations overheard as the result of illegally installed listening devices.

In recent years more and more jurisdictions have begun to protect communications between a husband and wife from being revealed by a third person when those communications were intended to be confidential. This has been the ruling regardless of how the communication was overheard.

ATTORNEY-CLIENT PRIVILEGE

The attorney-client relationship is another which is recognized as one in which there should be a confidential exchange of information. This is one of the oldest relations to be accepted under the privileged-communications doctrine. It is mentioned in the old Roman laws. It was adopted early in the English judicial procedure. Its adoption has been attributed to a number of reasons. One is that to maintain a confidential exchange between an attorney and his client makes for a more orderly court procedure. At one time persons brought their own cases into court and adversaries defended themselves. As time went on, court procedure grew steadily more complex. As a result, it was found that there should be officers of the court to assist the litigants in trying and defending their cases. These officers were, and are, known as barristers, attorneys, or lawyers. They are still considered to be officers of the court in a sense. It is through their efforts that the trials run more smoothly and the rules of evidence are more nearly followed.

Another reason given for the adoption of the privileged-communications rule in the attorney-client relationship is it prevents undue or excessive litigation. If clients are free to furnish all the facts in their knowledge, even though some are unfavorable, attorneys know whether there are sufficient facts to state a cause of action, or to take the case to trial. Also, it is only through the complete revelation of all the facts that attorneys are able to decide whether to take or reject cases. Clients, therefore, should have the freedom to discuss matters without fear that they will be revealed. Also, it has been held that for the thorough preparation of a case for trial the attorney must be in a position to learn everything the client knows about the case.

From a practical standpoint in criminal matters, public policy demands that the exchange of information between an attorney and a client be kept confidential because of the constitutional guarantee of the "right of counsel." If this guarantee is to be given its full force and effect, there must be a free exchange of communications without fear that information will work to the detriment of the client.

In order for communication between attorney and client to be within the privilege rule, it must meet certain qualifications. First, there must be an attorney-client relationship. Just when such a relationship is created and whether there is such a relationship has been a problem for the courts. It must be decided who is an attorney and who is a client. An attorney is defined as one who is authorized to practice law in a given state or nation. A client is one who goes to an attorney seeking professional services or advice. To be licensed, the attorney must have complied with certain rules of the legal profession set forth in the state statutes. These rules usually require that the attorney successfully pass a law examination in the particular state in which he or she wishes to practice. Upon doing so, he or she is furnished with a license to practice law in that particular state. Generally, the license must be renewed periodically, usually each year. It is possible for a person to be licensed to practice law in more than one state at a time. However, the right to practice in one state does not automatically permit the attorney to practice law in another without complying with the procedure to be properly licensed.

No problem is involved in the attorney-client relationship when a client consults an attorney who is properly licensed to practice law in the state in which the attorney consulted. This individual definitely falls within the definition of an attorney. But what about the person who has failed to renew his license to practice or is licensed in another state, or the person who has completed law school but has not taken the bar examination? Are communications furnished to these individuals privileged within the rule? In addition, what about the information given to one who the client thought was an attorney, but, in fact, was not, or the law clerk in an attorney's office? These are some of the questions that have plagued our courts. Here again, there are various approaches to the problem. Some states have tried to overcome these troublesome situations by including in their statutes all-encompassing definitions. For example, one state statute defined a lawyer as follows: "A person authorized, or reasonably believed by the client to be authorized, to practice law in any state or nation." Not all jurisdictions have gone quite this far in setting forth definitions of an attorney, or lawyer. As a result, it has created a particular problem about the application of the privilege rule when a person consults a lawyer who is licensed to practice in another state, but not in the one in which consultation occurs. Should information exchanged between them be considered a privileged communication? The decisions in this regard are quite limited and are split in their rulings, very much like those pertaining to a person who consults one mistakenly believed to be an attorney. The crux of the decisions seems to be the degree of care used by the client to determine whether the person consulted was actually an attorney licensed to practice in the jurisdiction consulted. Also, the intelligence of the person seeking legal assistance would have to be taken into consideration in measuring the degree of care used.

■ When Is the Attorney- Client Relationship Created?

The rules concerning the time when the relationship of an attorney and client is created have been quite universally established. It has been held that the moment a client consults an attorney on legal matters, the attorney-client relationship is created. This is true even though the attorney rejects the case. The right of a client to furnish preliminary information to an attorney to enable the attorney to decide whether to take a case must be protected, and this right to furnish preliminary information is a necessary part of the privileged-communications rule. If the rule were otherwise, a client would have to accept the first attorney who would handle a case for a fee without knowing any facts of the case. It has been held that there need be no agreement concerning payment, or fee, for the attorney-client relationship to be created.

COMMUNICATIONS MADE IN THE PRESENCE OF A THIRD PERSON. For a communication to come within the privilege rule, it must have been made to the attorney because of the relationship of attorney and client, and in privacy. If a communication is made in the presence of a third person, the privilege is not applicable. An exception to this is where the information is made in the presence of the attorney's secretary, clerk, or other employee. In this instance the privilege is still binding, not only on the attorney, but also on employees and any other person to whom a disclosure of information is reasonably necessary for the best interest of the client and the attorney. Such a person may be a private investigator who is assisting the attorney in obtaining information about the case or an accountant reviewing books in an alleged fraud case. This would also include an agent of the client who, while acting for the client, furnishes information to the attorney.

If communication is made in the presence of someone who came with the client, the privilege rule is not applicable to either the third person or the attorney. It is presumed under these circumstances that the client did not intend the communication to be a confidential one. On the other hand, if the person who accompanied the client was also seeking the services of the attorney in the same case, the privilege would be binding on all present. The privilege would also prevent the disclosure of confidential information overheard by an eavesdropper.

WHAT IS A COMMUNICATION BETWEEN ATTORNEY AND CLIENT? As in the case of the husband-wife relationship, it must be determined what is included in a privileged communication between an attorney and client. In other words does a privileged communication comprise oral and written statements only, or does it include acts? The decisions are somewhat split in this regard, but it is generally held that any information that is furnished the attorney by the client as a result of the professional status is considered to be a privileged communication. This includes oral and written statements and acts on the part of the client. If during the consultation with the attorney a client should display to the attorney a gun, a sack of money, or scars and marks, these too would fall within the privilege rule. These acts would have to have some connection with the case about which the attorney was being consulted.

However, the attorney should not be a depository for criminal evidence. In the case of *State ex rel. Sowers v. Olwell,* 64 Wash. 2d 838 (1964), the Supreme Court of the State of Washington described the obligation of an attorney who receives such evidence from his client as follows:

> The attorney should not be a depository for criminal evidence (such as a knife, other weapons, stolen property, etc.), which in itself has little, if any, material value for the purposes of aiding counsel in the preparation of the defense of his client's case. Such evidence given the attorney during legal consultation for information purposes and used by the attorney in preparing the defense of his client's case, whether or not the case ever goes to trial, could clearly be withheld for a reasonable period of time. It follows that the attorney, after a reasonable period, should, as an officer of the court, on his own motion turn the same over to the prosecution. . . .
>
> Although . . . the fact that the client delivered such evidence (a knife, gun, etc.) to his attorney may be privileged, the physical object itself does not become privileged merely by reason of its transmission to the attorney.

A client may make a complete confession to an attorney about a crime. If this confession was made during their consultation on the case, the attorney's lips are sealed. Irrespective of the confession, the attorney may still have the client enter a plea of not guilty and endeavor to get an acquittal for the client. This may seem to be a parody of justice. But it is justified in the eyes of many by the presumption that a person is innocent of a crime until proved guilty. It is the responsibility of the prosecution to prove guilt, and the defendant is entitled to a fair trial. Some lawyers take the attitude that an acquittal in a fair trial is proof of innocence. There are many lawyers who cannot in clear conscience go this far. They find a defendant who is guilty in a criminal matter difficult to defend and for that reason will not accept his case.

The privileged-communications rule does not apply when an attorney is consulted concerning the committing of a future crime or asked for advice on committing a crime or on concealing the defendant after a crime has been committed. If an attorney should become involved in the crime or conspire to commit a crime, there is no privilege between the attorney and associates in the crime.

■ Waiver of the Privilege

From a practical standpoint, the problem of the waiver of the privileged communication between an attorney and a client does not arise frequently enough in criminal matters to be of much significance. It should be stated in passing, however, that the privilege is that of the client alone, to waive or to claim. The privilege may be waived by the client in so many words of express consent for the attorney to testify, or it may be waived as the result of the client testifying in the case concerning matters told to the attorney. If the client waives the privilege of keeping matters discussed with an attorney confidential, the attorney may claim no privilege and may be compelled to testify concerning matters discussed. The privilege is established for the benefit of the client, not the attorney. This does not prevent the attorney from calling the privilege to the client's attention in the event that the attorney feels that the client is not aware of the special circumstances of privileged communications.

PHYSICIAN-PATIENT PRIVILEGE

The common law did not recognize the physician-patient privileged-communication rule, nor is it recognized in many states in this country. It is felt that the sealing of the lips of a physician when the public interest is at stake should not be permitted. But beginning with New York in 1828, a number of states have adopted rules relating to communications between a physician and a patient as privileged communications. These rules have been established to encourage the free disclosure by the patient of facts which would aid the physician in treating the patient.

Rules concerning physician-patient privileged communication vary considerably among the states, but it is generally accepted that for a communication between a physician and patient to be privileged the communication or information furnished by the patient must be one that would aid the physician in treating or prescribing for the patient. For this reason some states recognize the physician-patient privileged-communication doctrine in civil matters only and not in criminal proceedings. It is felt that there could be little or no communication concerning a criminal matter which would aid a physician in treating a patient. It is held that a physician would treat a gunshot wound in the same manner whether it was received accidentally or deliberately. In fact, some states by statute make it mandatory for a physician to inform the police if the physician has been consulted about a gunshot wound. There are also states which require a physician to report to police any information that the physician may receive indicating physical abuse of a child. In this regard, other states merely hold that a physician who does report information about child abuse cannot be held civilly liable. Irrespective of these rules, one state recognizes the privileged-communication doctrine in criminal matters but not in civil proceedings. Uniform Rule of Evidence 27 provides for communications between a physician and a patient to be privileged in civil matters and in the prosecution of misdemeanor charges. But for the communication to be privileged it must be one which the physician or patient reasonably believed to have been necessary or helpful in the treatment of the patient.

The privileged-communications rule between a physician and a patient includes not only what was said by the patient, but information gained by the doctor in observation and examination of the patient.

The privileged-communications rule in the physician-patient relationship, like that of the attorney-client, was established for the protection of the patient. The patient may waive the rule.

■ Psychotherapist-Patient Privilege

Before leaving the physician-patient privilege, some mention should be made of a new privileged-communications doctrine which is beginning to appear on the statute books in a few states, that is, the "psychotherapist-patient privilege." The use of psychotherapy is being accepted more and more as a scientific means of treating mentally and emotionally disturbed persons. As a result, a few states have laws which protect confidential communications exchanged between a patient and a psychotherapist.

A patient in this case is defined as any person who consults a psychotherapist for the purpose of the diagnosis or the treatment of a mental or emotional condition.

A psychotherapist is defined as a person who has been authorized to practice medicine and devotes a substantial portion of his time to the practice of psychiatry, or a person who is recognized by the laws of the particular jurisdiction as a certified psychologist.

Those states which have included this relationship within the privileged-communications doctrine have protected the confidences expressed by the patient which may assist in the diagnosis or treatment even though they may pertain to criminal matters. As was previously pointed out, it is generally believed that there is little in the way of communications that needs to be passed between a physician and a patient pertaining to criminal matters that would assist the physician in the treatment of the patient. However, in the case of the psychotherapist there may be a necessity for the patient to make a full disclosure of facts which may be causing some mental or emotional disturbance in order for proper treatment to take place. This disclosure could even entail the confession of having committed a crime. In these circumstances the communications are privileged.

There are a few situations in which the privileged-communications doctrine is not recognized between a psychotherapist and a patient. This includes instances when the patient is charged with a criminal act and the patient pleads insanity or diminished capacity as a defense for the criminal act. The privilege is not recognized if, after consultation with the patient, the psychotherapist has reasonable cause to believe that the patient is in such mental or emotional condition as to be dangerous to himself or herself, or to the person or property of another, and that disclosure of the communications is necessary to prevent the threatened danger.

Although this privileged-communication doctrine is established for the benefit of the patient, who may waive the privilege, one state permits the psychotherapist to claim the privilege even though waived by the patient.

CLERGY-PENITENT PRIVILEGE

At common law the exchange of information between a member of the clergy and a penitent was not recognized as being within the privileged-communication rule. Most jurisdictions today have included this relationship as another in which confidences should be kept secret. Because of our religious heritage, public policy demands that a person should be permitted to confess sins and seek spiritual guidance without the fear that those confessions will be revealed.

A member of the clergy has been described as a priest, minister, religious practitioner, or similar functionary of a religious denomination or organization. A penitent is one who seeks out the clergy in a religious capacity for the purpose of securing spiritual advice.

In the past it has been generally held that to fall within the privileged doctrine the communication must have been a confession, but a few jurisdictions today have included any "penitential communication" as a privileged communication. A penitential communication would be any communication between the penitent and the clergy which was made in confidence to assist the penitent in receiving spiritual aid. Just how far this could be carried is difficult to determine. For example, if a penitent should come to a minister and ask him to hide a gun or a sack of money which were instrumentalities of a crime, would this be a penitential communication? Probably not, unless the request was made in connection with the penitent's desire to repent and then to take some action toward absolution.

A majority of jurisdictions consider the clergy-penitent privileged-communications relationship primarily for the benefit of the penitent, and therefore hold that the penitent only may claim or waive the privilege. However, there are a few states which have granted the clergy the right to refuse to disclose a penitent communication, even though the privilege is waived by the penitent. This right has been granted to the clergy in some jurisdictions because certain religious denominations hold that it is a violation of the church principles for the clergy to reveal penitential communications.

It is generally held that for a penitential communication to come within the privileged-communications doctrine, the clergy and the penitent do not have to belong to the same faith. All that is necessary is that the penitent seek the clergy for the sincere purpose of repentance.

OFFICER-INFORMATION PRIVILEGE (OR OFFICIAL-INFORMANT PRIVILEGE)

The officer-informant privileged communication is based upon the common law. At common law a privilege existed which protected the government against compulsory disclosure of military, diplomatic, or other state secrets when it was in the best interest of the people to do so. This common-law privilege has been embodied in the statutes of the various states and has been enlarged upon to permit government officials to keep certain information confidential. The statutes creating this privilege usually state the following: "A public officer cannot be examined about communications made to him in official confidence when the public interest would suffer by the disclosure." Such a statute permits a law enforcement officer to withhold the identity of an informant under certain conditions. The purpose of this right was stated by the United State Supreme Court in the case of *Roviaro v. United States,* 353 U.S. 53 (1957). The Court in that case said:

> The purpose of the privilege is the furtherance and protection of the public interest in effective law enforcement. The privilege recognizes the obligation of citizens to communicate their knowledge of the commission of crimes to law enforcement officials and, by preserving their anonymity, encourages them to perform that obligation.

Although the Court spoke of the obligation of a person to report crimes to officials, generally there is no legal obligation as such to report knowledge of a crime. At common law it was a violation to have knowledge of a serious crime and not report it. It was known as "misprision of a felony." There is no such violation in most of the jurisdictions of this country. As a result, a person has no obligation to report knowledge of a crime to the authorities. Yet as was expressed in the Roviaro case, society realizes that there is a need to encourage those who have such knowledge to come forward and report it. It is known that there are many persons who have information about criminal activities and would like to report it, but for a number of reasons they are reluctant to do so unless it can be done in complete secrecy.

Although the officer-informant privilege has been recognized, no other privilege has been subjected to greater controversy by our appellate courts than that of the privilege between a law enforcment officer and an informant. The courts are constantly placing limitations on what is considered confidential and can therefore be withheld. Efforts are continuously being made to determine, on the one hand, what is in the best interest of the public and, on the other hand, what the defendant is entitled to in preparing a defense. With the emphasis being placed on the supremacy of individual rights over those of society, officers are finding that they must reveal more and more information that was furnished in confidence. This has been particularly true since the doctrine of "right of discovery" has been extended. Because of the effect of the right of discovery on officers, it will be discussed in detail in Chapter 10. In the meantime it may be well to consider some of the matters which officers may have to reveal, and those which fall within the purview of the privileged-communications doctrine.

It has been held that the identity of an informant who was a participant in a crime cannot be withheld if requested. Although the Court in the Roviaro case recognized the importance of keeping the identity of the informant, as well as his communication, confidential, the Court stated:

> The scope of the [officer-informant] privilege is limited by its underlying purpose. Thus, where the disclosure of the contents of a communication will not tend to reveal the identity of an informer, the contents are not privileged. Likewise, once the identity of the informer has been disclosed to those who would have cause to resent the communication the privilege is no longer applicable.
>
> A further limitation on the applicability of the privilege arises from the fundamental requirements of fairness. Where the disclosure of an informer's identity, or of the contents of his communication, is relevant and helpful to the defense of the accused, or is essential to a fair determination of a cause, the privilege must give way. In these situations the trial court may require disclosure and, if the Government withholds the information, dismiss the action.

There have been times when the government refused to disclose the identity of an informant, even though an action was dismissed, because it was felt that the continual flow of information from a particular informant was more important than the prosecution of the accused.

If an informant was an eyewitness to a crime for which the accused was brought to trial, the informant's identity must also be disclosed. If the information furnished by the informant was the only reason the law enforcement officer took action, the communication cannot be claimed as a privilege. There is some question whether a communication that is the basis for obtaining a search warrant is privileged or not. Some jurisdictions have held that where a search is made pursuant to a search warrant valid on its face, the prosecution is not required to reveal either the identity of the informant or the information which was the basis of the search warrant.

Attention is directed to the provisions required to obtain a search warrant. A search warrant cannot be issued unless there is probable cause to believe that the particular thing sought is in a certain place. The officer seeking the search warrant does not have to have actual knowledge; the application for the warrant can be based upon reliable information. It is highly possible therefore that the appellate courts may demand the revelation of the communication and/or the identity of the informant to justify the establishment of probable cause.

As a result of the right of discovery, the number of instances in which an officer must reveal the identity of the informant has deprived the officer-informant privilege of much of its significance. Also, this privilege has been further restricted by the Freedom of Information Act passed by Congress in 1966 and similar statutes passed by some state legislatures. The full effect that this type of legislation will have upon the officer-informant privilege is yet to be determined through court interpretations as cases are taken up on appeal. But it is known that the maintenance of confidential government records has become increasingly difficult, even to the identity of confidential informants.

■ Waiver of Privilege

The right of a government to withhold information when it is in the best interest of the public to do so is a privilege created for the government, which the government must claim or waive. Technically under these circumstances informants have no right to claim or waive the privilege. Since the identity of informants is withheld primarily for their benefit and safety, if an informant has no objection to disclosing identity, the privilege will undoubtedly be waived by the government.

NEWS REPORTER AND NEWS SOURCE

The protection of newspaper reporters against the compulsory disclosure of sources of information was not recognized at common law, nor is it recognized by the federal government or in a number of states. Yet efforts have been made by reporters to have adopted a privilege whereby they would not have to reveal sources of information or even to be compelled to appear before grand jury hearings or other judicial proceedings. They have alleged that this privilege is granted to them by the "freedom of the press" guarantee of the First Amendment to the United States Constitution and that, therefore, such privilege should be nationally recognized. It has been further alleged that unless such privilege is adopted under the First Amendment guarantee, the freedom of the press to collect and disseminate news will be undermined.

But the United States Supreme Court in the case of *Branzburg v. Hayes,* 408 U.S. 665 (1972), ruled that the First Amendment guarantee of freedom of the press did not afford any privilege to a newspaper reporter from appearing before a grand jury or other judicial proceeding, nor from revealing the identity of news and information sources. The Court in that case stated:

> The public through its elected and appointed law enforcement officers regularly utilizes informers, and in proper circumstances they may assert a privilege against disclosing the identity of these informers. But the purpose of the privilege is the furtherance and protection of the public interest in effective law enforcement. . . . [But] such informers enjoy no constitutional protection. Their testimony is available to the public when desired by grand juries or at criminal trials; their identity cannot be concealed from the defendant when it is critical to his case. . . .
>
> As noted previously, the common law recognized no such [news reporter] privilege, and the constitutional argument was not even asserted until 1958. From the beginning of our country the press has operated without constitutional protection for press informants, and the press has flourished. The existing constitutional rules have not been a serious obstacle to either the development or retention of confidential news sources by the press. . . .
>
> We see no reason to hold that [news] reporters, any more than other citizens, should be excused from furnishing information that may help a grand jury in arriving at its initial determinations.

It should be noted that the Branzburg decision merely held that the First Amendment guarantee of freedom of the press did not automatically grant a news reporter–source privilege. That decision did not bar Congress or state legislatures from passing statutes which would grant some protection to news reporters relating to their news sources. As a result a few states have by statute granted the newspaper reporter the privilege of not being held in contempt of court for refusing to reveal a source of information. These statutes have been adopted upon the allegation of news representatives that in recent years there has been an increase in mutual distrust and tension between the press and public officials. Therefore, there is now more need for the protection of a confidential news source, particularly where the press seeks news about minority cultural and political groups or dissident organizations suspicious of the law and public officials.

However this privilege is not without its complications. The first of these is the determination of those to whom the privilege is granted. The Court in the Branzburg decision recognized this problem. The Court stated that if the news reporter privilege were to be read into the First Amendment guarantee of the freedom of the press:

> The administration of a constitutional newsman's privilege would present practical and conceptional difficulties of a high order. Sooner or later, it would be necessary to define those categories of newsmen who qualified for the privilege, a questionable procedure in light of the traditional doctrine that liberty of the press is the right of a lonely pamphleteer who uses carbon

paper or a mimeograph just as much as the large metropolitan publisher who utilizes the latest photocomposition methods. Freedom of the press is a fundamental personal right which is not confined to newspapers and periodicals. It necessarily embraces pamphlets and leaflets. The press in its historic connotation comprehends every sort of publication which affords a vehicle of information and opinion. . . . The informative function asserted by representatives of the organized press in the present cases is also performed by lecturers, political pollsters, novelists, academic researchers, and dramatists. Almost any author may quite accurately assert that he is contributing to the flow of information to the public, that he relies on confidential sources of information, and that these sources will be silenced if he is forced to make disclosures before a grand jury.

The statutes which have been passed granting a news reporter protection against revealing the news source have been of little help in making the determination as to whom the protection is granted. These statutes provide, generally, that a publisher, editor, reporter, or other person connected with or employed upon a newspaper, magazine, or other periodical publication, or by a radio or television station, or who has been so employed, may not be held in contempt of court for refusing to reveal the source of any news which was obtained in connection with his or her employment. It is to be noted that these statutes do not define with any clarity what is a newspaper or what is a periodical publication. Apparently if a question should arise as to granting or not granting the privilege to a questionable news reporter, the decision would fall within the discretion of the judge of the proceedings involved.

The privilege is also complicated by the fact that it must be determined what is protected by the privilege. Is the information itself protected from disclosure by the news reporter or is it only the source of the information? The privilege, where adopted, has been adopted generally on a limited basis. It is the source of the information that is protected and not the information itself, as was stated in the case of *Lightman v. State*, 15 Md App. 713 (1969):

> The statutory newsman's privilege of Maryland does not protect against the disclosure of communications but extends the privilege only to the source of the information. It is not a privilege of the informer but only of the newsman, and where the newsman by dint of his own investigation personally observes conduct, the newsman himself is the source of the information and the privilege does not apply.

Thus, a news reporter may not refuse to appear before a judicial proceeding and furnish the requested information when commanded to do so without being held in contempt of court, but may refuse to reveal the source of that information without being held in contempt of court in those jurisdictions in which the privilege is recognized.

VOIR DIRE EXAMINATION (*VOIR DIRE* MEANING "TO SPEAK THE TRUTH")

The admissibility of the testimony of a witness frequently depends upon the competency of the person to be a witness. As has been pointed out, competency may be questioned because the witness produced is a child of tender years; or there may be some question about the witness being married to the defendant; or there may be a question about the mental stability of the witness. When these questions arise, a preliminary examination may be permitted in order to determine competency. This inquiry is legally known as *voir dire*. Questions may be asked of the witness to determine competency.

The questions that are asked during this examination must relate to the issue of competency and cannot be about the facts of the case. In other words, as has been previously stated, if the witness were a small child, the questioning would revolve around the child's understanding of and ability to relate those things that were seen; while testifying, the child may be questioned about knowing the necessity of telling the truth. The usual procedure, however, is for the side producing a small child, or a mentally retarded person, to establish competency before proceeding with the questioning about the facts of the case. Irrespective, the opposing side has the right to cross-examine the witness on *voir dire* in order to be fully satisfied of his competency. The judge also may inject questions.

If the question of competency concerns the witness's being a spouse of the defendant, it is usually raised in the form of an objection by the opposing side. It is not necessary to establish ahead of time that the marriage had been dissolved.

As will be discussed in Chapter 4, with an expert witness the *voir dire* to determine the qualifications of the expert is often quite lengthy.

It is the prerogative of the judge to decide whether a person is competent to be a witness. Once the judge decides that the person, be it a child or someone of possible mental instability, is competent, that person may testify. The jury will decide the weight that is to be given to the testimony.

SUMMARY

A witness is a person who makes a declaration under oath or affirmation in a trial proceeding. Most of the common-law restrictions against persons becoming witnesses have been abolished. Generally, today a person who can perceive correctly, retain facts, relate the perceptions in an understandable manner, and understand the necessity for telling the truth may become a witness.

In certain relationships public policy encourages the mutual exchange of confidences known as privileged communications. The following relationships are generally recognized: (1) husband and wife; (2) attorney and client; (3) physician and patient; (4) clergyman and penitent; (5) officer and informant; and (6) in some jurisdictions, newspaper reporter and news source. The confidential nature of these communications may carry over even after the relationship is severed. Except in the case of the husband-wife and clergyman-penitent relationships, the privilege may be waived entirely by one party to the relationship, but it must be by the one to whom the law has endeavored to grant the privilege, such as the client, the patient, or the officer.

In the husband-wife relationship the law not only endeavors to protect the exchange of confidential information between them, but also recognizes a privileged relationship which may prevent one from testifying against the other while the marriage is intact. Various jurisdictions have approached this problem differently in the effort to maintain the tranquillity of the home, and yet protect society from the criminal. Some jurisdictions will not permit either spouse to testify for or against the other without the consent of both unless one spouse is the victim of a crime committed by the other. Some jurisdictions permit a spouse who so desires to testify against the other, but neither spouse may be compelled to do so, except, again, where the defendant spouse has committed a crime on the victim spouse. A few jurisdictions grant no marriage-privileged relationship in criminal matters.

The competency of a witness may be questioned. In order to establish competency, a preliminary examination is permitted known as *voir dire*. Questions concerning the facts of the case may not be asked during *voir dire*; only those questions which pertain to the establishing of the competency of the witness may be asked.

QUESTIONS FOR REVIEW

1. Who is a witness?
2. What were some of the common-law restrictions against a person being a witness?
3. Are these common-law restrictions recognized today?
4. Under what circumstances may a child testify?
5. What reason is given for not permitting a wife to testify against her husband?

6. Name two exceptions where a wife may testify against her husband.

7. What is a privileged communication? Upon what is it based?

8. Name four categories of relationships which are generally recognized by the law as relationships in which privileged communications are encouraged.

9. List three different approaches that are made about one spouse's being able to testify against the other.

10. How does a spouse becoming a victim of a crime committed by the other change the rule in some jurisdictions?

11. In what way does the dissolution of the marriage make a difference about what a spouse may testify?

12. How does the physician-patient privilege differ from other privileges in its application in some jurisdictions?

13. What is the general limitation placed upon the communication under the clergyman-penitent privilege rules?

14. What are some of the matters that may have to be revealed in the officer-informant relationship?

15. What is the purpose of the *voir dire* examination?

LOCAL RULES

As there are differences among jurisdictions on some rules of evidence, the reader may wish to ascertain the answers to the following questions from the local prosecuting attorney, as suggested in Chapter 1.

1. What are the restrictions, if any, on competency of witnesses in this state of
   a. Children
   b. Persons who have been convicted of a crime
   c. One spouse testifying for or against the other

2. What are the restrictions as they pertain to the following privileged communications:
   a. Husband-wife privilege
      Is the privilege recognized if it involves a criminal matter?

Is an act as well as an oral or written communication recognized under the privileged-communications doctrine?

What is the ruling concerning remarks overheard by third persons?

b. Physician-patient privilege

Is the privilege recognized in criminal matters?

c. News reporter–news source

Does the state recognize this privilege?

d. Does this jurisdiction grant the right to claim the privilege to the clergy even though waived by the penitent?

Witnesses–Lay and Expert

BECOMING A WITNESS

A person becomes a witness because of having knowledge about the facts of a case to be tried. This knowledge may have been acquired through something seen, heard, smelled, or touched. A law enforcement officer who is called as a witness usually has gained knowledge through personal investigation of a case or of a special phase of it. Witnesses are called on during the course of a trial to relate their particular knowledge.

Witnesses are seldom surprised when they are called to testify, especially in criminal cases, because preceding most trials, law enforcement officers conduct extensive investigations and usually advise those they interview that they may be called. Although many people willingly serve as witnesses, others, for a variety of reasons, serve reluctantly: Some wish not to become involved; some fear reprisal; others fear cross-examination. Still others may wish to cooperate but are reluctant to lose time at work. Judges often allow trials to be continued without advance notice, necessitating that witnesses take another day from work to return each time a case is set for trial—a procedure that can become expensive for a wage earner.

An individual does not always have a choice, however, whether to appear as a witness. Anyone with information that may be of value in arriving at the truth in a trial may be compelled to be a witness. This compulsion in criminal trials is based on the provision in the Sixth Amendment to the Constitution that "the accused shall enjoy the right . . . to be confronted with the witnesses against him, . . . to have compulsory process for obtaining witnesses in his favor."

The Fourteenth Amendment made this constitutional right of an accused to be confronted with the witnesses against him applicable to the states by the United States Supreme Court in the case of *Pointer v. Texas,* 380 U.S. 400 (1965). In that case the Court stated:

> The Sixth Amendment is a part of what is called our Bill of Rights. In *Gideon v. Wainwright* in which this Court held that the Sixth Amendment's right to the assistance of counsel is obligatory upon the States, we did so on the ground that "a provision of the Bill of Rights which is fundamental and essential to a fair trial is made obligatory upon the States by the Fourteenth Amendment." . . . We hold today that the Sixth Amendment's right of an accused to confront the witnesses against him is likewise a fundamental right and is made obligatory on the States by the Fourteenth Amendment.
>
> It cannot seriously be doubted at this late date that the right of cross-examination is included in the right of an accused in a criminal case to confront the witnesses against him. . . . The fact that this right appears in the Sixth Amendment of our Bill of Rights reflects the belief of the Framers of those liberties and safeguards that confrontation was a fundamental right essential to a fair trial in a criminal prosecution.

■ Notifying the Witness

How does one know to appear in court as a witness? Official notification is by subpoena. The subpoena is an official document issued by a judge or the clerk of a court and served on the witness. In criminal cases it sets forth the name of the defendant to be tried, the name of the person to be the witness, and the time and place where the person is ordered to appear. If the person has papers, records, or other physical evidence needed for the trial, the person will be served with a *subpoena duces tecum.* This subpoena not only gives the information mentioned above, but in addition describes the material that the person is to bring to court.

A person does not have to be served with a subpoena to become a witness. A witness may appear voluntarily or at the oral request of an attorney representing either side. However, if a witness does not appear in accordance with an oral request, no penalty can be imposed. For this reason, the usual procedure is to serve a subpoena on each person desired as a witness.

■ Witness List

Before a trial, the attorneys representing each side will furnish to the clerk of the court a list of persons who are needed as witnesses. The clerk will either issue the subpoenas or have the judge issue them. In some jurisdictions, the prosecuting attorney and the public defender may issue their own subpoenas. Although in most states anyone may serve a subpoena, in criminal cases the subpoenas are usually given to an officer of the court—who may be a deputy sheriff, a constable, or a marshal—to be served on the person named in the subpoena. The service of the subpoena consists of personally handing the subpoena to the person. By so doing, the officer can verify that the person was aware of the necessity to appear. Failure to appear could cause the person to be held in contempt of court and subject to be fined or sentenced to a term in jail. It is the duty of all persons to testify when needed. Organized society is based on the civic contribution of its members. It is also considered to be an inherent right of our courts to compel a person to appear as a witness. Few circumstances will excuse anyone from attendance as a witness, because the needs of justice must be met and the convenience of the witness is of little consequence. Being a witness is deemed to be a civic duty owed by a person to society; therefore, the witness who attends a criminal trial is not always compensated. Usually, there is a limit placed upon how far a witness may be required to travel in order to testify without being compensated. Legally, a subpoena is valid anywhere within the state in which it is issued. But if a witness is required to travel from one county to another or within a prescribed distance, the witness is usually paid a mileage fee and some small remuneration for expenses involved.

The general practice is that when a witness resides in a county other than the one in which the subpoena is issued, the court issuing the subpoena will designate on the subpoena that the witness is material to the trial and will be compensated for appearing at the trial.

■ Out-of-State Witnesses

As pointed out, a subpoena is valid only within the state in which it is issued. Consequently, in the past, when a material witness in a criminal trial resided in another state, commanding an appearance created a problem. But today, most states have solved this problem by adopting the Uniform Act to Secure the Attendance of Witnesses from without the State in Criminal Cases. This act permits a court to issue a subpoena to an out-of-state witness and to have the subpoena sent to a court in that state. The witness will be commanded to appear in that court, where a hearing will be held to determine whether he or she is a material witness. If the decision is affirmative, the witness will be ordered to appear in the court where the original subpoena was issued. A witness who fails to appear as ordered may be held in contempt of court. Again, the witness is entitled to compensation for appearing.

■ Segregation of Witnesses

Although the defendant in a criminal trial is entitled to a public trial, it is not unusual to exclude the witnesses from the courtroom during the trial.

This is not considered to be a violation of the defendant's right to a public trial. The witnesses are excluded or segregated to prevent one witness from trying to corroborate the story of another irrespective of the truth. From a practical standpoint, a complete separation of the witnesses is almost impossible. They still may get together in the halls of the courthouse during recesses, or at other times when the trial is not in session.

The segregation of witnesses is not a necessity to the trial procedure. It may be done at the request of the attorney representing either side; or a judge who believes that the ends of justice would be better served by doing so may instigate the segregation.

LAY OR ORDINARY WITNESSES

Witnesses have been classified into two categories: (1) the lay or ordinary witness and (2) the expert witness.

The lay witness is a person who has some personal knowledge about the facts of the case and who has been called upon to relate this information in court. The law enforcement officer will usually fall within the category of the lay witness. The lay witness is permitted to testify about facts only, and may not state personal opinions except in a few instances. The restriction on opinions or conclusions may be most frustrating to the witness. Much of our daily conversation is made up of conclusions and opinions. People get into the habit of speaking in this vein, and when not permitted to do so on the stand, a witness becomes virtually tongue-tied. As a result, the manner or method in which a witness relates information becomes very important to the trial proceeding.

■ Methods of Interrogating Witnesses

Aiding witnesses in properly relating their story on the stand is one of the major functions of the attorneys involved in the trial of the case. As has been previously stated, leading questions, with a few exceptions, may not be asked of a witness during direct examination. During the direct examination the attorney may ask specific questions of the witness, but the desired answer cannot be indicated by the question asked. In other words, a question may be asked of the witness which may require only a "yes" or "no" answer, but it may not be asked in such a manner that the witness knows the answer desired. Asking specific questions which require only short replies is probably the best method of confining the testimony to the issues at hand, but it is a slow and time-consuming way to get the facts before the judge and jury. On the other hand, it does eliminate the striking from the record of much irrelevant material that may be otherwise given by the witness.

Another method by which the witness may be interrogated is the narrative form. In this method the witness is requested to state in his or her own words what happened in a particular instance. This permits the witness to tell the story in a logical sequence, and it is undoubtedly easier for the jury to follow evidence presented in this manner. But this method too has its drawback. The witness, not being fully informed on the rules of evidence, may testify concerning many things that are incompetent or irrelevant, bringing objections by the opposing side and requests to strike the testimony from the record. The judge must then admonish the jury to disregard the testimony. This procedure, too, can be very time-consuming. Also it is difficult for the jury to disregard something said by a witness even though it is stricken from the record and there is an admonition to not consider it.

There is another disadvantage to the narrative presentation so far as the direct examination is concerned. While telling his or her story, the witness may go into matters the attorney did not intend to include at that particular time. Or the witness may include irrelevant material, which would result in extensive cross-examination and could be detrimental to the case.

Even though both methods of examination have their weaknesses, it is necessary to use one or the other, or a combination of the two, in order to get the facts to the judge and jury. Both are time-consuming and account for the lengthy ordeals that many trials become.

On cross-examination the specific type of questioning is almost universally used. Usually, questions asked by the cross-examiner demand a "yes" or "no" answer. This is done for a purpose: The cross-examiner is better able to control the information related by the witness. It must be remembered that the witness under cross-examination is usually an adverse witness, who often develops an unconscious hostility toward the cross-examiner. If the cross-examiner does not exert control, the witness may take advantage of the situation and present additional information in behalf of one side of the case. This is an ever-present hazard of cross-examination. Although most witnesses have a dread of being cross-examined, the cross-examining attorney is probably more afraid than the witness, if the truth were known. Actually, the attorney has more to lose than the witness. Cross-examination is at best a dangerous procedure. The cross-examiner never knows what the answers will be and in most instances is bound by them, no matter how unfavorable. Very few attorneys are capable of clever cross-examination. Cross-examination therefore is frequently held to a minimum by attorneys, or it may be waived entirely.

If there is any chance of impeaching a witness's testimony by the cross-examination, the cross-examiner will attempt to do so. For an officer witness, the cross-examination can become very unpleasant. This is probably due to the fact that the officer is one of the more damaging witnesses so far as the defendant's case is concerned. Unfortunately for the officer, there are defense attorneys who will go to any length to confuse, belittle, or embarrass an officer on the stand in the effort to devaluate the testimony.

At the same time, this often works to the advantage of the prosecution. If an officer is able to maintain composure and control, the jury may feel more sympathetic toward the witness than toward the defense attorney. The officer should bear this in mind while testifying. This matter will be discussed in further detail in Chapter 13. So even though the officer dislikes the experience of a cross-examination, in most instances the defense attorney too would avoid it if it were not considered necessary to proper representation of the defendant.

WITNESS MUST ANSWER QUESTIONS. A witness must answer all questions the judge permits, whether the questions are in direct examination or cross-examination. Sometimes the witness is reluctant to answer a question that may be adverse to the side for which the witness has been called, particularly during cross-examination. But the witness must remember that the purpose of a trial is to arrive at the truth, irrespective of whom it may hurt. The witness does not have to answer a self-incriminating question. The guarantee of the Fifth Amendment to the Constitution of the United States and the provisions of the laws of the various states give to a witness, as well as a defendant, the right against self-incrimination.

REFUSAL TO ANSWER A QUESTION. Occasionally a witness will refuse to answer a question asked by an attorney. This is more likely to occur during cross-examination. As has been pointed out, a witness is usually favorable to one side and will answer its questions. The entire testimony of a witness who refuses to answer a question may be stricken from the record. This is based on the premise that the entire truth must be revealed by the witness, not just the portion believed beneficial to one side.

When an answer given to a question is not responsive, the unresponsive answer may be stricken from the record. An unresponsive answer is one that has no relation to the subject matter of the question or goes beyond the scope of the question asked and relates to some other matter. The mere fact that an answer does not come up to expectation is not sufficient grounds to have it removed from the record. Neither is receiving an unexpected answer, or one less favorable than was expected, grounds to have it stricken from the record.

When an answer is stricken from the record, the jury will be instructed to disregard the answer and not to consider it as evidence of the case.

If a witness absolutely refuses to answer a question and if the question is not incriminating, the witness can be held in contempt of court in addition to having his or her entire testimony stricken from the record.

■ Opinion Testimony of Lay Witnesses

The lay witness may relate only facts—not opinions—so that the truth can be brought out in the trial procedure. Yet, often the line between fact and opinion is very finely drawn. An opinion has been defined as an inference or conclusion drawn from a fact known or something observed. As it relates to the testimony of a lay witness, it would be an inference drawn from something the witness observed. There are situations which can only be intelligently described or expressed in the form of a conclusion or opinion. For example, a witness may state that the defendant was mad or angry when he came home. Is this a conclusion of the witness, or is it a fact? At first glance, it may appear to be definitely a conclusion. On the other hand, it is known that even a small child quickly senses anger or that a parent is displeased about something. This emotion is felt so keenly that it may be a fact. Then, too, how would one prove that the defendant was angry? The court may demand that a witness relate what was actually seen and heard. So the witness states that when the defendant came home his face was red, his mouth was drawn, his eyes were snapping, and he spoke in a loud, rough manner. Has anything really been gained by such a detailed description? Besides, is not the statement that the defendant's eyes were snapping, his face was red, or his mouth drawn, a conclusion? We see, therefore, that it is not easy to determine whether a matter is a fact or a conclusion of the witness.

The courts in their decisions have endeavored to set certain guidelines whereby a witness may relate information in the form of an opinion, but these have not always been easy to follow. It has been held that if the matter involved is of such a nature that it cannot otherwise be described to the jury, the lay witness may give conclusions or opinions. In other words, if there is no way of expressing the observation except in the form of a conclusion, the lay witness may relate testimony in that form. A state of emotion exhibited by a person would be difficult to relate to others except by giving an opinion as in the foregoing example. Is it not better to allow a witness to state that the defendant was angry than to endeavor to describe all the physical aspects of the defendant's face on returning home? The jury thoroughly understands the witness who says, "The defendant was angry when he came home," but on the other hand, a description could be entirely misconstrued by the jury. This same description of the defendant's appearance could well have been interpreted as one registering fear and not anger. This difference in the interpretation by the jury of the emotion involved could be the determining factor between a first-degree murder verdict and one of not guilty because it was believed that the killing was done in self-defense. So there are many experiences within the common knowledge of humanity which enable one to draw conclusions and relate them as such on the witness stand. Chief among these experiences are conclusions concerning emotions, as almost all persons are in a position to decide whether another is happy, sad, or angry. Thus when it is in the best interest of justice and when it assists the jury in the search for truth, the lay witness is permitted to state a conclusion or an opinion about certain common experiences.

In one case, the court made some interesting observations concerning situations about which a lay witness may express an opinion. These include:

> . . . questions of identity, handwriting, quantity, value, weight, measure, time, distance, velocity, form, size, age, strength, heat, cold, sickness, and health; questions also concerning various mental and moral aspects of humanity, such as disposition and temper, anger, fear, excitement, intoxication, veracity, general character, etc. . . . We identify men. We cannot tell how, because expressions of the face, gestures, motions, and even form are beyond the power of accurate description. Love, hatred, sorrow, joy, and various other mental and moral operations, find outward expression, as clear to the observer as any fact coming to his observation, but he can only give expression to the fact by giving what to him is the ultimate fact, and which, for want of a more accurate expression, we call opinion. [See *Holland v. Zollner,* 102, Cal. 633 (1894).]

Before a lay witness may express an opinion, a proper foundation must be laid to prove that the witness had adequate opportunity to observe the facts from which the witness is going to express an opinion. Attention is called to the fact that the opinion of the lay witness may be only about something that the witness observed, heard, or smelled and not in answer to some hypothetical question pertaining to the witness's opinion of the matter.

A great deal of liberty has been given to the trial judge in determining when a witness may relate an opinion. The appellate courts have stated that the trial judge is in a better position to make this decision in accordance with what is taking place at the time, and the appellate courts are therefore reluctant to reverse decisions of this kind unless there is a material error in judgment.

Some of the more commonly encountered opinions that may be expressed by a lay witness in criminal matters are discussed in further detail in the following sections.

STATE OF EMOTION. In criminal trials a lay witness is frequently called upon to express an opinion of the state of emotion of the accused or of the victim of a crime. It may be most important to know whether the accused was angry or excited at a particular time; or whether the victim was afraid, happy, or in love. If the lay witness had an opportunity to observe the accused or the victim at the pertinent time, the witness may express an opinion of the state of emotion of each.

SPEED OF VEHICLES. A lay witness who has observed a moving vehicle is permitted to state an opinion as to the speed of the vehicle. It is not necessary that the witness be able to drive in order to state an opinion as to the speed. It has been held proper for a witness to state that a vehicle was going very fast or that it was going faster than other vehicles in the area. However, it is doubtful if a witness with no experience in the operation of a vehicle could give an opinion as to the approximate miles per hour. Even if a trial judge did permit such an opinion to be stated, the jury probably would give but little weight to such an opinion. In some jurisdictions, a lay witness is permitted to state that a vehicle was going fast or very fast merely from hearing the sound of the vehicle pass an area. A lay witness may not give an opinion about speed merely from observing skid marks, as this falls within the purview of the expert witness. Neither may the lay witness state that a person was driving negligently or dangerously as this may be the very issue in question and must be decided by the jury.

AGE, IDENTITY, AND PHYSICAL CONDITION OF A PERSON. A lay witness may give an opinion of the estimated or approximate age of a person that the witness has observed. If a lay witness is acquainted with another person or has observed that person, the witness may express an opinion about whether a photograph is a good likeness of the individual. The witness may also state an opinion whether a voice heard over a telephone or through a closed door was that of someone with whom the witness was acquainted or had heard speak. It has been held permissible for a lay witness to state an opinion whether a person was intoxicated or not. Likewise, a lay witness may give an opinion about the general physical characteristics of a person. This includes such opinions as whether a person appeared to be strong, weak, feeble, or ill. As the opinion relates to the physical condition of a person in question, it is considered to be the better practice for the witness to state the facts upon which the witness based the opinion that the person was strong, weak, feeble, or ill. With this knowledge, the jury can more properly weigh the opinion. Generally, a lay witness may not give an opinion about a type of illness or any internal condition of a person. Lay opinions would be confined to things which could be observed and would not include inferences about internal disorders, except possibly that the person was suffering from a cold or some other commonly known illness which may manifest itself by external conditions.

OPINIONS ON MISCELLANEOUS MATTERS SUCH AS WEIGHT, COLOR, VALUE, ETC. Because of the familiarity of the average person with a great number of things in the nonscientific field, the lay witness may express an opinion on these matters. These include an opinion about the approximate weight, size, and color of an object. The witness may state an opinion on matters of taste, smell, and touch. The witness may, on a limited basis, give an opinion of the value of certain objects or property. If the value is a real issue in the case, to arrive at it may call for the services of an expert. A lay witness may also express an opinion concerning the approximate distance between two objects observed. It has been held proper for a child to state that something was very close. To evaluate an opinion expressed by a witness concerning distances, the witness is often tested by being asked to estimate distances between objects within the courtroom.

SANITY.   There are occasions when a lay witness may even express an opinion on the sanity of a person with whom he or she is intimately acquainted. But as a general rule, a lay witness may not express an opinion of whether the acquaintance knew the difference between right and wrong, as that is a fact that the jury is called upon to decide during a trial. In some jurisdictions, the lay witness may not express an opinion as to the sanity of a person but may merely express an opinion as to whether the person in question acted in a rational or irrational manner. The courts have stated that it is not necessary that the witness have any prior acquaintance with the person in order to give this opinion. This is based on the supposition that a rational person reacts in a certain normal manner and that an irrational person deviates from this normal manner. Anyone should be in a position to draw a conclusion whether a person appeared rational after observing the person for a short time. In order that a jury may better evaluate an opinion, it is considered proper procedure for the lay witness to relate as far as possible the actions and words from which the lay witness drew the conclusion as to a person's sanity or rationality.

OPINIONS ABOUT THE GENUINENESS OF HANDWRITING.   It may come as a complete surprise to the student to learn that, in some instances, a lay witness may state an opinion about the genuineness of the handwriting of another. The use of the lay witness in this regard stems from a historical background. At common law, both in England and in this country, it was frequently important to endeavor to authenticate a document or identify handwriting. In earlier days, handwriting experts were unknown, so the services of the lay witness were used through necessity. It was held that if a witness had seen another person write or had received correspondence or documents from the person, the lay witness could express an opinion about the genuineness of a writing. This kind of opinion must not be confused with the opinions that are expressed by the expert witness in the field of handwriting comparisons. The lay witness merely observes a questioned handwriting and, being familiar with the handwriting of the person, expresses an opinion whether it is genuine.

■ Terminology of the Lay Witness

In general conversation, people frequently start a statement with such phrases as "in my opinion," "it is my belief," or "I believe." At first glance, this would imply that the person using such phrases is expressing a conclusion. In reality the witness may be stating an actual fact. So terminology alone does not necessarily make a statement inadmissible on the witness stand. Upon the use of such a term by a witness, it may be necessary for the attorney conducting the examination to further question the witness to clarify that a fact is being stated and not a conclusion.

EXPERT WITNESSES

With the great advancement of science and with the wide variety of skilled occupations encountered today, a jury may be called upon to make judgments about many matters of which they have no personal knowledge or understanding; or, they may have some personal knowledge about the facts, but the conclusion which has to be drawn from those facts may require someone skilled in the field. To assist the jury in their search for the truth and in the best interests of justice, the services of the expert witness have been developed. As subject matters continue to become more technical and specialized, no doubt the expert witness will play an even more important role in trial proceedings in the future, so that one might think of the expert witness as an assistant to the jury. The expert witness gives the jury the benefit of knowledge of a particular science or skill by which the jurors are assisted in arriving at the truth. An expert is permitted to express an opinion concerning a particular set of facts or about some examination of evidence made. The jury may or may not accept the opinion.

■ Definition of Expert Witness

An expert witness is a person skilled in some art, trade, science, or profession. An expert must have a skill and knowledge that is beyond and above that of the average person. In this respect, therefore, an expert is in a position to assist the jurors because it is presumed that they would not under ordinary circumstances have this knowledge. Contrary to the belief of many persons, the expert witness does not have to be a person of great educational background or training. All that is necessary to qualify as an expert witness is knowledge in some trade or occupation which the ordinary person on the street does not have. The witness may have gained this knowledge by long-time work experience in the particular field. For example, a cement mason may have very little educational background, yet because of experience in the cement and concrete trade may qualify as an expert in that field. A mason may be in a position to express an opinion about how long it takes concrete to harden before it can be driven upon without doing damage. On the other hand, there are certain areas in which the expert witness may have to show extensive study and training. This would be true in matters pertaining to medical or scientific examinations.

It is possible to qualify as an expert witness through self-instruction and experience. Many of the crime-laboratory experts fall within this category. There are certain fields in which there are but few courses available or in which there has been very little written.

■ When an Expert May Be Used

In the past in order to utilize the services of an expert witness, two things had to be determined. First, was the subject matter under discussion a field in which the average person would have little or no knowledge? Second, did the witness have the qualifications necessary for an expert in the field? Today, the courts have begun to relax the necessity rule and hold that the opinion of an expert witness may be admissible when an opinion would be of assistance to the judge and jury in the trial of the case. Even though the necessity rule is being relaxed, the witness must still meet the qualification rule.

The student is probably more familiar with the crime-laboratory expert than any other expert, so the crime-laboratory expert will be used as an example in determining when an expert witness may be used. When the crime-laboratory examiner makes a bullet comparison or compares a latent fingerprint with a suspect's, the expert's opinion is necessary in the trial since the average person in the street is unable to analyze the findings without assistance. Thus the first qualification is met: An area has been established in which the services of an expert are needed by the jurors in reaching a verdict. Now we come to the second qualification: What is necessary to qualify as an expert in these fields? It is difficult to lay down any definite criteria. It would be somewhat unfair to require any extensive formal education in view of the fact that to date there is very little available in the way of academic training in the field of ballistics or fingerprints. Yet there are related subjects which could be studied. For example, in the case of the ballistics examiner, it would be to his advantage to have a knowledge of metals, physics, chemistry, and criminalistics, although there is no requirement that he must have studied these courses in order to qualify. It is possible for an examiner to qualify as an expert without any formal study in a higher educational institution. Under such circumstances the examiner would undoubtedly show extensive experience working under the supervision of another who is considered to be well versed in the field. However, if the examiner can show formal study as well as experience, the testimony will probably hold greater weight with the jury.

■ Qualifying the Expert: *Voir Dire*

An expert witness cannot just get on the witness stand and begin to testify concerning opinions and conclusions. The witness must be qualified as an expert. What is necessary to qualify as an expert witness has not been crystallized to date. However, it is established that the proposed expert must have exceptional knowledge beyond that of the average person on the street concerning the particular science, trade, skill, or occupation about which the proposed expert has been called upon to testify. Proving this knowledge rests upon the side producing the expert witness. Preliminary questions are asked of the witness about study, experience, and work in the field in an effort to show that the witness has the necessary knowledge to qualify as an expert. For example, consider a crime-laboratory technician who specializes in bloodstain examinations. The prosecuting attorney would call the technician to the stand and after asking the witness's name and occupation would probably ask about educational background, because college training in science, particularly in chemistry and biology, would certainly improve the image of the witness. In addition to the educational qualifications, the witness's work experience, including training under the supervision of other experts in the field, would be brought out. Also the length of time that the technician had been engaged in this particular kind of examination would be gone into, particularly if it were over a period of years. The more qualifications the prosecuting attorney can elicit, the more likely the expert is to impress the jury and the more inclined they are to accept the conclusions as accurate.

After the prosecuting attorney has finished questioning the witness about qualifications, the defense attorney may also question the witness. This preliminary examination by the attorneys is known as *voir dire*. The defense attorney may endeavor to show that the witness is not qualified as an expert—particularly if the technician is known to have had but little education in a scientific field where education is desirable or if the witness has had limited experience. Even if the defense attorney is not able to bar the witness from testifying as an expert, the attorney may seriously damage the effect of the testimony by the questioning. Consequently, a person endeavoring to qualify as an expert witness should be in a position to show as extensive skill and knowledge of the subject matter of the testimony as is possible.

If during the qualifying of the expert by the prosecuting attorney, it has been shown that the witness is a highly skilled individual, the defense attorney may waive *voir dire* entirely. However, this does not preclude the defense attorney from cross-examining the expert after the expert has given testimony on direct examination. Many times, a defense attorney has lessened the effect of the expert testimony through cross-examination. Here again, cross-examination of an expert witness becomes a difficult task for an attorney, because the attorney usually has very little knowledge of the field. For this reason, except for a few routine questions on the law of probability, the cross-examination may be limited.

The final determination whether a person qualifies as an expert witness or not is made by the trial judge, and unless the decision is beyond all reason, it will not be overruled on appeal. Once the witness is accepted by the judge as an expert witness, the weight given to the testimony is determined by the jury.

■ Testimony of the Expert Witness

The opinions and conclusions of the expert witness may be presented in either of two ways. After having made an actual examination of some piece of evidence, the expert may state conclusions as a result of the examination. Or the expert may be presented with a set of hypothetical facts from which he or she is asked to draw conclusions. This latter type of presentation is not used frequently in criminal cases. The testimony usually is the result of an actual examination of a piece of evidence. This is particularly true in the case of a crime-laboratory technician. A technician's appearance as an expert witness originates generally from an earlier examination of an article found at a crime scene. This does not preclude the defense attorney, or the prosecuting attorney either, from also presenting certain hypothetical questions to the expert.

For further clarification of the testimony by an expert witness through actual examination, assume that a laboratory technician experienced in bloodstain examinations is called upon to testify concerning stains which he has tested for blood, and that the object which the technician examined is a stained shirt found at a crime scene. During the examination, he made certain chemical tests of the stains and, as a result of these tests, concluded that the stains were blood. He then made other tests and from these formed the opinion that the blood was of human origin. After further tests to determine the blood group, the technician concluded that it was type A blood. The expert may express these opinions to the jury.

At first glance, the reader may assume that these are scientifically proven facts and not mere conclusions of the witness. It is scientifically accepted that blood will react to certain chemicals, that human blood will react in a different manner from animal blood, and that blood can be grouped. But it is merely a conclusion of the expert that the stains found on the shirt were human blood of type A. Because of alleged skill and knowledge of such matters, the witness may give opinions resulting from the examination for the benefit of the jury. They may or may not believe the opinions true, depending upon how well qualified they consider the witness to be and how convincing they find the testimony.

In the second method of presenting the opinions of the expert witness through the use of hypothetical questions, the expert witness will not have examined any evidence and will have no knowledge, either directly or indirectly, about the case. Instead, a set of hypothetical facts which have some relation to the matter at issue will be given to the expert, who will then be asked for an opinion, based on his experience and knowledge, of what would happen in the given circumstances. For example, a medical doctor may be placed on the witness stand and asked such a question as: "Assuming that a man had been in the habit of drinking four cans of beer each night before supper for over two years, would this in your opinion retard his reaction time?" After the question had been asked, the medical expert would express an opinion.

Some people in the legal field think that the hypothetical-question presentation has no part in jurisprudence. They hold that this kind of testimony has no actual connection with any part of the case and that any conclusion reached is at best merely a hypothesis arrived at by an imaginary set of facts that may not be associated with what is to be proved. Also it is asserted that it tends to promote biased testimony. It is stated that an expert is usually paid to appear and has an unconscious loyalty to the side that pays.

Either the prosecution or the defense may call expert witnesses, or the judge may request that an expert be called in for some purpose. This is particularly true if a question of insanity is involved or some physical ailment is alleged.

Some jurisdictions have included in their statutes the following provision, which is set forth in the Uniform Rule of Evidence 59:

> When it appears to the court, at any time before or during the trial of an action, that expert evidence is or may be required by the court or by any party to the action, the court on its own motion or on motion of any party may appoint one or more experts to investigate, to render a report as may be ordered by the court, and to testify as an expert at the trial of the action relative to the fact or matter as to which such expert evidence is or may be required.

■ Kinds of Expert Witnesses

It would be next to impossible to list all the kinds of expert witnesses that one may encounter. However, a few of the better-known areas in which experts appear in criminal cases will be reviewed.

AUTOPSY SURGEON. In homicide cases the cause of death must be established. This is invariably done by the autopsy surgeon. The surgeon will be called as an expert witness by the prosecution to give an opinion of the cause of death as a result of an examination of the body. Here again the reader may think that the cause is a fact, not an opinion; but can one ever be certain about the true cause of death? It is only after the autopsy surgeon has made a complete examination of the body that he can conclude that the death was due to stabbing and not to a heart attack, or that a death was due to strangulation and not to accidental drowning.

DOCUMENT EXAMINER. A document examiner is usually skilled in making comparisons of both handwritten and typewritten documents and would be able to qualify as a handwriting expert and an expert in the field of typewritten documents. As was pointed out in the study of the lay witness, there are times when the lay witness can testify concerning an opinion on handwriting. But this is confined to cases where the lay witness is familiar with a person's handwriting and after looking at a document expresses an opinion whether it is the writing of an acquaintance. The handwriting expert is seldom acquainted with the person whose writing he examines. Instead, the expert's examination is purely a comparison of two or more writings. He may compare two checks in an effort to determine whether in his opinion they were written by the same individual. Or he may have a sample of the known handwriting of a person to compare to a questioned check or document in an effort to form an opinion whether the questioned document was written by the person who gave the known handwriting sample.

An expert in the field of typewritten documents may examine a document and express an opinion about the make of the typewriter used to type the document; or he may examine a document and a known sample from a particular typewriter and express an opinion of whether the document was typed with that particular machine. He may also examine two questioned documents and express an opinion of whether they were written on the same typewriter.

A document examiner will in many cases be able to express an opinion identifying the manufacturer of the paper used and the approximate date of manufacture.

Although many persons consider themselves to be authorities on handwriting comparisons, it requires a great deal of study and experience to become an expert in this field. There is much that must be taken into consideration; yet to date there is little in the way of formal schooling in this field available. Thus this is one area in which extensive educational background in the particular skill may be difficult to show. Even so, juries are usually impressed by college degrees, even when it comes to this kind of examination and testimony. A general study in the field of criminalistics would thus undoubtedly give greater weight to the testimony of an expert witness.

FINGERPRINT EXPERT. Many officers may be confused over the demarcation between what a lay witness may testify to and what requires the testimony of an expert witness in the field of fingerprints. The officer who examines a crime scene or a piece of evidence for latent fingerprints is doing so as a lay witness. Although it takes a certain amount of skill and knowledge to properly develop latent prints, it is not a field in which one must qualify as an expert witness to state that latent prints were located and developed. If an officer has had considerable experience in developing latent prints, the prosecuting attorney may bring this out. If so, it is done merely to give more weight to the testimony and not for the purpose of qualifying the officer as an expert witness. In many large law enforcement agencies, the person who searches for and develops latent prints is frequently the fingerprint expert. However, most small departments must rely on the officer in the field to develop and lift the prints, which are in turn given to the expert for a comparison with a suspect's prints.

The services of the fingerprint expert come into the picture when it is necessary to make a comparison between a latent fingerprint found at a crime scene and the prints of a known suspect to determine whether the latent print is that of the suspect. If an identification is made, the examiner will in most instances be called as a witness to prove the basis upon which an identification was made. In these circumstances the examiner will have to qualify as an expert in the field of fingerprint examinations. Here again, little in the way of formal education is available to an expert, but the expert will have to show some study, training, and experience in order to qualify as an expert. This is an area, as is also that of handwriting comparisons, where a few persons with limited knowledge and experience have endeavored to qualify themselves prematurely, causing jurors to lack confidence in such comparisons. However, every effort is being made to overcome such attempted premature qualification in order not to deprive juries of valuable aid in their search for the truth.

SKID-MARK AND SPEED EXPERTS.   With the speed of motor vehicles ever increasing, more and more serious accidents occur. In many instances, there are few, if any, eyewitnesses to automobile accidents, so that the determination of the speed of the vehicles involved in accidents is not easily made, yet the speed is often an important factor of a case. Therefore, the expert in the field of determining the approximate speed of the vehicle from the skid mark left at the accident scene is often called upon to give an opinion on the speed of the vehicles. Through the use of calculus, computers, and scientific knowledge, the speed of a vehicle can be determined with a fair degree of accuracy from skid marks. Also, experts in the field of estimating speed and related matters are frequently called upon to state opinions concerning what may be safe speeds in accordance with certain road conditions. These opinions are usually based upon hypothetical questions. These questions are often phrased in the following manner: "Based on your training and experience, assuming ideal road conditions—for instance, in the middle of the summer, no snow, not wet—what would be the reasonable or safe speed in and about the area of the accident?" The expert would then give the jury the benefit of an opinion to assist them in arriving at whether a driver involved in a serious or fatal accident may be held criminally responsible.

BOOKMAKING AND NARCOTICS.   Officers who have had extensive experience in working on bookmaking cases may become qualified as experts in what is considered to be material and paraphernalia used by bookmakers.

Likewise, officers experienced in narcotic investigations may qualify on the methods used by drug addicts in making injections. They may also express their opinion about scars which they believe to have been made by such injections or whether certain paraphernalia found at a crime scene were used by those engaged in the use or sale of narcotics.

84

The narcotic content of a pill or powder, however, would have to be determined by a person skilled in the field of chemistry.

CRIME-LABORATORY EXPERT.   It is next to impossible to list all the areas in which individual experts in a crime laboratory may be involved. But a few of the more commonly encountered ones are in the fields of ballistics, spectroscopic examinations, the examination of hairs and fibers, soils, toxicology, glass and glass fractures, blood and other body fluids, paints, and chemicals.

FOOTPRINT EXPERT (SOMETIMES REFERRED TO AS SHOE-PRINT EX-PERT).   Footprints are admitted in evidence when their similarity to the shoes worn by a defendant justifies an inference that the prints were made by his shoes. To date there is not much that science can add to a comparison of a cast or photograph made of a footprint found at a crime scene with the shoe of a suspect. The similarities in any peculiar markings between the cast or photograph and the shoe, as well as a comparison of the size, may be made by the jury with as much proficiency as by a witness. Consequently, there is little in the way of scientific expert testimony in this field. Yet courts differ in their requirements of whether the testimony concerning the similarities must be given by an expert or may be given by a lay witness. Whether the testimony is given by an expert or a lay witness, a proper foundation must be laid. In order to identify the footprints with a suspect's shoe, the witness must specify the features upon which he bases his judgment of identity. Some courts hold that since this identity is in the form of an opinion, it may be expressed only by an expert witness. Other courts hold that a lay witness may point out the similarities between the cast and the shoe, and the jury may draw their own conclusions.

Even though expert testimony is not necessary in comparing footprints with a suspect's shoes, there are times when a footprint may have other significance to a case, and an analysis of the print may call for the service of an expert. It must not be overlooked that there are persons who are expert trackers or who have made a study of walking patterns. As experts, these persons can determine with considerable accuracy certain things by examining tracks at a crime scene, such as whether the suspect walked or ran from the scene, walked with a limp, was carrying something heavy, or was having difficulty with equilibrium. Any of these facts could be important in the prosecution of a case.

PSYCHOLOGISTS.   It is recognized that doctors specializing in psychiatry may state their opinion on the sanity of a person, but questions have arisen whether a psychologist may state an opinion on the sanity issue. It is known that sanity is a matter of mental illness and as such is not wholly within the realm of only the physician. Thus a psychologist who is trained and experienced in mental illnesses may qualify as an expert in this field and may express an opinion on the sanity of a person. Both psychiatrists and psychologists are permitted to give a jury the benefit of their knowledge and training by expressing an opinion as to whether a person examined by them knew the difference between right and wrong at the time a crime was committed.

EXPERTS ON OBSCENITY.   In the prosecution of charges of obscenity, it must be established whether a publication or performance was obscene. It has been held that the test for obscenity is whether the publication or performance violated contemporary community standards. Some courts have held that in order to establish contemporary community standards only the opinion of an expert in this field is admissible. Other courts hold that any evidence which tends to establish contemporary community standards is admissible, whether given by a lay witness or an expert witness. Courts following this latter approach feel that the lay witness is as informed on community standards and what is and what is not objectionable as the expert witness is. In applying the test, the extent of the community in which the test is to be applied must first be established, that is, whether the community is confined to a city, a county, or the complete state. Some states have passed statutes defining the community as the entire state. In other states, in the absence of statutory definitions, courts have been inclined to confine the community to a city and the immediate surrounding areas. After the community has been determined, it will be necessary to present evidence in an effort to prove that a particular publication or performance is without redeeming social value within that community.

POLYGRAPH EXAMINERS.   Concerted efforts have been made by those interested in polygraph examinations to have the results of these examinations admitted in evidence by the courts. Polygraph experts allege that the polygraph is now beyond the experimental stage and is a recognized scientific instrument capable of detecting truthfulness and falsehood. The courts have agreed that there has been substantial progress in improving the equipment and the operator techniques used in administering polygraph tests, but the courts, generally, are reluctant to accept results of polygraph examinations. This reluctance stems from the allegation of the courts that the results still lack the reliability necessary for full acceptance. It is alleged that too many factors can affect the reliability of the polygraph test. These factors include such matters as the emotional condition of the person being examined. Also, physical condition, such as high or low blood pressure, drunkenness, fatigue, or use of drugs, can cause unreliable results. The experts in the field readily admit that these factors can and do often affect the tests, but they allege that when these conditions exist, they will be taken into consideration and the results, if not reliable, will not be used. But when conditions are normal, as is true in most instances, it is stated, the results should be introduced in evidence for whatever assistance they may have in aiding the jury in arriving at a verdict. The courts have countered this argument with the allegation that juries often find it difficult to accept the polygraph results as only an opinion of the expert as to whether the person examined was falsifying or not, and not a proven fact. Some courts hold that this is true even though the judge instructs the jury that the polygraph result presented by the polygraph examiner is only an opinion and that the jury may accept the opinion or reject it as they see fit. The courts in a few jurisdictions have accepted the results of polygraphs on a limited basis. In one instance, a defendant was charged with forceful rape. The victim admitted being picked up by the defendant while she was hitchhiking, but claimed that after being picked up by the defendant, she was forcefully raped. The defendant admitted picking the victim up, but denied that he had sexual relations with her. The defendant, his attorney, the victim, and the prosecuting attorney all agreed that the defendant and the victim would be given polygraph examinations and that the results of the examinations could be introduced by the polygraph examiner. The polygraph examiner testified that as a result of his examinations of the defendant and the victim, it was his opinion that the victim was being truthful in her statements and the defendant was evasive. The defendant was convicted, but the conviction was reversed upon appeal because the judge failed to properly instruct the jury that the result of the polygraph examinations was only an opinion of the expert as to the credibility or truthfulness of the victim and the defendant and the opinion did not go to the point of fact on the guilt of the defendant.

In those jurisdictions in which the courts have not accepted polygraph results, some prosecuting attorneys have endeavored to have the courts accept in evidence the refusal of a defendant to take a polygraph test upon the grounds that the refusal proved guilty knowledge or consciousness of guilt. However, the courts have not generally accepted this refusal in evidence upon the grounds that an accused may refuse to take a polygraph test, not because he or she fears that it will reveal a consciousness of guilt, but because the test may record as a lie what is in fact the truth. The courts likewise have refused to accept in evidence a defendant's expressed willingness to take a polygraph test. The courts state that a guilty suspect may be willing to hazard taking the test in hope that the test will erroneously record innocence, knowing that even if the test does not reflect innocence the results of the test cannot be used as evidence.

VOICEPRINT EXPERT.   Individuals have been accepted by the courts as experts in the method of voice identification known as voiceprints. This method of voice identification consists of identifying or eliminating an unknown voice among several known by both listening to the voices and visually inspecting a spectrogram. Scientifically described, acoustical spectrography is a branch of science which consists of composing the voice or sound into harmonic components and obtaining a visual pattern of the sound. This pattern is called a spectrogram.

A voiceprint expert generally is utilized when a victim receives threatening calls about bombs, kidnapping, extortion, or other similar dangers and there is an opportunity to record the assailant's voice in some manner. Thereafter, if a suspect is located, his voice is also recorded, and the voiceprint expert will listen to the recordings and endeavor to determine similarities in the two recorded voices. The expert will also compare the voiceprint patterns displayed on the spectrograms. The expert will then form an opinion whether the threatening voice of an unknown individual is identical with that of the known suspect. The expert, if properly qualified and if called upon to do so, may thereafter express an opinion concerning the identity during the trial of the suspect.

Some courts have permitted the voiceprint expert to state an opinion on identity because it has been held that the voiceprint method of identification has reached a stage of acceptable reliability whereby the results are accepted as evidence. Some courts state that the test of admissibility of scientific testing is whether or not it has received general acceptance by recognized experts in the field. The experts in the field of voiceprint identification attest to its reliability.

It is interesting to note that the scientific voiceprint identification has entered the investigative field recently compared to the polygraph; yet the voiceprint identification has revealed general acceptance by the courts, whereas the polygraph results are accepted, if at all, on a very limited basis. Much speculation has taken place over the reason for this. Some allege that the voiceprint is an opinion on identification only and is not generally feared by the public. But the polygraph results amount to a confession of having committed a wrongful act, and there is therefore a general fear of the polygraph by the public as a whole, which has resulted in a general rejection of the instrument, however scientific it may be or however competent the operator. This public rejection has undoubtedly caused the courts to have some reservations about accepting polygraph results as evidence. Also, the courts in some jurisdictions have alleged that the experts in the field of the polygraph examination cannot agree among themselves as to the reliability of the tests, which makes the rejection of the results valid.

PHOTOGRAPHERS.   Except for certain scientific photographs, such as the spectrograph, micrograph, or x-ray, a photographer does not have to be an expert in the field of photography to have photographs admitted in evidence. (For further details see Chapter 12 on Photographic Evidence.)

REFRESHING RECOLLECTION
OR MEMORY

As we have seen, the witness, whether lay or expert, is frequently called upon to give much detailed information while testifying. To recall all details often becomes a tax on the memory. It may be well to consider what may be done to assist the witness to remember the things necessary to tell the story properly on the stand. So far as an officer is concerned, the officer should review the case file to become thoroughly familiar with it before the trial. The officer should go over the case with the prosecuting attorney. But because of the tension of the trial, even having done these things, sometimes an officer forgets a fact while on the stand. What may be done to help this situation?

Rules of evidence have been developed which permit a witness to refresh his or her memory or recollection while on the witness stand. There is some variation among jurisdictions about just what a witness may utilize for this purpose. Before a witness can use anything, it must be established that the witness has definitely forgotten and needs help. Establishing this fact is a comparatively simple procedure. About all that is necessary is that the witness express inability to recall a particular fact and a desire to refresh recollection of it. When the witness is an officer, the prosecuting attorney will probably ask whether the officer has in possession anything that would refresh recollection or help the officer to remember the fact. Or the prosecuting attorney may ask the witness whether seeing something pertaining to the case would assist in recalling the fact. If the witness indicates that it would, the judge is requested by the prosecuting attorney to permit the witness to review some document or article. The problem involved is just what the witness may review for this purpose.

At common law, and in many jurisdictions in this country, no restriction is placed upon what may be used to refresh one's memory. It may be a report, a photograph, a newspaper article, or an object. Anything that may cause memory to return is all that is necessary. Other jurisdictions have adopted a very strict view about what may be utilized. They have held that a witness may refresh memory only with something that was written by the witness or under the witness's direction and that was recorded at or about the time the event took place. A few other jurisdictions have taken a middle-of-the-road approach in determining what may be used by the witness. These jurisdictions hold that the witness may refresh memory from any writing or photograph, whether prepared by the witness or someone else; but the witness may not use an object.

It may be well to reflect upon these two viewpoints for a moment. Is one superior to the other in the search for truth during the trial? The advocates of the unrestricted rule hold that anything that refreshes the recollection should be utilized. It is the testimony and not the document or object which is the evidence. In fact, usually the writing is not even admitted into evidence when the memory is refreshed. Some critics of this view have asked how one can be certain that the memory has been refreshed. These critics should not overlook the fact that the witness is still subject to cross-examination upon the testimony. If the frailties of the memory were so great that it was not refreshed, this fact undoubtedly will be brought out during the cross-examination. It must be recalled that the opposing attorney has the right to make a complete examination of the document or the thing used to refresh the recollection. The attorney may object to its use or may use it to cross-examine the witness and thereby be in a position to determine whether it did in fact refresh the memory.

As stated, the strict view is to limit the refreshing of the memory to something written by the witness or under his direction, and it must have been written at or about the time that the event took place. There seems to be no really solid argument for this restriction. Some observers think that by this restriction an effort is being made to combine the rule concerning "refreshing the memory" and "past memory recorded." One must then consider what is meant by past memory recorded.

■ Past Memory Recorded

At times a witness is shown writing that fails to refresh his or her memory. The witness may still be unable to recall the facts. In these circumstances, the witness may have to be excused from the stand, or it may be possible to continue with some other portion of the testimony which is remembered. However, when a witness cannot recall a fact and has something written down concerning it, it may be possible to introduce this writing or its contents into evidence. If admitted, the writing or its content becomes part of the evidence in the case. Two general requirements must be fulfilled before the writing can be admitted: (1) The writing must be by the witness, or by another under his direction; and (2) the writing must have been made at or about the time the event occurred. The first requirement causes very little trouble in its interpretation, but the second one creates difficulty. Just when is "at or about the time" the event occurred? If an officer conducts an investigation and while doing so writes down findings, or if the officer records an interview while questioning a person, there is no doubt that this is "at the time." In these circumstances the officer may use the notebook to refresh his or her recollections, or if after reviewing the notes the officer still does not recall the facts, the notebook or its contents can be offered as evidence. It has met all the qualifications. This is probably why great emphasis has been placed on the officer's notebook in the past and on its continuing retention and preservation. The emphasis has been so great that many an officer's locker is so cluttered with old notebooks that it resembles the back room of a secondhand bookstore.

Even though the locker may become cluttered with old notebooks, the retention of the notebooks has become very significant in jurisdictions in which the defendant is granted a liberal right of discovery. The federal courts and the courts in some states have held that the right of discovery by the defendant includes the right to review the officer's notebook and/or investigative notes taken during interviews with suspects and prospective witnesses. This review is permitted even though the contents of the notes have been incorporated into an official investigative report. It has been further held that destruction of these notes is a violation of the defendant's right of discovery and could result in a reversal of a conviction upon appeal. The right of discovery will be discussed in detail in Chapter 10.

INVESTIGATIVE REPORT AS A MEANS OF REFRESHING MEMORY AND PAST MEMORY RECORDED. What about the officer's investigative report? Under the strict rule, may the report prepared by the officer, or under his or her direction, be used to refresh his recollection on the stand? Again there is no question about the report prepared by the officer, but what about one dictated to the police stenographer? There seems to be no question about this either, as it certainly is not the report of the typist but of the officer who dictated it. Occasionally, an efficient secretary will make so many corrections in grammar and phraseology that there is very little similarity between the way the officer talks and the way the report reads, but it is held that even this kind of report complies with the rule of "under his direction," particularly so long as the facts were not changed.

The problem now arises: How soon must the report be prepared or dictated to come within the rule of "at or about the time" the event occurred? There seems to be no reasonable criterion for measuring this time. Some jurisdictions have endeavored to overcome the problem by stating, "written at the time the event occurred, immediately thereafter, or at any other time when the facts were fresh in the writer's memory." The criterion here is that the event must be recorded when the witness was able to recall the facts and make an accurate record of them. For this reason the officer should write an investigative report or dictate it as soon as possible after the investigation took place. If it is dictated, the officer should read the typed report while the facts are fresh in his memory and attest to the accuracy of the report by signing it. When the officer does this, the report meets all the necessary requirements, even under the strict rule both for refreshing the recollection and for past memory recorded.

Our next question is: What about a report based on the investigation of more than one officer or where two officers worked together? In these circumstances each officer should prepare his or her portion of the report, or the officers should make separate reports. Each officer should review the report after it has been typed, and each should sign the report attesting its accuracy. Where two or more officers work together on the same portion of a case, the report should be prepared by them jointly, and each should read it and sign the report attesting its accuracy. In this way the report may be used without question by any or all of the officers involved. It may be used either to refresh the memory or as a record of past memory recorded if the officer cannot recall all the details after reviewing the report.

As to material used to refresh the memory, some jurisdictions have permitted the opposing attorney to examine the things used by a witness before the trial to refresh memory, as well as anything to be used while on the stand. At one time this practice created a certain amount of consternation among law enforcement agencies. It meant that if an officer admitted on the stand that he had reviewed his file on a case to refresh his memory before coming to testify, the defense attorney could demand to see the file. With the right of discovery, which is now so prevalently exercised by defense attorneys, the defense attorney has the right to see the file anyway. Little or no problem thus arises when the officer admits reviewing the file to refresh his or her memory before coming to the trial. In fact, the officer who is going to make a good witness must review the file.

■ Laying the Foundation for Past Memory Recorded

Even jurisdictions that do not adhere to the strict rule about what may be used to refresh the memory do adhere to strict requirements on past memory recorded. For example, if an officer does not recall certain facts about an investigation, the prosecuting attorney may show the officer a report made by the officer. If this report still does not refresh the officer's memory, the prosecuting attorney will undoubtedly wish to offer the report or its contents in evidence in lieu of the testimony, since no testimony is forthcoming. Before the report or its content can be offered in evidence, a foundation must be laid for its introduction.

This foundation consists of proving that the writing meets the requirements for admissibility. First, it must be shown that the writing was done by the witness, or in the case of our example, the officer. If it was not done by the witness, it must be shown that the writing was done under the officer's direction, for example, by dictation to a stenographer. The next requirement is that the writing must have been done at a time when the facts were fresh in memory of the witness, and the witness must now know that the writing was a correct report of the facts. The officer knows this because it was prepared at a time when the officer did recall the facts and they were so recorded. After meeting all these requirements, the writing or its content will be offered in evidence. The defense attorney may include some cross-examination of the witness, but little can be gone into on cross-examination because there has been no testimony. The entire story is the writing. In the case of a report by an officer, the defense attorney may question the officer about who made the report if it was not by the officer but under his or her direction, and the officer may be questioned about how soon the report was made; but other than this, there is very little that may be asked on cross-examination. If there should be some question about who made the report or when it was made, the defense attorney may object to its being admitted. Its admissibility is a matter for the judge to decide. If it is admitted, the jury can believe or disbelieve the report as they see fit. If a report is made sometime after the event occurred, it still may be admitted in evidence, but the jury may take the attitude that the officer could not recall all the details, and they may place but little weight on the report.

Even though the report itself is entered in evidence, the prosecuting attorney may ask the witness to read the report to the jury, or the prosecuting attorney may read it to the jury. This permits the facts to be brought to the jury at the proper time in a logical sequence of the trial proceedings.

A few jurisdictions will not permit a document to be introduced in evidence but only its content. The document will be read to the jury by the witness or the attorney involved, and the content will become the oral testimony of the witness. Even under this stricter rule of admissibility, the document itself may be introduced in evidence by the opposing side. The primary reason for not permitting the document to be introduced by the side producing the witness is that the jury is permitted to take all documents with them during deliberation. This would enable the jury possibly to give greater weight to the testimony of a witness who could not recall any of the facts than to the testimony of a witness who was able to testify from memory and whose testimony the jury would have to recall, since in most instances the transcript of the testimony would not be available to the jury.

SUMMARY

A person becomes a witness as a result of having some personal knowledge about the facts of a case to be tried. The person is officially notified to be a witness when a subpoena has been served on him or her. If the witness is to bring some document or record to court, the witness is served with a *subpoena duces tecum*, which describes the thing that the witness is to bring. Failure to comply with the subpoena may cause the person to be held in contempt of court.

Witnesses are classified into two categories: (1) lay or ordinary witnesses and (2) expert witnesses. Lay witnesses may relate facts only and not opinions, with a few exceptions. There are some experiences within the common knowledge of mankind from which a lay witness may draw conclusions and may give the jury the benefit of these conclusions. The expert witness is used as an aid to the jury in its search for truth. An expert witness is one having skill and knowledge beyond the average person in a certain art, trade, science, or profession. An expert may state conclusions from an examination made by the expert or from a set of hypothetical facts presented to the expert. The expert witness must qualify as such before being permitted to testify. This is done by *voir dire*.

A witness may refresh his or her memory while testifying. Jurisdictions vary about what may be used for this purpose. The majority of the states hold that the witness may use anything which will enable him to recall the facts. A few states restrict the use to something written by the witness or under his direction, and it must have been recorded at or about the time the event took place. After having refreshed his memory, the witness continues the testimony and the material used usually does not become evidence.

If, after reviewing the document, the witness still is unable to recall the facts, the document itself or its content may be offered in evidence. Before it is admitted, though, it must meet certain requirements. The document must have been written by the witness or under his or her direction, and at or about the time the event took place.

QUESTIONS FOR REVIEW

1. Why does a person become a witness?
2. What is the difference between a subpoena and a *subpoena duces tecum*?
3. What is meant by segregation of the witnesses?
4. What two methods of questioning are used to enable a witness to tell his or her story on the stand?
5. Name five situations in which a lay witness may give an opinion when testifying.
6. Who is an expert witness?
7. In order to utilize the services of an expert witness, what two things must be determined?
8. By what two methods may an expert arrive at his conclusions?
9. What is meant by the term "refreshing the recollection"?
10. What may a witness use to refresh his or her recollection?
11. How do "refreshing the recollection" and "past memory recorded" differ?
12. What foundation must be laid in order to use past memory recorded?

LOCAL RULES

As there are differences among jurisdictions on some rules of evidence, the reader may wish to ascertain the answers to the following questions from the local prosecuting attorney, as suggested in Chapter 1.

1. What may a witness use to refresh his or her memory while testifying? May it be an object as well as writing?
2. May the attorney for the opposing side demand the production of something used by the witness to refresh his or her memory prior to the time of the trial?
3. May whatever is used by the witness to refresh his or her memory be introduced in evidence?
4. What are the restrictions on what may be introduced in evidence as past memory recorded?
5. Is the writing itself admitted in evidence as past memory recorded or is only the reading of the contents of the writing admitted as evidence?

Credibility
and Impeachment

5

CREDIBILITY

Credibility means simply the weight that is given to the testimony of a witness. If a witness is able to impress the jury with ability to observe correctly, to retain observations, and to relate them convincingly on the witness stand, his or her credibility is undoubtedly good. In other words, the credibility of a witness is entirely dependent upon how much the jury believes the testimony, how much credit the jury gives it. A jury may believe the entire testimony, or it may believe part of it and not believe other parts. It is not unusual for a jury to disbelieve all the testimony given by a witness.

Although before testifying a witness takes an oath or affirms that he or she will tell the truth, witnesses are not always truthful. A witness may not tell the truth for a number of reasons. He may be unable to observe correctly, and thus may honestly believe that he saw something he did not see. Because of poor memory, original observations may become confused so that a witness gives an unintentionally inaccurate account of what was seen. A witness may have some interest in the case, sympathy for one side or a prejudice against the other, or may have some financial interest in the outcome. Any of these factors may cause a witness unconsciously to color testimony toward a particular side. In addition, some persons, for reasons of their own, intentionally falsify while testifying.

All these possibilities affect the credibility of the witness, particularly if the jury senses them or if their influence becomes apparent during cross-examination. If the jury is unaware of them, it may still believe the story as related by a witness, irrespective of how false or inaccurate the testimony may have been, and so far as that jury is concerned the witness's credibility is still good.

IMPEACHMENT

Impeachment is any attack made upon the credibility of a witness. It is an attempt made by the opposing side to devaluate the testimony of a witness in the eyes of the jury, so that it is given less weight. Many persons are under the mistaken belief that if impeachment occurs, the entire value of the testimony is lost. This is not necessarily true. It is possible for an attack upon the credibility of a witness to be so serious that the jury does disbelieve his or her entire testimony. On the other hand, the attack may create only a small doubt in the mind of the jury about the truthfulness of the story and merely lessen its effect. The attack may be on only a portion of the testimony, so that the jury may give a great deal of weight to one part of the story and little or no consideration to other parts. It is possible that the attack will fail entirely and that the effort to impeach the witness will backfire and actually strengthen the testimony. This is particularly true if an attorney displeases the jurors by the manner of attack. Or the witness may have been testifying honestly and truthfully, and an attack will merely emphasize the story in the minds of the jury. This frequently happens when an officer has convincingly and truthfully related a story and the defense attorney endeavors to attack the credibility of the officer. The officer should not be apprehensive of an effort to impeach his or her testimony, because the attack may work to the officer's advantage.

■ Methods of Impeachment

Attack on the credibility of a witness may be made in a number of prescribed ways, most of which are set forth in the statutes of the various states. The methods of impeachment are comparatively uniform. Generally, a witness may be impeached by showing that:

1. The witness has made prior statements inconsistent with his or her present testimony.
2. The witness's reputation for truthfulness, honesty, and integrity is bad.
3. The witness is biased or prejudiced because of emotional involvement in the case at hand.
4. The witness's ability to observe, retain, and/or relate is defective because of age, mental capacity, eyesight, hearing, or some other physical weakness.

Some jurisdictions have permitted impeachment by proof that the witness has been convicted of a crime. A few jurisdictions have allowed a witness to be impeached by a mere showing of bad conduct.

Some observers believe there is a growing tendency away from trying to impeach witnesses. This has not been the experience of the officer, who is usually the witness most damaging to the defendant's case. Frequent efforts are made to impeach officers. These efforts to impeach can become most unpleasant. For this reason, various methods utilized to impeach witnesses are discussed in detail under separate headings.

Before discussing the methods of impeachment, it may be well to consider the general procedure followed in making attacks upon the credibility of witnesses. In almost all instances, impeachment begins with cross-examination of the witness, and in some cases it must begin there. As pointed out in Chapter 1, the primary function of cross-examination is to safeguard the accuracy and completeness of the testimony. Certain points mentioned during direct examination are clarified; they are brought forth in greater detail, and their accuracy is measured. During this measurement of accuracy, it may be determined that the witness did not actually recall the details as they were and is now confused concerning them, and so the process of impeachment begins. Much of cross-examination is for the purpose of impeachment. Attempts to impeach a witness may be well founded. If a witness has inaccurately related facts on the witness stand, the inaccuracies should be brought out during the cross-examination and an attack upon the credibility of the witness is in order, but an attack made solely for the purpose of devaluating the testimony of a witness because the testimony is damaging to the side of the cross-examiner should be frowned upon.

If cross-examination is for impeachment purposes, a witness may be questioned on a number of matters seemingly having no relationship to the issues of the case. Even jurisdictions which adhere to the strict rule of confining cross-examination to matters mentioned during direct examination will permit considerable liberty in the asking of questions that affect credibility. If questions seem to be far afield, the cross-examiner may have to prove to the satisfaction of the trial judge that the questions are designed for impeachment purposes. How far the cross-examiner can go in questioning the witness is largely at the discretion of the trial judge.

In some instances, the effort to impeach a witness may not take place through cross-examination but through the use of the testimony of an impeaching witness. The testimony of an impeaching witness is often used in an attempt to prove that a witness has a bad reputation for truthfulness and honesty, and/or in an effort to prove bias or prejudice on the part of a witness who had previously testified. In many instances, efforts to impeach a witness may be made by a combination of cross-examination and impeaching witnesses.

PRIOR INCONSISTENT STATEMENTS. One of the more frequently used means of impeachment is to show that the witness has made prior statements inconsistent with those being made in present testimony. These inconsistent statements may have been made before the trial, or they may be answers during cross-examination which are inconsistent with those given during direct examination. In fact, one of the reasons for extensive cross-examination is to determine whether the witness will give inconsistent answers. This is not necessarily done to prove that the witness is a "liar," but to show that there may be some question about his or her ability to retain pertinent facts. If weakness in the retention power of the witness is shown by inconsistent statements, his credibility is placed in jeopardy.

In most jurisdictions if an effort is made to impeach the witness by proof of prior inconsistent statements, a proper foundation must be laid. This must be done for two reasons: (1) to prevent the witness from being taken entirely by surprise and (2) to give the witness the opportunity to make a logical explanation of the alleged inconsistency, thereby saving time spent in trying to prove the inconsistency. Alleged prior inconsistent statements made by the witness must be quoted to him or her, and the witness must then be asked whether he made such statements. The time, place, and persons present must also be called to his attention. These requirements further refresh his memory on the alleged inconsistency.

After the foundation has been laid, the witness may admit the prior statements and satisfactorily explain why a present statement is inconsistent with a previous one. The sufficiency of the explanation, however, will be determined by the jury. On the other hand, the witness may deny making any prior inconsistent statement, or may claim not to remember making any such statements. In either case, the cross-examiner will have to prove that such statements were made through the use of the cross-examiner's own witnesses. It will be a matter then of whether the jury believes the witness who is alleged to have made the inconsistent statements or the witnesses of the cross-examiner.

In a few jurisdictions it has been held that such a foundation need not be laid and the alleged inconsistent statements may be related by an impeaching witness, but under this procedure the impeached witness must be given an opportunity at a later time to explain any inconsistency that may have been alleged.

SHOWING BAD REPUTATION.   It is generally held that a witness cannot be impeached by merely proving that he has a reputation of being bad. The bad reputation must be limited to areas of truthfulness, honesty, and integrity. For example, a man may be continually drunk or a woman have loose morals, but both may be entirely truthful and honest in all their statements.

Impeachment by proof of bad reputation for truthfulness, honesty, and integrity is accomplished by the use of other witnesses and not by the witness who is testifying. These persons are frequently referred to as "character witnesses."

Legally speaking, reputation is what others think and say about a person. The witness who is to prove the reputation must be in a position to know what others say and think about a person. In these circumstances it is usually necessary to prove that the impeaching witness resides or works in the same area as the person to be impeached or travels in the same social circle. This is the responsibility of the side producing the impeaching witness and is known as "laying the foundation." Also, the reputation should be current at or about the time of the trial. Although there is no time limitation placed on just when a character witness must have knowledge of the reputation, if it is in the remote past, the effectiveness of the attack is considerably weakened. However, a witness's reputation of being a liar ten years ago could still devaluate his present testimony in the eyes of the jury. If the knowledge of the reputation is in the too distant past, the attack could fail entirely.

It was once generally held that what the character witness thought about the person being impeached was immaterial and not admissible, but this viewpoint has been changed in some jurisdictions. The rule followed in a few jurisdictions permits the character witness to express his or her own opinion about the honesty or dishonesty of the witness being impeached when the impeaching witness has an acquaintance with the witness. It is possible that opinions of those whose personal intimacy gives them first-hand knowledge of another's character are far more reliable indications of that character than reputation, which is little more than accumulated hearsay. The danger involved in admitting these opinions is no greater than in reputation evidence.

After a witness has been impeached for having a bad reputation for truthfulness, honesty, and integrity, the side producing the impeached witness may produce witnesses to prove that the impeached witness enjoys a good reputation for truthfulness, honesty, and integrity. However, evidence of good character of a witness cannot be shown until the character of the witness has been attacked. It is presumed that witnesses have a good reputation for truthfulness, honesty, and integrity. This presumption saves much trial time, for otherwise, before any witness could testify, extensive evidence might be produced to build up the witness in the eyes of the jury.

PROOF OF CONVICTION FOR A CRIME. Jurisdictions vary considerably in their rules about the impeachment of a witness who may have been convicted of a crime. However, all jurisdictions permit some attack to be made, although it is highly restricted in some states. Impeachment by proof of a conviction is based upon the assumption that a person may be of such bad character that he or she should not be believed while on the stand. It should be recalled by the reader that at common law convicted persons were not even competent to be witnesses because they could not be relied upon to tell the truth, but this restriction has been abolished in most of the states of this country.

A problem arises: What kind of conviction must be proved to attack the credibility of the witness? A few states hold that any conviction of crime is sufficient ground for making the attack. The grounds would include conviction of misdemeanors as well as felonies. If misdemeanors are included, should persons who have been convicted of traffic violations be subject to impeachment? The jurisdictions which permit impeachment by proof of prior convictions of both misdemeanors and felonies generally eliminate traffic violations as being outside the rule. A few jurisdictions permit attack to be made only if the conviction is for a felony or for misdemeanors which involve "moral turpitude." The difficulty with this rule is trying to determine the nature of a misdemeanor involving moral turpitude. Moral turpitude is a rather ambiguous term and subject to varied interpretation. A great deal of latitude is given to the trial judge in the determination of moral turpitude in states which permit this kind of impeachment. A few other states have overcome the problem by including in their codes a provision that a witness may be impeached only by proof of a conviction of a felony.

In addition to restricting the impeaching conviction to a felony, courts of a few states have further held that the felony must be one pertaining to honesty and integrity, such as robbery, burglary, theft, thereby excluding convictions that may have been for acts of violence, such as battery, rape, or murder. Some persons in the field of jurisprudence have criticized this latter restriction as being somewhat unrealistic. They hold that a person who has been convicted of a violent type of rape may not be any more inclined to testify honestly than one convicted of a theft. In some jurisdictions, either by statute or court decisions, it has been held that if a prior conviction is presented in an effort to impeach a witness, that prior conviction must not be in the too remote past. What is considered to be "in the not too remote past" has not always been definitely established. Some courts have held that six years is not too remote, but have been silent as to a period beyond that. Some states by statute have excluded conviction that is beyond a period of ten years.

Proof of a conviction may be accomplished by merely asking the witness upon cross-examination whether he or she has ever been convicted. If the witness admits the conviction, no further proof need be given. However, if the witness denies the conviction, proof is established by producing a copy of the conviction from the court where the conviction took place. The conviction need not be in the state where the testimony takes place, but may be in any state or federal court.

The next problem is: How far may an attorney go into the details of the conviction for impeachment purposes? Certainly the more serious or aggravated kind of crime would have greater effect upon the credibility of the witness, but it is generally held that the proof of conviction is restricted to the nature of the charge, that is, whether it was robbery, burglary, forgery, or forceful rape; the date and place of conviction; and most jurisdictions permit some inquiry about the sentence received.

There is a definite difference of opinion about the effect of a pardon upon the impeachment rule. Some states hold that the pardon does not prevent use of the conviction, but that the witness may mention the pardon and thereby attempt to overcome the attack on his credibility. Other states hold that if a pardon and/or a certificate of rehabilitation has been granted, the conviction may not be used to impeach the witness.

It should be pointed out that the proof of a conviction is merely an attack upon the credibility of the witness. As in the other methods of impeachment, proof of a conviction does not mean that the jury does not, or should not, believe the witness. It is possible for a convicted person to testify truthfully. Proof of a conviction is merely one way to show possibility of doubt about the truthfulness of the witness or that the witness's character is such that he should not be believed.

BAD CONDUCT NOT RESULTING IN A CONVICTION. At common law, cross-examination permitted an inquiry to be made into the general personal life of the witness as a check on credibility. This inquiry included questions about associates as well as acts of misconduct. However, self-incrimination was not required, that is, the witness did not have to subject himself to prosecution. Most jurisdictions in this country do not permit this type of questioning. It is believed that the danger of unduly embarrassing the witness or the risk of creating unfair prejudice outweighs any advantage to be gained by such an inquiry. In addition, specific acts of misconduct are probably of little consequence unless they affect the witness's ability to testify truthfully. However, a few jurisdictions allow inquiry to be made into the character of a person even to the extent of questions about specific acts of misconduct. This is done in an effort to prove the witness of such base character that the sanctity of the oath to tell the truth is meaningless and that the witness probably cannot be believed. Some jurisdictions allow only a limited inquiry to be made and restrict the questions to conduct which may affect the witness's veracity. For example, questions pertaining to illicit sexual relations on the part of the witness would not be permitted, as they would not pertain to veracity. On the other hand, questions whether the witness had filed a false insurance claim would be allowed, as this would be a matter involving truthfulness.

In states in which the inquiry about misconduct is allowed, the witness may be asked about the misconduct, but if he denies it, no evidence may be presented to prove the acts of misconduct. There may be further cross-examination of the witness in an effort to bring the misconduct to light, but if this questioning is still unproductive, the inquiry ends. It should be stated that the witness must answer the question about misconduct even though the answer may be embarrassing. The witness may refuse to answer only when the answer would be self-incriminating.

BIAS, PREJUDICE, OR MOTIVE. One very effective way to devaluate the testimony of a witness is to show that the witness entertains feeling for or against one side or the other in the trial. For example, a defense witness may be a close relative of the defendant, for whom favorable bias would be natural. Yet, aside from pointing out the close relationship by questioning the witness, it may be most difficult to prove bias. On the other hand, a witness who entertains a feeling of hostility or prejudice toward one side or the other may have expressed hostility to someone in so many words or may have committed acts which manifested this hostility. If so, these words or acts may be proved either through the witness or through other witnesses who have heard the words or seen the acts. For example, a defense witness may have made hostile remarks to an officer during the arrest of the defendant or may have attempted to strike the officer. Although this hostility on the part of a defense witness would not necessarily result in untruthful testimony, there could well be a prejudice against the prosecution which would color the testimony. If a witness has made statements showing hostility toward the police, the victim, or society generally, the prosecuting attorney may be permitted to ask him about these statements. If the witness admits making them, he is given an opportunity to explain them if he so desires. If he denies making the statements, the prosecution may present witnesses in an effort to prove that the statements were uttered by the witness or that a hostile act was committed.

Defense attorneys often try to prove that an officer is prejudiced against or hostile toward the defendant. These efforts usually result from some casual remark made by the officer during the arrest of the defendant. The remark may have been made to the defendant, to a relative, or to another officer and overheard. For this reason officers should be most circumspect in their remarks to a defendant or to a defendant's associates.

The attack upon the credibility of a witness by proof of bias, prejudice, or interest is permitted because any of these feelings could cause a witness to color testimony in favor of one side or the other. It is only natural to be inclined to testify according to one's emotional involvements. In weighing the testimony of a witness, the jury is entitled to know anything that may influence the witness in testifying. Much of the emotional involvement of the witness is proved by the cross-examination, but it is not restricted to the cross-examination, as it may be presented through other witnesses.

PROOF OF PHYSICAL OR MENTAL WEAKNESS. The testimony of a witness may be attacked in an effort to prove mental deficiency or physical weakness. The attack is usually made by the cross-examination of the witness rather than through other proof. Lack of mental capacity does not necessarily imply mental instability. It may be that the witness was intoxicated at the time that the witness is alleged to have learned the facts about which he or she is testifying. If so, there may be some doubt about the witness's ability to correctly observe the facts that he or she is endeavoring to relate. If the witness is a child, an attack may be made upon the ground that the child did not understand thoroughly what was taking place at the time of the incident. This attack may be made even though the child was found to be a competent witness. The mental capabilities of a witness may be subject to attack on grounds of old age having caused the power of retention to weaken, or mental retardation having caused a lack of understanding. As stated, mental capacity is not always a criterion of competency, but it may have an effect upon credibility.

An attack may be made upon a physical weakness which would prevent the witness from properly observing, hearing, or relating, so that less weight may be given to the testimony by the jury.

SELF-IMPEACHMENT. All too frequently, a witness will devaluate his or her own testimony without any attack having been made on the witness. This may be the result of conduct on the stand, such as the witness's attitude or manner of speaking. It may be because of his inability to testify convincingly. It is entirely possible for a witness who is testifying honestly and truthfully to hesitate, repeat, or become confused to such a point that the jury believes the witness is actually fabricating a story. For this reason the officer should be thoroughly familiar with the facts of the case through reviewing reports before going on the witness stand.

LACK OF RELIGIOUS BELIEF. The question has arisen from time to time of whether a witness could be impeached because of having a particular religious belief or because of no religious belief. Various states have answered the question by court decisions or by statutes. Most states follow the rule set forth in the Pennsylvania statute which provides that "no witness shall be questioned, in any judicial proceeding, concerning his religious belief; nor shall any evidence be heard upon the subject, for the purpose of affecting either his competency or credibility." However, a few states still hold that the credibility of a witness can be affected by evidence of disbelief in the existence of a God.

■ Rehabilitation of Impeached Witness

A question arises: When the credibility of a witness has been attacked by the adversary, does the side producing the witness have to stand idly by and do nothing to restore the witness's credit in the eyes of the jury? All jurisdictions permit some effort to be made to rehabilitate the attacked witness. The extent to which this may be done differs among the courts. As already learned, evidence of the good character of a witness is not admissible before an attack on that character. Once an attack has been made by the opposing side, the side producing the witness may present witnesses who can attest to the good character of the impeached witness. These witnesses must know of the good reputation of the impeached witness for veracity in the community in which he or she resides or works. Usually, when efforts are made to rehabilitate a witness by proof of good reputation, it must be a good reputation for truth and honesty and not just proof of a good reputation generally. However, in those jurisdictions in which impeachment is permitted by proof of acts of misconduct not resulting in a conviction, evidence that the witness has the reputation of being a person of good character may be admissible. It is doubtful, though, that proof of specific acts of good conduct would be admitted, as such evidence would not of itself prove good character.

When a witness has been attacked upon the ground of a conviction, rehabilitating witnesses may be produced to prove that, irrespective of the conviction, the witness has a good reputation for veracity. It must be remembered that the mere fact that a person has been convicted of a crime does not mean the person cannot testify truthfully.

There is a division of opinion about the support which should be allowed in cases in which the witness has been impeached by allegations of prior inconsistent statements. Generally, it is held that prior consistent statements made by the witness may not be admitted to corroborate or support present testimony. If the witness is inclined to falsify, the mere repetition of previous statements does not make his present testimony any more true. It has been held that when there is an allegation that the witness is now fabricating a story for some recently developed reason, the fact that the witness made similar statements in the past may be admissible to overcome this alleged recent influence, motive, or bias.

When an attack has been made on a witness and an effort is made to rehabilitate the witness, it becomes the prerogative of the jury to determine how much weight should be given to the testimony. It is possible to overcome the attack entirely by the rehabilitation, or the rehabilitation may fail, or it may cause a reevaluation of the testimony. The main principle to be remembered is that the impeached witness is entitled to have his or her character reinstated if this is warranted. Of course, there are witnesses who are of such bad character that little can be done to rehabilitate them. The rehabilitating witnesses, as well as impeaching witnesses, are subject to impeachment.

■ Impeaching One's Own Witness

Frequently, the remark is heard that one cannot impeach one's own witness. Is such a statement true, and if so, to what extent is it true? What is meant by it? And who is "one's own witness"? The answers to these questions vary from one jurisdiction to another. At common law the rule was most specific: One could not impeach one's own witness. The reason behind this rule is somewhat obscure. It was undoubtedly based upon the theory that in the search for the truth in a trial proceeding, one would not produce a witness that would not testify truthfully. And so the character and reputation of a witness were considered to be good or were vouched for in a sense by the side producing the witness. Consequently, they could not be attacked later if the witness did not testify as expected.

A few states still adhere to the strict common-law prohibition against impeaching one's own witness. The majority of the states have relaxed the rule to a degree and some have become very liberal in this regard.

Before going into the various applications of the rule in this country, it may be well to consider who one's own witness is. Each side in a trial prepares a list of witnesses to be called to testify. Through the testimony of the prosecution's witnesses, the elements of the crime are established and efforts are made to prove beyond a reasonable doubt the guilt of the defendant. In most instances, these persons have been interviewed by the investigating officer and their stories have been made portions of the investigative report. It is logical to presume that these persons related facts when interviewed and that they will repeat them on the stand. They become witnesses for the prosecution. The defendant's attorney will also have witnesses for the defense, such as alibi witnesses or character witnesses, through whom an effort will be made to establish the innocence of the defendant or to cast doubt on his guilt. These are the defendant's own witnesses.

Generally then, the witness belongs to the side calling him or her, but exceptions to this rule may arise. It may become obvious after the side calling him asks a few preliminary questions that the witness is not going to produce the testimony anticipated; therefore, no further examination is made of that witness. The opposing side may desire to call this person to testify in its behalf. In these circumstances, the witness becomes the witness of the opposing side and no longer of the side by which originally called. The question now is: May this witness be impeached by the side originally calling? Even states adhering to the strict rule of not permitting impeachment of one's own witness allow impeachment in this instance.

REASONS FOR IMPEACHING ONE'S OWN WITNESS.   It is presumed that a witness will testify favorably toward the side that calls him or her, as one does not usually call a witness who is expected to testify unfavorably. Why, therefore, should one wish to impeach one's own witness? Attorneys frequently find that witnesses cannot be depended upon to give the testimony anticipated, particularly prosecution witnesses when a family matter is involved. For example, take a case of aggravated assault on a victim by a member of the family. Immediately after the assault, the witnesses, while under the emotional impact of the assault, will truthfully relate unhesitatingly what they saw happen, even though it is detrimental to the defendant member of the family. However, between the time the assault occurred and the time of the trial, anger against the defendant may have subsided, the victim's wounds healed, and all is forgiven. As a result, the witness called by the prosecution may be reluctant now to testify adversely against the defendant, and may completely reverse his story on the witness stand. In these circumstances, the prosecution is placed in a most unfavorable position if the testimony is allowed to stand uncontested. Yet if the strict rule against impeaching one's own witness is followed, nothing can be done by the prosecution to overcome the testimony.

A few jurisdictions adhere to a comparatively strict rule of not permitting the impeachment of one's own witness but allow some deviation from the rule. These jurisdictions hold that the adverse testimony of a witness may be ignored and other witnesses may be called to overcome the testimony of the adverse witness by proving entirely different facts from those related by the unfavorable witness. The philosophy behind this suggestion may be well taken, but from a practical application it is not too sound. In the prosecution of criminal cases, witnesses are not too plentiful at best, and there is seldom a free choice of witnesses. Thus the efforts to overcome the testimony of an adverse witness by other witnesses may not be possible.

For this reason, the courts in many states have relaxed the rule that prohibited the impeachment of one's own witness. But not all jurisdictions agree on the grounds on which one's own witness may be impeached. In the past it was generally held that one's own witness could be impeached only upon the ground that the witness had made prior statements inconsistent with his present testimony, but this rule is being relaxed in some jurisdictions.

Even though many states still permit one's own witness to be impeached by proof of prior inconsistent statements, the states do not agree on the approach to the problem or on the proof required.

Many states have permitted impeachment of one's own witness by merely showing that the witness had made prior statements inconsistent with his present testimony. But the same proper foundation must be laid in these instances as in the case of the impeachment of an adversary's witness. In other words, in most jurisdictions one's own witness must have his prior statements quoted to him and must be reminded of the time and place of the statements and of the persons present. The witness must be permitted an opportunity to explain the alleged inconsistency, if possible.

A few jurisdictions have adopted a very strict rule in permitting the impeachment of one's own witness by proof of prior inconsistent statements. These jurisdictions hold that the prior inconsistent statements must have been in writing and subscribed to by the witness, or the statements must have been made under oath or affirmation. The relaxation of the rule to this extent only is not of great benefit to the prosecution in a criminal case because seldom would such statements be available or in existence. In jurisdictions adhering to this rule, it would be advisable for officers to take signed statements from prospective witnesses when it is anticipated that they may change their story on the witness stand. Some jurisdictions will not permit impeachment of one's own witness unless it can be shown that the testimony given by the witness came as a complete surprise and was damaging to the side that called the witness. What is surprise and what may be damaging are not always easily determined. It has been held that mere disappointment in the testimony of a witness, or the fact that the witness failed to come up to expectations, is not enough to permit impeachment.

In some jurisdictions all prohibitions against impeaching one's own witness have been abolished. It is held that the credibility of a witness may be attacked or supported by any party, including the party calling the witness. Therefore one's own witness could be impeached by the same means as a witness called by the opposing side.

■ Impeachment of the Defendant in a Criminal Trial

If the defendant takes the witness stand in his or her own behalf, the defendant is treated the same as any other witness. The defendant may be cross-examined by the prosecuting attorney and may be impeached. There are some persons in the field of jurisprudence who think that the defendant should be impeached by the same means as any other witness, even by the proof of a prior conviction. Others think that there should be some limitation upon impeachment of the defendant by proof of prior conviction because of the prejudice that may be created.

PROOF OF PRIOR CONVICTION. As a general rule, the criminal record of a defendant, as well as proof of other crimes or acts of misconduct committed by the defendant, may not be brought out during the trial. The primary reason is that these matters have no relation to the case at hand. If the defendant is to be convicted, it must be upon facts pertinent to the specific charge on which the defendant is being tried. Past record or misdeeds would have no bearing upon whether or not the defendant had committed this particular act, unless they went to prove motive or knowledge, or were a part of the present crime for which the defendant had been charged (for further details see Chapter 9). Generally, the courts are very strict in prohibiting testimony that indicates a past criminal record or past misdeeds by the defendant because a criminal record may cause prejudice in the minds of the jurors against the defendant. The jury may tend to believe that if the defendant has committed other crimes, he must be guilty of the one with which charged. Thus the defendant may be convicted on a past record and not on the evidence presented in the case at hand. At times, an officer has inadvertently included in testimony admissions made by the defendant concerning other crimes, which has resulted in the officer's being severely chastised by the judge. In some instances, judges have gone so far as to declare a mistrial because of alleged damage to the defendant. Although the jury could be admonished not to allow the testimony to affect their judgment, it is impossible to erase the testimony from the minds of the jurors. Consequently, officers should be most circumspect in mentioning misdeeds of the defendant irrelevant to the issues of the case. Because of this possibility of prejudice, a few jurisdictions hold that if the defendant takes the stand, the defendant should be shielded from the possibility of impeachment by proof of a prior conviction. The courts in these jurisdictions believe that the defendant should be permitted to testify without fear of prejudice of being impeached by proof of a prior conviction. But in many jurisdictions the defendant may be impeached by proof of a prior conviction because it is believed the defendant should not be permitted to appear falsely to be crime-free.

Uniform Rule of Evidence 21 takes a slightly different approach, stating: "If the witness be the accused in a criminal proceeding, no evidence of his conviction of a crime shall be admissible for the sole purpose of impairing his credibility unless he has first introduced evidence admissible solely for the purpose of supporting his credibility." In other words, this model rule suggests that unless the defendant has tried to show himself to be a person of good character, he should be shielded from impeachment by the record of a prior conviction. Many states have not adopted the Uniform Rules of Evidence. Most of those that have still permit the defendant to be impeached by prior convictions, but in some states the conviction must be a felony and not just a misdemeanor.

It is pointed out that if the defendant was not represented by an attorney during the prior trial and the defendant did not intelligently waive the right to an attorney, in some jurisdictions that prior conviction may not be used to impeach the defendant.

Even though the statutes of some states provide that a witness may be impeached by proof of prior conviction of a felony, some courts have placed restrictions on these grounds for impeachment when a defendant takes the stand in his own defense. The courts have held that if the prior conviction was too remote in time and the defendant has been leading a lawful life in the meantime, that prior conviction may not be used for impeachment purposes. Other courts have held that unless the prior conviction had some connection with veracity, it is not admissible for impeachment purposes. In other words, the prior conviction must have had something to do with lack of honesty and/or truthfulness attributing to such crimes as robbery, burglary, fraud, deceit, or perjury, and not be for crimes of violence such as aggravated assault, rape, or even murder. This latter restriction is based on the premise that any disclosure of a prior conviction is so detrimental to the defendant it must be made with great caution and for sufficient reason. A mere prior conviction of a felony which does not indicate that the defendant cannot be believed may not be disclosed for impeachment purposes. It is further held in some jurisdictions that even though the prior conviction was one pertaining to honesty and/or truthfulness, the prior conviction may not be used for impeachment of the defendant if the prior conviction was for the same crime for which the defendant is now on trial because of the strong prejudicial effect of such a prior conviction. Even though a defendant had been previously convicted of robbery, if the defendant is now on trial on a robbery charge and takes the stand in his own defense, that prior robbery conviction could not be used for impeachment purposes.

However the courts of some states have criticized this restriction placed upon the prosecution in an attempt to impeach the defendant. The courts have stated that this restriction permits the defendant to create a false impression of his veracity. As was stated in one case, no witness, including the defendant, who elects to testify in his own behalf is entitled to a "false aura of veracity." The general rule is that felony convictions bearing upon veracity are admissible for impeachment purposes. Therefore a witness, including the defendant, may be asked if the witness has been convicted of a felony, and then it is permissible to ask the witness the nature of the crime. However, as was pointed out by the courts, there is little, if any, authority that requires the witness to be asked the nature of the crime. Under these circumstances, the courts have stated that if it is believed that a defendant witness may be unduly prejudiced by impeachment by a felony conviction, the prosecuting attorney should be permitted to ask the defendant if he had been convicted of a felony, but the prosecuting attorney should be prohibited from going into any further details. If the defendant felt that the jury might imagine a crime more damaging than the one for which he was convicted, the defendant at his election could clarify the nature of the crime during the cross-examination or during redirect examination.

PRIOR INCONSISTENT STATEMENTS. Almost all jurisdictions allow impeachment of the defendant, as of other witnesses, by proof that he or she has made prior statements inconsistent with his present testimony. One of the effective ways to prove that the defendant has made prior inconsistent statements is the introduction of a signed confession given by the defendant or other proof of confession, such as a tape recording. The reader may wonder why these would be used for impeachment purposes and not during the presentation of the prosecution's case. There are times when the prosecuting attorney may not desire to use a confession or an admission because of numerous inaccuracies or falsehoods but may find them most beneficial for impeachment purposes. However, before a statement may be used for impeachment purposes, the prosecution must be in a position to prove that the confession meets the test for trustworthiness. It was implied by the United States Supreme Court in the case entitled *Miranda v. Arizona*, 384 U.S. 436 (1966), that unless a confession met all the rules handed down in that case, the confession was not admissible for any purpose, including impeachment. (For further discussion of the Miranda case see Chapter 7.) But in the case entitled *Harris v. New York*, 401 U.S. 222 (1971), the United States Supreme Court gave a different interpretation to the use of statements of a defendant when the Miranda warnings had not been given. The Court in the Harris case stated:

> Some comments in the Miranda opinion can indeed be read as indicating a bar to use of an uncounseled statement for any purpose, but discussion of that issue was not at all necessary to the Court's holding and cannot be regarded as controlling. Miranda barred the prosecution from making its case with statements of an

accused made while in custody prior to having or effectively waiving counsel. It does not follow from Miranda that evidence inadmissible against an accused in the prosecution's case in chief is barred for all purposes, provided of course that the trustworthiness of the evidence satisfies legal standards. . . .

It is one thing to say that the Government cannot make an affirmative use of evidence unlawfully obtained. It is quite another to say that the defendant can turn the illegal method by which evidence in the Government's possession was obtained to his own advantage, and provide himself with a shield against contradiction of his untruths. Such an extension of the Weeks doctrine would be a perversion of the Fourth Amendment. [See Chapter 8 for a full discussion of the case entitled *Weeks v. United States.*] . . .

[T]here is hardly justification for letting the defendant affirmatively resort to perjurious testimony in reliance on the Government's disability to challenge his credibility. . . .

Every criminal defendant is privileged to testify in his own defense, or to refuse to do so. But that privilege cannot be construed to include the right to commit perjury. . . . Having voluntarily taken the stand, petitioner was under an obligation to speak truthfully and accurately, and the prosecution here did no more than utilize the traditional truth-testing devices of the adversary process. . . .

Had inconsistent statements been made by the accused to some third person, it could hardly be contended that the conflict could not be laid before the jury by way of cross-examination and impeachment.

The shield provided by Miranda cannot be perverted into a license to use perjury by way of a defense, free from the risk of confrontation with prior inconsistent utterances. We hold, therefore, that petitioner's credibility was appropriately impeached by use of his earlier conflicting statements.

Irrespective of the Harris decision, the courts of a few states will not permit a confession to be used for impeachment purposes if the Miranda decision was not completely adhered to. It should be pointed out that state courts may not make United States Supreme Court restrictions more liberal than set forth in a United States Supreme Court decision, but the state courts may set forth more restrictive guidelines under their own police powers as provided by the Ninth and Tenth Amendments to the United States Constitution.

■ Illegally Obtained Evidence Usable for Impeachment

Mapp v. Ohio, 367 U.S. 643 (1961), established that illegally obtained evidence was not admissible in state courts to convict one of a crime. But this decision did not necessarily make illegally obtained evidence inadmissible for impeachment purposes. This fact was emphasized in the case of *Walder v. United States,* 347 U.S. 62 (1954), in which the United States Supreme Court held that illegally obtained narcotics could be used to impeach the testimony of the defendant. Although this case preceded the Mapp case, there was a rule excluding illegally obtained evidence as it related to federal cases long before the Mapp decision was handed down. In the Walder case the Court stated: "Although the Government cannot make an affirmative use of evidence unlawfully obtained, there is no justification for letting the defendant affirmatively resort to perjurious testimony in reliance on the Government's disability to challenge his credibility."

Again as in the case of the improperly obtained confession, state courts could restrict the use of improperly obtained evidence for impeachment purposes in spite of the Walder decision.

SELF-INCRIMINATION

As has previously been stated, when a person receives a subpoena to be a witness, he or she must obey the order to appear, willing or not. The witness is also required to answer truthfully the questions permitted by the judge to be asked, irrespective of whom the answers may hurt. There is one exception to this: The witness has the right to refuse to answer any question which will be self-incriminating.

Because of the extensive coverage of trials and hearings by the press and the communication of this coverage to the public through such media as newspapers, radio, and television, the privilege against self-incrimination comes as no surprise to the reader, as there is no more frequently invoked constitutional guarantee than this one. Yet confusion still reigns in the minds of many about just what the term "self-incrimination" comprises. For a better understanding of the discussion on the privilege against self-incrimination, it may be well to explain just what it means. This privilege permits a witness to refuse to answer any question if the answer would tend to show that he or she is guilty of a crime and would subject him to the danger of prosecution and conviction. He may refuse even though his answer may not be a complete admission of guilt. He may refuse if the answer merely connects him with a crime or would be a source through which evidence could be obtained to link him with a crime.

At times many citizens have become distraught when members of hoodlum gangs and members of subversive organizations have hidden behind this privilege seemingly to the detriment of society. They believe that the privilege has been extended far beyond its original intent. A historical review of the development of the privilege may therefore be in order.

As surprising as it may seem, the privilege was not included in the better-known English documents written to protect certain rights. It was not contained in the Magna Charta of A.D. 1215 or the English Bill of Rights of 1689, but efforts to prevent self-incrimination were prevalent in England as well as in the American colonies during the late 1600s and early 1700s. The American colonists were particularly disturbed by continually being brought before representatives of the Crown and extensively questioned about seditious statements and acts. And so it is little wonder that they included in our federal Constitution a guarantee against self-incrimination. In 1789, amendments to the Constitution were proposed setting forth certain rights guaranteed to the people of the United States. Included in the Fifth Amendment to the Constitution is, among other guarantees, the privilege against self-incrimination. This amendment states, "Nor shall [one] be compelled in any criminal case to be a witness against himself." Although this guarantee was originally effective only in federal proceedings, it has been included in the constitutions of all the states except Iowa and New Jersey. In these two states the same results have been achieved by other means—in Iowa by a due-process clause of its constitution, and in New Jersey by a statute. Irrespective of these constitutional provisions and state statutes, the Supreme Court of the United States has now held that the guarantee of the Fifth Amendment to the United States Constitution is applicable to the states through the due-process clause of the Fourteenth Amendment [see *Malloy v. Hogan*, 378 U.S. 1 (1964), and *Griffin v. California*, 380 U.S. 609 (1965)].

Some think that this privilege has interfered with our suppression of crime and subversion; that it protects the guilty, and not the innocent; and that it is built upon sentimentality, and not upon the basic needs of a good society. Even Justice Cardozo, in the case of *Palko v. Connecticut*, 302 U.S. 319 (1937), stated, "Today as in the past there are students of our penal system who look upon immunity [privilege against self-incrimination] as a mischief rather than a benefit, and who would limit its scope, or destroy it altogether. No doubt there would remain the need to give protection against torture, physical or mental . . . [but] justice, however, would not perish if the accused were subject to a duty to respond to orderly inquiry."

Irrespective of these thoughts, there are a number of reasons why the rule exists and will undoubtedly continue to be a part of our judicial procedure. One reason is that there is already in many instances a great reluctance on the part of witnesses to testify. If they were subjected to possible incrimination, this reluctance would be magnified. Also if the rule were otherwise, it would create a temptation to falsify and it would be a most difficult rule to enforce. Perhaps the basic reason for the rule in this country is that it is a safeguard of democracy, and so we find the courts jealously guarding the privilege against self-incrimination.

The privilege extends not only to a witness in a criminal trial, but to any kind of trial or official hearing. It is applicable to the defendant in a criminal trial as well as to witnesses. This is why the courts so closely scrutinize the admissibility of confessions and admissions; details will be discussed in Chapter 7 entitled "Confessions and Admissions."

■ Claiming the Privilege against Self-Incrimination

How far a witness may go in claiming the privilege against self-incrimination has created no end of problems. The witness is not the sole judge whether he or she may claim the privilege. Basically the decision is left to the discretion of the trial judge. If the question asked is obviously incriminating, the witness may refuse to answer, a refusal that will be upheld by the judge. If the question asked does not appear to be one which would incriminate the witness, the witness may still claim the privilege of not answering the question because he thinks that the answer would incriminate him. In order to determine whether the witness should be permitted to invoke this privilege (or "hide behind the Fifth," to use the vernacular), the judge may have to make some inquiry of the witness in an effort to determine why the witness thinks the answer would be incriminating. The weight of authority is that the witness may be compelled to answer a question when it is perfectly clear that it would not incriminate him even though he may think that it would. If the witness absolutely refuses to answer the question, he may be held in contempt of court. In making a determination whether a question is such that the answer may incriminate the witness, the judge will take into account the immediate setting of the testimony, in the light of other testimony, and what the likelihood of possible prosecution of the witness may be. In order to meet the test of possible incrimination, the judge must endeavor to determine whether there is any possibility that the witness has committed a crime and that the answer might in some way link the witness to that crime. The witness may not refuse to answer a question because he anticipates that the next question will be one which would incriminate him. The fact that the answer will incriminate someone else is not ground for refusal to answer the question. It has also been held that if the danger of prosecution is barred for some reason, such as the guarantee against double jeopardy, or by the statute of limitations, or by a grant of immunity, the witness may not claim the privilege. The mere fact that the answer to a question will embarrass or degrade the witness is not sufficient ground for refusing to answer.

Some people are concerned over the fact that a witness may not be aware of his right to refuse to answer a question which may be incriminating. It is difficult to imagine a person's being ignorant of this privilege in view of the wide publicity given to various congressional hearings and judicial proceedings in which it is invoked continuously by recalcitrant witnesses. For the protection of those who are not informed about this privilege, however, the trial judge is on the alert for this situation and is there for the protection of all. The judge will assume the responsibility for enlightening the witness in the event he is unaware of the privilege; therefore this worry seems to be a rather needless one.

Likewise, some people are very disturbed over the fact that if a defense witness claims the privilege against self-incrimination, the claim will automatically reflect on the defendant. If a witness invokes the privilege, the defense attorney can request the judge to instruct the jury to disregard the invocation of the privilege by the witness as being prejudicial to the defendant. But if the jury, being composed of ordinary, prudent persons, still entertains a prejudice, there is little that can be done about it. It is impossible to control everything that may place a defendant who has been charged with the commission of a crime in an unfavorable light.

■ Waiver of Privilege against Self-Incrimination

A witness may waive his or her privilege against self-incrimination. In other words, the witness may testify concerning matters that may incriminate him if the witness so chooses. This is his right, and his alone. The defendant may not object to such a waiver, or claim the privilege for the witness under the circumstances. Also, if the privilege is waived, it is waived for the entire matter. The witness may not testify about some of the facts which may benefit the defendant and then claim the privilege for those things which may be unfavorable to him during cross-examination.

■ Witness's Immunity against Prosecution

Many times in society's fight against crime and subversion, there is need to obtain from a witness facts of which the witness has knowledge; yet if the witness were to relate these facts, the witness might subject himself or herself to prosecution. The witness may, consequently, claim the privilege against self-incrimination, thereby depriving society of its protection against the criminal or subversive element. To overcome this difficulty, rules have been developed under which a witness may be granted immunity against prosecution if the witness furnishes facts which might otherwise incriminate him. When afforded this immunity, the witness can be compelled to answer questions; if the witness refuses to answer, the witness may be held in contempt of court.

The development of the immunity laws did not come easily or overnight. Many problems had to be solved. The major question was whether if one jurisdiction granted immunity against prosecution, the witness could still be prosecuted in another jurisdiction. For example, if a witness were given immunity by the federal government, could the witness still be prosecuted in a state court for a crime which the witness admitted to in the federal court? Or if state immunity were granted, could the witness be prosecuted by the federal government or in another state? Another question was: If a witness were given immunity against prosecution based on his testimony, would this immunity carry over to evidence that might be discovered if the discovery were made from the facts introduced through the testimony? Only through progressive changes in statutes and court interpretations have these problems been solved.

It has been decided by the Supreme Court that Congress has the authority to make laws granting immunity to witnesses against prosecution both by the federal and state governments [see *Ullman v. United States,* 350 U.S. 422 (1956)], and in *Murphy v. Waterfront Comm'n,* 378 U.S. 52 (1964), it was decided that if a witness is granted immunity against self-incrimination, neither his testimony nor any "fruits" therefrom may be used against him in any court. It appears from the wording of this case that if a witness is granted immunity in one jurisdiction and is compelled to testify, all other jurisdictions, whether state or federal, are barred from utilizing that testimony or the fruits therefrom against that witness. This viewpoint is based more upon the "exclusionary rule" than upon the power of any jurisdiction to grant an all-exclusive immunity. The courts have taken the approach that when a witness is granted immunity and is compelled to testify, the testimony is in effect evidence obtained illegally against the witness himself and as such any incriminating statements are not admissible against him. But whatever the basis may be for barring the use of the testimony, the results are the same, that is, total immunity.

PROCEDURE IN GRANTING IMMUNITY. Jurisdictions vary somewhat in the procedure whereby a witness is granted immunity against self-incrimination. In some states the witness is promised immunity from the time the person receives the subpoena to appear as a witness. In other states the witness is not afforded immunity until the witness claims the privilege against self-incrimination. If, at that point, the prosecuting attorney believes that the testimony warrants granting the witness immunity, the prosecuting attorney will so advise the witness and the judge. Then the witness will be ordered by the judge to answer the questions asked. There are some who think that the latter procedure is the better. This belief is based on the fact that the witness may always waive the privilege against self-incrimination and testify as he wishes; also, sometimes there may be danger in granting a witness wholesale immunity when testifying.

Although immunity is granted to a witness under either procedure, this does not prevent the witness from being prosecuted for perjury if the witness should intentionally furnish false information while testifying. The witness may also be held in contempt of court and ordered to jail if the witness is granted immunity and refuses thereafter to answer the questions asked.

The immunity afforded the witness is against prosecution only, and the witness may not refuse to testify even though he may suffer embarrassment, lose his job, or cause his life or that of his family to be endangered (see *Ullman v. United States*). There have been times when members of hoodlum gangs have preferred to be placed in jail for contempt of court rather than break the "hoodlum code of ethics" or chance being "done away with" by furnishing information about criminal activities. How long a witness may be held in jail for refusing to testify is not clear, but presumably the witness can be detained until he agrees to testify. In one case a witness was held several months [see *In re Grand Jury Investigation of Sam Giancana*, 352 F.2d 921 (1965)]. As was stated in the Giancana case, the imprisonment of the witness for contempt of court in refusing to testify is not a form of punishment but a way of coercing the witness to furnish the evidence needed for the best interest of society.

■ Defendant's Privilege against Self-Incrimination

Although a person can be compelled to be a witness, this compulsion does not apply to the defendant in a criminal trial. The defendant cannot be compelled to take the witness stand. There was a time at common law, as we have already learned, when the defendant could not take the stand even when wishing to do so. Today the defendant may take the stand in his own defense if he chooses, but there is no requirement that the defendant must, even though he may be in the best position to furnish the information needed in arriving at the truth. The defendant has the right to remain completely silent. In a few jurisdictions it was formerly held that if the defendant did not take the stand in his own defense, the failure to explain or to deny by his testimony any facts or evidence against the defendant could be commented upon by the prosecuting attorney and/or the judge. But the United States Supreme Court held in the case of *Griffin v. California,* 380 U.S. 609 (1965), that permitting the prosecuting attorney and/or the judge to comment upon the defendant's failure to take the witness stand in his own defense was indirectly forcing the defendant to be a witness against himself in violation of the Fifth Amendment guarantee against self-incrimination.

■ What Is Not Self-Incrimination

The privilege against self-incrimination relates primarily to "testimonial compulsion." The courts have generally held that if the defendant is required to perform certain physical acts, or to give physical evidence, they are not considered to be self-incrimination. This viewpoint was reaffirmed by the Supreme Court in *Schmerber v. California*, 384 U.S. 757 (1966). In writing the majority opinion in that case, Justice Clark stated that the withdrawal of blood by a physician to determine whether the accused was intoxicated did not violate the Fifth Amendment guarantee against self-incrimination, nor was there any "protection against compulsion to submit to fingerprinting, photographing, or measurements, to write, or speak for identification, to appear in court, to stand, to assume a stance, to walk, or to make a particular gesture. . . . Compulsion which makes a suspect, or an accused, the source of 'real or physical evidence' does not violate it [self-incrimination guarantee]." (For further discussion of the Schmerber decision see Chapter 8.)

SUMMARY

The credibility of a witness is entirely dependent upon how much a jury believes the witness while testifying—how much weight the testimony carries with a jury. Although a witness swears or affirms to tell the truth while on the stand, a number of factors may cause the witness not to testify truthfully.

If there is an indication that the witness is not testifying truthfully, efforts may be made to impeach the witness. Impeachment is any attack made upon the credibility of the witness; it is any effort made to devaluate the testimony. This attack upon the credibility may be made in a number of ways, and the methods are comparably uniform throughout the United States. A witness may be impeached by showing that

1. The witness has made prior inconsistent statements.
2. The witness's reputation for truth, honesty, and integrity is bad.
3. The witness is biased or prejudiced for some reason.
4. The witness's ability to observe, retain, and relate is defective.

One of the primary purposes of cross-examination of a witness is impeachment. A witness may devaluate his testimony by his own conduct while on the stand; the demeanor of the witness may create doubt in the mind of the jury about his truthfulness.

Although an effort may be made to impeach a witness by the adversary, the side producing the witness may present evidence to rehabilitate him. Although at common law one could not impeach one's own witness, this restriction has been abolished in most of the states in this country. Generally speaking, one's own witness is the witness of the side which originally called the witness to testify. It may be necessary to impeach one's own witness because of a change in his attitude or statements between the time of the crime and the trial. At common law a defendant was not a competent witness, but this rule has also been abolished in this country, and the defendant may testify in his own behalf if he so desires. If the defendant does become a witness, the defendant may be impeached.

A person properly subpoenaed must appear as a witness and must answer the questions asked him unless the answers are incriminating. Answers which would subject the witness to punishment or forfeiture are considered incriminating. A witness may be granted immunity against self-incrimination. In this event the witness must answer the questions asked or the witness may be held in contempt of court. A defendant in a criminal trial cannot be compelled to be a witness. In fact, the defendant does not have to take the witness stand in his own behalf, although it may appear to be advantageous for him or her to do so. The defendant's failure to take the stand may not be commented upon by the prosecution. Self-incrimination refers to compulsion to testify and not to the performance of certain physical acts.

QUESTIONS FOR REVIEW

1. What is meant by the credibility of a witness?
2. What is meant by impeachment of a witness?
3. Name the methods by which a witness may be impeached.
4. Explain what foundation must be laid in most jurisdictions in order to impeach a witness by prior inconsistent statements.
5. Name some of the things that may cause a witness to be biased or prejudiced that would affect his or her trustworthiness.
6. What are some of the things that may cause a witness not to be able to observe, retain, and/or relate correctly?
7. How do jurisdictions differ in the impeaching of a witness by former convictions?
8. What is meant by the term "self-incrimination"?
9. What effect does immunity against self-incrimination have?
10. What is considered not to be self-incrimination?

LOCAL RULES

As there is some variation in the rules of evidence among jurisdictions, the answers to the following questions should be obtained from the local prosecuting attorney as suggested in Chapter 1.

1. May a witness be impeached by proof of the conviction of a crime? If so, what are the restrictions, i.e., misdemeanor and felony, or felony only?
2. May a witness be impeached by proof of acts of misconduct not amounting to a conviction for a crime?

3. If the witness has received a pardon for the conviction, may he or she still be impeached?

4. Must a foundation be laid before a witness may be impeached by proof of prior inconsistent statements, i.e., must the witness be reminded of the time, place, and persons present?

5. If a witness may be impeached by proof of a crime, may the witness be asked about the sentence imposed?

6. May the defendant in a criminal trial be impeached by proof of a conviction of a crime?

7. May one's own witness be impeached? If so, what are the restrictions, if any?

The Hearsay Rule – Its Exceptions

6

Even a person with the most limited knowledge of judicial procedure is aware of the rule that, generally, hearsay evidence is not admissible in a trial proceeding. However, this has not always been true. There was a time when a person could be convicted of a crime merely upon the presentation of rumors about him. Although the necessity of a rule against the admission of hearsay evidence was a concern of judges for many centuries, it was not until the middle of the seventeenth century that courts began to take a really dim view of such evidence. In the early 1700s the rule against the presentation of hearsay evidence, as it is known today, became a reality.

A number of reasons could be cited for the rule against the admissibility of hearsay evidence, but perhaps the most cogent is that determination of the truthfulness of hearsay is not easy. As we have previously learned, one of the greatest guarantees of the trustworthiness of a witness is a thorough cross-examination. If the declarant of a statement is not available for cross-examination, this guarantee is denied. From the standpoint of the defendant in a criminal case there is a much more practical reason for the rule, and that is his right "to be confronted with the witnesses against him," a right guaranteed in the Sixth Amendment to the Constitution of the United States. A similar provision is included in the constitutions or the statutes of the various states. This guarantee of confrontation has been included as one of the rights of an accused for three reasons:

1. It affords the accused the opportunity of cross-examination.

2. It is supposedly more difficult for a witness to falsify when in the presence of the accused.

3. The judge and the jury may observe the demeanor of the testifying witness and so be in a better position to determine the weight to be given to the testimony.

These reasons have all been listed as sufficient to exclude hearsay evidence and a fourth reason might be cited: The hearsay statement was not made under oath, so that at the time it was made, there was no legal pressure to ensure a truthful statement.

DEFINITION, HISTORY, AND EXCEPTIONS

To give a clear and concise definition of hearsay is not easy. To define it in a simple manner, we might call it a "rumor." It has been referred to as "secondhand information." It is information that has been told to a witness by someone else. If admissible, it would be a statement made by a witness on the stand which was told to him or her by someone outside of court. The legal definition of hearsay, like that of reasonable doubt, becomes wordy and confusing, but the legal definition in Uniform Rule of Evidence 63 is being quoted in order that the reader may appreciate the difficulties so often encountered in giving workable definitions of legal terms. Rule 63 defines hearsay as "evidence of a statement which is made other than by a witness while testifying at a hearing offered to prove the truth of a matter."

Hearsay need not necessarily be false; in fact, in a great many instances it is a true statement, but it is the establishment of the truthfulness of the hearsay which becomes the problem, and because of this problem it is generally excluded from evidence. Let us review some of the efforts which are made to have only true statements presented in evidence. In trying to accomplish this, (1) there must be witnesses who are competent, that is, witnesses who have the ability to perceive, retain, and relate truthfully; (2) before taking the stand a witness must swear or affirm to tell the truth; and (3) there is the right of cross-examination to assist in determining the truthfulness of the statements made. In addition, while testifying, the demeanor of the witness can be studied to aid in deciding whether the witness is telling the truth. When a statement is made by one outside a court proceeding, none of these guarantees of trustworthiness and accuracy are available. To cite an example to illustrate the problems involved in determining the truthfulness of hearsay: Assume that a defendant has been charged with bank robbery, and a witness takes the stand and testifies that a neighbor told the witness that the defendant robbed a bank. In this case the witness has no personal knowledge about the acts of the defendant, knowing only what the neighbor said. In other words, the information that the defendant robbed a bank is strictly hearsay. Even though the witness is telling the truth about what the neighbor said, the accuracy of the facts is dependent upon the neighbor, who is not in court. It is possible that the information given by the neighbor is true, but it may not be. It is conceivable that the neighbor may have obtained the information he repeated from another person, so that the truthfulness of the statement is now dependent upon a third individual. Up to this point we have not even considered who the neighbor is, not that it really matters. But the neighbor, if called to testify, may not even be a competent witness for some reason, perhaps being a child of tender years or a senile person, without the ability to perceive the situation correctly, or being of bad reputation for telling the truth. Another danger in admitting hearsay evidence is that the witness may not be accurately relating what was heard; yet since the original declarant is not present to correct any inaccuracies, the hearsay would stand as related. Thus it can readily be seen that hearsay can be dangerous and may give little assistance to the jury in its search for the truth and is therefore objectionable. Since the usual safeguards for trustworthiness are lacking in hearsay evidence, the rule excluding it was developed.

Although hearsay is not usually admissible in a judicial proceeding, certain exceptions to this rule have been established through necessity. This necessity usually results because the original declarant is not available to testify for some reason, and the information is such that in the best interest of justice it should be introduced in order that the facts of the case may be determined. If the information is to be forthcoming, it must be brought to the trial through the lips of someone other than the original declarant. When exceptions to the hearsay rule are admitted in evidence, a unique method of meeting the test of trustworthiness has been developed for each exception, a method which acts as a substitute for the other established safeguards, such as the oath and the right of cross-examination.

To reiterate, in order to introduce hearsay into evidence as one of the exceptions to the rule, three requirements must be met:

1. Generally, the original declarant must be unavailable to testify.
2. The declaration must shed some light on the establishment of the facts of the case and the information cannot be presented through any other source.
3. There must be some test of the trustworthiness of the statement in lieu of the oath and the right of cross-examination.

Although many exceptions to the hearsay rule have been developed through the years, only those frequently encountered in criminal matters will be considered for more detailed discussion. Those included are (1) dying declarations, (2) spontaneous declarations, (3) former testimony,

(4) business records, (5) pedigree, (6) past memory recorded, (7) confessions, and (8) admissions.

There is no particular significance in the order in which these exceptions will be discussed, but in view of the changes that have taken place as a result of Supreme Court decisions and the problems involved in the admissibility of confessions and admissions, one entire chapter will be devoted to these exceptions to the hearsay rule.

DYING DECLARATIONS

A dying declaration as an exception to the hearsay rule is the most restricted of all in its admissibility. Most jurisdictions limit the introduction of dying declarations to homicide cases. Dying declarations have been legally defined as that "evidence which is the act or declaration of a person, made under a sense of impending death, respecting the cause of his death." States adhering to the strict rule of admissibility of dying declarations permit the declarations to be introduced only in those trials in which the defendant is charged with the murder of the declarant, and the statements which are admitted must be confined to those which pertain to the circumstances surrounding the injuries received by the victim-declarant and which ultimately brought about his or her death. Dying declarations were developed as an exception to the hearsay rule because of the extreme necessity of getting the facts before the jury. Many cases arose in which the killer and the victim were the only ones present at the time that the assault took place, and so only they knew what happened. It was thought that if after the assault the victim should live long enough to make some declaration concerning his injuries, the declaration should be introduced in evidence at the trial against the slayer; otherwise the slayer might go free to prey upon others, and justice would not be done. It is this necessity that may account for the strict limitation in the use of dying declarations in the majority of jurisdictions. There is a trend toward a relaxation of the rule of confining the admissibility of dying declarations to homicide cases only.

■ Test for Trustworthiness

Regardless of any changes that may be taking place in the introduction of dying declarations, one requirement is uniformly demanded by the courts: The test for trustworthiness must be rigidly met. As was mentioned in the beginning of the discussion on the admissibility of exceptions to the hearsay rule, each must meet some test for trustworthiness. Dying declarations have a unique test, which is that the declaration must have been uttered at a time when the declarant had given up all hope of recovery and thought that death was near at hand. This requirement is based upon the premise that a person under the fear of impending death is in a mental state that will prevent falsifying. This exception to the hearsay rule originated at a time when religion had a dominant influence upon the courts. It was considered that anyone under a sense of impending death and about to meet the Maker would be afraid to tell a falsehood and that this mental state was equal to the solemnity of the oath. Although today religion plays a much lesser role in the lives of many, the courts still recognize this exception on the theory that the awful realization of impending death and the uncertainty of the hereafter creates a most solemn occasion when one would not be in the frame of mind to fabricate a story.

The major problem created by this exception is the determination of the state of mind of the declarant at the time of making the statements. In other words, were the injuries of such severity that the declarant was under the impression that death was imminent as a result of them? This does not mean that the declarant must be in a final death struggle. The declarant does not have to say in so many words, "I know that I am going to die." Belief in the imminence of death may be shown by the declarant's requesting the final rites of the church, by concern that the family be properly cared for, or by the expression of a desire to see the family once more.

It should be emphasized that the belief of the declarant is essential to the admissibility of the declarations. It may be perfectly obvious to all present that the declarant has no chance of survival. The declarant may have even been told by the doctor that death is near, but unless the declarant is convinced that it is, the test of trustworthiness is not met. It is the solemnity of impending death that supposedly places the declarant in a frame of mind to say only what is true.

It has been held that if there is any lingering hope of recovery, declarations of the injured person are not admissible as the declarations do not meet the test for trustworthiness. In one case an injured man stated: "I believe that I am very near death and that I may not recover." The declarations made by this person concerning his injuries were held to be inadmissible because of the lingering belief of recovery. However, in another case in which a husband and wife were both injured by the same assailant, their statements were held to be admissible. In that case the husband stated: "We are dying, help us," and he then gave information concerning the identity of the assailant. While on the way to the hospital in an ambulance, the wife stated: "Please hurry, I am dying." She then gave information concerning the identity of the assailant. The declaration of both the husband and wife were held to be admissible as dying declarations. So the demarcation between what is a lingering hope of recovery and the complete abandonment of recovery seems most finely drawn.

It is not necessary that the declarant die immediately after making declarations for them to be introduced in evidence. There is no specified time after making the declarations within which the declarant must die for them to be admitted. Neither is there a prescribed time after the assault took place that the declaration must be made. It is neither the time of death nor the time when the declaration was made that is of importance, but the frame of mind of the declarant at the time the declarations were made. In fact, after making a declaration under the thoughts of impending death, the condition of the declarant may improve, and the declarant may thereafter entertain hope of recovery. But so long as at the time the declarations were made the declarant was without hope of recovery, the test of trustworthiness is met. Of course, the declarant must thereafter die. Otherwise there could be no charge of homicide, so the problem would not even arise. In those jurisdictions in which the rule has been relaxed to allow dying declarations to be admitted in any judicial proceeding, the declarant must also have died; otherwise he would be available to testify.

■ Strict Rule—Homicide Cases —Declaration of Victim Only

The strict rule on the admissibility of dying declarations holds that the declarations may be admitted only in homicide cases, and in addition, the declarations admitted must be those of the victim whom the defendant is charged with slaying.

The declarations may not be uttered by someone other than the victim. Even though a dying declaration is made by another who may have also been involved in the altercation or who may have witnessed it, the declaration is not admissible. For example, a mother may enter a room and see her daughter being beaten to death, and as a result the mother may suffer a heart attack. The mother may know that she is dying, and with this knowledge she may tell others who murdered her daughter; but this statement may not be introduced in evidence against the slayer of the daughter, because it was that of a witness of the crime and not the victim.

Many writers on evidence think that this is a senseless restriction. But those who argue in favor of the limited use of the dying declaration do so upon the ground that the introduction of any hearsay evidence is dangerous, and therefore the strict-admissibility rule is in the best interests of justice, particularly in cases in which the death penalty may be imposed. They further assert that only because of the extreme necessity involved are the dying declarations even of the victim considered admissible.

As stated, there has been some relaxation of the strict rule on admissibility of dying declarations in some jurisdictions. Statutes have been passed in some states permitting the introduction of dying declarations not only in homicide cases but also in civil matters, such as wrongful death suits where the cause of death of the declarant is in question. A few other states have materially relaxed the rule on admissibility of dying declarations and have followed the provisions of the Uniform Rules of Evidence. Rule 63 (subsection 5) of these Rules provides, briefly, that a statement made voluntarily when the declarant was under a belief of impending death with no hope of recovery is admissible as an exception to the hearsay rule. This rule abolishes all restrictions on admissibility as long as the statement meets the test of trustworthiness.

Returning to the example of the mother who saw her daughter being beaten to death, the statement of the mother concerning the identity of the slayer, while under the belief of impending death from a heart attack, would presumably be admissible under this rule during the trial of the accused for the murder of the daughter. The mother in this case is only a witness and not the victim. The mother's dying declaration is admissible even though she was only a witness to the slaying and not the victim.

DYING DECLARATION MUST PERTAIN TO THE CAUSE OF DEATH. For a dying declaration to be admissible under the strict policy of admissibility, it must not only be made by the victim of the assault, but the subject matter of the declaration must be confined to facts about the injuries which ultimately caused the death. The statements may include things which took place just prior to the actual assault as well as those which happened closely enough thereafter to be considered as an integral part of the event. A recital of past happenings or threats on the part of the assailant would not be admissible, unless they assisted in the identification of the assailant. Dying declarations may include not only the facts of how the injuries were received or inflicted, but information which identifies the assailant, as this, in a sense, also pertains to the cause of death. The declarant does not have to identify the assailant by name, but any descriptive data which assist in the identification may be admitted. For example, a victim of a fatal stabbing may make a statement that while walking in the park, she was grabbed by a man with a beard and long hair who was wearing a red shirt, and when she screamed, he stabbed her. All this statement would be admissible if it were made by the declarant under a sense of impending death because all the statement is an integral part of the event. Where she was at the time that the injury was inflicted, the act of grabbing, and the scream followed by the stabbing are all facts surrounding the injury from which the declarant died. The description of the assailant is a part of the event and pertains to identification.

■ Form of the Dying Declaration

There is no prescribed form which a dying declaration must follow to be admissible. It may be an oral or a written statement, or it may be made by a sign or a nod of the head. The declaration may come as a voluntary statement on the part of the victim-declarant made at a time that all hope of life had been abandoned. It may be a very simple statement, such as, "John shot me." The declaration may be the spoken answer to a question asked of the victim, or it may be that the victim, asked whether he knows who injured him, merely nods his head. The next question may be one that would identify the assailant, such as, "Was it John?" to which the victim again would nod. It is also possible that the victim-declarant may be asked to point to the person who assaulted him, and the victim may merely indicate the assailant by the act of pointing. When a declaration is an act and not an actual statement made by the victim, it may become necessary to prove that the victim's mental condition was not perceptibly affected or impaired by the injuries inflicted. The main point to be remembered is that once it is established that the declarant has abandoned all hope of recovery, utterances made concerning his injuries are admissible whether the statements are volunteered by the victim or instigated by another.

In the introduction of dying declarations at a trial it is logical to assume that the same witness who proved that the declarant was under the knowledge of impending death at the time the declarations were uttered would also present the declarations concerning the cause of death, but the frame of mind of the declarant and the statements pertaining to the injuries do not have to be presented by the same witness for the declarations to be admissible.

In other words, one witness may present facts to prove that the declarant was under the impression of impending death and another witness may present the declaration of the deceased which related to the cause of the declarant's death, but the declarations concerning the cause of the injuries causing the ultimate death must have been made when there was still no belief of recovery. The time lapse between the declarant's impression of impending death and the declaration as to the cause of the injuries or the identity of the assailant must not be too great.

The primary problem involved with the use of one witness to prove the state of mind of the declarant and another witness to prove the declaration concerning the cause of the injuries or the identity of the assailant is whether there was a change about the belief of impending death during the time involved.

■ Who May Utilize Dying Declarations

From a practical standpoint, dying declarations are almost always introduced by the prosecution to aid in the proof of guilt. However, there is no restriction which prohibits the defendant from introducing dying declarations in defense. In those jurisdictions adhering to the strict rule of admissibility it is difficult to visualize a situation where the defendant would be in a position to use a dying declaration unless he or she could produce a witness who had heard the deceased victim state that the fatal injury had been inflicted by someone other than the defendant.

■ Weight To Be Given to Dying Declaration

It is primarily the responsibility of the trial judge to determine whether the utterances of a victim meet the test of trustworthiness, that is, whether the victim was under the impression that death was close-at-hand. Once the dying declaration has been admitted in evidence, the jury decides the weight to be given to it. A jury may give great weight to a declaration because of the solemn occasion under which it was given, and the jury may become emotionally involved in the pathos of the situation, believing that in these circumstances no one would utter anything but the truth. On the other hand, the jury may think that when the utterances were made, the declarant was in a state of shock—the body was racked with pain, and the mind was filled with many things—so that the memory may have been shaken. In this case the dying declaration may be given but little weight by the jury.

In a few jurisdictions, even though the judge permits the declarations to be introduced as dying declarations, the jury may also measure the test for trustworthiness. If the jury was under the impression that the declarations were made when the declarant had not given up all hope of recovery, the jury may disregard the declarations entirely. The problem involved with this procedure is that many persons believe that as long as there is life all hope of recovery is never abandoned. Thus, the introductions of dying declarations could be most restrictive.

Dying declarations are admissible even though there is other evidence to prove the homicide. The dying declarations are introduced in order to corroborate the other evidence introduced.

Inasmuch as most jurisdictions still adhere to the very strict rule on the admissibility of dying declarations as an exception to the hearsay rule, it may be well to reiterate the requirements which must be met in order for these declarations to be introduced in evidence:

1. The charge must be one of homicide.
2. The declaration must be made by the one whom the defendant is charged with slaying.
3. The declaration must be about the cause of the injuries, which may include facts that will assist in establishing the identity of the assailant.
4. The declaration must have been made at a time when the declarant was under a sense of impending death.

In jurisdictions in which the restrictions have been relaxed, the primary qualification which must be met is the test for trustworthiness, that is, the declaration must have been made at a time when the declarant had no hope of recovery. Also, the rule still holds that the declarant must be unavailable as a witness because of death.

SPONTANEOUS DECLARATIONS (*RES GESTAE*)

It is a known fact that many times spontaneous reactions or utterances resulting from unusual events or happenings can be most revealing. This fact has been recognized by the courts, and another exception to the hearsay rule was established as a result. In certain circumstances spontaneous declarations or utterances may be admitted in evidence even though they are hearsay. Such declarations have been admitted as another exception to the hearsay rule because of their assistance in arriving at the truth. Although this exception is generally known as the spontaneous-declarations exception, it has been referred to as the "*res gestae* exception."

Perhaps in no other area in the rules of evidence is there a term more ambiguous and confusing than that of *res gestae*. Many writers on evidence, including the great authority Wigmore, think that the term *res gestae* should be removed from our legal phraseology. Irrespective of this viewpoint, the term continues to weave its way into arguments for the presentation of certain evidence. Literally, the term means "the things done." This meaning has been the explanation for the admissibility of certain evidence which may seem to be hearsay or which may appear at first glance to be inadmissible. It must not be thought by the reader that evidence admitted under this doctrine is improper. The doctrine permits the introduction of evidence which assists in clarifying or explaining what happened in a particular case and which is considered to be an integral part of a crime or event. This may include declarations, conduct, or physical objects so closely related to the event that they are considered parts of the event itself. It is probably for this reason that spontaneous utterances made during a shocking experience have been termed by some students of evidence as the *res gestae* exception to the hearsay rule. This only adds to the confusion already caused by the term *res gestae*.

Although spontaneous utterances can be, and usually are, considered a portion of the *res gestae* of an event, spontaneous utterances are only a small portion of what may fall within the realm of *res gestae*. Many writers on evidence and distinguished judges disapprove referring to spontaneous declarations as the *res gestae* exception to the hearsay rule. As a result, most works on evidence refer to this exception of the hearsay rule as the "spontaneous-declarations exception."

■ Spontaneous Declarations Defined

Spontaneous declarations are also known as "spontaneous utterances," "spontaneous exclamations," and "excited utterances." Spontaneous declarations are utterances made as the result of some sudden and shocking event, such as an accident or crime. The primary requirement for these utterances to be admissible under an exception to the hearsay rule is that there must have been some event startling enough to produce such nervous excitement that the utterance was a natural and involuntary reaction to the occurrence. When these utterances assist in explaining what happened in a particular case, they are admitted in evidence. They are admitted through the testimony of a witness present at the time the utterances were made and who is now testifying about what was said by the declarant of the spontaneous utterances.

The following are examples of excited utterances which would no doubt be admissible as spontaneous declarations. A wife observing her husband shot by a member of the family may run from the home screaming, "John just killed my husband"; or the husband may stagger from the house in a dazed condition and state, "John shot me"; or a woman may see a car drive through an intersection against the red light and may scream, "That man drove right through that red light." Anyone who overheard these excited utterances may introduce them in evidence, as these statements assist in arriving at the truth in each situation.

■ Test for Trustworthiness

Since spontaneous declarations are treated as another exception to the hearsay rule, the test for trustworthiness of the declaration becomes important to its admissibility. This exception also has its own unique test for truthfulness. The test stems from the involuntary spontaneity of the declaration. To be admissible in evidence the declaration must have been made as a spontaneous reaction to a shocking event and must have been uttered so simultaneously with the event that there was no time to fabricate a story.

A major problem involved in the admissibility of spontaneous declarations is the determination of the time element involved. How soon after the event took place must the excited utterance be made to be admissible? It has been held that the utterance does not have to be at the exact moment of the event producing the shock, but the utterance must come before there was any opportunity to reflect upon the event or before there was any possibility of misrepresenting.

The true spontaneous utterance is an involuntary and unprompted reaction to an event, and any declaration made in response to an inquiry for an explanation of what took place will usually take the utterances out of the realm of spontaneous declaration. It is possible for one to say something to the question "What happened?" and have the reply still fall within the rule of a spontaneous declaration. Whether a response to a question asked would be admissible as a spontaneous declaration would depend largely upon how soon after the event took place the question was asked and the state of shock of the declarant at the time the question was asked.

In one case the declarations made by a victim of a robbery were held admissible even though the declarations were in response to inquiries. The victim-declarant was knocked unconscious after being robbed. The victim was taken to the hospital still in a state of unconsciousness some 45 minutes later. An officer requested the emergency room nurse to ask the victim what had happened to him. About 20 minutes after arriving at the hospital, the victim regained consciousness for about 4 or 5 minutes. During this time the nurse asked the victim what had happened to him. He replied either, "I was beaten" or "I was robbed." He was next asked if he knew who attacked him and replied, "No." Then the nurse asked, "Was there more than one?" He replied that there was more than one. She then asked if there were more than two, and the victim said, "Maybe two or three." The appellate court upheld the admission of all the statements made to the nurse as spontaneous declarations. The appellate court stated that neither the lapse of time between the event and the declarations nor the fact that the declarations were elicited by questioning deprives the statements of spontaneity if it appears that the declarations were made under the stress of excitement and while the reflective powers were still in abeyance. The court stated that the victim was unconscious for most of the time between the beating and the nurse's questioning and did not have the power to reflect on his answers [(see *Peo. v. Washington,* 459 P2 259 (1969)].

Returning to the test for trustworthiness, was there sufficient lapse of time between the event and the inquiry for the declarant to reflect upon what happened and thereby be able to misrepresent the facts? Or, disregarding the time element, was the declarant still in such a state of mind that he was not likely to have told a falsehood? It is almost impossible to form any criteria for measuring either time lapse or state of mind, as conditions could well vary from one person to another as well as from one situation to another.

The primary test of trustworthiness is not so much the time factor as it is the state of mind of the declarant. Was the utterance made while the mind was still so dominated by the nervous excitement of the event that the power to reflect was inoperative? If so, the utterance is admissible.

UTTERANCE MUST PERTAIN TO THE EVENT JUST PRECEDING IT. The second requirement for a spontaneous declaration to be admissible is that it must relate in some way to the event which just preceded the utterance. The utterance must in some way explain what has just taken place, and it may not pertain to things that happened the day before, or at some other time, such as threats previously made.

■ Availability of the Declarant as a Witness

This exception to the hearsay rule is unusual in that there is no hard-and-fast requirement that the declarant of the spontaneous declaration be unavailable to testify for the utterance to be introduced in evidence. In fact, some students of evidence think that the spontaneous declaration may have more reliability than testimony of the declarant given while on the witness stand. This opinion is based upon the fact that the declarant may not even recall having made the utterance, or may have been in such a state of shock as not to be able to accurately recall what took place. If the original declarant is not called upon to testify, generally it is not necessary to explain or give any reason for not calling the declarant. Even if the original declarant is called upon to testify, his or her spontaneous utterance may be related by another witness who heard the utterance. This might take place particularly if the opposing side should make an allegation that the declarant had falsely testified.

There are times in which an utterance of a victim of a homicide may be introduced as a spontaneous declaration, when the utterance does not meet the test for trustworthiness as a dying declaration. But, of course, the utterance would have to meet the test for trustworthiness of a spontaneous declaration.

■ Criticism of the Admissibility of Spontaneous Declarations

Some authorities criticize the introduction of spontaneous declarations. They contend that because the declarant was in a state of shock, his mind may have been numbed to reality, and he or she may have uttered not a true observation but a mere opinion. Also it has been contended that a person in nervous excitement often receives a misconception of what is taking place and therefore cannot accurately relate what happened. However, as long as the utterance meets all the requirements of a spontaneous declaration, the courts generally permit such a declaration to be introduced for whatever value it may have in arriving at the truth.

■ Requirements for Admissibility of Spontaneous Declarations Summarized

To summarize the requirements that must be met in order for an excited utterance to be admissible as an exception to the hearsay rule as a spontaneous declaration: The utterance (1) must have been made as a natural reaction to some startling event; (2) must have been made so contemporaneously with the event that there was no opportunity to fabricate a story; and (3) must have some relationship to the event which just preceded the utterance.

FORMER TESTIMONY

The testimony given by a witness at a prior proceeding is admissible in a subsequent trial in certain circumstances as an exception to the hearsay rule. As with the other exceptions, there are specific requirements which must be met before the former testimony may be introduced in evidence. The essential requirement for the admissibility of the former testimony is the present unavailability of the witness who gave the former testimony. To further clarify this exception to the hearsay rule, assume that a witness at a former trial related facts in his knowledge about the case which was being tried, and thereafter the matter is to be tried again for some reason, and the testimony of the witness is important to this second trial, but the witness is now unavailable to repeat the facts previously given. The only way to get these facts before the jury in its search for the truth in the second proceeding is to get the former testimony before them. Because of this necessity, another exception to the hearsay rule was established under which the former testimony may be admitted. However, other requirements must be met besides the unavailability of the witness before this former testimony may be introduced in evidence. These requirements are spelled out rather specifically in the statutes of the various states. Although they vary somewhat from one jurisdiction to the next, the primary requirements are the same. The rules are more strict in criminal matters than in civil, principally because of the constitutional guarantee of the right of the accused to be confronted with the witnesses against him. It may be well at this point to reiterate the requirements generally necessary for the admissibility of former testimony, and then consider each requirement in detail for better understanding. The first and primary requirement which must be met and which is uniformly required by all jurisdictions is the present unavailability of the witness who gave the former testimony. In criminal matters, the next major qualification which must be met is that the defendant in the subsequent proceeding must be the one, or one of those, who was involved in the prior hearing or trial where the former testimony was given. The third qualification is that the issue, or the charge, must be the same, or substantially the same, as in the prior matter.

■ Unavailability of the Witness

Since the primary prerequisite for the introduction of former testimony at a subsequent judicial proceeding is the unavailability of the witness, there must be proof that the witness is now unavailable to testify; thus the question arises what is necessary to prove that the witness is unavailable. The courts have generally accepted three causes as sufficient proof of unavailability. These are (1) death of the witness; (2) insanity; or (3) inability, after due diligent search, to locate the witness. A few jurisdictions have included a fourth cause, the subsequent incompetence of the witness. Before introduction of former testimony, a foundation must be laid to prove that the witness is not now available to testify because of one of these reasons. This proof is generally established through the testimony of witnesses who have some actual knowledge why the former witness is not now available to testify.

UNAVAILABILITY BECAUSE OF DEATH. If a witness should die between the time the witness gave the former testimony and the time that the witness is again needed as a witness in a second proceeding, some proof of death must be offered in order to establish that the witness is not now available to testify. The proof of death may be established by a friend or relative of the former witness who knows of his or her own knowledge that the former witness is dead, or the death may be proved by the presentation of a death certificate which has been properly certified by the official in charge of the vital statistics in the jurisdiction where the death occurred. Either of these methods would be considered proper foundation for the introduction of the former testimony.

UNAVAILABILITY BECAUSE OF INSANITY. Although the courts have included the insanity of the witness as a sufficient cause to prove unavailability, this cause is not without its complications. It must be remembered that insanity is not a bar to competency in many jurisdictions, the insanity going only to the credibility of the witness. Just what proof is necessary to establish unavailability for this cause is not certain. It is presumed that if between the time of the first trial and the second proceeding the witness became so mentally unbalanced as to lose all reasoning power and the ability to relate intelligently, the condition would be sufficient foundation to introduce the former testimony in any jurisdiction.

UNAVAILABILITY BECAUSE OF INABILITY TO LOCATE. The most prevalent cause offered for the introduction of former testimony is being unable to locate the former witness after a diligent search has been made. This cause, too, is not without problems. The chief problem is how far one must go in the search for the witness in order to prove that the witness is now unavailable. In other words, what is due diligent search? There is no set criterion that must be met to prove that due diligent search has been conducted, but it is definitely accepted that there must be some concerted effort made to locate the witness. The following procedures have been suggested as means of measuring whether there was due diligence exerted in the search. First, it has been held that there must have been a subpoena issued for the appearance of the witness sufficiently in advance of the date of the appearance for a proper and diligent search to be made in the effort to locate the witness. It must be shown that during the search a check was made at the last known address of the witness as well as at other addresses where the witness is known to have stayed, and at other logical places where the witness may be located, including place of employment. A check of the current telephone book and city directory must have been made, as well as efforts to determine whether the witness gave a change of address to any source. Inquiry should have been made of friends and relatives to ascertain information which would lead to the witness's present whereabouts. If proof can be presented that efforts to locate the witness were made and the search was without results, a sufficient foundation has been laid to introduce former testimony.

It is likewise true that establishing that a witness was purposely hiding to avoid testifying will be accepted as proof of unavailability.

UNLOCATED WITNESS OUT OF STATE. It was formerly the rule that if during the search for the witness it was established that he or she was out of the state, this was sufficient to prove unavailability. However, this is no longer true. Most states have now adopted the Uniform Act to Secure the Attendance of Witnesses from without the State in Criminal Actions, as described in Chapter 4. Thus the out-of-state witnesses may now be commanded to appear at the trial. So if the witness is out of state, a concerted effort must be made to bring the witness back before his or her prior testimony may be used. This is true even if it is established that the witness is in jail in another state. This was particularly emphasized by the United States Supreme Court in the case entitled *Barber v. Page*, 390 U.S. 719 (1968). In that case a witness testified against the defendant at the preliminary hearing, but by the time of the trial the witness was in prison in another state. During the trial, proof was presented that the witness was out of state and in prison. The trial judge then permitted the former testimony given at the preliminary hearing to be introduced against the defendant at the trial. He was convicted, but the United States Supreme Court reversed the conviction on the grounds that the defendant had been denied the right of confrontation by the witness, since it was not shown that any effort had been made to have the witness brought back to testify.

UNAVAILABILITY BECAUSE OF ILLNESS. A witness's suffering from serious and prolonged illness may be a sufficient cause to prove unavailability, so that former testimony may be introduced. Many factors must be taken into consideration in permitting former testimony to be admitted in the case of illness or physical incapacity. If the illness or physical incapacity is of a temporary nature, the judge, in lieu of using the former testimony, may grant a continuance of the trial until the witness is available. In one case the judge permitted the former testimony to be introduced over the objections of the defense when the witness was pregnant with complications having set in. The appellate court held that this disability was of such temporary nature that a continuance should have been granted. In another case, between the time a man testified at a preliminary hearing and the time of the trial, the witness suffered from a cerebral thrombosis which incapacitated him from speaking. The prognosis was that the witness would not recover his speech facility for another eight-week period, if that soon. The court permitted the prior testimony given at the preliminary hearing to be introduced in evidence at the trial over the objection of the defense. The appellate court upheld the introduction of the prior testimony on the ground of the unavailability of the witness.

The situation wherein a witness has become temporarily incapacitated between the time of giving prior testimony and the present proceedings poses a serious dilemma to the trial judge. If the judge permits the prior testimony to be introduced over the objections of the defense, the defendant may be successful upon appeal by alleging that right of confrontation was denied. On the other hand, if the judge grants a continuance of the present trial over the objections of the defense until an incapacitated prosecution witness is available to testify at the present trial, the defendant may successfully claim on appeal that his or her right to a speedy trial was denied. It appears therefore that the estimated length of the incapacity plays an important factor in making the determination of whether to permit the introduction of the prior testimony or grant a continuance.

REFUSAL TO TESTIFY AND LAPSED MEMORY. It has been held that when a witness refuses to testify at a second proceeding, this refusal is sufficient to meet the requirement of unavailability. In one case, after testifying at the preliminary hearing, a key prosecution witness refused to testify at the trial because of having received a number of threatening phone calls and letters as a result of testifying at the preliminary hearing. This man refused to testify at the trial because of fear for his own safety and that of his family. The witness continued his refusal to testify even though he was held in contempt of court. His prior testimony was then introduced over the objections of the defense. The introduction of the prior testimony was upheld by the appellate court upon the grounds that the refusal to testify met the requirement of unavailability.

In another case a prosecution witness testified at a first trial, but after the conviction was reversed and the defendant was retired, the witness refused to testify during the second trial upon the grounds that she would incriminate herself. The trial judge at the second trial permitted the prior testimony to be introduced in the second trial upon the ground that the witness had the right to claim the guarantee against self-incrimination and therefore was unavailable to testify. The introduction of the prior testimony under the circumstances was upheld by the appellate court.

It has also been held that if between the time that a witness gave testimony in a first proceeding and the second proceeding the memory of the witness completely fails, the prior testimony can be introduced. This procedure has been criticized by some as lending itself to possible perjury, as a witness may easily feign collapsed memory in order to avoid testifying at a second proceeding. So sufficient proof would have to be presented of the failed memory before the prior testimony could be introduced.

UNAVAILABILITY BECAUSE OF INCOMPETENCE. A few states allow the introduction of former testimony when, between the time that the prior testimony was given and the subsequent trial, the witness has become incompetent or disqualified. This is particularly true in criminal matters when the witness has become incompetent because of a marriage with the defendant subsequent to giving the prior testimony.

■ Test for Trustworthiness

For some unknown reason the courts in the past seem to have been more concerned with the constitutional guarantee of confrontation of the witnesses before the accused in the former-testimony exception to the hearsay rule than in any other exception. Yet the test for trustworthiness in this instance is probably more nearly complete and more realistic than in any of the other exceptions. In order to introduce testimony which has been given previously, the former testimony must have been given in a judicial proceeding in which the witness testified under an oath or affirmation to tell the truth; and there must have been the opportunity to cross-examine the witness. Although it is not necessary that actual cross-examination took place in order for the former testimony to be admitted, there must have been the opportunity to cross-examine if the opposing side wished to avail itself of it. It is also generally accepted that the former testimony must have been reduced to writing in the form of a transcript or other official record. When these requirements have been met, the only advantage of confrontation over this exception to the hearsay rule is the present opportunity for the jury to observe the demeanor of the witness on the stand.

It may be well to consider some of the kinds of judicial proceedings in which the former testimony was given in order for it to be introduced in a subsequent trial. As already stated, in criminal matters the former proceeding must have been one in which the defendant in the present trial was also the defendant, or was one of the defendants; also, the issues or charge involved in the prior proceeding must have been substantially the same as those in the present one. In these circumstances it stands to reason that in a criminal case the prior proceeding is fairly well limited to a preliminary hearing, or a previous trial which resulted in a hung jury, or an instance where a new trial was granted for some reason, such as the decision of the trial judge or a reversal on appeal.

A problem arises in the prior proceeding if it was a preliminary hearing in which the accused was not represented by an attorney. May the testimony of a witness at the preliminary hearing now be used at the trial because of the unavailability of the witness? In the past it has been generally accepted that so long as the defendant himself had the opportunity to cross-examine the witness, the former testimony was admissible. However, this problem was settled by *Pointer v. Texas*, 380 U.S. 400 (1965), in which the Supreme Court held that the testimony given at a preliminary hearing could not be introduced at the trial inasmuch as the defendant was not represented at the preliminary hearing by an attorney, and so was denied the right of cross-examination then and the right of confrontation now. For this reason judges now insist that the defendant be represented by counsel at a preliminary hearing, unless the defendant has waived the right to the assistance of counsel after that right has been carefully explained to the defendant by the judge.

DEPOSITIONS

The next problem is whether a deposition taken from a person who is now unavailable to testify may be introduced in evidence on the same basis as former testimony. First, it may be well to review what constitutes a deposition. It is an out-of-court written statement of a person who has some knowledge of the facts pertaining to a case to be tried. A deposition has been legally defined as "a written declaration, under oath, made upon notice to the adverse party, for the purpose of enabling the adversary to attend and cross-examine." This declaration is usually in question-and-answer form and is much the same as if it were actually related on the witness stand. At the time that this declaration is made, both sides have the right to be present. In a criminal matter, a member of the district attorney's staff is present as well as the defense attorney. The defendant may also be present. The deposition is taken before a judge or other official having the authority to execute the oath or affirmation since the declaration must be given under oath or affirmation and there must the opportunity to cross-examine the person giving the declaration. The deposition is taken in lieu of the personal appearance of the individual in court as a witness because there is some sufficient reason why the witness cannot appear. The customary reason for the unavailability of such a person is an infirmity that prevents the personal appearance in court, or a hardship case where the witness is planning to leave the state and cannot return to testify at the trial. Only about one-third of the jurisdictions permit the use of depositions in criminal matters; the others, including the federal government, still prohibit the introduction of depositions in criminal proceedings by the prosecution because of the right of the accused "to be confronted by the witnesses against him." Some criticize this strict exclusionary rule of depositions because they state it is the only way in which pertinent facts may be brought before a jury in many cases.

The introduction of the deposition in evidence, in those jurisdictions where it is permitted, is not to be confused with the introduction of prior testimony. A deposition is taken in those instances where the testimony of a witness is material to the proceeding but for a sufficient reason that witness cannot appear in person at a trial or a hearing. In these circumstances there is no prior testimony which can be introduced. The deposition becomes the first testimony of the witness, and is utilized in lieu of the personal testimony at the court proceeding.

BUSINESS RECORDS

The admissibility of business records, or business entries, as they are also called, in evidence is one of the older exceptions to the hearsay rule. Since at common law a party to a suit could not be a witness, there were many times that the only way the person could get his or her side of the case presented was through the production in court of business records, or shopbooks. As a result, another exception to the hearsay rule was developed; it was originally known as the *shopbook rule*. This exception is still recognized today of necessity, and it meets a satisfactory test for trustworthiness, based upon the principle that businesses in the normal course of events maintain complete and accurate records. In addition, these records are usually audited periodically by outside sources, and the records are made by persons who have no reason to falsify. Although business records play a very small part in the trial of criminal cases, they are introduced occasionally, so that a cursory discussion of this exception to the hearsay rule is in order.

■ Categories of Business Records

Business records may be divided into two general categories: (1) private business records and (2) public records. Although some writers on evidence endeavor to distinguish between the two so far as exceptions to the hearsay rule are concerned, there seems little to be accomplished in trying to treat them as separate exceptions to the hearsay rule. Both are based upon the same general principle for trustworthiness mentioned above, as the public official also has a desire for accuracy in his or her records and under normal circumstances there is no reason for the public official to falsify. However, there is a difference in the ways the records are introduced in evidence.

LAYING FOUNDATION FOR INTRODUCTION OF PRIVATE BUSINESS RECORDS. Generally, before any hearsay evidence can be admitted in evidence, there must be a showing that the declarant of the hearsay statement, or the person who has actual knowledge of an event, is not available to testify. The business-records exception has deviated from that rule to a degree. Although there may be someone, someplace, who has actual knowledge of the transaction in a business record, producing this person to testify is often impracticable, if not impossible. So, in a sense, the declarant is still unavailable. It has been held that because of the complexities and volume of business today, requiring a person who has actual knowledge of a business transaction to appear as a witness would seriously handicap the economy, and very little would be gained by the personal appearance of such a witness that could not be accomplished by the record. For example, it if were necessary to prove that a long-distance telephone call had been made, it would be impractical to try to locate the operator who may have assisted in making the call; in addition, with automatic dialing, there may be no living being who would have personal knowledge that a call was made. Consequently the production of a witness may be impossible, and the only information about the call may be the record. Even if the telephone operator were produced to testify, in most instances the operator would not remember the call, or, even if remembering it, probably could add nothing that would not be reflected in the record. Generally, therefore, it is not necessary to prove why the declarant was not produced as a witness prior to the introduction of business records.

A foundation must be laid, though, to have private business records introduced. Certain requirements must be met. It is not necessary that the person in charge of the records produce them in court, but they must be produced by someone who is acquainted with the records and business procedure of the particular company whose records are to be introduced. Generally, for the introduction of the records, the witness producing them must be in a position to prove that (1) the company maintains records in the normal and regular course of business, and that the records produced are a part of those regularly kept; (2) the entries in the records are made at, or about, the time the transactions take place; (3) the entries are made from reports, memoranda, sales slips, or other documents prepared by someone who had actual knowledge of the transactions; and (4) the records produced are the original records, though photographic reproductions have been generally accepted in lieu of the originals.

The Uniform Rules of Evidence (Rule 63, section 13) is somewhat less strict in the requirements for admissibility of business records, and this rule has been adopted in a number of states. Rule 63 provides that "writings offered as memoranda or records of acts, conditions or events to prove the facts stated therein, [are admissible] if the judge finds that they [the writings] were made in the regular course of business at or about the time of the act, condition or event recorded, and that the source of the information from which made and the method and circumstances of their preparation were such as to indicate their trustworthiness."

The private business records most likely to be introduced in criminal trials are those of hotels, public utilities, hospitals, insurance companies, and banks, but the records of many other kinds of private businesses may be introduced from time to time.

PUBLIC RECORDS.   Public records may be introduced in the same manner as those of a private business, that is, an official from the public office will produce the public records in court and will lay the same general foundation that is required for the introduction of private records. But in most instances, it is not necessary for a public official to appear as a witness. The record is usually introduced by the attorney who wants it placed in evidence. The attorney will offer a copy of the public record with a certificate that it is an accurate copy signed by the official in charge of the records and sealed with the official seal.

The only requirement is that there be a statute which authorizes the public office to keep records and the official in charge to furnish certified copies. It has been held that to require an official to appear in court each time a public record is needed would work a handicap upon public officials and would materially interfere with the volume of business which must be conducted on a daily basis. It has also been held that permitting a certified copy of the record to be produced without the personal appearance of an official is not a violation of the defendant's right of confrontation. To be classified as a public record it is not necessary that the record be one which is open to public inspection.

The public records most frequently introduced in criminal trials are court records, vital-statistics records, motor-vehicle-department records, and those of similar public agencies.

As restrictions against the introduction of business records as an exception to the hearsay rule are relaxed, greater use may be made of public records, particularly those of law enforcement agencies. This increase in use was manifested in one case. In that case an undercover agent of the police department made a purchase of narcotics from the accused defendant. The purchase was turned over to an officer who in accordance with his usual procedure placed the substance purchased in an envelope which he sealed, initialed, and dated. The envelope was then placed in an evidence locker to which only the officer and a laboratory technician had a key. The technician removed the envelope later and analyzed the contents as heroin. The technician resealed and initialed the envelope and placed it in the evidence locker. Thereafter the defendant was indicted partially upon the testimony of the officer. Between the time of the grand jury hearing and the trial, the officer died. During the trial the envelope bearing the date and the initials of the deceased officer was offered in evidence by a fellow officer to assist in proving the guilt of the defendant. The other officer of the department was permitted to testify that the deceased officer in the regular course of his duties followed the procedure of placing substances purchased by undercover agents into an envelope which he sealed, initialed, and dated. He then placed the envelope in an evidence locker in order that the contents might be later analyzed by a laboratory technician. The fellow officer also testified that he was acquainted with the handwriting of the deceased officer and recognized initials and date on the envelope as the writing of the deceased officer. The trial judge permitted the introduction of the record under the business-records exception to the hearsay rule. The introduction of the records was upheld by the appellate court, which court stated that the procedure followed by the deceased officer was a practical procedure developed by the police, a procedure that had stood the scrutiny of defense counsel in many narcotic cases that have been before the courts. The written record was made as a part of a government activity in the regular course of business at or near the time of the act and the sources of information and method and time of preparation were such as to indicate its trustworthiness. The court further stated that a qualified witness testified as to the identity and the mode of preparation of the record, as well as identifying the writing and initials of the deceased officer and testifying concerning the procedure followed for the handling of narcotics seized as evidence.

It is to be noted that the introduction of the transaction in this case followed more closely that of the introduction of private business records than that generally followed in the introduction of public records. Irrespective, this case is illustrative of the possible greater use that can be made of police records under emergency circumstances during which, otherwise, a dismissal of a charge might take place when an officer is unavailable because of death.

PEDIGREE OR FAMILY HISTORY

Only during the last half-century has any concerted effort been made to keep official records of vital statistics. Earlier, to establish the birth, marriage, or death of a person, it was often necessary to revert to some type of hearsay information, and thus one of the oldest exceptions to the hearsay rule was developed, that of establishing the pedigree or family history of a person. The pedigree exception to the hearsay rule plays a very small role in the trial of criminal cases today because of the requirement in most states that official records of vital statistics be maintained. However, because many transient individuals have no official vital statistics available to prove their family history, and pedigree often can be accomplished only through hearsay information, this exception to the hearsay rule will be briefly discussed.

MATTERS WHICH RELATE TO FAMILY HISTORY. Matters generally accepted as included in family history or pedigree pertain to birth, marriage, divorce, death, legitimacy, race, ancestry, relationship by blood or marriage, or other similar facts. These matters are likely to be significant in the prosecution of defendants charged with such crimes as incest, bigamy, or sexual relations with a female under the age of consent, known in some jurisdictions as statutory rape.

■ Test for Trustworthiness

If there is no official record available to prove a fact concerning family history, it is permissible for a witness who has actual knowledge of the event in question to testify in an effort to establish the fact. For example, if the date of birth of a child is in question and there is no record of the birth, a person who was present at the birth could testify concerning this event in the family history. This information would not be hearsay, and the pedigree exception would not arise. The problem arises when there is no record and nobody now available to testify who has actual knowledge of the event. There are many instances, though, when other persons are available who have information which has been passed on to them by individuals who had personal knowledge of the family history. May these persons testify in order to prove some event in the family history? In some circumstances they may, but certain requirements must be met in order to fulfill the test for trustworthiness. First, the original declarant must be unavailable to testify; and second, the original declarant who made the statement about the family history must be one in a position to know accurate facts about the family. It is generally held that the original declarant must have been a member of the family, either by blood relationship or marriage. However, if the original declarant was not a member of the family but was so intimately associated with the family that he had accurate information, this declarant's statement overheard by another may be related on the witness stand by the one who overheard it to assist in proving family history.

■ Hearsay Writings to Prove Family History

In addition to the admissibility of the testimony of witnesses who may have hearsay information about family history, it has been held that certain types of other hearsay evidence may be admissible to prove family history, such as entries made in a family Bible or other family books, charts, or records; engravings on rings; information on family portraits; or engravings on tombstones.

The test for trustworthiness in proving family history is based on the information's being furnished or recorded at a time when there was no reason to falsify.

PAST MEMORY RECORDED

As previously pointed out in Chapter 4, there are times when a witness on the witness stand is shown a document he or she has prepared that fails to refresh memory sufficiently to enable the witness to testify about the facts contained in the document. In these circumstances, the document itself is frequently introduced in evidence in lieu of the testimony of the witness. The courts permit the document to be introduced as another exception to the hearsay rule—the test for trustworthiness again being based upon the fact that the document was prepared by the witness or under his or her direction at a time when the facts were fresh in the memory of the witness and made at a time when there was no reason to falsify. The witness must be in a position to verify that the facts contained in the document were correctly recorded.

If the contents of the document are read into the court record at the time of the trial, the contents become the oral testimony of the witness, and generally the contents under these circumstances are not considered to be hearsay. A few jurisdictions will not permit the document to be introduced by the witness except on the request of the opposing side.

SUMMARY

Hearsay, which is defined as a statement made by one other than the witness testifying, is generally not admissible in evidence. The reason for this exclusion is that it lacks trustworthiness. A second reason may be given so far as criminal trials are concerned and that is the right of an accused "to be confronted with the witnesses against him." Through necessity, exceptions to this rule have been developed, but each exception has had to establish a unique test for trustworthiness in order to be admissible.

Although there are many exceptions to the hearsay rule, those most frequently encountered in criminal trials are (1) dying declarations, (2) spontaneous declarations, (3) former testimony, (4) business records, (5) pedigree, (6) past memory recorded, (7) confessions, and (8) admissions.

DYING DECLARATIONS. A dying declaration has been defined as "an act or declaration of a person made under the sense of impending death, which declaration tends to explain the circumstances surrounding his injuries which resulted in his ultimate death." Most jurisdictions restrict the use of dying declarations to criminal cases in which the charge is homicide and the defendant is charged with killing the declarant of the dying declaration. A few jurisdictions permit the use of dying declarations in civil matters, particularly when the cause of death is in issue, and a few have made no restriction on the use of dying declarations. In those few adhering to open use of dying declarations, the declaration may be introduced so long as it is pertinent to the issues and was made under the sense of impending death and the declarant is now deceased and so unavailable to testify.

SPONTANEOUS DECLARATIONS. Spontaneous declarations are utterances made as a result of some sudden and shocking event and made so simultaneously with the event that there was no opportunity to reflect upon it or to fabricate a story. The chief problem involved in the introduction of spontaneous utterances is how soon after the event took place the utterance must have been made to be admissible. It is generally accepted that if the declaration was made prior to any opportunity to reflect, it is admissible. The utterance must pertain to the event which just preceded it and must have been a spontaneous reaction to that event. Generally, if the declaration was forthcoming in response to a question asked of the declarant, the utterance will be excluded, but the mere fact that an inquiry was made is not fatal to the admissibility. If the person making the utterance was still in a state of shock, the response may still be considered sufficiently spontaneous to be admissible. Most jurisdictions do not require that the original declarant be unavailable to testify in order to introduce spontaneous declarations.

FORMER TESTIMONY. In some circumstances, the testimony given by a witness at a prior judicial proceeding may be introduced at a subsequent one. In order for the former testimony to be admissible, certain requirements must be met. The main, and uniformly accepted, prerequisite is that the person giving the former testimony must now be unavailable for sufficient reason. The reasons for unavailability usually considered to be sufficient are (1) death; (2) insanity; (3) not being found after due diligent search; and (4) in some jurisdictions, subsequent incompetence or disqualification of the witness. In addition to unavailability of the witness, the former testimony must have been given under an oath or affirmation to tell the truth, and there must have been an opportunity to cross-examine the witness at the prior proceeding. In criminal matters there are the additional requirements that the former testimony must have been given in a matter in which the defendant of the present proceeding was the defendant, or one of the defendants, of the prior matter and that the charges must have been the same, or substantially the same, as in the present case.

BUSINESS RECORDS. Business records fall into two categories: (1) private business records, or business entries; and (2) public records, or documents. In order to introduce private business records, someone familiar with the business customs of the company must introduce the records. This person must prove that the company kept records in the regular course of business and that the record produced is one of these records; that the entry was made at or near the time of the transaction; that the entry was made from memoranda prepared by one having actual knowledge of the transaction; and that the record is the original or a photographic copy of the original.

Public records are usually introduced merely by presenting a certified copy of the record.

PEDIGREE OR FAMILY HISTORY. Family history pertains to matters of birth, marriage, divorce, death, legitimacy, race, ancestry, relationship by blood or marriage, and other similar facts.

In order to introduce hearsay evidence to prove family history, the original declarant must be unavailable; the original statement about the family history must have been made by a member of the family, either by blood relationship or through marriage; or the statement may have been made by one intimately associated with the family who knew the accurate family history.

Writings in family Bibles or books, on family portraits, engravings in rings, or engravings on tombstones may be introduced to prove family history.

PAST MEMORY RECORDED. When a document contains facts which the witness is unable to recall sufficiently to be able to testify, it may be introduced in evidence and admitted as another exception to the hearsay rule.

QUESTIONS FOR REVIEW

1. Define "hearsay."
2. Why is hearsay evidence usually not admissible?
3. Why were exceptions to the hearsay rule developed?
4. List the eight exceptions to the hearsay rule most frequently encountered in criminal trials.
5. Describe the test for trustworthiness for each of the six discussed in this chapter.
6. What restriction has been placed on the introduction of dying declarations in most jurisdictions, and in what way is this restriction being changed?
7. In what circumstances may former testimony be introduced in a criminal trial?
8. What constitutes sufficient cause of unavailability of a witness in order to introduce former testimony?
9. Name the two kinds of business records which fall under the business-records exception, and explain how each is introduced in evidence.
10. What matters are included in family history?

LOCAL RULES

There are some differences among jurisdictions on certain rules of evidence; therefore the reader should ascertain the answers to the following questions from the local prosecuting attorney, as suggested in Chapter 1.

1. What are the restrictions on the use of a dying declaration?
2. In determining unavailability of a witness in order to use prior testimony, is subsequent incompetence or disqualification sufficient to establish unavailability?
3. May depositions be introduced in evidence in a criminal case?

Confessions and Admissions

7

CONFESSIONS AS AN EXCEPTION TO HEARSAY RULE

No exception to the hearsay rule is better known than that of confessions, nor has any exception been more closely scrutinized by the courts or had more revolutionary changes made in the rules pertaining to its admissibility than confessions. A confession has been described as the most convincing form of evidence for the prosecution in establishing guilt beyond a reasonable doubt. It is likewise one of the most damaging pieces of evidence against the accused. It is little wonder therefore that an accused makes great efforts to prohibit the introduction of a confession in evidence during a trial.

Perhaps no chapter in this study on evidence has greater importance to the officer than this one on confessions. Even though the subject of "Exclusionary Rule—Searches and Seizures" may seem of equal value, it will be learned that unless a confession is properly obtained, evidence discovered by it will be excluded during a trial. Because confessions are so often subjected to close scrutiny, considerable space is being devoted to them.

Because improper methods have been used to induce confessions, courts have for some time taken a rather dim view of confessions as evidence. As a result, the Supreme Court has established very strict rules pertaining to the admissibility of confessions. The transitions made in the requirements for admissibility, as expressed in the decisions of the Supreme Court, are worthy of consideration and will be discussed in this study on confessions.

149

■ Definition of a Confession

A confession has been defined as a statement or acknowledgment of guilt made by a person accused of a crime. This definition standing alone does not make the statement hearsay. The confession becomes hearsay when the person to whom it was made endeavors to relate it on the witness stand. It then falls into the category of a statement made out of court to the witness by another person. The truthfulness of the statement, or confession, is dependent upon the original declarant and not the witness relating it. In the usual situation the confession is given by the defendant who is on trial where the confession is being introduced. Although the original declarant is in court, he or she cannot be compelled to testify. Consequently, if the information contained in the confession is to be made available to the jury in its search for the truth, hearsay evidence must be reverted to. In this way the necessity rule to utilize hearsay evidence is met.

■ Test for Trustworthiness

The use of confessions as an aid to convict persons of crimes is almost as old as the human race. The fact that confessions were hearsay was of little importance because, as has been pointed out, there was a time when hearsay evidence was used extensively. History has revealed that many of the confessions used in the past to convict persons were coerced through various forms of torture, such as the rack and screw or the application of red-hot irons to the bare flesh. Many of these confessions were false, for it is a known fact that a person under excruciating pain will promise anything, or confess to a crime, just to get immediate relief, with little thought given to the consequences of such a promise or confession made under pain. As time went on and hearsay evidence began to be excluded, confessions were still admitted as one of the exceptions to the hearsay rule, but like the other exceptions a test for trustworthiness had to be developed. The test established was a more or less assumed one. It was assumed that under normal circumstances a person would not confess to having committed a crime unless it were true. However, for this test to be applicable, it was held that the confession had to have been given freely and voluntarily.

For a confession to have been freely and voluntarily given, the person making the confession must have been in a position to exercise complete mental freedom at the time of the confession. The courts have become most strict in their interpretation of what will affect this complete mental freedom and have ruled that the slightest pressure applied to induce the confession will be considered as an interference with mental freedom and will cause the confession to be excluded.

As confessions were admitted as an exception to the hearsay rule, the courts at the beginning were primarily concerned with whether the confessor had been subjected to any physical abuse to induce the confession. It was recognized later that other things might affect freedom of the mind, such as psychological pressures upon the accused before or during interrogation, which might also act as an inducement to make confession. Psychological pressure has been interpreted as any act or statement which may place the accused under a mental strain, such as a threat of violence, a threat of action to be taken against members of his family, deception, a promise of reward, or duress.

An interesting definition of a voluntary confession was given in *State v. Anderson,* 208 N.C. 771 (1935):

> Confessions . . . are called voluntary when made neither under the influence of hope or fear, but are attributable to that love of truth which predominates in the breast of every man, not operated upon by other motives more powerful with him, and which, it is said, in the perfectly good man, cannot be countervailed.

Requirement that the confession must be given freely and voluntarily serves a dual function. First, unless the confession is so given, there may be a doubt about its trustworthiness; and second, unless it is given freely and voluntarily, the accused's right against self-incrimination may be violated.

■ Additional Requirements Established

Until about the middle of the twentieth century, the admissibility of confessions was entirely dependent upon meeting the test for trustworthiness, that is, whether the confession was freely and voluntarily given. If it was, the confession was admitted in evidence against the accused. Then in 1943 the Supreme Court rendered the decision in the famous McNabb case (see pp. 162-164), and an entirely new approach was made to the admissibility of confessions. Admissibility did not depend on the voluntariness of the confession or its trustworthiness but was based on whether certain legal procedures were followed, and a whole new set of requirements for admissibility of confessions began to emanate from Supreme Court decisions. These new requirements were the result of applying the guarantees embodied in the Fifth and Sixth Amendments to the United States Constitution and making these guarantees applicable to the states as well as to federal officers. The Fifth Amendment guarantees to the accused the right not to be compelled in a criminal matter to be a witness against himself, and the Sixth Amendment—among other provisions—gives him the right of counsel.

In view of the importance of these procedural requirements to the admissibility of confessions, each will be discussed in detail hereinafter. For now, in brief, it will suffice to state that for a confession to be admitted in evidence, the accused must not only have been in a position where he or she was able to exercise complete mental freedom in making the confession, but the accused must have been advised in detail of his or her constitutional rights, and the accused must have thereafter intelligently waived these rights. The accused must have been advised that he had the right to remain silent and that if he made any statements, they could be used against him, that the accused was entitled to have an attorney present during the interview and if the accused did not have the funds with which to employ an attorney, counsel would be provided. If after all these rights had been explained in detail to the accused and he had intelligently waived his rights to remain silent and to have the assistance of an attorney, any statements he made might be introduced in evidence against him. However, if the accused had been arrested and he was not arraigned without unnecessary delay, the confession might still be excluded, as was set forth by the McNabb decision.

These more recent rules of admissibility of confessions are, for the most part, the result of Supreme Court decisions handed down after reviews of criminal trials in which confessions were introduced against the accused in an effort to prove guilt. Most of the cases reviewed were of local state trials.

HISTORICAL BACKGROUND OF REQUIREMENTS. There was a time in our history when the United States Supreme Court was not greatly concerned with the manner in which trials in the local courts were conducted. It was thought that the procedure followed and the admissibility of evidence were within the police power of the states, and so long as the defendant was given a fair trial, it was assumed that the defendant had been afforded due process of law. But there has come about a change in the philosophy of the Supreme Court, so that now a very close inspection is made not only of the conduct of the federal courts and federal law enforcement officers, but of local courts and local officers as well.

To present a more understandable picture of how and why this change in attitude of the Supreme Court came about, it may be well to digress momentarily and review some of the developments of the United States Constitution, particularly amendments highly applicable in criminal matters. After the United States Constitution was drafted in 1787, some statesmen asserted that amendments should be added to guarantee the people certain rights to protect them from a strong, oppressive central government which might develop. In 1789, twelve amendments were proposed, ten of which were ratified in 1791. These first ten amendments are known as the Bill of Rights, because they guarantee to the people certain rights against possible oppression by the federal government.

Of these first ten amendments to the Constitution, the Fourth, Fifth, and Sixth set forth certain guarantees to an accused in criminal matters and have played an important part in the interpretation of rules of evidence and the determination of what may or may not be admitted in evidence. The Fourth Amendment deals primarily with searches and seizures of evidence; the Fifth Amendment, among other rights, states that no person shall be "twice put in jeopardy of life or limb"; and in relation to confessions, this amendment provides that no person "shall be compelled in a criminal matter to be a witness against himself." The Sixth Amendment entitles an accused person to a "speedy and public trial, by an impartial jury; . . . to be informed of the nature and cause of the accusation; to be confronted with the witnesses against him; to have compulsory process for obtaining witnesses in his favor; and to have the assistance of counsel for his defense." Although the Eighth Amendment plays an important role in criminal procedure, it has little application in the field of evidence as such. This amendment prohibits excessive fines, or bail, and cruel and unusual punishment.

These amendments were designed primarily for the control of the federal government and its officers. The Tenth Amendment reserved to the people, or to the states, certain powers, which are sometimes referred to as the "police powers" of the states. Under these powers the states regulated their own officers and the conduct of their criminal trials.

In 1868 the Fourteenth Amendment was added to the Constitution, placing some control upon the states and their officers. This amendment states that no state shall "deprive any person of life, liberty, or property, without due process of law," and it has been the basis for most of the restrictions placed upon local officers by the Supreme Court in recent years. The Court has held that if any effect is to be given to the due-process clause of the Fourteenth Amendment, the guarantees embodied in the Fourth, Fifth, Sixth, and Eighth Amendments must be honored by all courts throughout the land. As a result of this viewpoint, these amendments have now been made applicable to the states as well as the federal government. This change in attitude did not come overnight. As will be pointed out in later discussions, there were justices of the United States Supreme Court who for a long time thought that the Supreme Court should not dictate to the states how to run their courts, but one by one decisions have been handed down by the Court whereby the Fourth, Fifth, Sixth, and Eighth Amendments are now all applicable to the states through the due-process clause of the Fourteenth Amendment. These decisions have for the most part eliminated any major differences in the admissibility of evidence among the states. The guidelines are generally the same whether the evidence is being admitted in a state court or a federal court. The conduct of the law enforcement officer—whether federal or local—in obtaining evidence or securing a confession is comparatively uniform throughout the United States.

As the Supreme Court began its review of state trials, two areas were of particular concern. One was the manner in which local officers obtained confessions, and the second was the method used in making searches and seizures of evidence. These reviews were the result of appeals made by defendants who had been convicted in the state courts. Their appeals were based on the contention that in the local courts they had been denied due process of law as provided by the Fourteenth Amendment. This allegation gave the Supreme Court jurisdiction to review the admissibility of the evidence which had been introduced in the state courts. If the Supreme Court concluded that the defendant had been denied due process of law, the conviction was reversed. The state courts found that they were no longer able to enjoy the local autonomy that they once had in determining the admissibility of evidence, but that they must now abide by the rules and regulations set forth by the United States Supreme Court or find that their convictions would be reversed; thus a new philosophy was born governing the admissibility of evidence in criminal matters, that of the Supreme Court making independent reviews of the conduct of local officers and of the admissibility of their evidence.

In fairness to the state courts and local trial judges, it should be pointed out that they have been concerned for many years over improperly induced confessions, and where they have come to light, the confessions have been excluded. It has been a well-established policy in local courts that when a confession was introduced by the prosecution and the defendant made an objection to its admissibility on the ground of some impropriety in the inducement, it became the burden of the prosecution to prove that it was freely and voluntarily given. If the trial judge concluded that it was properly obtained, the judge would admit it in evidence, and if the jury agreed with the judge that it was voluntarily given, they could give the confession the consideration that they felt it deserved. If the defendant was convicted, he could take his case to the state appellate courts for review. If they agreed that the confession was properly obtained, the conviction would stand. If they did not agree, the conviction would be reversed and the case sent back for retrial. In the past when this procedure was followed, it was assumed that the defendant had been afforded due process of law. It was after the conviction had been affirmed by the state appellate courts that cases were taken on appeal by defendants to the United States Supreme Court upon the contention that due process of law had not been granted. In this way the reviews by the Supreme Court began, and the new guidelines on the admissibility of confessions were established. Some of the more prominent, and often-cited, cases will be set forth below, and exact quotations from the decisions will be included in order that the thinking and reasoning behind them may be better understood.

CONFESSIONS OBTAINED THROUGH PHYSICAL FORCE

It is unfortunate that there was a time when a law enforcement officer, eager to solve a crime and get a conviction, was not beyond extorting a confession from an accused by the use of physical force. As a result the term "third degree" came into the discussion of confessions, and this term still permeates the language of appellate court decisions on confessions. It was vividly used by Chief Justice Warren as late as 1966 in writing his opinion for the majority in the Miranda decision. When such conduct came to the attention of the courts, the law enforcement officer was placed in a most unfavorable light, and the courts began to take a dim view of the use of confessions as evidence against an accused. Therefore, the courts have for some time excluded confessions obtained through the use of violence or inhuman treatment to the accused. The exclusion of such confessions went beyond the fact that they did not meet the test for trustworthiness, for the exclusion was also exercised as a way of disciplining the officer. The courts have stated in so many words that if an officer acts in this way, even though the confession is true, the court will not be a party to such conduct and will not permit an accused to be convicted by such evidence.

In one of the first state court decisions involving confessions to be reviewed by the United States Supreme Court, the confessions were obtained through the use of physical force. This is the much-quoted case of *Brown v. Mississippi,* 297 U.S. 278 (1936). In this case the Supreme Court reversed a murder conviction of three Negro defendants who had been convicted in the local court primarily on the basis of their confessions.

According to the facts in this case, a deputy sheriff, accompanied by other persons, took one of the defendants to the crime scene, where he was questioned about the murder. He denied guilt and was hanged by a rope from a limb of a tree for a period of time. He was then let down, after which he again denied his guilt. He was next tied to the tree and whipped. He still refused to confess and was finally permitted to return home. He was later seized again and whipped until he confessed. The other two defendants were laid over chairs and whipped until they confessed. During the trial the confessions were allegedly admitted before the manner in which they were obtained was brought out. The case was taken to the Supreme Court of the United States, where it was argued that by the introduction of these confessions, the defendants had been denied due process of law.

The Supreme Court held that inasmuch as the confessions had been induced by brutal treatment, the defendants had been denied due process of law, and the conviction was reversed. The appeal was made strictly upon the contention that due process of law had been denied, and the guarantee against self-incrimination contained in the Fifth Amendment was not argued. At the time of this case, it was still considered that the Fifth Amendment was applicable only to federal officers, and not to state procedure. It was not until later decisions were handed down by the United States Supreme Court that the self-incrimination clause of the Fifth Amendment was held to be applicable to the states through the due-process clause of the Fourteenth Amendment. But the Brown case set the stage for independent reviews by the United States Supreme Court of state trials involving confessions, and this resulted in a close scrutiny by that Court of the conduct of local officers in obtaining confessions. Although the Court itself has admitted that inhuman treatment of an accused person is rare today, it still is skeptical of the procedure used by officers in interrogating suspects, and some most restrictive rules have been created.

Not only will actual physical mistreatment of the accused cause a confession to be excluded, but any discomfort suffered by the accused during the interrogation will also cause statements made to be inadmissible. Such discomforts include lengthy interrogations during which the accused was made to stand, or biological relief was not permitted, or the accused was not allowed to rest. In one recent case the confession of an accused was excluded because it was alleged that at the time he was interrogated, he was still tired from an extradition trip, even though he was permitted rest during the trip. The appellate courts have interpreted all these acts as affecting the complete freedom of the mind while giving the confession.

However, the mere fact that an interrogation extended over a long time does not necessarily make it fatal to the admissibility of a confession given. But the prosecution must be in a position to prove that every consideration was given to the accused during the questioning, and that nothing interfered with his mental freedom during the time.

APPLICATION OF PSYCHOLOGICAL PRESSURE

As the caliber of peace officers improved, physical violence against an accused to induce a confession was no longer condoned by the officers themselves, and such tactics began to rapidly disappear. Yet the courts continued to review methods used by officers in obtaining confessions, and the Supreme Court maintained a close inspection of state cases to make certain that due process had been followed. The courts next became concerned with other pressures which may have been used to induce confessions and which may have affected the complete mental freedom of the accused in making confessions. These pressures have been referred to as "psychological pressures," and another evolutionary phase in the admissibility of confessions came into being: excluding confessions induced by the application of mental stress on the accused.

Psychological pressure, or "mental stress," takes on many forms. It may be a verbal threat to inflict violence on the accused, or a gesture indicating that violence will take place. Mental stress may result from a mere suggestion that if the accused will confess, "things will go easier for him"; or it may be some other promise or reward, such as a promise that no action will be taken against the accused's wife, or that every effort will be made to assist the family of the accused to get welfare aid if the confession is given; or the mental stress may be created by a threat of action to be taken against the family of the accused, such as placing his children in a juvenile home unless a confession is forthcoming.

The psychological pressure may also result from fear, as when an alarming number of officers are present during an interrogation, or the accused is held for an unduly long time without contact with his family in strange surroundings. However, the fact that the accused was in custody, or at the police station, at the time a confession is given will not of itself exclude the confession.

Just four years after the Brown case, the Supreme Court reviewed another state case in which psychological pressure in the inducement of the confession became an issue. This was the case of *Chambers v. Florida*, 309 U.S. 227 (1940). In the Chambers case there was no allegation of physical violence having been inflicted upon the accused, nor even a threat thereof, but the Supreme Court still read coercion in the inducement of the confessions because of the procedure used in obtaining them. The pressure was brought about by protracted questioning while the defendants were being held in jail without contact with the outside world.

The facts of the Chambers case are that four young blacks were convicted of murder primarily upon confessions that they had given. This case was carried to the Supreme Court of the United States on the basis that the defendants had been denied due process of law. As in the Brown case, it was alleged that the defendants were convicted on confessions improperly admitted in the trial court against them. The Supreme Court reversed the convictions on the grounds that the confessions had been coerced and the defendants therefore had been denied due process of law.

The facts are that the murdered victim, an elderly white man, was robbed and murdered about 9 p.m. on a Saturday night at his home 12 miles from Fort Lauderdale, Florida. The crime was described by local authorities as a "most dastardly and atrocious act, which aroused great and justified public indignation." As a result, from 9:30 p.m. on Saturday to 9:30 p.m. Sunday, between 25 and 40 blacks, including Chambers and the 3 others who were convicted with him, were picked up and placed in jail for questioning about the killing.

On the following Monday, Chambers and some of the others who had been arrested were transferred from the local jail at Fort Lauderdale to Miami, allegedly to prevent mob violence, but they were returned the next day to Fort Lauderdale, where they were questioned "persistently and repeatedly" until the following Saturday night, at which time confessions were given.

The problem presented to the Supreme Court in this case was not one involving the trustworthiness of the confessions, but one of voluntariness. The trial court of Florida held that the confessions were given voluntarily. They therefore were admitted in evidence, and the admissibility was upheld by the Florida Appellate Courts. The United States Supreme Court took the view that protracted questioning of the defendants in unfriendly surroundings and without outside contact showed sufficient pressure to make the confessions involuntarily given, and the conviction was reversed.

This case marked the beginning of a new attitude of the Supreme Court on the admissibility of confessions. The Court took into account that brutality was becoming a thing of the past; yet, the Court stated, it took cognizance that other pressures of a more subtle nature might be applied to induce a confession and, consequently, there was all the more reason why an "independent examination" should be forthcoming concerning the manner in which a confession was obtained.

As a result of the Chambers case, the Supreme Court in its reviews became concerned not only with the possibility of physical force being applied to induce a confession but with psychological pressures as well. Just what would be classified as psychological pressure was still unknown at that time, and it was only as a result of subsequent decisions by various appellate courts that "psychological pressure" began to be clarified. It was soon learned that anything that caused mental stress to the accused in the inducement of the confession would be categorized as psychological pressure and cause the confession to be excluded.

Following the Brown and Chambers decisions, more and more requests were made by defendants for the Supreme Court to review their cases upon the allegation that confessions had been improperly admitted against them in the state courts. Another of the more frequently quoted cases in which the problem of psychological pressure was an issue is *Ashcraft v. Tennessee,* 322 U.S. 143 (1944). In this case the Supreme Court held that protracted questioning of the defendant was sufficiently coercive to make the confession involuntarily given. In the Ashcraft case the questioning of the defendant probably exceeded that of psychological pressure and reached physical abuse. Ashcraft was convicted in the state courts of Tennessee of the murder of his wife, and he was sentenced to 99 years in prison. The facts are that on June 6, 1941, Zelma Ashcraft, the wife of the defendant, left her home by automobile to visit her mother. Later that same afternoon, her dead body was found, and she had several cuts on her head. Ashcraft was taken into custody on Saturday, June 14, 1941, and was questioned continuously until 9:30 the following Monday morning, when he confessed to a plot of having his wife killed. It was admitted during the trial that Ashcraft had been questioned in relays because the officers conducting the interrogation became tired and needed rest, but Ashcraft was not permitted to sleep or rest during the questioning until after he had given the confession.

Justice Black in his majority opinion was very critical of the trial court for permitting the introduction of a confession obtained in this manner, and he stated that it was difficult to see how it could be considered that this confession was voluntarily given. He further stated that the mere fact that a jury and two state courts had considered the confession voluntarily given did not "foreclose" the United States Supreme Court from making an independent examination in an effort to determine whether the confession had been induced in such a manner that it was in violation of the due-process clause of the Fourteenth Amendment to the Constitution. He said: "The Supreme Court of the United States stands as a bar against the conviction of any individual in an American court by means of a coerced confession."

It was the majority opinion of the Court that the confession was involuntarily given and, therefore, the defendant had been denied due process of law. The conviction was accordingly reversed.

At the time of this decision, there was still a concern on the part of some of the justices about how far the Supreme Court should go in "policing" the state courts on the admissibility of evidence. Three justices dissented from the majority opinion in the Ashcraft case, and Justice Jackson in his dissenting opinion stated: "The burden of protecting society from most crimes against persons and property falls upon the state." He believed therefore that since the trial court and the appellate courts of Tennessee had come to the conclusion that the confession in the Ashcraft case was voluntarily given, the Supreme Court of the United States should not interfere with that decision and the Supreme Court had no supervisory powers over the state courts.

Justice Jackson did not condone the manner in which the confession was obtained, and stated that if it had been a federal court in which it was introduced he would agree with the majority and rule it involuntarily given. His only concern was the powers of the United States Supreme Court. His dissent had but little effect on the majority of the Court, as the Supreme Court continued its independent review of state court trial procedures and the admissibility of evidence in state courts.

In the Ashcraft case the facts revealed that there was protracted questioning of the defendant to a point where physical exhaustion had undoubtedly set in. It is difficult to determine whether this procedure should be classified as inhuman treatment or as psychological pressure applied to induce the confession. But we now come to a line of cases in which there is no indication of any physical mistreatment, not even to the point of protracted questioning, but cases in which the pressure applied to induce the confession is purely psychological. One of the more interesting cases is *Spano v. New York*, 360 U.S. 315 (1959), in which the psychological pressure was one of playing on the sympathy of Spano through deception. Although a number of cases were decided between Ashcraft in 1944 and Spano in 1959, the Spano case reflects the thinking of the justices of the United States Supreme Court about the application of any kind of pressure which may affect the freedom of the mind in making a confession.

The facts of the Spano case are that Spano, a man twenty-five years of age, a junior high school graduate of Italian descent, was convicted of murder in New York. On January 22, 1957, Spano was drinking in a bar, and while he was there a former professional boxer who weighed 200 pounds took some of Spano's money from the counter. As this man left the bar, Spano followed him outside in an effort to recover his money. A fight ensued, and the man knocked Spano down and kicked him in the head several times. After this, Spano walked to his apartment, obtained a gun, and then proceeded to a candy store this man was known to frequent. The man was in the candy store, and Spano fired five shots in his direction. Two of the shots entered his body, causing his death. The only witness to the shooting was a young man who was supervising the store at the time. After the shooting, Spano disappeared for a week.

On February 3, 1957, Spano telephoned a close friend of his who was a rookie police officer. Spano told the officer that he, Spano, had taken a terrific beating from the murder victim, and being dazed, he, Spano, did not know what he was doing when he shot at the victim. Spano further stated that he was going to get a lawyer and give himself up. The officer relayed this information to his superiors. The following day, Spano, accompanied by an attorney, surrendered to the police. After cautioning Spano against answering any questions, the attorney left, and Spano was immediately taken to a room and interrogated. Spano, in accordance with his attorney's instructions, refused to answer any questions. The questioning, however, was continued, and Spano persisted in his refusal to answer. He requested to see his attorney, but the request was denied. Those in charge of the investigation thought that Spano's friend, the rookie officer, could be of assistance. The friend was called and was told to inform Spano that the telephone call made to him by Spano had caused him a "lot of trouble." The officer was instructed to try to win sympathy from Spano for his (the officer's) wife and children. The rookie officer played his part, but Spano still refused to answer any questions. It was not until the fourth effort was made by the rookie officer to gain the sympathy of Spano that he finally agreed to tell the authorities about the shooting. Spano did make a confession, which was introduced in evidence against Spano over the objections of the defense attorney, who alleged that the confession had not been voluntarily given. The trial judge admitted the confession and instructed the jury that they might rely on the confession if they found it to have been voluntarily given. A guilty verdict was returned, and Spano was given the death penalty. The conviction was affirmed by the New York Court of Appeals, and the case was then taken to the United States Supreme Court on the grounds that Spano had been denied due process.

The majority opinion, written by Chief Justice Warren, reflects the thinking of the Supreme Court on the use of deception as a means of psychological pressure to induce a confession. A portion of Chief Justice Warren's opinion is quoted as an illustration of the reasoning of the Court in this case. Justice Douglas wrote a separate opinion in which he agreed with the majority, but Justice Douglas was particularly concerned with the fact that Spano had requested to see his attorney during the period of the questioning and had been refused. Justice Douglas's thinking in the Spano case was a forerunner of the decision handed down in the Escobedo case, which will be discussed later.

Chief Justice Warren, in writing the majority opinion which reversed Spano's conviction, stated:

> This is another in the long line of cases presenting the question whether a confession was properly admitted into evidence under the Fourteenth Amendment. As in all such cases, we are forced to resolve a conflict between two fundamental interests of society; its interest in prompt and efficient law enforcement, and its interest in preventing the rights of its individual members from being abridged by unconstitutional methods of law enforcement. Because of the delicate nature of the constitutional determination which we must make, we cannot escape the responsibility of making our own examination of the record.

Following the Spano case two years later was the case of *Rogers v. Richmond,* 365 U.S. 534 (1961), in which the Supreme Court further expressed its opinion about deception. In this case Rogers was found guilty of murder by a jury in a Connecticut superior court, a conviction which was affirmed by the Connecticut Supreme Court, but which was reversed by the United States Supreme Court.

The facts in this case are: Rogers, the defendant, while lodged in jail pending a trial, was questioned concerning a killing which had taken place in the area. The interrogation commenced at approximately 2 p.m. on the day Rogers was arrested and continued throughout the afternoon and evening. During the interrogation Rogers was allowed to smoke and was brought a sandwich and some coffee. He was at no time subjected to violence, nor was there a threat of violence.

After Rogers had been intermittently questioned without success by a team of at least three police officers from 2 p.m. to 8 p.m., the assistant chief of police was called in to conduct the interview. When Rogers persisted in his denial that he had done the shooting, the assistant chief pretended, in Rogers' hearing, to place a telephone call to police officers, directing them to stand in readiness to bring in Rogers' wife for questioning. After the passage of approximately one hour, during which Rogers remained silent, the assistant chief indicated that he was about to have Rogers' wife taken into custody. At this point Rogers announced his willingness to make a confession, which was introduced against him during the trial.

The United States Supreme Court held that the Connecticut trial court erred in holding that the confession in this case was voluntarily given, and that the Connecticut Supreme Court was wrong in affirming the conviction as they "failed to apply the standard demanded by the Due Process Clause of the Fourteenth Amendment for determining admissibility of a confession."

It was stated in the majority opinion that:

> Our [the United States Supreme Court] decisions under the Fourteenth Amendment have made clear that convictions following the admission into evidence of confessions which are involuntary, i.e., the product of coercion, either physical or psychological, cannot stand. This is so not because such confessions are unlikely to be true, but because the methods used to extract them offend an underlying principle in the enforcement of our criminal law: "That ours is an accusatorial and not an inquisitorial system—a system in which the State must establish guilt by evidence independently and freely secured, and may not by coercion prove its charge against an accused out of his own mouth."

The reversal in this case was based upon the fact that there had not been complete freedom of the mind on the part of the accused in making his confession. It was stated that the behavior of the law enforcement officials was such as to overbear the will of the accused. The fact that the accused spoke the truth is beside the point.

EXCLUSION OF CONFESSIONS BECAUSE OF DELAY IN ARRAIGNMENT

For many years it has been considered to be a serious breach of an accused person's rights to delay arraigning him, but in the past a delayed arraignment was not the basis for the exclusion of a confession. However, this was changed as a result of the famous McNabb decision handed down by the United States Supreme Court in 1943 (see *McNabb v. United States*, 318 U.S. 352). This decision created an entirely new approach to the exclusion of confessions. The Court in the McNabb case was not concerned with the voluntariness of the confession, but with whether certain judicial procedures were followed, that is, whether the accused was arraigned "without unnecessary delay." If not, there had been a violation of the rights of the accused, so that any confession given before the arraignment should be excluded from evidence.

The McNabb decision had far-reaching effects on law enforcement throughout the nation. Although this decision pertained to the action of federal officials, the Court pointed out that the states also have requirements that arrested persons be arraigned without unnecessary delay. The implication was that the ruling in the McNabb case would be held applicable to local officers should it be put to a test in a United States Supreme Court review.

The facts of the McNabb case are that three McNabb brothers were convicted in the United States District Court of the Eastern District of

Tennessee on a charge of second-degree murder for killing a United Alcohol Tax Unit officer. This conviction was reversed by the United States Supreme Court primarily upon the grounds that the McNabb brothers had not been properly arraigned within the prescribed time, and consequently the confessions given by them during the period of time that they were being illegally held were improperly admitted against them.

In this case several Alcohol Tax Unit officers made a raid upon a cache of illegal whiskey which allegedly belonged to the McNabb brothers. During the raid one of the officers was shot and killed. Thereafter the McNabb brothers were taken into custody on the charge of killing the officer. They were held in jail for several days and were interrogated intermittently. There was no allegation of mistreatment or psychological pressure being applied to induce the confessions. The McNabbs were not permitted to see their relatives and they did not have an attorney, but there was no showing that they had requested an attorney. The only wrong committed by the federal officers was that there was a lapse of six days between the time of the arrest and the time of the arraignment. During this time confessions were obtained.

The case was appealed to the United States Supreme Court on the ground that the confessions which were admitted in evidence against the McNabbs were in violation of the constitutional guarantee against self-incrimination. No mention was made in the appeal of the failure to arraign the defendants without unnecessary delay. However, the Supreme Court in its decision bypassed the guarantee against self-incrimination, and decided the case entirely upon the failure of the federal officers to abide by a Federal Rule of Criminal Procedure passed by Congress which provides that "an officer in making an arrest shall take the arrested person without unnecessary delay before the nearest commissioner."

The wording of the majority opinion in this case, a portion of which is being quoted, emphasizes how strongly the majority of the justices disapproved the failure to arraign the McNabbs within a reasonable time. The Court stated:

> The circumstances in which the statements, admitted in evidence against the McNabbs, were secured reveal a plain disregard of the duty enjoined by Congress upon federal law officers. . . . The record leaves no room for doubt that the questioning of the McNabbs took place while they were in custody of the arresting officers and before any order of commitment was made. Plainly, a conviction resting on evidence secured through such a flagrant disregard of the procedure which Congress has commanded cannot be allowed to stand without making the courts themselves accomplices in wilful disobedience of law.

After this decision was rendered by the Supreme Court, the question in the mind of law enforcement, and particularly of federal, officers was whether all confessions taken prior to arraignment would be excluded, or only those obtained through long and extensive questioning without the aid of friends, relatives, or counsel. Fortunately, some of the problems were solved by the decision handed down one year later in *United States v. Mitchell*, 322 U.S. 65 (1944). In this case the defendant was convicted of burglary in Washington, D.C. The conviction was affirmed by the United States Supreme Court. The facts are that in August and October 1942, two houses in the District of Columbia were broken into and property from each was stolen. Police investigation led to one Mitchell, who was taken into custody at his home at 7 p.m. on Monday, October 12, 1942, after which he was taken to the police station. Within a few minutes after his arrival there, he admitted his guilt and advised the police officers where a number of stolen items could be located. Mitchell was held thereafter for eight days before he was arraigned. Mitchell was convicted primarily upon the confession of guilt and as a result of the property recovered about which Mitchell had told officers. The United States Supreme Court held in this case that the confession was not obtained after lengthy interrogation but almost immediately after arrest. The fact that the defendant was held eight days thereafter before being arraigned did not act as a bar to admitting the confession. This case therefore did clarify the fact that the delay in arraignment alone would not vitiate the confession so long as the delay was not for the purpose of eliciting the confession.

The next case of importance in relation to the admissibility of confessions from a procedural standpoint is *Mallory v. United States*, 354 U.S. 449 (1957). Mallory was convicted of rape in the District of Columbia and was given the death penalty. The conviction was reversed by the United States Supreme Court. The victim in this case was raped in the basement of the apartment house in which she lived. She had gone to the basement to wash some clothes; she had difficulty in detaching a hose, and Mallory, who lived in the same building, detached it for her and left. Shortly thereafter, a masked man appeared and attacked the victim. She described the man as having the same general features as those of Mallory. Efforts to locate Mallory failed as he disappeared from the apartment building about the time of the rape. He was arrested the next afternoon along with some of his relatives. The relatives were questioned first, and about 8 p.m. Mallory was questioned and after an hour and a half of steady interrogation he admitted his guilt. He thereafter repeated his confession to other officers. At 10 p.m. the same day the officers tried to locate a United States commissioner for the first time in order that Mallory could be arraigned. A commissioner could not be located, and so Mallory was held overnight and arraigned the next morning. In the meantime his confession was reduced to writing, and he signed it sometime about midnight that same day. The next morning Mallory was arraigned. During his trial the signed confession was introduced into evidence. The defendant was convicted largely as a result of this confession.

The Court in this case stated:

> The scheme for initiating a federal prosecution is plainly defined. The police may not arrest upon mere suspicion but only on "probable cause." The next step in the proceeding is to arraign the arrested person before a judicial officer as quickly as possible so that he may be advised of his rights and so that the issue of probable cause may be promptly determined. The arrested person may, of course, be "booked" by the police. But he is not to be taken to police headquarters in order to carry out a process of inquiry that lends itself, even if not so designed, to eliciting damaging statements to support the arrest and ultimately his guilt.
>
> The duty enjoined upon arresting officers to arraign "without unnecessary delay" indicates that the command does not call for mechanical or automatic obedience. Circumstances may justify a brief delay between arrest and arraignment, as for instance, where the story volunteered by the accused is susceptible of quick verification through third parties. But the delay must not be of a nature to give opportunity for the extraction of a confession. . . .
>
> The circumstances of this case preclude a holding that the arraignment was "without unnecessary delay."
>
> We cannot sanction this extended delay, resulting in confession, without subordinating the general rule of prompt arraignment to the discretion of arresting officers in finding exceptional circumstances for its disregard. In every case where the police resort to interrogation of an arrested person and secure a confession, they may well claim, and quite sincerely, that they were merely trying to check on the information given by him. Against such a claim and the evil potentialities of the practice for which it is urged stands the rule on arraignment as a barrier.

The Mallory decision did not change the picture materially. It was recognized by the Court that "booking" procedure was a necessary function of police work, and that a reasonable period of time before arraignment was permissible for this process. The problem for law enforcement officers was just how much delay would be tolerated for the booking procedure before the arraignment took place, and what would be the effect on the admissibility of any statements made by the accused during that time. It was stated in the Mallory decision that any delay in arraignment made solely for the purpose of eliciting a confession would cause the confession to be excluded.

It must be remembered that the McNabb rule of excluding confessions because of a delay in arraignment is applicable only to federal officers and that, to date, this rule has not been applied to the states. Most states have not adopted the McNabb rule, so that a mere delay in arraignment will not exclude a confession. However, this rule could be invoked if it were proved that the delay in arraignment was solely for the purpose of seeking a confession. Also the delay might affect the voluntariness of the confession in certain instances.

RIGHT OF COUNSEL
AND RIGHT TO REMAIN SILENT

Another revolutionary change in the requirements for the admissibility of confessions was established by *Escobedo v. Illinois,* 378 U.S. 478 (1964). In substance, the United States Supreme Court stated in this decision that any time a suspect is taken into custody and interrogated by an officer, the suspect is to be warned of his right to remain silent, and if a request is made for the assistance of counsel, it is to be granted. If these rules are not abided by, any statements made by the suspect will be excluded from evidence.

In brief, the facts of this case are that Escobedo was arrested on a charge of having murdered his brother-in-law. Escobedo refused to make any statements to the police, and his attorney had him released later in the day on a writ of habeas corpus. Thereafter the police received some additional information verifying that Escobedo was responsible for the murder, and he was again arrested and taken to the police station. Upon his arrival there, Escobedo requested permission to see his attorney, who had in the meantime arrived at the station. The attorney also requested permission to talk with Escobedo. Both requests were denied. Escobedo was then interrogated by the police. During this time he made additional requests to see his attorney, which were also denied. While being interrogated Escobedo made some incriminating statements to the police, statements which were used against him during his trial for murder.

Escobedo was convicted of murder, a conviction upheld by the Illinois Supreme Court, and the case was then taken to the United States Supreme Court upon the contention that Escobedo had been denied due process of law because he had not been afforded the right of counsel as provided by the Sixth Amendment. The attorneys for the state of Illinois argued that the right-of-counsel guarantee of the Sixth Amendment granted the right of assistance at the time of trial and not prior thereto. The United States Supreme Court gave a different interpretation to this guarantee, and held that the right of counsel starts at the moment that an "investigation begins to focus on a particular suspect." At this moment the suspect had to be warned of his right to remain silent and had to be allowed to talk to his attorney if he requested to do so. Otherwise any statements made by him could not be used against him in court. Since Escobedo was denied these rights, his conviction was reversed by the Supreme Court, and a new rule on admissibility of confessions was created.

Because of the significance of this case upon law enforcement in the interrogation of suspects, a portion of the decision is being quoted in order that the reasoning of the Court may be better understood.

The Supreme Court stated:

> The interrogation here was conducted before petitioner [Escobedo] was formally indicted. But in the context of this case, that fact should make no difference. When petitioner requested, and was denied, an opportunity to consult with his lawyer, the investigation had ceased to be a general investigation of "an unsolved crime." Petitioner had become the accused, and the purpose of the interrogation was to get him to confess his guilt despite his constitutional right not to do so. . . .
>
> Petitioner, a layman, was undoubtedly unaware that under Illinois law an admission of "mere" complicity in the murder plot was legally as damaging as an admission of firing of the fatal shots. The guiding hand of counsel was essential to advise petitioner of his rights in this situation. This was the stage when legal aid and advice were most critical to the petitioner. It was a stage surely as critical as arraignment and the preliminary hearing. What happened at this interrogation could certainly affect the whole trial.

The Court further stated:

> In Gideon v. Wainwright [372 U.S. 335 (1963)] we [the Supreme Court] held that every person accused of a crime, whether state or federal, is entitled to a lawyer at trial. The rule sought by the State here [in the Escobedo case] however, would make the trial no more than an appeal from the interrogation; and the right to use counsel at the formal trial would be a very hollow thing if for all practical purposes the conviction is already assured by the trial examination. . . . It is argued that if the right to counsel is afforded [to the accused] prior to indictment, the number of confessions obtained by the police will diminish significantly, because most confessions are obtained during the period between arrest and indictment, and any lawyer worth his salt will tell the suspect in no uncertain terms to make no statement to police under any circumstances. This argument, of course, cuts two ways. The fact that many confessions are obtained during this period points up its critical nature as a stage when legal aid and advice are surely needed. The right to counsel would indeed be hollow if it began at a period when few confessions were obtained. There is necessarily a direct relationship between the importance of a stage to the police in their quest for a confession and the criticalness of that stage to the accused in his need for legal advice. Our Constitution, unlike others, strikes the balance in favor of the right of the accused to be advised by his lawyer of his privilege against self-incrimination. . . .

> We have learned the lesson of history, ancient and modern, that
> a system of criminal law enforcement which comes to depend on
> the confession will, in the long run, be less reliable and more
> subject to abuses than a system which depends on extrinsic evi-
> dence independently secured through skillful investigation.

The reverberations caused by this decision, as by the McNabb case,
were felt across the nation. Law enforcement officials, prosecutors, and
many judges thought that the Supreme Court had placed undue restrictions upon law enforcement, and for all practical purposes had eliminated
the chances of obtaining confessions from accused persons. Even some of
the Supreme Court justices were not in agreement with the interpretation
of the majority, as this was a 5-to-4 decision. However, this decision became
the law of the land, and it had to be followed if confessions were to be
admitted in evidence. Law enforcement officers and prosecutors knew this
and would comply. But complying with this decision was not without its
problems. The warning to remain silent and the right of counsel were to be
made operative "when [in the language of the decision] the investigation is
no longer a general inquiry into an unsolved crime but has begun to focus
on a particular suspect." Just when this point is reached is not easily determined in many instances. Also, when does the case pass from the investigative stage to the accusatory stage? The solution to this question was most
puzzling to those who endeavored to operate under the Escobedo rules.

Two years later the United States Supreme Court in *Miranda v.
Arizona,* 384 U.S. 436 (1966), endeavored to provide answers to the problems created by the Escobedo case. In their efforts to clarify the problems
of the Escobedo case, the Court established additional restrictions on the
admissibility of confessions by granting to the accused further protection of
the right of counsel and the right to remain silent.

Whether the United States Supreme Court in the Miranda case intentionally created further restrictions upon the admissibility of confessions or
whether the Court merely endeavored to clarify what they tried to accomplish by the Escobedo case is not known for sure. But in either event,
further restrictions were imposed upon law enforcement officers as to
how they may interrogate accused persons.

The Court held in the Miranda case that for a confession to be admissible, officers must abide by a prescribed set of rules specifically set forth in
that decision. In brief, these rules provide that if a suspect is in custody, or
if he is deprived of freedom of action in any way, he must be advised that
(1) he has the right to remain silent; (2) if he gives up this right to remain
silent, anything he says can and will be used as evidence against him in
court; (3) he has the right to consult an attorney and to have that attorney
present during the interrogation by the peace officer; and (4) if he is unable
to afford an attorney, he is entitled to have an attorney appointed to represent him during the course of the interrogation, free of charge.

The Miranda case was one of four cases decided by the Supreme Court at the same time, each based primarily upon the same issue, that is, the right of the accused to have the assistance of counsel during the custodial interrogation. These decisions are referred to as the "Miranda rule." In writing the majority opinion, Chief Justice Warren was not unmindful that serious criticism had been directed toward the Supreme Court as a result of the Escobedo case. In fact, the Chief Justice went so far as to quote some of the criticisms in his Miranda opinion. He undoubtedly anticipated further repercussions from the Miranda decision, which may account for the fact that this is one of the longest decisions handed down by the United States Supreme Court in a criminal case.

Because of the impact of the Miranda decision on law enforcement, a portion of it is worthy of quoting verbatim to show the thinking of the majority of the Court.

Chief Justice Warren stated:

> The cases before us [meaning the Miranda case and the other three companion cases] raise questions which go to the roots of our concepts of American criminal jurisprudence: the restraints society must observe consistent with the Federal Constitution in prosecuting individuals for crime. More specifically, we deal with the admissibility of statements obtained from an individual who is subject to custodial police interrogation and the necessity for procedures which assure that the individual is accorded his privilege under the Fifth Amendment of the Constitution not to be compelled to incriminate himself. . . .
>
> The constitutional issue we decide in each of these cases is the admissibility of statements obtained from a defendant questioned while in custody and deprived of his freedom of action. In each, the defendant was questioned by police officers, detectives, or a prosecuting attorney in a room in which he was cut off from the outside world. In none of these cases was the defendant given a full and effective warning of his rights at the outset of the interrogation process. In all cases, the questioning elicited oral admissions, and in three of them, signed statements as well which were admitted at their trials. They all thus share salient features— incommunicado interrogation of individuals in a police-dominated atmosphere, resulting in self-incriminating statements without full warnings of constitutional rights. . . . An understanding of the nature and setting of this in-custody interrogation is essential to our decisions today. . . .
>
> In dealing with statements obtained through interrogation, we do not purport to find all confessions inadmissible. Confessions remain a proper element in law enforcement. Any statement given freely and voluntarily without any compelling influences is, of course, admissible in evidence. The fundamental import of the privilege while an individual is in custody is not whether he is

allowed to talk to the police without the benefit of warnings and counsel, but whether he can be interrogated. There is no requirement that police stop a person who enters a police station and states that he wishes to confess to a crime, or a person who calls the police to offer a confession or any other statement he desires to make. Volunteered statements of any kind are not barred by the Fifth Amendment and their admissibility is not affected by our holding today.

To summarize, we hold that when an individual is taken into custody or otherwise deprived of his freedom by the authorities and is subject to questioning, the privilege against self-incrimination is jeopardized. Procedural safeguards must be employed to protect the privilege, and unless other fully effective means are adopted to notify the person of his right of silence and to assure that the exercise of the right will be scrupulously honored, the following measures are required. (1) He must be warned prior to any questioning that he has the right to remain silent; (2) that anything he says can be used against him in a court of law; (3) that he has the right to the presence of an attorney; and (4) that if he cannot afford an attorney one will be appointed for him prior to any questioning if he so desires. (5) Opportunity to exercise these rights must be afforded to him throughout the interrogation. (6) After such warnings have been given, and such opportunity afforded him, the individual may knowingly and intelligently waive these rights and agree to answer questions or make a statement. But unless and until such warnings and waivers are demonstrated by the prosecution at trial, no evidence obtained as a result of interrogation can be used against him.

The Miranda decision did clarify to a degree what the Court meant in the Escobedo case when they spoke of an investigation being focused on a particular suspect. The Court in the Miranda decision stated that this was any time that a suspect was in custody or otherwise deprived of his "freedom of action in any way." The Miranda case still left a problem hanging for the law enforcement officer, that is, just what would be interpreted as depriving a person of his "freedom of action in any way"?

In the case of *Oregon v. Mathiason*, 50 L. Ed. 2d. 714 (1977), the United States Supreme Court held that a suspect who voluntarily came to a police station and furnished incriminating information was not deprived of his freedom of action in such a way as to make the Miranda warnings necessary.

The facts of the Mathiason case reflect that an officer was furnished with the name of a suspect by a burglary victim. The officer left a note at the home of the suspect advising him that the officer wished to discuss something with him. The suspect came to the police station, where he was met by the officer in the hallway of the station. They shook hands and the suspect was advised that he was not under arrest. They then entered an office, and the door was closed. The suspect was advised that it was believed he was involved in a burglary. The suspect admitted taking the property involved in the burglary. This admission came within five minutes of the suspect's arrival at the police station. Thereafter the suspect was advised of his Miranda rights and a taped confession was taken from the suspect. He was again advised that he was not under arrest, and he was released to return to his home. He was later charged with the burglary, and his confession was introduced against him during the trial which resulted in his conviction. Upon appeal, the Oregon Supreme Court reversed the conviction on the ground that the interrogation was conducted under a custodial atmosphere, making the Miranda warnings necessary before the interrogation could begin.

The case was appealed to the United States Supreme court, which Court disagreed with the Oregon Supreme Court and upheld the conviction. The United States Supreme Court held that the interrogation of the defendant was not a custodial interrogation making the Miranda warnings necessary before the interrogation could begin. The Court in that case stated:

> Our decision in Miranda set forth rules of police procedure applicable to "custodial interrogation." By custodial interrogation, we mean questioning initiated by law enforcement officers after a person has been taken into custody or otherwise deprived of his freedom of action in any significant way. Subsequently we have found the Miranda principle applicable to questioning which takes place in a prison setting during a suspect's term of imprisonment on a separate offense, and to questioning taking place in a suspect's home, after he has been arrested and is no longer free to go where he pleases.
>
> In the present case, however, there is no indication that the questioning took place in a context where respondent's freedom to depart was restricted in any way. He came voluntarily to the police station, where he was immediately informed that he was not under arrest. At the close of a one-half hour interview respondent did in fact leave the police station without hindrance. It is clear from these facts that Mathiason was not in custody "or otherwise deprived of his freedom of action in any significant way."
>
> Such a noncustodial situation is not converted to one in which Miranda applies simply because a reviewing court concludes that, even in the absence of any formal arrest or restraint on freedom of movement, the questioning took place in a "coercive environment." Any interview of one suspected of a crime by a police officer will have coercive aspects to it, simply by virtue of the fact that the police officer is part of a law enforcement system which may ultimately cause the suspect to be charged with a crime. But police officers are not required to administer Miranda warnings to everyone whom they question. Nor is the requirement of warn-

ings to be imposed simply because the questioning takes place in the station house, or because the questioned person is one whom the police suspect. Miranda warnings are required only where there has been such a restriction on a person's freedom as to render him "in custody." It was that sort of coercive environment to which Miranda by its terms was made applicable, and to which it is limited.

The Miranda decision does not require that the Miranda warnings be administered with each contact between an officer and a person. It has been held that in general on-the-scene questioning of citizens in the fact-finding process to determine in general what happened in a case does not demand that all persons interviewed be advised of the Miranda rights. It has been held also that spontaneous incriminating statements made by a person contacted by an officer are admissible. Also, incriminating statements made in response to an officer's inquiry in emergency situations concerning the health and/or safety of another are admissible. As was stated in one case: "While life hangs in the balance, there is no room to require admonitions concerning the right to consult and to remain silent. It is inconceivable that the Miranda court or the framers of the Constitution envisioned such admonishments first to be under the facts presented in an emergency."

The Miranda decision made it quite clear that if the accused's freedom of movement was interfered with in any way, the accused had to be advised of his or her Miranda rights before the interrogation could begin. The Escobedo case merely stated that if the accused requested an attorney and his request was denied, any statement made by him would be excluded. The Escobedo case made no provision for advising the accused of his constitutional guarantee of right of counsel. The Miranda case so stated that after the right to remain silent and the right of counsel have been explained to the accused, the accused must intelligently waive these rights. The general interpretation of this requirement is that the accused must make a definite statement that he understands his rights and that he waives them before any statements made by him will be admissible. It was also pointed out that even though the accused begins to make statements, he may exercise his right to remain silent, or his desire to consult an attorney at any time, and if he does so, the interrogation must terminate. Some jurisdictions have held that once the accused has indicated that he desires to remain silent or to consult an attorney, the interrogation may not be reinstituted except by the request of the accused. It cannot be instigated by the officer. Does this mean that the officer cannot even ask the accused at a later time if he, the accused, wishes to discuss the matter further? The rulings are not entirely clear on this point, but it appears to be a rather harsh rule that would not permit an officer to attempt further interrogation, particularly in light of additional facts that may have developed through subsequent investigation. This problem was partially resolved by the United States Supreme Court in the case of *Michigan v. Mosley*, 423 U.S. 96 (1976). The Court in that case did sanction a subsequent questioning of Mosley after he had indicated that he did not wish to further discuss the charge for which he had been arrested. The facts of that case reflect that the defendant Mosley was arrested early in the afternoon in connection with several robberies. The arresting officer took Mosley to the robbery detail office and advised Mosley of his Miranda rights. The officer began to question Mosley about the robberies. But Mosley stated that he did not want to answer any questions about the robberies, whereupon the officer promptly ceased the interrogation and Mosley was placed in a jail cell. At no time did Mosley indicate that he wished to consult with an attorney.

About 6 p.m. of the same day, another officer had Mosley brought to the homicide detail office for the purpose of questioning him about a murder which had taken place during a robbery. Mosley was again advised of his Miranda rights and was then questioned about the murder. Mosley at first denied any involvement in the murder but later made a statement implicating himself. The interrogation lasted approximately 15 minutes, and at no time did Mosley ask to consult with an attorney or indicate that he did not want to discuss the homicide.

Mosley was charged with the murder, and his attorney made unsuccessful efforts to prevent the incriminating statements made by Mosley from being used during the trial. Mosley was convicted, but the Michigan Court of Appeals reversed the conviction upon the ground that the interrogation of Mosley about the murder was in violation of the Miranda rules, since Mosley had previously stated that he did not wish to answer any questions. The Michigan Supreme Court declined to hear an appeal on the case, whereupon the case was appealed to the United States Supreme Court, which Court agreed to hear the case because of the important constitutional question involved.

The question in this case was whether the conduct of the police that led to Mosley's incriminating statement did in fact violate the Miranda guidelines so as to render the statement inadmissible in evidence against Mosley at his trial. The solution to this question according to the Court turned almost entirely on the interpretation of a single passage in the Miranda decision.

> "Once warnings have been given, the subsequent procedure is clear. If the individual indicates in any manner, at any time prior to or during questioning, that he wishes to remain silent, the interrogation must cease. At this point he has shown that he intends to exercise his Fifth Amendment privilege; any statement taken after the person invokes his privilege cannot be other than the product of compulsion, subtle or otherwise. Without the right to cut off questioning, the setting of in-custody interrogation operates on the individual to overcome free choice in producing a statement after the privilege has been once invoked."

This passage states that "the interrogation must cease" when the person in custody indicates that "he wishes to remain silent." It does not state under what circumstances, if any, a resumption of questioning is permissible. The passage could be literally read to mean that a person who has invoked his "right to silence" can never again be subjected to custodial interrogation by any police officer at any time or place on any subject. Another possible construction of the passage would characterize "any statement taken after the person invokes his privilege" as "the product of compulsion" and would therefore mandate its exclusion from evidence, even if it were volunteered by the person in custody without any further interrogation whatever. Or the passage could be interpreted to require only the immediate cessation of questioning, and to permit a resumption of interrogation after a momentary respite.

It is evident that any of these possible literal interpretations would lead to absurd and unintended results. To permit the continuation of custodial interrogation after a momentary cessation would clearly frustrate the purposes of Miranda by allowing repeated rounds of questioning to undermine the will of the person being questioned. At the other extreme, a blanket prohibition against the taking of voluntary statements or a permanent immunity from further interrogation, regardless of the circumstances, would transform the Miranda safeguards into wholly irrational obstacles to legitimate police investigative activity, and deprive suspects of an opportunity to make informed and intelligent assessments of their interests. Clearly, therefore, neither this passage nor any other passage in the Miranda opinion can sensibly be read to create a per se proscription of indefinite duration upon any further questioning by any police officer on any subject, once the person in custody has indicated a desire to remain silent.

A reasonable and faithful interpretation of the Miranda opinion must rest on the intention of the Court in that case to adopt "fully effective means . . . to notify the person of his right of silence and to assure that the exercise of the right will be scrupulously honored." The critical safeguard identified in the passage at issue is a person's "right to cut off questioning." Through the exercise of his option to terminate questioning he can control the time at which questioning occurs, the subjects discussed, and the duration of the interrogation. The requirement that law enforcement authorities must respect a person's exercise of that option counteracts the coercive pressures of the custodial setting. We therefore conclude that the admissibility of statements obtained after the person in custody has decided to remain silent depends under Miranda on whether his "right to cut off questioning" was "scrupulously honored."

A review of the circumstances leading to Mosley's confession reveals that his "right to cut off questioning" was fully respected in this case. Before his initial interrogation, Mosley was carefully advised that he was under no obligation to answer any questions and could remain silent if he wished. He orally acknowledged that he understood the Miranda warnings and then signed a printed notification of rights form. . . .

This is not a case, therefore, where the police failed to honor a decision of a person in custody to cut off questioning, either by refusing to discontinue the interrogation upon request or by persisting in repeated efforts to wear down his resistance and make him change his mind. In contrast to such practices, the police here immediately ceased the interrogation, resumed questioning only after the passage of a significant period of time and the provision of a fresh set of warnings, and restricted the second interrogation to a crime that had not been a subject of the earlier interrogation.

The Court stated: "For these reasons, we conclude that the admission in evidence of Mosley's incriminating statement did not violate the principles of Miranda v. Arizona."

In the Mosley case, the suspect was questioned about an entirely different charge than that for which he was arrested and originally interviewed. The court was silent as it related to a subsequent interrogation concerning the same charge once a suspect has indicated he does not wish to answer any questions about the charge. It was noted in a footnote to the Mosley decision that the "vast majority of federal and state courts presented with this problem have concluded that the Miranda case does not create a per se prohibition against any further interrogation of a suspect once he or she has indicated a desire to remain silent. The controlling factor concerning the admissibility of statements made after a refusal to waive the Miranda rights is whether the subsequent interrogation was such that the freedom of the will of the suspect was respected."

In another case, a state court upheld the admissibility of incriminating statements made by a suspect after he refused to waive his Miranda rights. The facts of that case reveal that a suspect was arrested on a charge of burglary. The arresting officers immediately and routinely advised the suspect of his Miranda rights, and the suspect advised he did not wish to waive his rights. The suspect was transported to the police station and placed in a cell. Two days later, the suspect was brought to an interrogation room where he was again advised of his Miranda rights. Still later, the suspect advised that he was willing to talk about the charge, and he gave a confession about the burglary. The confession was introduced against the suspect during the trial over the objections of his attorney. The defendant was convicted, and the case was appealed on the grounds that the defendant's Miranda rights had been violated when he was questioned after previously advising that he did not wish to waive his rights. The appellate court upheld the conviction concluding that the Miranda rights had not been violated. The court stated that the first warnings were given during a field arrest and not during a formal interrogation. Even though the interrogation was initiated by the police solely to obtain a statement from the accused, there was no reason why the accused could not "freely, knowingly, and intelligently elect to speak without counsel at interrogation." In fact, the court in that case quoted from another decision stating: "There is no reason why, once having requested counsel and the request having been recognized by a cessation of interrogation, the accused cannot later elect to proceed without counsel if that election is freely, knowingly, and intelligently made."

It would appear from the Mosley decision as well as from the decisions of the appellate courts of a number of states that a suspect may be further questioned even though the suspect has expressed a desire to "cut off the questioning." The controlling factor appears to be whether the officer fully respected the suspect's right to stop the questioning at the time, and that there was a sufficient lapse of time between the "cut off" and the second questioning so as not to wear down the resistance of the suspect in an effort to make the suspect change his or her mind about conversing about the charge.

EVIDENCE DISCOVERED THROUGH IMPROPER CONFESSION EXCLUDED

The Miranda decision also reemphasized that not only will any statements made by the accused be excluded when his or her rights have been violated, but so will any evidence discovered as a result of such statements. This, however, is not a new philosophy on the part of the United States Supreme Court, because this Court, as well as many state courts, has for some time held that evidence discovered through improperly obtained statements would be excluded. It has been held that if a confession is poisonous (improperly obtained), the evidence discovered is nothing more than the "fruits of the poisonous tree" and will likewise be excluded. If the confession is inadmissible, so is the evidence discovered from the confession. It has been held also that a confession which is the product of illegally obtained physical evidence is inadmissible. In other words, if physical evidence unlawfully seized is displayed to an accused and causes the accused to confess, that confession is not admissible.

Another problem which has been presented to the courts is whether everything learned from a confession that was improperly obtained must be excluded from evidence. This problem was met to a degree by the United States Supreme Court in the case of *Michigan v. Tucker,* 417 U.S. 433 (1974). In that case, the Court held that the testimony of a witness whose identity was obtained through the questioning of a suspect who had not been fully informed of his Miranda rights was admissible. The facts of that case reflect that the accused was arrested on a charge of rape and seriously assaulting the raped victim. Before the interrogation of the suspect, he was asked if he wanted an attorney and whether he understood his constitutional rights. He advised that he knew his constitutional rights, and he was told that anything he said could be used against him in court at a later time. Since this arrest took place before the Miranda decision was handed down, the suspect was not advised that if he could not afford an attorney one would be provided for him free of charge.

During the interrogation of the suspect, he was questioned about his activities on the night of the rape, and he stated that he spent the evening with a friend, one Robert Henderson. Henderson was later interviewed in an effort to verify the story of the suspect, and Henderson stated that the suspect was with him only a short time on the evening of the rape and that on the day following the rape, he had seen the suspect, and the suspect had made some incriminating statements to him concerning the rape charge.

Although the arrest of the suspect in this case took place before the Miranda decision, the trial took place after that decision was handed down, whereupon the statements made by the suspect concerning his activities were not introduced against him during the trial because he had not been fully advised of his constitutional rights. Henderson, however, was called upon to testify concerning the incriminating statements made to him by the suspect. Unsuccessful efforts were made by the suspect's attorney to prevent Henderson from testifying upon the ground that Henderson's identity was fruit of the poisonous confession, that is, a confession obtained when the accused had not been fully informed of his constitutional rights. The accused was convicted of the charges, and his conviction was affirmed by the appellate courts of Michigan. He appealed to the United States Supreme Court upon the ground that the identity of Henderson was the result of an improperly obtained interrogation in violation of his Miranda rights. The Court stated: "This Court has already recognized that a failure to give interrogated suspects full Miranda warnings does not entitle the suspect to insist that statements made by him be excluded in every conceivable context." The decision pointed out that in the *Harris v. New York* case, the "Court was faced with the question of whether the statements of the defendant himself, taken without informing him of his right of access to appointed counsel, could be used to impeach defendant's direct testimony at trial." The Court also stated: "It does not follow from Miranda that evidence inadmissible against an accused in the prosecution's case in chief is barred for all purposes, provided of course that the trustworthiness of the evidence satisfies legal standards. . . . We believe that this reasoning is equally applicable here."

CONFESSION GIVEN AFTER AN UNLAWFUL ARREST MAY BE EXCLUDED

Another problem presented to the courts since the Miranda decision is whether a confession given following an unlawful arrest is admissible when the accused was advised of his or her Miranda rights. In other words, is a confession given after an unlawful arrest so much the product of the unlawful arrest that the confession becomes a fruit of the poisonous tree, or will advising the accused of his or her Miranda rights and a waiver of those rights remove the taint of the unlawful arrest and make the confession admissible? This question was partially answered by the United States Supreme Court in the case of *Brown v. Illinois,* 422 U.S. 590 (1975). In that case the Court held that incriminating statements made by Brown after an unlawful arrest were inadmissible even though Brown had been advised of his Miranda rights. The Court held that the statements were the fruits of a poisonous tree, that is, the unlawful arrest. However the Court stated that their decision in the Brown case was a limited one in that they did not agree with the Illinois Supreme Court, which held that advising the accused of his Miranda rights always purged the taint of the unlawful arrest, thereby making any incriminating statement by the accused admissible. The United States Supreme Court did not rule that all statements made after an unlawful arrest would be inadmissible, but there would have to be sufficient intervening circumstances to purge the taint of the unlawful arrest. The Court stated:

> It is entirely possible, of course, as the State [of Illinois] here argues, that persons arrested illegally frequently may decide to confess, as an act of the free will unaffected by the initial illegality. But the Miranda warnings, alone and per se, cannot always make the act sufficiently a product of free will to break, for the Fourth Amendment purposes, the causal connection between the illegality and the confession. They cannot assure in every case that the Fourth Amendment violation has not been unduly exploited. . . .
>
> The question whether a confession is the product of a free will must be answered on the facts of each case. No single fact is dispositive. The workings of the human mind are too complex, and the possibilities of misconduct too diverse, to permit protection of the Fourth Amendment to turn on such a talismanic test. The Miranda warnings are an important factor, to be sure, in determining whether the confession is obtained by exploitation of an illegal arrest. But they are not the only factor to be considered. The temporal proximity of the arrest and the confession, the presence of intervening circumstances, and particularly, the purpose and flagrancy of the official misconduct are all relevant. The voluntariness of the statement is a threshold requirement. And the burden of showing admissibility rests of course, on the prosecution.

It would appear from the Brown decision that if an accused were advised of his Miranda rights and he chose to waive those rights and made incriminating statements, those statements may be admissible even though the accused had been unlawfully arrested. However, the burden would be on the prosecution to prove that the incriminating statements were not the product of the unlawful arrest but were made with a complete freedom of the will.

CONFESSIONS STILL ACCEPTABLE AS EVIDENCE

There is no doubt that the Miranda decision has made obtaining confessions more difficult and their admission as evidence more uncertain. But this decision did not abolish the use of confessions as evidence. In fact, the Court in the Miranda case specifically pointed out that "confessions remain a proper element in law enforcement."

Also, as many commentators and courts have recognized, there is a compulsion to confess to crime. Wigmore states the point colorfully:

> The nervous pressure of guilt is enormous; the load of the deed done is heavy; the fear of detection fills the consciousness; and when detection comes, the pressure is relieved; and the deep sense of relief makes confession a satisfaction. At that moment, he will tell all, and tell it truly. To forbid soliciting him, to seek to prevent this relief, is to fly in the face of human nature. A psychiatrist explains the phenomenon of confessions in terms of subconscious but overpowering guilt feelings and desire for punishment. There is an impulse growing more and more intense suddenly to cry out his secret in the street before all people, or in milder cases, to confide it at least to one person, to free himself from the terrible burden. The work of confession is thus that emotional process in which the social and psychological significance of the crime becomes preconscious and in which all powers that resist the compulsion to confess are conquered.

It is well that the courts still recognize that a confession freely and voluntarily given has a place in law enforcement and in the protection of society. There are many crimes committed where even after the most clever, intelligent, and scientific investigation is conducted, practically no evidence is discovered to aid in the identity of the perpetrator or assist in his conviction. This is particularly true in murder cases because in most instances the murderer and the victim are the only ones present at the time of the slaying, and frequently there is no physical evidence at the scene except the dead victim. The killer frequently disposes of the murder weapon miles from the scene. The identification and the successful prosecution of a slayer become most difficult. It is only by interrogation of a suspect that positive identity can be made and material evidence can be discovered. This does not mean that coerced confessions should be permitted or condoned, but proper interrogation should continue to be allowed if society is to be protected.

■ Procedure for Introduction of Confessions

A confession is introduced through the testimony of the officer to whom it was made. If the defense attorney objects to the introduction of a confession in evidence because it was improperly obtained, a preliminary inquiry will be held by the trial judge to determine whether the confession should be admitted. At one time in most jurisdictions this inquiry was heard by both the judge and jury. If the judge decided that the confession was involuntarily given, he would exclude it. If there was some doubt about the voluntariness, he would admit the confession and instruct the jury that they should decide the issue. If they believed that the confession was involuntarily given, they should disregard it.

The United States Supreme Court in *Jackson v. Denno,* 378 U.S. 368 (1964), held that this procedure denied the defendant the right of a fair trial. It was pointed out that although the jury is instructed to disregard a confession they believed to have been involuntarily given, this is not easily done. The United States Supreme Court asked, when a confession is solidly implanted in the jury's mind, as in the Jackson case, even though the jury finds the confession involuntarily given,

> does the jury . . . then disregard the confession in accordance with its instructions? If there are lingering doubts about the sufficiency of the other evidence, does the jury unconsciously lay them to rest by resort to the confession? Will uncertainty about the sufficiency of the other evidence to prove guilt beyond a reasonable doubt actually result in acquittal when a jury knows the defendant has given a truthful confession?
>
> It is difficult, if not impossible, to prove that a confession which a jury has found to be involuntary has nevertheless influenced the verdict. . . .
>
> In those cases where without the confession the evidence is insufficient, the defendant should not be convicted if the jury believes the confession but finds it to be involuntary. The jury, however, finds it difficult to understand the policy forbidding reliance upon a coerced, but true, confession. . . . That trustworthy confession must also be voluntary if it is to be used at all, generates natural and potent pressure to find it voluntary. Otherwise the guilty defendant goes free.

Therefore, the Court concluded that "It is both practical and desirable that in cases to be tried hereafter a proper determination of voluntariness be made prior to the admission of the confession to the jury which is adjudicating the guilt or innocence."

Since the *Jackson v. Denno* decision, courts have followed one of two methods in determining the admissibility of a confession. One is known as the Massachusetts procedure. Under this procedure when an objection is made to the introduction of a confession, a preliminary inquiry is held by the trial judge to determine whether the confession was voluntarily given. This inquiry is made out of the hearing of the jury. If the judge concludes that the confession was properly obtained, he will admit it, but he must instruct the jury that they have the final power to determine whether the confession was voluntarily given. The jury then makes their own independent determination on the voluntariness of the confession. The Jackson case did not rule out this procedure as it was held that the jury would be permitted to consider only those confessions which the judge deemed to have been voluntarily given. As was pointed out by Justice Harlan in his dissent in the Jackson case, it is difficult to make a distinction between the procedure ruled improper in the Jackson case and the Massachusetts procedure.

The other procedure, which is followed in some jurisdictions, requires the trial judge to hold a preliminary inquiry out of the hearing of the jury, and to make the final determination whether the confession was voluntarily given or not. If the judge admits it, the jury will determine only the weight that will be given to the confession.

The advocates of the Massachusetts procedure argue that it is the better procedure because it is traditional to submit disputed facts to the jury for their determination. Those in favor of the judge's making the final determination hold that this is the better procedure because otherwise the judge could easily "pass the buck" to the jury when there was a difficult decision to make. Also, the Massachusetts procedure still places on the jury an impossible task of disregarding a confession they may believe to have been involuntarily given.

Under both procedures all that is necessary in order to have an inquiry made as to the admissibility of a confession is for the defendant to indicate opposition to the confession's being introduced in evidence. During such inquiry or hearing, the prosecuting attorney has the burden of proof that the confession was properly obtained. The prosecuting attorney must present evidence through the testimony of witnesses that the confession was voluntarily given and that all the other rights and procedures were followed in properly obtaining the confession. Whether the judge presiding over the inquiry has to be convinced beyond a reasonable doubt or only by a preponderance of the evidence was answered by the United States Supreme Court in the case of *Lego v. Twomey*, 404 U.S. 477 (1972), in which the Court stated: "When a confession challenged as involuntary is sought to be used against a criminal defendant at his trial, he is entitled to a reliable and clear-cut determination that the confession was in fact voluntarily rendered. Thus, the prosecution must prove at least by a preponderance of the evidence that the confession was voluntary. Of course, the States are free, pursuant to their own law, to adopt a higher standard." (The states, that is, may require that the proof be beyond a reasonable doubt.) The demarcation between proof beyond a reasonable doubt and proof by a preponderance of the evidence is not always easily determined. Preponderance of evidence has been described as evidence of great weight or evidence that is more credible and convincing as to the truth when weighed against the evidence presented by the opposition. Reasonable doubt is that as defined in Chapter 1.

At this inquiry the defendant is permitted to offer evidence in an effort to contradict the evidence presented by the prosecution. If the judge decides that the confession was not properly obtained, the confession will be excluded and the trial will have to be conducted without the benefit of the confession. If the judge concludes that the confession was properly obtained, the judge will permit the confession to be introduced during the trial. If the defendant is convicted, the defendant may appeal, and the appellate court will make an independent review concerning the manner in which the confession was obtained. If the appellate court concludes from the record of the case that the confession was improperly obtained, the conviction will be reversed.

■ Reversal Regardless of Other Evidence

The United States Court has also held that when an improperly obtained confession is introduced against an accused during a trial and he is convicted, the conviction must be reversed even though there is other sufficient evidence to substantiate the conviction. This is based upon the theory that it is impossible to determine the weight and influence that the confession had in bringing about the conviction. As was stated by the Supreme Court in *Payne v. Arkansas*, 356 U.S. 560 (1958), although the prosecution contended that there was sufficient evidence besides the confession to sustain the verdict of guilty,

> where as here, a coerced confession constitutes a part of the evidence before the jury, no one can tell what credit and weight the jury gave to the confession and under these circumstances this Court has uniformly held that even though there may have been sufficient evidence, apart from the coerced confession, to support a judgment of conviction, the admission in evidence, over the objection, of the coerced confession, it vitiates the judgment because it violated the "due process" clause of the Fourteenth Amendment.

ADMISSIBILITY OF SECOND CONFESSION AFTER FIRST WAS IMPROPERLY OBTAINED. A problem which frequently presents itself is whether a second confession which meets all the requirements for admissibility may be introduced in evidence after a first confession has been improperly obtained. The appellate court decisions on this point are comparatively few in number, but the general opinion is that, in most instances, the second confession will not be admissible because it is the poisonous fruit of the first confession. However, the mere fact that the first confession was improperly obtained is not always fatal to the admissibility of the second one. But a very strict test must be met before it is admitted. The second confession must have been given under such circumstances that all the evil forces which induced the first confession were gone and were not an inducement for giving the second one.

It is known that once an accused has given a confession, irrespective of the circumstances under which it was given, securing a second one is a relatively simple matter. Once he has told his story, the advantages in remaining silent are no longer present. As was stated by Justice Jackson in *United States v. Bayer*, 331 U.S. 532 (1947),

> after an accused has once let the cat out of the bag by confessing, no matter what the inducement, he is never thereafter free of the psychological and practical disadvantages of having confessed. He can never get the cat back in the bag. The secret is out for good. In such a sense, a later confession always may be looked upon as fruit of the first. But this Court has never gone so far as to hold that making a confession under circumstances which preclude its use, perpetually disables the confessor from making a usable one after those conditions have been removed.

In the Bayer case, the defendant, an army officer, while being illegally detained, confessed to accepting bribes. Six months later while no longer in custody, he again confessed, a confession which was introduced against him. The Supreme Court held that the second confession was properly obtained and was admissible against the defendant. Attention is called to the fact that there was a lapse of six months between the first confession and the second, which may account for a more liberal attitude toward admissibility, as undoubtedly all influences which may have been involved in obtaining the first confession were gone long before the second confession was obtained. It is to be noted that the Bayer decision was handed down in 1947, long before the United States Supreme Court began to adopt strict rules concerning the admissibility of confessions. It is only a conjecture as to the attitude of appellate courts on this issue today, but undoubtedly courts in general would take a very dim view in admitting a second confession properly obtained following one improperly obtained. A considerable amount of proof would have to be presented to overcome the taint of the first improperly obtained confession in order for a second to be admissible.

■ Wording of Confessions

There is no prescribed wording for a statement to fall within the category of a confession. As was learned from the definition of a confession, it is an acknowledgment of guilt by one accused of a crime. This acknowledgment may be merely an affirmative answer to a question. In other words an accused may be asked: "Did you kill Richard Roe?" If the accused says: "Yes," this would be a complete acknowledgment of guilt, and so would be classified as a confession. Or the confession may be a simple statement on the part of an individual. The accused may merely state: "I killed Molly Brown with a hatchet." On the other hand, the confession may be a very lengthy acknowledgment in which the accused relates in detail every phase of the crime. This may include the facts leading up to the commission of the act, the details of the act itself, and the actions on the part of the accused after the commission of the crime, such as the method of getaway or the disposal of the fruits of the crime and other related matters.

Although the majority of the states make no requirement that the confession be reduced to writing, from an evidentiary standpoint, it is preferable that the confession be written and signed by the accused. In Texas there is a statute which requires that the confession be in writing and signed by the accused unless "taken before an examining court in accordance with law." This statute also requires that the written statement show that the accused has been warned that he does not have to make a statement and that if he does, it can be used against him. The United States Supreme Court decisions would seem to make these requirements, although not included in the statutes of other states, the unwritten law of all states.

In view of the Miranda decision, many prosecuting attorneys have suggested that an accused person being interrogated be advised along the following lines: "(1) You have the right to remain silent. If you talk about this case, anything you say can and will be used against you. (2) You have the right to consult an attorney and to have your attorney present while you are being questioned. If you cannot afford an attorney, one will be provided for you without cost to you. (3) You can talk about the case without consulting an attorney or having one present if you so desire. (4) Do you wish to talk to me about this case, or do you prefer to remain silent? (5) Do you want to talk to an attorney, or do you want to talk to me without an attorney? and (6) Do you understand what I mean by saying that you have the right to remain silent and that you have a right to an attorney?"

If the interrogation of the accused is recorded by an electronic device, each of these questions and each answer should be included at the outset of the interrogation. If the interrogation is to be recorded by a stenographer, and in question-and-answer form, these questions and the answers should be included at the beginning of the statements. If the interrogation is to be written in a summary narrative form of statement, a preamble should be included as the first paragraph of the statement of the accused which should read in substance as follows: "I, (the name of the accused), make this voluntary statement to officer (name of officer or officers conducting the interrogation). I make this statement without threats or promises being made to me. I have been advised of my right to remain silent. I have also been advised of my right to consult an attorney, and to have that attorney present during the time that I am being questioned by the officer. I was also advised that if I could not afford an attorney, one would be provided for me free of charge. I was advised that if I did say anything, it could be used against me in court. I wish to state that I understand my right to remain silent and my right to an attorney, but I waive these rights and wish to make the following statements to (officer's name)."

In addition to setting forth this preamble to the confession, it is suggested that as a concluding paragraph, the accused in his own handwriting place at the end of the confession a statement to the effect: "I have read the foregoing statement, and it is true and correct to the best of my knowledge and belief." The accused should then sign the confession, and the signing should be witnessed by another individual besides the one to whom it is given. If the accused cannot read, a statement should be included that the confession was read to the accused in the presence of (setting forth the names of those present during the reading). Those persons present should sign the statement that the confession was read to the accused in their presence.

If corrections are made in the confession, they should be made by the accused in his own handwriting and initialed by him. He should also initial each page of the statement if it consists of more than one page. This will overcome any allegation on the part of the accused that other pages which he had not seen were added to the confession.

The written confession may be in question-and-answer form, or it may be a narrative of what the accused stated. Most courts feel that the question-and-answer form is the better, as it more truly reflects the exact statements of the accused. This form of reducing the statement to writing is a time-consuming one, and without stenographic assistance becomes an arduous task. For that reason, some officers prefer a narrative form of statement, which is a summary of the facts as related by the accused. The difficulty with the narrative statement is that too frequently it is in the words of the officer and not those of the accused. In reading the statement, the jury may be inclined to think that the officer may have put words in the mouth of the accused and the statement was not in fact that of the accused. With a tape recorder, there is little need to worry about stenographic assistance at the time a confession is given, as it can be placed on tape and transcribed and signed at a later time.

In reducing any confession to writing the officer is faced with the problem of including only those facts relevant to the crime for which the accused is to be tried. If the written statement includes too many irrelevant details or other incriminating evidence, the written confession may be objectionable at the time of the trial and thereby be excluded.

If a suspect is willing to talk freely about the case as well as other matters and the interrogation is being recorded, the entire conversation should be recorded, and thereafter a second statement should be obtained including only those matters relevant to the case at hand.

■ Confession Implicating a Codefendant

Officers frequently encounter a situation where a crime is committed by two or more defendants: one defendant confesses to the crime, implicating the other; the other defendant refuses to give a confession. A problem arises when the defendants are to be tried jointly. May the confession be introduced? This problem was encountered in the case of *Bruton v. United States*, 391 U.S. 123 (1968), in which the United States Supreme Court held that the confession could not be introduced in a form which implicates the codefendant who did not confess to the crime. Although this case pertained to federal procedure, it has been cited as a precedent in some states, thereby preventing the introduction of such a confession.

Various procedures have been suggested to overcome this problem. The following rules laid down by the courts in some jurisdictions state that when the prosecution proposes to introduce into evidence a confession of one defendant that implicates a codefendant, the trial court must adopt one of the following procedures:

1. It can permit a joint trial if all parts of the confession implicating any codefendants can be and are effectively deleted without prejudice to the defendant giving the confession.
2. The trial court may grant a severance of trials if the prosecution insists upon using the confession and it appears that effective deletions cannot be made.
3. If a severance is not judicially feasible and effective deletions cannot be made, the confession must be excluded from evidence.

These rules create a problem for an officer in his interrogation of a suspect if the interrogation is being electronically recorded as a confession. Again, it is probably advisable to permit the suspect to talk freely of his activities as well as those of his associates, and thereafter either record a second statement or have his statement taken down stenographically and delete the names of the associates or other defendants.

This procedure may be done by merely having the suspect tell of his or her own activities, admit to being one of those who had robbed a store, and not mention the names of others who participated in the robbery. By deleting the identity of codefendants, the confession can be introduced during a joint trial without prejudice to the codefendants. Otherwise, as was stated in the aforementioned rules, either the confession may not be introduced or it becomes necessary to have separate trials.

These rules are applicable even if the charge is one involving a conspiracy. It has been held that the conspiracy has ended by the interrogation time, and the statements of a coconspirator are not binding on the other conspirators once the conspiracy has ended.

PROOF OF THE CRIME
IN ADDITION TO CONFESSION

It is generally conceded in this country that a person cannot be convicted of a crime upon a confession alone. There must be some proof of the crime in addition to the acknowledgment of guilt by the accused, some outside proof of the corpus delicti, that is, proof that a crime has been committed. The amount of proof required varies among the states. Some jurisdictions require only a slight amount of proof that a crime was committed, whereas other jurisdictions demand a substantial amount of evidence to prove that a crime was committed. It is generally held that the proof of the corpus delicti does not have to connect the confessor with the crime, but merely prove that a crime was committed.

It is possible to theorize upon the reason for the rule of requiring additional proof of a crime beyond a confession, but little could be gained by such discussion. It suffices to state that the best interests of justice demand that we not convict persons who may be innocent of having committed a crime. Not infrequently, people who suffer from mental instability confess to imaginary crimes. For reasons of their own, people confess to crimes committed by others. Seldom would such a person be brought to trial, as police interrogation would reveal the confession to be lacking in authenticity.

ADMISSIONS

Up to this point we have been concerned with the introduction of a confession against the defendant in a criminal trial as part of the proof of guilt. It has been learned that a confession is a complete acknowledgment of guilt of the crime for which the defendant is being charged. The problem now is: What use, if any, can be made of statements by an accused which do not amount to an acknowledgment of guilt but do link the accused with a crime or are in some ways incriminating? Statements of this nature are known as "admissions." They, too, are a form of hearsay, and are admissible as an exception upon the same basis as confessions. It is sometimes difficult to draw a line between a statement which is con'idered to be an admission and one which is a confession. The definition of a confession states that it is a *complete* acknowledgment of guilt, which would indicate that anything less would be an admission. We might think of an admission as a junior confession. The admission may be a comparatively simple acknowledgment by the accused of being at the crime scene or being acquainted with the victim of a crime. This coupled with other evidence could be most incriminating. For example, in the Escobedo case, Escobedo and one DiGerlando were both being questioned by the police about the murder of Escobedo's brother-in-law, Manuel. Escobedo denied any knowledge of the crime, until he was confronted with DiGerlando, when Escobedo stated: "I didn't shoot Manuel, you did it." This was the first admission by Escobedo that he had any knowledge of the murder, and, coupled with other statements, it was incriminating.

The next problem is one of the admissibility of admissions. An admission, like a confession, can be fatal to the cause, or defense, of an accused. Consequently, the courts are inclined to apply the same rules of admissibility to admissions as to confessions. In other words, the test for voluntariness must be met as well as a compliance with the prescribed judicial procedure for the accused before the admission can be used as evidence in the proof of guilt.

■ Acts as Admissions

One has a tendency to think only of oral declarations of an accused as admissions, but acts have also been classified as a form of admission. An admission, as defined in the broad sense, is any act or declaration of an accused which is inconsistent with his present allegation of innocence; thus acts on the part of the accused such as trying to escape detection and arrest or to hide a crime have been held to be admissions and may be introduced against the accused at a trial. However, these acts as admissions probably fall more logically under the subject matter of "consciousness of guilt," and in order to avoid repetition, they will be discussed under the heading of "Consciousness of Guilt" in Chapter 9.

■ Admission by Silence (Accusatory Statements)

Silence on the part of an accused who in ordinary circumstances would speak out may be of great significance. The problem is whether this silence of an accused may be introduced in evidence as an admission of guilt. Much depends upon the conditions under which the silence took place. If a person makes a statement in front of another accusing him of committing a crime and no reply or denial is made, this is considered to be an implied admission of guilt. This presumption is based upon the premise that one does not ordinarily remain silent in face of an accusation of having committed a crime unless the accusation is true.

Remaining silent in the face of an accusation has been referred to as a "tacit admission," that is, an admission implied by silence.

In passing, it should be noted that a few writers in the field of evidence have made a distinction between admissions as such and "admissions by silence." They have categorized admissions by silence as a separate exception to the hearsay rule and classified them under the heading of "accusatory statements." It is immaterial whether we consider them as admissions or accusatory statements because the rules pertaining to admissibility are the same. In the light of the Escobedo and Miranda decisions the use of admissions by silence is very restricted in the field of evidence.

There was a time when if a person were accused of a crime by a law enforcement officer and no denial was made of the accusation, this failure to deny, or the remaining silent, could be introduced against the accused at a criminal trial. It is now a well-established rule of evidence that one accused of a crime has the right to remain completely silent in front of a law enforcement officer or any officer of the court. Under this rule, the silence may not be introduced against the accused. To date, this rule apparently does not exclude accusatory statements made by others. For example, assume a mother enters her daughter's home and finds her lying dead on the floor with her husband standing over her holding a gun. The mother asks, "Why did you kill her?" and the husband makes no reply. This silence could be most important, because in ordinary circumstances the accused person would have made a denial of the killing unless it were true. Assuming then that the husband was charged with the murder of his wife, the accusatory statement of the mother-in-law could be introduced as well as the silence on the part of the defendant. This silence could carry an implication of guilt. It should be pointed out that the accusatory statement and silence on the part of the accused may be introduced in evidence by anyone present at the time, and does not have to be by the one making the accusation. It is not the accusation that is evidence, but the silence on the part of the accused. The accusation is introduced merely for the purpose of showing that a statement was made that would ordinarily require an answer or a denial.

For the silence of one accused of a crime by a private person to be admissible, the accusation must have been made in circumstances which would ordinarily call for a denial unless the accusation were true. It was held in one case that the silence of a suspect who was in custody of the police was inadmissible when accused by the victim. It was held that since a suspect has the absolute right to remain silent in the presence of an officer, remaining silent in the circumstances was within the suspect's constitutional rights.

If an accused makes any denial of an accusation, the accusatory statement and the denial are both inadmissible, as they serve no purpose for either the prosecution or the defense. The denial would be considered a "self-serving statement" that adds nothing to a defendant's present allegation of innocence.

On the other hand, if the accused makes a statement not amounting to a denial, the reply may be introduced. To return to our example, assume now that when the mother asks the husband: "Why did you kill her?" the husband replies: "Who, me?" this is not a denial, and the inference of guilt may be as significant from this reply as if he had remained silent. Had he replied: "I do not know," this would amount to an admission of guilt, and could be introduced as such.

The accused husband is entitled to present evidence in his behalf to explain his silence. He may say that he was in such a state of shock at finding his wife dead that he did not hear his mother-in-law speak or that he was in such a state of shock that he could not reply. It then becomes a matter for the jury to decide to whose testimony they will give the greater weight.

DEFENDANT'S SILENCE BY NOT TAKING THE WITNESS STAND. As was pointed out in Chapter 5, there was a time when if a defendant in a criminal trial did not take the stand to explain or deny some point in issue, this failure to do so could be commented upon by the prosecuting attorney and/or the judge to the jury, and the jury was entitled to draw an inference that might be unfavorable to the defendant because of the silence. But as was stated by the United States Supreme Court in the case of *Griffin v. California*, to permit such comments was in a way forcing the defendant to be a witness against himself in violation of the Fifth Amendment. It was held that the right of an accused to remain silent in the presence of law enforcement officers is equally applicable to an accused before a judge and jury during trial. As a result of the Griffin decision, comments may not be made either by the prosecuting attorney or the judge concerning the failure of a defendant in a criminal trial to take the stand in his or her own behalf. The Court pointed out that there may be reasons why even one innocent of the charge may not wish to take the stand. As was stated by the Court, the defendant may be fearful of being impeached by prior convictions which may be more prejudicial than silence in not taking the stand. Even though comments may not be made concerning a defendant's failure to take the stand, the jury may still draw an unfavorable inference of possible guilt from it.

However, not all comments by the prosecuting attorney and the judge concerning the silence of the defendant during a trial are barred by the Griffin decision. If the defendant decides to take the stand to testify in self-defense, the right to remain silent is considered to have been waived. If the defendant fails during his or her testimony to explain some damaging evidence presented by the prosecution, this failure or silence by the defendant may be commented upon by the prosecuting attorney and by the judge in his instructions to the jury. It has been held that a defendant may not take the stand in his or her own behalf and merely testify concerning those matters which are favorable and stop short of explaining incriminating evidence presented by the prosecution about which the defendant is fully informed without comments being permitted on that silence. The jury is then entitled to draw an unfavorable inference from the silence.

SUMMARY

One of the best known exceptions to the hearsay rule, and the most closely scrutinized by the courts, is confession.

A confession has been defined as a complete acknowledgment of guilt of a crime. It was admitted as an exception to the hearsay rule upon the premise that one would not confess to committing a crime unless it were true. However, it must be shown that the confession was voluntarily given. The test for voluntariness is that the confession was given in a state of complete mental freedom. The use of either physical mistreatment or psychological pressure in the inducement of a confession will cause it to be excluded from evidence, as the accused would not be considered under complete mental freedom.

In addition to the accused's having complete mental freedom at the time that the confession was given, it must be proved that certain prescribed judicial procedures and constitutional rights were afforded the accused before the confession may be introduced. In other words, the accused must have been arraigned without unnecessary delay, permitted the right of counsel, and advised of the right to remain silent.

A confession which is the product of unlawfully seized evidence or an unlawful arrest is generally inadmissible, as is a confession by one defendant against a codefendant.

An admission is an act or declaration by an accused which is in some way incriminating to the accused. The incriminating declaration must meet the same requirements as a confession to be admissible.

Admissions by silence, also sometimes referred to as an exception to the hearsay rule by the term accusatory statements, may be introduced if the silence was in the presence of anyone other than a law enforcement officer or an officer of the court, such as a prosecuting attorney. The accusatory statement must be one which in ordinary circumstances would require a reply. When it is such a statement and no reply is made, there is an inference of guilt. The failure of an accused to take the witness stand in his or her own behalf may not be commented upon by the prosecuting attorney or the judge. The jury may make their own inference from the failure of the defendant to testify. If the defendant testifies and fails through remaining silent to explain or deny damaging evidence, that silence may be commented upon by the prosecuting attorney and judge.

QUESTIONS FOR REVIEW

1. Define a confession.
2. What is the test for trustworthiness that must be met for admissibility of confessions?
3. Give some examples of psychological pressures.
4. How did the McNabb decision change the requirement for admissibility of confessions?
5. List the requirements that must be met for admissibility of confessions as set forth in the Miranda decision.
6. What is the effect on the admissibility of a confession which is the product of unlawfully seized evidence or the product of an unlawful arrest?
7. What procedures are suggested to be followed when a confession given by one defendant against codefendants is offered in evidence?
8. How does the procedure in determining the admissibility of a confession under the *Jackson v. Denno* decision differ from that of the Massachusetts procedure?
9. How do confessions and admissions differ?
10. What are the rules on admissibility of admissions?
11. What are accusatory statements and what are their significance in the field of admissions?
12. When may the silence of a defendant in a criminal trial be commented upon by the prosecution and judge?

LOCAL RULES

United States Supreme Court decisions have made the rules on the admissibility of confessions and admissions comparatively uniform throughout the United States, but the reader may wish to get the answer to the following questions from the local prosecuting attorney.

1. What procedure is followed in determining the voluntariness of a confession, i.e., the Massachusetts procedure or the procedure whereby the trial judge makes the final determination?
2. Must the prosecution establish the voluntariness of a confession beyond a reasonable doubt or only by a preponderance of the evidence?

The Exclusionary Rule – Searches and Seizures

8

WHAT IS THE EXCLUSIONARY RULE?

The exclusionary rule is very simple. It merely provides that illegally obtained evidence will be excluded from use in a criminal trial. Generally speaking, this rule excludes the introduction into evidence of physical objects found in connection with the investigation of a case as the result of an improper search or obtained by an improper seizure. However, as learned in Chapter 7, the rule may also exclude a confession when that confession was the product of an unlawful arrest or improperly seized evidence. The rule is court-created and came into being by the decision handed down by the United States Supreme Court in the celebrated case of *Weeks v. United States*, 232 U.S. 383 (1914). The rule was made effective only on federal officers, and many of the states had no exclusionary rule until it was made applicable to the states by the United States Supreme Court in the Mapp case (see p. 199) in 1961.

The exclusionary rule is easily understood, and few have any serious quarrel with its primary purpose, but the extent to which the rule has been carried by the courts and the legal technicalities involved have made abiding by the rule and implementing it an almost impossible task for the officer and the prosecuting attorney. The implementation of the rule has been further complicated by the "expectation of privacy" doctrine, which will be discussed in detail.

■ The Common-Law Rule

At common law the fact that evidence was illegally obtained did not exclude it from being admitted in court against the accused. It was held that if evidence was relevant to the case and aided in proving that the defendant was guilty, it should be admitted. The courts did not concern themselves with how the evidence was obtained. For many generations, courts in the United States operated under a similar viewpoint. For a long time not too much sympathy was wasted on the wrongdoer. If he had broken the laws of society, he should be punished. If there was evidence available which would prove him guilty, it should be used. If the accused had been wronged by trespass or other illegal act in the search and seizure of the evidence presented against him, he could sue the offender in a civil action and recover appropriate damages.

■ Development of the Exclusionary Rule

The exclusionary rule is unique to the American system of justice. Neither the English nor the Canadian legal system, both highly regarded, has adopted our exclusionary rule. Not until 1885 did any court in this country display concern over evidence illegally obtained being admitted in court. In that year the United States Supreme Court gave some thought to the matter, but no formal action was taken until the Weeks case was decided in 1914. This decision placed in operation an exclusionary rule applicable to federal officers. The Court held that illegally seized evidence was in violation of the Fourth Amendment to the Constitution and therefore was not admissible in a federal court. This amendment provides:

> The right of the people to be secure in their persons, houses, papers, and effects, against unreasonable searches and seizure, shall not be violated, and no warrants shall issue but upon probable cause, supported by oath or affirmation, and particularly describing the place to be searched, and the persons or things to be seized.

As stated by the United States Supreme Court in the case of *Stone v. Powell*, 428 U.S. 465 (1976):

> [The Fourth] Amendment was primarily a reaction to the evils associated with the use of the general warrant in England and the writs of assistance in the colonies, and was intended to protect the "sanctity of a man's home and the privacies of life," from searches under unchecked general authority.

To state its purpose simply, this amendment was adopted to prevent a general unauthorized invasion by government agents into the homes and

places of business of the people of this nation in an effort to obtain incriminating evidence. This amendment was originally designed to control
the conduct of federal officers. The states were free to make their own
rules on searches and seizures and the admissibility of evidence.

At the time of the Weeks decision, none of the states had an exclusionary rule in operation. It was not until Prohibition days that people generally began to worry about the possibility of illegal searches and seizure of
evidence. A number of persons who considered themselves pillars of society were not in sympathy with the prohibition law and did not abide by it.
Consequently, they were many times in possession of illegal liquor, and a
search of their home or automobile would have revealed that they were
violating the law. The concern of these people over the possibility of illegal
searches and seizures manifested itself by the adoption of the exclusionary
rule by some of the states. Among the first to adopt this rule were Michigan, Illinois, and Indiana during the early 1920s. Thereafter other states
followed suit and adopted an exclusionary rule by statute or constitutional
provision or as a result of a state supreme court decision. It was not until
the decision in *Mapp v. Ohio*, 367 U.S. 643 (1961), was handed down by the
United States Supreme Court that the exclusionary rule was placed in
operation for all the states. This decision will be discussed in further detail.

At the time that the Mapp decision was rendered, only about one-half
the states had adopted an exclusionary rule. In states where the exclusionary rule was already in existence, the Mapp decision made very little
change in the operational procedures of law enforcement officers in conducting searches and seizures. But in states where there was no exclusionary rule until the Mapp case created one for them, the impact of the case
was seriously felt. Until that time there was little thought about how evidence was obtained, as it was usable in court so long as it aided in proving
the guilt of the accused. As the result of the exclusionary rule, officers
found that much of their method of operation had to be changed or their
evidence would be excluded.

The historical development of the exclusionary rule and the buildup to
the Mapp decision makes an interesting study. Returning to the Weeks
case, the facts are that following Weeks's arrest by state officers on a charge
of violating a lottery statute, a search was made of Weeks's residence by the
state officers without the knowledge or consent of Weeks. The officers were
able to enter the residence because a neighbor had told them where the key
was kept. During the search various papers and letters were discovered
which indicated that Weeks had been using the United States mails to
transport lottery tickets. These papers were turned over to a United States
marshal. Thereafter a United States marshal and some state officers returned to the home of Weeks and were admitted by an unidentified person.
A further search was conducted, and additional papers were located indicating a violation of the mail statutes. All these papers were admitted in the
federal court against Weeks over the objection of his attorney. The United
States Supreme Court held upon appeal by Weeks that the admission of the

papers obtained by the United States marshal in cooperation with the state officers was a violation of the Fourth Amendment and should have been excluded. However, it is interesting to note that the Court held that the papers which were seized by the state officers working on their own were properly admitted, since the Fourth Amendment was applicable only to the federal government officers and not the local officers. As a result of this latter viewpoint there was developed what became known as the "silver-platter rule." This rule undoubtedly derived its name from a comment made by Justice Frankfurter who stated: "So long as the state officers handed the evidence to the federal officer on a silver platter, it was admissible." The silver-platter rule meant that if the federal officer got the evidence legally from the state officer, it was admissible, and the federal courts would not go into the collateral issue of how the state officer obtained the evidence.

Irrespective of the freedom given federal officers by the silver-platter rule, other restrictions were placed upon them. Six years after the adoption of the exclusionary rule by the Weeks case, the *Silverthorne Lumber Co. v. United States*, 251 U.S. 385 (1920), case was decided, and an additional restriction was placed upon federal officers and the admissibility of evidence. It was decided in the Silverthorne case that not only was illegally obtained evidence not admissible, but any information gained as a result of an illegal search was also inadmissible. So the poisonous-fruit doctrine was established. This doctrine has been reiterated many times in recent decisions. The doctrine merely states that if the search itself is illegal, it is the same as a poisonous tree, and any information gained as a result of the illegal search is also illegally obtained, and is considered the poisonous fruit of a poisonous tree.

The Court in the Silverthorne case did not close the door on all information that may be gained through an illegal search. As the Court stated, if the same information, or knowledge, was also gained through an independent source other than the illegal search and this fact could be proved in court, the information would be admissible through this source, but not through the illegal search.

The federal courts continued to operate under the silver-platter rule until *Elkins v. United States*, 364 U.S. 206 (1960), in which the United States Supreme Court stated that this rule was no longer acceptable. It was held that if the evidence was illegally obtained by a state officer, it was inadmissible, even though it was legally turned over to a federal officer. The test to be applied was: If the evidence was obtained by a state officer in such a manner that if it had been done by a federal officer it would be considered illegally obtained, the evidence turned over to the federal officer is inadmissible.

As previously stated, these rules were all applicable only to federal officers, and the states were still free to establish their own rules of conduct pertaining to searches and seizures and admissibility of evidence without interference by the federal government, and many states did not see fit to adopt the exclusionary rule. But there was a growing concern by many whether the accused was being granted due process of law when illegally obtained evidence was admitted against him in state courts. This issue came to a head in *Wolf v. Colorado*, 338 U.S. 25 (1949). For the time being, this case settled that the states were still free to establish their own rules of admissibility. In the Wolf case a local officer and others without a warrant searched a doctor's office and seized certain records, which were the basis upon which a criminal charge was brought against the doctor, and which were introduced in the court trial against him resulting in his conviction. Although the United States Supreme Court expressed concern over the fact that illegally obtained evidence was admitted in the Wolf trial, the majority of the justices did not see fit to invoke the Fourth Amendment upon the states as of that time. However, they did express the opinion that

> the security of one's privacy against artibrary intrusion by the police—which is at the core of the Fourth Amendment—is basic to a free society. It is therefore implicit in the concept of ordered liberty and as such enforceable against the State through the Due Process Clause. . . . Accordingly, we have no hestitation in saying that were a State affirmatively to sanction such police incursion into privacy it would run counter to the guaranty of the Fourteenth Amendment.

But the Court concluded that the state had not sanctioned such action in the Wolf case, and the exclusionary rule should not be imposed upon the states. The Court further stated: "We hold, therefore, that in a prosecution in a state court for a state crime the Fourteenth Amendment does not forbid the admission of evidence obtained by an unreasonable search and seizure." It was pointed out that this was particularly true when the person wronged by the illegal seizure had a remedy available to him through civil action against the wrongdoer. As a result of the Wolf case, as previously pointed out, about one-half of the states continued to admit illegally seized evidence until the *Mapp v. Ohio* decision was handed down in 1961 by the United States Supreme Court.

Three dissenting justices of the United States Supreme Court in the Wolf case were of the opinion that the evidence in that case should have been excluded because it violated the unreasonable-search-and-seizure clause of the Fourth Amendment and so should have been made applicable to the state court through the due-process clause of the Fourteenth Amendment. This dissenting viewpoint started a trend by the United States Supreme Court toward making a close inspection of the manner in which evidence was obtained and its admissibility in state court trials. Between the time of the Wolf case and the Mapp decision, the United States Supreme Court made a number of reviews of state court convictions in which it was alleged that due process had not been granted because illegal evidence was admitted.

One frequently cited case in this regard is *Rochin v. California*, 342 U.S. 165 (1952), in which the state's conviction of Rochin on a charge of possession of narcotics was reversed by the United States Supreme Court. In the Rochin case local officers received information that Rochin was selling narcotics. The officers entered Rochin's room and saw Rochin sitting on the bed. Beside the bed was a nightstand upon which the officers saw two capsules. When Rochin was asked about the capsules, he immediately placed them in his mouth. Efforts were made to extract them from his mouth, but the officers were unsuccessful, and Rochin was taken to a hospital. At the request of one of the officers a doctor forced an emetic solution through a tube into Rochin's stomach against his will. This solution caused Rochin to vomit up the two capsules, which were analyzed and found to be morphine. Rochin was convicted of possessing narcotics. The case was taken to the United States Supreme Court on appeal, and the Court reversed the conviction upon the ground that Rochin had been denied due process of law as provided by the Fourteenth Amendment to the Constitution. The Court stated that the method used by the officers in obtaining the two capsules of morphine was conduct which "shocked the conscience," and when methods used in obtaining evidence reach this stage, there has been a violation of the due-process clause.

In the Rochin case the Court did not bring in the Fourth Amendment's prohibition of unreasonable search and seizure, but confined their remarks entirely to that of "due process," so that there was no effort to invoke the Fourth Amendment on the states at that time. The chief problem created by the Rochin case was: What conduct would be acceptable and what would shock the conscience? There seemed to be no criteria, and so each case would have to be decided on its own facts.

The Rochin case was followed two years later by *Irvine v. California*, 347 U.S. 128 (1954), in which the United States Supreme Court again had to decide whether the conduct of local officers had violated the due-process clause. In this case local officers made several entrances into Irvine's home to install a secret microphone. A microphone was first installed in the living room, then changed to the bedroom, and later to a bedroom closet. Officers monitored conversations for nearly a month through this device, and through the information received, Irvine was brought to trial and convicted on a bookmaking charge. During the trial, information obtained through the microphone was introduced in evidence against Irvine. The case was taken on appeal to the Supreme Court on the ground that Irvine had been denied due process of law because of the introduction of evidence illegally obtained against him. The Supreme Court affirmed the conviction on the ground that although the conduct of the officers in this case was repulsive, it was not so shocking to the conscience that it came within the Rochin decision, and consequently there was not a violation of the due-process clause.

In 1961 the Mapp decision was handed down, making the Fourth Amendment applicable to the states through the due-process clause of the Fourteenth Amendment. The Court stated: "We hold all evidence obtained by searches and seizures in violation of the Constitution is, by that same authority, inadmissible in a state court." This decision overruled the doctrine in existence since the Wolf case, and established the rule that the federal government could dictate to the states what evidence would be admissible and what would not. As was stated by the Court in the *Stone v. Powell* decision:

> The Mapp majority [of the Justices] justified the application of the rule to the States on several grounds, but relied principally upon the belief that exclusion would deter future unlawful police conduct. . . . The primary justification for the exclusionary rule then is the deterrence of police conduct that violates Fourth Amendment rights.

In the Mapp case Darlee Mapp was convicted for having in her possession obscene materials, a conviction which was affirmed by the Ohio Supreme Court. The case was thereafter appealed to the United States Supreme Court. The facts of this case are briefly: Miss Mapp resided on the top floor of a two-family dwelling in Cleveland, Ohio. Acting upon information that a suspect in a bombing case was hiding in the home of Miss Mapp and that policy paraphernalia was hidden there also, the city police went to Miss Mapp's home and asked permission to make a search of her place. Miss Mapp called her attorney and then refused to admit the officers unless they had a search warrant. The officers left, but returned later and again sought admittance. Miss Mapp failed to come to the door, and the officers broke the outer door to the residence and had started up the stairs when they were met by Miss Mapp. She asked to see their search warrant. One of the officers displayed a paper purporting to be a search warrant. Miss Mapp grabbed the paper, and a scuffle ensued. The paper was retrieved by one of the officers, and the officers then searched Miss Mapp's apartment and found the obscene material which brought about her conviction. The United States Supreme Court held that this invasion of Miss Mapp's residence and the subsequent search was an unreasonable search and seizure, and as such was in violation of the Fourth Amendment to the Constitution, and that "the exclusionary rule is an essential part of both the Fourth and Fourteenth Amendments [and that it] is not only the logical dictate of prior cases, but it also makes very good sense." With that statement a new philosophy was adopted by the Supreme Court, and the exclusionary rule became the law of the land and was made an operating principle in all states.

■ Philosophy of Exclusionary Rule

Many arguments have been presented by those involved in the administration of justice concerning the right and the wrong of the exclusionary rule. It has been asserted that this rule permits many persons guilty of crimes to go free to prey again upon society, and that it hampers the law enforcement officer in the protection of society against the criminal. The courts themselves recognize that evidence which assists in arriving at the truth must be excluded only after careful consideration, but strong arguments have been presented for the rule. It has been stated that the right of privacy is basic to a free society; it is one of the constitutional guarantees which must be recognized and upheld, and to permit an invasion of that privacy to obtain evidence illegally, whether by a federal or a state officer, would be ignoring a fundamental right of free people. Illegally obtained evidence is not excluded from a trial proceeding because it is untrustworthy but because of the misconduct of a government official, a law enforcement officer, which the courts will not condone.

It is possible that the future will bring about some modification of the exclusionary rule, particularly in instances in which an officer acted in the good faith belief of conforming with the law. In fact, modifications have been suggested by many highly qualified legal scholars, among whom are justices of the United States Supreme Court. Chief Justice Burger made such suggestions in both the *Bivens v. Six Unknown Federal Narcotics Agents*, 403 U.S. 388 (1971), and the *Stone v. Powell* decisions. Chief Justice Burger in the *Stone v. Powell* decision stated:

> It seems clear to me that the exclusionary rule has been operative long enough to demonstrate its flaws. The time has come to modify its reach, even if it is retained for a small and limited category of cases. . . .
>
> In evaluating the exclusionary rule, it is important to bear in mind exactly what the rule accomplishes. Its function is simple— the exclusion of the truth from the factfinding process. The operation of the rule is therefore unlike that of the Fifth Amendment's protection against compelled self-incrimination. A confession produced after intimidating or coercive interrogation is inherently dubious. If a suspect's will has been overborne, a cloud hangs over his custodial admissions; the exclusion of such statements is based essentially on their lack of reliability. This is not the case as to reliable evidence—a pistol, a packet of heroin, counterfeit money, or the body of a murder victim—which may be judicially declared to be the result of an "unreasonable" search. The reliability of such evidence is beyond question; its probative value is certain. . . .
>
> As Mr. Justice White correctly observes today in his dissent, the exclusionary rule constitutes a "senseless obstacle to arriving at the truth in many criminal trials." He also suggests that the rule be substantially modified so as to prevent its application in those many circumstances where the evidence at issue was seized by an officer acting in the good faith belief that his conduct comported with existing law and have reasonable grounds for this belief.

Irrespective that suggestions were made as far back as 1971 that the exclusionary rule be modified, the courts are still strictly applying the exclusionary rule whether the officer acted in good faith or whether there was intentional misconduct. Chief Justice Burger pointed out in the Bivens case that an officer acting in good faith and one showing intentional misconduct were two different situations and should not be treated in the same manner. He gave as an analogy:

> Freeing either a tiger or a mouse in a schoolroom is an illegal act, but no rational person would suggest that these two acts should be punished in the same way. . . . Yet for over 55 years, and with increasing scope and intensity, . . . our legal system has treated vastly dissimilar cases as if they were the same.

Modifications may still be long in coming because the courts still cling to the theory that only by the exclusion of evidence can police misconduct be deterred. As pointed out by Chief Justice Burger in the Stone decision: "Despite its [the exclusionary rule] grave shortcomings, the rule need not be totally abandoned until some meaningful alternative could be developed to protect innocent persons aggrieved by police misconduct. With the passage of time, it now appears that the continued existence of the rule, as presently implemented, inhibits the development of rational alternatives. The reason is quite simple: incentives for developing new procedures or remedies will remain minimal or nonexistent so long as the exclusionary rule is retained in its present form." Also as stated by Chief Justice Burger in the Bivens case: "The deterrence theory underlying the Suppression Doctrine, or Exclusionary Rule, has a certain appeal in spite of the high price society pays for such a drastic remedy."

On the other hand, as pointed out further by Chief Justice Burger:

> Notwithstanding its [the exclusionary rule] plausibility many judges and lawyers and some most distinguished legal scholars have never quite been able to escape the force of Cardozo's statement of the doctrine's anomalous result: "The criminal is to go free because the constable has blundered. . . . A room is searched against the law, and the body of a murdered man is found. . . . The privacy of the home has been infringed, and the murderer goes free." *People v. DeFore,* 242 NY 13 (1926).

Even though some modification of the exclusionary rule does take place, undoubtedly there will always be some penalty attached to evidence which is seized as a result of misconduct or even in instances in which very poor judgment was utilized. The courts will in all probability interpret such seizure as unreasonable within the meaning of the Fourth Amendment. It must be remembered that neither the Mapp decision, nor the exclusionary rule, nor the Fourth Amendment, abolishes all searches and seizures. The exclusionary rule, in conformance with the provisions of the Fourth Amendment, only excludes evidence obtained through an "unreasonable search and seizure." However, the problem is that in many instances there is a very fine line between what is considered to be a reasonable search, and what is deemed to be unreasonable. This is clearly shown by the number of split decisions of the appellate courts in their reviews of cases involving search and seizure. Little wonder then that an officer, caught in this web of complexities, might become confused in an effort to conscientiously apply the rules of reasonable search and seizure. And the necessity to make split-second decisions as a crime unfolds makes the officer's role even more difficult.

It is impossible to set forth positive criteria that will assist in determining what is a reasonable search and seizure and what is not in all instances. Yet every effort will be made to discuss the guidelines as they now stand, so that the officer may exercise the best judgment possible in conducting searches and seizures in order that the evidence will not be excluded at the time of the trial.

SEARCH AND SEIZURE

Search and seizure are generally thought of in connection with obtaining physical evidence, but they may also pertain to the receipt of information through wiretaps, recording devices, inspection of papers, and even conversations. But the discussion here will be confined primarily to the search for and taking of physical objects by a law enforcement officer during the investigation of a crime. As has been pointed out, whether or not these objects discovered and taken may be used as evidence in a judicial proceeding is entirely dependent upon whether the search for and the seizure of the objects were reasonable or unreasonable.

Although there is a tendency by a number of persons to use the terms "search and seizure" as if they are one act, legally and technically, this is incorrect; a search is one act and a seizure is another. It is possible to make a search and not a seizure, or there may be a seizure without conducting a search.

The legality of a seizure is usually dependent upon the legality of the search, but it is possible to have an illegal seizure stem from a legal search. This is particularly true when things other than those described in a search warrant are taken, as will be pointed out in that section of this chapter dealing with search warrants.

■ What Is a Search?

In the past a search has been generally described as looking, or prying, into hidden places in an effort to locate an object or objects intentionally concealed or put out of sight. The mere observation of what was in open and full view was not considered to be a search. For example, if an officer stepped up to a car and saw through the window stolen merchandise or a gun, this observation was not considered to be a search. Nor was it considered to be a search if while standing on the sidewalk in front of a house, an officer saw the fruits of a crime through a partially opened door. But for these observations to be lawful under the exclusionary rule, the officer must have been lawfully upon the property from which the observations were made and in general not trespassing. The officer must not have violated the rules pertaining to the right of expectation of privacy, as interpreted by the courts, when the observations were made.

■ What Is a Seizure?

Although a seizure has been defined as forcibly taking an object, or grabbing it, this definition may give a false connotation. It is believed that the term would be more meaningful in the sense used here to state that a seizure is taking possession of an object to the exclusion of the former possessor, and usually against his will, but it does not have to be with force. For example, an officer may take a gun from a suspect using no force, but the officer takes exclusive possession, probably against the will of the suspect.

There may be a seizure of property from a person even though the property was not owned by the one from whom it was taken. In fact, this is the situation when stolen property is taken from a suspect. Even if the property is stolen, it may not be admitted in evidence against an accused unless that property is seized by the officer by means considered to be reasonable.

■ Ways of Making a Reasonable Search and Seizure

Through court decisions and the enactment of laws, three methods have been developed whereby a search is generally accepted as being reasonable, and property seized as a result of these means of search may be admitted in evidence against an accused person. These methods are (1) a search made as a result of a valid consent given, (2) a search made pursuant to a search warrant, and (3) a search made incidental to a lawful arrest. Even though these methods of search are generally acceptable, they are not without their complications. Involved in each method are a number of legal technicalities which must be abided by or the search may still be deemed unreasonable. Each method will be discussed in some detail. However, space will not permit complete discussion of all the ramifications of the laws as they pertain to search and seizure, for in no other field of evidence has more been written than on the subject of search and seizure.

SEARCH BY VALID CONSENT

If a person gives consent to be searched, or to have his or her property searched, it would logically seem awkward for that person to question the legality or reasonableness of the search at a later time. Yet there are a number of things which affect the giving of the consent which in turn may affect the legality of the search. For a search to be legal the consent must have been given by a person capable of consenting, that is, by a person of sound mind, or one old enough to comprehend the meaning of the consent. Also the person who gave the consent must have been in control of the premises to be searched, and the consent must have been freely and voluntarily given.

Whether or not a consent was voluntarily given may depend on many things. Any showing that the consent was induced by a threat, promise, duress, fear, or deceit will affect the validity of the consent. Just how far an officer may go before it is considered to be a threat or duress or how little he or she can do before it falls within these conditions is still a matter of conjecture. However, it has been held that the mere fact that the accused was under arrest or in jail at the time that he or she gave the consent is not of itself a threat or duress, nor is the request of an officer in uniform to make a search of a place deemed to be duress. However, if there should be a sudden show of force by a large number of officers appearing at a place to be searched, it may be alleged that fear induced the consent because of the large number of officers present at the time consent was given. It is therefore deemed inadvisable to have more than two officers present at the time a request for permission to search is made.

It is the responsibility of the trial judge to determine whether the consent was voluntarily given. The judge will make his or her decision from the facts presented by the prosecution about the manner in which the consent was obtained, and thus the circumstances under which the consent was obtained can be most important to the prosecution of the case because the admissibility of the physical evidence will be completely dependent upon the validity of the consent. If there is doubt about the voluntariness of the consent, the search will be considered an unreasonable one, and the exclusionary rule will be put in operation.

■ Warning That Consent May Be Withheld

Jurisdictions are split about whether a person must be forewarned of his or her right not to give consent to a search for the search to be lawful. The United States Supreme Court and the appellate courts of a number of states hold that such forewarning is not necessary as long as the consent is otherwise freely and voluntarily given. The United States Supreme Court in the case of *Schneckloth v. Bustamonte*, 412 U.S. 218 (1973), stated:

> Our decision today is a narrow one. We hold only that when the subject of a search is not in custody and the State attempts to justify a search on the basis of his consent, the Fourth and Fourteenth Amendments require that it demonstrate that the consent was in fact voluntarily given, and not the result of duress or coercion, express or implied. Voluntariness is a question of fact to be determined from all the circumstances, and while the subject's knowledge of a right to refuse is a factor to be taken into account, the prosecution is not required to demonstrate such knowledge as a prerequisite to establishing a voluntary consent.

The courts have stated that mere asking of permission to make a search carries with it the implication that the person can withhold permission for the search. The courts have pointed out that the request for permission to make a search is for the purpose of obtaining physical evidence and not a form of a confession, which requires the Miranda forewarnings. The courts have further pointed out that even if a search leads to incriminating physical evidence, it does not make the consent a form of testimonial evidence coming from the lips of an accused.

It is to be noted that in the Schneckloth decision the United States Supreme Court referred to the fact that the person giving consent was not in custody, leaving unanswered the question as to the attitude that courts might take in instances in which a request for permission to make a search was made from a person in custody. This question was partially answered by the United States Supreme Court in the case of *United States v. Watson*, 423 U.S. 411 (1976), in which the United States Supreme Court upheld a search by consent when the consent was given by a person while in custody. The Court stated: "He [Watson] had been arrested and was in custody, but his consent was given while on a public street, not in the confines of the police station. Moreover, the fact of custody alone has never been enough itself to demonstrate a coerced confession or consent to search." The Court left the impression that perhaps a forewarning might be required if the consent was requested of the person in custody within the police station. The lack of such forewarning could be taken into consideration by the courts in determining the voluntariness of the consent. As one state appellate court stated, the police would be "well advised" to forewarn a person of the right to withhold consent in "close cases." If a person were in custody within the police station when the request for permission to make a search was made, the case could be classified as a close one requiring a forewarning.

Irrespective of these holdings, the courts of a few states feel that, as with a request for a confession, a request for permission to make a search must be preceded by a forewarning that the person may withhold permission for the search.

■ Form of Consent

No formal wording is necessary for a consent to be considered freely and voluntarily given, but there should be some affirmative statement made, and not a mere failure to object to the search. Silence alone is not deemed to be a consent. It is possible that silence followed by some action or gesture would be tantamount to consent. For example, if an officer should go to a house and ask the occupant for permission to search the premises and if, after the request was made, the occupant stepped back and motioned the officer into the building, this would be considered a consent to search.

Although a consent may be given either orally or in writing, it is deemed highly desirable that the consent be reduced to writing and signed by the person giving it. This precludes the person from later alleging that consent was not given for the search. It is suggested that the following preamble be made the first paragraph of a written consent to search: "I, (name of person giving consent), give my free and voluntary consent to have a search made of the premises located (address of place to be searched). I give this consent without any threat or promise being made to me." (In jurisdictions in which a warning of the right to withhold consent must be given, the following should also be included in the written consent: "I have been advised of my constitutional right to refuse to permit a search to be made.") This written consent should be signed and dated by the person giving it, and witnessed by someone other than the officer receiving it. Whether any additional data are included in the written consent should be left to the discretion of the officer at the time. It should be pointed out that if a valid consent is given for a search, any attack on a seizure of property pertinent to a crime will not be effective unless the search was extended beyond the scope of the consent. It must be remembered that a consent is a right of the person giving it, and it may be limited in area or purpose or it may be withdrawn. In view of the right to withdraw a consent, a troublesome problem has arisen in connection with a search commenced as the result of a freely and voluntarily given consent. May the consent be withdrawn as the officer approaches the spot in which incriminating evidence may be located? Decisions on this point are limited, and there is a difference of opinion among appellate court justices on this point. Some hold that if the consent was voluntarily given, the person may not suddenly withdraw that consent as the officer approaches a place where incriminating evidence is concealed. Others hold that the consent is an absolute right and may be withdrawn at any time or point during a search. In jurisdictions following the latter ruling, if the consent is withdrawn as the officer approaches the incriminating evidence, the officer has no alternative but to discontinue the search. The officer may have to resort to other means in order to conduct the search further, such as having a search warrant issued or making an arrest. Unless the officer is in a position to use these means, the officer may be completely stymied in the continuation of the search.

The fact that a consent to make a search was freely given does not permit continual and repeated invasion of the premises thereafter. How soon the search has to be made after the consent is given depends largely upon the circumstances, but as a practical matter, it is suggested that the search be made as soon as possible, for the consent may be withdrawn at any time. Although the courts have not established any prescribed time within which a search must be made after a consent is given, if there was an undue delay between the consent and the search, the court might interpret the delay as tantamount to a withdrawal of the consent, and declare the search unreasonable.

■ Who May Give Consent

If the search is to be of a person, the person who is to be searched is the one to give the consent, except, of course, in case of a person of unsound mind, or a child too young to know the meaning of the consent, then it may be given by the parent or guardian. If on the other hand the search is one to be made of premises, the consent must be given by the person in possession and control of the premises. It is not always easy to determine who this person is. If the place to be searched is a residence, the occupant of that residence would be the proper person to give the consent. If there is more than one occupant of the residence, any one of the occupants present at the time may give consent to a search. This would be true even if the accused was one of the occupants, and the consent to the search was given by an occupant other than the accused. The spouse of an accused person, when they occupy the same dwelling, may give valid consent for a search. But it has been held that teenage children of an accused are not in a position to give consent for a search. It has also been held that where there are co-occupants and permission to make a search is granted by one of the occupants away from the residence, a search may not be made over the objection of the occupant present. This is based on the fact that each occupant is entitled to a degree of privacy, and that this privacy should not be at the complete mercy of the other. This may seem contrary to what was just said about any occupant being able to give consent to a search. The difference is that any occupant present may give consent for a search to be made, and if there is no objection, the search is a reasonable one, but if the occupant present objects, the search would be unreasonable because the occupant present has actual control at the time.

The ability to give consent to search premises is largely dependent upon the control that a person has over the particular premises in question. A servant within a household who has free access to the premises, and who has a key and may come and go at random, has been held to be a proper person to give permission for a search, whereas a workman in the house who is there temporarily to do a certain job could not give consent to a search.

The general weight of authority is that a hotel or motel manager, or an employee such as a desk clerk, does not have the right to give consent for a search of a guest's room as long as the guest is current in rent. A few times, a search of a room has been held to be reasonable when an officer believed in good faith that the manager, or an employee, had authority to give consent to the search. The lack of authority by a hotel manager, or a clerk, to give consent for a search of a guest's room was specifically spelled out by the United States Supreme Court in *Stoner v. California,* 376 U.S. 483 (1964). In this case the hotel clerk gave officers permission to search the hotel room of Stoner, and evidence discovered during the search was used against Stoner in a state trial. The state's attorney argued that the search was reasonable because the officers believed that the night clerk had the authority to give consent for the search. The Supreme Court held that there was no basis for the contention that the officers had any honest belief that the hotel clerk had the authority to grant permission to search the room. The Court stated:

> Our decisions make it clear that the rights protected by the Fourth Amendment are not to be eroded by strained applications of the law of agency or by unrealistic doctrines of "apparent authority."
>
> It is important to bear in mind that it was the petitioner's [Stoner's] constitutional right which was at stake here, and not the night clerk's nor the hotel's. It was a right, therefore, which only the petitioner could waive by word or deed, either directly or through an agent. It is true that the night clerk clearly and unambiguously consented to the search. But there is nothing in the record to indicate that the police had any basis whatsoever to believe that the night clerk had been authorized by the petitioner to permit the police to search the petitioner's room.
>
> It is true that when a person engages a hotel room he undoubtedly gives implied or express permission to such persons as maids, janitors or repairmen to enter his room in the performance of their duties. But the conduct of the night clerk and the police in the present case was of an entirely different order. . . .
>
> No less than a tenant of a house, or the occupant of a room in a boarding house, a guest in a hotel room is entitled to constitutional protection against unreasonable searches and seizures. That protection would disappear if it were left to depend upon the unfettered discretion of an employee of the hotel.

However, if during the cleaning of a room, a maintenance person observes an object which involves the occupant in a crime, and it is seized by the maintenance person and voluntarily turned over to the police, it is admissible in court. But if the officer directs the maintenance person, or manager, to go to the room for the purpose of endeavoring to seize evidence of a crime, it has been held that such evidence is not admissible. The management in this instance would be acting as a representative of the law enforcement agency and would not have any more authority to seize the evidence than the officer. Only when a private person acting entirely on his or her own, and not at the direction of the police, seizes physical objects and turns them over to the authorities are they admissible in evidence. It is held that the search-and-seizure guarantee of the Fourth Amendment is applicable to constituted authority and not to private persons. So long as the private person is acting on his or her own, the manner in which the object was seized by the private person is not important to the admissibility of the object in evidence.

■ Fortuitous Finds

If consent is voluntarily given to search premises for a particular object, and during the search something else is found, that object may be admissible in evidence if it was found within the scope of the consent given. However, as has been previously pointed out, a consent to search may be a limited one. For example, if a person should give consent for an officer to search a house for television sets, and in making the search the officer should find other stolen electrical appliances, these appliances would undoubtedly be admissible in evidence, because this discovery would be within the scope of the consent. However, if a stolen gun were located in a small dresser drawer, the gun probably would be excluded because the search of a small dresser may be considered by the court as going beyond the scope of the consent. It would be a stretch of the imagination to expect to find large electrical appliances in a small drawer.

SEARCH PURSUANT TO A SEARCH WARRANT

As has been pointed out before, the Fourth Amendment to the Constitution guarantees to the people the right to be secure against unreasonable searches and seizures. The framers of this constitutional provision realized that there would be times when reasonable searches and seizures would be necessary and expedient for the protection of the people, for instance, when a crime had been committed and the perpetrator of that crime attempted to conceal himself or the fruits of the crime. Therefore some right had to be available to those in authority to find that person, or thing, in order that the criminal might be brought to justice. So the right to make a reasonable search pursuant to a search warrant was recognized. A search warrant allows an invasion of privacy by governmental sanction, and because this invasion is permitted, strict rules were included in the Fourth Amendment pertaining to the issuance of a search warrant in order to prohibit arbitrary use being made of this permission. These rules must be carefully adhered to or the search may still be deemed unreasonable and the seized evidence excluded. The constitutional provision states that "no search warrant shall be issued except on probable cause, supported by oath or affirmation, particularly describing the place to be searched and the persons and things to be seized." Even though a search warrant is issued, unless all these rules are followed, the property seized in connection with the search warrant may still be excluded from evidence.

■ Definition of Search Warrant

A search warrant is a written order issued upon probable cause by a magistrate, in the name of the people, to a peace officer directing him or her to search a particular person or place, and to seize certain described personal property and bring it before the magistrate.

■ Grounds for Issuing Search Warrant

Although the grounds for the issuance of a search warrant may vary slightly from one jurisdiction to another, generally they are the same. A search warrant may be issued when (1) the property has been stolen or embezzled; (2) the property is in the possession of a person with the intent to use it as a means of committing a public offense, or when the property is in the possession of another to whom it may have been delivered to prevent its being discovered; (3) the property consists of any item which tends to show that a felony has been committed, or tends to show that a particular person has committed a felony; or (4) the property or things were used as the means of committing a felony.

■ Procedure to Obtain Search Warrant

An officer may not merely go to a magistrate and request that a search warrant be issued for the search of a person or a place. The officer must be in a position to show that there is sufficient reason or probable cause to believe that one of the foregoing grounds for the issuance of a search warrant exists. This belief must be set forth in a written document known as an affidavit. This affidavit is the very heart of a search warrant, and the validity of the search warrant is dependent upon the facts set forth in it. First, it must contain sufficient facts to enable the magistrate to determine that there is reasonable probable cause to issue the search warrant. If the magistrate does not think that the officer has enough facts to establish probable cause, the magistrate will refuse to issue the search warrant. But rather than refuse outright to issue the search warrant, the magistrate may question the officer in order to determine whether there is sufficient reason to believe that the items are at the place where they are alleged to be, or to obtain further description of the things to be seized in order to meet the "rule of particularity" (to be discussed hereinafter). These questions and answers will be reduced to writing and made a part of the affidavit filed by the officer. If, after this questioning takes place, the magistrate is convinced that there is sufficient probable cause, the magistrate will issue a search warrant.

Sample of Search Warrant

IN THE _____ COURT OF THE _____ JUDICIAL DISTRICT, COUNTY OF _____, STATE OF_____.

The people of the State of _____ to any Sheriff, Constable, Marshal or Police Officer in the County of _____:

Proof, by affidavit, having been this day made before me by (1) (name of officer to be inserted here) that: (2) (there is just, probable, and reasonable cause for believing) that: (3) (insert here the facts which show probable cause as reflected in affidavit).

You are therefore commanded, in the daytime (4) (if warrant is to be served other than daytime insert "or any time of the day or night") to make immediate search of the (5) (insert description of place to be searched) in the County of _____, State of _____, for the following property: (6) (insert description of property to be seized), and if you find the same or any part thereof, to bring it forthwith before me at the _____ Court, _____ Judicial District, County of _____, State of _____.

Given under my hand and dated this _____ day of _____, 19_____.

_____

_____

Judge of the _____ Court of _____ Judicial District,

County of _____ State of _____

Sample of Affidavit in Support of Search Warrant

IN THE _____ COURT OF THE _____ JUDICIAL DISTRICT, COUNTY OF _____, STATE OF _____.

Personally appeared before me this _____ day of _____ _____, 19_____, the affiant, (name of officer) a peace officer, who, on oath, makes complaint, and deposes and says that he or she has and there is probable and reasonable cause to believe, and that he or she does believe, that there is now on the premises located at and also described as (insert description of property) the following personal property, to wit: (insert description of property).

Your affiant says that there is probable and reasonable cause to believe and that the peace officer does believe that the said property constitutes: stolen property, and property used as a means of committing a felony.

Your affiant says that the facts in support of the issuance of the search warrant are as follows: (insert information to establish sufficient probable cause for believing the things to be seized are at the place described; this may be from reliable information received or from an independent investigation by the officer).

That based upon the above facts, your affiant prays that a search warrant be issued for the seizure of said property, and that the same be brought before a magistrate and disposed of according to law.

(signature of officer, the affiant)

Residing at _____

Subscribed and sworn to before me
this _____ day of _____, 19_____.

_____
Judge of the _____ Court,
_____ Judicial District,
County of _____, State of
_____

■ Probable Cause

Although the Fourth Amendment provides that no search warrant shall be issued except upon probable cause, it does not spell out what probable cause or reasonable cause is (the courts use the terms "probable cause" and "reasonable cause" interchangeably). The definition of probable cause has been developed primarily through court decisions and interpretation.

Probable cause as it pertains to search warrants has been held to exist when there is a set of facts which would cause an ordinarily prudent man to reasonably believe that the grounds alleged for the issuance of the search warrant are sufficient to justify the belief. In other words, if it is alleged that certain stolen property is believed to be at a particular place, there must be enough facts presented to cause an ordinary prudent person to think that the stolen property is at that place. The test may be: "Did the officer at the time he or she filed the affidavit have enough reliable facts in his or her possession to reasonably believe that a law was being violated on the premises to be searched?"

SOURCE OF INFORMATION.   It is not necessary for the officer seeking a search warrant to have actual knowledge of his or her own that a particular thing sought is where it is alleged to be in order to establish probable cause. The officer's information may stem from a variety of sources. The officer may receive it from a superior officer, from a confidential informant, from an anonymous telephone call, from a reliable person in the community, from another officer who is an expert in a particular field, such as in narcotics or bookmaking, or the officer may have gained the information from personal observations. The source of the information is often hearsay in nature; it does not have to be the kind of information that would be admissible in a trial. But it must have been supplied by a source that a person of ordinary prudence would accept as reasonably trustworthy.

CONFIDENTIAL INFORMANT OR ANONYMOUS SOURCE.   Many times when information is furnished to an officer, it is deemed advisable to keep the identity of the informant confidential. The informant does not have to be identified in the affidavit in order to establish probable cause for issuing a search warrant, but there must be enough facts set forth to determine the reliability of the information furnished. There must be facts stated which would cause an ordinarily prudent person to believe the information to be true. This is usually accomplished by relating that prior information furnished by this same informant had been found to be true and reliable. It may be necessary to set forth the number of times information had been furnished, or over how long a period reliable information had been given, to assist the magistrate in making a determination that there is reasonable cause to believe the informant. The information furnished by an unnamed informant should be set forth in the affidavit in as much detail as possible in order to establish the probable cause, but it is not necessary to include information which would tend to identify the informant, particularly if it would tend to subject the informant to bodily harm.

It has been held that information furnished by an anonymous telephone caller is sufficient to establish probable cause, if the officer recognizes the voice of the caller and can state that this same caller has furnished other reliable information in the past.

If information is supplied by an informant whose reliability has not been established, it may be possible to determine the reliability of information by verifying certain other information given by the informant, such as facts concerning other crimes, or identities of certain criminals. If this cannot be done, the officer may have to use the information furnished as a source of investigative leads and establish probable cause resulting from the officer's investigations. In these circumstances the officer would be establishing probable cause from his or her own observations and knowledge, and not that of an informant. However, this knowledge must have been gained through proper conduct, and not by an illegal entry, trespass, or other violation of the law.

JUDICIAL REVIEW OF PROBABLE CAUSE. Although a search and seizure were made pursuant to a search warrant, it does not mean that the search and seizure will be considered to have been reasonable in all instances. The appellate courts have been making a careful review of the issuance of search warrants to make certain that they are issued with sufficient probable cause. It must be remembered that the search warrant permits official invasion of one's privacy. The invasion may take place only with sufficient probable cause, and the probable cause must be weighed and determined by a magistrate who stands between the officer, who is charged with protecting society, and the privacy of the individual. Consequently, the magistrate must function as a neutral and detached person in the performance of his or her duties. Thus the magistrate must have enough facts upon which to determine if there is sufficient probable cause to issue a search warrant. This was particularly pointed out in the case of *Aguilar v. Texas,* 378 U.S. 108 (1964).

The facts of this case reveal that in the affidavit filed by the police officers it was stated: "The affiants [the police officers] have received reliable information from a credible person and do believe that heroin, marijuana, barbiturates and other narcotics and narcotic paraphernalia are being kept at the above described premises for the purpose of sale and use contrary to the provisions of the law." Based on this affidavit, a search warrant was issued, a search was made of the described premises, and narcotics were found. The defendant was arrested and convicted of possession of narcotics. The defendant appealed his conviction on the ground that the affidavit failed to establish sufficient probable cause to justify the issuing of a search warrant. The conviction was reversed by the United States Supreme Court, which stated that the affidavit was faulty, since it could not be shown how the reliable person obtained his information. There must be facts showing not only the reliability of the informant but also the source of the informant's information. Only by this means can the magistrate determine whether there is sufficient probable cause to support a search warrant. The Court stated: "Although the reviewing court will pay substantial deference to judicial determination of probable cause, the court must still insist that the magistrate perform his 'neutral and detached' function and not serve merely as a rubber stamp for the police." As a result of the Aguilar case, the courts now generally require that the information furnished by an informant be based upon the personal knowledge of the informant and not based upon hearsay information.

If a reviewing court believes that the search warrant was issued without sufficient probable cause, the search pursuant to such a search warrant will be deemed an unreasonable one, and any evidence seized will be inadmissible in court. Consequently, a conviction based on such evidence will be reversed.

On the other hand, if the appellate court believes that there was sufficient probable cause to issue a search warrant, the search pursuant to the warrant will be deemed reasonable. The magistrate is given a great amount of discretionary power in making the determination concerning the sufficiency of probable cause.

■ Description of Property to Be Searched

The Fourth Amendment to the Constitution provides that the place to be searched and the things to be seized must be particularly described, which is sometimes referred to as the "rule of particularity." Just *how* particularly described is not spelled out; so again court decisions have set forth certain guidelines, but these seem to vary somewhat, especially in the description of personal property to be seized. Again the purpose of the description being particularly set forth must be considered. It is to prevent an indiscriminate blanket authority to search a place or an area and to effect a wholesale seizure without some control. Consequently, the courts look very carefully at the description of the place to be searched. If it is not specifically designated, the magistrate may fail to issue the search warrant. If the premises to be searched are a dwelling house, the description should be somewhat as follows: premises located at 129 Main Street, Walnutville, Maine, consisting of a one-story dwelling, with an attic, a basement, a detached garage, and tool shed (if the grounds surrounding the residence and outbuildings are to be included in the search, notation should be made in the search warrant to that effect). If the occupant of the premises is known, the occupant's name should also be included in the description of the premises to be searched.

■ Discovery of Other Property

The rule is that only those things described in the search warrant may be seized. The seizure of other things is considered to be an unreasonable seizure, and will cause them to be excluded from evidence. A problem arises then of what action an officer should take when, during a search pursuant to a search warrant, the officer discovers other things, such as stolen property, or things that mere possession of is a crime, none of which is described in the search warrant. Can this property be seized by the officer? The general consensus is that once the officer is legally within the premises, the officer does not have to be blind to other things that may be observed on the premises even though those things are not described in the search warrant. If the officer sees things of which mere possession is a crime, the officer should be able to seize them.

The general rule is that the officer may seize the property and deprive the possessor access to it, thus preventing the possessor from using or destroying it. Whether this property may be introduced in evidence against the possessor is still in doubt in many jurisdictions. This property was not listed in the search warrant, and any property seized but not described may be considered to be an unreasonable seizure. However, the appellate courts of some states have decided that unlisted contraband property may be admissible. These courts hold that with the issuance of the search warrant, the judgment has already been made by the magistrate to permit a serious invasion of a person's property. No legitimate interest, other than formal legal technicalities, is gained by imposing artificial restrictions on the officer or by making the officer return to the magistrate to obtain a second search warrant in order to seize the contraband located while properly executing the first search warrant, thereby making the contraband admissible. The United States Supreme Court in the case of *Cady v. Dombrowski,* 413 U.S. 433 (1973), upheld the admissibility of evidence not listed in the search warrant but which was seized while executing a search warrant of a vehicle.

However, in those jurisdictions in which it has not been definitely decided that the property seized which is not listed in the search warrant is admissible, the officers may have to obtain a new search warrant for the newly discovered contraband to be admissible. Therefore, to be on the safe side, upon the discovery of such property, an officer should be stationed on the premises to guard the property to prevent its removal or destruction while another officer obtains a search warrant for the newly discovered property. This may appear to be a useless gesture, but as the appellate courts continue to closely scrutinize the issuance of search warrants and review the property seized as result of search pursuant to search warrants, it may mean the difference between a conviction being upheld and a reversal upon appeal. If the possessor is present and an arrest can be made at the time for the possession of this property, it is possible to seize the property incidental to that arrest. The search is a legal one, and the fact that it preceded the arrest in this instance would not be an unreasonable search and seizure. If the possessor is not present so an on-the-spot arrest can be made for the possession, a search warrant should be obtained. Little difficulty should be experienced in obtaining the search warrant under these circumstances, because probable cause can be positively established. The probable cause is the result of the officer being legally upon the premises, and through the officer's own observation he or she knows that the property is on the premises. The officer is also in a position to specifically describe the premises to be searched even to the room, shed, or other place, as well as particularly to describe the things to be seized. Thus all the requirements for a valid search warrant can readily be complied with.

■ Night Service of Warrant

Generally, a search warrant may be served only during the daytime. However, if there are good reasons for permitting the search to be made at night, they should be set forth in the affidavit. A sufficient reason would be that there might be a further concealment of the property, or a nighttime destruction of the property which would defeat the purpose of the search warrant. If the magistrate agrees with the officer, the magistrate will designate on the search warrant that it may be served either during the day or night. Daytime has been defined as the period of time between sunup and sunset, but some jurisdictions have held that daytime is anytime that there is sufficient natural light to conveniently see, or for normal objects to be clearly seen.

Also, in some states the legislature has extended what are considered reasonable hours within which to serve a search warrant. The statutes of those states read generally as follows: "Upon a showing of good cause, the magistrate may, in his discretion, insert a direction in a search warrant that it may be served at any time day or night. In the absence of such a direction, the warrant shall be served only between the hours of 7 o'clock a.m. and 10 o'clock p.m." It is to be noted that this is an extension of what is ordinarily interpreted as daytime.

■ Who May Serve Warrant

A search warrant may be served by a peace officer only and not a private person. A search warrant may be served by any one of the officers, or class of officers, mentioned in the search warrant. If a particular officer is named in the search warrant and no others, that officer, or someone who is aiding him or her while that officer is present, must serve the warrant.

It is generally presumed that the officer will have the search warrant in his or her possession at the time the officer is going to execute the search, but not all states have statutes requiring this. The usual practice is that when a search is made in pursuance of a search warrant, the officer executing the search shows the original search warrant to the occupant of the premises to be searched, and furnishes the occupant with a copy of the warrant and the affidavit, before the search. If there is no one present at the time of the search, a copy of the search warrant and affidavit should be posted in a conspicuous place inside the premises searched.

■ Use of Force in Execution of Warrant

The generally accepted procedure for the execution of a search warrant is for the officer to announce to the occupant of the premises to be searched his or her identity as an officer and the officer's authority to search the premises. If after making this announcement the officer is not admitted, the officer may break into the premises in order to make the search. An officer may use the amount of force reasonably necessary to carry out the search. The officer may restrain persons who try to interfere with the search, and in some cases the officer may even arrest the ones who interfere. The officer may break into locked rooms and closets if admittance is not otherwise granted. But the search warrant does not give the officer blanket authority to do excessive or extensive damage to the premises in conducting the search.

There are times when it has been held that announcing the officer's purpose prior to entering the premises is not necessary. If the officer has reasonable cause to believe that his or her life, or that of others, may be in danger, the officer does not have to announce his or her presence or the purpose of the visit prior to entering the premises. The officer may also enter the premises without prior announcement and request for admission if there is reason to believe that evidence may be destroyed by such announcement. If the officer has an honest belief that the premises to be searched are unoccupied, no announcement need be made, and the evidence seized is admissible, even though it turns out that there were occupants in the premises at the time.

FORCE ON PERSON IN EXECUTION OF WARRANT. When searching a person in pursuance to a search warrant, an officer is entitled to use the amount of force reasonably necessary to seize the evidence, but the officer may not go so far as an act which may "shock the conscience" of the community. An officer may use the force necessary to force open the hand or even the mouth of a person to seize evidence, but may not pump the stomach of an accused in order to retrieve evidence.

■ Time Limit on Length of Search

There is no time limitation placed on the length of the search, but the search warrant does not permit a search to continue indefinitely. However, any search must be thoroughly made, and can be time-consuming. The kind of premises to be searched and the kind of property or evidence sought are determining factors in the length of time that a search may reasonably take. To give an example: If electrical appliances are to be sought in a private residence, the search would probably be over in a few hours at the very most, while a search for stolen automobile parts in an automobile-parts warehouse or a junkyard could easily extend into several days.

Also, there is no limitation on the number of officers that may make the search, but again, to avoid criticism and possible attack, it is suggested that the number of officers used should be commensurate with the situation. Again, the search of a private residence under ordinary circumstances should require fewer officers than that of a huge warehouse.

One must bear in mind that the search warrant permits an invasion of a person's privacy. Though a valid search warrant makes the invasion a reasonable and legal one, the appellate courts could very well take the view that the search went beyond the limits of reasonableness if discretion in length of time, number of officers, and treatment of persons and property was not used.

■ Time Limit on Execution of Warrant

Even though a search warrant is issued for the search of a person or place, it does not permit the officer to hold the warrant indefinitely before making the search. The statutes usually spell out specifically the time within which the search must be executed. The usual length of time is ten days from the date of issue. If the search is not made within that time, the search warrant becomes void, and if the officer still wishes to make a search, the officer will have to obtain a new search warrant, as in most jurisdictions the time cannot be extended.

In some jurisdictions, there is no prescribed time within which the search warrant must be executed. The law of those jurisdictions merely provides that the search warrant must be served within a "reasonable time." This leaves much to speculation about what will be deemed within a "reasonable time." Is it a day, a week, or a month, or just how long? In most instances, the facts of the case will be the determining factor. However, seldom will the time for service be extended beyond a two-week period.

■ Return of the Search Warrant

After a search has been made pursuant to a search warrant, a return must be made to the magistrate who issued the search warrant. This return is a separate document in most instances. It gives a list of the property seized in connection with the search. Only the property described in the search warrant and seized should be listed on the return. Should additional property which is not described in the search warrant be seized, this property should be listed on a separate document. Otherwise, an attack may be made on the entire search, and the evidence might be excluded. The officer will maintain custody and control of the property seized until the court orders proper disposition of it.

■ Attack on the Search Warrant

The mere fact that a search warrant was issued and property seized in pursuance to the warrant does not prevent an attack from being made by the defendant on the search warrant. If the attack is successful, the property may be excluded from evidence, or a conviction may be reversed upon appeal. If an attack is made, the burden is upon the defendant to prove that the search warrant was invalid, or improperly issued, or that some other defect or improper procedure resulted. The attack may be made on any of several grounds. The defendant may allege that there was insufficient probable cause for the issuance of the search warrant; that the place to be searched or the thing to be seized was not "particularly" described; or that it was not properly executed, for example, that there was an unreasonable breaking and entering without prior request for admission into the premises, or that excessive force was used in the execution, or that the warrant was not executed within the prescribed time.

SEARCH AND SEIZURE
INCIDENT TO AN ARREST

The third method by which a reasonable search may be made is incident to an arrest (or sometimes referred to as incidental to an arrest); however, for this search to be reasonable, the arrest must be a lawful one. If the arrest is made in compliance with a warrant of arrest, very little difficulty is encountered about it being a lawful arrest. But where the arrest is made without a warrant, the lawfulness of the arrest is frequently the subject of attack, and if the attack is successful and the arrest is found to be unlawful, any property seized incident to that arrest will be excluded from evidence. When an arrest is made without a warrant of arrest, the factor determining the lawfulness of the arrest is whether there was sufficient probable cause or reasonable cause to support the arrest. In other words, was there sufficient reason to believe that the person arrested was guilty of a crime? Probable cause as it relates to an arrest has been stated to exist "if a man of ordinary caution or prudence would be led to believe and conscientiously entertain a strong suspicion of an accused's guilt." The use of the "ordinary cautious or prudent man" test for probable cause was explained by the United States Supreme Court in *Brinegar v. United States,* 388 U.S. 160 (1949), in which the Court stated:

> The rule of probable cause is a practical, nontechnical conception affording the best compromise that has been found for accommodating these often opposing interests [i.e., the rights of the accused versus the protection of society]. Requiring more would unduly hamper law enforcement. To allow less would be to leave law-abiding citizens at the mercy of the officer's whim and caprice.

Therefore if facts exist that would cause a person of ordinary prudence to believe that an offense has been committed, there is sufficient probable cause for a lawful arrest, and a search may be made incidental to that arrest and will be deemed a reasonable one, that is, within certain limitations to be discussed hereinafter.

There are those who feel that the ordinary-prudent-person test is somewhat unrealistic, and a few appellate courts have adopted a slightly more liberal viewpoint. These courts have held that in view of the officer's experience and training, the officer is in a better position to determine what is a reasonable ground for believing that a crime has been committed than the ordinary prudent person is. However, the Supreme Court apparently was trying to avoid this very test as a criterion, and made it the belief of an ordinary prudent person in an effort to curb the possible overzealousness of a police officer. Because of the Supreme Court's opinion about the ordinary-prudent-person test, most jurisdictions follow it. As a result, one of the most difficult decisions that an officer has to make in line with his or her duties is whether the action which unfolds before the officer would cause an ordinary prudent person to entertain a conscientious belief that a crime has been committed. In many cases, even the appellate judges disagree among themselves whether there was sufficient probable cause to make an arrest. It is little wonder therefore that the officer is often caught in another web of legal technicalities from which there seems to be no escape. There is not much that can be set forth in the way of guidelines to assist the officer in making the determination of how an ordinary prudent person would think. However, mere suspicion by the officer is usually not enough to establish probable cause, for what would cause an officer to be suspicious might not cause an ordinary prudent person to think a crime had been committed.

Although there may be probable cause to make an arrest, the arrest may still not be a lawful one, since the arrest may have been carried out in an unlawful manner. For example, an entry into a residence to effect the arrest may have been by unlawful means because no request for admittance was made before breaking into the residence, and so any search incident to that arrest would be an unreasonable one. However, not all entries made without a prior request for admittance are unlawful. Many jurisdictions hold that if lives could be placed in danger or evidence quickly destroyed as a result of a prior request for admittance before entering a building to make an arrest, such a request is not necessary, and the arrest will be deemed a lawful one [see *Ker v. California,* 374 U.S. 23 (1963)].

■ Reason Search Permitted

The reason a search is permitted incidental to an arrest is that there may be evidence of the crime within the immediate control of the accused which may be destroyed if not quickly seized. Also, there may be weapons with which the arrested person may injure the arresting officer, or with which the accused may make an escape. A search made at the time of the arrest to safeguard life or evidence is deemed to be a reasonable search, and the evidence seized is admissible. Evidence of the crime would include not only the things taken or fruits of the crime, but instrumentalities which may have been used in committing the crime, such as a mask used in a robbery.

■ Search and Arrest Must Be Contemporaneous

For a search incidental to an arrest to be reasonable, the search must be made contemporaneous with the arrest, and not made at some later time.

The search must be a part of the same transaction as the arrest. Otherwise, the search is not a search incidental to the arrest. Any substantial delay in making the search incidental to the arrest makes a search warrant necessary; otherwise the evidence obtained without the search warrant is generally inadmissible. In one case in which the search took place one hour after the arrest, it was held to be improper and unreasonable, as it was not contemporaneous with the arrest. However, in the case of *United States v. Edwards,* 415 U.S. 800 (1974), the United States Supreme Court upheld the admissibility of evidence obtained several hours after the arrest was made. The defendant was arrested at approximately 11 p.m., taken to a local jail, and placed in a cell. His clothing was not taken from him until the next morning, and an examination of the clothing revealed incriminating evidence, which was used during the trial to convict him. The Court stated: "It is plain that searches and seizures that could be made on the spot at the time of arrest may legally be conducted later when the accused arrives at the place of detention." The Court pointed out that both the defendant and his clothing had been in the custody of the police during the entire time, and that the police did no more on the morning following the arrest than they were entitled to do incident to the usual custodial arrest and incarceration.

It is to be noted that the Edwards case is an entirely different situation from that where an arrest is made in a home or place of business when there is no custody and no control over the place by the police and when a search must be made contemporaneous with the arrest.

■ Area Which May Be Searched

The general rule is that when a person is arrested, a search may be made of the person and that which is under his or her "immediate control." The extent of the area under the arrested person's immediate control is not always easily determinable. Again it is necessary to return to the reason behind the search to establish some type of criterion, that is, to seize evidence that may be quickly destroyed, or to seize weapons by which injury or escape may be accomplished, but even this does not supply all the answers as to what may be considered within the immediate control of the accused.

Most of the guidelines are the results of appellate court decisions. The courts have adopted a much stricter view when a search is made of a residence than of other premises. This strictness is based on the belief that the Fourth Amendment to the Constitution was designed primarily to prohibit invasion of the privacy of homes, rather than other areas.

In *Chimel v. California,* 395 U.S. 752 (1969), the United States Supreme Court set forth some guidelines on the area that may be searched incident to an arrest, but even that case has left some questions about the *extent* of the area. The facts of the Chimel case reveal that Chimel was arrested in his residence on a charge that he had burglarized a coin shop. Incident to the arrest, the entire house was searched, including the attic and garage. The search took between 45 minutes and an hour to conduct. Items found in the bedroom and sewing room were taken and introduced against Chimel at his trial. He appealed his conviction on the grounds that the arrest was unlawful. The United States Supreme Court upheld the arrest on the grounds that there was sufficient probable cause to make the arrest, but held that the search of the entire residence incident to that arrest went beyond the area that was within the immediate control of the accused, and the conviction was reversed.

The Court stated:

> When an arrest is made, it is reasonable for the arresting officer to search the person arrested in order to remove any weapons that the latter might seek to use in order to resist arrest or effect his escape. Otherwise, the officer's safety might well be endangered, and the arrest itself frustrated. In addition, it is entirely reasonable for the arresting officer to search for and seize any evidence on the arrestee's person in order to prevent its concealment or destruction. And the area into which an arrestee might reach in order to grab a weapon or evidentiary items must, of course, be governed by a like rule. A gun on a table or in a drawer in front of one who is arrested can be as dangerous to the arresting officer as one concealed in the clothing of the person arrested. There is ample justification, therefore, for a search of the arrestee's person and the area "within his immediate control"—construing that phrase to mean the area from within which he might gain possession of a weapon or destructible evidence.

> There is no comparable justification, however, for routinely searching rooms other than that in which an arrest occurs—or, for that matter, for searching through all the desk drawers or other closed or concealed areas in that room itself. Such searches, in the absence of well recognized exceptions, may be made only under the authority of a search warrant. The "adherence to judicial processes" mandated by the Fourth Amendment requires no less.

> The rule allowing contemporaneous searches is justified, for example, by the need to seize weapons and other things which might be used to assault an officer or effect an escape, as well as by the need to prevent the destruction of evidence of the crime—things which might easily happen where the weapon or evidence is on the accused's person or under his immediate control. But these justifications are absent where a search is remote in time or place from the arrest.

The language of the Court in the Chimel case still saddles the officer with the problem of how far the officer may go in a search incident to an arrest. May the officer open any drawers within the room where an arrest is made, or may the officer open all of them? May the officer open a closed door within the room? The Chimel case gave no answer to these questions.

■ Search of Vehicles

The Chimel case provided little in the way of guidelines in regard to searching a vehicle incident to an arrest. After the arrest of an individual in an automobile, may the entire vehicle, including the trunk compartment, be searched incident to the arrest, or must the search be confined to the front seat of the vehicle and that area which could be reached by the accused? Based on some court decisions, there seems to be a more relaxed rule relative to vehicle searches than searches of homes or offices. This relaxation of the rules is based on the mobility of a vehicle making possible a greater opportunity for the destruction or loss of evidence if a complete search is not made on the spot and at the time of the arrest. Also, because of the emergency circumstances, obtaining a search warrant is most impractical. Decisions have upheld search of the entire vehicle even when the accused was arrested standing beside the vehicle. However, in most incidents, it is generally held that to justify a search of the entire vehicle there must have been a good faith belief by the officer that the vehicle contained contraband.

United States Supreme Court cases have upheld warrantless searches of vehicles on grounds other than searches incidental to an arrest, and these cases could act as possible guidelines for reasonable searches and seizures. In *Cooper v. California,* 386 U.S. 58 (1967), the United States Supreme Court upheld the search and seizure of incriminating evidence in connection with an impound search of a vehicle. Cooper was convicted of selling heroin. The conviction rested in part on the introduction in evidence of a small piece of a brown paper sack seized by police without a warrant from the glove compartment of an automobile, which, upon Cooper's arrest, had been impounded and was being held in a garage. The car had been seized in accordance with a law requiring the seizure of a vehicle used in the transportation of narcotics. The search of the automobile occurred a week after the arrest of Cooper. Cooper appealed his conviction on the ground that the search of the automobile was unreasonable, since it was not incident to the arrest, and he cited *Preston v. United States,* 376 U.S. 364 (1964), to uphold his contention.

The United States Supreme Court upheld the conviction and held that the search of the automobile was reasonable. The Court conceded that the search was not made incident to an arrest, but held that the police had seized the automobile to impound it and kept it according to the law until forfeiture proceedings were concluded. This did not take place until more than four months later. The Court stated:

> It would be unreasonable to hold that the police, having to retain the car in their garage for such a length of time, had no right, even for their own protection, to search it. It is no answer to say that the police could have obtained a search warrant, for the

relative test is not whether it is reasonable to procure a search warrant, but whether the search was reasonable. Under the circumstances of this case, we cannot hold unreasonable under the Fourth Amendment the examination or search of a car validly held by officers for use as evidence in a forfeiture proceeding.

Also in the case of *Chambers v. Maroney*, 399 U.S. 42 (1970), the United States Supreme Court upheld the search of an automobile at a police garage after an arrest had been made of the occupants in another place. The search was not based on an arrest but was upheld on the ground that the police had reasonable cause to believe that the automobile contained contraband. In this case four individuals were arrested in a station wagon on a charge of armed robbery of a service station attendant. The station wagon was driven to the police station. In the course of a thorough search at the station, the police found two .38 caliber revolvers concealed in a compartment under the dashboard. Some small change and a card bearing the name of the service station attendant who had been robbed were found in the glove compartment. These items were introduced in evidence against Chambers, and he was convicted of armed robbery. On appeal he contended that the search of the station wagon was unreasonable and cited the Preston case as a precedent. The United States Supreme Court stated:

> In Preston, the arrest was for vagrancy; it was apparent that the officers had no cause to believe that evidence of crime was concealed in the auto. . . . Here the situation is different, for the police had probable cause to believe that the robbers, carrying guns and the fruits of the crime, had fled the scene in a light blue station wagon . . . there was probable cause to arrest the occupants of the station wagon that the officers stopped; just as obviously was there probable cause to search the car for guns and stolen money.
>
> In terms of the circumstances justifying a warrantless search, the Court has long distinguished between an automobile and a home or office. In *Carroll v. United States*, 267 U.S. 132 (1925), the issue was the admissibility in evidence of contraband liquor seized in a warrantless search of a car on the highway. After surveying the law from the time of the adoption of the Fourth Amendment onward, the Court held that automobiles and other conveyances may be searched without a warrant in circumstances which would not justify the search without a warrant of a house or an office, provided that there is probable cause to believe that the car contains articles that the officers are entitled to seize. The Court expressed its holding as follows: "We have made a somewhat extended reference to these statutes to show that the guaranty of freedom from unreasonable searches and seizures by the Fourth Amendment has been construed, practically since the beginning of the Government, as recognizing a necessary difference between a search of a store, dwelling house or other structure in

respect of which a proper official warrant readily may be obtained, and a search of a ship, motor boat, wagon or automobile, for contraband goods, where it is not practicable to secure a warrant because the vehicle can be quickly moved out of the locality or jurisdiction in which the warrant must be sought.

"Having thus established that contraband goods concealed and illegally transported in an automobile or other vehicle may be searched for without a warrant, we come now to consider under what circumstances such search may be made. . . .

"[T]hose lawfully within the country, entitled to use the public highways, have a right to free passage without interruption or search unless there is known to a competent official authorized to search, probable cause for believing that their vehicles are carrying contraband or illegal merchandise.

"The measure of legality of such a seizure is, therefore, that the seizing officer shall have reasonable or probable cause for believing that the automobile which he stops and seizes has contraband liquor therein which is being illegally transported."

The Court also noted that the search of an auto on probable cause proceeds on a theory wholly different from that justifying the search incident to an arrest: "The right to search and the validity of the seizure are not dependent on the right to arrest. They are dependent on the reasonable cause the seizing officer has for belief that the contents of the automobile offend against the law."

In enforcing the Fourth Amendment's prohibition against unreasonable searches and seizures, the Court has insisted upon probable cause as a minimum requirement for a reasonable search permitted by the Constitution. As a general rule, it has also required the judgment of a magistrate on the probable cause issue and the issuance of a warrant before a search is made. Only in exigent circumstances will the judgment of the police as to probable cause serve a sufficient authorization for a search. Carroll holds a search warrant unnecessary where there is probable cause to search an automobile stopped on the highway; the car is movable, the occupants are alerted, and the car's contents may never be found again if a warrant must be obtained. Hence an immediate search is constitutionally permissible. . . .

On the facts before us, the blue station wagon could have been searched on the spot when it was stopped since there was probable cause to search and it was a fleeting target for a search. The probable cause factor still obtained at the station house and so did the mobility of the car unless the Fourth Amendment permits a warrantless seizure of the car and the denial of its use to anyone until a warrant is secured. In that event there is little to choose in terms of practical consequences between an immediate search without a warrant and the car's immobilization until a warrant is obtained. The same consequences may not follow where there is unforeseeable cause to search a house. But as Carroll held, for the purposes of the Fourth Amendment there is a constitutional difference between houses and cars. . . .

It was not unreasonable in this case to take the car to the station house. All occupants in the car were arrested in a dark parking lot in the middle of the night. A careful search at that point was impractical and perhaps not safe for the officers, and it would serve the owner's convenience and safety of his car to have the vehicle and the keys together at the station house.

Another after the arrest–station-house search of a vehicle was condoned by the United States Supreme Court in the case of *Harris v. United States,* 390 U.S. 234 (1968). In the Harris case the defendant was arrested for robbery as he entered his car. The car was towed to the police station as evidence because it had been seen at the robbery site. According to the regulations of the police department involved, whenever a car was impounded, the vehicle had to be searched thoroughly and valuables removed. During the search for this purpose, the officer observed a registration card bearing the name of the robbery victim. This card was introduced in evidence against the defendant, and he was convicted. The conviction was appealed on the ground that the search was unreasonable. The United States Supreme Court upheld the conviction on the ground that the police had a right to impound the car and were entitled to search it for valuables. An officer who was lawfully in the vehicle did not have to be blind to objects falling in his view.

■ Exploratory Search Illegal

For a search incidental to an arrest to be reasonable, the search must logically be for things related to the crime for which the person was arrested. An officer may not make a general or "exploratory" search in effort to establish other crimes. However, if during the search for evidence pertaining to the crime for which the accused was arrested, evidence of other crimes is discovered, that evidence may be seized. It has been held that an officer does not have to be blind to contraband and evidence of other crimes just because they do not relate to the arrest. It has also been held that an arrest of the driver of a vehicle for a traffic citation alone does not justify a search of the vehicle, as such search would not reveal any evidence of the crime for which the traffic arrest was made. However, if the arrest were made for drunken driving, a search could be made of the vehicle for liquor, and if things were found involving the driver with other crimes, such things would be admissible.

Whether a search is reasonable and within the scope of the arrest depends a great deal on the facts of the case. As in the previous example, if a person is arrested for possession of stolen television sets, a search in small dresser drawers may be beyond the scope of the arrest and be considered merely exploratory in nature, but at the same time, the search may be justified upon the grounds that weapons are being sought with which the accused, or others, may cause injury to the arresting officer or aid the accused in making an escape. The finding of other objects implicating the accused in crime would be admissible, as the search would not be exploratory in nature.

■ Blood Samples and Drunken Driving

The extent to which an officer may go in obtaining physical evidence from the accused at the time of the arrest or thereafter frequently presents a problem, and this has been particularly true in cases of arrests for drunken driving, when it is desired that a blood sample be obtained for purposes of chemical analysis for alcoholic content. Does drawing blood from the accused invade privacy, and is this illegal seizure of evidence? The answer to this question was squarely met in *Breithaupt v. Abram,* 352 U.S. 432 (1957). In this case, local police took a blood sample from an unconscious person who had been the driver of a vehicle involved in a fatal automobile accident. A manslaughter conviction was returned against the driver partly based upon the blood sample taken, which showed the driver to have been intoxicated. The United States Supreme Court upheld the conviction. In doing so, the Court stated that taking the blood was done in a medically approved manner and as such did not shock the conscience. Therefore the seizure of the evidence was not unreasonable.

Justice Clark, who wrote the majority opinion, stated that the sample of blood was taken under the protective eye of a physician, and that the blood-test procedure has become routine in our everyday life. There was no coercion or brutality involved. He further pointed out that

> as against the right of an individual that his person be held inviolably even against so slight an intrusion as is involved in applying a blood test of the kind to which nearly millions of Americans submit as a matter of course nearly every day, must be set the interests of society in the scientific determination of intoxication, one of the great causes of the moral hazards of the road. And the more so since the test likewise may establish innocence, thus affording protection against the treachery of judgment based on one or more of the senses.

The right to withdraw blood by an approved method was reaffirmed in *Schmerber v. California,* 384 U.S. 757 (1966), decided by the United States Supreme Court in 1966. The facts in this case were that Schmerber, the accused, was involved in an automobile accident in which he and his passenger were injured. Because of the odor of alcohol on the breath of the accused, the investigating officer requested that a blood sample be taken from him at the hospital while he was under treatment for his injuries. A sample was taken by a physician over the objections of the accused. The blood analysis report was admitted in evidence against the accused, and he was convicted of drunken driving. The Supreme Court upheld the conviction in this case.

The defendant appealed the case to the Supreme Court on the contention that he had been denied due process of law because taking his blood was a violation of his guarantee against self-incrimination, and also was a violation of the Fourth Amendment as it was an illegal seizure of evidence, and so the blood analysis should have been excluded because of these two alleged violations.

Justice Clark in writing the majority opinion held that the guarantee against self-incrimination embodied in the Fifth Amendment did not relate to obtaining physical evidence but to communication or testimony (see page 116). Justice Clark also overruled the contention that there was a violation of the Fourth Amendment. He pointed out that there was sufficient probable cause to make an arrest of the defendant on the charge of drunken driving, and that an arrest did take place and that it has been consistently held that a search may be made incidental to a lawful arrest. Evidence of the crime may be seized as a result of that search. This search and this seizure are permitted because the evidence may otherwise be destroyed. In this case, the defendant could not destroy the evidence himself, but it is a medically known fact that the alcoholic content of the blood would eventually dissipate, and unless a sample were taken at the time, it would be of little or no evidentiary value later; therefore, the seizure of the evidence was proper as an incident to the arrest. The next problem was whether the seizure was reasonable in order to prevent it from being a violation of the guarantee against unreasonable search and seizure as provided by the Fourth Amendment; that is, was the blood taken in such a manner that it did not shock the conscience of the community. Justice Clark pointed out that the blood sample was taken in a medically approved manner, and as such did not "shock the conscience or offend the dignity of the community." Therefore, the seizure of the evidence was a reasonable one. However, it has been held that undue force may not be used to subdue a defendant in order to take blood in a medically approved manner.

■ Refusal to Give Samples—Admissible Evidence

Although it has been held that the giving of blood samples, handwriting exemplars, or speaking for identification is not a violation of the privilege against self-incrimination, there is no way to force an accused to furnish this evidence. However, an accused who refuses to give the evidence should be advised that it is not a violation of the privilege against self-incrimination and that there is no constitutional right to refuse to furnish the requested evidence. The accused should also be advised that refusal to give the evidence can be used against him or her in court.

Except in the case of postindictment identification lineups, the accused is not entitled to the assistance of counsel in giving physical evidence. But if counsel has been appointed for the accused, the counsel should be advised of any contact made with the accused for the purpose of obtaining physical evidence.

SEARCH WITHOUT AN ARREST

A problem which frequently presents itself to the officer is whether an officer may at any time temporarily detain a person for interrogation purposes and make a search of that person short of an actual arrest. Many times, an officer has definite reason to believe that a person has been involved in some illegal act, yet the officer does not have sufficient probable cause to make an arrest; however, because of his duty to protect society he feels that some action should be taken on his part. But just how far may he go in detaining a person and making a search? This problem has been resolved in some states by statute, and in others by court decisions and interpretation. These statutes and court decisions have authorized the officer to stop a person who is in a public place and question him about his identity, and ask for an explanation of his actions. This detention can be made only when the officer has reasonable grounds to believe that the person has committed a crime, is committing one, or may be about to commit a crime. Reasonable grounds to believe may fall short of sufficient probable cause to make an arrest. Yet the demarcation between reasonable cause to believe and sufficient probable cause to arrest is, in many instances, most difficult to distinguish.

In addition to being able to stop and question a person's identity, the officer may, if he honestly believes his life to be in danger, search the person for weapons. If during this search evidence is found connecting the person with a crime, an arrest may be made and a complete search made incidental to that arrest.

The right of an officer to search an individual, short of an arrest, received the sanction of the United States Supreme Court in the case of *Terry v. Ohio*, 392 U.S. 1 (1968). The facts of this case reveal that an officer, after watching three men for some time, one of whom was Terry, became highly suspicious that they were about to commit a robbery. He was also fearful that they were armed. He stopped the men and identified himself. After questioning them for a few minutes, he grabbed Terry and "patted down" his outer clothing. He felt a gun in the overcoat pocket of Terry, and so he removed the coat in order to recover the gun. He also found a gun on one of the other men as a result of a pat-down search. Terry and the other man were arrested and charged with carrying concealed weapons. They appealed their conviction to the United States Supreme Court on the ground that the search was in violation of the Fourth Amendment, since it was an unreasonable search because there was insufficient probable cause to make an arrest.

The Supreme Court engaged in a considerable discussion over the right of an individual to be free from governmental intrusion but concluded that there are times when an officer may make a search for weapons in circumstances that lack probable cause for an arrest. The Court stated:

> The sole justification of the search in the present situation is the protection of the police officer and others nearby, and it must therefore be confined in scope to an intrusion reasonably designed to discover guns, knives, clubs, or other hidden instruments for the assault of the police officer. . . .
>
> We conclude that the revolver seized from Terry was properly admitted in evidence against him. At the time he [the officer] seized Terry and searched him for weapons, the officer had reasonable grounds to believe that Terry was armed and dangerous, and it was necessary for the protection of himself and others to take swift measures to discover the true facts and neutralize the threat of harm if it materialized. The policeman carefully restricted his search to what was appropriate to the discovery of the particular items which he sought. Each case of this sort will, of course, have to be decided on its own facts. We merely hold today that where a police officer observes unusual conduct which leads him reasonably to conclude in light of his experience that criminal activity may be afoot and that the persons with whom he is dealing may be armed and presently dangerous; where in the course of investigating this behavior he identifies himself as a policeman and makes reasonable inquiries; and where nothing in the initial stages of the encounter serves to dispel his reasonable fear for his own or others' safety, he is entitled for the protection of himself and others in the area to conduct a carefully limited search of the outer clothing of such persons in an attempt to discover weapons which might be used to assault him. Such a search is a reasonable search under the Fourth Amendment, and any weapons seized may properly be introduced in evidence against the person from whom they were taken.

Even though the United States Supreme Court has given sanction to stop and search in situations with less than probable cause for arrest, the officer is still presented with the problem of what the appellate courts will accept as a sufficient reason to stop a person; and this is particularly true when it involves the stopping of a person in a vehicle. In other words: What will constitute sufficient suspicious circumstances to justify a stop? What facts must be present to make the officer believe that the officer's own life or others' lives may be in danger? There are no specific guidelines which will help to answer these questions, but it has been held that mere unusual movements of a person in a vehicle are not sufficient to justify stopping the vehicle and questioning the occupants.

Another problem presented to the officer is: How far may the officer proceed in identifying an object to determine if it is a weapon? The officer must have reason to believe that an object he touches during the pat-down search is a weapon before investigating further. Thus, any soft object, however bulky, may not justify further investigation. In one case an officer removed an object from the pocket of a person during a pat-down search and recognized it as a cigarette package. Opening the package, the officer found that it contained marijuana. The individual was arrested for possession of marijuana, and a conviction was obtained. The conviction was reversed on appeal, since it was held that once the object was identified as a cigarette package and not a weapon, the fear was gone, and the officer had no right to open the package. Yet in another case, during a pat-down search an officer felt an object in the leather boot of an individual stopped for questioning. Upon the removal of the object, the officer saw that it was a clear plastic bag containing marijuana. The individual was arrested and convicted for the possession of marijuana. The conviction was appealed upon the ground that the officer exceeded the pat-down search. The appellate court upheld the conviction on the contention that many criminals carry weapons in their boots, and because of leather not being pliable, the officer was justified in removing the object to determine whether it was a weapon. Once the object was removed, the officer did not have to be blind to the fact that the object was not a weapon and was in fact contraband.

■ Expectation of Privacy

There was a time when it was believed that the Fourth Amendment guarantee against unreasonable search and seizure related to areas of privacy, and unless there was an intrusion of the area there was no unreasonable search and seizure. However, that concept has been changed. It is now held that the Fourth Amendment protects people and not areas. This change was particularly pointed out in *Katz v. United States,* 389 U.S. 347 (1967). Katz was convicted of transmitting wagers in interstate commerce through the use of a pay telephone booth to which FBI agents had attached an electronic listening device that had recorded conversations of Katz which were used to convict him. On appeal, it was contended that there had been an unreasonable seizure of the conversations of Katz, since his privacy had been invaded. The United States Supreme Court upheld the contention of Katz and reversed the conviction. The Court stated:

> The Fourth Amendment protects people, not places. What a person knowingly exposes to the public, even in his own home or office, is not a subject of Fourth Amendment protection. . . . But what he seeks to preserve as private, even in an area accessible to the public may be constitutionally protected. . . .
>
> It is true that the absence of penetration was at one time thought to foreclose further Fourth Amendment inquiry for that Amendment was thought to limit only searches and seizures of tangible property. But the premise that property interests control

the right of the Government to search and seize has been discred-
ited ... we have expressly held that the Fourth Amendment
governs not only the seizure of tangible items, but extends as well
to the recording of oral statements overheard without any technical trespass under local property law. Once this much is acknowledged, and once it is recognized that the Fourth Amendment
protects people and not simply areas against unreasonable
searches and seizures, it becomes clear that the reach of that
Amendment cannot turn upon the presence or absence of a physical intrusion into any given enclosure.

With the United States Supreme Court in the Katz decision adopting
the viewpoint that the Fourth Amendment protects persons and not places,
the expectation-of-privacy doctrine was greatly extended, and compliance
with the exclusionary rule became even more complicated. The problems
which have resulted are: What will the courts consider to be within the
realm of reasonable expectation of privacy, and what will be considered to
be an invasion of that privacy by an officer? Again there are no specific
guidelines which can be set forth, as justices of the appellate courts cannot
agree among themselves to the answers to many of these problems. In the
past, it was generally accepted that if an officer observed an object of
contraband or an unlawful act that was in open view (sometimes referred to
as the "open field doctrine"), there was no expectation of privacy and thus
no invasion of privacy. However, now, this is not always true under the Katz
doctrine. Even though something is observed in open view, the officer in
making the observation must have been lawfully upon the premises from
which the observation was made. Determination of whether an officer was
lawfully upon the premises is not always easily made. It has been held that
if the observation was made by an officer from a place where members of
the general public with legitimate business might be expected to be, the
officer would not be invading the expectation of privacy. For example, if
the officer made the observation from a hallway in an apartment house or a
hotel, in most instances, it would be considered that the officer was lawfully
upon the premises. Or one may expect a visitor to be on the front porch of
a dwelling but not on the lawn beside the dwelling, far away from normal
paths for visitors. There have been cases in which the observation of an
officer who walked down a driveway to look into a neighboring yard was
upheld, even though permission had not been directly received from the
occupant of the premises from which the observation was made. In such
cases the courts have held that the driveway was used by service people as
well as delivery persons and there was therefore no reasonable expectation
of privacy.

On the other hand, there have been cases in which the courts have held
that the expectation of privacy was invaded even though an officer was
lawfully upon the premises from which the observation was made. For
example, in one case an officer stationed himself in the plumbing access

area of a public restroom, where he was able to view an unlawful act between two male individuals. The court held that even though the unlawful act was committed in a doorless stall of a public restroom, the officer has no right to retreat to a clandestine position in order to "peer" into areas of reasonable expectation of privacy. In another case, an officer received permission to enter a small area between a garage and a fence in order to look into a neighboring yard. The court in that case held that the officer "squeezed" himself into an area not generally used by persons; thus he invaded the expectation of privacy of the neighbor. It has been held that making observations from a neighbor's second-story bedroom window is not an invasion of the expectation of privacy. Also, the use of a flashlight to illuminate dark areas has been sanctioned as not being an invasion of the expectation of privacy.

ENCLOSED-AREA OBSERVATIONS. Problems have arisen in connection with the reasonable expectation of privacy of areas or yards enclosed with a wooden fence or a concrete block wall, the height of which is usually restricted to not more than 6 feet. Is there a reasonable expectation that activities within such enclosures would not be observed at some time by a neighbor or others? A young lady sun bathing in the nude may have a right to expect that her activity would not be invaded by a neighbor climbing a ladder to observe her; yet it may well be expected that a neighbor may have a visitor more than 6 feet tall who could easily observe the activities in an adjoining yard even though enclosed with a 6-foot wall. So the individual who is raising opium poppies in an enclosed backyard may have a reasonable expectation of privacy against the police climbing a ladder in a neighbor's yard to observe the poppies. Yet is it not reasonable to expect that the neighbor may at some time climb a ladder to trim a hedge or get on the roof to retrieve a toy, during which time the neighbor would have a full view of the activity in an adjoining yard? In other words, is the officer who climbs on a ladder to observe activity in an adjoining yard invading the reasonable expectation of privacy, when the 6-foot-4 officer could easily observe activities in such an enclosure? The answers to these questions are generally determined by the facts of each individual case.

AERIAL OBSERVATIONS. Similar problems have been presented in relation to aerial observations of enclosed areas. An old adage provides that the owner of a plot of land owns "the sky above and the earth below." The courts have in some cases taken a similar view by holding that the expectation of privacy is not earthbound and state that "the Fourth Amendment guards the privacy of human activity from aerial no less than terrestrial invasion." However, in some cases, aerial observations have been upheld, but whether there was an invasion of privacy from aerial observation or not must be decided upon the facts of each case. For example, in one case, an officer received information that large marijuana plants were being grown in an enclosed corral. It was not possible to view the enclosed area from the public right-of-way in the area; so some officers rented a helicopter to fly over the enclosure. The court held that there was an invasion of the reasonable expectation of privacy. The court reasoned that, since the corral was in a rural area not near an airport, and, since there were no known crop-dusting or insect-abatement programs being conducted in the area, the occupants of the corral had a reasonable expectation of privacy, which was in a rural area not near an airport and since there were no known in another case, the court upheld the observation of officers from an airplane when they were able to observe a three-quarter acre of marijuana growing in a hidden valley. The court held that it was not reasonable for the occupants of the field of marijuana to think that the field would not be flown over at some time by passing aircraft, even though the field was in a hidden valley. Also, in another case, the court upheld an aerial observation of an enclosed automobile-wrecking yard. The officers were seeking a stolen automobile, which was believed to be in the enclosure. The officers requested a police helicopter to fly over the wrecking yard in an effort to observe the vehicle, which was seen by an officer in the helicopter. The court upheld the observation from the helicopter upon the ground that the wrecking yard was in an urban area patrolled by police helicopters, and there was no reasonable expectation that the helicopter would not at some time pass over the area of the enclosure and be able to view that which was in the open as so far as aerial viewing was concerned.

LOOKING INTO TRASH CONTAINERS. The courts in some jurisdictions have held that the placement of one's trash containers at the curbside in front of a dwelling or in the alley behind a house for collection is not necessarily an abandonment of one's trash to the police or general public to the point that there is no reasonable expectation of privacy. Looking into such containers by the police has been held to be an invasion of privacy. However, it has been held in some instances that the police looking into apartment house trash containers, used in common by a number of tenants, when there was reasonable cause to believe that they contained incriminating evidence was not an invasion of privacy. The courts in these instances have held that an apartment house tenant has less reason to believe what is deposited in such common trash containers will remain private than does a home dweller who provides and uses his own individual cans. Trash placed in such containers is especially likely to be tampered with. Although unwelcome, the intrusion into these containers is not totally unexpected, and the common usage of such containers by a large number of tenants diminishes the reasonable expectation of privacy. On the other hand, some appellate courts have held that even though a tenant places trash in an apartment house or communal trash receptacle, there is still a reasonable expectation of privacy against the trash being examined by police officers without a search warrant.

OBJECTING TO
INTRODUCTION OF EVIDENCE

If a defendant believes that evidence has been illegally obtained, the defendant must object to its use by the prosecution in court at the earliest opportunity. The objection is usually made in the form of a written request to the trial judge requesting that the evidence be excluded from use against the accused. The written form is legally known as a "motion to suppress evidence."

The defendant's attorney may file this motion to suppress evidence almost immediately after the arrest and before the preliminary hearing or the grand jury hearing. The motion to suppress evidence will set forth the reason why the defendant thinks that the evidence was illegally obtained. The objection may be based upon the fact that the consent was not voluntarily given or that the search went beyond the scope of the consent. The objection may be an attack on the search warrant, or in the case of a search incidental to an arrest, the objection may be that there was insufficient probable cause to make the arrest, in which case the arrest would be illegal and the search and seizure would be unlawful. The defendant may claim that the search incidental to the arrest extended beyond the area under the immediate control of the accused, which also would make the search and seizure unlawful.

A hearing is usually held on the motion to suppress evidence prior to the trial; the prosecution may present evidence in an effort to prove that the evidence was legally obtained, and the defendant will present evidence why it should be excluded. If the judge agrees with the defendant, the evidence will be excluded, but if the judge decides that the evidence was legally obtained, it will be admitted against the accused during the trial. The admission of such evidence over the objections of the defendant causes cases to be reviewed by the appellate courts. If the appellate court thinks the evidence was illegally obtained and should have been excluded, the conviction will be reversed in most instances.

If the defendant does not file a motion to suppress evidence prior to the trial, in most jurisdictions the defendant may still object to the introduction of the evidence during the trial. The defendant must be given every opportunity to determine whether evidence which is offered was legally obtained. The defendant may question the prosecution's witnesses and may present witnesses in his or her own behalf. He may question the officers who made the arrest concerning the sufficiency of their probable cause to make the arrest. This often results in the necessity of revealing the identity of informants. The officer may be examined about the method used to induce the defendant to consent to a search of person or premises. If there are any irregularities in obtaining the evidence, it will undoubtedly be excluded. The burden is primarily upon the prosecution to prove that the evidence was legally obtained.

FRUITS OF THE POISONOUS TREE

The exclusionary rule not only excludes illegally obtained evidence, but it also excludes any information received by an illegal act or from illegally seized evidence. This is known as the "fruits-of-the-poisonous-tree" doctrine. This doctrine holds that if an act is illegal, it is a poisonous tree, and any information obtained from that illegal act is the fruit of the poisonous tree, and is consequently also unlawfully obtained and must be excluded. The fruit-of-the-poisonous-tree doctrine was placed into operation upon federal officers by the Silverthorne Lumber Company case (see page 196), but it was only after the Mapp decision that it became operative on the states. The courts have adopted the viewpoint that the taint of an illegal act will carry over to the information received from that act. For example, it has been held that if there was an illegal entry into the premises of an accused, statements made by the accused as a result of that illegal entry will be excluded as fruits of the poisonous tree. This was specifically pointed out in *Wong Sun v. United States,* 371 U.S. 471 (1963), in which the United States Supreme Court stated:

> The exclusionary rule has traditionally barred from trial physical, tangible materials obtained either during or as a direct result of an unlawful invasion. It follows from our holding in Silverman v. United States [365 U.S. 505] 1920 that the Fourth Amendment may protect against the overhearing of verbal statements as well as against the more traditional seizure of "papers and effects." Similarly, testimony as to matters observed during an unlawful invasion has been excluded in order to enforce the basic constitutional policies. . . . Thus, verbal evidence which derives so immediately from an unlawful entry and an unauthorized arrest as the officer's action in the present case is no less the "fruit" of official illegality than the more common tangible fruits of the unwarranted intrusion.

In *Davis v. Mississippi,* 394 U.S. 721 (1969), the United States Supreme Court held that fingerprints taken of an illegally detained suspect may not be used against the suspect.

The courts have also held that evidence discovered as a result of an improperly obtained confession will be excluded as being fruit of the poisonous tree.

It has been stated, however, that not all evidence which may come to light as the result of some illegal act will have to be excluded because of the fruit-of-the-poisonous-tree doctrine. If the prosecution can convincingly prove that the evidence would have been discovered from some other independent source, the evidence may be admissible. This viewpoint was mentioned also by the Supreme Court in the Wong Sun decision.

LINEUP IDENTIFICATION

Up to this point, the discussion of the exclusionary rule has been based on the Fourth Amendment guarantee against unreasonable search and seizure. Now the exclusionary rule must be considered from a different approach, based on the right to assistance of counsel embodied in the Sixth Amendment. In the case of *United States v. Wade,* 388 U.S. 218 (1967), the United States Supreme Court held that evidence of a pretrial lineup identification was inadmissible if the defendant was denied the right of counsel at the pretrial lineup. In the Wade case, the facts reflect that a bank was robbed on September 21, 1964, by a man with a small strip of tape on each side of his face. After forcing the bank employees to fill a pillowcase with money, the robber left with an accomplice who was waiting outside the bank in a stolen car. On March 23, 1965, Wade was indicted for robbing the bank. He was arrested on April 2, 1965, and counsel was appointed for him on April 26, 1965. Fifteen days later, an FBI agent, without notice to Wade's lawyer, arranged to have the bank employees observe a lineup made up of Wade and other prisoners. Each person in the lineup wore strips of tape on his face and was directed to say something like "put the money in the bag." The employees identified Wade.

At the trial, the employees again identified Wade as the robber. Wade's attorney moved for a judgment of acquittal on the grounds that the lineup without notice to and in the absence of the attorney was a violation of the Fifth Amendment privilege against self-incrimination and the Sixth Amendment right to assistance of counsel. The motion was denied, and Wade was convicted. He appealed his case to the United States Supreme Court, and the conviction was reversed on the grounds that Wade's Sixth Amendment guarantee to assistance of counsel had been violated, since he had been denied the right of counsel at the pretrial lineup.

In reversing the conviction the Court stated:

> [T]he confrontation compelled by the state between the accused and the victim or witnesses to a crime to elicit identification evidence is peculiarly riddled with innumerable dangers and variable factors which might seriously, even crucially, derogate from a fair trial. The vagaries of eyewitness identification are well known; the annals of criminal law are rife with instances of mistaken identification. . . . A major factor contributing to the high incidence of miscarriage of justice from mistaken identification has been the degree of suggestion inherent in the manner in which the prosecution presents the suspect to witnesses for pretrial identification. . . .
> Since the presence of counsel itself can often avert prejudice and assure a meaningful confrontation at trial, there can be little doubt that for Wade the postindictment lineup was a critical stage of the prosecution at which he was as much entitled to such aid of counsel as at the trial itself.

Thus the Wade decision made the exclusionary rule operative from a new angle. That decision held that, because of the possible undue suggestive manner in which confrontations between accused persons and victims or witnesses takes place, the accused is entitled to the assistance of counsel at such confrontations. If counsel were not present during the confrontations, the accused's Sixth Amendment guarantee to the assistance of counsel had been violated, and evidence of such identification would be excluded during the trial.

The Court in upholding the lineup as not being a violation of the Fifth Amendment stated: "The prohibition of compelling a man in a criminal court to be a witness against himself is a prohibition of the use of physical or moral compulsion to extort communication from him, not an exclusion of his body as evidence when it may be material."

■ **On-the-Scene Identifications
and Preindictment Confrontations**

Many times, shortly after a crime is committed, a suspect is taken into custody. The most expedient way to substantiate that the suspect is the perpetrator of the crime or to eliminate the suspect is to have an immediate confrontation between the suspect and the witness, or the witnesses. In view of the Wade decision, the question that was presented to the law enforcement officer was: Did all identification procedures necessitate a formal lineup with counsel for the accused present, or because of the emergency of a situation, could the suspect be presented to the witness then and there?

In the *Stovall v. Denno* case, 388 U.S. 293 (1967), the United States Supreme Court gave sanction to an identification confrontation between a victim of an armed robbery and a suspect without counsel for the accused present. But there was an emergency existing, since it was not known how long the victim might live, and she was the only one who could either identify or eliminate the suspect. But what about cases in which there is no emergency? In the case of *Kirby v. Illinois*, 406 U.S. 682 (1972), this question was answered. The United States Supreme Court upheld a "station-house" confrontation between two suspects and the victim of a robbery where the suspects were not represented by counsel.

The facts of this case reflect that one Willie Shard was robbed by two men. Two days later, the police arrested two suspects, one of whom was Kirby, and took them to the police station. Thereafter Shard was brought to the station. Immediately upon entering the room in the police station where the suspects were seated at a table, Shard positively identified them as the men who had robbed him. No lawyer was present in the room, and neither suspect had asked for legal assistance or been advised of any right to the presence of counsel.

More than six weeks later, the suspects were indicted for the robbery. Upon arraignment, counsel was appointed to represent them, and they pleaded not guilty. A pretrial motion to suppress Shard's identification testimony was denied, and at the trial Shard testified as a witness for the prosecution. In his testimony, he described the identification of the suspects at the police station and identified them again in the courtroom as the men who had robbed him. Kirby was convicted, and he appealed his conviction to the United States Supreme Court on the Wade decision, that he was denied the right of counsel at the confrontation.

In upholding the station-house confrontation, the Court reemphasized that a postindictment confrontation between a defendant and a victim, or witness, to a crime is at a critical stage of the prosecution, and so the defendant is entitled to the assistance of counsel. But the Court stated: "When a person has not been formally charged with a criminal offense, Stovall strikes the appropriate constitutional balance between the right of a suspect to be protected from prejudicial procedures and the interest of society in the prompt and purposeful investigation of an unsolved crime." Therefore the Court concluded that until the suspect is formally charged with a crime, he is not entitled to the assistance of counsel at an identification confrontation.

It appears from the wording of the Kirby case that as long as there is no formal charge placed against an accused, the identification confrontation can be either an informal type as in the Kirby case or the more formal lineup procedure, and the accused is not entitled to have the assistance of counsel present.

■ Suspect Entitled to Counsel after Being Formally Charged

Attention is called to the fact that the Kirby decision held that once the accused is indicted or otherwise formally charged with a crime, the accused is entitled to have the assistance and presence of counsel at any identification confrontation; otherwise, evidence of such identification is not admissible, nor is a courtroom identification permissible if it is based on a lineup conducted in violation of the constitutional standards, i.e., the denial of the assistance of counsel. It is generally accepted that an accused is formally charged when an indictment has been returned by a grand jury or an information or a complaint has been filed. It has been held that an unnecessary delay in formally charging an accused in order to conduct a lineup will cause the identification evidence from such a lineup to be inadmissible. In one case, an accused was arrested on a charge of robbery, but an identification lineup was not conducted until six days later, at which time the accused was identified as the robber. Immediately after the identification was made, the accused was formally charged by the filing of a complaint. The court rejected the identification evidence on the ground that the accused had not been arraigned without unnecessary delay, in violation of the accused's constitutional rights.

Although the accused is entitled to have an attorney present at any identification confrontation after being formally charged, the attorney has no right to prevent the confrontation, nor does the accused have a right to refuse to participate in a lineup or other types of identification confrontations. If the accused does refuse to participate, either on the advice of counsel or without it, the accused should be advised that refusal can be used by the prosecution in court, the refusal being an indication of consciousness of guilt.

SUMMARY

The exclusionary rule provides that illegally obtained evidence will be excluded in a trial proceeding. The *Mapp v. Ohio* decision of the United States Supreme Court made this rule applicable to all the states. The exclusionary rule makes the Fourth Amendment to the Constitution applicable to the states through the due-process clause of the Fourteenth Amendment. Although this rule is applicable to all evidence which is unlawfully obtained, most of the problems arise through unreasonable searches and seizures.

The exclusionary rule does not abolish all searches and seizures, only unreasonable ones. Three kinds of searches have been held as reasonable: (1) search by consent; (2) search by search warrant; and (3) search incidental to lawful arrest.

A search has been defined as "looking, or prying into, hidden places in an effort to locate some object which has been intentionally concealed or put out of sight." A seizure is taking possession of an object to the exclusion of the former possessor and usually against that person's will.

For a search by consent to be a reasonable one, the consent must have been voluntarily given. Consent any way induced by force, threat, promise, duress, or deceit will affect the validity of the consent, and in turn the reasonableness of the search and the seizure. The ability to give consent is largely dependent upon the control that a person has over the particular premises to be searched. Consent to search may be limited or withdrawn.

For a search pursuant to a search warrant to be reasonable, the search warrant must be valid, and the execution of the search must also conform to the prescribed rules and regulations. Before a search warrant may be issued, the officer must submit an affidavit setting forth information which establishes reasonable cause to believe that the things sought are at a particular place. The place to be searched and the objects to be seized must be specifically described. A search warrant must be served within a reasonable time, or a prescribed time as set forth by statute. Reasonable force may be exerted in executing a search warrant. Generally, before forceful entry can be made for the execution of a search warrant, a request for admittance must be made, but if there is a danger that the evidence will be destroyed, or if danger to the officer may be caused by requesting admittance, some jurisdictions have permitted entry to be made without prior request for admittance.

The third method by which a reasonable search and seizure may be made is incidental to an arrest. Basic to the reasonableness of such a search is the lawfulness of the arrest. If it develops that the arrest was unlawful, a search incident to that unlawful arrest is also unlawful, and any evidence seized will be excluded, and cannot justify the arrest. The person arrested may be searched and the area within immediate control of that person may also be searched. The search must be contemporaneous with the arrest and may not be remote in time or place. The purpose of a search incident to an arrest is to seek weapons by which the accused may cause harm to the officer, and to seek evidence pertaining to the crime for which the accused was arrested. The courts have generally been less restrictive in applying the exclusionary rule in the search of vehicles because of the mobility of a vehicle and the greater chance of the loss or destruction of evidence.

The United States has sanctioned the temporary detention of persons in public places when there is reason to believe that they may be involved in a crime. This detention is for the purpose of ascertaining their identity and explaining their actions at the time. A search for the weapon may be made at the time if the officer has reason to think his or her life may be in danger.

The courts have held that the Fourth Amendment protects persons and not places, and if an officer invades an area of reasonable expectation of privacy, any evidence discovered as a result of that invasion is inadmissible. The United States Supreme Court has held that once an accused is formally charged with a crime, the accused is entitled to the assistance of counsel at any identification confrontation proceeding.

QUESTIONS FOR REVIEW

1. What does the exclusionary rule of evidence provide?
2. What case made this rule applicable to all of the states?
3. What types of searches and seizures are deemed to be illegal according to the Fourth Amendment?
4. By what three methods may lawful searches and seizures be made?
5. What may affect the giving of a consent?
6. Who may give consent for a search?
7. What is a search warrant?
8. What must be included in the affidavit supporting the search warrant?
9. How soon must a search warrant be executed?

10. For a search incidental to an arrest to be reasonable, what is required of the arrest?
11. What may be taken during a search incidental to an arrest?
12. What area may be searched incidental to an arrest?
13. What is the fruit-of-the-poisonous-tree doctrine?
14. What was the significance of the Katz decision?
15. What were the problems created by the Katz decision?
16. What is the purpose of a pat-down search?
17. When is such a search permissible?
18. When is an accused entitled to the assistance of counsel during an identification confrontation?

LOCAL RULES

As the result of United States Supreme Court decisions, the rules on the exclusionary rule and searches and seizures are comparatively uniform throughout the United States, but there are a few minor differences in the rules as they pertain to search warrants and other procedures. Therefore the reader should get the answers to the following questions from the local prosecuting attorney for the rules in the jurisdiction.

1. On what grounds may a search warrant be issued?
2. Must the officer be in possession of the search warrant when the search is made pursuant to a search warrant?
3. Must the officer announce his or her presence and purpose before breaking into a building in all instances when executing a search warrant?
4. What are the definitions of day and night as they relate to the service of a search warrant?
5. Within what period of time must a search warrant be executed after it has been issued? If not executed within that time, may the time for service be extended or must a new search warrant be obtained?
6. To make the consent valid, must a warning be given that the right to consent to a warrantless search may be withheld?
7. May contraband which was seized but not listed in a search warrant be admitted in evidence?

Circumstantial Evidence
9

DIRECT EVIDENCE VERSUS CIRCUMSTANTIAL EVIDENCE

For years evidence has been classified as direct evidence and circumstantial or indirect evidence, yet many writers make no effort to distinguish between the two, as they think that such a distinction has no practical value. In fact, this opinion was expressed by the court in *Rodella v. United States*, 286 F.2d 306 (1960), in which it was stated: "Any attempted differentiation between direct and circumstantial evidence at times becomes indistinct and in law, unimportant." Yet the terms direct and circumstantial evidence continue to weave their way into the language of our statutes and court decisions, making some explanation of these terms in order, although, occasionally, the demarcation between them may be difficult to see.

■ Direct Evidence Defined

Direct evidence has been described as the testimony of witnesses who looked on while an act was being committed. In a criminal trial, direct evidence would be the facts presented by a witness who saw the accused actually commit the crime. Legally, direct evidence has been defined as that evidence which proves the facts in dispute directly, without an inference or a presumption being drawn from any other set of facts. Evidence is declared to be direct and positive when the very facts in dispute are communicated by persons who have actual knowledge of the facts by means of their senses. For example, if, in a murder case, a person saw the accused actually shoot the victim, that person's testimony would be direct evidence of the shooting and would bear directly on the dispute about the guilt of the accused.

245

■ Circumstantial Evidence Defined

Circumstantial evidence is an indirect approach to proving the facts in dispute. Circumstantial evidence is sometimes called "presumptive evidence" because certain facts may be presumed, or inferred, to have taken place when other facts are proved to have happened. Legally, circumstantial, or indirect, evidence has been defined as evidence which tends to establish the facts in dispute by proving another set of facts from which an inference or presumption can be drawn in an effort to prove the facts in dispute. One or more inferences may be said to arise reasonably from a series of proved facts. Returning to the murder case, if no one saw the accused commit the murder, efforts would have to be made to prove his guilt beyond a reasonable doubt by proof of other facts from which an inference of guilt could be drawn.

To prove a murder charge, evidence may be presented that a witness overheard a heated argument between the accused and the victim, then heard a shot, and thereafter saw the accused with gun in hand run from the room in which the victim was found dead. From these facts, an inference could be drawn that the accused was guilty of the murder. It may appear at first glance that these facts are direct evidence, as, in each instance, the witness heard or saw something. The testimony is direct evidence about what was heard and seen, but is only circumstantial evidence about the fact in issue—that is, the guilt of the accused—because what the witness heard and saw does not prove directly that the accused shot the victim. It only presents a set of circumstances from which a strong presumption of guilt can be drawn. This presumption is drawn because in most instances when this set of facts is present, the accused is guilty of murder. The accused may also present circumstantial evidence in an effort to prove innocence. The accused may endeavor to show that the deceased was "out to get" him or her and that the accused shot in self-defense.

■ Why Use Circumstantial Evidence?

One frequently hears people claim not to believe in circumstantial evidence. Such remarks usually mean that most people do not understand what circumstantial evidence is or its significance in the prosecution of cases. Circumstantial evidence has a definite place in the trial of cases. It is admissible because, many times, it is the only means by which the truth of what happened can be determined. A great number of crimes are committed without eyewitnesses, particularly in crimes of murder and burglary, so the only way of proving guilt is through circumstantial evidence. Circumstantial evidence can be as convincing in proving guilt as direct evidence, and in many cases equally, if not more, reliable. Most of the scientific evidence presented by crime-laboratory technicians is nothing more than circumstantial evidence; yet its reliability is most satisfactory and convincing. A latent fingerprint developed on a safe that the accused is charged with burglarizing is the strongest kind of proof that the accused touched that safe.

The philosophy by which circumstantial evidence is utilized is based upon the fact that human experience has been that when a given set of circumstances takes place, the results of those circumstances are usually the same each time they happen. In other words, human experience has shown that when a person overhears a heated argument between two people, hears a shot, sees an individual running from a room with a gun in his hand, and finds a deceased victim in the room, the individual seen fleeing is usually guilty of murder. Given this same set of circumstances again, the inference which can be drawn is again that the fleeing person is guilty of murder.

Except in some jurisdictions when the charge is perjury or treason, it has been held that circumstantial evidence alone is sufficient to support a conviction. However, it may take a greater amount of circumstantial evidence to prove guilty beyond a reasonable doubt. In most cases, both direct and circumstantial evidence are introduced.

■ Relevancy of Circumstantial Evidence

Whether direct or circumstantial evidence is to be introduced, the rules of admissibility are the same. The evidence must be presented through witnesses who have some knowledge about the facts of the case, and, for the evidence to be admissible, it must be relevant to, or have some connection with, the issues in dispute. In the case of direct evidence, the connection can usually be readily recognized, but the relevancy of circumstantial evidence is often hidden, and the connection of circumstantial evidence with the proof of the fact in issue may have to be explained by the attorney endeavoring to introduce it before the judge will admit it. For example, the appearance of an accused person's clothing immediately after a crime has been committed may not seem, at first glance, to have any connection with establishing guilt. But if the charge against the accused is murder or aggravated assault, the fact that the accused's clothing indicated he had been in a struggle could be material in proving guilt. The state of mind of a murder victim may be important to prove that the victim was afraid of the accused, and thus be indicative of guilt.

The relevancy of circumstantial evidence is based primarily on logic, reasonableness, good sense, and good judgment. If circumstantial evidence tends to explain in a reasonable manner what happened and aids in proving the truth of issues in dispute, it is considered relevant.

At times, a single circumstance may be offered in evidence from which no logical inference can be drawn, but coupling it with other circumstances may make it relevant to the issues in dispute. For example, evidence presented that an accused is an expert shot with a rifle may not have any particular significance even in a murder case, but if it is proved that the murder victim was killed from a great distance with a rifle, the fact that the accused had the ability to commit such an act could create an inference of guilt.

How far one may go in the introduction of circumstantial evidence depends a great deal upon how remote the relevancy, or connection, with the issues the circumstantial evidence is. If it is too remote or would consume too much time in its presentation or create undue prejudice, it may be excluded. The trial judge is given a great deal of latitude in determining whether circumstantial evidence will be admitted or excluded. However, a number of rules on admissibility of circumstantial evidence have been developed over the years which act as guidelines for judges. Some of these rules will be discussed.

As to circumstantial evidence being too remote to establish guilt, the United States Supreme Court held in one case that the mere presence of the accused at a still where illegal liquor was being made was not enough to prove guilt, but his presence there coupled with other activity showing some connection with the still might be admitted to prove guilt.

■ Circumstantial Evidence Used in Many Ways

Circumstantial evidence is used in many ways in the prosecution of criminals. In a great number of cases, the entire presentation of evidence against the accused consists only of circumstantial evidence because there were no eyewitnesses to the crime to present direct evidence. For example, if an accused were being tried for burglary, all the evidence presented by the prosecution might be nothing more than a series of events from which the jury could draw an inference of guilt. The first fact might be the testimony of an officer that he had arrested the accused during the night near a store that had been burglarized. The officer might add to the testimony that the accused had had in his possession at the time articles known to have been taken during the burglary of the store. This testimony does not directly place the accused in the store, nor does it put the accused in the position of actually burglarizing the store. However, from this set of events, or facts, there is a strong suspicion of guilt already created. There may be added to these facts testimony that latent fingerprints developed in the store were identified as those of the accused. With this additional bit of evidence, the case against the accused becomes stronger. There may be added information that a small piece of glass found in the pant cuff of the accused fit in place with those taken from a broken window of the burglarized store. None of these facts individually or collectively directly prove that the accused is the burglar, yet, as a whole, they probably are as strong in establishing guilt beyond a reasonable doubt as if a witness had testified: "Yes, I saw the accused break into the store and burglarize it."

In fact, this series of circumstances may be considered by the jury to be more convincing than the direct evidence of a witness who testified to seeing the accused burglarize the store. The jury may think the witness is not reliable, but a strong inference of guilt can be drawn from the circumstantial evidence, and thus the mere fact that the only evidence available is circumstantial does not mean that it cannot establish a strong case against the accused.

Circumstantial evidence may be used to corroborate direct evidence presented by the witnesses. Returning to the example of a witness who testified, "Yes, I saw the accused break into the store and burglarize it," circumstantial evidence of latent fingerprints developed inside the store and glass fragments in the pant cuff of the accused may corroborate the direct evidence.

Many other uses are made of circumstantial evidence, but one of the more frequent is to connect the accused with the crime, that is, to identify the accused as the one who committed the act. In the effort to establish identity, evidence may be introduced that the accused has committed other crimes with the same *modus operandi* or that he had the ability and means with which to commit the crime in question. Circumstantial evidence may be introduced to overcome an allegation that a homicide was committed in self-defense, or by accident, or to prove premeditation. Circumstantial evidence may also be presented by a defendant in an effort to prove innocence. Some of the more prominent uses of circumstantial evidence in criminal cases will be discussed in further detail.

ADMISSIBILITY OF
PREVIOUS CRIMES AND MISCONDUCT

A person who goes around committing acts of misconduct and crimes is more likely to be guilty of the crime of which accused than one who does not. Therefore, revealing to the jury the past acts of misconduct and crimes committed by a defendant in a criminal trial could create a strong suspicion of guilt. But generally, evidence of prior acts of misconduct and crimes of the defendant, which are not a part of the charge for which he is now being tried, may not be introduced during the trial. As was stated in Chapter 5, this restriction has been established for several reasons. First, the mere fact that the accused has committed other acts of misconduct or crimes does not necessarily mean the accused is guilty as charged. It has been held that the defendant in each case is entitled to go to trial with a clean slate, and is to be tried on the facts of the case at hand and not on past record. It has also been stated that prior misconduct and crimes introduced against the defendant may so prejudice the jury that the defendant will not get a fair trial. The jury may be inclined to automatically assume that a defendant is guilty of the crime of the present charge because of past acts.

There are times, however, when prior acts of misconduct or crimes committed by the accused may be introduced during a criminal trial because they are pertinent to the issues and may assist the jury in arriving at the truth. They are strong bits of circumstantial evidence which indicate guilt of the accused. Specific rules have been developed about when these past acts may be admissible.

It has been held that evidence of prior acts of misconduct or crimes by the accused may be introduced when they tend to show a plan, scheme, system, design, or a characteristic behavior pattern of the accused similar to that for which the accused is on trial. It was stated in an early New York case entitled *People v. Molineux*, 168 N.Y. 264 (1901):

> Generally speaking, evidence of other crimes is competent to prove the specific crime charged when it tends to establish (1) motive; (2) intent; (3) the absence of mistake or accident; (4) a common scheme or plan embracing the commission of two or more crimes so related to each other that proof of one tends to establish the other; (5) the identity of the person charged with the commission of the crime on trial.

■ Other Crimes Prove Intent or Motive

Prior acts of misconduct or crimes frequently become the reason or motive for the repetition of that same act or crime or may be an indication that a particular act was intended and not an accident. Although there is a tendency to use the terms "intent" and "motive" interchangeably in general conversation, legally they are not the same. Intent is a state of mind; it expresses mental action which is usually coupled with an outward physical act to bring about a particular result. Motive is the reason behind an act. It is the inducement to act or commit a crime. Intent is a necessary element of most crimes. Being a state of mind, it is not easily proved, and must usually be proved by circumstantial evidence. A motive may be proved whereby the intent is inferred from the motive. Past acts of misconduct or crimes are frequently introduced in evidence to prove a motive for the crime for which the defendant is on trial.

One of the most bizarre cases in which motive became an issue is *People v. Lisenba*, 14 Cal. 2d 403 (1939), in which the defendant was charged with the murder of his wife. Prior acts of misconduct were admitted to prove motive for the murder for which the defendant was tried. Briefly, the facts are that the defendant, using the last name of James, employed a manicurist, Mary, to work in his barbershop. A short time thereafter, James married the manicurist and immediately took out an insurance policy on her life with a double-indemnity clause for accidental death. Shortly thereafter, James conspired with a friend to help him kill his wife and make the death appear an accident in order to collect on the double-indemnity clause of the insurance policy. James induced his friend to obtain two rattlesnakes, which James planned to use to bring about his wife's death, so that the death would appear to be an accident. After obtaining the rattlesnakes, James tied his wife's arms behind her, taped her mouth, and strapped her to the kitchen table. He placed one of her feet in the box of rattlesnakes, and one of the snakes struck her foot. James and the friend then left the house. Upon their return, James found that the venom had not had any serious effect on his wife. He then decided to drown her in a fishpond in a manner to make it appear that she had accidentally fallen into the pond. The wife was carried to the pond, and her head and shoulders were placed beneath the water, where she was held until she drowned. James thereafter went out to dinner with another friend and his wife. After returning home, James made a pretense of searching for his wife, came back from the yard, and stated that his wife had apparently fallen into the fishpond and drowned. An autopsy was performed and the drowning was confirmed. An investigation at that time failed to reveal the facts of the wife's death.

James in the meantime endeavored to collect on the insurance policy, but payment was refused on the ground that the accidental death was under suspicion. This suspicion was based on the fact that three years before, James, under the name Lisenba, had married a woman in Colorado and had immediately taken out an insurance policy on her life with a double-indemnity clause. Thereafter, while on a ride to Pike's Peak, Lisenba and his wife were allegedly in an automobile accident. The facts of this alleged accident were brought out during the trial of James for the murder of his wife, Mary. The facts were that James had gone on a ride with the first wife up Pike's Peak, and while riding along the road, James had struck his wife severely on the back of the head. He then jumped from the car and pushed it over an embankment, thinking that his wife was dead from the blow on the head. James hiked to a service station for help to report the accident. He told the service station attendant that his wife and he had been driving up the Pike's Peak road, that he had lost control of his car, and that his wife had been killed. The attendant returned to the scene with James and found the car had rolled over an embankment. Although the wife was not dead, she had received a serious blow on the back of the head, and a hammer with blood on it was found in the car. The wife recovered from the blow on the head and told what had taken place. But before any prosecutive action could be brought, the wife was found mysteriously drowned in the bathtub of her home.

The prior acts of misconduct of James, consisting of taking out an insurance policy with a double-indemnity clause, the attempt to kill his wife and make it appear an accident, and the mysterious drowning, were all admitted in evidence against James during the trial for murder of his wife Mary, because these prior acts of misconduct reflected a motive for the present murder, as well as a common scheme or design.

Another case in which prior acts of misconduct were introduced against a defendant to prove common scheme or plan was one in which the defendant was charged with rape. The facts were that the victim had gone to the defendant for medical advice, and the defendant was accused of having given the victim a hypodermic injection which caused her to become semiconscious. While in this condition, the defendant had sexual relations with the victim. The defendant took the stand in his own defense and denied the charge. The prosecution was permitted to introduce the testimony of three other women who testified that they had also gone to the defendant for medical advice and aid, that he had given them injections rendering them semiconscious, and that while they were semiconscious, he had sexual relations with them. The court held that the testimony of the prosecution witnesses was admitted to show a common scheme or plan. It was evidence to establish that the defendant had raped three women by the use of drugs at different times. In each instance, the woman came to his office either as an employee or a patient; each had been administered a drug into a vein, after which the rape occurred. Each woman testified she would not have had, nor did she have, intercourse without the drug.

Evidence of the commission of acts similar to the alleged crime committed is admissible to show common scheme or plan, or *modus operandi*. Particularly, evidence of similar acts to show *modus operandi* is admissible in rape cases.

■ Other Crimes Prove Lack of Mistake or Accident

Evidence of other crimes, or acts of misconduct, may be admitted to prove that the accused had knowledge, or should have had knowledge, that the act committed was a crime and not a mistake, accident, or innocent act. For example, it has been held that if a defendant is charged with the crime of possession of marijuana and endeavors to prove innocence by alleging ignorance that the material found in his or her possession was marijuana, the prosecution is permitted to show that the defendant had been previously convicted of possession of marijuana in order to prove that the defendant did have knowledge, or should have had knowledge, that the material found in his or her possession was marijuana. Likewise it has been held that when a man is charged with the murder of his wife, evidence of illicit relations with another woman and his efforts to obtain a divorce from his wife are admissible to overcome an allegation that the wife's death was accidental. Evidence of acts of incest between a father and his daughter may be shown when the father is charged with the murder of his daughter and there is evidence that the daughter was trying to break the relationship with the father. Prior lewd acts with young boys by an accused were held to be admissible when the accused was charged with molesting children, to refute the accused's contention that his touching the children was an innocent act. Other acts of misconduct or crimes by an accused may be introduced to prove passion or a propensity for unnatural sexual relations.

■ Other Crimes to Prove Identity

During the trial of a criminal case, not only must the fact that a crime has been committed be proved, but it must be established that the defendant was the one who committed the act, unless he or she admits committing the act and claims self-defense. Proving that the defendant is the one who committed the crime for which he or she is on trial is not always easily accomplished, particularly if the defendant alleges mistaken identity or claims an alibi defense. Prior crimes known to have been committed by the defendant sometimes may be introduced in evidence in an effort to prove that the defendant committed the crime for which he or she is on trial. But because of the highly prejudicial effect that the admission of prior crimes by a defendant may have on a jury, strict rules have been adopted concerning the introduction of prior crimes. The courts have held that the mere fact that prior crimes and the one for which the accused is on trial have certain marks of similarity is not enough because many crimes of the same nature committed by different individuals may have marks of similarity. Some courts have gone so far as to hold that the manner in which the prior crimes were committed, that is, the *modus operandi,* and the currently charged crime must be so unusual and distinctive as to be like a signature. Other courts have held that there does not have to be a unique or nearly unique similarity between the prior crimes and the present one for the prior crimes to be admissible, but there must be a reasonable number of distinctive signature-like features between the two for the admissibility of the prior crimes. Whether there are such distinctive features between the prior crimes and the presently charged one is within the sound discretion of the trial judge, and unless that discretion is abused the judge's decision will be upheld on appeal. For example, a defendant was charged with murder. During the trial, it was brought out that the defendant was alleged to have agreed to take the victim to her home and that, instead of taking her home, he drove her to a lonely spot where he ripped her clothing off and had sexual intercourse with her twice, while a male companion sat and watched. The defendant is alleged thereafter to have killed the woman.

The prosecution was permitted to introduce a female witness's testimony that six years previously the defendant, in company with another man, had invited her with her girl friend to go to a restaurant. Instead of taking them to the restaurant, the defendant drove to a lonely spot and, after parking, ripped off all of her clothes and had intercourse with her twice. The witness testified that he was in possession of a knife and threatened to kill her. In presenting this testimony, the prosecution contended that the rape in the present murder trial was an important element of the crime of murder in the first degree, and in view of the striking similarities between the present offense and the one committed six years previously, the evidence of the prior crime was relevant to prove common scheme or common *modus operandi.* It was pointed out that in each instance the defendant had a male companion with him; he invited the woman to go one place and took her to another; he ripped off all the woman's clothing and had intercourse twice; and the acts took place in a parked car while a companion was present. The appellate court upheld the introduction of the prior crime as being relevant to prove a common scheme and plan to commit rape, thus aiding in the identifying of the defendant as the perpetrator of the murder for which he was being tried.

In another case, prior crimes were introduced during a murder trial in an effort to assist in identifying the defendant as the person who had committed the murder. The victim was found by her husband lying face down dead in a bathtub filled with water. The victim was fully clothed except for her shoes. The cause of death was attributed to strangulation with a cord or rope. She had also been struck on the head with a blunt object, and there was a puncture wound in her abdomen. She was not known to have been sexually molested. There were indications that her wrists and ankles had been tied. In the bathtub with the body were a piece of rope, several towels, a blanket, and a piece of sheet which had been ripped from the bed. In the living room lying beside a chair, which was for sale, was a flashlight that was ordinarily kept in the garage. There was no indication of a forced entry into the home and no signs of a struggle. The victim was known to have advertised a chair for sale by placing a 3- by-5-inch card in a supermarket bearing her telephone number. She was also known to have been saving some money from a part-time job, to be used for a vacation, which money was missing.

During the trial, another young woman was permitted to testify that she had placed a 3-by-5 card bearing her telephone number in a supermarket advertising a bed for sale. A few days later, the witness testified, the defendant made arrangements through a telephone call to visit her to view the bed. Upon his arrival, the victim had ushered the defendant into the bedroom, where he examined the bed. During the conversation about the bed, the defendant stated that he had lost the stem to his watch. While the woman was on her hands and knees looking for the watch stem, the defendant grabbed her from behind, placing a hand over her mouth, and with the other hand, he placed a knife at her throat. He ordered her to lie on her stomach and tied her wrists and ankles with a piece of cord he had brought with him. He stated that he needed money desperately. The victim advised him where she kept some money in a book, which the defendant took. He then announced that he wanted to have sex with her, but he was unable to achieve an erection. He then began to drag her toward the bathroom, stating that he wanted to wash up. She heard water running in the bathtub. The defendant returned to her and tried to suffocate her by wrapping some bath towels around her head. He told her that as soon as she stopped breathing, he would leave. A short time later, she was still breathing, and he stabbed her four times and dropped a flower pot on her head. The witness concluded by testifying that the defendant was frightened off by a door slamming.

In addition to this testimony, the prosecution introduced evidence of four other offenses committed by the defendant approximately twenty years previously, for which he was convicted. In all those offenses, the victims were women who were robbed and sexually assaulted in their own homes. The women had advertised items for sale by posting ads in newspapers. In each instance, the defendant came to the home of the victim on the pretense of examining the item for sale, and each time told the victim that he had lost the stem to his watch, subdued the victim by grabbing her from behind, threatened each with a knife, and bound her wrists and ankles with a cord or rope that he had brought with him. One victim obtained a flashlight to use in the search for the watch stem. In none of the cases was the defendant able to have an orgasm.

The defendant was convicted of murder and appealed his case upon the ground that the trial judge abused his discretion in permitting testimony concerning the other crimes known to have been committed by the defendant. The conviction was upheld by the appellate court, which stated that there were enough distinctive signature-like features between the murder charge and the other crimes committed by the defendant to permit those crimes to be introduced to assist in establishing the defendant as the one who committed the murder. [See *People v. Wein,* 69 Cal. App. 3d 79, (1977).]

It has been held that a jury is entitled to know of other crimes committed by a defendant when there are sufficient distinctive marks of similarity with a present charge in order that the jury may draw an inference that if the defendant committed the other crimes, he probably committed the one for which he is on trial. On this basis, the other crimes are admissible.

When evidence of prior acts of misconduct or crimes committed by the accused is presented, it must be in good faith. The acts must have been actually committed, and the presentation may not be based upon a mere rumor that they were committed. The acts must be subject to some proof, but that proof does not have to be beyond a reasonable doubt. The proof may be presented through the testimony of witnesses who have knowledge that the acts were committed by the accused. Such testimony has been held to be sufficient proof.

It is realized that there is a definite danger to the cause of the defendant in the presentation of these acts, but there must be a balance of interests involved. The defendant should not be subjected to undue prejudice, but neither must society be endangered by mere technicalities when the proof of other crimes or misconduct becomes a part of the issues at hand in the search for truth. On this basis, prior crimes and misconduct are admissible.

MEANS OR CAPABILITY TO COMMIT A CRIME

Circumstantial evidence is often introduced to prove that the accused had the means with which to commit a particular crime or that he had the capability of committing it. Perhaps the most illustrative example of this was brought out in the Warren Commission report of the assassination of President Kennedy. In the effort to substantiate that Lee Harvey Oswald was the perpetrator of that crime, it was shown that Oswald had a high-powered rifle equipped with a telescopic sight and that this gun was one with which a crime of this nature could be accomplished. It was also shown that Oswald was considered to be an expert shot while in the Marines and was known to have had target practice after his discharge. Had Oswald been brought to trial, his means and capabilities would have undoubtedly been introduced against him.

CONSCIOUSNESS OF GUILT

Although individuals may react differently from time to time, people follow a more or less standard pattern of behavior. Frequently, a person who has committed a crime will deviate from his or her usual pattern of conduct. When this occurs, proof of uncustomary acts, statements, or appearance may be introduced to show consciousness of guilt. It has been held that any act from which the inference of consciousness of guilt can be drawn is admissible.

If an accused person were seen fleeing from the scene of a crime, this fact could be introduced in evidence as a part of the proof of guilt, because the usual tendency for a person who has committed a crime is to flee from the scene. The fact that the defendant was in a highly emotional state immediately after a murder which he was accused of committing may be introduced to show consciousness of guilt. The fact that the accused attempted to evade arrest, to escape, or to disguise his appearance by growing a beard or dyeing his hair may also be introduced. The fact that the accused denied his identity to the police or started using a fictitious name immediately after a crime was committed would be evidence of consciousness of guilt. The failure to appear for trial; the refusal to submit to a sobriety test when accused of drunken driving; an attempt to conceal evidence; the refusal to participate in a lineup or refusal to furnish handwriting exemplars; or an attempt to bribe witnesses are all circumstances which would indicate that the accused is guilty of a crime.

CHARACTER OF THE DEFENDANT

If the defendant in a criminal trial has a reputation of bad character, this reputation may be some indication of guilt because one usually acts in accordance with one's reputation; the reputation of the defendant may therefore be pertinent to the issues. But the prosecution is not permitted to introduce evidence that the defendant is a person of bad character in order to prove guilt. Two reasons have been advanced for this prohibition. First, there is no presumption that the defendant in a criminal trial is a person of good character, and much trial time is saved by not requiring the prosecution to show that he is bad. Second, and probably the more realistic reason, if evidence is presented that the defendant has a reputation for being bad, it may subject him to undue prejudice. There is always danger that the jurors may convict the defendant on his reputation rather than on the facts of the case.

On the other hand, the defendant may present evidence of alleged good character in an attempt to prove innocence. Such evidence is an effort to show that the accused is not the kind of person who would commit the crime of which he has been accused. It has been held that the good character of the defendant must have some bearing upon the crime, or it must show traits in opposition to the type of crime which the defendant is accused of having committed. For example, if the defendant were charged with robbery, evidence that the defendant has a reputation for being honest would be admissible as it would be in opposition to the charge, but if the defendant were charged with child molesting, a reputation for being an honest person would not be pertinent and would not be admissible. A defendant charged with aggravated assault might endeavor to prove innocence by showing a reputation for being a quiet and peaceful person, thereby attempting to show that the assault was done in self-defense.

■ Proving Good Character of the Defendant

The good character of the defendant must be shown through witnesses, referred to as "character witnesses," who are in a position to know the reputation of the defendant. Character and reputation are not the same. Character is what a person is morally, and reputation is what others say about a person. It is assumed that a person's character is what that person's reputation indicates it is. As previously stated, to prove the reputation of a person, a witness must be in a position to know what others say about the person. For the defendant to prove good character, character witnesses who know what others say about the defendant in the community in which the defendant resides or works must testify to such knowledge. It must be the general reputation reflected among a certain class of persons. For example, a gambler may have a good reputation among his associates for being entirely honest because he pays all of his gambling debts, and he may have the reputation of being a generous person. However, in the community in which he resides he may have a bad reputation because he is considered to be a leech on society and a "bum."

In proving the good character of a defendant, a character witness must be in a position to know the general reputation of the defendant, and the witness may not attempt to prove good character by merely relating specific good acts of the defendant. The character witness may tell of residing in the same community as the defendant for a number of years and never hearing anything bad about the defendant. This type of testimony is permitted upon the assumption that if the defendant were bad, something would have been said in the community to that effect.

For any weight to be given to the testimony of a character witness, the witness should have recent knowledge of the defendant's reputation; that is, the knowledge should be as of, or about, the time that the crime was committed. If the knowledge of the reputation is in the too distant past, it may be of little consequence to the jury.

A few jurisdictions not only permit a character witness to relate the reputation of the defendant as the witness has heard it, but allow the character witness to state a personal opinion about the good or bad character of the defendant, when the witness is personally acquainted with the defendant.

■ Prosecution's Proof of Defendant's Bad Character

Once the defendant has endeavored to prove to be a person of good character, the prosecution may present evidence to show that the defendant is of bad character. The defendant has placed character in issue, and the prosecution is permitted to meet this issue, or to refute the defendant's contention of being good, by proving that the defendant is in reality bad.

To overcome the defendant's efforts to prove a reputation for being a good person, the prosecution may attempt to impeach the character witness. This impeachment effort may follow any one of the previously discussed impeachment methods, or the prosecuting attorney may endeavor to devaluate the character witness's testimony by asking the witness about certain acts of misconduct in which the defendant has engaged.

Although the defendant's character witness may not prove good character by relating good deeds done by the defendant, the prosecution is permitted to test the knowledge of the character witness by asking whether the witness has heard of specific acts of misconduct by the defendant. These questions may be asked by the prosecuting attorney, if asked in good faith, that is, if the prosecuting attorney is in possession of information that the defendant has committed acts of misconduct or if the prosecuting attorney knows statements have been made that the defendant committed acts of misconduct. The prosecuting attorney may not just make up a rumor in an effort to test the character witness. In fact, when questions are asked by the prosecuting attorney about acts of misconduct by the defendant, the trial judge may require the prosecuting attorney to present evidence that the questions are asked in good faith by having the prosecutor identify the source of information and give evidence of its reliability. This preliminary inquiry by the trial judge is not made in the presence of the jury.

Although the prosecuting attorney may ask the character witness about acts of misconduct by the defendant, the courts have adopted rather strict rules pertaining to the manner in which the questions may be asked. The prosecuting attorney may ask the witness "whether he has heard of" the acts of misconduct, but may not ask "whether he knows of" the acts of misconduct. To ask the witness "whether he knows of" the misconduct implies that the defendant has in fact done the act of misconduct, and the jury may convict the defendant on a bad record rather than on the facts of the present case. To ask the witness "whether he has heard of" the misconduct indicates a rumor only and not a fact and is considered not to be so prejudicial to the defendant, who may not actually have committed the misconduct, inasmuch as proof beyond a reasonable doubt does not have to be presented to the judge before the judge permits such questioning. Also, by asking the character witness "whether he has heard of" rather than "whether he knows of" the misconduct may result in a more nearly correct response from the character witness. The witness may have "heard of" the misconduct, but he may not have knowledge of, or "know of," the misconduct.

There are people who think that to permit the prosecution to indulge in a wholesale background inquiry about the prior misconduct of a defendant is highly prejudicial in all instances and should not be allowed. On the other hand, it must be remembered that the defendant does not have to place his character in issue by attempting to prove to be of good character, particularly if the defendant knows, better than anyone else, that the good character does not exist. The defendant is aware that the prosecution cannot show bad character or prior acts of misconduct until he, the defendant, opens the issue, and so he does it at his own risk. It is only right that the prosecution should be entitled to overcome the defendant's allegation that he is a good person when he is not. It is considered to be in the best interests of justice to permit some inquiry to be made of the defendant's character witnesses to determine their reliability as well as to establish the true character of the defendant. In addition to being asked whether the witness has ever heard of acts of misconduct or prior crimes, the witness may be asked whether he had heard of the prior convictions of the defendant.

Although a character witness may be asked whether he or she has heard of specific acts of misconduct committed by the defendant, it is generally held that neither good nor bad character can be proved by specific acts alone. Likewise a character witness may be asked whether he or she has heard of the prior convictions of the defendant, but the prosecution may not present other independent proof of the prior convictions merely for the purpose of showing the defendant to be a person of bad character.

When a character witness is asked whether he or she has heard about a defendant's prior conviction, the problem presents itself whether it may be any prior conviction, or whether the prior conviction must have some similarity to the crime for which the defendant is now on trial. For example, if the defendant is on trial for robbery, would a prior conviction for incest have any bearing on the defendant's character so far as a robbery charge is concerned? The courts seem to be somewhat divided on this issue. Many courts permit the character witness to be asked whether he or she has heard of any prior conviction regardless of its nature. This is permitted because the character witness is attesting to the good reputation of the defendant and the prosecution should be allowed to test the credibility of the character witness on personal knowledge of the reputation. Any prior conviction should have an effect upon the reputation of the defendant regardless of the charge. A few courts have taken the view that unless the prior conviction has some similarity to the present charge, the character witness may not be asked about it. This view is taken on the ground that the prior conviction is not otherwise material to the present issues. The opponents of this view think that it is too restrictive and gives the defendant an undue advantage, because the defendant may have any number of prior convictions, but unless there is a similarity in traits, the character witness cannot be asked about them. Thus it would not be known whether the character witness had never heard of them or did not think them material to the reputation.

Another question arises: How far back into the personal history may the prosecution go in asking about the prior conviction? There seems to be no set rule in this regard. However, if the prior conviction was in the too remote past, it may have but little impact upon the jury in trying to prove that the defendant is not of good character. It is possible that if the prior conviction was in the too remote past, the judge might not permit evidence of the prior conviction to be introduced. It was held in one case that the defendant's reputation for violence seven years before he committed the acts for which he was being prosecuted was too remote, and evidence of that reputation was excluded.

When the prosecuting attorney is permitted to ask the defendant's character witness whether he or she has heard about the past acts of misconduct or prior convictions of the defendant, the witness is placed in a rather precarious position. If the witness admits hearing of the past misconduct and still tries to prove that the defendant has a good reputation, the jury may have some doubt about the good character of the witness. If, on the other hand, the witness denies ever hearing of the rumors, the jury may think the witness is not very well informed of the defendant's reputation or that the witness is not reliable.

Not only may the prosecuting attorney endeavor to prove the bad character of the defendant by devaluating character witnesses for the defendant, but he may also present his own witnesses to disprove the defendant's good reputation, and in some jurisdictions, if the witnesses are acquainted with the defendant, they may express their own opinion about the character of the defendant. It then becomes a matter of whose witnesses the jury will believe.

■ Amount of Proof to Show Good or Bad Character

There is no set number of witnesses needed to prove either good or bad character. Much is dependent upon the weight given to the testimony of the character witnesses. In any event, the trial judge will usually allow a reasonable number of witnesses on both sides in order that some determination may be made by the jury. The judge will limit the number after a certain point; otherwise, the presentation of character witnesses could go on indefinitely.

CHARACTER OF VICTIMS

■ Homicide Victim

When one person is killed by another, the character of the deceased victim is generally unimportant. The crime of murder still stands whether the deceased victim was good or bad. In these circumstances the prosecution is not required to present any evidence concerning the character of the deceased. However, there are times when the character of the victim of a homicide may become an issue in a trial. For example, when the defendant is charged with murder, the defendant may endeavor to show that the killing was done in self-defense. The defendant may try to prove a reputation of being peaceful and quiet, and that the deceased had the reputation of being violent and aggressive. When this kind of evidence is introduced by the defendant, the prosecution may present witnesses to prove just the opposite. The prosecution may prove that the defendant had the reputation of being bad-tempered and the deceased was reputed to be meek and mild.

When the defendant tries to prove that he acted in self-defense, he must prove not only that the deceased had a reputation for violence, but also that the defendant knew of this reputation. Knowledge of the reputation is necessary if the defendant is going to allege thinking that his or her life was endangered. However, the bad character of the deceased may still be introduced by the defendant even though he had no knowledge of it in an effort to prove that the deceased was the aggressor and that the defendant acted in self-defense. The character of the deceased is proved in the same manner as that of the defendant, that is, by witnesses knowing the general reputation of the deceased, or again in some jurisdictions, by persons acquainted with the deceased who could express their opinion about the deceased's character. A few jurisdictions permit evidence of specific acts of violence to prove that the deceased was a dangerous person. Most jurisdictions restrict the introduction of specific acts of violence to those previously committed on the defendant, and not upon third persons. However, if the defendant saw the deceased commit acts of violence upon third persons, evidence of these acts is generally admissible to prove that the defendant thought that his life was in danger.

Most jurisdictions will permit the defendant to offer evidence concerning threats made by the deceased against the defendant, and these threats do not have to have been communicated to the defendant. The threats are introduced to show the state of mind of the deceased and assist in proving that the deceased, not the defendant, was the aggressor, and that the defendant may have acted in self-defense.

■ Victim of Assault

The character of the victim of an assault case may also be put in issue when the defendant alleges that the assault was committed in self-defense. The same rules of admissibility are applicable as in admitting evidence of the character of a homicide victim.

■ Victim in Sex Cases

When a defendant is charged with forceful rape, most jurisdictions permit the defendant to introduce evidence that the victim voluntarily submitted to his advances. This evidence may include proof that the victim has a reputation of being promiscuous or unchaste. This evidence is allowed on the theory that if she was permissive with others, she may have been permissive with the defendant. Some courts take the viewpoint that the mere fact that a victim was known to have had sexual relations with another man on a number of occasions does not imply that she consented to the acts of the defendant, and consequently evidence of relations with other men is not pertinent. The legislatures of some states have passed statutes prohibiting the introduction of evidence by the defendant concerning the sexual conduct of a rape victim in an effort to prove that she consented to the act of intercourse, unless the conduct satisfies some requirement for an attack on the credibility of the victim. These statutes are based on the fact that many rape victims are subjected to such embarrassing cross-examination by the defense concerning their sexual conduct that many forceful rape attacks were not being reported.

If seduction is the charge, evidence of prior sexual intercourse by the victim is admissible because the chaste character of the victim is a necessary element of the crime.

If the charge is statutory rape (under the age of consent), the character of the victim is not important. A few jurisdictions permit the defendant to offer as a defense the fact that he had an honest belief that the victim was of age to give consent. But even in this situation, there is some doubt whether the character of the victim would be relevant, unless it were in some way indicative that the defendant thought that the victim was of age to give consent.

■ State of Mind of Homicide Victim

When the defendant has been charged with murder and he offers as a defense that the killing was an accident or was in self-defense, evidence may be presented by the prosecution which may reflect the state of mind of the deceased. Statements made by the victim that she was afraid of the defendant may be introduced. For example, if a husband is charged with the murder of his wife, statements of the wife to others that she was afraid of her husband or statements concerning threats made by him to kill her are held to be admissible. These statements are hearsay statements, but they are not offered as proof of the act, but to prove the state of mind or emotional feeling of the victim. They are offered to overcome the allegation that the killing was by accident or in self-defense. Such statements may also be introduced to aid in proving that the accused was the one who was responsible for the murder.

A defendant may likewise present statements of the deceased which were threats to kill the defendant. These statements may be offered to substantiate the defendant's contention of acting in self-defense.

SUMMARY

Direct evidence is evidence that proves the facts in dispute directly through the testimony of witnesses who saw the crime committed.

Circumstantial evidence establishes the facts of the case from inferences which may be drawn from the proof of another set of facts. A conviction may be based upon circumstantial evidence alone except when the charge is treason or perjury.

Circumstantial evidence to be admissible must be relevant to the issues in dispute. It must in some way logically prove the facts. If circumstantial evidence is too remote, would require too much time in its proof, or would create undue prejudice, it will be excluded.

Circumstantial evidence may be used in many ways. An entire case may be presented by circumstantial evidence, or circumstantial evidence may be used to substantiate and corroborate direct evidence. Circumstantial evidence of character may assist in proving innocence or guilt. Circumstantial evidence of other crimes or misconduct may be admitted to show intent and motive, plan and design; to overcome an allegation that an act was an accident or a mistake; or to prove identity. The prosecution may not introduce evidence of the bad character of the defendant until the defendant has tried to prove innocence by evidence of good character.

Circumstantial evidence about the character of a victim of certain crimes may be introduced to prove an act was committed in self-defense or to prove guilt. Evidence that tends to show consciousness of guilt may be admitted to prove guilt. The fact that the accused had the ability and means with which to commit the crime in question is admissible.

QUESTIONS FOR REVIEW

1. Explain how direct and circumstantial evidence differ. Give an example of each.
2. On what is the relevancy of circumstantial evidence based?
3. List four ways in which circumstantial evidence may be used.
4. Why is the prosecution prohibited from introducing the bad character of the defendant until after the defendant has tried to show good character?
5. By what methods may the prosecution show the bad character of the defendant?
6. In what way does the character of the victim of certain crimes become important?
7. In what situation may the prosecution offer evidence of prior crimes or acts of misconduct by the defendant?
8. List four ways an accused person may indicate consciousness of guilt.

LOCAL RULES

The rules on the admissibility of circumstantial evidence are comparatively uniform throughout the United States; however, there is a slight variation among jurisdictions on the proof of the character of both a defendant in a criminal trial and a murder victim. Therefore, the reader should ascertain the answers to the following questions from the local prosecuting attorney for the rules in the reader's jurisdiction.

1. In attempting to prove the good or bad character of a defendant or a murder victim, may the character witness who is personally acquainted with the defendant or victim express his or her opinion about the character or must his or her testimony be confined to what others say about the character?

2. In attempting to prove that a murder victim had a reputation for violence, may testimony of specific acts of violence be related by the character witness, and if so, must those acts of violence have been committed on the defendant only, or may they have been committed on anyone?

Documentary Evidence and the Right of Discovery 10

DOCUMENTS AS A KIND OF EVIDENCE

Documents, or writing, are another kind of evidence by which facts are presented during a judicial proceeding. A document, or writing, includes handwriting, typewriting, printing, photostating, photographing, and every other means of recording any form of communication or representation—including letters, words, pictures, sounds, symbols, or any combination thereof. Documents have been classified as (1) public and (2) private. Public documents have been further categorized as (1) laws; (2) judicial records; (3) other official documents, such as records of drivers' licenses, marriage applications, and birth certificates; and (4) public records of private writings, such as records of deeds and mortgages. Private documents are the private writings of individuals, such as letters, memorandums, suicide notes, or wills.

Although private documents generally play a more significant role in the trial of civil matters, there are times when they become an important part of a criminal case. For example, an extortion note may be necessary to prove a charge of extortion; a suicide note or a threatening letter may be a part of the proof in a homicide case; or the "date book" of a call girl may be presented in a prostitution trial. However, these articles may fall more properly in the category of real evidence than in that of documents.

■ Authentication

A document to be introduced in evidence must be presented by a witness. This witness must have a knowledge of the document, and what it is. The witness must be able to attest to the fact that the document is genuine and is what it purports to be. The witness will also relate the connection of the document with the issues of the case. After this has been done, the document will be offered in evidence. This is known as laying the foundation for the introduction of the document in evidence or the authentication of the document. If the judge agrees that the document is genuine and is connected with the issues of the case, the judge will admit it, and the document will then speak for itself.

■ Best-Evidence Rule

When the contents of a document become an important part of a trial, the document itself must be introduced to prove its contents. This provision is known as the *best-evidence rule*. Legally, the rule provides that "there can be no evidence of the contents of a writing other than the writing itself." This rule means that if information is to be offered during a trial concerning what is contained in a document, the best evidence, or best proof, of the contents of the document is the document itself, and so it must be introduced. The document introduced must be the original document, and it must be proved to be genuine. To prove the genuineness of a document or writing, the witness must be in a position to know that the signature is of the person it purports to be, or if there are alterations on the face of the document, that the alterations are a part of the original document, and not something that was added or changed for fraudulent pur-purposes.

The best-evidence rule was adopted many years ago, and for good reasons. The first reason was that it came into being at a time when the only way in which copies of a document could be made was to copy the wording and symbols by hand. It was known that copying by hand brought in a great likelihood of mistakes and inaccuracies, and, further, it opened the door to possible fraud and deceit. Another reason for requiring the original document and not something that was added or changed for fraudulent testimony to relate the contents, there was a danger of misinterpretation as well as the possibility of omitting important portions of the contents during the testimony because of faulty memory.

■ Primary versus Secondary Evidence

When an original document is produced in court, it is known as the primary evidence of what the document contains. When the original is introduced, no problem arises, as compliance with the best-evidence rule has taken place. Although the best-evidence rule is considered to be sound, there are occasions when it is either impossible or impractical to produce the original document in court, and so exceptions to the best-evidence rule had to be adopted. The courts have established certain guidelines whereby the contents of an original document may be presented by producing a copy of the original or by oral testimony of its contents. When other evidence is substituted for the original document, the substitute is known as secondary evidence.

The following are the most frequently encountered situations in which secondary evidence of the contents of a document or writing may be introduced: (1) when the original document has been destroyed or lost; (2) when the original document is in the possession of the adverse party and after a notice to produce it, the adverse party fails to do so; (3) when the document or record is in the custody of a public officer; or (4) when the original documents are voluminous and cannot be examined without a great loss of time, and merely a summary of their contents will suffice.

Whenever secondary evidence is offered in lieu of the original document, the necessary foundation must be laid before the secondary is admitted. Three things have to be shown: (1) that there has been a writing in existence; (2) that the secondary evidence is a genuine copy of the original; and (3) the reason why a copy is being offered in evidence instead of the original.

■ Lost or Destroyed Documents

When it is alleged that the original document cannot be produced because it was lost, there must be a showing that an effort was made to locate the lost document before the secondary evidence is admissible. The amount of search necessary will vary depending upon the kind of document involved and its importance to the case. At least, it must be shown that contact was made with the last person known to have had the document, or with persons most likely to know its whereabouts, and, further, that the last place where the document was known to be was searched without result.

It has been held that a document which is out of the state, or beyond the reach of the court, falls within the same category as a lost document. But there should be some showing that a reasonable effort was made to obtain the original document unless it can be proved that such an effort would have been fruitless.

It has likewise been held that when it can be proved that the original document is in the hands of a third party who for some reason refuses to cooperate and release the document, secondary evidence may be admitted on the same basis as if the original were lost.

When a person offers secondary evidence of the contents of a destroyed document, it must be proved that the destruction was not intentionally made by the side offering secondary evidence to prevent use of the destroyed document as evidence.

In the instance of a lost or destroyed document, if there is no copy of the original, oral testimony may be given about the contents of the writing by one having knowledge of the original contents.

■ Adverse Party Refuses to Produce Original

When an original document is in the hands of a defendant in a criminal trial, notice must be given to the defendant to produce the original before secondary evidence may be substituted for the original. There is no particular form necessary for this notice; it may be merely an oral request to produce the document, but reasonable time must be given for the production. If the defendant denies having the document, notice to the defendant to produce it is not necessary. It has been held that if the production of a document would cause self-incrimination, the defendant does not have to produce it. This provision does not prevent secondary evidence from being admitted to prove the contents of the writing.

■ Document in Custody of Public Officer

Although original public records could in most instances be produced in court, it is deemed impractical to do so in most cases. This practice is based on the fact that there is too much danger that an original record will be lost or destroyed. Consequently, secondary evidence in the form of a copy of an original is admissible to prove the contents of the record, but the copy must be authenticated. The secondary evidence is usually authenticated by a statement attached to the copy in which the officer in custody of the record certifies that the document is a true copy of the original. This is known as a certified copy of the original document.

Sometimes in criminal cases, it is necessary to prove prior convictions of a defendant in another state, or other court proceedings. In such cases, the record generally must be certified by the clerk of the court attesting that the document is a true copy of the original, and in addition, the presiding judge of the particular jurisdiction must also certify that the attestation of the clerk is in due form. This kind of copy is sometimes referred to as an "exemplified copy" of the original. Attestation of both the clerk and the judge is deemed necessary because the record is most important to the issues of the case, and, therefore, someone in addition to the officer in custody of the record should attest to the accuracy of the copy.

■ Original Documents Too
Voluminous to Examine

There are occasions when information from the records of a business may be important to the issues of a case. This occurs more frequently in civil matters than in criminal trials. However, in either event, it has been held that unless each item in business records is necessary to prove the fact in issue, a summary of the business records may be substituted as a matter of expedience for the original records. To produce the entire records of a company and examine them completely in court would be time-consuming and impractical; so when a summary of the records will suffice, it is admissible in lieu of the original records.

■ What Is an Original Document?

Where there is only one original document and it is produced in court, the best-evidence rule has been satisfied, and no problem arises. But many times, a number of copies of a document are made simultaneously, such as carbon copies, printed copies, or mimeographed documents, and the best-evidence rule comes into operation. What is the original document? Would any one of these be considered an original, and if so, what about a photographic copy, or a copy made by a duplicating machine? Should these be treated as originals, or must the original be produced? The answer to these questions is still somewhat uncertain. However, as far back as 1938 in *United States v. Manton*, 107 F.2d 834 (1938), the court held that photographic reproductions of checks had the same probative value as the original documents, and that the fear of fraud or mistake upon which the best-evidence rule rests was not present in such reproductions; therefore the reproductions should be accepted as though they were the original documents.

The rule in the Manton case appears to be logical, and many jurisdictions have adopted the rule that when a reproduction is made by carbons, print, or other reproduction devices, and is authenticated as a genuine reproduction, it is admissible without having to account for the original.

■ Parol-Evidence Rule

Coupled with the best-evidence rule is another rule of evidence referred to as the *parol-evidence rule*. This rule merely prohibits, with certain exceptions, the introduction of any additional or outside evidence to vary the terms of a written agreement, will, or deed. This rule has practically no applicability whatsoever to criminal trials, and it is deemed unnecessary to discuss the rule other than to state what it is.

WHAT IS RIGHT OF DISCOVERY?

The right of discovery, or the right of inspection, in criminal matters is of comparatively recent origin, and, like many other rules of evidence, it stems primarily from court decisions and not from statutes. The right of discovery is a right afforded to the adversary in a trial to examine, inspect, and copy the evidence in the hands of the other side. The right of discovery in criminal matters was designed basically for the benefit of the defendant and not the prosecution, and it is granted solely for the purpose of enabling the defendant to properly prepare his defense. It allows the defendant to examine certain pieces of evidence held by the prosecution upon the theory that this examination is necessary for the accused to meet the charge on which he or she is to be tried.

■ Right Not Recognized in Common Law

There were no rules in the common law which permitted the accused to order the prosecution to produce the evidence held against him in order that he might inspect it. It was contended that to allow the accused to know the evidence against him would enable him to fabricate a story in his own behalf and to obtain perjured testimony to substantiate that defense. Many jurisdictions in this country still have not adopted the right of discovery in criminal cases. But as the accused is being continuously granted more privileges and protection, it is thought to be only a matter of time until all states will be required to give the defendant in a criminal case some right to examine the evidence held by the prosecution prior to the time it is offered in evidence against the defendant. A discussion of the right of discovery is a timely subject, even in those jurisdictions still not recognizing this right.

■ Right Gained Only after Struggle

Although the merits of the right of discovery in criminal matters were argued pro and con for many years, little was gained by those seeking the right until about the 1950s, and it was only after a long and difficult struggle that anything was accomplished. Many strong and convincing arguments were presented against giving the accused the opportunity to inspect the evidence in the hands of the prosecution and the law enforcement agency involved. Because of the strength of these arguments, some jurisdictions still have not granted the right, whereas others have relaxed the rule to some extent, and yet others have afforded the defendant a most liberal right to examine the evidence held by the prosecution.

■ Arguments against Right of Discovery

In order to prevent the defendant in a criminal trial from inspecting the evidence held by the prosecution, all the arguments presented at common law were reiterated along with many others. It was argued that granting the defendant the right of discovery would be contrary to our adversary system of justice, the adversary system being one in which each side, that is, the prosecution and the defense, presents its evidence to assist in arriving at the truth, and each side comes to trial on an equal basis. It has been contended that the defendant already has every advantage, and granting the defendant the right of discovery would only make the balance all the more in the defendant's favor. As the defendant enters the trial, he is entitled to the presumption of innocence until proved guilty, and this guilt must be proved by the prosecution beyond a reasonable doubt. The jury in most jurisdictions must return a unanimous verdict. The defendant has the right to remain silent, and such silence may not be commented on. Also, because of the belief of many justices that to compel the defendant to reveal his evidence would be a violation of the guarantee against self-incrimination, the right of discovery is a "one-way street." It has also been pointed out that the cooperation of witnesses in criminal matters is difficult to obtain at best, but if witnesses knew that the accused would be entitled to their names and addresses before the trial, many of those who had information of value to the prosecution would be hesitant to come forward because of fear, and those who did furnish information might be threatened by the defendant, so that they would change their stories or disappear entirely. It was also argued that to permit the defendant in a criminal trial to pry into the files of a law enforcement agency would enable the defendant to identify those who were informing against the criminal world.

Justice Vanderbilt expressed his viewpoint against the right of discovery very vividly in *State v. Tune*, 13 N.J. 203 (1953), in which he stated:

> In criminal proceedings long experience has taught the courts that often discovery will not lead to honest fact-finding, but on the contrary to perjury and suppression of evidence. Thus the criminal who is aware of the whole case against him will often procure perjured testimony in order to set up a false defense.... To permit unqualified disclosure of all statements and information in the hands of the State would go far beyond what is required in civil cases; it would defeat the very ends of justice.

For these many reasons it was believed that the right of discovery in criminal matters should be denied.

◼ Arguments in Favor of Right of Discovery

As convincing as the arguments against the right of discovery may have been, many believed that the accused should be able to inspect the evidence that was to be presented against him. Their strongest argument was that this right was necessary in order that the defendant might properly defend himself. It was felt that an accused is "entitled to a fair trial and an intelligent defense in light of all relevant and reasonably accessible information" in order to properly defend himself. Some courts have gone so far in implementing the right of discovery to hold that the prosecution must disclose items of substantial and material evidence known to the prosecution, which evidence is favorable to the defense, even in the absence of a request for a disclosure. It has been contended that the defendant's attorney frequently does not enter the case until all the investigation has been completed by the law enforcement officers and a confession has been obtained, and only by the right of discovery will the defense attorney know what has taken place. It is further argued that the officer now has developed many scientific skills which can catch the defendant completely by surprise and against which defense cannot be made unless the accused knows of them prior to the trial; that the prosecution has unlimited resources available to it to obtain witnesses and other evidence unavailable to the defendant; and that the prosecution has in the past withheld evidence which would have assisted the defendant had it been brought forth, and that only through the right of discovery will the defendant be able to learn of this evidence.

Although there are those who still think that the arguments against the right of discovery by the accused are stronger than those in favor of it, there has been a gradual relaxation of the rule prohibiting the accused from examining the evidence held by the prosecution. It is argued that in our form of society and justice there is no desire to convict an accused through concealment and surprise, and that a criminal trial is not a place in which to play games, but one in which to seek the truth. From this argument, the right of discovery in criminal cases was born.

■ Problems Involved in Granting Accused Right of Discovery

As judges and legislators began to entertain the view that the accused was entitled to the right of discovery, many problems arose. The primary one was the balance between "fairness to the accused" and the "protection of society" against the criminal. In weighing this balance the first question asked was: To what extent should the accused be permitted to examine the evidence held by the prosecution; that is, just what should the accused be allowed to see, everything or only a limited number of items? If a limited number of things, then what should they include? The next question was: When should the accused be permitted to examine the evidence? Should the right be granted only at the time of the trial or immediately after the arrest and long prior to the trial?

Differing opinions have been expressed in answer to these questions, and in attempting to arrive at some equitable solution to the problems involved, various jurisdictions have established a wide divergence in the rules adopted pertaining to the right of discovery.

Although a relaxation of the doctrine prohibiting discovery began to take place, no wholesale permission was given to the accused at the beginning to examine the evidence held by the prosecution, and the right of discovery was fairly well confined to the period of the trial. However, in most jurisdictions in which the right of discovery has now been granted, the accused has the right to examine the evidence prior to the trial. This pretrial right of discovery has been adopted because it enabled the accused to better prepare a defense, which was the whole basis for the grant of the right of discovery in the first place.

RIGHT OF DISCOVERY
THROUGH PRELIMINARY HEARING

It should be pointed out that the accused has had some right of discovery for years in many jurisdictions through the right of an accused to a preliminary hearing, and even today in states in which the right of discovery per se has not been adopted, the accused still has a chance to learn something of the adverse evidence from the preliminary hearing, or "preliminary examination." It is impossible to hold a preliminary examination without the prosecution revealing a portion of its case. There must be sufficient evidence presented to convince the magistrate that there is a substantial doubt of the innocence of the accused in order for the accused to be bound over for trial. In fact, prior to the adoption of the right-of-discovery doctrine, the prosecuting attorney was caught on the horns of a dilemma. The prosecutor had to present a reasonable amount of evidence to bring about a doubt of innocence but did not want to reveal all the case because the defense might be able to fabricate a story to meet the evidence held by the prosecution. But since the defendant is entitled to learn of the evidence now by the right of discovery, there is every advantage to presenting as much evidence as possible at the preliminary hearing, because the witnesses are usually more willing to cooperate and testify more truthfully immediately after the crime has been committed than months later when the trial may take place. Once the witnesses have testified under oath at the preliminary hearing, it is difficult for them to change their stories at the time of the trial.

Even in jurisdictions where an accused is brought to trial by an indictment and not through a preliminary hearing, the accused still has some pretrial discovery. In most instances, the accused is entitled to a copy of the grand jury transcript, which sets forth the testimony of witnesses appearing before the grand jury.

■ Growth of the Right of Discovery

Although the accused had a limited right of discovery through the preliminary hearing, there were those who thought that this was not sufficient to enable the defense to properly prepare a case, and so the right of discovery was developed and adopted in many states.

One of the first statutes granting the right of discovery to an accused was that adopted by the federal government in 1946, which was included in Federal Rule of Criminal Procedure 16. This statute provided:

> Upon a motion of a defendant at any time after the filing of the indictment or information, the court may order the attorney for the government to permit the defendant to inspect and copy or photograph designated books, papers, documents or tangible objects, obtained from or belonging to the defendant or obtained

from others by seizure or by process, upon a showing that the items sought may be material to the preparation of his defense and that the request is reasonable. The order shall specify the time, place, and manner of making the inspection and of taking copies or photographs and may prescribe such items and conditions as are just.

Irrespective of the existence of this rule, it was not until the famous case entitled *Jencks v. United States,* 353 U.S. 657 (1957), was handed down by the United States Supreme Court that attention was really focused on the right of discovery. As a result of this case, the right of discovery is frequently referred to as the Jencks rule. Jencks, a labor union official, was convicted of violating a federal law by filing an alleged false affidavit in which he denied that he had ever been a member of the Communist party. During the trial, two witnesses working in connection with the FBI testified that they had observed Jencks engaging in Communist party activities. Upon cross-examination, these witnesses admitted that they had made reports to the FBI about the actions of Jencks. The defense attorney made a motion to the court requesting that these reports be produced in order that he could inspect them. The motion was denied by the trial judge on the grounds that there was no showing that there was any inconsistency between the reports made to the FBI and the testimony of the witnesses.

After Jencks was convicted, the case was appealed to the United States Supreme Court on the ground that Jencks was denied due process because of the failure of the government to produce the reports requested. The Supreme Court reversed the conviction and stated that the denial to order the production of the reports was in error. The Court held that a defendant in a criminal trial is entitled to inspect all reports in the hands of the government which touch on matters about which witnesses might testify.

Because of the broad wording of the majority opinion in the Jencks case, which seems to grant an unlimited right to the defendant in a criminal case to examine all government reports, consternation reigned for a short time because it was feared that much confidential information pertaining to the security of the nation might have to be revealed if prosecution were attempted. In fact, Justice Clark in his dissenting opinion in the Jencks case stated: "Unless the Congress changes the rule announced by the Court today, those intelligence agencies of our Government engaged in law enforcement may as well close up shop, for the Court has opened their files to the criminal and thus afforded him a Roman holiday for rummaging through confidential information as well as vital national secrets." A few months later, Congress did pass legislation tempering the effects of the Jencks decision to a degree. The federal statute passed by Congress in substance required the government to produce upon demand any signed statement of a witness in the possession of the United States government which related to the subject matter of the witness's testimony. But the statute further provided that if the government claimed that any statement ordered to be produced contained matter not relating to the testimony, it was to be examined by the trial judge, who would delete any matter which did not relate to the testimony, and the remainder of the statement was to be furnished to the defendant.

Following the Jencks case, a number of states adopted some right of discovery by the defendant either through court decisions or statutes.

PRETRIAL DISCOVERY

As stated, at first the right of discovery was confined to the trial period, but now most jurisdictions allowing any right of discovery have extended the right to pretrial discovery. There is still some difference of opinion about just when the right should be exercised. Some jurisdictions have not permitted any discovery until after the preliminary hearing, whereas others allow the right to be exercised any time after the arrest. It is argued by the defense that the right should commence as soon as possible and before the preliminary hearing. This argument is based upon the fact that the defense counsel has the right of cross-examining the prosecution witnesses during the preliminary hearing, and so should be entitled to inspect the statements and other evidence in order to properly cross-examine the witnesses. It should be noted that Federal Rule of Criminal Procedure 16 on the right of discovery and inspection was changed in 1966. As adopted in 1946, it provided that the defendant may request an order for the production of certain evidence any time after the filing of an "indictment or information" against the defendant. However, in the 1966 revision no mention is made of the time when inspection may take place, which implies that it may be as soon as possible and prior to the filing of an indictment or information. This rule undoubtedly will be a criterion for judges of the various states in the future, absent some court decision directly on the point.

Even though the defendant fails to exercise his right of pretrial discovery in those jurisdictions permitting it, this does not preclude the defense from requesting the right to examine the evidence held by the prosecution at the time of the trial.

■ Matters Which May Be Examined

Jurisdictions vary considerably in what evidence may be examined by the defendant. Some jurisdictions still limit the right of discovery solely to statements made by the defendant to law enforcement officers. Some states have included the right to discovery of scientific reports held by the prosecution, such as reports from a crime laboratory or an autopsy report. A few jurisdictions permit the defendant, or the defendant's attorney, to inspect almost every bit of evidence in the hands of the prosecution or the law enforcement agency involved. Included in the right of discovery are:

1. Statements of the accused, including the right to hear any recordings made of conversations with the accused.
2. Statements of prospective prosecution witnesses.
3. Names and addresses of prospective witnesses.
4. Names and addresses of certain informants, particularly when probable cause for the arrest may stem from such informant, or if the informant was a participant in the crime or a witness thereto.
5. Notes and documents made by witnesses, including the peace officer, used to refresh their memory prior to testifying.
6. Notebook used by the officer during the course of the investigation of the case.
7. Photographs of the defendant shown to the victim of a crime for identification purposes.
8. Scientific reports, such as crime-laboratory reports.
9. Photographs pertaining to the crime.
10. Real evidence collected during the investigation.

■ Defendant's Right to Identity of Informants

There are learned persons in the field of jurisprudence who still are skeptical of the alleged advantages of the right of discovery in criminal matters. This skepticism is based upon the fact that the courts are not dealing with the most ethically motivated member of society when granting an accused the right to know the case against him. It is known that it is not unusual for a defendant to do everything possible in his or her own behalf from falsifying testimony to doing away with prosecution witnesses and informants—all of which may not be in the best interests of the community and its protection from the criminal world.

One area in which the right of discovery has worked detrimentally to law enforcement is the compelled disclosure in many cases of the identity of confidential informants. As was pointed out in Chapter 3, the right of discovery afforded the defendant has practically abolished the privileged-communication doctrine between the officer and the informant. The courts hold that the disclosure of an informant's identity is required if it appears from the evidence that the informant is a material witness on the issue of the defendant's guilt or innocence. Because of the privileged-communication doctrine, the courts cannot compel the officer to disclose the identity of the informant. But if the failure to disclose the identity would deny the defendant the right of a fair trial, the charge against the defendant must be dismissed. The guidelines as to whether an informant is a material witness are not clearly established. The courts have ruled that if an informant participated in the crime or was an eyewitness to the crime, the informant is a material witness. The burden is upon the defendant to prove that "in view of the evidence" the informant is a material witness. It has been held that this burden is discharged when the defendant demonstrates a reasonable possibility that the informant, whose identity is sought, could give evidence on the issue of guilt or innocence of the defendant. It has been stated that no one knows what the informant, if produced in court, may give in the way of testimony. The informant might contradict or persuasively explain away the prosecution's evidence. It is the deprival of the defendant of the opportunity of producing evidence which might result in the acquittal of the defendant that is the basis of the disclosure order or a dismissal of the charge. However, it has been held that the defendant must show more than a mere speculation that the informant has information that will bear upon the defendant's innocence or will aid in some way.

■ Procedure for Pretrial Discovery by Defendant

Generally, an oral request made by the defense attorney to either the prosecuting attorney or the law enforcement agency to inspect the items in their possession is sufficient to obtain permission to do so. However, the defense attorney may make a formal request to exercise this right of inspection. If so, the attorney will file an affidavit with the court requesting the right to examine certain items being held by the law enforcement agency or the prosecution and will state the reasons for wishing to examine the evidence. It has been held that it may not be just a fishing expedition in effort to see what is being held against the defendant with the hopes that it may be beneficial to the defense. However, about all the defense attorney has to state is that the inspection of the prosecution's evidence is deemed necessary for the preparation of the defense, and in most instances the right of discovery is placed into operation and the judge will issue an order for pretrial discovery. The defense attorney must list in the affidavit the evidence requested for examination. The pretrial order of discovery is generally similar in form to a *subpoena duces tecum*.

In most instances when a request is made by the defense for a pretrial discovery, either formally or informally, the prosecuting attorney prefers to be consulted before any disclosure for examination is made. In this way, the prosecuting attorney can better control that which must be released for examination.

■ Rule in England

It is argued that there is no right of discovery in England; yet the courts of England operate under a rather strict rule so far as the preliminary hearing is concerned. It is held that no evidence may be presented against the accused at the trial which has not been introduced during the preliminary hearing. As a result of this rule, the defendant in England has almost as complete a right of discovery as if the right itself were adopted. The defendant has every opportunity to prepare the defense, and cannot be subjected to surprise, as no evidence may be introduced at the trial that the defendant does not know about. It has been argued on the other side that the prosecution may withhold certain evidence and not introduce it at the preliminary hearing, and that this withheld evidence may be material to the defense of the accused.

PROSECUTION'S RIGHT OF DISCOVERY

After defendants in criminal cases were granted the right of discovery in many jurisdictions, prosecuting attorneys have been endeavoring to obtain, either through court decisions or statutes, similar rights. But strong arguments have been presented by defense attorneys and some appellate court justices against granting the prosecution the right of discovery. The most convincing argument against granting such a right is that it would violate the accused's right against self-incrimination. It has been held that to compel the defendant to produce his evidence is compelling him to be a witness against himself. The supreme court of one state has held that the prosecution must "shoulder the entire load of their burden to prove the defendant guilty beyond a reasonable doubt without the assistance of the defendant's silence or his compelled testimony. Any demand for discovery by the prosecution which might conceivably lighten the burden of the prosecution would be in violation of the accused's Fifth Amendment right against self-incrimination." [See *Prudhomme v. Superior Court of Los Angeles County*, 2 Cal. 3d. 224 (1970).] Although the court in that case stated that they were not abolishing all right of discovery by the prosecution, it is most difficult to determine what may be discovered by the prosecution that would not conceivably lighten the burden of the prosecution. The decision in that case has been criticized by many in the justice system, even by some appellate court justices, as being too restrictive upon the prosecution. It has been argued that the right of discovery by the defendant is based upon the fundamental proposition that the defendant is entitled to a "fair trial and an intelligent defense in the light of all relevant and reasonably accessible information." To deny the people, or the prosecution, an equal right to access to "relevant and reasonably accessible information is denying the people the right to a fair trial and due process of law, and not only this, but the search for the truth, the only purpose of a criminal trial, is frustrated." It is stated also that "the search for the truth is not served but hindered by the concealment of relevant and material evidence."

It has also been claimed by those opposing the right of discovery by the prosecution that the right would violate the attorney-client privileged-communications doctrine. It is to be noted that one argument presented by defense attorneys against the prosecution's right of discovery is the claim that if the names and addresses of defense witnesses are known to the prosecution and law enforcement officers, the witnesses will be subjected to possible harrassment. This argument was apparently borrowed from the prosecution's attempt to deny the defendant the right of discovery on the same grounds.

Although strong efforts have been exerted to prohibit prosecutors from obtaining the rights of discovery, some rights have been granted in several jurisdictions. Perhaps that granted to federal prosecutors through Rule 16 of the Federal Rules of Criminal Procedure as amended in 1966 is one of the more liberal. This rule provides that if the defendant is granted the right of discovery by the trial judge, the government attorney may also request the defendant to permit the "government to inspect and copy or photograph scientific or medical reports, books, papers, documents, tangible objects, or copies or portions thereof, which the defendant intends to produce at the trial and which are within his possession, custody or control, upon a showing of materiality to the preparation of the government's case and that the request is reasonable." This rule did not give the government the right to statements made by the defendant, which would be a violation of the guarantee against self-incrimination.

Rule 16 has been upheld by the United States Supreme Court. In the case of *United States v. Nobles*, 422 U.S. 225 (1975), the Court stated:

> The dual aim of our criminal justice system is that guilt shall not escape or innocence suffer. To this end, we have placed our confidence in the adversary system, entrusting to it the primary responsibility for developing relevant facts on which a determination of guilt or innocence can be made. . . .
>
> The need to develop all relevant facts in the adversary system is both fundamental and comprehensive. The ends of criminal justice would be defeated if judgments were to be founded on a partial and speculative presentation of facts. The very integrity of the judicial system and public confidence in the system depends on full disclosure of all the facts, within the framework of the rules of evidence. To ensure that justice is done, it is imperative to the function of courts that compulsory process be available for the production of evidence needed either by the prosecution or by the defense.

In order to give some assistance to prosecuting attorneys, about one-third of the states have granted prosecuting attorneys the right to know whether a defendant is going to offer as a defense an alibi, that is, whether the defendant plans to establish innocence by the fact of being someplace else when the crime was committed.

Some of these states make it mandatory that the defendant inform the prosecuting attorney of the alibi defense, whereas others require it only if the prosecuting attorney makes a request for the information. Also the jurisdictions differ in the amount of information the defendant must give. A few states require that the defendant only furnish information of the city or county in which he alleges he was at the time the crime was committed. Other states hold that the defendant must not only set forth the city or county in which he claims he was, but a specific address within that city or county. Some states have gone even further in their demands for information which must be given to the prosecution, and require the defendant to furnish the names and addresses of the witnesses whom he intends to call to assist in establishing the alibi.

Those states which have adopted the alibi right of discovery have done so upon the basis that the right saves time and money. It is held that if the defendant has an alibi and it can be verified, the case will be dismissed. The right also prevents the prosecution from being taken by surprise and consequently requesting a continuance until the matter can be investigated. It is a known fact that a defendant can very easily and quickly manufacture an alibi defense which is most difficult to disprove, particularly when introduced near the end of a trial. The right of discovery prevents the allegation of many such false alibis because when it is known that the information can be investigated, the defendant is reluctant to offer a false alibi.

The right of the prosecution to know of the intended alibi defense has been challenged as being a violation of the defendant's right against self-incrimination. But the United States Supreme Court in the case of *Williams v. Florida*, 399 U.S. 78 (1970) upheld the Florida rule on the prosecution's right of discovery on the alibi defense. In that case the Court stated: "We decline to hold that the privilege against compulsory self-incrimination guarantees the defendant the right to surprise the State with an alibi defense." The Court further stated:

> We need not linger over the suggestion that the discovery permitted the State against the petitioner [the defendant] in this case deprived him of due process or a fair trial. Florida law provides for liberal discovery by the defendant against the State, and the notice-of-alibi rule is itself carefully hedged with reciprocal duties requiring state disclosure to the defendant. Given the ease with which an alibi can be fabricated, the State's interest in protecting itself against an eleventh hour defense is both obvious and legitimate. . . . The adversary system of trial is hardly an end to itself; it is not yet a poker game in which players enjoy an absolute right to always conceal their cards until played. We find ample room in that system, at least as far as due process is concerned, for the instant Florida rule, which is designed to enhance the search for the truth in the criminal trial by insuring both the defendant and the State ample opportunity to investigate certain facts crucial to the determination of guilt or innocence.

Most prosecuting attorneys as well as law enforcement officers believe that the right of discovery by the prosecution could well be granted in other areas besides that of the alibi. Those areas proposed include the right to know if the defendant is going to claim that:

1. The arrest was unlawful.
2. There was unlawful search and seizure.
3. The confession was improperly obtained.
4. The defendant was not guilty by reason of insanity.
5. The act was committed in self-defense.

In some jurisdictions, the prosecuting attorney will have some advance notice of the aforementioned defenses by a pretrial motion to suppress evidence. However, not all jurisdictions permit a motion to suppress evidence prior to the trial. In those jurisdictions it would be of great assistance to know in advance the defense that is to be presented.

DEFENDANT'S RIGHT TO ORIGINAL INVESTIGATIVE NOTES

A problem has arisen concerning the defendant's right of discovery as it pertains to the original investigative notes of an officer. The problem is whether a defendant's right of discovery has been violated when an officer destroys his or her original notes, in accordance with departmental policy, after the information contained in those notes has been incorporated in an official report. The majority of the courts in the past have held that there is no basis for the contention that the officer or the prosecution would withhold information or otherwise frustrate the defendant by the destruction of the original notes as a matter of routine practice. However in the case of *United States v. Harris*, 543 Fed. Rptr. 2d 1247 (1976), the United States Court of Appeals for the Ninth Circuit held that "the FBI must hereafter preserve the original notes taken by agents during interviews with prospective government witnesses or an accused. The preservation of such evidence is necessary in order to permit courts to play their proper role in determining what evidence must be produced pursuant to the Jencks Act or other applicable law." The court further stated: "We reject the contention of the government that the good-faith destruction of rough notes in accordance with normal agency procedure is justifiable. Notes taken by FBI agents in interviews either with prospective government witnesses or, as in this case, with the accused, constitute potentially discoverable materials."

In those jurisdictions in which the defendant is given a liberal right of discovery, this decision could act as a precedent for other courts and make the preservation of the original notes significant.

SUMMARY

Documents are another kind of evidence. They are divided into two categories: (1) public and (2) private. In order to introduce a document in evidence, someone familiar with the document who knows that it is genuine must so testify as a form of authentication of the document. The best-evidence rule provides that there shall be no evidence of the contents of a document except the document itself. There are times when the original document cannot be introduced. In such circumstance, other evidence may be admitted to prove the contents of the document. This is permissible when (1) the original has been lost or is unavailable; (2) the original is in the hands of the adverse party; (3) the document is in the hands of a public official; or (4) the documents are voluminous. To introduce the secondary evidence, it must be shown that there was an original document in existence; that the secondary evidence is a genuine copy of the original or that the person giving oral testimony knew the contents of the original; and the reason why the original is not being offered.

The right of discovery is the right of one side to a trial to examine, inspect, and copy the evidence in the hands of the other. In criminal matters it was developed primarily for the benefit of the defendant in order that the defense might be properly prepared. Not all jurisdictions give the defendant the right of discovery. A few jurisdictions, including the federal government, grant the right of discovery not only to the defendant, but also to the prosecution. Prosecuting attorneys in some jurisdictions are entitled to information concerning any alibi defense the accused may plan to use. Both sides may make an oral request for the right to inspect evidence held by the other side, but if not granted, a court order must be obtained compelling the production of the evidence for examination. This order must be based upon an affidavit setting forth the reasons why the inspection is necessary.

QUESTIONS FOR REVIEW

1. How are documents classified?
2. What is the best-evidence rule?
3. Name the four exceptions to the best-evidence rule.
4. What must be shown before secondary evidence may be introduced?
5. What is the right of discovery?
6. Why was the right of discovery granted to the defendant in criminal matters?
7. What are some of the arguments presented against the right of discovery?

8. In what ways do states differ in what the defendant may inspect under the right of discovery?
9. What rights have been given to the prosecution pertaining to discovery?
10. What effect has the right of discovery had on the privileged-communications doctrine between the law enforcement officer and his informant?
11. What procedure is followed in exercising the right of discovery?

LOCAL RULES

Many jurisdictions do not recognize any right of discovery in criminal matters. Those that do vary considerably in the procedure followed. For this reason the reader should ascertain the answers to the following questions:

1. Does this jurisdiction recognize the right of discovery in criminal matters, and if so, to what extent?
   a. What may the defendant examine?
   b. At what time during the prosecuting procedure may the examination take place?
   c. Does the prosecution have any right of discovery?

Physical Evidence

11

WHAT IS PHYSICAL EVIDENCE?

As previously pointed out, evidence is categorized into kinds for better understanding. One kind is *physical evidence*, or material objects. In a criminal trial, physical evidence may be a gun, a knife, bloodstained clothing, a latent fingerprint, or a photograph. Physical evidence has also been referred to as "demonstrative," and "real evidence." Some authorities have endeavored to distinguish between demonstrative and real evidence. They describe real evidence as the actual object itself, or the real thing, whereas demonstrative evidence is classified as a model or reproduction of the real thing, for example, a plaster of paris cast or a photograph. However, the reader generally will find that the terms physical evidence, real evidence, and demonstrative evidence are used interchangeably.

Facts are received in evidence during a trial proceeding through three channels: (1) witnesses, (2) documents, and (3) inspection. Physical evidence falls within the inspection channel. Physical evidence is a particularly satisfactory kind of evidence. Once it is introduced, it speaks for itself. The jury does not have to rely upon the testimony of some witness to explain what was found and describe it. The jury can hold, feel, inspect, and examine the object and glean from it the information which it contains.

■ Physical Evidence Must Be Relevant

For physical evidence to be admissible, it must have some connection with the facts of the case: It must be relevant to the issues of the trial, and it must assist in proving the facts in dispute. It has been held that if an object is a part of the transaction of the crime, or a part of the *res gestae*, and assists in explaining and unfolding the story of the case, the object may be introduced in evidence and exhibited to the jury. This is true even though the object may excite the jurors or inflame their minds.

As we speak of physical evidence, the term *res gestae* presents itself again. If the term has any significance, it means the explanation of why certain objects are admitted in evidence that would not otherwise have been introduced. As stated in the discussion on spontaneous declarations, the term *res gestae* has been used loosely to describe those statements, but the term is more universally thought of in connection with the introduction of physical evidence.

■ Laying Foundation for Admissibility

Before any physical object may be admitted in evidence and exhibited to the jury, proof must be presented that the object is in some way connected with the issues in dispute. A foundation must be laid to prove the relevancy of the object. This is accomplished through testimony of a witness familiar with the object and the facts of the case, who can relate the connection of the object with the facts. This procedure is sometimes referred to as the authentication of the evidence.

In the presentation of the physical evidence in a criminal trial, the burden of authentication generally falls upon the officer because an officer usually discovers the object while investigating the crime, and so knows its connection with the crime and the accused. The officer may be aware of the connection because he or she discovered the object at the scene of the crime, or he or she may have removed it from the accused at the time of the arrest. Other witnesses besides the officer may have to assist in the authentication because the officer will not have knowledge of all the connecting facts. For example, if the accused were charged with robbing a man of his wallet and money and an officer arrested the accused and removed from his possession a wallet, the officer would be able to connect the wallet with the accused, but the victim of the robbery would have to identify the wallet as the one taken in the robbery in order to connect it with the crime.

INTRODUCING PHYSICAL EVIDENCE.   It may be well to review a few of the details involved in proving the connection of an object with the facts of a case. Returning to the example about the accused being charged with robbing a man of his wallet and money, the prosecuting attorney will undoubtedly want to introduce the wallet into evidence. Although the wallet may have but little monetary value while the contents consisted of several thousand dollars, the wallet is a part of the *res gestae*, or the things done, and as such may be introduced in evidence. Although the victim could testify about the robbery and what was taken and the officer could relate the facts about the arrest and the discovery of the wallet in the possession of the accused without the wallet being introduced in evidence, the introduction of the wallet and exhibition of it to the jury emphasize the facts of the case and substantiate the oral testimony. Also in most jurisdictions the physical evidence may be taken to the jury room for further examination during the deliberation to assist the jury in remembering facts as they were presented during the trial.

The sequence in calling witnesses to present physical evidence is not too material. In the example, the prosecuting attorney may first call the victim of the robbery to the stand to establish that a robbery did in fact take place. While relating his story, the victim will tell about his wallet containing money having been taken. At this point, the prosecuting attorney may show the wallet to the victim, and he will identify it as the one taken during the robbery. The prosecuting attorney may at this time offer the wallet in evidence. The defense attorney may object to the introduction of the wallet upon the ground that there is no proof of its connection with the accused. The judge may agree with the defense counsel, and the wallet will be excluded from evidence. Even though the wallet is not entered in evidence at this time, the prosecuting attorney will request that the wallet be marked for identification purposes. When an object is marked for identification purposes only, it is not evidence and may not be considered by the jury. It is so marked for more orderly court procedure in referring to it and for security against misappropriation. After the victim has related his story, the officer will be the next logical witness and will tell about arresting the accused and finding the wallet. The prosecuting attorney will again offer the wallet in evidence, and it will be admitted because it has been connected with the crime and the accused. The wallet may now be exhibited to the jury and examined by them.

It is possible that the wallet may have been admitted when it was identified by the victim as the one taken during the robbery. The judge may have overruled the objection by the defense attorney that it had not been connected with the defendant. It is true that the wallet had not been connected with the defendant at that point, but the wallet was identified as the one taken during a robbery, and it was a part of the transaction of the crime, and as such assists in proving the crime. The officer's testimony will establish the connection of the wallet with the defendant when the officer identifies the wallet as the one found on the defendant. The wallet now has an evidentiary value in proving the guilt of the defendant.

Theoretically, until an object is admitted in evidence, the jury must disregard it. However, such disregard is not easily accomplished because in most instances the laying of the foundation for the introduction of the object takes place in the presence of the jury. In the event the object is not admitted, it is almost impossible for the jury to erase from their minds the memory of the object. Once the object is introduced, the jury may consider it from all angles and give it the weight they think that it deserves. They may examine and inspect it at the time it is introduced, and the attorneys during their closing arguments to the jury may refer to it.

ATTACKING PHYSICAL EVIDENCE. Because of the impact physical evidence has on a jury, the defense attorney will often do all within his or her power to prevent an object from being introduced as evidence. The defense attorney may attack the introduction of the object from several angles, attempting perhaps to prove that the object has no connection with the defendant or the case at hand or challenging the officer's ability to positively identify the object as the one that the officer found. The defense attorney may endeavor to show that the object was tampered with or that it became contaminated in such a way that it does not carry the proof for which it is intended. When these attacks are successful, the success usually stems from improper handling of the investigation of a crime, which includes the collection, identification, and preservation of physical evidence. It is only reasonable, therefore, that some discussion be devoted to the collection, identification, and preservation of physical evidence. Before delving into this subject, however, it may be well to consider some of the sources of physical evidence as well as some of the kinds of objects which may be considered as a part of a crime, or transaction, and thereby be relevant to the issues of a case.

SOURCES OF PHYSICAL EVIDENCE

The sources of physical evidence are varied. Usually, the most lucrative source is the place where the crime was committed. Here material may be discovered which will aid in proving what happened, and it may assist in the reconstruction of the crime. Frequently, objects are located which will aid in the identification of the perpetrator of the crime, such as a latent fingerprint.

Another source is the suspect. The suspect may be wearing the clothing of the victim of a crime, may be in possession of the wallet or a watch of the person robbed, or may still have the gun which shot the fatal bullet in a murder case. The place of abode of the suspect is also a source where much physical evidence may be located. Here may be found the blood-stained clothing worn by a suspect during a murder or a knife used in an aggravated assault.

Frequently, a criminal will discard many objects connected with a crime along his getaway route, or he may dispose of articles which have no value to him, such as a safe taken in a burglary. Such things may be found anyplace, so that it is impossible to list all the sources in which some object of a crime may be located.

■ Kinds of Physical Evidence

As with sources of physical evidence, it is impossible to list all the kinds of physical evidence which may be considered to be a part of the transaction of a crime, because there could be as many kinds as there are objects in existence. However, kinds of physical evidence, as a matter of convenience, may be classified under three general headings: (1) the fruits of the crime, such as loot taken in a burglary, or money and jewelry taken in a robbery; (2) instruments used in committing the crime, such as a gun used in a homicide, or a knife used to threaten a victim of a robbery; and (3) objects which assist in identifying the accused or aid in connecting the accused with the crime, such as a latent print developed at the crime scene, or footprints of the suspect, or clothing worn by the perpetrator during the commission of the crime. Any object discovered during the investigation which falls within one of the categories mentioned above should be admitted in evidence with little difficulty so far as proof that it is a part of the *res gestae* is concerned. The only problem which may arise is the proper authentication of the object with the transaction. It is here that collection, identification, and preservation play their paramount role.

■ Protecting the Crime Scene

One of the first things a new officer learns is the necessity of protecting the scene of a crime. The preservice student also hears this continually throughout his or her training. Even so, this important function cannot be overemphasized. Unless the scene is properly protected until it can be searched and the physical objects collected, much valuable evidence may be lost, destroyed, or not discovered. Improper protection of a crime scene may mean the difference between objects being admitted or excluded. The mechanics of protecting a crime scene will not be included in our discussion here, as this falls more properly in the field of criminal investigation, and/or criminalistics.

The author is aware that to protect a crime scene is much easier said than done. This is true for many reasons. Some crime scenes do not lend themselves to ready protection because of the extent, or nature, of the area involved, and, all too frequently, crowds have already begun to gather by the time the officer arrives, and it is not easy to control or remove them. This is why upon the arrival at the scene, the officer may feel an overwhelming temptation to rush in and start collecting everything in sight that may in any way be associated with the crime. But in no circumstances should one yield to this impulse, for many things must be taken into consideration before the actual search for physical evidence can begin. Approaching the scene, the officer's first concern must be to determine whether there are any victims that require immediate aid. Next comes an appraisal of the extent of the area to be protected. The officer should endeavor to remove all persons not authorized to be there, make arrangements for the scene to be photographed from all angles before anything is moved in order that a proper record of the scene may be made, and at the same time put into motion the protective measures that may be necessary to secure the scene. Not until these things have been done is the officer ready to start the search, the collection, and the identification of physical evidence. Only then may an officer devote entire attention to this highly important phase of the work.

RECORDING THE CRIME SCENE. Before the collection of physical evidence from a crime scene, the scene itself should be recorded. This can best be done by photography augmented by the officer's notes. This record should be made before moving or handling anything, except victims who may need medical attention.

SKETCHING. Many prosecuting attorneys like to utilize a sketch of a crime scene during the trial of a case. This is particularly true in homicide cases. They feel that a sketch can better reflect physical objects found at a crime scene in their relative positions. For this reason it is often necessary for an officer to record the crime scene with a sketch in addition to his or her notes and photographs.

As useful as a sketch may be in the prosecution of a case, it is not without its complications from both the standpoint of production and introduction of the sketch in evidence. One problem involved in sketching a crime scene is that the officer must enter the crime scene and examine it extensively in order to make measurements. The measuring should be done before anything is moved. Unless extreme care is taken during the measuring procedure, evidence could be destroyed or obliterated. Sketching is a time-consuming procedure, and if done properly it requires a certain degree of talent and skill that few officers perfect.

There are a few basic requirements that should be met for a sketch to be a satisfactory record of the crime scene. First, the sketch should be drawn to scale with the dimensions indicated on the sketch itself, for example, that 1 inch equals so many feet. If the sketch is drawn to scale, it will not be necessary to include measurements within the sketch itself. It is desirable not to include these measurements so the details of the scene will be less cluttered. The sketch must reflect the compass points, and north should be at the top of the sketch. Although it is not critical to the sketch or its admissibility in evidence if north is not at the top of the sketch, it would be less confusing to the jury if north were at the top of the sketch, since this is the normal way one reads a map. The physical objects found in the crime scene should be listed. It is better that a number be placed by the object within the scene and a legend, or list, identifying the object according to the appropriate number be put below the sketch. The sketch must reflect the identification of the officer who prepared the sketch and the date it was prepared.

A sketch may be used by the prosecuting attorney merely for the purpose of giving the jury an overview of the crime scene in order that they may follow the testimony more clearly, or the sketch may be introduced in evidence. If the sketch is to be introduced in evidence, a few facts must be

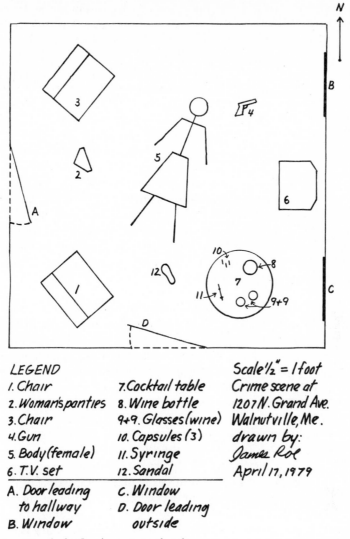

LEGEND

1. Chair	7. Cocktail table	Scale ½" = 1 foot
2. Woman's panties	8. Wine bottle	Crime scene at
3. Chair	9+9. Glasses (wine)	1207 N. Grand Ave.
4. Gun	10. Capsules (3)	Walnutville, Me.
5. Body (female)	11. Syringe	drawn by:
6. T.V. set	12. Sandal	James Roe
		April 17, 1979
A. Door leading to hallway	C. Window	
B. Window	D. Door leading outside	

Fig. 11-1. Rough draft crime scene sketch.

considered. The sketch to be introduced is seldom, if ever, the one prepared by the officer at the time the crime scene is originally recorded. This is true for several reasons. First, the officer is not generally equipped to make a scaled sketch in detail at the time of the initial investigation. Second, the pressure of other matters that must be handled will not permit the necessary time to be given to a detailed sketch during the recording of the scene. This necessitates making a rough draft sketch from which the officer will reproduce a scaled sketch at a later time for the trial. The problem which now arises is: Was the reproduced sketch made while the facts were still fresh in the officer's mind so that the reproduction was accurate?

Probably not, and so the officer must rely upon his or her rough draft sketch, drawn at the time of the initial investigation. Is this rough draft also to be introduced in evidence, or just the reproduced sketch? The procedure may vary from one jurisdiction to another, but irrespective of what procedure is followed, the officer will in most instances have to refer to his or her original rough draft to reproduce an accurate sketch. In these circumstances it may be well to preserve the original rough draft sketch in order to verify the accuracy of the reproduced sketch. This is one time when original notes in the form of a drawing should be preserved.

A sketch introduced in evidence becomes a part of the testimony of the witness. It is a form of pictorial communication. It is introduced on the same basis as a map, a photograph, or a model. It is a form of physical evidence which augments the oral testimony.

Although a sketch is made of a crime scene, the scene should be photographed first because a picture can be made without entering the crime scene. Because of the important role that photography is playing in the recording of crime scenes and in the prosecution of cases, Chapter 12 is devoted entirely to photographic evidence.

COLLECTING PHYSICAL EVIDENCE. Having discussed the preliminary steps, we consider for a moment the actual search of the scene and collection of the objects there. It is not our function in a book on criminal evidence to list the mechanics of either the search or the picking up of the objects at the scene. This is more appropriately covered in other branches of the field of police science. But in passing, it must be reiterated that the officer in conducting the search, as well as in collecting physical objects, should bear in mind two things. First, as the officer searches the scene and picks up objects, the officer must be in a position to present satisfactory proof at the time of the trial that the object has a connection with the transaction or the crime for which the accused is being tried. Second, the officer must be able to positively identify the object at the time of the trial as the one which he or she found at the scene. The officer must also be able to establish that the object has not been tampered with or altered in any way so that it will be excluded, or so that if admitted its evidentiary value will be lessened. The way the officer handles the objects as he or she collects them can become most important to their admissibility in a court trial. It is necessary to discuss in detail this phase of his or her work, so that the officer may avoid some of the pitfalls which may otherwise be encountered.

CONNECTING OBJECTS WITH ISSUES OF TRIAL

As already learned, objects which are a part of the transaction of the crime may be introduced in evidence and exhibited to the jury. But it must be proved that the object offered as evidence is a part of the transaction. To do this, someone must be in a position to state on the witness stand that the object was connected with the crime. The officer who investigated the case may or may not be able to do this, depending upon certain circumstances. It must be remembered that the officer can testify only to what he or she did and saw. The officer can only describe the crime scene as it was upon his arrival. Also, it must be realized that the officer is seldom the first one on a crime scene, so that the proof that a particular object was a part of the scene may be dependent upon someone other than the officer. It becomes most important therefore that the officer obtain the names and addresses of those present upon his or her arrival at the crime scene and that the officer ascertain whether the scene is in its original state or whether anything has been removed, tampered with, or handled. The person who originally discovered the crime scene can be a very important link in the chain of proof that a particular object has a connection with the crime for which the accused is being tried.

Once it is proved by someone who was first on the crime scene that it was still intact and in its original status when the officer arrived, the officer may testify in detail concerning the discovery of the objects and prove their connection with the crime. Otherwise, the defense attorney may successfully attack the introduction of an object on the lack of proof that it is a part of the transaction in issue.

■ Identification of Object as the One Found

Although the connection of an object with a crime scene or as a part of the transaction at hand is seldom difficult, the presentation of proof that a particular article offered in evidence is the one found by the officer sometimes becomes complicated. Also, it is often equally difficult to prove that the object examined or analyzed has not been changed, tampered with, or contaminated between the time of its discovery and the analysis. When these things cannot be proved, the object will in most instances be excluded from evidence. It behooves the officer therefore to be fully cognizant of the procedures which may be followed in order that the necessary proof may be presented and the value of the physical evidence not be lost forever.

Three procedures may be followed by the officer that will enable him or her to positively identify an object as the one the officer found, and to establish that it has a relation to the case at hand:

1. The officer may keep the object in his or her complete and exclusive custody and control from the time it was found until it is presented in court.
2. The officer may maintain a complete and accurate record of the chain of possession.
3. The officer may mark the object in some distinctive manner making it readily recognizable later.

IDENTIFICATION BY CUSTODY AND CONTROL. One of the most positive means whereby the officer can identify an object to be introduced in evidence is for the officer to keep the object in his or her possession or exclusive control from the time the officer picks it up at the crime scene until he or she produces it in court. Yet from a realistic standpoint this means is the most impracticable for a number of reasons. First, it is almost impossible for an officer to maintain any object under his or her exclusive control. Available storage facilities for such items alone make a most difficult means of identification. Second, and probably more important, the object is in most instances of such a nature that it must come into the hands of others. It may be necessary to examine it for latent fingerprints, or it may have to be examined by an expert in the crime laboratory. There is a third reason why this means of identification is impractical, and that is the right of discovery by the defendant. This right gives to the defendant the privilege of reviewing the physical evidence which may be introduced during the trial. Consequently, the officer may lose control of objects during this review by the defendant.

Inasmuch as there may be instances when the officer is not required to release physical evidence to another, some consideration should be given to what is entailed in complete custody and control of objects. Obviously, complete custody and control does not mean that the officer must carry the object at all times, but it does mean that from the time the officer picks it up at the crime scene until it is produced in court, the object must be continuously under his or her exclusive control. In other words, after picking up the object at the scene of the crime, the officer must transport it to the station, or to another place where the officer will store it, and it must be kept where no one else has an opportunity to handle the object outside his or her presence. This necessitates a locker, or cabinet, to which only the officer has the key or access. This complete custody and control further implies that if the object is to be viewed or examined by another, the officer must be present. All of this makes for a very clumsy system of identification, and other means have been developed which are more workable.

IDENTIFICATION BY CHAIN OF POSSESSION. As pointed out, by the very nature of some objects found at a crime scene by an officer, they must pass into the hands of others besides the finder. This is particularly true when an object must be examined by a crime-laboratory expert. In such a circumstance, the officer loses complete custody and control of the object. When this takes place, the officer must know to whom the object was released, when it was released, and the purpose for which it was released. In other words, the officer must maintain *the chain of possession*.

Specifically, what is meant by the chain of possession? It is merely the knowledge, or a record, of each person who has come into possession of a physical object found at a crime scene from the time it was discovered until it is presented in court. This record is important for two basic reasons:

First, it may be the only way to prove that an article presented in court is the one that was found at the scene, and is thus a part of the transaction; second, this record may be the only way to establish that the thing examined and analyzed by the expert was the one found in connection with the crime or that it had not in some way been altered or tampered with between being found and being analyzed. If this proof is not available, the object, as well as the analysis made by the expert, may be excluded from evidence.

As an example of how the doctrine of chain of possession works and how it can be most important to the prosecution of a case, assume that an officer, whom we shall call A, finds a knife on a suspect in a murder case. On this knife is a stain which is believed to be blood, and A desires that the stain be examined by a laboratory expert to determine whether this stain is blood, whether it is of human origin, and the blood type. A gives the knife to officer B to take to the police station, where it is to be sent to the crime laboratory. On arrival at the station, finding that officer C is going to the crime laboratory with some other physical evidence, B gives the knife to C to take also. C takes the knife to the laboratory and turns it over to clerk D. D gives the knife to the expert E, who makes a scientific examination of the stains on the knife. E concludes from examination that the brownish stains are blood of human origin, and that the blood is of the AB grouping, which is a rare type and is the same type as that of the victim of the murder. This knife and the analysis of the expert become most important to the prosecution of the suspect. In the meantime, officer A asks officer F, who is going to the laboratory, to pick up the knife and return it to the station. F does pick up the knife and returns it to the station, and places it in the evidence room until the time of the trial. On the day of the trial, A gets the knife from the evidence room and takes it to court. There may be something distinctive about this knife which enables A to positively identify it as the one A took from the suspect even though it has been out of A's possession, but how can A possibly state in convincing manner that the stains which were on the knife when it was taken from the suspect are the same ones examined by the expert? A cannot do so because this knife has gone through several hands, and it cannot be proved that someone did not use it for some purpose between the time it was found and the time it was examined, or that the blood examined was the blood that was on the knife originally. Since this proof is not available, the knife as well as the analysis may be excluded from evidence. However, if all the persons who came in contact with this knife are known and are available to testify concerning their part in the transaction and can establish that the knife had not been tampered with, the knife and the analysis will undoubtedly be admitted in evidence.

It accordingly becomes mandatory that a record be maintained listing persons coming in contact with the object which is to be produced in court, particularly when scientific analysis is to be made. It must be proved that there was no tampering with, alteration of, or substitution of, the object between the time it was found in connection with a crime and the time the analysis was made by the expert in the crime laboratory. Also, as was pointed out in Chapter 6, an accurate record of the chain of possession may enable material evidence to be introduced during a trial that might otherwise be inadmissible if some of the persons handling the evidence should become unavailable at the time of the trial.

Although an accurate and complete record is maintained of the chain of possession of physical evidence, it is still highly advisable that the objects go through as few hands as possible. First, the fewer persons who come in contact with the physical evidence, the less the chance that it will be tampered with, altered, or lost entirely. Second, probably most important is that each person who comes in contact with the physical evidence may have to be called as a witness to establish the fact that the evidence analyzed was in fact found in connection with the crime now in issue. The production of a long line of witnesses to prove a relatively small segment of the case can be time-consuming as well as boring to the jury, who could well lose interest in the case, so that the value of the physical evidence would be lost entirely. Also, when a number of witnesses are required to prove a point, there is always a possibility that one witness in the chain may be unavailable at the time of the trial. The unavailability of any one witness may be enough to exclude the object from being introduced. So returning to our example of the officer finding the knife with the stains believed to be blood, it would have been a much better procedure for the officer to have maintained possession of this knife until able personally to take it to the crime laboratory and turn it over directly to the blood-analysis expert. This procedure could have eliminated three potential witnesses—that is, officer B, who took the knife to the station; officer C, who transported the knife to the crime laboratory; and clerk D, who accepted the knife from C. It would have been just as well if officer A had obtained the knife from the crime laboratory after the analysis, though once the analysis is completed the object may be treated somewhat differently. Before analysis, proof must be presented that no tampering, contamination, or substitution took place between the finding of the object and the analysis. After the analysis, all that is necessary is that the officer who found the object be able to recognize it at the time it is produced in court. However, there are many objects which do not lend themselves to ready recognition, and so the chain of possession even after an analysis should not be overlooked.

MARKING OBJECTS
FOR IDENTIFICATION

Obviously, the identification of physical evidence by means of complete custody and control is not always practical, and identification by maintaining a record of the chain of possession sometimes breaks down because of a missing link or inaccuracy. Therefore, the officer may wish to resort to other means which will enable the officer to recognize an object at the time of trial as the one he or she found in connection with a particular crime. The most efficient and most desirable method is the marking of the object by the officer who discovered it in an identifying manner in order that the officer may recognize it later. The marking should take place at the time the object is removed from its original position. The mark should be a distinctive one the officer will recognize as the one the officer placed on the object. It is also desirable that objects be marked at the time they are found even though the officer plans to maintain complete custody and control of the object, or even though an accurate record of the chain of possession is maintained. In these circumstances should there be an unexpected release of the object to another or an incompleteness in the record of chain of possession, the officer could still recognize the object and connect it with the crime in issue. Even if an object is not to be examined scientifically or to be released to another, the officer should mark it so that when the officer is on the witness stand there will be no doubt in his or her mind that it is the one he or she found, and the officer can also eradicate any doubt on the part of others that the object produced in court is the one he or she found. In most instances there is a considerable lapse of time between the discovery of physical evidence and its production in court. The officer may feel at the time of the discovery that he or she will readily recognize it in the future. This does not always take place, and there may be an allegation by the defense of some possible substitution of the object for another, so that the officer must be in a position to dispel any doubts that the object produced in court is other than the one found in connection with the transaction at hand. The best way for the officer to be able to do this is to mark the object at the time it is found for future identification and recognition.

As acceptable and convincing as marking for identification is, it is not without its complications. First of all, marking physical evidence can be a time-consuming procedure, and the pursuit of the many other responsibilities at a crime scene frequently does not allow the time necessary to do this job thoroughly. Also, many objects found at a crime scene do not lend themselves to ready marking, such as objects with hard surfaces, soil specimens, hairs, and fibers. These objects may have to be transported to the station where proper tools for marking are available. Irrespective of the problems, the importance of marking of physical evidence cannot be overemphasized.

If it becomes impossible for the officer properly to mark an object at the crime scene, the officer must maintain that object under his or her exclusive control until he or she can mark it. This may necessitate carrying the object with him or her and locking it in the trunk compartment of his or her squad car or in some other place to which the officer alone has access. It is not possible to outline the exact way in which the various objects found at a crime scene should be marked, but because of the unique problems which present themselves in marking certain objects, a few guidelines are being listed. One fact must be taken into account by the officer when any object is marked—the marking must be done in such a way as not to interfere with any scientific examination that is to be performed in connection with the object. Every effort must be exerted not to obliterate any latent prints that may be on the object. The officer should bear in mind that there is nothing in the rules of evidence which requires that the marking for identification purposes be extensive. The mark can consist of a small, distinctive scratch which will enable the officer to recognize it at a later time as the one the officer placed on the object. It is preferable that the officer place his or her initials on the object if possible, and the initials should be inscribed in script instead of printing. The mark of an "X" should be avoided. The data which usually accompany the identification of an object, such as where, when, and by whom found, may be written on a tag to be attached to the object.

Even though an object is marked for identification, it must not be overlooked that a record of the chain of possession is often most important. This is particularly true when physical evidence must be examined by an expert. Again it must be proved that the evidence was in the same condition when examined as when found at the crime scene.

◼ Where and How to Mark Specific Objects

The following items are some of those frequently encountered in crime scenes, and the proper marking of each becomes an important function of the officer on finding them.

FATAL BULLETS (OR PROJECTILES). As a gun barrel is bored during manufacturing, the boring tool becomes worn with use. This results in each barrel having its own distinctive striation markings. As the projectile passes through the barrel, those markings are transferred to the projectile. If the projectile is not too badly damaged upon impact, a ballistics expert can identify the projectile as having been fired from a particular gun.

In homicide cases when the deceased met death by gunshot, the bullet which caused the death can become a most important piece of evidence to the successful prosecution of the case; therefore the procedure to be followed in the recovery, as well as the marking, of the bullet, may be crucial in the investigation of the case. When the fatal bullet is still in the body of the deceased, its removal is usually the responsibility of the autopsy surgeon, but it is most desirable that an officer be present during the removal of the bullet to see that it is done without damage to the rifling striations, and so that the chain of possession may not be broken. Upon removal of the bullet, the officer should mark it on the base with his or her initials and thereafter pack it with cotton and place it in a suitable container for preservation, so that it can be scientifically examined by the ballistics expert and later be presented in court. In addition to marking the bullet itself, the officer should include with the container a tag or some other evidence-data sheet,

Fig. 11-2. Photograph of two shell casings taken through the eyepiece of a comparison microscope.

which will give the name of the victim from whom it was removed, the surgeon who removed it, the date and place where the removal took place, and the name of the ballistics expert who examined the bullet.

SHELL CASINGS. In addition to the projectile portion of a shell, the casing also contains much information which may assist in identifying it with a particular gun. The most significant part of the casing from the standpoint of identification is the firing-pin indentation. Ejector and extractor markings may also be of help in some instances in identifying the shell casing as having been shot from a particular weapon. High-powered guns frequently make impressions from the breech or barrel; these identifying characteristics should also be taken into consideration. Because of this possible aid in the scientific examination, the shell casing should be marked by the officer on the inside wall of the casing.

In the case of fired shells, little is to be gained by a latent fingerprint examination, as the firing of the shell and heat therefrom usually obliterate any latent prints, but in major cases, an officer should never overlook the possibility of fingerprints on the smooth hard surface of a shell casing.

UNFIRED CARTRIDGES. Unfired cartridges should be marked on the nose of the bullet, and thought should be given to the possibility of latent prints on the shell casing of these cartridges.

OBJECTS BEARING SERIAL NUMBERS. Many objects bearing serial numbers are connected with crimes. Some officers tend to consider the recording of the serial number in their notes as sufficient identification for future reference. Although this may be adequate for recognition of the object at a later date in most instances, attention is called to the fact that in the manufacture of many objects the sequence of serial numbers is often repeated. This repetition is known to occur in the manufacture of guns in some countries, and to circumvent any difficulty at the time of trial concerning the positive identification of a gun or other objects bearing serial numbers, it is advisable that the officer place on the object some identifying mark of his or her own, in addition to recording the serial number. There is a great deal of comfort and security while on the witness stand in being able to positively identify an object without having to refer to any other data or notes.

GLASS OBJECTS. Glass objects, such as liquor bottles or drinking glasses, have a surface upon which latent prints are probably more easily developed than almost any other surface. Glass is also a difficult surface upon which to place a permanent identifying mark; therefore it is not easy to mark such objects without disturbing the latent prints that may be contained thereon. Because prints are seldom developed on the base of such objects, it is suggested that the identification marks be made on the base, and that a grease or wax pencil, or a felt marker, be used. Liquor bottles may be marked on the cap and on the label near the point where the cap screws on, as little in the way of latents are developed in these areas. Unless a mark is scratched into the surface of the glass itself, it may be rubbed off easily.

There are times when the level of liquid found in a bottle becomes important during a trial, and it may be advisable to make a small mark to indicate this level upon the discovery of any bottle or container. Care must be taken when it is desired that the object be examined for latent prints because the mark could very well be placed on a latent print. It may be advisable for the officer who discovered the object containing liquid to be present during the latent-print examination and then make a mark indicating the level of the contents after the examination is completed.

CLOTHING. Although a few writers on criminalistics have indicated that latent prints may be developed on some fabrics, from a practical standpoint at present little, if anything, is attempted in trying to develop latent prints on cloth in the average crime laboratory. It is felt that the officer need not be concerned over handling clothing, so far as latent-print examinations are anticipated. However, there are many other scientific examinations that may be made of clothing. It is known that clothing can carry many bits of telltale evidence that can be of particular significance to the successful prosecution of a case. It may have hairs and fibers adhering to it which can be identified with the suspect, or it may have bloodstains, semen deposits, bullet holes, or powder burns, all of which may help to build a case against the defendant. The clothing itself, as well as the things contained on it, may be introduced in evidence; therefore the marking for identification as well as the handling of this material is important.

When preparing to mark clothing, the officer must bear in mind that it should be handled as little and as gently as possible because microscopic pieces of evidence may be lost or destroyed. Clothing containing damp stains, particularly blood, should be spread out to dry at room temperature before being folded or wrapped. Care should be exerted not to permit it to come in contact with other objects during the drying process if it is to be examined for hairs and fibers. If clothing is suspected of containing semen deposits, it should be very carefully handled, as the most satisfactory proof that a stain is semen is the discovery of spermatozoa by microscopic examination. Spermatozoa become very fragile when dry and a separation of the head and tail can make positive identification difficult.

All clothing should be placed in a clean container as soon as possible after the officer acquires it. Transparent plastic bags, similar to those used by cleaning establishments, make excellent containers because the clothing can be viewed by witnesses and others needing to do so without having to remove them from the sealed container. Each piece of clothing should be placed in a separate container, and in no circumstances should the clothing of a suspect and a victim be allowed to come in contact with each other.

Before placing clothing in a container, the officer should mark it for future recognition. Pants should be marked on pockets or on the label; coats may be marked on the inside sleeve lining or on the label; hats or caps on the inside of the band; shirts and blouses on the label, inside the collar, or on the tail; and shoes on the inside of the tongue or inside lining. Any other items of clothing that may be encountered may be marked in any obscure place which will not interfere with any scientific examination. Clothing may best be marked with ink, and India ink is preferred. Wherever possible the entire garment should be submitted to the crime laboratory for examination. If for some reason the garment cannot be obtained by the officer intact, every effort should be made in its removal from the victim or suspect not to make cuts through stains, holes, or tears that may be significant to the examination.

LATENT PRINTS. In many cases one of the most damaging pieces of evidence against the defendant is a latent print which has been developed and identified as the defendant's. The courts have long recognized fingerprints as our most positive means of identification.

The officer should be on the constant alert for objects at a crime scene which may bear latent fingerprints. Upon being located, these objects should be handled as carefully and as little as possible. Unless absolutely necessary for mailing to a crime laboratory, they should not be wrapped, because rubbing, or friction, of the wrapping material may completely destroy latent prints that may be on the object. It is best to transport such an object by placing it in a box in such a manner that it does not roll around or get broken, or by putting it in a clean paper sack; plastic types of containers which have a tendency to adhere to objects should be avoided because of the possibility of obliteration of latent prints.

Fig. 11-3. Photograph of a latent fingerprint developed on a water glass.

Once a latent print is developed, it should be photographed, then lifted. Both the photograph and the lift, as well as the object upon which the prints were developed, become physical evidence. In fact, the object and the developed prints should both be made available for introduction in evidence. Frequently after a lift is made from an object, the print is still visible; in this case, it is highly desirable to bring the object to court with the visible print, as it enables the jury to see for themselves the print still on the object.

At the time the print is photographed, the officer should place his or her initials on a slip of paper and include this identification within the photograph. After the lift is made, the lift also should be identified by the officer who developed the print and made the lift.

It is most important for the officer who finds an object upon which there may be latent prints to maintain the chain of possession of the object from the time it is found until it is examined for latent prints, because it must be proved that the suspect did not have an opportunity to place any prints on the object subsequent to its discovery at the scene of the crime.

In identifying a suspect by a comparison of the suspect's known fingerprints with a latent print, the number of points of similarity necessary to make the identification often arises. Although legal discussions indicate any number between nine to fifteen points of similarity, there seems to be no exact number; much would depend upon the latent print which was developed. Many unusual patterns have been encountered, particularly in the core portion of whorls patterns. When such a latent print is found, the fingerprint comparison expert would undoubtedly feel confident in making an identification with even less than nine points of similarity and would in all probability be able to convince a court that an exact number of points of similarity is unnecessary.

DOCUMENTS. The investigator often comes in possession of many documents, particularly forged checks, which are material to the prosecution of cases. It is consequently well to give some consideration to marking documents for identification as well as handling them generally in order that the information which they contain may not be lost. The examination of documents for evidentiary material is confined primarily to the written content, that is, for an interpretation of what it may tell about the writer, the handwriting, the typewriter, or the check protector which may have been used. However, the fact that these documents, even forged checks, may have latent prints impregnated in them should not be overlooked.

It is realized that canceled checks pass through many hands, and the number of latent prints which may be on such checks could be numerous and in most instances useless. Yet the author knows of an actual case in which a latent print developed on a canceled forged check resulted in a plea of guilty to a forgery charge being entered by the accused. In this case a number of forged checks were being cashed in supermarkets. A suspect

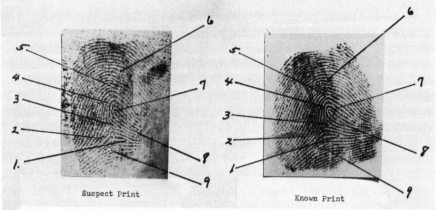

Suspect Print   Known Print

Fig. 11-4. Photograph depicting points of similarity between suspect print and known print.

using the same name as the maker of the forged checks was located. On being questioned concerning the checks, the suspect denied any knowledge whatsoever of the checks. The forged checks were processed for latent prints, and one of the prints developed was identified as being that of the suspect. On being presented with this evidence, the suspect admitted the forgeries, and entered a plea of guilty.

Inasmuch as the latent prints contained on documents may be significant, the documents should be handled in a way as not to obliterate the prints. It should be remembered that latent prints on paper are absorbed by the paper itself, so that it is almost impossible to destroy them by rubbing, or friction contact; but they can be completely destroyed by carelessly placing another print on top of one already on the paper. This fact must be kept in mind while handling documents. Documents should be placed in transparent plastic or cellophane containers as soon as possible. If such containers are not readily available, placing the document between two pieces of paper or in a large envelope is a satisfactory means of preservation, but this latter method does not allow ready examination without removal of the document from the container, while using a transparent container will. Care should be exercised in placing the document in the container so that the handler does not put his or her prints over those that may already be on the document. The document should be handled with rubber surgical gloves or with tweezers; or if these articles are not available, the officer can lift the document by holding the extreme corner edges.

The document should be marked by the officer for identification by using his or her initials. The mark should be placed on the reverse side from the writing to be compared. If there is writing on both sides, the officer should place his initials in small letters at an extreme edge, or corner, of each document. All additional data which the officer deems necessary to have available concerning the document may be put on a slip of paper and placed in the container with the document. This allows the identifying marks to be kept to a very minimum and eliminates the hazard of obliterating latent prints that may be on the document.

It is advisable to photograph documents that may be processed for latent prints because some processing procedures discolor the document so much that the written content may be made obscure. It is suggested that the prosecuting attorney be consulted before the document is processed for latent prints in order to determine whether the prosecuting attorney wishes to chance the possibility of the writing being obliterated.

A document should not be folded or its appearance changed in any way before examination by the document examiner.

■ Unmarkable Objects

Up to this point we have concerned ourselves with the mechanics of actually placing some distinctive mark on an object found in connection with a crime. But there are many objects discovered during the investigation of a case which by their very nature do not permit marking for future recognition. These are such things as hairs, fibers, soil samples, paint specimens, liquids, and powders. It therefore becomes necessary to devise other means of identification. The only practical way is to place such objects in a suitable container and to mark the container. Since the container becomes the significant portion of the identification, it is well to list a few suggested containers that may be utilized. The kind of container used is largely determined by the object to be placed in it. But whatever the container may be, one factor must be taken into consideration: The container must be as nearly sterile as possible. Otherwise there may be contamination of the object which could seriously affect the examination, or an allegation of possible contamination may be brought out during cross-examination and could devalue the evidence.

There was a time when it was suggested that an officer obtain pillboxes to be used as containers for physical evidence. This suggestion was made because these boxes were always readily available from any drug store and were as sterile as a container could be, but the pillbox is almost a thing of the past. However, pills and capsules are still dispensed in glass or plastic containers which are suitable for preserving small physical objects that may be collected at a crime scene. These containers can be easily sealed by use of adhesive tape upon which the officer may place identification. Transparent plastic sandwich bags, which are readily available, may also be effectively used as containers. Envelopes should be avoided for small objects such as hairs, fibers, saw filings, and powders because most envelopes are not completely sealed at the corners, and often the officer may find later that much of the specimen has been lost through the openings. If an envelope is to be used, the small object, or specimen, should first be wrapped in a carefully folded paper, using what is known as the "druggist fold." This consists of folding the paper over one-third, then the other one-third over that, and repeating the process on the sides. After being completely folded in this manner, the corners are all closed, preventing any of the specimen from spilling out.

Even though the container is properly identified by the officer when the specimens are placed in it, the chain of possession of these containers bearing the specimens must be accurately kept because of the possible allegation that someone may have opened the container and substituted some other object for that which was originally found. If for any reason it is necessary to place an object in a different container, the original one should be preserved, as it may be the only thing which will enable the officer who found the object to identify it in court.

■ Tagging Physical Evidence

Although the officer places some distinctive identifying mark upon an object when the officer removes it from a crime scene, there are additional data which should accompany the object from the time of its discovery until it is presented in court. It is deemed not only impractical, but inadvisable, to maintain these data on the article itself. They are best recorded on a tag or slip of paper attached to the article or the container in which it is kept.

It is realized that the officer will have notes or other official records which will give information concerning physical evidence. It is still deemed

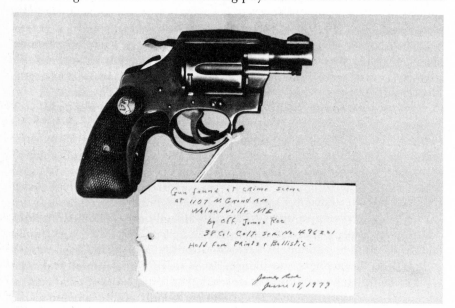

Fig. 11-5.   Gun with front view of field evidence tag attached.

highly desirable that an evidence tag, or other written data, be included with the article itself. Such a record enables the officer to quickly refresh his or her memory concerning the article at the time of the trial; it will assist in maintaining a more accurate and complete record of the chain of possession.

There is no particular uniformity in the way the data are to be recorded, nor is there any specific requirement of what should be included in the record. It is suggested that each law enforcement agency have available for the officer's use some kind of evidence tag which can be readily attached to physical evidence and that this tag include sufficient information to assist the officer in associating it with the transaction at hand. The evidence tag should contain (1) the case number; (2) the name of the defendant; (3) the name of the victim; (4) the name of the officer who found the object; (5) the date, time, and place where found; (6) a brief description of the article (this is important in event the tag should become detached from the object and also because there are some objects which cannot be recognized from appearance alone); (7) the signature of the officer finding the object; (8) the person to whom released and reason or purpose for the release; (9) the date and time of release; and (10) the ultimate disposition of the object, that is, to whom it is to be returned after it has satisfied its purpose in court, or what is to be done with it if not used as evidence.

When the physical evidence is returned after having been released by the finding officer to another person, the officer should examine it to make certain that it is the proper evidence. The officer should make a record of the return date, verify the identifying marks, and note any change in the appearance of the evidence. This is particularly true when the physical evidence has been examined by a laboratory expert, because the laboratory expert may have removed a portion of the physical evidence or changed its appearance in some way. By examining the evidence upon its return, the officer will not be caught by surprise on the witness stand and will also be prepared to explain any change which took place.

STORAGE OF PHYSICAL EVIDENCE

With a little experience, the average officer becomes quite proficient in collecting, marking for identification, and tagging physical evidence; but all too frequently much of the value which could be derived from the evidence is lost because of the storage procedure. Many law enforcement agencies are cramped for space or have inadequate facilities, so that there is little opportunity for proper storage of physical evidence. As a result, officers may place objects found at crime scenes on top of lockers and file cabinets, or place them in some large closet along with hundreds of similar items.

When the time for trial comes, the officer finds it difficult to testify convincingly that he had complete custody and control of an object, or that there was an accurate record of chain of possession, or that there was no tampering with the evidence. Any of these circumstances may cause the object to be excluded from evidence.

Each law enforcement agency should give serious thought to the storage of physical evidence. This is even more true than ever before as the rules on the admissibility of evidence become more stringent. Today officers and prosecutors have to rely more on scientific investigations and the presentation of physical evidence than at any time in our history, so that no chances should be taken on physical evidence being lost or excluded because of improper storage. Each department should have a separate room for the storage of physical evidence. This room should be kept locked at all times, and the key held by the watch commander. In the room should be separate cabinets with individual locks, the key to which is kept under the exclusive control of the officer using the locker for the storage of evidence. This is particularly true when evidence is to be scientifically examined; otherwise the officer may not be able to prove that the evidence analyzed is in the same condition as when found.

It is recognized that there are objects which do not have to be under the complete custody and control of one person. This is often true after a piece of evidence has been scientifically examined. It is important that the object be available for use in court and that the officer be able to identify it as the one connected with the case at hand. Nevertheless, objects should still be stored in an evidence room where they can be retained as nearly as possible in their original shape and appearance. When objects are to be stored for a considerable period of time, it is advisable to place them in cartons, or otherwise wrap them, in order to prevent dirt, dust, and the elements from changing their appearance. The cartons, or wrapping, should be sealed, with proper identifying data on the outside of each package, from which each carton's contents may be readily learned. Such storage will prevent unauthorized handling as well as aid in keeping objects from being soiled or losing their original appearance. There have been times when articles were excluded from evidence because of marked alterations in appearance. If the physical evidence is going to create confusion instead of clarifying what happened, it will be excluded.

Because of the shortage of personnel and the routine nature of many investigations, it is not practical to assign two officers to investigate all crimes. But it is deemed advisable in major cases, such as homicides, to have two officers present when the physical evidence is collected and marked for identification. In these circumstances either could testify concerning the object and its connection with the case. Otherwise, if only one officer has knowledge of the physical evidence, and if the officer should become unavailable, this evidence would undoubtedly be inadmissible, and its value lost to the prosecution of the case.

MAILING PHYSICAL EVIDENCE

In many outlying areas there are no crime laboratories readily available, and the only practical way of transmitting physical evidence to a crime laboratory for scientific examination is by mail. To maintain the chain of possession of the evidence, the officer finding the object should wrap the object, seal the container, and properly initial it. Included on the outside of the package should be a cover letter describing the object to be examined and the desired examination. With this data given, the package can be delivered to the person who is to make the examination, thereby eliminating others from having to come in contact with the evidence. After the object has been wrapped, sealed, and initialed by the officer, the whole package, including the cover letter, should be wrapped with an outer wrapping suitable for mailing. The outer wrapping should be addressed to the crime laboratory, and notation that it contains evidence placed on the outside of the package. It is also advisable that a letter be sent to the crime laboratory under separate cover, advising the laboratory that a package is in transit; this letter should also describe the object being transmitted and the desired examination. The crime laboratory thus can be on the alert for the package, and the number of persons handling the package can be curtailed. The package should be sent by registered or certified mail.

PREPARATION OF PHYSICAL EVIDENCE FOR USE IN COURT

It is a generally accepted fact that the display of physical evidence to a jury is beneficial to the prosecution of a case, yet much of the impact of this evidence is lost because very little thought is given to the manner in which it is exhibited. Many persons find it repulsive to touch much of the physical evidence in criminal cases, and consequently the jurors pass up the opportunity to really examine the objects as they are introduced in court. It is suggested therefore that thought be given to placing the various objects in some kind of suitable containers with transparent tops. In this way the jurors may pass the object from one to another without being reluctant to take the object. Officers become so accustomed to handling firearms that it is difficult for them to realize that there are people who recoil at handling guns; thus it is well that guns also be displayed by placing them in a box or mounting them on a board. Though a fatal projectile may appear perfectly clean, there are those who prefer not to touch something that has brought about the death of a human being. The projectile should be laid on cotton and placed in a small plastic box, so that the jurors may observe it without hesitancy. Even a plaster of paris cast to which dirt and debris are still adhering is not the most pleasant thing to handle. The cast, and the shoe which is alleged to have made the track from which the cast was formed, should be placed in a container for better inspection by the jury. With the use of a little ingenuity and planning, physical evidence can be most effectively displayed to the jury, and its value as evidence greatly enhanced.

It must be remembered that physical evidence emphasizes and substantiates the officer's testimony and that in most jurisdictions the jury may take the physical evidence with them while deliberating to enable them to better recall the testimony of the officer.

GRUESOME OBJECTS

Often the physical evidence collected at the scene of a crime, particularly in murder cases, is repulsive to look upon. It has been held that unnecessarily exhibiting gory objects which may inflame the minds of the jurors should be avoided. But the mere fact that some object may excite the jurors or cause them to recoil is not enough to exclude it from evidence when it is a part of the transaction of the crime, or a part of the *res gestae*, and aids the jury in arriving at the truth. As was stated in the case of *State v. Moore*, 80 Kan. 232 (1909), "a court cannot arrange for lively music to keep the jury cheerful while the state's case in a murder trial is being presented, and gruesome evidence cannot be suppressed merely because it may strongly tend to agitate the jury's feelings."

In one case a passbook in the pocket of the deceased victim of a homicide had been pierced by a bullet. The passbook was introduced in evidence over the objection of the defense counsel, who alleged that the passbook would excite the jury and prejudice them against his client. The passbook was held to be admissible because it became important to the case in order to show the direction of the bullet which pierced it.

It is generally accepted therefore that gruesome objects may be introduced to substantiate the prosecution's case. The bloody clothing worn by a victim at the time of a homicide or the bloodstained instruments used in committing a homicide are admissible as a part of the *res gestae*. A pipe, allegedly wielded by the defendant as the lethal weapon and found in the grave of the murdered victim, was admitted in evidence in one case. In the Lisenba case, a box containing two rattlesnakes was admitted during the murder trial of Lisenba. These snakes were identified as the ones purchased by an accomplice of the defendant and used by the defendant to strike the murder victim in an effort to bring about her death. The admission of these snakes was upheld by the United States Supreme Court as being a part of the *res gestae* [see *Lisenba v. California*, 314 U.S. 219 (1941)].

The judge may exclude gruesome objects after allowing a reasonable number to be introduced. It is held that unnecessary display of gruesome objects which may inflame the minds of the jurors should be avoided. But to prohibit entirely the introduction in evidence of gruesome objects connected with a crime would give undue protection to the accused. Otherwise, the more atrocious and gory the crime, the more the accused would be able to prevent the evidence from being admitted.

PHYSICAL OBJECTS
NOT PRODUCED IN COURT

It is generally considered that physical evidence has its advantages in arriving at the truth during a trial proceeding, but there is nothing in the rules of evidence stating that it must be produced or introduced in evidence. All that is required is that the defendant be afforded a fair trial. In the prosecution of criminal cases, the district attorney has the prerogative of determining whether physical evidence is to be presented. Since he is in a better position than an officer to know what will aid the prosecution and what the trial judge may exclude, the district attorney may select some objects and eliminate others.

There are times when some physical object is too large to be produced in court, yet, if it were available, it would create an impact upon the jury. One example which came to the attention of the author was a large truck used in connection with a crime. To all outward appearance this truck was loaded with rough lumber from a sawmill, but in reality it was a huge box containing a trapdoor. This contrivance was conceived in a kidnapping with the idea of using it to hold the victim until the ransom was paid. If this truck could have been produced in court, it would have materially assisted in convincing the jury that the contraption was devised for some diabolical purpose. When physical evidence is pertinent to the issues of the case and is too large to be produced in court, it may be photographed, and the photographs exhibited in lieu of the actual object. This point will be further emphasized in the chapter on "Photographic Evidence."

VIEWING OF CRIME SCENE BY JURY

Photographs of crime scenes are frequently displayed to jurors in order that they may more clearly follow the testimony of the witnesses. However, there are times when a jury is taken as a body to the scene of a crime to view the physical aspects of the scene. This is done in those cases where it is anticipated that there will be much testimony about the scene itself and when it is believed that the jury will have a better understanding of the issues involved if the crime scene is viewed by them. Whether or not the jury is permitted to view the crime scene is entirely dependent upon the trial judge. The judge must decide whether viewing the scene is worth the effort and time necessary. Often it is held that little is to be gained by actually viewing the scene that cannot be accomplished through a series of photographs. Also in many instances the scene may have changed materially and actually may be misleading to the jury: therefore viewing the scene will not be permitted.

Generally, the viewing of the scene by the jury is not considered to be independent evidence in criminal matters but as an aid to the jury in following the testimony. However, a few jurisdictions have held that viewing a crime scene is a form of independent evidence even in criminal matters. In these circumstances the judge, the prosecuting attorney, the defendant, and the defendant's attorney should be present at the time of the viewing.

Even though viewing the scene is not considered in some jurisdictions to be evidence, it is most difficult for the jury to completely erase from their minds certain conditions they may have observed. Because of the harm that may be done and the misconduct which may take place, a judge may be most reluctant to permit a jury to be taken to view a crime scene.

SUMMARY

Physical evidence is material objects connected with a crime. It is also referred to as real evidence and demonstrative evidence. It is considered to be a particularly satisfactory form of evidence because once it is introduced, it speaks for itself. The jury may handle it and inspect it. To be admissible, it must be a part of the transaction of the crime, or a part of the *res gestae*. It must assist in unfolding the story of what happened in the case.

In order to introduce an object in evidence a foundation must be laid to prove that the object is connected with the case at hand. This is called authentication. The authentication is accomplished by having someone familiar with the object and its connection with the case take the witness stand and relate the connection. Usually this is done by the person who discovered the object at the crime scene.

Physical evidence may be found at any place where some elements of the crime occur. This may be where the crime was committed, along the getaway route, on the suspect, in the suspect's car or home. Physical evidence may be (1) fruits of the crime, (2) instrumentalities used in committing the crime, or (3) objects which aid in identifying the accused with the crime.

Before collection of physical evidence, the crime scene should be protected to prevent evidence from being destroyed, lost, or tampered with. The crime scene should be recorded, preferably by photography, before any object is removed.

For a witness to connect an object with the issues of a case, the witness must be able to identify the object as one found in connection with the crime. This may be done by (1) maintaining complete custody and control of the object, (2) recording the chain of possession, or (3) marking for future recognition.

Objects should be marked in a manner not to destroy the objects' value for scientific examination. In addition to being marked, they should be tagged with data concerning the person who found them, as well as where and when found, what they are, and to whom released

Gruesome objects which are a part of the transaction of the crime may be introduced in evidence even though they may inflame the mind of the jury.

Careful consideration should be given to the storage of physical evidence as well as to preparing it for exhibition to the jury during the trial of the case.

Physical evidence does not have to be produced. When an object is too large to be produced in court, a photograph of it may be introduced in lieu thereof. The jury may view a crime scene, but the viewing is generally not considered to be a part of the evidence of the case.

QUESTIONS FOR REVIEW

1. What is physical evidence? Give some examples.
2. By what other terms is physical evidence known?
3. Why is physical evidence considered to be a very satisfactory type of evidence?
4. What foundation must be laid before physical evidence may be introduced?
5. What are the lines of attack that may be made against the introduction of physical evidence?
6. List the sources of physical evidence.
7. What objects may be considered to be connected with a crime or a part of the transaction?
8. Why is the protection of the crime scene important?
9. How may a crime scene best be recorded?
10. Name three ways by which an officer may recognize an object at the time of the trial as the one the officer discovered in connection with a crime.
11. Explain the meaning of the term "chain of possession."
12. List six items which present unique problems in marking, and explain how each should be marked, and why.

13. Explain why it is important to properly prepare physical evidence to be exhibited in court.
14. How may objects too large to be produced in court be displayed to the jury?
15. What facts must a trial judge take into consideration before permitting a jury to view a crime scene?

LOCAL RULES

There is very little, if any, difference among jurisdictions in the rules on admissibility of physical evidence, except in regard to viewing the crime scene.

1. Is viewing the crime scene considered to be evidence?

Photographic Evidence

12

PHOTOGRAPHS AS EVIDENCE

Although most courts have accepted photographs as another form of evidence, some writers have endeavored to distinguish between photographs which are actually evidence in and of themselves and those which act as a form of a "silent witness" to augment the testimony of a person on the stand. It is the author's belief that any attempt to draw such a distinction merely confuses the issue and has no practical significance. Consequently, this discussion on photographs will proceed from the premise that photographs of a crime scene, or any pertinent segment thereof, are as much a form of evidence as a gun used in a murder or a knife in an assault case.

Photographs have been described as a particularly satisfactory form of demonstrative evidence because of their power to communicate all details to the jury. It is seldom possible for a jury to view a crime scene, and there are many times when the physical evidence connected with a case cannot be brought into the courtroom because of its size, because of deterioration, or for other reasons, yet to be able to view the scene or the physical evidence would materially assist the jury in determining what happened in a case. In these instances a photograph is often substituted for the physical evidence or the actual scene.

To introduce a photograph in evidence, certain legal steps must be followed. Because of these requirements and because of the extensive use made of photographs as an aid to the prosecution of cases, it is deemed advisable to devote an entire chapter to the subject of photographic evidence. However, no effort will be made to include data concerning the operating principles of a camera or the mechanics of taking a photograph except as they may facilitate the admissibility of the photograph in evidence. The discussion, therefore, will be confined to the rules of evidence

317

as they have been developed through the years pertaining to the introduction of photographs as evidence during a trial proceeding.

Photographs used as evidence vary greatly in subject matter. A photograph may be of a crime scene where a burglary took place; it may be of an intersection where a traffic fatality occurred; it may show the body of a murder victim, the wounds of an assault victim, or a latent fingerprint developed at a crime scene. The rules of admissibility are basically the same, yet there are some special rules applicable in certain situations which become of particular importance. These will be discussed under individual headings throughout this chapter. It will not be possible to cover every type of photograph that may be taken in connection with a crime, but those which may be generally introduced will be discussed.

◼ Historical Approach

The acceptance of photographs as a form of physical evidence by the courts required a certain amount of education. There was some resistance to their acceptance at the beginning. Defense attorneys cried that photographs would inflame the minds of the jurors and thereby deny the accused a fair trial. Judges tended to accept this cry of prejudice and were reluctant to accept photographs as evidence. It was thought that here was something new and novel in the field of jurisprudence, and that if photographs were permitted to be used as evidence, any conviction obtained might be overruled on appeal because of a prejudicial error in admitting photographs that may have inflamed the jurors' minds. Fortunately, progressive judges recognized that a photograph is a scientific aid available to both the prosecution and the accused which would materially assist the jury in determining what happened in a particular case. They therefore held that photographs should be admitted, but even these judges realized that certain rules had to be followed before a photograph could be properly admitted. A review of the rules developed and the reasons for them may be of significant value to the officer in remembering and abiding by them. Before going into the rules themselves, a historical summary reflecting the first use of photographs as evidence may make these rules more realistic and understandable.

When an officer appeared in court for the first time with a photograph to be introduced in evidence, it was not easy to get it admitted. There was the cry of prejudice on the part of the accused, and there was the assertion of "this is what happened and the way it looks" on the part of the prosecution. Caught in the middle of these diametrically opposed views was the judge who had to make the decision. As was stated above, if he admitted the photograph and a conviction was obtained, the conviction might be reversed on appeal because he had permitted prejudicial evidence to be introduced, and thus he would be told in effect that he had erred. On the other hand, the judge readily recognized that the officer who was trying to introduce the photographs had in his possession an object which would tell

the story of what happened much more clearly than any words or testimony, so that it would be deplorable to deny the jury the right of this
valuable explanation. The judge was inclined to permit the photographs to
be admitted, but he had to base the decision upon some logic, and so he
began to draw upon his legal knowledge for some precedent to allow the
photographs to be introduced.

As the judge began to think back upon trial procedures, he recalled
that he had permitted officers to go to the chalkboard while testifying and
draw diagrams of a crime scene to further explain their story; he had
permitted drawings and diagrams prepared in advance of the trial to be
used by a witness to augment the testimony. These had been accepted in
evidence, so why not admit a photograph, which is a product of science and
not subject to the human inaccuracies of a drawing, map, or diagram? Here
in the form of a photograph was a mirrorlike reflection of the scene, or the
thing about which the testimony was concerned. Yet it was this scientific
realism which almost prevented the photograph from ever being accepted.
The photograph was not in the same category as a drawing or map, for a
map or drawing was an impersonal thing and caused no feeling within the
jurors. Also they could accept the fact that certain human inaccuracies
would come about in the drawings, but a photograph was a different matter. A photograph was lifelike, it reflected what was in front of the lens, and
since it was a scientific reproduction, it was accepted as true in all respects.
Yet from a practical standpoint, it was also recognized that not all photographs were necessarily accurate representations of what happened. Many
factors may enter in to cause inaccuracy, and when the photographs are not
true representations, the photographs will not be admitted in evidence.

FIRST RULE OF
ADMISSIBILITY—RELEVANCY

For a photograph to be admissible in evidence it must be relevant to, or
have some connection with, the facts of the case. It must tend to prove some
issue in dispute. Relevancy does not present too serious a problem to the
law enforcement officer so far as photographs are concerned. An officer's
photographs are almost always related in some way to the charge on which
the accused is being tried, and little time need be spent on this rule other
than to mention it in passing.

SECOND RULE OF ADMISSIBILITY
—ACCURATE REPRESENTATION

The primary purpose of the introduction of a photograph in evidence
is to give a clearer understanding of what happened in a particular case to

assist the jurors in arriving at the truth. Consequently, the second rule of admissibility is: The photograph to be admissible must be an accurate representation of the thing it endeavors to explain. In other words, the photograph must be a true picture of the scene or object depicted. If it is not, the photograph will be excluded because it will only create confusion rather than clarity.

To achieve accuracy, a crime scene should be photographed as soon as possible after its discovery and before there have been any changes or alterations of the scene. If objects have been removed, positions changed, or other things added, the photograph will not be an accurate account of the scene, and being inaccurate, it may not be admissible in evidence. Although some change in the crime scene may not be fatal to admissibility, if the change is such that the explanation of the change is more confusing than clarifying to the jury, the judge will undoubtedly refuse to admit the photograph in evidence. Unless there are injured persons or animals at a crime scene that require immediate removal, no change or entry should be made in a crime scene until it can be properly photographed. Only when a scene is unchanged can one testify to the accuracy of the photograph.

■ Proof of Accuracy

Once a photograph is introduced in evidence, it speaks for itself, but it must be introduced through a witness who is in a position to attest to the accuracy of the photograph. There is no presumption that a photograph is a true and correct reproduction. This attestation of the correctness of a photograph is known legally as a verification or authentication of the photograph. This verification may be accomplished by any person who witnessed the scene and can testify to the accuracy of the photograph. The witness does not have to be the photographer who took the picture. The witness attesting to the accuracy of the photograph does not even have to have been present when the photograph was taken. The only thing necessary is that the witness should have seen the scene depicted in the photograph, and therefore be in a position to testify that it is an accurate reproduction of what the witness saw.

■ Photographer Most Logical One to Verify Accuracy

Although anyone familiar with a crime scene may verify the accuracy of a photograph depicting the scene, the most logical person to verify its accuracy is the person who took it. Although generally it is not important how a photograph was taken, there are times when questions may come up in this regard, and some judges have permitted questions about how a photograph was taken. Such questioning is usually allowed on the contention that it is necessary to the effort to establish accuracy of the photograph.

When this is permitted, the photographer may be the only one who can supply the answers. However, it should be repeated that in most instances how the photograph was taken and what equipment was used are of little or no consequence. There is no legal requirement that any particular type of camera be used. It matters little whether the photograph was taken with an inexpensive, simple Instamatic camera, or an elaborate, complicated one. The main requirement is that the photograph be an accurate representation. No doubt a better camera in most instances reflects greater detail, but distortions can occur irrespective of the equipment.

Inasmuch as judges have permitted questions to be asked concerning how a photograph was taken and the equipment used, it is thought that the officer taking the photographs should have some knowledge of the equipment and the mechanics of taking the photograph. Some departments have developed photographic forms upon which the needed information may be recorded at the time photographs are taken. These forms are frequently referred to as "photographic data sheets."

Sample of a Typical Photographic Data Sheet

Case or file no.: _____ Photographer: _____

Thing photographed: _____

Date and time photographed: _____

Place where photographed: _____

Kind of camera used: _____

Kind of lens: _____ Kind of film used: _____

Shutter speed: _____ Lens opening: _____

Height of camera: _____ Direction photograph shot: _____

Recording the data required for such a form can be a time-consuming process, and often when taking photographs time is of the essence, and it is practically impossible to keep a record at the time the photographs are taken. A review of the data required will reveal that most of them are comparatively constant, and most of them can be completed immediately after the series of photographs are taken and still be within the scope of proper legal procedure. The only reason for the sheet is to enable the officer at the time of testifying to have a fresh recollection about how the photograph was made, and so the sheet may still be filled out at about the time the event took place. If experienced in photography, the officer may be able to furnish all the necessary data without having to revert to a data sheet, and filling one out would be unnecessary. However, the less-experienced photographer may need to refresh memory while testifying, and the data sheet is a material aid.

Generally, shutter speed, aperture opening, kind of light source, and lens speed are of little consequence. Also the kind of lens used—that is, whether it was a normal, telephoto, or wide-angle lens—may be of significance only if there should be an allegation of distortion, but this too could take place regardless of the kind of lens. Usually the height of the camera when the photograph was taken is not important unless a photograph is introduced to show the visibility of a driver in a vehicle involved in an accident. In this case, the camera should be held at the approximate eye level of the driver of the vehicle to depict what his visibility would have been as he approached the point of impact. The height of the camera can also be of importance when efforts are made to show the relative position of objects within a crime scene. The more directly a photograph can be taken looking straight down on the scene, the more correctly the actual position of objects within the scene will appear. Other than in these two situations, the height of the camera when the photograph is taken will be of little consequence.

The direction in which a photograph is taken may be very important during a trial when the location of dead bodies, entrances and exits of buildings, or other objects in a crime scene become a point of issue. A record of direction on a data sheet could be of material assistance to the officer at the time of the trial.

PHOTOGRAPHER NEED NOT BE AN EXPERT. There is no legal requirement that the taker of a photograph to be used as evidence have any particular amount of experience in photography for the photograph to be admissible. There is no doubt that an expert photographer is more likely to get a better photograph under adverse conditions than an inexperienced one, but the important thing is the accuracy of the photograph and not the experience of the photographer. In fact, if so inclined, a clever, experienced photographer could more easily manipulate a camera to reflect things advantageously than an inexperienced one. It must be remembered that the veracity of the witness verifying the accuracy of the photograph is of first importance. If the jury believes the witness, the photograph will be considered from that standpoint. If they do not believe the witness, the photograph may be given little weight regardless of its accuracy.

In an effort to verify the accuracy of a photograph, a less-experienced officer should not try to go into many technical explanations of how the photograph was taken. Even an experienced photographer, being asked technical questions concerning the speed of light, refractions, and other technical subjects, need feel no embarrassment in courteously advising the judge that no effort is being made to qualify as an expert, in which circumstance the judge will usually request that the line of questioning be discontinued, and will admit the photograph or reject it for reasons other than the experience of the photographer.

Even the most experienced police photographer should avoid endeavoring to qualify as a photographic expert in order to get photographs introduced in evidence. First, it is not necessary, and second, it may cause the officer to be placed in a very embarrassing position and the photographs to be rejected. This does not mean that the prosecuting attorney may not try to show that the officer has had considerable experience in photography in an effort to prove that the photographs should carry a great deal of weight. There is a vast difference between proving ability in the field of photography and qualifying as an expert.

Frequently, an officer will verify the accuracy of a photograph by stating that he knows that it is an accurate reproduction of the crime scene because he took the picture. Next it may be necessary to prove that the officer knows that it is the photograph he took. This may be done in one of three ways. First, the officer may maintain complete possession of the film and photograph until it is produced in court. Second, the officer may maintain a chain of possession of the film and photograph. Third, the officer may place some identifiable object within the crime scene.

■ Verification by Continual Possession

Many law enforcement agencies today are equipped with a photographic darkroom where an officer who has taken photographs can process the film and print the pictures. In this way, complete custody and control of the film and prints can be maintained and a photograph can be verified in court as the one the officer took because the officer has had continual possession of it.

Not knowing the film-processing procedure, the officer may still be able to maintain custody and control of the film by staying in the darkroom with the technician who does the developing and printing process.

Many officers who develop their own film find it advantageous to place their initials on the developed negative in the extreme lower left- or right-hand corner. The negative, as well as the prints from that negative, will carry the identification of the officer, which will facilitate identifying the photograph on the witness stand. This identification is helpful to the officer even though continual possession of the photographs has been maintained from the time of developing until they are produced in court. It also alleviates part of the problems involved if the continual possession is interrupted.

Marking the negative should be most carefully done so as not to obscure an important detail in the picture. The marking may be made by using a regular fluid-ink fountain pen or by scratching the initials in the emulsion with a very sharp instrument.

Identification by continual possession is probably the most impractical means of identification because of the need of others to view photographs connected with a case, so that it is next to impossible to maintain the complete custody and control of photographs.

■ Verification by Chain of Possession

As stated, an officer may stay in a darkroom while the film is being processed by another and still maintain continual possession, but this means tying up the officer's time unnecessarily in most instances. To avoid this waste of time, many departments have devised a system to maintain a record of the chain of possession. After taking the photographs, the officer places film in an envelope specially designed for this purpose. The envelope will have spaces on it for the name of the photographer, the date taken, the case or file number, the name of the person to whom the film was released to be developed, and the date released. After the film has been developed, the negatives and prints are returned to the officer who took them and the proper notations again made on the envelope.

Although the officer who took the photographs should be the only one called upon to testify to the accuracy of the photographs, it is conceivable that the laboratory technician may also have to appear should there arise some question whether the photographs were the ones the officer took, which again means tying up two departmental employees in order to get the photographs introduced in evidence.

■ Verification by Identifiable Object in Scene

Perhaps the most practical means of identifying a photograph as the one the officer took is to place a recognizable object within the crime scene before taking the photograph. Placing an object in the scene may seem to be contrary to the admonition about taking a photograph of a crime scene before any changes or alterations are made in it, but if the recognizable object is intelligently selected and carefully placed within the camera range, no difficulty should be encountered in having the photograph admitted in evidence. The object placed in the scene should be clearly placed there for identification purposes and not be something which may be confused with a part of the crime scene.

In placing an object in the crime scene for identification purposes three matters must be given consideration: (1) What should be used? (2) Where should it be placed? and (3) What identification data should be included?

WHAT SHOULD BE USED FOR IDENTIFICATION PURPOSES. The most practical object to be placed in a crime scene is a small chalkboard or slate. It is obvious to everyone that such an object is for identification purposes only, and it should not be confused with something that may have been in the original crime scene. When the photograph is taken close to the scene or article, such as a footprint, a small 3- by 5-inch card with proper notations on it may suffice as an object for identification purposes. A business card giving the officer's name and department placed in the close-up scene would be permissible, but the officer definitely should not place a badge or other objects for identification in the scene.

WHERE OBJECT SHOULD BE PLACED. Careful thought should be given to where the identification board is to be placed in the crime scene.

Fig. 12-1.   Photograph of crime scene depicting location of body and positioning of the identification data board.

Particular care should be used when the scene must be searched for evidence because any entrance into the scene for the purpose of placing the identification board may result in a small piece of evidence being destroyed or obliterated. It is not necessary that the identification board be placed in the center of the picture. It is preferable to place the board just within camera range in either the lower right- or left-hand corner. Even if the board is slightly out of focus, it will not affect the identifiability of the photograph. Care should be taken in placing the board within the scene in order that an allegation cannot be made that the board may be hiding some detail of the crime. This usually can be overcome by first photographing the scene at a distance and progressively moving forward in order to get greater details, advancing the identification board into the scene as additional photographs are taken.

WHAT IDENTIFICATION DATA SHOULD BE INCLUDED ON THE BOARD.   The identification data written on the board placed in the crime scene should be kept to a bare minimum. Actually all that is necessary is enough to identify the board as the one the officer placed in the scene. The original purpose of this board must be kept in mind, that is, to facilitate recognition of the photograph as the one the officer took. All that needs to be included are the officer's initials written in script. The officer may find it advantageous to include the date on the identification board. This will ensure a ready recall of the date that the photograph was taken while the officer is testifying. If the case number is known by the photographer at the time of photographing the crime scene, there is no legal objection to this being included. Any additional information beyond this may just result in trouble for the officer at the time of trial.

It is inadvisable to include the time of day the photograph was taken inasmuch as the exact time cannot readily be determined and has little, or no, value so far as the photograph is concerned. The officer can testify to the approximate time of day, and that is all that is necessary, and even that usually has but little significance. There have been occasions when an officer has included the time that the photograph was taken on the identification board, only to find that within the camera range was a clock which showed a different time. Defense attorneys can make a big issue of the alleged inaccuracy of such a photograph.

It is definitely a dangerous procedure to include on the board any statement about the kind of crime involved because, too often, the actual charge for which the accused is tried may not be the one expected at the time the photographs were taken. All too frequently, the author has seen photographs taken of a dead body in which there was included on the data board the word "suicide," and later the death was determined to be a homicide and the photographs were offered as evidence in the trial of the accused murderer. Although this would not necessarily be fatal to admissibility, it does create an embarrassing situation for an officer to allege suicide on a photograph which turns out to be a murder. Likewise, the author has had occasion to see some photographs of a crime scene in which the

Fig. 12-2. Close-up photograph of coffee table depicting objects on it.

Fig. 12-3. Photograph of shoemark found at a crime scene depicting measurement with identification included.

charges "robbery-rape" were written on the identification board. As the facts later developed, rape was not committed and the accused was tried only on a robbery charge. The defense counsel objected to the inflammatory allegation of rape being included in the photographs and was successful in getting them excluded from evidence.

Some police photographers make a practice of including a number on their identification board, and number each photograph taken in sequence. Other photographers have equipped their cut film holders with small plastic numbers which appear on each negative. There is no legal objection to this procedure, and in fact it facilitates connecting the photographs with the investigative notes and/or photographic data sheets.

There are those who have criticized the practice of numbers appearing on photographs on the basis that difficulty may be experienced when all the photographs taken are not produced in court. There seems to be little reason for this concern, because there is no legal rule which requires that all physical evidence, or all witnesses who have some knowledge of the case, be produced during a trial. In most instances a photographer will take more photographs than will be needed in court because of the feeling that one taken from a different angle may be better, or the wish to make certain that there was not a malfunction of the equipment. All of this could be easily explained should the problem arise; also, there is no reason why all the photographs could not be produced if the issue comes up, as the additional photographs would undoubtedly just place greater emphasis on the point in issue.

■ Placing of Measurement Devices in the Scene

Many times the size of an object, a hole, or an opening photographed may be of particular significance. The most practical way to show size is to place a ruler or other standard measuring device near the object or opening photographed. Some departments have adopted gummed tape upon which is printed standard measure in inches. This device is particularly advantageous when small objects are to be photographed. In placing the measuring device beside any object, it should be placed in such a position that there is some space between the object and the measuring device in order to overcome any allegation that something was being hidden. The space need be only slight.

There should be no advertising matter or other written data on the measuring device except for identification data, such as the officer's initials and the name of the department.

POSED PHOTOGRAPHS

There are times when a photograph cannot be taken before alterations are made in a crime scene or before objects are removed, and thereafter an effort is made to reconstruct the scene to photograph it in as nearly as possible its original state. This kind of photograph has been termed a "staged" or "posed" photograph. For example, if a dead body is removed before the scene is photographed or a gun is picked up from the scene, someone will assume the position of the body in the crime scene or a gun will be replaced in its alleged original position.

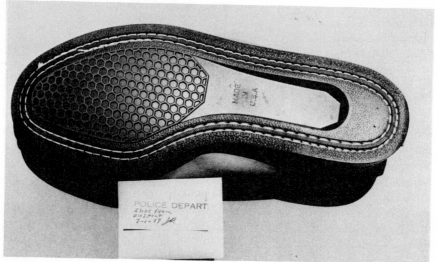

Fig. 12-4.   Photograph of a shoe found in possession of a suspect.

Although there is no rule stating that such a photograph is not admissible, there are problems involved. Often questions arise during the trial of a case when the exact position of a murder victim or the exact location of a gun is highly important. Only a photograph taken of the crime scene before any alterations or changes were made may reveal the answer to these questions, so that a posed photograph may only add to the confusion rather than clarify the issue. In these circumstances the photograph probably would not be admitted. However, there are times when only relative positions or locations of objects in a crime scene are of importance, and a reconstructed scene photographed for this purpose, if properly explained, would undoubtedly be admissible. It would be necessary, however, for someone who saw the original crime scene to take the witness stand to verify the accuracy of the reconstructed scene. It has been suggested that if a posed photograph is taken and if the original object, or an exact duplicate, cannot be used, something entirely dissimilar be used. This would avoid confusion. For example, if there was a gun in the actual crime scene, and another gun of a different make or caliber is placed in the staged scene, the jury may have difficulty in distinguishing the gun about which the testimony is related and the one photographed, whereas if a stick or other marker is used, the jury can quickly determine that it is the position of the object and not the object which is important.

■ Reenacted Crime Scene Photographs

With the advent of the movie camera and videotape television, officers have found that there are times when an accused person is willing to reenact the way he committed a crime. A movie made of the reenactment of a crime by the accused can be most beneficial in bringing the facts before the jury. Such a motion picture is admissible so long as constitutional guarantees of the accused are not violated. The motion picture is admissible even though it is a reenacted version, because it is presumed that the accused is in the best position to know how the crime was committed, and acting it out becomes a form of verification.

GRUESOME PHOTOGRAPHS

The mere fact that a photograph may be unpleasant or gruesome to look upon does not render it inadmissible. As previously pointed out, crimes of violence often result in repulsive scenes from which the normal person would withdraw. Photographs of such scenes can be most distasteful, but as long as the photographs are relevant to the issues of the case they are admissible. Photographs of murder victims, or of persons who have been subjected to aggravated assault, may be most unpleasant to view, but such photographs may be important in proving what happened and therefore may be admissible.

The fact that a photograph of a mutilated body would inflame the jury more than one less gruesome in nature is not enough to exclude it from evidence. If the rule were otherwise, the more brutal the crime, the more the accused would be protected by the exclusion of a gruesome photograph.

NUDE PHOTOGRAPHS

The mere fact that a photograph may reflect a part of a human body that would not ordinarily be exposed to public view does not render it inadmissible. However, there are a few words of caution that should be given in photographing nude persons. If a homicide is discovered, and the victim is nude, the scene should be photographed just as it is. No effort should be made to cover any portion of the body before the scene is properly photographed from all angles. If, because of some local ruling on preserving the dignity of the deceased or to prevent embarrassment to relatives, it is deemed advisable to cover that portion of the body which may expose the sex organs, it may be so done, and then additional photographs taken. But at least some photographs should be taken just as the crime scene is discovered. These unaltered photographs may bring the answers to questions that arise during the trial. Also, the chance of destroying other physical evidence while attempting to cover the body is always a hazard.

If, on the other hand, the victim of a battery is alive and there are injuries on portions of the body which would not generally be exposed to public view, certain precautions should be considered before photographing such a person in the nude, especially a female.

Seldom, if ever, is a victim of an attack permitted to display wounds on certain portions of the body in the courtroom. If these wounds are to be viewed by the court and jury, it must be by photographs. Again, if the photographs are relevant to show the extent and location of injuries received, they are admissible even though they are taken of a person in the nude. However, if certain portions of the body do not have to be depicted and are not pertinent to the case, it is suggested that the portion not generally exposed to public view be covered.

Also, it is deemed inadvisable for a male officer to photograph any portion of a live female victim's body which usually would not be visible in average attire. Although no rule excludes such photographs from evidence if otherwise relevant, the embarrassment to the officer that could result from such photographs does not warrant their being taken. If it is considered to be necessary to have photographs of this nature taken, it is suggested that the services of a female officer be used. Even though the female officer may have a very limited knowledge of photography, it is possible to have the photographic equipment set up for her, and permit her to snap the picture when the victim disrobes the pertinent portions of her body after the male officer has left the room. It is recognized that people are becoming more liberal in their attitudes toward photographs of females in the nude, but many very conservative persons still serve on juries who may take a very dim view of a male officer photographing a nude female victim. It was brought to the author's attention that on one occasion an officer found himself in a most embarrassing situation on the witness stand when he endeavored to introduce some photographs taken of a rather well-developed thirteen-year-old girl who had been severely beaten on the back and buttocks. Although the mother of the victim and the police matron were present when the photographs were taken, the defense counsel made a most embarrassing issue of a male officer's photographing a nude young lady. In this way efforts were made to impeach the officer's testimony. It is with this case in mind that the precaution is given about male officers photographing nude live female victims.

In another case with which the author is familiar, a wife was the victim of repeated assaults made upon her by her husband. After one particularly aggravated beating, the victim bore severe wounds and bruises over her entire body, and she suggested that she be photographed in the nude by an officer in order that the photographs might be used as evidence against her husband, whom she wanted prosecuted. The photographs were taken, and thereafter, as a result of a political entanglement in the community, the victim accused the police of forcing her to pose in the nude for photographs, creating a most uncomfortable position for not only the officers involved but the entire department.

It has been suggested that perhaps a medical doctor should be required to take such photographs. There is some doubt whether a male doctor has any more authority to take the photographs than a male officer, and a doctor's acting as photographer may not result in any less embarrassment in the long run. Although treatment by a medical doctor would undoubtedly entitle the doctor to view the wounds wherever located on the body, treatment would not necessarily give him any authority to photograph them. On the other hand, if the victim were willing to have her wounds photographed so they could be presented as evidence of her suffering and the doctor agreed to take the photographs, they certainly should be admissible as long as otherwise pertinent. However, they should be admissible if they were taken by a male officer in like circumstances. The side issues that may arise bring forth this admonition about photographing live female nude victims.

MOTION PICTURES AS EVIDENCE

Motion pictures and videotape television are introduced in evidence on the same basis and principles as still photographs. Motion pictures are in reality still photographs of action taken in sequence before the camera and displayed on the screen in the same manner. In fact, with proper equipment any one of the series of motion pictures may be viewed individually as a still photograph.

There have been judges who were reluctant to accept in evidence any motion-picture film which had been spliced. This reluctance was based on the theory that there might have been some effort made to alter the motion picture. Such a conclusion is far from practical because the accuracy of any photograph is only as reliable as the photographer who took it, or the person verifying its accuracy, whether it is a motion-picture film or a still photograph. A clever photographer could make any series of pictures in any sequence he so desires and never have a splice show on the film; thus the fact that a film has been spliced does not in any way attest to its accuracy or inaccuracy. The better view would be to encourage proper editing of the film before any effort is made to display it in court. Any portion not pertinent can be cut out, scenes can be rearranged in more logical sequence for better understandability, and the splicing of a film should not become an issue or be of significance.

COLORED PHOTOGRAPHS

Colored photographs are equally admissible in evidence as black-and-white photographs, and they are admitted on the same basis. Although colored photographs have not been utilized as evidence extensively to date, it is only a matter of time until they will entirely replace black-and-white photographs as evidence. This is only natural, as we can see crime scenes and physical evidence in all the colors of the spectrum and not just in black and white and shades of gray.

The primary reason that color has not been used more to date is not rules of evidence but the expense involved and the complicated problems of temperature control during the process of developing colored pictures. Only the larger law enforcement agencies are generally equipped to process color film, and those that are not have to send film away for processing, which means losing the control and chain of possession of the film. Also, color rendition was not always true and reliable, and there was a reluctancy to introduce colored photographs. But as film becomes more economical to purchase, as true color rendition becomes a reality, and developing processes simpler, color photographs will be a part of almost every criminal trial. Therefore, a few guidelines in the use of colored photographs are in order.

■ Slides versus Prints

Photographic evidence in color may be presented in court in one of two ways. It may be produced through color slides projected on a screen in the courtroom, or through the use of colored prints. Both methods have their advantages and disadvantages.

◼ Colored Slides

Colored slides, which sometimes are referred to as colored positive transparencies, may vary in size, but the usual dimension is 35-millimeter film size, and most departments utilize the 35-millimeter camera for color photography.

When the 35-millimeter slide is desired for evidentiary purposes, it is usually processed by an outside photographic company. This necessitates sending the film away for processing. There are those who feel this practice undesirable inasmuch as the chain of possession is lost, but from a practical standpoint, this may not be too serious. As previously mentioned, all that is necessary to verify the accuracy of a photograph is for a witness acquainted with the scene depicted in the photograph to state that it is a true and accurate representation. The photographer does not have to testify concerning the photograph in most instances, and so it should matter little who has been in possession of the film so long as someone can testify to its accuracy. If the photographer feels inclined to give the verification, the identification board previously discussed may be placed within view of the camera, and this will facilitate recognition of the slide as the one the photographer took, irrespective of the loss of possession.

The 35-millimeter camera is a handy and practical camera to utilize for color photography and it is also economical, but there is a disadvantage to the use of colored slides as evidence because they can create problems. As mentioned, the defense attorney is entitled to view all photographs offered in evidence before they are admitted; also, the judge must review them in order to make a decision whether the photographs are to be admitted. All of this should be done out of sight of the jury. This means that the jury must be excused during this proceeding or some other procedure must be followed whereby the slides may be viewed without the jury having to be recessed during this time. Some departments have had small prints made of each slide to be utilized, and these can be viewed without having to excuse the jury while the arguments whether the slides are to be admitted are being presented. Prints can become expensive if many slides are to be introduced, but if there are to be a large number of slides offered, it may be practical to have the jury excused while all the slides are viewed at one time by the judge and the defense counsel.

There is an advantage to the color slide in that it may be projected on a screen and viewed by the entire jury at one time, whereas prints must be viewed by jurors individually.

◼ Colored Prints

Probably at the present time, the greatest disadvantage in attempting to use colored prints as evidence is the equipment cost involved. In order to develop colored prints properly a considerable amount of equipment is necessary. Unless there is proper temperature control during the processing and the necessary equipment for measuring tonal quality is available, true color rendition is almost impossible. If prints are made by outside commercial companies, the cost is almost prohibitive to small departments. The future will undoubtedly overcome most of the present disadvantages experienced in the use of colored prints as evidence.

■ Proof of Color

Many times, the color of an object becomes most important during the trial of a case, for example, when there is a transfer of paint from one car to another in fatal accidents. When this occurs, it is advantageous to the officer to have some additional verification that a slide or print is a true color rendition of the thing photographed besides the officer's own statement to that effect. To accomplish this, many departments maintain a color chart which is photographed, and the print or slide, as the case may be, of this chart is displayed to the jury along with the chart itself. In this way the jury can judge for themselves the trueness of the color rendition.

PRINTS TO BE USED AS EVIDENCE

Whether the prints to be offered as evidence are black-and-white prints or colored ones, no required legal size must be met. The size of the print depends largely upon the use to be made of it. The generally accepted size is an 8- by 10-inch enlargement. This size print has certain advantages. It is large enough to bring out sufficient detail, it is easy for the jurors to handle, and it fits into the court file conveniently.

If a print is to be used by a witness during testimony to point out or explain certain facts, such as fingerprint or handwriting comparisons, the print should be enlarged to a size that may be readily seen by the jury as they are seated in the jury box. This may necessitate the print being enlarged to as much as 36 inches square. Although some expert witnesses in presenting fingerprint comparison testimony do not feel it necessary to utilize photographs, this is possibly a mistake because by using photographs the jury themselves can see the similarities between a latent print and that of the accused. Although the jury may not know anything about fingerprints, they still are able to appreciate the viewed similarities.

As to the weight of paper to be used in making prints to be introduced in evidence, there are no set rules; nor is any specified kind of finish required. However, a few practical suggestions are in order. It has been found that double-weight paper is more convenient for the jurors to handle, and less damage is done to the prints as they are passed among the jurors. Also, prints made on paper with a gloss or semigloss surface tend to give a more graphic effect to crime scene photographs than those of mat or softer tone finishes.

Fig. 12-5. Photograph of an intersection depicting the driver's visibility of the intersection.

■ How Many Photographs Should Be Taken?

No set number of photographs should be taken for evidentiary purposes; nor are there any set criteria for what photographs should be taken. In photographing any crime scene, enough photographs should be taken to tell the story of what happened. Undoubtedly the more serious the crime committed, the more the crime scene should be photographed.

In a homicide case, it may be well to include a photograph of the general area where the homicide took place. If the homicide was committed in a residence, a photograph of the street in front of the house is often used advantageously during the trial. The exterior of the house itself should be photographed, as well as an overall shot taken of the room in which the homicide actually took place. A photograph should be taken of the body showing the exact position in which it was found and its location in the room; close-up shots should be taken of the body depicting the wounds; and photographs should be taken of all other pertinent objects that may have a connection with the crime, including possible entrances and exits.

In a traffic-accident case, at least one shot should be taken in the direction in which each vehicle was traveling. Photographs should be taken showing the visibility of the drivers as they approached the point of impact. Close-up shots should be taken showing the damage to the vehicles, and photographs of skid marks should be included. The photographs of the skid marks may better be photographed from the direction opposite that in which the vehicles were traveling, as they are usually more pronounced nearer the point of impact and can be more clearly followed.

■ Preparing Photographs for Trial Use

Before going to court, the officer should review the photographs that the officer plans to introduce. By this review, the officer will make certain of having the photographs needed, and will make sure the photographs have been properly printed. Sometimes in the haste of printing, photographic negatives are placed in the enlarger with the emulsion away from the paper, which prints everything in reverse order. This can be most embarrassing if discovered for the first time on the witness stand.

It is permissible for the officer who plans to introduce photographs in evidence to initial the back of the prints before their introduction. In fact, this initialing is advisable unless there is some identification within the photograph itself which will enable the officer to readily recognize the photographs on the stand. However, no marks should be placed on the face of the photograph before taking the witness stand. If it becomes necessary to point out something within the picture or indicate it with a mark, marking should be done only at the time of the trial. Also in no circumstances should any effort be made to retouch or alter in any way either a negative or a print. This does not imply that portions of a negative may not be cropped as an enlargement is made to bring out details in a small portion of the negative. There is no legal requirement that the entire negative must be included in all prints. It may be well to have one print of the entire negative to offset possible allegation that there was an attempt to hide or change the appearance of a scene.

It is also perfectly permissible to dodge in certain portions of a negative in making the enlargement so long as it is done merely to bring out the details of the negative and is not done to intensify a portion of a negative to mislead.

■ Use of Filters

Filters used in connection with cameras have a function in the field of photography, but there is some doubt that they should be used except by the truly experienced photographer in taking photographs to be used as evidence. The average person is not well informed on the use of filters and the purposes they serve. If it is brought out during a trial proceeding that filters were utilized in taking the photographs, some doubt of the accuracy of the photographs could creep into the minds of the jurors. Filters generally serve very little purpose in law enforcement photography, and the harm that could be done outweighs almost any advantage. The law enforcement photographer would be wise to forget about filters and use a camera equipped with a normal lens, except, of course, when infrared film is being used, when a filter is often a necessity.

Filters on the camera lens are not to be confused with filters that may be utilized on enlargers in the darkroom in connection with certain types of photographic papers. The use of this kind of filter is nothing more than a good photographic technique to bring forth the best that a negative has to offer in the printing process.

■ Film to Be Used

The kind of film, as well as the equipment used, is relatively unimportant in law enforcement photography. The main objective is to get as good a representation of the thing photographed as possible. This can be best accomplished by standardizing the camera and the film used. By becoming familiar with the photographic equipment and film a photographer becomes proficient.

Although a number of kinds of film may be used advantageously to get desired results, a panchromatic film of average emulsion speed will handle almost any problem encountered in law enforcement photography so far as black-and-white photographs are concerned. For colored photographs, it may be necessary to become more selective, depending upon the nature of the subject matter to be photographed and whether slides or prints will be made.

DEVELOPING PROCESS.   The kind of chemicals used in the developing process as well as the time necessary generally is of little consequence in the introduction of photographs in evidence. Except when chain of possession may be involved, very little, if any, testimony concerning the developing process should be necessary for the admissibility of photographs in evidence.

X-RAY PHOTOGRAPHS

X-ray photographs must be introduced in a different manner than ordinary photographs. X-ray photographs involve a technical field and depict that which is not visible to the eye. These photographs must be introduced through expert witnesses. The first expert witness will be the one who took the photographs. The competency of the witness as well as the accuracy of the machine will have to be established. Also, the procedure for taking the photographs may have to be explained. Usually the x-ray photographs will have to be interpreted by another expert witness who is capable of reading them.

SUMMARY

Photographs are being used extensively as evidence to assist juries in arriving at the truth. To be admissible, a photograph must be relevant to the issues of the case and must be an accurate representation of the thing depicted. A witness who has seen the crime scene, or the thing depicted, must verify the accuracy of the photograph. The witness may be anyone familiar with the scene and does not have to be the photographer. The photographer is the most logical person to introduce the photographs. Questions may be asked about how the photograph was taken, and the photographer is the only one who would know the answers. Generally, how a photograph was taken and the equipment used are not important.

An officer may verify that a photograph was the one taken by maintaining complete custody and control of the film and print, by a record of the chain of possession, or by placing some identification within the scene when it is photographed.

A crime scene should be photographed as soon as possible after discovery before any changes or alterations are made in it. A ruler or other standard measuring device should be placed in certain scenes when size is of significance.

Motion pictures are admissible upon the same basis as still pictures. Color photographs are being used more and more extensively. The introduction of colored slides presents some difficulty because of the right of the defense attorney and the judge to view the slides prior to their admission.

Photographs to be introduced in evidence need not meet any particular legal size. The generally accepted size is an 8- by 10-inch enlargement. The number of photographs to be taken depends largely upon the crime involved. The officer should review the prints before going to court to make certain that the photographs have been properly prepared.

QUESTIONS FOR REVIEW

1. What are the first and second rules of admissibility for photographs as evidence?
2. Who may verify the accuracy of a photograph?
3. Why is the photographer the most logical person to introduce a photograph in evidence?
4. What are some of the questions that may be asked concerning how a photograph was taken?
5. When may the height of the camera be important when a photograph is taken?
6. Name the three methods of identifying a photograph on the witness stand as one the officer took.

7. What data should be included on the identification board in a photograph?
8. What is the rule on the admissibility of gruesome photographs?
9. What is the policy on taking photographs of nude persons?
10. Upon what basis are motion pictures admitted?
11. Relate some of the problems involved in the introduction of colored slides in evidence.
12. What is the generally accepted size of a photograph to be used as evidence?

LOCAL RULES

The rules on the admissibility of photographs as evidence are basically the same throughout the United States.

How to Testify Effectively

13

THE OFFICER'S ROLE

As emphasized throughout this study, the law enforcement officer plays a paramount role in the successful prosecution of the criminal. During the investigation of a crime, the officer interviews witnesses who can prove the elements of the crime and assist in proving the defendant guilty beyond a reasonable doubt. The officer also collects and preserves most of the real evidence, performing these investigative duties with ease and efficiency. But most officers would like to avoid their final function before the file on a case can be closed, testifying at the trial. Like other witnesses, most officers become apprehensive about appearing in court.

Being nervous about testifying at a trial is natural. It is a new and strange experience to most people. The timid feel conspicuous and uncomfortable on the witness stand. Nearly all witnesses fear being embarrassed, especially during cross-examination; being contradicted by another witness; and being unable to remember an important detail. Being human, the officer is not immune to these worries, and a new officer is especially apprehensive about a first appearance as a witness in a trial. Even the most experienced officer may feel some tension when called to testify because he realizes that what is said on the stand—and how it is said—may make the difference between conviction and acquittal.

Most of these fears can be eliminated—or greatly lessened—by the observation of a few simple rules, and the officer can testify effectively and convincingly.

It is impossible to list everything an officer should know to become a good witness and to explain every situation that may arise during a trial proceeding, but one very simple rule—and the most important one—will eradicate most of the worries of an officer: Testify truthfully. The officer who tells the truth need have no concern about being tripped on cross-

examination, being contradicted, or not being corroborated by other witnesses. It is important to remember that the witness's role is to tell a chapter
in the story of the case or whatever he or she knows about the facts. The
officer who testifies truthfully, fully, and fairly will have nothing to fear, will
soon become oblivious to the strangeness of the courtroom surroundings,
and will be the kind of witness expected and desired.

PROBLEMS OF NEW OFFICER

Those who have been involved in trials over a long period of time
frequently forget that there are many things a new officer may wish to
know after receiving that first subpoena to appear as a witness. The more
experienced officer, having become acclimated to the trial procedure and
adjusted to being a witness, may fail to inform the new officer of many
important details, and the new officer may be reluctant to ask questions
because of not wishing to reveal ignorance or apprehension. Little things
may become major issues: What do I wear? Where do I appear? What do I
do when I get there? What do I take with me? The list of worries grows
as the date for the appearance draws nearer with these questions still
unanswered.

■ Notification to Appear

As pointed out in Chapter 4, prospective witnesses are usually notified
that they are to appear as witnesses by having a subpoena served on them.
It tells them where and when to appear in court. The officer may receive a
subpoena, the same as any other witness, or may merely receive a call from
the prosecuting attorney advising that he or she is needed as a witness in a
particular case. Many prosecuting attorneys think that the formality of
having a subpoena issued for an officer is unnecessary. The usual advantage of serving a prospective witness with a subpoena is that it is a court
order demanding the presence of the person in court as a witness. It is not
needed for an officer, who does not have to be compelled to appear. On the
other hand, in heavily populated areas, prosecuting attorneys may find it
convenient to have subpoenas issued for all witnesses, including officers.
The prosecutors thus eliminate individual calls to the officers involved and
are less likely to overlook a necessary officer.

WHAT TO DO BEFORE THE TRIAL

On receipt of notice to appear as a witness, the officer should be sure to
do a number of things before appearing in court. One cardinal rule, which
should have been observed long before receipt of the notification, is that

the officer must give all the facts of the case to the prosecuting attorney. An officer may be reluctant to reveal certain weaknesses in a case or may fail to advise the prosecuting attorney of a problem. These matters should have been discussed with the prosecuting attorney when the officer sought to have a complaint filed against the accused, but if weaknesses or problems have been overlooked, they should be brought to the prosecutor's attention before the trial. It is dangerous to ignore them in the hope that a case can be successfully prosecuted without their coming out.

The officer should be completely familiar with the facts of the case. Usually, a considerable period of time elapses between the investigation and the trial. The officer meanwhile will have investigated other cases, and will find it impossible to remember all the details that must be related during testimony unless the case file is reviewed. Well in advance of appearing in court, the officer should ascertain from the prosecuting attorney just what he or she is expected to testify about. A new officer should discuss the case with superior officers, who will be able to advise how to present effectively the facts and the physical evidence.

An officer responsible for the introduction of physical evidence should make certain the evidence is available and the officer should prepare it for proper presentation. The officer should make necessary arrangements to be available on the trial date. Nothing should interfere with being in court on the date and at the time scheduled by the court. The officer may need to change shifts and make certain his superiors are notified of the subpoena so they can have his beat or assignment covered while he is gone.

◼ What to Wear in Court

Some old-timers in law enforcement have been heard to remark that they do not care what an officer wears to court so long as the officer testifies effectively. In a sense, this attitude may seem logical. But when an officer enters the courtroom, the jury begins to make its appraisal and may be favorably—or unfavorably—impressed immediately. Overall appearance —particularly the manner of dress—makes the first impact. A witness who is well groomed, neat, and pleasant in appearance makes a more favorable first impression than one who walks into the courtroom wearing flashy colors and unpressed clothes. The first impression may be a lasting one that overshadows testimony. It would therefore be foolish for an officer to handicap his testimony by wearing inappropriate attire to court. Modern law enforcement agencies make a great effort to have officers dress according to the customs of the time and the place when they are witnesses.

If an officer wears a uniform at work, the uniform is perfectly permissible in court. However, more and more prosecuting attorneys are suggesting that the officer appear in court in civilian clothing rather than in uniform. Their suggestion is based on the idea that jurors tend to associate the officer in uniform with traffic citations they have received. To some jurors, the uniform and badge may represent authority which they resent. These things could affect the weight given to an officer's testimony. In some small departments it is not possible for the officer to be relieved of duty long enough to change from uniform into civilian clothing, so that appearing in court in uniform is a necessity. As stated earlier, there is nothing improper or legally incorrect about an officer wearing a uniform to testify. However, one word of caution is in order. The uniformed officer's sidearm is considered a part of regulation attire, but some judges object to a gun in a courtroom. The prosecuting attorney will usually know the feelings of the judge on this point, and the officer who finds it necessary to wear a uniform to court should find out in advance the attitude of the judge toward wearing a gun in court. This precaution could save the officer from a most embarrassing situation—appearing in court with a gun, and being admonished by the judge for doing so. Even though a judge may have no objection to an officer's wearing a gun in the courtroom, it is considered in better taste in most areas not to have a gun showing if the officer is wearing civilian clothing, and it is definitely inadvisable to wear a "sap" in the courtroom. Wearing one only tends to substantiate what many would like to believe—that the police are brutal. Even though the nightstick, or baton, is a part of the regulation attire of an officer in uniform, it is suggested that it not be worn in the courtroom when testifying.

If the officer is going to appear in court wearing civilian clothing and is undecided how to dress, the prosecuting attorney's attire is usually a good example to follow as this is the person who will generally set the pace for the proper mode of dress for the area and the occasion. In most instances, the officer should plan to wear conservative business clothing. A man should consider a white or soft-pastel-colored shirt, such as tan or light blue, and a modest tie. Although he may substitute a conservative sport coat and pants for a business suit, he should avoid a sport shirt open at the collar unless the area and climatic conditions dictate otherwise.

A woman officer should also dress conservatively. She should wear hose and shoes of a style that will not cause comment. She should not wear flashy jewelry and her hairstyle should be in good taste for a court appearance. Most judges do not permit women to wear hats in a courtroom, particularly when testifying. An officer may carry gloves during her appearance, but should not wear them. She should be careful to avoid wringing or twisting her gloves during testimony.

The officer certainly should not wear part of a uniform with civilian clothing. Whether in uniform or civilian clothes, the officer should wear well-shined shoes and clothing that is clean and neatly pressed. Pockets should not bulge with pencils, notebooks, and other items which may distract from testimony. If an officer in court appears casual, unkempt, and careless, the jury may assume the officer's work to be of the same caliber and give little weight to the testimony.

Whether a man or woman, the officer should have a clean handkerchief to use while on the stand. It is very annoying to many jurors for a witness to sit and sniff during the entire time that testimony is being related. It is equally disconcerting to see an officer pull from a pocket or handbag a well-used handkerchief or a dirty cleaning tissue to wipe nose or brow.

■ Where to Appear and What to Do

When the officer receives a notice to appear in court, whether it is by subpoena or by a telephone call from the prosecuting attorney, the officer is usually advised exactly where and when to appear. If the officer is to appear the first day of the trial, the officer must go to the designated courtroom and wait for further instructions. It may be that the case will be continued. If so, the judge will advise the witnesses that they are excused but are to return on a certain date. Generally, this is the only notice the witness will receive for the new appearance date. If the prosecuting attorney has advised that the officer does not have to appear until some time after the trial has started, the officer should be in court at the appointed time, and should in some way notify the prosecuting attorney of being available to testify. This can be done by so advising the prosecuting attorney when court is not in session, or through the bailiff or court clerk when court is in session.

In many instances, witnesses are excluded from the courtroom during a trial. If not present at the beginning of the trial, the officer should determine before going into the courtroom whether the witnesses have been excluded, in order not to violate the judge's order. If the witnesses have been excluded and the officer goes into the courtroom and sits down, the officer may be severely reprimanded by the judge; or the officer's presence, unless discovered immediately, may be the cause for a mistrial.

In summary, it is mandatory that the officer be where he or she is supposed to be at the right time. There is no excuse for being late or not showing up for a court appearance, regardless of how many continuances have been granted or may be anticipated.

CONDUCT BEFORE AND DURING COURT SESSION

Before court time and during recess periods, many persons are walking around in the vicinity of the courtroom or waiting for court to convene. Some of these individuals are prospective jurors, and inasmuch as jurors frequently formulate opinions of witnesses before they ever take the witness stand, officers should be most discreet and circumspect about their language, conversation, and conduct, both in the courtroom and outside. This is particularly true if the officers are in uniform and can be readily identified as officers. An ill-advised remark about the case, a political figure, or an ethnic group or loud and boisterous conduct by an officer may so prejudice a juror that anything the officer says on the stand will be disregarded.

If witnesses are not excluded from the courtroom, officers should avoid carrying on conversations or passing notes and papers among themselves while the trial is in progress. The officer must not display emotion as a spectator in the courtroom. It is only natural for the officer who has investigated the case thoroughly to be convinced that the defendant is guilty. Otherwise, the prosecuting attorney would not have brought the case to trial; but during the trial proceedings the officer must assume a completely neutral position. The officer must not give the impression to the jury of being prejudiced against the defendant or trying to "railroad" the defendant into jail. If not entirely careful, an officer's facial expressions when the prosecuting attorney wins a point or the defense attorney scores will convey to the jury the feelings of the officer. Any indication of partiality should be avoided because there are some jurors who are not favorably disposed toward law enforcement officers at the outset. Their feelings may be aggravated by little things, which only build the unfavorable impression all the more and lessen the effect of the officer's testimony. The officer should remember that the trial is a serious affair, and at all times, both on the stand and off, should show the greatest dignity, poise, and decorum possible.

Many officers have found to their regret that certain actions which they have engaged in during trial recesses have worked to their disadvantage. It is not a good practice to engage in conversation with the defense attorney during recesses. There have been times when an officer has been recalled to the witness stand to repeat some ill-timed remark made to a defense attorney during a recess period. The officer should also avoid contact with the defendant. Frequently, the officer's is the only familiar face that the defendant may see, and the defendant out on bail may attempt to engage the officer in friendly conversation. Although the officer is to be impartial during the trial, jurors do not understand a seeming bond of friendship between an officer and the defendant after they have heard the officer relate some disgusting facts about the defendant's conduct. For example, an officer who had testified very effectively in a sex perversion case concerning the misconduct of the defendant, after completing testimony and leaving the witness-box, stepped up to the defendant, patted the defendant on the back, and said within the hearing of the jury, "Good luck, old pal." This is not the way to reflect impartiality in a criminal case.

There should be no communication between an officer and any member of the jury. This may be difficult if the officer is well acquainted with one of the jurors and they have not seen each other for a long time.

Yet if there is any conversation between the officer and the juror during the trial, it may be a sufficient cause for a mistrial. Any renewal of friendship between the juror and the officer should take place after the trial is completed and a verdict has been rendered.

■ Conferring with the Prosecuting Attorney

Any conference with the prosecuting attorney concerning the officer's testimony should take place prior to the trial date. The officer should not take up the time of the prosecuting attorney during the progress of the trial except on an emergency matter. It should be remembered that the officer is only one of many witnesses with whom the prosecuting attorney must deal, and the prosecuting attorney must deal with many matters besides what the officer is to testify about. A prosecuting attorney who wishes to confer with the officer will so indicate. Otherwise, the officer should stay away, so that the prosecuting attorney may concentrate on the matters at hand. Also, the officer should not borrow the prosecutor's file to review the investigative reports.

■ Being Called to the Stand

If witnesses are not excluded from the courtroom, the officer may gain many important points on how to, or how not to, testify effectively by listening to the trial as it progresses. From the demeanor of the judge and the manner of cross-examination by the defense attorney, a great deal can be learned about how the prosecuting attorney wishes the witness to testify on direct examination, and other pointers can be picked up on how to become a good witness. Also the officer will be there when his turn comes to testify.

If witnesses are excluded from the courtroom, the officer should remain in the immediate area in order to be ready to testify when needed. This is not the time to take a coffee break.

When called as a witness, the officer should walk to the front of the courtroom toward the witness-box in a dignified and professional manner, not swaggering and not stopping en route to greet old friends among the spectators. On going through the swinging gate which separates the spectator area from the area where the attorneys' tables are located, the officer should ease the gate closed and not let it bang. In going to the witness-box, if room will permit, the officer should avoid walking between the judge's bench and the attorneys' table.

■ Taking the Oath

Procedures differ among courts on the exact place where the oath is administered. In some courts it is administered just before the witness gets into the witness-box and while the witness is still standing in front of it. In other courts, the witness is permitted to get into the witness-box, and then is asked to stand and be sworn. If possible, it is well to determine in advance the position where the oath is given. In any event, the officer should stand erect during this procedure, with right arm extended about shoulder height, and the forearm up at a 90-degree angle, the palm toward the person administering the oath, and the fingers together pointed up.

After the oath has been given, the officer should reply with the words, "I do." This reply should be made in a sincere, firm voice loud enough for the jury to hear, but it is not necessary to bowl the jury over with a thunderous "I do."

Once a witness has been given the oath, it is usually not necessary for it to be given a second time if the witness is called back to the stand during the same trial.

ON THE WITNESS STAND

After the oath has been administered, the officer should take a seat on the witness stand and sit up straight, with both hands folded in the lap or placed on the arms of the chair. The officer should not slouch or slump or sit on the edge of the chair. Scratching or rubbing the nose, pulling the ear lobes, cleaning fingernails, or continually clearing the throat should be avoided. The officer should not chew gum or have a cough drop or any other obstruction in the mouth while testifying. One must be especially alert to avoid these distracting mannerisms, as many are done unconsciously because of the tension of testifying.

■ Voice and Grammar

While testifying, the officer should use a normal conversational tone, sufficiently loud to be heard at all times. It is most embarrassing to an officer for a judge to say, "Speak up, no one is going to hurt you." As questions are being asked by the attorneys, the officer should look at the attorney asking the question, but the officer should direct the answer to the jury. It is the jury, not the attorney, who renders the verdict, and it is they who must know the facts. If the trial is a court trial, some judges prefer that the officer direct answers to the judge, but generally it is permissible to direct the answer to the attorney asking the question. Many courtrooms today are equipped with microphones for the use of witnesses when testifying. If so, the officer will have to talk into the microphone rather than turn toward the jury.

Law enforcement officers are seeking professional status, and every effort is being made to improve their image in the public eye. Yet all too frequently officers overlook the way they speak; the terms and words chosen and the grammar used do not reflect professional standards. Therefore it behooves officers to do all within their power to improve their manner of speaking. This effort should be made in the daily routine of duty, and not just when on the witness stand. It is almost impossible to be careless about speech in daily life and then to make a favorable impression on the witness stand. To many jurors the use of improper grammar is most annoying, particularly when used by one who should know better, such as a law enforcement officer. When an officer's testimony is permeated with terms such as "have went," "have came," "have took," "ain't," or "irregardless," the jury tends to assume that the officer is as ignorant or careless about work as about speech; therefore little weight is given to the testimony.

The author is not implying that an officer must have the equivalent of a master's degree in English to speak or testify effectively, but with the educational facilities available and the many books in print on correct speech and grammar, the officer today has little excuse not to be grammatically correct in speech.

PROFANITY AND VULGARITY. The officer is in constant contact with the criminal world, where profanity and vulgarity are parts of normal speech. Too often, the officer uses the same vocabulary as the criminal in daily conversations, and when on the witness stand, finds to great embarrassment that some of these vulgar or profane terms inadvertently slip into the testimony. It must be remembered that neither profanity nor vulgarity should be used by a witness while testifying unless the witness is asked by the attorney to repeat the exact words used in a conversation. In this situation the exact words should be used, even though they may be vulgar or profane, because they have an evidentiary value.

JARGON. Persons in all walks of life use a form of occupational jargon which, in most instances, is meaningless to those outside the occupation. The officer is no different from anyone else in this way. He uses initials or numbers when speaking of certain violations, and has a vocabulary in which the terms of the criminal have been adopted. This occupational jargon, as well as language of the hoodlum, should be avoided when testifying as the jury, not being familiar with the terms, will lose the entire meaning of the officer's testimony. For example, officers frequently refer to a suspect's room or home as a "pad"; call marijuana "hay"; and use code section numbers when referring to certain violations. In one state, the vehicle code section making drunken driving a violation was section 502. Officers facetiously referred to this violation as "five-o-deuce," and this term became so much a part of the language of one officer that he used the term while testifying. The defense attorney challenged his remark concerning the alleged violation. The officer became so confused that he could not recall the correct code section, and ended by making a ridiculous spectacle of himself. The author is not trying to eliminate all occupational shortcut terminology or take all humor out of life, but an officer who frequently adopts slipshod language and jargon will find it most difficult to change when conversation must take on a serious note, as it must while testifying.

■ References to the Accused

An officer in testifying will undoubtedly have to refer to the accused. It is very easy for the officer's voice to carry an inflection showing prejudice against the accused. This is particularly true when the accused has been exceptionally overbearing and uncooperative. The officer's voice should not change pitch in referring to the accused, and references should be made to "the defendant" or to "Mr.," "Miss," or "Mrs." (followed by the accused's last name).

Many jurors tend to be sympathetic toward the accused, and any indication that the officer is prejudiced may be so much resented by the jurors that they devaluate the testimony of the officer.

■ Answering Questions on the Stand

The first few questions asked of the officer by the prosecuting attorney will be identification questions, such as the officer's name, address, and occupation. These are simple questions to answer, and the officer may blurt out the answers quickly, in a bored manner. The court reporter and jury may miss some of the answers, and the officer will be asked to repeat the answers to the simplest questions asked during the whole trial. The officer should pace answers to these questions at the speed of the rest of the testimony. However, the officer should not be so hesitant in giving name, address, and occupation as to seem too frightened to speak or think. The officer should give this information in normal conversational tones and not appear bored with the whole procedure. These questions and answers are necessary for the record of the trial proceedings. The mere fact that the officer is sitting in the witness-box wearing a uniform which may carry name and place of employment does not make this information a part of the record.

As the prosecuting attorney begins the interrogation of the officer concerning the facts of the case, the defense attorney will undoubtedly make objections to some of the questions asked. When an objection is made, the judge may sustain it (which means that the question may not be answered) or overrule it (which authorizes the officer to answer the question). Before answering any question, whether it is during direct examination or cross-examination, the officer should allow sufficient time for an objection to be made. It is actually to the advantage of the officer to wait a second or two before answering, taking an opportunity to think about the question and form an intelligent answer. But it is not necessary for the officer to look at the defense attorney after each question is asked by the prosecution to see whether an objection is forthcoming. If an objection is made to a question asked, it does not matter how eager the officer may be to give the answer; the officer *must* wait for the judge to rule upon the objection. Nothing irritates a judge more than to have an officer persistently answer questions before a ruling can be made on an objection. If the objection is overruled and the officer does not recall the question or does not quite understand it, the officer should ask that it be repeated. The officer should not guess what was asked.

As the direct examination progresses, the officer frequently has a tendency to relax and settle down because the prosecuting attorney is an ally and everything is going well. Then come the defense attorney and the cross-examination. The officer immediately sits erect and eases out on the edge of the chair to meet the enemy, all of which gives the impression of two prizefighters squaring off at each other. It is suggested therefore that the officer sit upright in the chair and give the impression of being alert during the entire time on the stand. In this way the officer will not manifest any change in attitude as the cross-examination begins. There is no reason to fear or to fight the defense attorney if the officer has testified truthfully during the direct examination. Not all defense attorneys are "out to get" officers. The defense attorney is duty-bound to properly represent the defendant. The cross-examination is one of the defense attorney's functions. The officer should continue in the same conversational tone during the cross-examination, should not become emotional or sarcastic, and should not make wisecracks or argue with the defense attorney.

A few defense attorneys in overzealous efforts to represent the defendant can become most disagreeable in their cross-examination of officers. It becomes difficult to maintain composure in this circumstance, but it is important; otherwise, the officer is playing right into the hands of the defense attorney. If a quick temper is displayed on the stand, the defense attorney may take advantage by alleging that a confession was given only because of fear of the officer, or that a consent to search was obtained through fear of the officer's emotion. If the jury has seen this temper reflected on the stand, they may be inclined to believe the defense attorney. On the other hand, if the officer can remain calm during an attempted browbeating session with the defense attorney, the officer will undoubtedly receive the respect of the jury, and the defense attorney's tactics will actually work to the advantage of the officer.

When asked a question, whether on direct examination or cross-examination, the officer should answer that question as concisely, accurately, and clearly as possible. The officer should not volunteer information. By volunteering information, the officer may unnecessarily open up an area for cross-examination or may bring out matters which the prosecuting attorney planned to emphasize at a later point in the trial. Frequently during cross-examination, the defense attorney will continue to look at the officer after the officer has completed the answer. Officers sometimes think that the attorney is waiting for more information and will add to the testimony. This is when an officer often gets into difficulty because he may make some inane remark which will allow additional cross-examination. All questions should be answered as completely as possible, and when this has been done, the officer should stop and wait for the next question. If more is wanted or needed, it will be asked for.

During the direct examination, the officer who thinks that the prosecuting attorney has overlooked something may mention it to the prosecuting attorney at the first opportunity. It may be necessary to wait until the first recess; but the officer should not volunteer it on the stand. The prosecuting attorney may have left the particular testimony out purposely. After completing testimony, if the officer sincerely believes that there was a very important point overlooked, it is permissible to mention it to the prosecuting attorney when leaving the stand. If the prosecuting attorney thinks that the testimony is important enough, he or she may recall the officer to the stand. If the prosecuting attorney chooses to continue to disregard the point, the officer should not argue. It is the prosecuting attorney's responsibility to guide the prosecution of the trial, and not the officer's.

Officers should be most careful during their testimony not to mention other crimes, or criminal records, of the accused unless that point has been directly asked. It must be recalled that other acts of misconduct, crimes, and criminal records of the defendant may be revealed only under very limited circumstances. Referring to such matters during the testimony by the officer may cause a mistrial to be declared. Sometimes after relating a conversation with an accused, the prosecuting attorney or defense attorney may ask the officer whether that was all that was said by the defendant. Generally, the answer to this question should be confined to "no" or "that is all that was said pertaining to the case." Too often, when asked this question, particularly by the defense attorney, the officer thinks that it opens up the opportunity to relate other acts of misconduct or crimes which the defendant admitted committing, but many judges consider any evidence of other crimes admitted so prejudicial to the defendant that a mistrial will be declared, and the officer may be severely reprimanded.

■ When the Officer Forgets Testimony

Although the officer should become as familiar as possible with the facts of the case, the officer is not expected to be able to recall certain minute details, such as serial numbers, measurements, or license numbers. It is recognized that the officer will have investigated a number of other cases, and may not recall some of the details of the present case. If this should happen, the officer should not feel any embarrassment. If unable to remember, the officer should advise the judge of this fact and ask permission to refresh his or her memory. What the officer may use to refresh memory was covered in Chapter 4. As pointed out in that chapter, the most logical document to use in refreshing memory is a copy of the investigative report that the officer made at a time when the facts were still fresh in the memory of the officer.

It must be remembered that any memory-refresher the officer uses while on the stand may be examined by the defense attorney. If the officer uses a notebook for this purpose, the defense attorney may peruse the entire notebook. For this reason the officer should utilize a loose-leaf notebook in order to remove only those pages which pertain to the case at hand, and to take them to court to refresh memory if the need arises. It must be recalled also that there are some jurisdictions which permit the defense attorney to examine anything the officer uses before the trial to refresh the memory about the facts of the case. Here again, if the officer refers to a notebook for this purpose, the defense attorney may examine the entire notebook unless those pages pertaining to the case may be removed and furnished to the defense. It has been held that it is not an error to permit the defense attorney to see only those pages relating to the defendant's case, and not the remainder of the notebook.

■ Cross-Examination

Defense attorneys differ in their approach to witnesses upon cross-examination. Some attorneys assume a very friendly attitude toward the witness. The defense attorney may be very complimentary to an officer. Each question may be posed in a manner to give the impression that it is a privilege to be permitted to make such an inquiry of the officer. This may lull the officer into a state of complacency or false security, so that the officer becomes overconfident and, as a result, may make careless remarks when answering the questions on cross-examination. Still other attorneys endeavor to browbeat witnesses, or assume an unfriendly attitude toward them, particularly when cross-examining officers. Insinuating remarks may be made by the defense attorney in an effort to devaluate the officer's testimony. When these things occur, the officer may be taxed to the extreme to maintain composure. The officer who cannot remain composed may become emotionally involved to the point of doing or saying things which are detrimental to the prosecution of the case. This may be the very thing the defense attorney hoped would happen. In no circumstances should the officer become engaged in a verbal altercation with the defense attorney.

Various kinds of questions are asked of an officer by the defense attorney. Frequently, questions are asked in which the defense attorney will demand a yes or no answer. Some questions cannot intelligently be answered with a yes or no, for example: "Have you stopped beating your wife?" This question implies that the witness has beaten his wife in the past and that the only fact now involved is whether he is still doing it or has stopped. It can be readily seen that if the witness never beat his wife, either a yes or no would be incorrect and not a truthful statement. An officer who encounters a question which cannot be intelligently answered with a yes or no should so inform the judge. If the judge insists on a yes or no answer, there is no choice but to answer with yes or no depending upon which is the more nearly correct. The prosecuting attorney will give the officer the opportunity to more fully explain the answer during redirect examination.

A question that often disturbs a new officer is one from the defense attorney such as: "Have you discussed this case with anyone?" Many persons think that there is something legally wrong or improper in discussing the facts of a case with anyone. Any witness, whether an officer or any other witness, who has not discussed the case with the prosecuting attorney is not properly prepared to testify intelligently. As previously pointed out, the case should be discussed by the officer with his or her superiors, and perhaps with the other officers who were involved in the case, to make certain that each knows what to testify about and the real evidence to present. The fact that the case has been discussed with others before the trial does not mean that a story has been fabricated or that the testimony is going to be falsely related. The officer should readily admit discussing the case with superiors and the prosecuting attorney, but should explain that he or she was not told what to say, except to relate the facts truthfully and accurately.

Many times, a defense attorney will ask an obviously absurd question, but this question may be designed to elicit an equally absurd or curt answer for some reason known only to the defense attorney. Such questions should be answered with the same courtesy and seriousness as all others. A question may be asked in an ambiguous or misleading manner, such as, "Do you wish the jury to believe," et cetera. If a question is asked in a misleading or ambiguous way, the officer should ask that it be clarified. Sometimes questions are asked in rapid sequence with the hope that the officer will make quick answers which may result in inaccuracy. The officer should not be hurried into making answers. If the officer needs time to regain composure, the officer may request that the question be repeated. Likewise, if the officer did not hear the question, or did not follow it, the officer may ask that it be repeated, but should not request each question to be repeated or the judge may suggest that the officer listen to the question as it is asked. Repeating questions is time-consuming, and judges resent unnecessary delays of a trial's progress.

If the officer does not know the answer to a question, the officer should have no hesitancy in stating, "I do not know." Neither should the officer be reticent about answering a question which may seem to be favorable to the defendant. The officer will gain more respect and favor with the jury if the officer tells his or her entire story in an impartial and impersonal manner than if the officer appears emotionally inclined against the defendant.

One mistake often made by an officer during cross-examination is to try to determine the motive behind a question asked by the defense attorney. In doing so the officer may gear the answer to what the officer believes is the motive and thus fail to give a direct and concise answer to the question. The officer may even include material that is not pertinent or may give an entirely irrelevant answer because of thinking about an alleged motive rather than the question asked. Any time an officer tries to maneuver with a defense attorney instead of adhering to the truth with short, concise answers, the officer will end up in serious trouble and do much to lose the case for the prosecution.

AFTER TESTIFYING

After completing testimony, both direct and cross-examination, the officer should make certain that he or she is excused before leaving the courthouse. It may be that the prosecuting attorney or the defense attorney will wish to recall the officer.

REVIEW CASE AFTER VERDICT

Having testified in the best manner possible, an officer should not take an acquittal personally. An officer who failed to testify properly should endeavor to determine the faults and correct them to assist others not to make the same mistakes. Whether an acquittal is granted or a conviction obtained, the officer should review the case to determine mistakes made in the testimony, the collection and preservation of the evidence, and the interviews with witnesses. The officer should examine all facets of the case in an effort to continually improve techniques. Only by so doing will the officer continue to grow as a witness, as an investigator, and as a professional officer.

SUMMARY

The role of the officer is most important in the successful prosecution of a criminal case. The officer's appearance, manner, and attitude may make the difference whether much or little weight is given to the testimony. The officer must remember that a trial is a serious affair. A defendant's life may even be at stake. The officer's conduct should be serious and dignified, whether in the courtroom or outside it.

Before the trial, the officer should become completely familiar with the details of the case. The officer should discuss it with the prosecuting attorney, fellow officers who are also involved in the case, and superiors. The officer should prepare the real evidence that the officer is to introduce. The officer should make the necessary arrangements for the court appearance in order to be at the designated place at the designated time.

The officer should be dressed in a clean, neatly pressed uniform, or in conservative civilian clothing. Shoes should be shined. Unless the prosecuting attorney engages in such informality, the officer should not wear sport clothes. If civilian clothing is worn, the officer's gun should be concealed.

The officer should testify in a normal conversational tone and should not volunteer information beyond answering the question. An officer may refresh his or her memory when testifying, but must request permission from the judge to utilize something with which to do so. The defense attorney may examine whatever is used.

An officer may encounter defense attorneys who have a variety of approaches to cross-examining witnesses; some appear friendly, and some have a tendency to browbeat. Many different kinds of questions are asked during cross-examination. Some demand a yes or no answer, some are ambiguous, and some misleading. Other questions tend to impeach so as to upset the officer emotionally, and still others are fired rapidly to shake up the officer's composure.

The officer's recess conduct and conversation should be most discreet. The officer should avoid contact with the defendant and the defense attorney. No contact whatever should be made with any member of the jury.

The officer should make certain to be excused from further testifying before leaving the courtroom area.

After the trial is completed, the case should be reviewed for strong points and weaknesses in the testimony, the investigation, the collection and preservation of evidence, and the interviews with witnesses.

QUESTIONS FOR REVIEW

1. What action should the officer take before the trial?
2. Describe how an officer should be dressed when going to testify.
3. Demonstrate how an officer should stand while taking the oath.
4. To whom should the officer direct answers while testifying?
5. When an objection is made to a question, the officer should answer quickly in the event an objection is sustained and he or she does not get a chance to get the information related. What is wrong with this statement?
6. Why is volunteering information not advisable?
7. What action may an officer take if unable to recall a detail while testifying?
8. What are some kinds of questions which may be en-

countered during cross-examination, and what action should be taken?

9. Why is the officer's conduct during trial recesses important?

10. What must an officer determine after testifying and before leaving the court?

11. What action should be taken upon the completion of the trial?

LOCAL RULES

The only variation among jurisdictions in testifying effectively would be what is acceptable attire for the officer when testifying in a particular area.

Appendix

Throughout this book many references have been made to case decisions, and in each instance a case citation has been given. To assist the reader in understanding the significance of the case citation, this appendix has been added.

In addition to trial courts, each state has appellate courts. These appellate courts exist to assure that justice is rendered. In a criminal case if the defendant is convicted, he may appeal his case if he feels that some error was made during the trial of the case. As it relates to the defendant, the grounds for appeal are numerous. A defendant may allege that evidence was introduced against him which had been illegally seized, that a confession was admitted which had been improperly obtained, or that there was misconduct by the prosecuting attorney or a juror during the trial. If there is any basis for the defendant's contention of error, the case will be heard by an appellate court.

Usually the appeal will be heard by a district court of appeal, which is known by various names depending upon the state in which the court is located. Each state also has a court of "last resort," which in most states is known as the state supreme court. It is possible in many instances for a case to be appealed to the state supreme court after it has been heard by the district court of appeal. If there should be some United States constitutional question involved, the case may be appealed to the United States Supreme Court.

The decisions of all these courts are published in official publications. In addition to the official publications, various publishing companies publish the decisions in their own reporter systems. In order to locate these decisions, each is given a citation, or reference number. For example, the *Miranda v. Arizona* decision carries the official citation of 384 U.S. 436 (1966), which means that, in the official records of the United States Supreme Court, this case can be found in volume 384 of the United States Supreme Court decisions on page 436. The figure in parentheses (i.e., 1966) denotes the year that the decision was handed down by the United States Supreme Court. In addition to the official records, this case may be found in the *Supreme Court Reporter* which is published by the West Publishing Company. The Miranda citation for the *Supreme Court Reporter* is: 86 S. Ct. 1602. The Bancroft-Whitney Company also publishes the United States Supreme Court decisions in a publication known as the *United States Supreme Court Reports, Lawyers' Edition*. The Miranda decision for this publication would be 16 L. Ed. 2d 964. To assist judges and attorneys in locating court decisions, all three citations are frequently listed in referring to the case. For example, the *Miranda v. Arizona* decision may be cited as: *Miranda v. Arizona*, 384 U.S. 436, 86 S. Ct. 1602, 16 L. Ed. 2d 694 (1966). This gives judges and attorneys three sources in which to locate the Miranda decision.

The official citations for the supreme court decisions of the various states usually carry the name of the state, or its abbreviation, in the citation. For example, a decision of the Michigan Supreme Court would carry a citation such as *Hubert v. Joslin*, 285 Mich. 337 (1937). The citation of a district court of appeal would carry the abbreviation of the state involved and the abbreviation of the word appellate (App.) in the citation. For example, an Alabama appellate court decision would be cited as *Craven v. State*, 22 Ala. App. 39 (1927).

As in the case of the United States Supreme Court decisions, besides the official publications, the state supreme court decisions and appellate court decisions are published in other publications. For example, the California Supreme Court decisions and Appellate Court decisions are published in a publication known as the *California Reporter*, published by the West Publishing Company. For example, in the case of *People v. Sudduth*, the official citation would be carried as 65 Cal. 2d 543 (1966); the *California Reporter* citation would be listed as 55 C.R. 393 or as 55 Cal. Rptr. 393.

Judges and attorneys often are interested in the supreme court decisions of states other than the one in which they are practicing. To assist the judges and attorneys in this regard, the West Publishing Company publishes state supreme court decisions in publications known as the *National Reporter System*. This system groups certain states in areas and publishes their decisions in a series of volumes. The *Atlantic Reporter* includes the supreme court decisions of the following jurisdictions: Connecticut, Delaware, Maine, Maryland, New Hampshire, New Jersey, Pennsylvania, Rhode Island, and Vermont. The following is an example of an *Atlantic Reporter* citation: *Commonwealth v. Bishop*, 228 A. 2d 661 (1967).

The *North Eastern Reporter* includes the states of Illinois, Indiana, Massachusetts, New York, and Ohio. A citation of this system carries the initials "N.E." The *North Western Reporter* carries the reports of Iowa, Michigan, Minnesota, Nebraska, North Dakota, South Dakota, and Wisconsin. The initials "N.W." denote this system. The other systems have similar initial designations. The *Pacific Reporter* covers the states of Alaska, Arizona, California, Colorado, Hawaii, Idaho, Kansas, Montana, Nevada, New Mexico, Oklahoma, Oregon, Utah, Washington, and Wyoming. The *South Eastern Reporter* includes the states of Georgia, South Carolina, North Carolina, Virginia, and West Virginia. Included in the *Southern Reporter* are the states of Alabama, Florida, Louisiana, and Mississippi. The *South Western Reporter* includes the states of Arkansas, Missouri, Kentucky, Tennessee, and Texas.

Thus returning to the Sudduth case, this decision may be cited as: *People v. Sudduth*, 65 Cal. 2d 543, 55 C.R. 393, 421 P.2d 401 (1966). The third citation is the *Pacific Reporter* citation for this case. As in the case of the United States Supreme Court decisions, by citing a decision in this form, judges and attorneys have access to a decision from several sources.

In each instance the number preceding the abbreviation of the reporter involved denotes the volume in which the case decision is located. The number following the abbreviation of the reporter is the page on which the decision begins. The year in which the decision was handed down is usually in parentheses, and it may follow the citations or precede them. It is to be noted that after the abbreviation of the reporter involved sometimes the figure "2d" or "3d" appears. This denotes that after a number of volumes of a particular reporter was published, a second or third series was commenced.

Table of Cases

Index

DATE DUE